THE
ELDER SENECA

DECLAMATIONS

IN TWO VOLUMES

TRANSLATED BY

M. WINTERBOTTOM

FELLOW OF WORCESTER COLLEGE, OXFORD

VOLUME 2

CONTROVERSIAE

BOOKS 7–10

SUASORIAE

CAMBRIDGE, MASSACHUSETTS
HARVARD UNIVERSITY PRESS
LONDON
WILLIAM HEINEMANN LTD
MCMLXXIV

American ISBN 0–674–99511–2
British ISBN 0–434–99464–2

Printed in Great Britain

CONTENTS

LIBER SEPTIMUS

Seneca Novato, Senecae, Melae filiis salutem.

1   Instatis mihi cotidie de Albucio: non ultra vos
differam, quamvis non audierim frequenter, cum per
totum annum quinquiens sexiensve populo diceret
⟨et⟩[1] ad secretas exercitationes non multi inrump-
erent; quos tamen gratiae suae paenitebat: alius
erat cum turbae se committebat, alius cum paucitate
contentus erat.   Incipiebat enim sedens, et si quando
illum produxerat calor exsurgere audebat.   Illa in-
tempestiva in declamationibus eius philosophia sine
modo tunc et sine fine evagabatur; raro totam
controversiam implebat: non posses dicere divisionem
esse, non posses declamationem; tamquam decla-   267M
mationi multum deerat, tamquam divisioni multum supererat.   Cum populo diceret, omnes vires
suas advocabat et ideo non desinebat.   Saepe decla-

---

[1] *Supplied by Kiessling*

2

BOOK 7

PREFACE

SENECA TO HIS SONS NOVATUS, SENECA AND MELA
GREETINGS

You keep on at me every day about Albucius.   I 1
shall not put you off any longer, though I didn't hear
him very often; in a whole year he would speak five
or six times in public, and on his private exercises few
intruded.   But those who did regretted showing him
this attention;   he was one man when he entrusted
himself to a crowd, another when he contented himself with a small audience.   He used to start off sitting
down, and if his passion carried him on he would
venture to get up.[1]   His celebrated philosophical
observations,[2] which were quite out of place in
declamation, then wandered on without restraint and
without end.   He rarely completed a whole *controversia*;   you couldn't call it a division—or a declamation: for a declamation, it lacked much, for a division
it had much that was superfluous.   But whenever he
spoke in public he used to summon up all his powers,

---

[1] We learn the same from Suet. *Gr. Rhet.* 30.3.
[2] Cf. *C.* 1.3.8; 1.7.17; 7.6.18.

3

mante illo ter bucinavit, dum cupit in omni controversia dicere non quidquid debet dici sed quidquid
potest. Argumentabatur moleste magis quam subtiliter: argumenta enim argumentis colligebat, et,
quasi nihil esset satis firmum, omnes probationes
probationibus aliis confirmabat.

2   Erat et illud in argumentatione vitium, quod
quaestionem non tamquam partem controversiae
sed tamquam controversiam implebat. Omnis
quaestio suam propositionem habebat, suam ex-
secutionem, suos excessus, suas indignationes, epilogum quoque suum. Ita unam controversiam
exponebat, plures dicebat. Quid ergo? non omnis
quaestio per numeros suos implenda est? Quidni?
sed tamquam accessio, non tamquam summa.
Nullum habile membrum est si corpori par est.

Splendor orationis quantus nescio an in ullo
alio fuerit. Non hexis magna, sed phrasis. Dicebat
enim citato et effuso cursu, sed praeparatus. Ex-
temporalis illi facultas, ut adfirmabant qui propius 268M
norant, non deerat, sed putabat ipse sibi deesse.
Sententiae, quas optime Pollio Asinius albas vocabat,
simplices, apertae, nihil occultum, nihil insperatum
3 adferentes, sed vocales et splendidae. Adfectus
efficaciter movit, figurabat egregie, praeparabat

---

[1] The phrase is puzzling. The trumpet blew at the end of
each watch of the night (*vigilia*), and each watch consisted of
three hours. It is difficult, however, to imagine that Albucius
spoke so long, and at night.

and so he didn't stop. Often while he was speaking
the trumpet would blow three times,[1] for in every
controversia it was his wish to say not what ought to be
said but what is capable of being said. He argued
laboriously rather than subtly; he used argument to
prove argument,[2] and as though there were no firm
ground anywhere confirmed all his proofs with further
proofs.

His argumentation had the further fault that he 2
would develop a question not as part of a *controversia*
but as a *controversia*. Every question had its own
statement, its treatment, its digressions, its appeals to
anger, even its epilogue. Thus it was that he set
himself a single theme, but actually spoke a number
of themes. You may ask: shouldn't every question
be developed in all its detail? Of course, but as an
adjunct, not as the whole. No limb is manageable if
it is as large as the body.

He had distinction of style perhaps unequalled by
anyone else. He had no great facility,[3] but consum-
mate diction. For he spoke in a swift onrush, yet
with premeditation. He wasn't without the ability
to extemporise, according to his more familiar friends,
but *he* thought he was. His epigrams, which Asinius
Pollio excellently called " white," [4] were simple,
open, bringing no hidden or unexpected point with
them, merely resonant and brilliant. He was effective 3

---

[2] Or: " amassed argument upon argument."

[3] For *hexis* see Quintilian 10.1.1: it is the assured ability to
compose that arises from constant reading and study.

[4] Perhaps with a pun on the declaimer's name, as a variant
on the usual *candidus* (cf. e.g. Quintilian 10.1.73 on the un-
affected Herodotus).

suspiciose. Nihil est autem tam inimicum quam manifesta praeparatio; apparet enim subesse nescio quid mali. Itaque moderatio [1] est adhibenda, ut sit illa praeparatio, non confessio. Locum beate implebat. Non posses de inopia sermonis Latini queri cum illum audires: tantum orationis cultae fluebat. Numquam se torsit quomodo diceret, sed quid diceret. Sufficiebat illi in quantum voluerat explicandi vis; itaque ipse dicere solebat, cum vellet ostendere non haesitare se in electione verborum: cum rem animus occupavit, verba ambiunt.

Inaequalitatem in illo mirari [2] licebat. Splendidissimus erat; idem res dicebat omnium sordidissimas—acetum et puleium et †dammam et philerotem† [3] lanternas et spongias: nihil putabat esse quod dici in declamatione non posset. Erat autem illa causa: timebat ne scholasticus videretur. Dum alterum vitium devitat, incidebat in alterum, nec videbat nimium illum orationis suae splendorem his admixtis sordibus non defendi sed inquinari; et hoc aequale omnium est, ut vitia sua excusare malint quam effugere. Albucius enim non quomodo non

269M

---

[1] *Warmington suggests* malitiae. Moderatio . . .
[2] inequalitatem—mirari *M:* (i)ndequalitate(m)—mirari non *ABV*.
[3] *These words appear only in the excerpta MSS, and should probably be deleted.*

---

[1] Bornecque compares *C.* 1.2.16 and other places where Albucius gave a " figure " to the whole plan of his declamation.
[2] Cf. *C.* 1 pr. 21: " magis nocent insidiae quae latent."
[3] Cf. Lucr. 1.832: challenged by Cicero, e.g. *Nat. Deor.* 1.8.
[4] Cf. Hor. *Ars Poet.* 311: " verbaque provisam rem non

at rousing emotion, excellent at figures,[1] skilled at allusiveness in his preparation. Now nothing is more prejudicial than obvious preparation:[2] for it makes it clear that something bad lurks beneath. So you must be restrained, so that it remains preparation without lapsing into explicit statement. He could fill out topics lavishly. No-one could complain of the poverty of Latin[3] if he heard Albucius— such was the flow of his polished language. He never agonised over how to say things, merely over what to say. He had the gift of developing a topic to the extent he desired; and so he himself used to say, in order to illustrate his lack of hesitation in the choice of words: "When my mind has taken hold of something, the words come eagerly flocking round."[4]

It was legitimate to be surprised by his unevenness of quality. He was full of polish—yet he could name the most sordid possible things, vinegar and flea-mint and lanterns and sponges: there was nothing, he thought, that one could not mention in a declamation. The reason was this: he was afraid of being thought a 4 schoolman.[5] While avoiding one fault he fell into another, and failed to see that his exceedingly brilliant style was not safeguarded but polluted by the admixture of these vulgarities. And indeed it is equally true of all men that they prefer thinking of excuses for their vices to keeping clear of them.[6] Actually Albucius wasn't seeking to avoid being a

invita sequentur," itself a variant on Cato's "rem tene, verba sequentur."
[5] Both fact and motive are given by Suet. *Gr. Rhet.* 30.3.
[6] Cf. Sen. *Ep.* 116.8: "We prefer excusing our vices to excising them."

esset scholasticus quaerebat, sed quomodo non videretur. Nihil detrahebat ex supervacuo strepitu;
haec sordida verba ad patrocinium aliorum adferebat.
Hoc illi accedebat inconstantia iudicii: quem proxime
dicentem commode audierat imitari volebat.
Memini omnibus illum omissis rebus apud Fabianum
philosophum, tanto iuveniorem quam ipse erat, cum
5 codicibus sedere; memini admiratione Hermagorae
stupentem ad imitationem eius ardescere. Nulla erat
fiducia ingenii sui, et ideo adsidua mutatio; itaque
dum genera dicendi transfert et modo exilis esse volt
nudisque rebus haerere, modo horridus et valens
potius quam cultus, modo brevis et concinnus, modo 270M
nimis se attollit, modo nimis se deprimit, ingenio
suo inlusit et longe deterius senex dixit quam
iuvenis dixerat; nihil enim ad profectum aetas ei
proderat, cum semper studium eius esset novum.
Idiotismos est inter oratorias virtutes res quae raro
procedit; magno enim temperamento opus est et
occasione quadam. Hac virtute varie usus est:
saepe illi bene cessit, saepe decidit. Nec tamen
mirum est si difficulter adprehenditur vitio tam vicina
virtus. Hoc nemo praestitit umquam Gallione nostro
6 decentius. Iam adulescentulus cum declamaret,
apte et convenienter et decenter hoc genere utebatur;
quod eo magis mirabar quia tenera aetas refugit

---

¹ That is, he used the vulgar words to get him off the charge
of being a schoolman that might have resulted from high-
falutin' words; cf. *defendi* above.

8

schoolman—merely being thought one. He wouldn't cut out any of his superfluous noise; these sordid words he brought in to back up others.[1] He was also afflicted by vacillation of taste; he wanted to imitate the last attractive speaker he had heard. I recall him sitting with his notebook at the feet of Fabianus the philosopher, who was so much younger than he, all other business neglected. I recall him breathless 5 with admiration for Hermagoras, burning to imitate him. He had no confidence in his own talents, and so kept chopping and changing. He would swop styles of speech, sometimes wanting to be lean and stick to the bare facts, sometimes bristling and strong rather than pretty, sometimes brief and balanced: sometimes he went too high, sometimes too low. Thus he made a mock of his abilities, and spoke far worse as an old man than he had as a youth. His age made no contribution to his progress, for his enthusiasms were always new. The pursuit of vulgarism [2] is one of the virtues of style that rarely succeeds; one needs great restraint and the right moment. His record in the employment of this quality was variable; he was often successful, often a flop. And it is not surprising that a virtue so close to a fault [3] should not be easy to master. But no-one employed this trick more appropriately than my friend Gallio. Already in his 6 youthful declamations he could use this manner fittingly and suitably and with propriety: I used to be the more surprised because a tender age normally

[2] For its proper use see Quintilian 8.3.21–3.
[3] For the doctrine of neighbouring faults in general, see Adamietz on Quintilian 3.7.25. For its application to style cf. esp. Demetr. *Eloc.* 114.

omne non tantum quod sordidum sed quod sordido simile est.

Raro Albucio respondebat fortuna, semper opinio: quamvis paenituisset audisse, libebat audire. Tristis, sollicitus declamator et qui de dictione sua timeret etiam cum dixisset: usque eo nullum tempus securum illi erat. Haec illum sollicitudo fugavit a foro, et tantum unius figurae crudelis eventus. Nam in quodam iudicio centumvirali, cum diceretur iurisiurandi condicio aliquando delata ab adversario, induxit eiusmodi figuram qua illi omnia crimina 7 regereret. Placet, inquit, tibi rem iureiurando tran- 271M sigi? Iura, sed ego iusiurandum mandabo:[1] iura per patris cineres, qui inconditi sunt, iura per patris memoriam; et executus est locum. Quo perfecto surrexit L. Arruntius ex diverso et ait: accipimus condicionem; iurabit. Clamabat Albucius: non detuli condicionem; schema dixi. Arruntius insta- bat. Centumviri rebus iam ultimis properabant. Albucius clamabat: ista ratione schemata de rerum natura tolluntur. Arruntius aiebat: tollantur; pot- erimus sine illis vivere. Summa rei haec fuit: centumviri dixerunt dare ipsos secundum adver- sarium Albucii si iuraret; ille iuravit. Albucius

---

[1] mandabo *Gertz:* dabo.

shuns everything that resembles vulgarity, let alone vulgarity itself.

Albucius was rarely lucky—but always well thought of. However sorry one was to have been to hear him, one was glad to go again. He was a gloomy, anxious declaimer, one who worried about his performance even at the end of a speech—in fact no moment was free of care for him. And it was this anxiety that drove him away from the forum—and in particular the cruel outcome of one single figure.[1] Once, at a trial in the centumviral court,[2] because he was told that the terms of an oath had on one occasion been prescribed by his adversary, he brought in a figure involving an oath which enabled him to make all the charges recoil on him. " You want," he asked, " to settle the point 7 by means of an oath? Swear—but *I* will dictate the oath. Swear by the unburied ashes of your father. Swear by your father's memory." And he finished the topic. When he had finished, Lucius Arruntius got up on the other side, and said: " We accept the terms, he will swear." Albucius screamed: " I wasn't putting forward terms—I was using a figure." Arruntius insisted. The centumviri were at the end of their business, and in a hurry. Albucius cried: " At this rate figures are banished from the world." Arruntius said: " Let them go: we shall be able to survive without them." The outcome of the matter was this: the centumviri said they would decide for Albucius' opponent if he would swear; he did swear.

[1] This story is told by Suet. *Gr. Rhet.* 30.5 and Quintilian 9.2.95.
[2] Which dealt largely with property cases and became very important under the empire.

non tulit hanc contumeliam, sed iratus calumniam
sibi imposuit: numquam amplius in foro dixit; erat
enim homo summae probitatis, qui nec facere iniuriam
nec pati sciret.

8 Et solebat dicere: Quid habeo quare in foro
dicam, cum plures me domi audiant quam quemquam in foro? Cum volo dico, dico quamdiu volo,
adsum utri volo. Et quamvis non fateretur, delecta- 272M
bat illum in declamationibus quod schemata sine
periculo dicebantur. Nec in scholasticis tamen
effugere contumelias poterat Cestii, mordacissimi
hominis. Cum in quadam controversia dixisset
Albucius: quare calix si cecidit frangitur, spongia
si cecidit non frangitur? aiebat Cestius: ite ad illum
cras; declamabit vobis quare turdi volent, cucurbitae
9 non volent. Cum dixisset Albucius in illa ⟨de⟩ [1]
fratre qui fratrem parricidii damnatum in exarmata
nave dimisit: " inposuit fratrem in culleum ligneum,"
Cestius eandem dicturus sic exposuit controversiam:
quidam fratrem domi a patre damnatum noverca
accusante, cum accepisset ad supplicium, imposuit
in culleum ligneum. Ingens risus omnium secutus
est. Sed nec ipsi bene cessit declamatio; paucas
enim res bonas dixit. Et cum a scholasticis non
laudaretur, nemo, inquit, imponit hos in culleum

---

[1] illa de *Schultingh:* illo.

---

[1] Literally, " inflicted on himself the penalty for *calumnia*,"
i.e. having brought a malicious charge (cf. *C.* 2.1.34 n.). The
self-imposed penalty was not to appear in court—as it would
have been in fact (cf. *Dig.* 3.2.1; A. H. J. Greenidge, *The
Legal Procedure of Cicero's Time* [Oxford, 1901], 468 *seq.*).

Albucius couldn't take this insult; in his anger he condemned himself,[1] and never again spoke in court. For he was a man of the highest integrity, who was incapable of doing an injury—or putting up with one.

In fact, he used to say: " What reason have I to speak in court?—more listen to me at home than listen to anyone else in court. I speak when I like; I speak as long as I like;[2] I appear for whichever party I like." And though he wouldn't admit it, he enjoyed declaiming just because he could use figures without danger. But not even in scholastic exercises could he escape insult from the biting tongue of Cestius. Albucius had said in one *controversia*: " Why is a cup broken if it falls—but not a sponge?" Cestius said: " Go to him tomorrow. He'll give you a declamation on why thrushes fly, but not pumpkins." In the *controversia* on the man who set his parricide brother adrift in a disabled boat, Albucius had said: " He put his brother in a wooden sack."[3] Cestius, about to declaim the same *controversia*, put the theme thus: A man put his brother, who had been convicted privately by his father on a charge made by his step-mother, and whom he had received for punishment, into a wooden sack. Universal shouts of laughter followed; but Cestius too didn't fare well in the declamation— he said few good things. When he got no compliments from the schoolmen, he said: " Why does nobody put these people in a wooden sack and send

[2] In court there were restrictions on the time of speeches (cf. Tac. *Dial.* 19.5). Compare Montanus' remarks on the freedom of declaimers in *C.* 9 pr. 2.

[3] For the sack as part of the equipment for punishing a parricide, see n. on *C.* 3.2.

ligneum, ut perveniant nescio quo terrarum, ubi calices franguntur, spongiae non franguntur?

Video quid velitis: sententias potius audire quam iocos. Fiat: audite sententias in hac ipsa controversia dictas.

I

AB ARCHIPIRATA FILIO DIMISSUS

Mortua quidam uxore, ex qua duos filios habebat, duxit aliam. Alterum ex adulescentibus domi parricidi damnavit; tradidit fratri puniendum: ille exarmato navigio imposuit. Delatus adulescens ad piratas archipirata factus est. Postea pater peregre profectus captus est ab eo et remissus in patriam. Abdicat filium.

1 ALBUCI SILI. De fratre nec iudicare audeo nec loqui: uno nomine ⟨ei⟩[1] et gratias ago et gratulor, quod patrem servare potuit mori iussus. *Tanta*

---

[1] *Supplied by Kiessling.*

---

[1] Cf. *C.* 1 pr. 22.
[2] The " parricide " was attempted murder (cf. §§7 and 26), and from §§8–9, 11 and 15 it would seem that the step-mother was responsible for the charge (cf. 7 pr. 9). This makes an exact parallel with the case of Tarius, who tried his son privately for plotting against his life and invited Augustus to be a member of the tribunal (Sen. *Clem.* 1.15). It seems clear

them somewhere in the world where cups get broken
but not sponges?"

I can see what you want—to hear epigrams, not
jokes.[1] Very well, you may hear the epigrams that
were spoken on this very *controversia*.

1

The Man who was Released by his Son, the Pirate Chief

A man whose wife had died, and who had two
sons by her, married again. He convicted one of
the youths privately for parricide;[2] he handed
him over to the other son to be punished, and the
brother put him on a disabled boat.[3] The youth
drifted into the hands of pirates, and became a
pirate chief. Later the father set out abroad and
was captured by the son and sent back to his
country. He disinherits his other son.

For the son

ALBUCIUS SILUS. I do not venture to judge my 1
brother or speak of him; I thank him and felicitate
him for one and the same reason—that he had it in
him to save his father after being condemned to death

from *Clem.* 1.15.7 (unless Seneca is being merely rhetorical)
that it was still at this date theoretically open to the father to
impose the traditional penalty by drowning in a sack. For
the father's power of domestic jurisdiction see e.g. B. Nicholas,
An Introduction to Roman Law (Oxford, 1962), 67: though
observe Latro's doubts in §16, Glycon's in §26.
[3] The rigging was removed. For this punishment, cf. the
treatment of *delatores* in Plin. *Pan.* 34.5–35.1 (Bonner adds
Caesar's threat in Suet. *Jul.* 66).

tempestate confusus neque aestimare *quicquam neque dispicere potui.* Plura tibi crimina, pater, fortuna torquente, quam quae videris ipse nosse indicabo. Solutum mihi fratrem tradideris an alligatum, nescio: quantum ad meum stuporem attinet, etiam fugere potuit; *nec satis memineram tale ministerium mihi pater an noverca mandasset, ministerium an poenam esse voluisset, vindictam parricidii an parricidium. Insui culleo fratrem iubes? Non possum,* pater. *Non ignoscis? an non credis? Ego contendo ne te quidem posse* si quis tibi dixisset tyrannus: veni, tuis manibus filium insue. In hoc opere potes oculis tuis, potes manibus uti? potes audire inclusi filii gemitum? Si 274M potes, timeo ne innocentem damnaveris; si non potes, quid frater in fratrem non posset patrem 2 testem dedi. Quid accusas quod inpunitatem fratri dederim, quom[1] fato consilium meum victum sit? A me frater ut viveret non impetravit, ut fugeret non impetravit: nihil aliud impetravit quam ut aliter quam in culleo moreretur. Malam causam habeo, ut inter fratres. Ubi spes? In gubernaculo? nulla est. In remigio? ne in hoc quidem est. In

---

[1] quom *Kiessling after Gronovius:* in quo(d).

---

[1] The mental storm (as in the next epigram but one: cf. §§6, 17) that affected the son when he was ordered to punish his brother.

[2] Cf. Ovid's remarks in *C.* 2.2.10. The epigram may be continuous with the next; in any case the "crimes" confessed are the son's actions that showed pity for his brother.

[3] That is, if he could act so cruelly, he is equally capable of

by him.—Bewildered by such a great storm,[1] I could not weigh or discern anything.—I will confess to more crimes,[2] father, under the torture of fortune, than you yourself seem to know of.—I don't know whether you handed my brother over to me free or bound; as far as my confused state was concerned, he could have escaped, even. I couldn't properly recall whether it was my father or my step-mother who had imposed such a task on me, whether they meant it to be a task or a punishment for me, a penalty for parricide or a parricide.—You tell me to have my brother sewn into a sack? I cannot do it, father. Don't you forgive me? Or don't you believe me? My contention is that even you could not do it if some tyrant had said to you: "Come on, sew your son in with your own hands." Can you use your eyes and hands for such a task? Can you bear to hear the groans of your son trapped inside? If you can, I fear that it is an innocent man you have convicted; if you cannot, I have given my father as a witness of what a brother could not do to a brother.[3]—Why do you accuse me of letting my brother go safe when in fact my plan was defeated by chance? My brother did not persuade me to let him live, or to let him escape; he only got me to let him die otherwise than in the sack. I have a bad case, as far as I and my brother are concerned.[4] —What hope has he? In the rudder? There is none there. In the oars? None there, either. In

having convicted his son wrongly; if he could not, he gives support to the case of the disinherited son.

[4] Because he did not wish to save him: but his case is good as regards his father, for he did not wish to disobey orders— cf. below "Am I to justify . . ." (and Gallio in §12).

comite? *nemo repertus est naufragi comes.* In velo? in antemna? *omnia* [paene][1] *instrumenta circumcisa sunt, adminiculum spei nullum* est. *Patri sum excusandus an fratri?* De filio tuo hoc respondeo: Quamdiu in patrio solo morari licet, civis est: proiectus in mare quidquid post exilium et naufragium vel facit vel patitur, ab omni foedere vitae communis abstractus, poenarum eius pars est, non nequitiae opus est. Sed aliis querentibus te ipsum testem dabo, non esse

3 piratam. Ego illi terrae, ego lucis conspectum, ego etiam mortis humanae facultatem abstuli; Fortuna ipsa, quae miserita eius est, nihil tamen illi praeter mare reliquit. "Moriendum est mihi; pater iussit: neque ego te deprecor ne moriar, nec tibi licet non facere quod iussus es. Inter patrem iratum et fratrem moriturum arbitrium pietati tuae necessarium suscipe: sanguinem meum patri 275M refer, culleum mihi remitte; volo mori, sed pura manu tua; *hoc pietatis tuae munus ad inferos perferam, licuisse mihi per fratrem aliter quam parricidae mori."*

4 ASINI POLLIONIS. Aequas mihi praebete aures: dabo vobis etiam damnatum absolvendum. "*Vivit*" inquit "*frater*"; *non* credo. "*Servavit*" inquit "*me*"; *fecisti ut crederem.* Haec est summa rerum gestarum: *in ea domo in qua facile parricidium creditum*

---

[1] *Deleted by C. F. W. Müller and Madvig.*

---

[1] Specifically, become a pirate.
[2] i.e. the pirate.

a companion? No-one has been found to accompany the doomed mariner. In the sail? In the yard-arm? All the gear has been stripped away, there are no grounds for hope.—Am I to justify myself in my father's eyes—or my brother's?—My reply as to your son is this: " As long as he can stay on his native soil, he is a citizen; once he has been cast on the seas, whatever he may do [1] or suffer after exile and ship-wreck, cut off from every convention that binds men's lives together, is part of his punishment, not the action of a wicked man. But if others complain I will bring you yourself as witness that he is no pirate."—*I* 3 deprived him of the sight of land and light, and even of the means to a man's death. Chance itself, though it pitied him, left him nothing besides the sea.—" I must die. My father has ordered it. I do not beg you to save me from death, and you cannot avoid carrying out your orders. You are between an angry father and a brother doomed to die; take the course that family duty demands. Let my father have my blood—but let me escape the sack. I am prepared to die—but without soiling your hands. This is the mark of *your* affection that I shall take to the shades below, that my brother allowed me to die otherwise than as a parricide."

ASINIUS POLLIO. Let me have a fair hearing: I will 4 present you with one [2] who, though convicted, deserves acquittal.—" Your brother is alive." I don't believe it. " He saved me." You have made me believe.[3]—This is the sum of events. In a house where there was ready belief for parricide *I* could not

[3] Because the son knows how affectionate his brother is: cf. §5 Argentarius.

est, ego fratrem occidere non potui, frater patrem.
" Quid mihi cum ista tabula ? Semel mori volo."

Q. HATERI. *Emicabant densis undique nubibus fulmina* et terribili fragore *horridae tempestates absconderant diem:* imbres undique et omnia procellis saevientia; expectat, inquam, parricidam mare. *Intumuerat* subitis tempestatibus *mare iustis quoque navigiis horrendum.* Fateor, fateor, dixi: fratrem tibi, si innocens est, Fortuna, commendo. Inveni relictum etiam a naufragis navigium,[1] fragmentum, infelix [etiam][2] navigaturis omen, quod si quis gubernator vidisset, iter suum distulisset. Naufragus a litore emittitur.

5 MARCELLI AESERNINI. *Habes, inquam, frater, si innocens es, navigium, si nocens, culleum. Non feci parricidium et—quam facile erramus homines!—factum putavi.* Deliberabam an parerem patri: " *frater,*" inquit " *tu primus in domo parricidium facies.*"

ARGENTARI. Quod iusseras factum est: periit 276M frater. "Vivit" inquit " et me dimisit"; bono argumento probatur vivere. Utrasque ad caelum

---

[1] *The words* inveni—navigium *appear in the MSS after* facies (§5): *they were transposed by Kiessling.*
[2] *Deleted by the editor.*

---

[1] The doomed son, seeing the boat, prefers a quick death. The speaker emphasises his own cruelty, to show he obeyed his father (for the embarrassments of such a defence cf. §9).
[2] For another storm cf. *C.* 8.6. This was a favourite topic for declamatory *descriptio* (commented on by [Dion. Hal.] *Rhet.* 10.17). Typical instances are Sen. *Agam.* 466 *seq.*; Curt. 4.3.16 *seq.*; Luc. 5.597 *seq.* The motif is discussed e.g. by M. P. O. Morford, *The Poet Lucan* (Blackwell, 1967), cc. 3–4.

kill my brother—and my brother could not kill my father.—" What have I to do with this plank? I want to die once." [1]

QUINTUS HATERIUS. Everywhere the clouds were thick: from them flashed thunderbolts, and with horrid din dreadful storms had hidden the day; everywhere rain, everything raging with hurricanes. [2] The sea, I said to myself, is waiting for a parricide.—The sea had swollen with sudden squalls; it boded ill even for properly equipped vessels. [3] I confess it, I confess it, I said: " I commend my brother to you, Fortune— if he is innocent." I found a boat ignored even by the shipwrecked, a carcass of a boat, an evil omen for aspiring voyagers, a boat that a helmsman would have taken one look at—and put off his journey. He is sent off from the shore already shipwrecked.

MARCELLUS AESERNINUS. " Brother, you have a 5 boat, if you are innocent—if you are guilty it is no more than a sack." [4]—I committed no parricide— and, so easily do men err, I thought a parricide had been committed. [5]—I was trying to decide whether to obey my father. " Brother," he said, " *you* will be the first parricide in the family."

ARGENTARIUS. Your orders have been carried out. My brother is dead. " He is alive—and has let me go." That is a *good* proof he is alive.—He raised his

---

[3] It is possible that a secondary meaning is " ships sailing in a good cause ": cf. §10 and *S*. 3.2. For the idea of the luck of a ship depending on the character of those sailing in her cf. e.g. [Lys.] 6.19; Hor. *Od.* 3.2.26 *seq.*; Acts 28.4.

[4] Cf. Sen. *Tro.* 510–12: " If fate helps the wretched you have a means to live; if it denies them life, you have a tomb," and the previous note.

[5] By his brother.

manus sustulit: " si nihil umquam impie cogitavi, ⟨si⟩ patrem meum etiam damnatus diligo, di immortales, veri rerum [1] omnium iudices, adeste." Si aliter sentiret, infelicia sibi imprecatus est maria: sic navem suam rexit.

6 BLANDI. *Iacebat in litore navigium, quod etiam integrum infeliciter vexerat. Credam parricidam si tibi proficiscenti navigium suum reddidit. Subito mihi non* sentienti *ferrum cum animo pariter excidit;* torpent manus, *et nescio qua perturbatione tenebrae stupentibus offunduntur oculis. Intellexi quam difficile esset parricidium facere, etiam quod imperaret pater. Ita mihi quae sola miseros in domo nostra respicis, Fortuna, succurras,* ita mihi contingat aut honeste degere [2] aut mori, ita ex domo nostra ego sim ultimus reus, ut ille iurabat meliorem se novercam habuisse quam fratrem.

7 CORNELI HISPANI. Fateor, volui occidere; sed tunc intellexi quam difficile esset parricidium. " Ego " inquit " patrem occidere volui? ne nunc quidem possum." *Pater* noster *navigavit* sereno die, *tranquillo mari, auspicato itinere, integra nave. Quid hoc est? felicius navigavit damnatus quam qui damnaverat.* " Vade " inquit; " patrem te habere mihi non licuit, habebo patronum; revertere." Magnum pietatis

---

[1] veri rerum *Gertz:* uerum.
[2] degere *Heinrich:* dicere.

---

[1] There was no rudder: and he left the direction to the gods.
[2] That is, if the pirate gave his father the " disabled boat " for his return journey: cf. Triarius in §8.
[3] Again, the speaker stresses his own cruelty to show he had not disobeyed.

hands to heaven. " If I have never had any wicked thought, if I love my father even after being convicted, help me, immortal gods, true judges in all things." He prayed that the seas should be cruel to him if his feelings were otherwise; that was how he steered his ship.[1]

BLANDUS. There lay on the shore a boat that even 6 when sound had been an unlucky craft to sail in.—I will believe him a parricide if he gave you his craft when you set out.[2]—Suddenly, without my being conscious of it, I lost my senses—and my sword went at the same time. My hands went limp, my eyes drooped, and an indescribable perturbation drowned them in darkness. I realised how difficult it was to do a parricide—even one that a father ordered.—So may you aid me, Fortune, who alone watch over the wretched in our house; so may I live honestly or die, so may I be the last member of our household to face trial—I declare that he swore he'd found his step-mother more favourable than his brother.[3]

CORNELIUS HISPANUS. I acknowledge it, I wanted 7 to kill him; but then I realised how difficult parricide was.—" Did I want to kill my father? " he [4] said. " Even now I cannot do it."—Our father set sail [5] on a clear day, sea calm, trip well-omened, ship sound. Yet—the condemned man sailed with better fortune than the man who had condemned him.—" Go," he said, " I could not have you as my father—I shall have you as my advocate.[6] Go back."—It is a great

---

[4] The pirate son, after capturing his father.
[5] On his outward voyage: despite the good omens he fell in with pirates.
[6] Cf. Varius Geminus' *colour* in §26.

argumentum filio carus pater etiam post supplicium. *Utrum vobis videtur innocentiam apud piratas didicisse, an ne apud piratas quidem perdidisse?*

ARELLI FUSCI patris. Potuit patrem occidere: 277M ecquem testem timebat? Abdicatus a patre quo me conferam? In maria? Non possum: iratos habeo piratas. Cum traditus est mihi frater imperatumque ut sumerem supplicium, si qua est fides, temptari me putavi an possem parricidium facere.

8 PORCI LATRONIS. *Perieras, pater, nisi in parricidam incidisses.*

TRIARI. In naufragio navigabat. Parum est quod non occidit patrem, immo etiam integra nave dimisit. Etiam pirata dicitur: iterum falso crimine male audit.

CESTI PII. *Erat navigium, immo fuerat,* sed[1] *putre, resolutis compagibus, infelix omen navigationis.* "Insue me culleo: certe sentiam maria, non et videbo." *Scissa quoque vela fecerant sinus et armatas classes naufraga praecesserat ratis: scires navigare qui servaturus esset patrem. O crudelis et pertinax noverca!* post omnia devicta *nihilominus saevit. Maria iam quiescunt, praedones* iam *miserentur,* irati iam *parcunt.* Ibamus praeter sepulchrum matris, ille mortem

---

[1] *The words* etiam integra—fuerat sed *appear in the MSS after* patrem *below. They were transposed by Kiessling.*

sign of filial affection that a son regards his father as
dear even after capital punishment.—Do you think
he learnt his innocent ways from the pirates—or preserved them even in their company? [1]

ARELLIUS FUSCUS SENIOR. He [2] could have killed
his father; had he any witness to fear?—If I am disinherited by my father, where am I to betake myself?
To sea? I cannot—there are angry pirates to fear.—
When my brother was handed to me and I was told to
punish him, I thought (if you can believe me) that I
was being tested out to see whether *I* was capable of
parricide.

PORCIUS LATRO. You would have perished, father, 8
if you hadn't fallen into the hands of a parricide.

TRIARIUS. He was sailing in a wreck.—Not only
did he not kill his father—he even sent him off in a
sound ship.—He is called a pirate, too—slandered by
a false charge all over again.

CESTIUS PIUS. It was, or rather had been, a boat;
but it was rotten, the seams gaping, a bad omen for
the voyage. " Sow me in the sack; at least I shall
feel the sea without having to see it as well."—The
sails, though torn, had billowed out, and the wreck of
a vessel had got ahead even of properly rigged fleets;
you might think the helmsman a man destined to save
his father.—Cruel and stubborn step-mother! All
else has been overcome—*she* still rages. By now the
seas are still, pirates pity, the angry relent.—We went
past our mother's tomb—he fearing death, I fearing

---

[1] The latter, of course: the son was never capable of
parricide.

[2] The pirate son: his pirate companions would not have
told the tale.

timens, ego scelus. Expectate, iudices, an fortuna nobis obiciat[1] scelus. Iacebat navigium pervetus 9 et attritum salo, vix unius capax animae. *Veni ad vos victoriam pulchram petiturus, ut probem me parricidam.* Non occidisti, inquit, fratrem. Noverca, audi[2] iucundissimam vocem: fateor me parri- 278M cidam, occidi fratrem; tutus sum, pater, si hoc probavero? Imposui in exarmatam navem: non est ⟨hoc⟩[3] occidere? Novercae quidem numquam satis privignus occiditur. *Multas rerum natura mortis vias aperuit et multis itineribus fata decurrunt,* et haec est condicio miserrima humani generis, quod nascimur uno modo, multis morimur: laqueus, gladius, praeceps locus, venenum, naufragium, mille aliae mortes insidiantur huic miserrimae animae. Et hoc occidere vocatur, sed diutius. Si quis nunc stat in turba, hoc dicit: huic quisquam parcat, qui fratrem suum 10 occidit et occidisse se probat? Componis in domo par, ut alter scelere sit parricida, alter ministerio. Inpositus est in navem frater. Qualem navem? Scitis nihil esse periculosius quam etiam instructa navigia: parva materia seiungit fata. Quid vero si non ruden- tibus committitur illa anima, non velis, non guber- naculo defenditur? Exarmata navis est, utroque

---

[1] iudices an—obiciat *Müller:* iudiam (uideam *V*)—obiciet.
[2] audi *Gronovius:* audiui.
[3] *Supplied by Kiessling.*

---

[1] The implication is: my story, that follows, will show that Fortune, in favouring the disabled boat, signalled her approval of my brother's action—and my own.

to commit a sin.—Wait to see, judges, whether
fortune reproaches us with a wicked deed.[1]—There
lay the boat, ancient, eaten away by the waves,
scarcely able to hold a single life.—I come before you 9
to win a glorious victory, by proving myself a parricide. "You did not kill your brother." Step-
mother, hear an utterance that will delight you: I
confess I am a parricide, I killed my brother. Am I
safe, father, if I prove this? I put him in a boat
stripped of its rigging; is not this to kill? For a
step-mother a step-son can never be killed enough.
Nature has opened many routes to death, our fates
hasten downwards along countless ways:[2] and this is
mankind's wretched lot, that we have one way to be
born—but many to die: the noose, the sword, a precipice, poison, ship-wreck and a thousand other deaths
lie in wait for this wretched life. This too may be
termed killing—but over a longer period. Someone
in the crowd here must be saying: "Can this man be
spared?—he has killed his brother, and is proving that
he did so."—You are matching a pair of gladiators 10
from within one house—one a parricide by his own
action, the other by the service asked of him.[3]—Yes,
my brother was put on a boat. What sort of a boat?
You know that nothing is more dangerous than a
boat, even an equipped one. It has only a small
width of wood to keep you from your fate.[4] But what
if that life is entrusted to no rigging? What if it is
protected by no sail, no steering? The ship is un-

[2] Cf. *C.* 1.8.6 n.
[3] Part of the narrative, rhetorically addressed to the father.
[4] For this topic see Sen. *Ep.* 49.11 and Mayor on Juv. 12.58,
14.289.

patens latere; inponitur miser in naufragium, navigio
per se pessum ituro pondus insuper ⟨additur⟩.[1]
Ecce navem divinitas armat: subito visa sunt vela,
subito navis coepit erigere se et attollere. Magnum
praesidium in periculis innocentia. Saevum mare
volvitur, procellae spumante impetu latera navigii
urgent, pulsatur undique navis periculis: innocentia 279M
11 tamen tuta est. *O maria iustiora iudiciis! o mitiores
procellae patre!* Quam eiec⟨it is vos servav⟩istis [2]
animam! Nec hoc tantum divinitus gestum est,
quod pervenit tutus in portum: excipitur classe
praedonum. Habet [3] pater mentem navigandi:
capietur iudex ut illum paeniteat sententiae suae.
" Damnare me noverca parricidii potuit; parricidam
facere ne damnando quidem potuit. Cognosce innocentiam meam in mari quam domi noluisti." Com-
plexu, osculis prosecutus est: sic patrem parricida
dimisit ?

12   Iuni Gallionis. Multa non adgnosco: frater domi
damnatus est, ego in publico; illi obiectum est quod
parricidium fecerit, mihi quod non fecerim; ille
negabat, mihi novo patrocinio utendum est: " fratrem occidi "; in ea domo in qua parricidia damnantur
haec innocentia est. Video vos invitos audire hoc
genus defensionis: malo itaque me vobis innocentem
probare quam patri. Fratrem non occidi, non potui

---

[1] insuper additur *Müller:* insui(t).
[2] eiecit is vos servavistis *Hertz:* effecisti(s).
[3] habet *ed.:* habeat.

equipped, gaping on either side. The wretched
youth is put on board a wreck, a further weight is
added to a boat that would founder even of its own
accord. Look, the boat is equipped by heaven;
suddenly sails have appeared, suddenly the ship
begins to ride higher and right itself. Innocence is a
great shield in danger. The sea rolls savagely, hurricanes press the ship's sides with the rush of their
spray, the boat is beaten on every side by dangers;
but innocence is safe. O seas that are more fair than 11
trials! O hurricanes more clement than a father!
You saved a life that *he* cast out.—This was not the
only act of providence, that he came safe to port: he
was picked up by a pirate fleet.[1]—The father takes a
mind to voyage; the judge will be captured, so that
he may repent the verdict he gave.—" My step-
mother was able to get me convicted of parricide: not
even by convicting me could she make me commit
one. Realise my innocence at sea—you refused to at
home." [2]—He saw him on his way with kisses and
embraces. Is that how a parricide let a father go ?

Junius Gallio. There is much that seems new to 12
me. My brother was convicted by a private tribunal,
I am tried in public. He was reproached with committing parricide, I with not committing it. He
denied the charge; I have to use a novel defence: " I
killed my brother." In a house where parricides get
convicted, this counts as innocence. I can see you
are unready to listen to this kind of defence. And so
I prefer to prove myself innocent in your eyes rather
than my father's. I did not kill my brother—I could

---

[1] The point lies in the unexpectedness of the last words.
[2] Words of the pirate son, sparing his father.

fratrem occidere; idem timuimus, idem doluimus, idem flevimus, eundem patrem habuimus, eandem matrem, eandem novercam; mitioris natura pectoris 13 sum, mollioris animi. Non idem omnibus mortalibus natura tribuit ingenium: animus ⟨huius⟩[1] durior est, illius clementior; apud piratas quoque invenitur qui non possit occidere. Putatis me electum ne alius 280M occideret? Si mater nostra viveret, puto, illi tradidisset: quod proximum fuit, mihi tradidit. Utrum vobis videtur per manus fratris punire filium voluisse, an ablegare privignum? Pudet me patrocini mei; timeo, ne, cum coepero narrare quid fecerim, dicatis: certe negabas posse te hominem occidere.

14 MUSAE. Traditus est frater puniendus mihi potissimum. Quo istud proposito, pater, feceris apud plerosque disputationem habet: ego, si quid mitius illo tempore voluisti fieri, non intellexi; imposui multum recusantem et insui culleo postulantem. Obicis mihi molliorem animum: alius mitior est [plus][2] quam debet, alius saevior quam necesse est, mediis alius adfectibus inter utrumque positus totus in sua potestate est. Quidam et accusare et damnare possunt et occidere, quidam tam mites sunt ut non possint in caput ne testimonium quidem dicere.

[1] *Supplied by Faber.*
[2] *Deleted by Müller.*

---

[1] i.e. perhaps my father let me do the punishment *expecting* I would show mercy; cf. §15 " Don't you think that pity . . ." and Passienus' *colour* in §22.

not kill my brother. We had the same fears, the same griefs; we shed the same tears, had the same father, the same mother, the same step-mother. I am, by nature, too gentle-hearted, too soft in temperament. Nature has not given every man the same character. 13 One man's temperament is harsher, another's kinder: even in a pirate fleet there can be found a man incapable of killing.—Do you think that I was chosen to prevent another doing the killing? [1] If our mother had been alive, I suppose, he would have handed him over to her. As it was, he handed him over to me— the nearest he could get.—Do you think he wanted to punish his son by his brother's hand, or to get rid of a step-son? [2]—I am ashamed of my line of defence; I am afraid that when I begin the narration of what I did, you may say: "Surely you said you are incapable of killing a man?"

Musa. My brother was handed over for punish- 14 ment to me, by preference. There is much dispute what your intention was in doing this, father. If you wanted some kinder course taken on that occasion, *I* did not realise it. I put him on the boat struggling wildly and demanding to be sewn in the sack.—You reproach me with too soft a character; some people are gentler than they should be—some harsher than they need be; some, with moderate emotions, and placed between the extremes, are wholly under their own control. Some are capable of accusing, convicting, killing; some are so gentle that they cannot bring themselves to endanger life even by giving evi-

---

[2] i.e. or was it the step-mother who was behind it all? *ablegare* implies that the father did not intend the killing of the son, merely his removal.

THE ELDER SENECA

Non possum hominem occidere: hoc vitium et apud piratas invenitur. Alii vivere sine rei publicae administratione non possunt, aliis in privato latere et extra omnem invidiam secessisse praecipua tranquillitas est, aliis non potest persuaderi ut matrimonio obligentur, aliis ut careant; sunt qui castra timent,
15 sunt qui cicatricibus suis gaudent. In tanta morum varietate videte quantulum sit quod excusem: non ambitioni, non inertiae veniam peto; misericors sum, non possum occidere hominem. Gratulare, pater, naturae meae: numquam eiusmodi filius parricidium faciet. Hoc vitium a te traxisse videor: an *non putatis misericordem qui quem damnavit puniendum fratri dedit? Centurio Luculli Mithridaten non potuit occidere* —dextra simul ac mens elanguit—*pro bone Iuppiter,* 281M *Mithridaten quam non dubium parricidam!*

Pompei Silonis. *Gaude, pater: neuter ex filiis tuis parricidium fecit.* Dimisi a portu naufragum. *Narra, pater, quomodo te dimiserit sic dimissus.* Vis, pater, scire accusator nocentior sit an reus? Conice in alteram navem novercam; illa faciat vota, precetur: si neminem innocentem accusavit, si privignum immerentem non oppressit, in eos piratas incidet qui sciant [1] captos dimittere.

---

[1] sciant *ed.* (sic sciant *Bornecque*)*:* nesciant.

dence in court. *I* am not capable of killing a man; one finds this fault even among pirates. Some cannot live without holding office, others find especial peace in retirement to private life, far from all cause for unpopularity. Some cannot be persuaded to be tied by marriage, others cannot be persuaded to forgo it. Some fear the camp; others revel in their scars. When attitudes are so various, observe how little *I* 15 have to apologise for. I do not have to beg pardon for ambition or lack of ambition. I feel pity—I cannot kill a man. Congratulate me, father, on my temperament; a son like this will never commit parricide. I must have inherited this fault from you —or don't you think that pity influences someone who handed over the son he convicted to be punished by his brother?—Lucullus' centurion could not kill Mithridates—mind and hand were simultaneously paralysed: and Mithridates, heavens above, was a quite undoubted parricide![1]

POMPEIUS SILO. Rejoice, father. Neither of your sons has committed parricide.—I despatched him from the port already wrecked. Tell us, father, how one who was thus despatched despatched *you*.— Father, do you want to find out if the accuser or the accused is the more guilty? Put the step-mother in a second boat; let her make her vows, say her prayers. If she accused no innocent man, if she did not persecute an undeserving step-son, she will fall into the hands of pirates who know how to let captives go.

[1] Cf. *C.* 7.3.4. For the centurion who almost killed Mithridates after the battle of Zela see Appian *Mithr.* 89; for his matricide *ibid.* 112.

16   Altera pars. Musae. Parricida meus in mari regnat.

Sepulli Bassi. *Nega nunc parricidam fuisse quem scis esse piratam.*

Gavi Sabini. Facinus indignum! damnatus parricida post poenam potuit dicere patri suo: "morere."

Divisio. Latro in has quaestiones divisit: an licuerit illi quod iubebat pater facere. Non licet, inquit, fratrem necare; ⟨nec iure⟩[1] ille damnatus erat: non enim iudicio publico ceciderat. Ignosce si diligentior sum cum videam hominem tam facile damnari: timeo ne quis me parricidi postulet—facile est. Si dicenda erit domi causa, etiam nocens absolutionem sperare potero: in foro quid respondebo? "occidi fratrem"? Parricidam me quidam vocant

17 quod non adfui reo. Si licuit, an debuerit. *Nocens est iste, sed mihi frater est. Naturae iura sacra sunt* 282M *etiam apud piratas.* Quid de me tu iudicaturus es si fecero? puto, difficulter postea in me parricidium credes. Etiamsi debuit parere patri, an ignoscendum sit illi si non potuit? Fatebor, inquit, quod fortasse offensurum est aures: [fratrem offensurum est][2] patri parere volui, ⟨volui⟩[3] fratrem occidere, non potui. Obortae sunt subito tenebrae, deriguit animus, sublapsum est intercepto spiritu corpus.

---

[1] *Supplied by Heinrich.*
[2] *These words were rightly deleted in A.*
[3] *Supplied by Thomas; the exact form of this sentence is uncertain.*

The other side

Musa. My parricide son is ruler of the waves.　　16

Sepullius Bassus. Say this man was no parricide
—now that you know he is a pirate.

Gavius Sabinus. What a wicked deed! That a
condemned parricide should have been in a position
after he had been punished to say to his own father:
" Die! "

Division

Latro's division was into the following questions:
Was he allowed to do what his father told him to?
" I am not allowed to kill my brother. He had not
been legally convicted, for he had not lost his case in a
public tribunal. Forgive me if I go into details when
I see a man so easily convicted. I am afraid I may be
accused of parricide: it is so simple. If I have to
plead my case at home before my father, I shall have
hopes of acquittal even if I am guilty. But what shall
I reply in court? ' I killed my brother '? Some
people call me parricide because I did not speak up
for my brother when he was accused." If he was 17
allowed to, should he have? " He is guilty, but he is
my brother. The ties of nature are sacrosanct—even
with pirates. What will your judgement be on *me*
if I do it? I suppose you will find it difficult to
believe *me* a parricide after that." [1] Even if he ought
to have obeyed his father, should he be forgiven if he
could not do it? " I will confess something that may
offend you: I wanted to obey my father, I wanted to
kill my brother—but I could not do it. A sudden
darkness came over me, my mind went numb, my

[1] Ironical.

35

Non possum fratrem occidere. Pone hoc loco piratam: non poterit. Quidam occidere hominem
†tantum† [1] non possunt; quorundam adversus hostes
deficit manus. Fratris quoque beneficium non est
tam magnum, pater, quam putas: non ille te noluit
occidere, sed non potuit. Novissimas illas partes
fecit: quamvis non occiderit, si tamen puniit damnatum, an abdicari non debeat. Dicit enim pater:
si non poteras, negasses, et misisses ad me non posse
18 te. Hoc loco dixit Latro rem valde laudatam:
" *Dixisses* " inquit " *te non posse.*" *Ita tu nesciebas?*
putasti me posse occidere? Quid ergo sic loquebaris
tamquam unum parricidi condemnasses? Deinde,
an punierit fratrem. Hic descriptio supplicii, quod 283M
dixit gravius etiam culleo fuisse, et adiecit hodie
⟨quoque⟩ [2] illum poenas dare inter barbaros inclusum,
per quos necesse est illi patria, populo, lare carere;
sed ne per illos quidem necesse est parricidium
facere.

Hac divisione usi sunt quibus placuit damnati
causam non defendere et tantum suam agere; alia
usi sunt quibus placuit et illius causam defendere,
inter quos et Geminus Varius fuit, qui aiebat adulescentem optimam causam habere si non occidit
fratrem etiam nocentem, meliorem tamen si non
19 occidit innocentem; patitur autem materia. Fecit
ergo has quaestiones Geminus et quibus idem placuit:
an abdicari non debeat, etiamsi nocentem fratrem

---

[1] tantum] cognatum *Müller* (" a relative ").
[2] *Supplied by Müller.*

breath was cut off, my body collapsed. I cannot kill
my brother. Put a pirate in this position: *he* will not
be able to. Some cannot kill a . . . man; some find
their hands fail when they raise them against an
enemy. Even what my brother did for you, father,
is not as great as you think: he didn't *not* want to kill
you—but he could not do it." The final parts Latro
made: Granted he did not carry out the killing, ought
he to be disinherited if he did *punish* the convicted
man? For the father says: " If you couldn't do it,
you should have said so, and sent word to me that you
could not." Here Latro said something that was 18
much admired: " ' You should have said you could
not.' Didn't you know, then? Did you think me
capable of killing? Why then did you talk as if you
had convicted only one son of parricide? " Then:
Did he punish his brother? Here came a description
of the punishment, which, Latro said, was worse even
than the sack. He added that even today he is being
punished, shut up among barbarians who force him to
do without country, people, home: but not even *they*
insist on him committing parricide.

This was the division employed by those who
decided not to defend the case of the convicted son,
but merely to plead the case they were given; a
different one was used by those who wanted to defend
the other son too, among them Varius Geminus, who
said that the youth has an excellent case if he didn't
kill his brother, despite his guilt, but an even better
case if the man he failed to kill was innocent—and the
theme does allow that. So these were the points 19
raised by Geminus and those who were of the same
mind: Ought he to be disinherited even if he failed to

non occidit. Hic dixit: *non licuit, non debui, non potui.* An innocentem non occiderit. Bellam rem hoc loco Geminus dixit, cum coepisset per omnis numeros fratrem tamquam reum defendere: Dicet, inquit, aliquis: " tam sero defendis? " Non potui citius: hodie primum res in forum delata est. Novissime: an etiam nocentem satis punierit.

20   De colore inter maximos et oratores et declamatores disputatum est, utrumne *aliquid deberet dici in novercam* an nihil. Passienus et Albucius et praeter oratores *magna novorum rhetorum manus in hanc partem* 284M *transit;* fuerunt et qui in novercam inveherentur; *fuerunt et illi qui non quidem palam dicerent, sed per suspiciones et figuras, quam rem non probabat Passienus et aiebat minus verecundum esse aut tolerabile infamare novercam quam accusare. Quidam principia tantum habuerunt in sua potestate, deinde ablati sunt impetu. Excusatius est autem in malum colorem incidere quam transire.*

Latro illum introduxit colorem rectum in narratione, quo per totam actionem usus est: non potui occidere. Et cum descripsisset ingenti spiritu titubantem et inter cogitationem fratris occidendi concidentem, dixit: noverca, aliud quaere in privignum tuum crimen; hic parricidium non potest facere.

21   Cestius colore alio usus est. Transiebamus, inquit, secundum matris sepulchrum. Invocare coepit

---

[1] Or " straightforward."

38

kill a guilty brother? Here Geminus said: " It was
not allowed, I should not, I could not." Was the man
he failed to kill in fact innocent? Geminus said a
pretty thing here, after he had started a full defence
of the brother, as though it was he who was on trial:
" Someone will say: Do you defend him so late in the
day? I could not do it sooner; this is the first time
the matter has been brought before the courts."
Finally: Did he punish him sufficiently even if he was
guilty?

The greatest orators and the greatest declaimers 20
were undecided about the *colour*; should any attack
be made on the step-mother? Passienus, Albucius
and, beside the orators, a great party of recent declaimers went into the no lobby. There *were* some
who did inveigh against her, and others who, without
open assaults, employed hints and figures. This displeased Passienus, who said it was more shameful and
intolerable to smear a step-mother than to accuse her.
Some could only keep control of their opening
remarks, then got carried away by the onrush of their
eloquence. However, it is more excusable to come
on a bad *colour* unawares than to make a deliberate
passage to it.

Latro introduced an honourable [1] *colour* in his narration, and used it throughout his speech: " I could not
kill." After describing with great spirit the son
staggering and fainting at the thought of killing his
brother, he said: " Step-mother, look for another
charge against your step-son; *this* man is incapable of
parricide."

Cestius used a different *colour*. " We were passing 21
by our mother's tomb. He began to call on her shades.

39

manes eius. Motus sum. Et puerili sensu colorem
transcucurrit: quid facerem? inquit: occidere pater
iubebat, mater vetabat. Et cum colore dixit: haec
mecum cogitavi: non est imperatum ut manu occiderem, non ut laqueo, non ut mari; eligere supplici
genus liberum est.

Fuscus Arellius hoc colore usus est: temptari
me putavi a patre; uno, inquam, supplicio alterum
filium punire, alterum experiri volt.

Albucius in argumentis plura posuit et omnes fere
colores contrectavit. In narratione hoc colore usus
est: [et]¹ dixit: hoc unum mihi praesta beneficium:
sine me ⟨non⟩ ² tamquam parricidam mori.

22   Argentarius, tamquam non frater esset huius con-   285M
sili inventor, dixit: cogitavi quid facerem; tandem
inveni quomodo parricidium vindicarem sine parricidio.

Passienus hoc colore usus est: Non putavi patrem
velle utique occidi filium. Videbatur mihi omnia
misericordiae praeparasse: quod domi cognoverat,
quod inter suos. Fratri, inquam, tradidit: age, si
parcere uoluisset, cui tradidisset?

Pollio Asinius dixit in novercam; itaque illo colore
usus est: cogitavi mecum quid liceret, quid oporteret.
Si tantum, inquam, nefas commissum est, nullae
meae partes sunt: ad expiandum scelus triumviris

¹ Deleted by the editor.
² Supplied by Faber.

----

¹ Cf. above §§2, 3.

40

I was moved." And he raced over the *colour* with a childish idea: " What was I to do? My father was ordering me to kill, my mother was forbidding me." He also used a *colour* to say: " These were my thoughts: I wasn't ordered to kill by hand, with a noose, with the sea; I am free to choose the method of execution."

Arellius Fuscus used this *colour*: " I thought I was being tested out by my father. ' He wants to use a single penalty to punish one of his sons and test out the other.' "

Albucius put a good deal into the proofs, and touched on virtually all *colours*. In his narration he used this one: " He said: ' Grant me this one boon: allow me to die—otherwise than as a parricide.' " [1]

Argentarius said—as though it wasn't the con- 22 demned brother who was the author of the plan: " I wondered what to do: at last I found a way of punishing parricide without committing it."

Passienus used this *colour*: " I didn't think my father really wanted his son killed. I thought he had made every preparation to show clemency, for he had held the trial at home and among relatives. ' He handed him over to his brother,' I said to myself. ' Well, if he had wanted him spared, whom *would* he have handed him to?' " [2]

Asinius Pollio attacked the step-mother, and so used the *colour*: " I pondered what I could do, what I ought to do. If, I said to myself, so great a crime has been committed, it's no affair of mine. To expiate wicked deeds one requires triumvirs,[3] the place of

[2] Answer: to me. Cf. §13.
[3] The *tresviri capitales*, who carried out death-sentences.

opus est, comitio, carnifice. Tanti sceleris non magis privatum potest esse supplicium quam iudicium.

Marcellus dixit: ita si iste parricidium fecit, ideo et ego faciam? et illam quam supra sententiam rettuli: habes, inquam, frater.

23 Varius Geminus et ipse dixit: nolui occidere. Egregie, inquam, noverca inter privignos divisit odium; aliter alium adgressa est: alteri parricidium obicit, alteri mandat. Et hac illum figura defendit in narratione: Interrogavi fratrem: Apud quem praetorem causam dixisti? " Apud nullum " inquit. Quis accusator fuit? " Nemo." Quis testis? immo qui testes? uni enim etiam de minore scelere non creditur. " Nemo " inquit. Quis de te pronuntiavit? " Nemo. Quid porro? " inquit " ego si reus fuissem, ad te non misissem? "

Sepullius Bassus hoc colore usus est: non habui parricidae instrumenta, non culleum, non serpentes: parricidam tamen in maria proieci.

24 *Hispanus duro colore usus* est: *Hoc, inquit, supplicium* 286M *tamquam gravius elegi.* Quid? iste, inquam, insuetur et statim omnem sensum supplici effugiet? Immo sollicitus pendeat et, quod ne insuti quidem parricidae patiuntur, ipse poenam suam spectet; nihil speret, timeat omnia. Peius debet quam ceteri parricidae mori: a patre damnatus est. Et hoc

---

[1] §5.
[2] To ask for help: the idea is that the son was not properly tried (cf. Latro in §16).
[3] One element, at least, of the traditional punishment.

assembly, the executioner. For such a great crime the punishment can be no more private than the trial."

Marcellus said: " So if *he* did a parricide, must *I* do one too ? " He also spoke the epigram I mentioned above: [1] " Brother, you have . . ."

Varius Geminus, too, said: " I didn't want to kill. 23 I said to myself: our step-mother has made an excellent division of her hatred between her step-sons; she has attacked each in a different way, reproaching one with parricide, and enjoining parricide on the other." And he used this figure to defend him in his narration: " I asked my brother before which praetor he had pleaded his case. ' None,' he said. ' Who was the accuser ? ' ' No-one.' ' Who was the witness ?—or rather witnesses, for a single one isn't believed even on a lesser charge.' ' No-one.' ' Who passed sentence on you ? ' ' No-one. Why go on ? If I had been on trial, wouldn't I have let you know ? ' " [2]

This was Sepullius Bassus' *colour*: " I didn't have the equipment for a parricide—the sack and the serpents. But I *did* throw the parricide to the mercy of the seas." [3]

Hispanus used a harsh *colour*. " I chose this 24 punishment because it was crueller. Shall he, I said to myself, be sewn up in a sack and immediately lose all perception of his punishment ? Rather let him be anxious and in suspense; let him be a spectator of his own penalty—something not even parricides in sacks suffer. Let him have no hope, every fear. He deserves a worse death than other parricides; it was his father who convicted him." And the *colour* he

43

colore per totam declamationem usus est, ut diceret hoc se tamquam gravius elegisse. *Displicebat color hic prudentibus. Quam enim spem habet absolutionis si nec paruit nec pepercit?*

Haterius hoc colore usus est: Diu mecum disputavi. Parricida est quem non testis protrahit, non index coarguit? Quid ergo? innocens ⟨est⟩ [1] quem condemnat pater? Invenioque poenam simillimam rei: [2] mersam, non tamen ex toto perditam ratem, quae vel punire fratrem posset vel absolvere.

25 Triarius et ipse quasi sententiam de fratre ferri voluisset egit et dixit: tandem ad caelum manibus levatis " quidquid est " inquam " quod terris imperat, quod regnat profundo, quidquid est quod ex sublimi res spectat humanas, invoco: damnatus alto committitur; di, iudicate post patrem!" Haec sententia dicebatur ex Graeco translata, sed Graeca corruptior est: Πόσειδον, ἀμετρήτων δέσποτα βυθῶν, τὴν ἐνάλιον κληρωσάμενε βασιλείαν, ἀνάγεται πατροκτόνος· μετὰ πατέρα δίκασον.

A parte patris, quod ab archipirata dimissus est, 287M sic Cestius: poenam, inquit, putavit mihi hanc esse morte graviorem. Et sic posuit in narratione: rogabam ut occiderer; non impetravi.

26 Varius Geminus ait: in hoc *me dimisit*, non quia

---

[1] *Supplied by Gertz.*
[2] rei *Otto:* reo.

used all through his declamation was to say he had
chosen this method as being harsher. Men of dis-
cernment were displeased by this *colour*: what hope
of acquittal has he if he neither obeyed his father nor
showed mercy to his brother?

Haterius used this *colour*: " I disputed with myself
for a long while. Is he a parricide whom no witness
tells on, no informer denounces? But then is he
innocent whom a father condemns? And I found a
penalty very suitable for the situation: a boat that
had been sunk but not altogether destroyed, that
could either punish my brother or acquit him."

Triarius, too, pleaded as though he had wished a 25
verdict to be passed on the brother. He said:
" Finally, raising my hands to the heavens, I said:
Whatever it is that reigns on earth, whatever it is that
rules the deep, whatever it is that from on high looks
on the affairs of man, I invoke it. The condemned
man is entrusted to the deep. Gods, do you judge,
now that his father has judged! " This epigram was
a translation from the Greek; but the Greek is in
worse taste: " Poseidon, master of the measureless
depths, who drew by lot the kingdom of the sea,[1] the
parricide is setting sail; judge, now that his father
has judged."

On the father's side, as to the release of the father
by the pirate chief Cestius said: " He thought that
this was a harsher punishment for me than death."
And he similarly put into the narration the words:
" I asked to be killed; I did not have my wish
granted."

Varius Geminus said: " He let me go not because 26

[1] When the three sons of Kronos divided up the world.

45

me volebat salvum esse, sed *ad patrocinium suum, ut, quia non* nunc *occiderat, videretur nec ante voluisse.*

Latro dixit: *quis porro me uno miserior est,* qui *vitam parricidae debeo?*

Diocles Carystius elegantem sensum in prooemio posuit pro adulescente cum diceret causas se abdicationis non invenire, luxuriae se occasionem non habuisse, parricidium sibi non obici, etiam contrario se nomine laborare: fortasse, inquit, queritur quod captum non redemerim. Adiecit: οὐκ ἔδει [1] λύτρων· παῖς ἦν. Et cum tractaret in ultima parte debere patrem etiam vitia liberorum ferre, utique in unico, adiecit: πεπείρασαι, πάτερ, ὅτι καὶ πονηρὸς ἐνίοτε υἱός ἐστιν εὔχρηστος.

Artemo in descriptione tempestatis laudatus est; et belle accessit ad eam: τὴν τοῦ εὐπλοήσαντος ἀναγωγὴν ἄκουσον, et cum de ipso navigio diceret, pulchre coepit: σκάφος ἔρημον, ἀνόστου τύχης, et ultimam descriptionis sententiam proposuit: ναυαγὸς ἀπὸ λιμένων ἀνήχθη,[2] et ad partem narrationis eleganter transit: διήγησαι νῦν, πάτερ, πῶς ⟨σ'⟩ ἀπέλυσεν οὕτως ἀπολυθείς.

288M

Glycon dixit: ἰδία κριτοῦ ἑνὸς οὐκ ἀρκεῖ καταδίκη· [3] ἐπὶ ναυαγίᾳ εἰς ναῦν ἐστεθείς· [4] εὑρίσκει τὸ μηδὲν ἀδικεῖν τύχην.

---

[1] ἔδει *ed.:* ΕϹΙΧΕ.
[2] ἀνήχθη *Gertz:* ΑΝΝΧΟΝ.
[3] ἰδία—καταδίκη *Gertz:* ΙΑΕΑ—ΚΑΤΑΜΚΝ.
[4] *If this sentence is correctly restored, it is not complete.*

he wanted me to be safe, but with an eye to his own defence —hoping that, because he hadn't killed me on this occasion, he might be thought not to have wanted to before either."

Latro said: " Who, moreover, is more wretched than I alone, who owe my life to a parricide ? "

Diocles of Carystos, for the youth, placed a choice idea in his proem: he said he could find no grounds for disinheritance; he had had no opportunity for debauchery, he was not being reproached with parricide, in fact the charge that he was faced with was quite the opposite. " Perhaps," he said, " his complaint is that I did not ransom him when he was captured." He added: " He needed no ransom-money: it was his son." And when he was at the end of his speech, handling the point that a father ought to put up even with the faults of his children, particularly an only child, he added: " You have learned by experience, father, that sometimes even a wicked son has his uses."

Artemo was praised for his description of a storm. He passed to it elegantly: " Hear now how the lucky sailor put to sea." And when he was talking of the actual boat, he started nicely: " A boat that had been abandoned, fated never to return home." And the last epigram in his description was: " He left the harbour a wrecked man." He made a neat transition to one part of his narrative: " Tell us now, father, how it was that one who set sail thus set you—free." [1]

Glycon said: " The private judgement of a single judge is insufficient.—. . . set on board ship to suffer shipwreck . . .—Innocence finds good fortune."

[1] So, in Latin, in §15.

27   Soleo dicere vobis Cestium Latinorum verborum
inopia ⟨ut⟩ [1] hominem Graecum laborasse, sensibus
abundasse; itaque, quotiens latius aliquid describere
ausus est, totiens substitit, utique cum se ad imitationem magni alicuius ingeni derexerat, sicut in
hac controversia fecit. Nam in narratione, cum
fratrem traditum sibi describeret, placuit sibi in
hac explicatione una et infelici: nox erat concubia,
et omnia, iudices, canentia ⟨sub⟩ [2] sideribus muta
erant. Montanus Iulius, qui comes fuit ⟨Tiberii⟩,[3]
egregius poeta, aiebat illum imitari voluisse Vergili
descriptionem:

> nox erat et terras animalia fessa per omnis,
> alituum pecudumque genus, sopor altus habebat.

At Vergilio imitationem bene cessisse, qui illos
optimos versus Varronis expressisset in melius:

> desierant latrare canes urbesque silebant;
> omnia noctis erant placida composta quiete.

Solebat Ovidius de his versibus dicere potuisse fieri 289M
longe meliores si secundi versus ultima pars absci-
deretur et sic desineret:

> omnia noctis erant.

---

[1] *Supplied by Müller.*
[2] *Supplied by Schultingh.*
[3] *Supplied by Kiessling.*

48

I often tell you that Cestius, being a Greek, was 27
handicapped by a lack of Latin words, while over-
flowing with ideas. And so, whenever he ventured
on some more extravagant sweep of description, he
would get stuck, especially when he had set himself
to imitate some great genius. This is what happened
in our present *controversia*. In his narration, when he
was describing how his brother was handed over to
him, he was satisfied with this one unhappy vignette:
" It was dead of night, and all singing things, judges,
were silent beneath the stars." Julius Montanus,
who was a friend of Tiberius and an outstanding poet,
said that Cestius had intended to imitate Virgil's
description:

" It was night, and over all the earth tired crea-
    tures,
  Birds and beasts, were held in deep sleep." [1]

Virgil, however, had (according to Montanus) been
fortunate in *his* imitation, for he had rendered for the
better those excellent lines of Varro:

" Dogs had ceased to bark, the cities were still,
  Everything was settled in the quiet calm of night." [2]

Ovid used to say of these verses that they could have
been much better if the last part of the second line
were cut out and it finished thus:

" Everything was of night." [3]

[1] *Aen.* 8.26–7.
[2] Varro Atacinus frg. 8 Morel; the first line is also quoted
by Sen. *Ep.* 56.6. Varro was translating Apoll. Rhod.
3.749–50.
[3] A typically Ovidian turn of phrase; cf. *Met.* 1.292:
" omnia pontus erat."

49

Varro quem voluit sensum optime explicuit, Ovidius in illius versu suum sensum invenit; aliud enim intercisus versus significaturus est, aliud totus significat.

II

Popillius Ciceronis Interfector

De moribus sit actio.

Popillium parricidii reum Cicero defendit; absolutus est. Proscriptum Ciceronem ab Antonio missus occidit Popillius et caput eius ad Antonium rettulit. Accusatur de moribus.

1   Bassi Sepulli. Si accusasset Cicero Popillium, viveret. *Occidit Ciceronem Popillius:* puto, *iam creditis occisum ab isto patrem.* Ut uno ictu pereat, tantum dabo: pro Cicerone sic liceat pacisci?

Gavi Sabini. Quod unum potuimus effecimus, ut veniret tempus quo Popillius Ciceronem desideraret.

---

[1] There was an *actio de moribus* at Rome, but it was restricted to divorce cases. Bonner (p. 124) suggests that " the position envisaged may be that of the summoning of Popillius by the censors." Compare also *RLM* p. 349.36.

Varro developed the idea *he* wanted excellently, while Ovid found in Varro's verse an idea of his own. The abbreviated line will mean something different from the complete one.

2

POPILLIUS, KILLER OF CICERO

An action may lie for misconduct.[1]

Cicero defended Popillius on a charge of parricide; he was acquitted. When Cicero was proscribed, Popillius was sent by Antony to kill him, and he brought back his head to Antony. He is accused of misconduct.[2]

Against Popillius

SEPULLIUS BASSUS. If Cicero had *accused* Popillius, he[3] would still be alive.—Popillius killed Cicero; I imagine you are now prepared to believe that he killed his father.—" I will give such-and-such an amount for his death at a single blow ":[4] may one bargain thus for Cicero?

GAVIUS SABINUS. We have done the only thing in our power—ensured that a time came when Popillius

---

[2] The accusation is imaginary, like Cicero's defence of Popillius for parricide (see §8). Our sources are more certain than Seneca himself was that Popillius did kill Cicero: for the evidence (including *S.* 6.20) see M. Gelzer, *Cicero* (Wiesbaden, 1969), 408. For more on the last days of Cicero, see *S.* 6–7.

[3] i.e. Cicero—Popillius would have been convicted.

[4] These words allude to Cicero's own in *Verr.* 5.118, where he pictures Verres' lictor saying to a Sicilian: " Ut uno ictu securis adferam mortem filio tuo, quid dabis? "

" Popilli, potes " inquit " Ciceronem occidere; potes vel patrem."

PORCI LATRONIS. Prorsus *occisurus Ciceronem debebat incipere a patre.* " *Antonius* " inquit " me *iussit.*" *Non pudet te, Popilli? Imperator te tuus credidit posse parricidium facere. Abscidit caput, amputavit manum,* 290M effecit ut *minimum in illo esset crimen quod Ciceronem occidit.* Facinus indignum! Felicissime licet cedat actio, id solum proficiemus, ut qui Ciceronem occidit tantum erubescat. *Pro di boni! occisum Ciceronem malos mores voco.*

2   ALBUCI SILI. Caedit cervices tanti viri et umero tenus recisum amputat caput. I nunc et nega te parricidam. *Hoc unum* tamen *feliciter* fecisti, *quod ante occidisti patrem quam Ciceronem. Facilius pro parricida iudicem movit quam pro se clientem. Ad vos hoc, patroni, exemplum pertinet: nullos magis odit Popillius quam quibus plurimum debet.* Ubicumque estis, iudices, qui in istum reum sederatis, ecquid paenitet absolvisse?

ARGENTARI. Impius est, ingratus est, audeo dicere: parricida; sensit qui defenderat. Respice forum: hic sub Cicerone sedisti; respice rostra: hic supra Ciceronem stetisti. Quantum eloquentia

---

[1] To defend him on this charge: cf. §5 " Nor do I despair . . ."

[2] i.e. Antony.

[3] It may be relevant that Cicero was named *pater patriae* for his suppression of Catiline. But the main idea is that of " working up " to a major crime via lesser ones (for which see 7.3.1 n.).

felt the need of Cicero.[1]—" Popillius," he [2] said,
" you are capable of killing Cicero—you are capable
of killing even your father."

PORCIUS LATRO. Since he was destined to kill
Cicero, he obviously had to start with his own father.[3]
—" Antony ordered me to." Aren't you ashamed,
Popillius? Your general thought you capable of
parricide.—He cut off his head, severed his hand,
made sure the least of his crimes would be to have
killed Cicero.—What an outrage! However successfully the suit goes for us, our only gain will be that
Cicero's killer merely—blushes.—Good God, that I
should call the death of Cicero " misconduct "!

ALBUCIUS SILUS. He struck the neck of the great 2
man, cut it right through to the shoulder and
removed the head. *Now* go and say you are no
parricide!—Your only fortunate act was to kill your
father before you killed Cicero.[4]—Cicero found it
easier to move the judge on behalf of a parricide than
to move his client on behalf of himself.—This is a
precedent affecting you, defence-counsel; Popillius
hates no-one more than those to whom he owes most.
—Wherever you are, judges who sat in trial on this
defendant, aren't you sorry you acquitted him?

ARGENTARIUS. He is wicked, ungrateful and, I
dare to say it, a parricide; his counsel has felt to his
cost how true that is.—Look at the forum: here you
sat at Cicero's feet.[5] Look at the rostra: here you
stood over Cicero.[6]—How powerful was Cicero's

---

[4] Who was thus alive to defend you.

[5] While he defended you.

[6] Cicero's hands and head were displayed on the *rostra* in
the forum (see e.g. *S.* 6.26).

tua, Cicero, potuit! Popillius de moribus reus est. *Abscidit cervices* loquentis: haec est absoluti clientis post longum tempus salutatio. *Parce iam*, quaeso, *Popilli: nihil tibi nisi occidendum* Ciceronem *mandavit Antonius.* Duo fecit parricidia, quorum alterum audistis, alterum vidistis.

3 Cesti Pii. Si dixero: " adulescentia turpis est, infamis pueritia," respondebit: iam ista Cicero defendit. Non *pudet ⟨te⟩*,[1] *Popilli? accusator tuus vivit.* " Quid tam commune quam spiritus vivis, terra mortuis, mare fluctuantibus, litus eiectis ? " Parricida, sic etiam tu perisses.   291M

Fulvi Sparsi. *Non credidisset Popillium facturum Antonius nisi in mentem illi venisset illum* et *parricidium fecisse.* Facinus indignum! A me defenditur Cicero, cum Popillium Cicero defenderit.

Mentonis. Non magis quisquam alius occidere Ciceronem potuit praeter Popillium ⟨quam quisquam alius Popillium⟩ [2] praeter Ciceronem defendere. Parricidam quom vivos negarit Cicero, occisus ostendit. Fortunam Ciceronis! Antonius illum proscripsit, qui accusatus est, Popillius occidit, qui defensus est. Si damnatus esses, carnifex te culleo totum [3] insuisset. Video quid respondeat: non credet Antonius occisum Ciceronem a Popillio nisi ei signum attulerit.

---

[1] *Supplied by Müller and Gertz (comparing E).*
[2] *Supplied by Thomas.*
[3] totum *V, Shackleton Bailey:* teo tum *AB.*

---

[1] i.e. but for Cicero's skill, Popillius would not have lived to be tried on this charge.
[2] Famous words of Cicero from the early speech for Sextus Roscius (72), describing elements foregone by the parricide

eloquence! Popillius is charged with misconduct.[1]—
He cut Cicero's neck while he was still speaking; this
is the greetings an acquitted client gives after a long
interval.—Stop there, please, Popillius; Antony
merely told you to kill Cicero.—He has done two
parricides: you have heard tell of one, seen the other.

CESTIUS PIUS. If I say: " Your adolescence is 3
shameful, your boyhood a disgrace," he will reply:
" Cicero has already defended that."—Do you feel
no shame, Popillius? It is your *accuser* who still lives.
—" What is so commonly shared as breath by the
living, earth by the dead, sea by the storm-tossed,
shore by those cast up? " [2] Parricide, you too
would have died like that.

FULVIUS SPARSUS. Antony would not have believed
Popillius would do it if he hadn't recalled that he had
also done a parricide.—What an outrage! I have to
defend Cicero—yet Cicero defended Popillius.

MENTO. No-one but Popillius could have killed
Cicero—just as no-one but Cicero could have defended
Popillius.—The man who the living Cicero said was
no parricide was shown to be one by Cicero dead.—
What luck Cicero had! Antony, who had proscribed
him, he had accused; Popillius, who killed him,
he had defended.—If you had been convicted, the
executioner would have sewn you in the sack unmutilated.—I see what he may reply: " Antony will
not believe that Popillius killed Cicero unless he takes
him back a proof."

undergoing punishment. Cicero himself criticised them in
Orat. 107 (cf. Quintilian 12.6.4). They are imitated in *Decl.*
p. 181 Ritter. When Cestius says " like that," he means:
" in the manner alluded to in that passage of Cicero."

4 TRIARI. Praesta Ciceroni quod propinqui Catilinae, quod amici Verris, quod ⟨clientes Clodi⟩[1] praestiterunt: proscriptum transi. Ne a mortuo quidem manus abstinet, lacerat occisum. Popilli, hoc parricidium tertium tuum est.

POMPEI SILONIS. Numquid magis exonerare te possum? praesta Ciceroni quod Antonius.

CORNELI HISPANI. Dic: Antoni, ego istud scelus facere possum: et patrem occidi. Securi erant amici Ciceronis postquam ad illum Popillius missus est.

ARELLI FUSCI patris. Potuisti Ciceronem occidere? At quam nobis bene persuaserat Cicero parricidium te facere non posse! Occidisti tu Ciceronem loquentem: numquid, inquit, est aliquis ex tuis verendus index? an nemo Ciceroni timendus est qui cum Popillio venit? 292M

5 Q. HATERI. Qui modo Italiae umeris relatus est, nunc sic a Popillio refertur? Proposito in rostris capite Ciceronis, quamvis omnia metu tenerentur, gemitus tamen populi liber fuit.

IULI BASSI. " Proscriptus " inquit " erat Cicero." Pater certe tuus proscriptus non fuit.

BLANDI. *Di manes Popilli senis et inultae patris, Cicero, te persecuntur animae, ut quem negasti parricidam sentias.*

CAPITONIS. Deduxi ad vos reum omnium quos terra sustinet nocentissimum, ingratum, inpium,

¹ *Supplied by Kiessling.*

¹ i.e. the intimates of Cicero's worst enemies spared him: why should a friend harm him?
² Popillius is asked to kill without mutilation, as Antony had ordered (for Antony requiring mutilation, however, see §12).

56

TRIARIUS. Grant Cicero the boon that Catiline's 4
relatives, Verres' friends, Clodius' clients granted
him:[1] now that he is proscribed, pass him by.—His
hand spares not even the dead—it mutilates the man
it has killed. Popillius, this is your third parricide.

POMPEIUS SILO. Can I lighten your burden further? Give Cicero what Antony gave him.[2]

CORNELIUS HISPANUS. Say: "Antony, I can do this
deed; I killed my father too."—Cicero's friends were
unworried when it was Popillius who was sent to him.

ARELLIUS FUSCUS SENIOR. Were you capable of
killing Cicero? Yet how well Cicero had persuaded
us that you could not commit parricide!—You killed
Cicero as he said: " Need you fear that any of your
companions will inform on you?[3] Or should Cicero
fear no-one who comes in the company of Popillius? "

QUINTUS HATERIUS. Once he was carried back on 5
the shoulders of Italy;[4] is he now carried back by
Popillius—thus?—When Cicero's head was displayed
on the rostra, though fear gripped all, yet the groans
of the people were free.[5]

JULIUS BASSUS. " Cicero had been proscribed."
Surely your father had not.

BLANDUS. The ghost of the elder Popillius, the un-
avenged spirit of his father, harry you, Cicero, so that
you may feel the blow of one you said was no parricide.

CAPITO. I have brought before you a defendant
who is the most guilty man alive on earth, ungrateful,

---

[3] If, that is, he let Cicero go (as Latro suggests in §9).

[4] Allusion to Cicero's triumphal return from exile in 57 B.C.
(cf. *post Red.* 39).

[5] Haterius here quotes Cicero's own words (*Phil.* 2.64).

percussorem, bis parricidam; nec tamen timeo; patroni viderint: nemo a Popillio nisi post beneficium occiditur. Ne damnationem quidem istius despero; non enim a Cicerone defenditur. Timeo ne causae non satis faciam. Maior causa est occisum a Popillio Ciceronem queri quam fuit aliquando pro-
6 bare non occisum patrem. Ciceronem quisquam potuit occidere qui audiit ? *Minturnensis palus exulem Marium non hausit; Cimber etiam in capto vidit imperantem;* praetor iter a conspectu exulis flexit; qui in crepidine viderat Marium in sella figuravit. Non possumus de Popillio queri: eodem loco patronum habuit quo patrem. *Cn. Pompeius terrarum marisque domitor Hortensi se clientem libenter professus est; et Hortensius bona Pompei, non Pompeium defenderat.* Romulus, horum moenium conditor et sacratus caelo parens, non tantam urbem fecit quantam Cicero
7 servavit. Metullus Vestae extinxit incendium, Cicero 293M Romae. Glorietur devicto [1] Hannibale Scipio, Pyrrho Fabricius, Antiocho alter Scipio, Perse Paulus, Spartaco Crassus, Sertorio et Mithridate Pompeius: nemo hostis Catilina propius accessit. Fertur ad-

---

[1] devicto *Bursian:* reuocato.

---

[1] In the sense that the crime is even more outrageous and incredible.
[2] Cf. *C.* 1.1.3. For Marius' adventures in 88 B.C. see e.g. Vell. Pat. 2.19, Val. Max. 2.10.6. The German slave sent to kill him recognised him because he had been imprisoned by him in the Cimbric wars. According to Plut. *Mar.* 40.3 *seq.* Sextilius, praetor of Africa, banned Marius from entering the province.

wicked, an assassin and double parricide. But *I* have no fears—it is his defence counsel who should beware: Popillius only kills those who do him a service. Nor do I despair of his being convicted; he isn't being defended by Cicero.—I fear I may not do the case justice. It is a more serious matter [1] to complain of Cicero's killing at the hands of Popillius than it was in time past to prove that he did not kill his father.— Could anyone who had heard Cicero speak bear to kill 6 him? The marsh of Minturnae did not engulf the exiled Marius; [2] the German saw the general even in the guise of a captive; the praetor diverted his course to avoid seeing the exile; one who had seen Marius in the gutter thought of him as he was in his official seat. —We cannot complain of Popillius; he treated his defender as he had treated his father.—Pompey, conqueror on land and sea, willingly avowed himself Hortensius' client; and Hortensius had defended Pompey's property, not his person.[3]—Romulus, founder of these walls and deified parent of our city, did not make the city so great as it was when Cicero saved it.[4]—Metellus put out the fire in the temple of 7 Vesta,[5] Cicero the fire in Rome. Let Scipio glory in the defeat of Hannibal, let Fabricius triumph over Pyrrhus, the second Scipio over Antiochus, Paulus over Perses, Crassus over Spartacus, Pompey over Sertorius and Mithridates. No enemy came closer [6]

[3] For this defence (86 B.C.) see Cic. *Brut.* 230.
[4] From Catiline in 63 B.C., when the burning of Rome was threatened.
[5] See *C.* 4.2.
[6] i.e. to Rome; all the other enemies stopped short of the city.

prensum coma caput et defluente sanguine hunc
ipsum inquinat locum in quo pro Popillio dixerat.

BUTEONIS. Quanta est vis[1] eloquentiae! probavit
ab eo non occisum patrem a quo occidi poterat etiam
Cicero.

MARULLI. Si inimicus essem patronis, optarem
ut reus absolveretur. Turpe iudico in ea civitate
Ciceronem non defendi in qua defendi potuit etiam
Popillius.

8 *Popillium pauci ex historicis tradiderunt interfectorem
Ciceronis et hi quoque non parricidi reum a Cicerone
defensum, sed in privato iudicio:* declamatoribus placuit
parricidi reum fuisse. Sic autem eum accusant tamquam defendi non possit, cum adeo possit absolvi ut
ne accusari quidem potuerit.

Latroni non placebat illum sic accusari quomodo
quidam accusaverunt: obicio tibi quod occidisti
hominem, quod civem, quod senatorem, quod con-
sularem, quod Ciceronem, quod patronum tuum.
Hac enim ratione non adgravari indignationem sed
fatigari. Statim illo veniendum est ad quod properat
auditor; nam in reliquis adeo bonam causam habet
Popillius ut, detracto eo quod patronum occidit, nihil
negoti habiturus sit; patrocinium eius est civilis belli 294
necessitas. Itaque nolo per illos reum gradus
ducere quos potest tutus evadere. Licuit enim in
bello et hominem et[2] civem et senatorem et consu-

---

[1] quanta est vis *Gertz:* quanta(e) fuit.
[2] hominem et *Gertz:* cum *AB (om. V).*

than Catiline.—He carried the head by the hair, and with the dripping blood polluted this very spot where it had spoken for Popillius.

BUTEO. How mighty is eloquence! It proved that the man who could kill even Cicero did not kill his own father.

MARULLUS. If I were an enemy of the defence counsel, I should pray for the acquittal of the defendant.—It is shameful, to my mind, for Cicero not to be defended in the city where even Popillius could find a defender.

Few of the historians have told us that Popillius was the killer of Cicero, and even they didn't represent him as having been defended by Cicero for parricide, but rather in a private suit. It was the declaimers who decided that he had been tried for parricide. But they accuse him in such a way as to suggest he cannot be defended: yet he can be acquitted—in fact he could not even have been accused.

Latro didn't approve of him being accused as some accused him: "I charge you with killing a man, a citizen, a senator, a consular, Cicero, your defender." He said that by this method indignation was not piled up but fatigued. "One must come at once to the point to which the listener is hurrying; for as to the rest Popillius has so good a case, that, leaving aside the fact that it was his defence counsel that he killed, he is going to have no trouble; his defence is the necessity arising from the circumstances of the civil war. So I don't want to lead the defendant through stages where he is capable of getting safely off. He *had* a right to kill a man, a citizen, a senator, a con-

larem occidere, ne in hoc quidem crimen est, quod
Ciceronem, sed quod patronum. Naturale est autem
ut, quod in nullo patrono fieri oportuit, indignius sit
factum in Cicerone patrono.

9   Latro accusavit illum de moribus, primum quod
sic vixisset ut causam parricidi diceret, deinde quod
patronum suum occidisset. Et fecit has quaestiones:
an non possit eo nomine accusari ⟨quo⟩ absolutus
est. " Si quis " inquit " volet hodie parricidi me
postulare, non poterit. Quomodo quod crimen obici
non potest puniri potest? " An in bello civili acta
obici non possint. Honeste dixit, cum hunc locum
tractaret, Varius Geminus: *si illa*, inquit, *tempora
in crimen vocas, dicis non de hominis sed de rei publicae
moribus.* Si potest quod civili bello actum est obici,
an hoc obici debeat. Hanc quaestionem in illa divisit:
an, etiamsi necesse ei fuit facere, non sit tamen
ignoscendum. Ad quaedam enim nulla nos debet
necessitas conpellere. Hoc loco Latro dixit summis
clamoribus: *ita tu, Popilli, si Antonius iussisset, et
patrem tuum occideres?* Deinde an non fuerit illi
necesse. Potuisti excusare te, potuisti praemittere
aliquem ad Ciceronem, ut sciret et fugeret; necesse 295M
certe non fuit manum caputque praecidere mortuo.

10   Colorem pro Popillio Latro simplicem habuit:
necessitate coactum fecisse; et hoc loco illam sen-

sular—in war-time. There is no charge to be found, either, in the fact that the victim was Cicero—merely in the fact that Cicero had defended him. But it is natural that what would have been wrong in the case of any defence counsel should be particularly wicked where Cicero was the counsel in question."

Latro accused him of misconduct first for living 9 such a life as to have to face a charge of parricide, then for killing his advocate. And he distinguished these questions: Can he be accused of something of which he has been acquitted? "If anyone wants to accuse me of parricide today, he will not be able to.[1] How can there be punishment of a crime if it cannot be made the subject of a charge?" Can deeds done in the civil war be the subject of a charge? Varius Geminus well said on this topic: "If you are calling those times to account, you are talking not of a man's conduct but of the state's." If acts done in the civil war can be made the subject of a charge, ought this one to be? This was how he sub-divided this question: Even if he had to do it, should he be forgiven? For to some things we should not be driven by any compulsion. At this point Latro, amid great enthusiasm, said: "Would you then, Popillius, kill even your father if Antony had ordered it?" Then: *Had* he to do it? "You could have excused yourself, you could have sent someone else on ahead to Cicero, so that he could have known you were coming and escaped. And you certainly did not have to cut the dead man's head and hand off."

Latro had a straightforward *colour* for Popillius— 10 that he had acted from necessity. This was where he

[1] Once tried, a case could not be brought again.

63

tentiam dixit: *miraris si eo tempore necesse fuit Popillio occidere quo Ciceroni mori?*

Albucius dixit in poenam Ciceronis ⟨ab Antonio⟩ [1] electum amicissimum Ciceroni, quasi exprobraturus per hoc illi fortunam esset. Molestius, inquit, feret se a Popillio occidi quam occidi.

Marcellus Aeserninus eundem colorem aliter induxit. Cogitabat, inquit, secum Antonius: Quod Ciceroni excogitabo supplicium? Occidi iussero? Olim iam adversus hunc metum emunivit animum: scit mortem nec inmaturam esse consulari nec miseram sapienti. Fiat aliquid novi, quod non expectat, quod non timet; non indignatur cervicem hosti porrigere, indignabitur clienti. Popillium aliquis vocet, ut sciat quantum illi defensi rei profuerint.

11   Silo Pompeius hoc colore usus est: Offendebar, inquit, proscriptione et quaedam liberius loquebar. "Non miror; Ciceronis cliens es: tanto magis occide Ciceronem tuum." Et dixit non suae infirmitatis sententiam: uterque, inquit, sed diverso genere punitus est: *Ciceronis proscriptio fuit occidi, mea occidere.*

Marullus, praeceptor noster, sic narravit: *iussit,* inquit, *imperator, iussit victor,* iussit qui proscribebat: *ego illi negare quicquam possem cui nihil poterat negare res publica?*

Blandus hoc colore: Volui, inquit, me excusare;

[1] *Supplied by Gertz.*

spoke the epigram: " Are you surprised Popillius had to kill—at a time when Cicero had to die? "

Albucius said that Antony had chosen a close friend of Cicero to punish him, as though in this way to make his fortune a gibe at him. " He will be more distressed to be killed by Popillius than just to be killed."

Marcellus Aeserninus brought in the same *colour* differently. " Antony was wondering: What punishment shall I invent for Cicero? Shall I have him killed? But he has long since fortified his mind against fear of that. He knows that death is not premature for an ex-consul or wretched for a wise man.[1] Let us have something new, that he neither expects nor fears. He does not resent offering his neck for an enemy to sever—but he will resent offering it to a client. Let someone call Popillius, so that Cicero may learn how much profit there was for him in defending the guilty."

Pompeius Silo used this *colour*. " I was offended, 11 he says, by the proscriptions, and made some over-free remarks. ' I'm not surprised—you are Cicero's client; so much the more must you be the killer of your friend Cicero.' " And he used an epigram that avoided his customary feebleness: " Both of us were punished—in different ways. Cicero's proscription was to be killed—mine to be the killer."

My teacher Marullus narrated like this: " The orders were given by the general, the victor, the proscriber; could *I* deny anything to a man to whom the state could deny nothing? "

Blandus' *colour*: " I wanted to excuse myself. I

[1] So Cicero in *Cat.* 4.3 and *Phil.* 2.119: see *S.* 6.12.

dixi: " Cicero me defendit"; respondit: " Scio; me accusavit. I ergo, ut sciat plus sibi Antoni accusationem nocuisse quam Popilli defensionem 296M profuisse."

12   Buteo hoc colore: " vocetur, inquit, ille Ciceronianus [ille][1] cliens, amicus; excogitavi quomodo Cicero sua periret manu."

Cestius hoc colore: Durissima, inquit, mihi militia in Antoni castris fuit ob hoc ipsum, quod Ciceronis eram cliens; difficillimae mihi expeditiones mandabantur. Tunc quoque vocatus sum quasi ad poenam: " i," inquit " occide Ciceronem; nec credam, inquit, nisi attuleris caput"; magisque admiratus est potentiam suam quod Ciceronem Popillio non licebat ⟨non⟩ occidere.

Fuscus Arellius hoc colore usus est: Antoni se partem secutum ut, si quid posset, Ciceroni prodesset; facta proscriptione ad genua se Antoni procidisse, deprecatum esse pro Cicerone; offensum Antonium dixisse: " eo magis occide quem mori non vis." Hic color displicebat Passieno, quia †ad testem ducit†;[2] nam, si hoc fecit Popillius, non tantum quod defendat non habet sed habet quod glorietur.

13   Hispo Romanius vehementi colore usus est et duro; patronum enim dedit Popillio et dixit aliter se causam acturum Popilli, aliter Antoni; pro Popillio dicturum: occidere nolui, coactus sum; pro Antonio dicturum: occidi Ciceronem oportuit. Et dixit locum, aliter

---

[1] *Deleted by Müller.*
[2] *No convincing emendation of these words has been suggested.*

said: ' Cicero defended me.' The reply was: ' I know—he accused *me*.[1] Go then, so that he may learn that accusing Antony has harmed him more than defending Popillius helped.' "

Buteo's *colour*: " ' Send for that client and friend 12 of Cicero. I have discovered how Cicero can die by his own hand.' " [2]

Cestius' *colour*: " My service in Antony's camp was very hard just because I was indebted to Cicero; I used to get sent on the most difficult assignments. So on this occasion—I was summoned as though for punishment. ' Go,' he said, ' kill Cicero. And I shan't believe it till you bring back the head.' He had the greater admiration for the extent of his own power because he saw that Popillius could not but kill Cicero."

This was the *colour* used by Arellius Fuscus: Popillius had followed Antony's party in order to help Cicero if he could. When the proscriptions took place, he fell at Antony's knees, and begged mercy for Cicero; Antony was offended, and said: " Kill him—the more because you want him to live." This *colour* displeased Passienus, because it †leads to a witness†. If Popillius did do this, he not only has nothing to defend—he has something to boast of.

Romanius Hispo used a forcible and tough *colour*. 13 He let Popillius have an advocate, and said that he would conduct the cases of Popillius and Antony differently. For Popillius he would say: " I didn't want to kill him. I was made to." For Antony: " Cicero had to be killed." And he produced a

---

[1] Antony alludes to the Philippics.
[2] i.e. by the hand of one who owed so much to him.

non potuisse pacari rem publicam quam si ille tur-
bator oti e re publica sublatus esset. Solus ex
declamatoribus in Ciceronem invectus est. Quid?
ille, inquit, cum Antonium hostem iudicaret et omnis 297M
Antoni milites, non intellegebat se et Popillium
proscripsisse? Hic color prima specie asperior est,
sed ab illo egregie tractatus est.

Varius Geminus dixit: cum imperasset mihi
Antonius, passus sum ne aliquis P. Clodi cliens
mitteretur, qui contumeliis adficeret antequam occideret, qui vivum laniaret.

14   Argentarius dixit: Vocatus veni; post proscriptionem Antonius terribilior erat factus etiam suis.
Iussus sum Ciceronem occidere: quid facerem?
non parere uno modo poteram, si me occidissem:
hoc nec Cicero poterat.

A parte accusatoris illo loco quo Popillius venit
nemo non aliquid voluit novi dicere. Latro ait:
praecluserat fores; nemo ad proscriptum recipie-
batur, Popillius, ut venit, admissus est.

Cestius dixit: ut renuntiatum est Ciceroni, ait:
Popillio semper vaco.

Hispanus Cornelius fecit etiam querentem Ciceronem: Popilli, tam sero?

Albucius ait: quid est, Popilli? ecquid tuto lateo?
numquid mutandus est locus?

---

[1] For more historical accounts of the circumstances see
S. 6.17 seq.

passage in which he said that the state couldn't have been pacified unless that disturber of the public peace had been got rid of. He was the only declaimer who inveighed against Cicero. "Surely, when he judged Antony, together with his whole army, a public enemy, he realised that he had proscribed Popillius too?" This *colour* is at first sight rather hard to stomach, but it was excellently handled by Hispo.

Varius Geminus said: "When Antony gave me his orders, I put up with it for fear some client of Publius Clodius' should be sent to insult him before he killed him, to mutilate him while he still lived."

Argentarius said: "I came when I was sent for. 14 After the proscription Antony had become more formidable even for his own men. I was told to kill Cicero. What was I to do? I could disobey in only one way—by killing myself; and even Cicero could not bring himself to do *that*."

For the accuser everyone wanted to say something novel at the point where Popillius came to Cicero.[1] Latro said: "He had barred the doors. No-one was being admitted to the proscribed man—but when Popillius arrived, *he* was let in."[2]

Cestius said: "When Cicero had the message, he said: 'I always have time for Popillius.'"

Cornelius Hispanus even made Cicero complain: "Popillius, you're so late."

Albucius said: "'What is it, Popillius? Am I not safe in my hiding-place? Must I change my ground?'"

---

[2] This and the following epigrams depend on Cicero thinking Popillius still his friend.

Inepte Sabidienus [1] Paulus, qui induxit Ciceronem cum maxime ⟨pro⟩ Popillio orationem legentem.

Et Murredius non est passus hanc controversiam transire sine aliqua stuporis sui nota. Descripsit enim ferentem caput et manum Ciceronis Popillium et Publilianum dedit: Popilli, quanto aliter reus Ciceronis ⟨tangebas caput⟩ [2] et tenebas manum eius!

III

TER ABDICATUS VENENUM TERENS

Ter abdicatus, ter absolutus conprensus est a patre in secreta parte domus medicamentum terens; interrogatus quid esset, dixit venenum et velle se mori, et effudit. Accusatur parricidi.

1 CESTI PII. *Dic quid commiserim.* Nescis? *certe nec secreta* te *fallunt.* Dimittat me: intellegetis cui paraverim. Dic quid ante commiserim: nisi forte contentus es reo obicere parricidium, parricidae nihil.

---

[1] Sabidienus *Prosopographia Imperii Romani 3.151*: sabidiebus.

[2] *Supplied by Thomas.*

---

[1] As suppliant. This play on words is what constitutes the Publilian element (see *C.* 7.3.8 *seq.*).

[2] There is a very similar case in *Decl.* 17, where the son is ordered to drink the poison: see also *Decl.* 377, and Juvenal's "fusa venena silent" (7.169).

[3] Because I'll drink the poison.

Sabidienus Paulus incongruously represented Cicero as just then reading his speech in defence of Popillius.

Murredius, too, did not let this *controversia* pass without some mark of his dull wit. He described Popillius bearing the head and hand of Cicero, and gave this saying *à la* Publilius: "Popillius, how differently you touched Cicero's head and held his hand when you were on trial!"[1]

3

THE THRICE-DISINHERITED SON CAUGHT POUNDING UP POISON

A son who had been three times disinherited and three times reprieved was caught by his father pounding up drugs in a secluded part of the house. Asked what it was, he said it was a poison and that he wanted to die. Then he poured it away. He is accused of parricide.[2]

For the son

CESTIUS PIUS. Tell me what I have done. Don't [1] you know? Surely even my secret thoughts don't escape you.—Let him let me go—then you will realise whom I prepared it for.[3]—Tell me what I did earlier—unless perhaps you are satisfied to accuse this defendant of parricide without accusing the parricide of anything else.[4]

---

[4] It was a common argument that parricide can only occur as the last of a long series of crimes: cf. *Decl.* p. 8.5 Lehnert: "nemo inde coepit quo incredibile est pervenisse" and p. 308.14; *Decl.* p. 418.21 Ritter.

THE ELDER SENECA

ARGENTARI. Volo mori quia reus fui. Quid ergo? nemo reus vivet? Vivet cui sordidatus adsederit pater. Revertar ad venenum, quoniam iniqua Fortuna nullo me periculo defungi semel passa est.

ALBUCI SILI. Quare ergo non moreris? Non iuvat me mori si quem alium iuvat. *Ut intervenit, in illas cogitationes abii: ergo quisquam tam infelix fuit? ergo quisquam me magis odit quam ego? Misereri mei coepi.*

2 VARI GEMINI. "Ter" inquit "abdicatus es." Videris mihi, pater, obicere quod tamdiu vivam. 299^M Quod venio, quod pro me loquor, nolite mirari: tam iucundum est innocentibus defendi quam miseris mori.

CORNELI HISPANI. Scio quosdam periclitantis illa iactare: nunc primum causam dico. Haec ego dicere non possum; ter reus fui, nec dubito quin vobis in odium venerim, cum ipse me oderim.

PORCI LATRONIS. *Ter causam dixi; accessit ad haec supplicia mea venenum; teneo; hoc si tibi satis non est, vivam.*

3 Altera pars. ALBUCI SILI. Testor deos immortales hoc me tribus iam abdicationibus cavisse, ne in domo mea venenum deprenderem. Parricidi reus vivit

---

[1] To arouse pity for his son in court: but the father had been the accuser, not the defender. Argentarius reports the conversation of father and son at the time of the poison incident.

CONTROVERSIAE 7. 3.1–3

Argentarius. " I want to die, because I have been on trial." " What, will no man who is put on trial survive? " " Yes, if his father sits by his side, in shabby clothes." [1]—I shall return to the poison—since harsh Fortune hasn't let me get quit of any danger once for all.[2]

Albucius Silus. " Why then don't you die? " I do not enjoy dying if another enjoys it.—When he interrupted me, I drifted off into these thoughts: " Well, was anyone ever so unlucky? Can it be that anyone hates me more than I hate myself? " I began to feel pity for myself.

Varius Geminus. " You have been three times 2 disinherited." Your charge, father, seems to be that I have lived such a long time.—Don't be surprised that I am here, that I speak up for myself; the innocent are as glad to defend themselves as the unfortunate to die.

Cornelius Hispanus. I know that some men on trial boast: This is my first speech in court. *I* cannot say this; I have three times been on trial, and I don't doubt you have come to hate me—I hate myself.

Porcius Latro. I have stood trial three times over; to these penalties has been added poison—I have it here. If that will not suffice for you, I will live.[3]

The other side

Albucius Silus. I call the immortal gods to witness 3 that in thrice disinheriting my son I was taking care that I should not find poison in my house.—Accused

[2] Allusion to his constant disinheritances.
[3] That being worse than death.

73

qui abdicatus mori voluit. In quam angusto domus
meae fortuna posita est! aut patri pereundum est
aut filio. Quid habes quare mori velis? Vivunt orbi,
vivunt naufragi, vivunt etiam quibus contigerunt
liberi ter abdicati. *Cum se mori velle dicat, vitam
rogat. Teneo parricidam*, quod apparet, *etiam in
suam mortem paratissimum.*

CORNELI HISPANI. Nolite mirari si debitas vires
dolori meo non exhibuero: tribus iudiciis experti
estis patres accusare non posse.

4   VIBI RUFI. *Cum tantum sit quod fateris, quantum
est quod negas?* Tu *venenum quaesisti,* tu *venenum
emisti,* tu *venenum intulisti in eam domum in qua habebas
inimicum patrem.* Recte vitam odisses si iam ⟨tum⟩ [1]
tibi parricidium obiecissem. Vis scire quid pecca-
veris? *Indica quis* tibi *vendiderit: dicetur illi: tu
*[illi] [2] *venenum vendebas? tu* ter *abdicato* vendebas?
sine dubio *nesciebas cui daturus esset.* Ita hoc ego   300M
iudicio fili mortem moror? Si me cum isto includitis
moriar, ut hanc vobis faciam invidiam quam iste mihi
facere voluit.

VARI GEMINI. *Quaeritis* filius meus *venenum cui
paraverit? non bibit.*

POMPEI SILONIS. " Mihi " inquit " paravi." Et
hoc est patri parare. Absolutus mori volt, reus
vivit.

[1] *Supplied by C. F. W. Müller.*
[2] *Deleted by Thomas.*

---

[1] For the argument, cf. *Decl.* p. 311.7 Lehnert.
[2] At the time of the disinheritance cases.

of parricide, he lives—though he wanted to die when he was disinherited.[1]—To how small a compass is the fortune of my house reduced! Either father or son must die.—Why should you want to die? The bereaved live, the shipwrecked live, even those who are afflicted with thrice-disinherited sons live.— Though he says he wants to die, here he is begging for life.—I have here a clear case of parricide: he is quite ready to cause his own death as well.

CORNELIUS HISPANUS. Don't be surprised if I don't show the vehemence that suits my griefs; you have found out from three judgements that fathers are incapable of accusing.

VIBIUS RUFUS. Since what you confess is so great, 4 what is the enormity of the crime you deny?—You looked for poison, bought it, brought it into the house where your father was your enemy.—You would have been right to hate life if even then [2] I had charged you with parricide.—You wish to know what your fault was? Tell us who sold it you. We will say to him: Did you sell poison? Did you sell it to a son who had three times been disinherited? Doubtless you didn't know whom he intended it for.—Then by this trial I am delaying my son's death?—If you [3] make me live in the same house as him, I shall die— and make you as odious as he wanted to make me.[4]

VARIUS GEMINUS. Are you trying to find out whom my son prepared the poison for? *He* didn't drink it.

POMPEIUS SILO. " I prepared it for myself." That is equivalent to preparing it for your father.— Acquitted he wants to die, accused he lives.

[3] The judges.
[4] i.e. by suicide.

75

THE ELDER SENECA

Musae. " *Habuit* malum medicamentum *Mithridates*." Quis enim alius debebat habere quam parricida? " *Habuit* " inquit " *Demosthenes venenum* et bibit." Idem ego tibi pater quod Demostheni Philippus?

5 Porci Latronis. Cum abdicarem, si quid obieceram aiebat: numquid deprendisti? Non iam habebitis quod multum de eo dubitetis: *quod negat parricidium, quod confitetur veneficium est.* " Mori " inquit " volo." Vivo patre et hoc parricidium est. Miser aeque timui ne biberet venenum quam ne daret.

Arelli Fusci patris. " *Mihi* " inquit " *paravi venenum* "; *ne quis dubitet an alium possit occidere.*

Iuni Othonis patris. Reus est parricidi qui mavolt mori quam patrem videre. Quomodo voltis magis probem vobis illum mori noluisse? non volt mori. " Mori " inquit " volui." Quare? quia ter vicisti? Si mihi creditis, parricidium facere voluit; si isti, a me parricidium fieri voluit. Qualis est reus cuius hoc unum patrocinium est, indignum se vita fuisse? *Dico tam invisum illi patrem fuisse ut occidere voluerit: ipse fatetur tam invisum* sibi fuisse *ut occidere* [1] *voluerit.*

---

[1] ⟨se⟩ occidere *is usually read. But there seems to be a play on* occidere *and* occidere.

MUSA. " Mithridates had a noxious drug." Who
else but a parricide should have had one ? [1] " Demosthenes had a poison, and drank it." [2] Am I, your
father, to you what Philip was to Demosthenes ?

PORCIUS LATRO. When I was disinheriting him, 5
whatever I charged him with he said: " Did you
catch me at it ? " *Now* you will have little hesitation about him; what he denies is parricide, what he
confesses is poisoning.—" I want to die." While your
father is alive, that too counts as parricide.—Alas, I
was as afraid of his drinking the poison as of his
giving it to me.

ARELLIUS FUSCUS SENIOR. " I got the poison ready
for myself." Let there then be no doubt that he is
capable of killing another.

JUNIUS OTHO SENIOR. The man who prefers death
to putting up with the sight of his father is guilty of
parricide.—How do you want me to prove more con-
clusively to you that he did not want to die ?—he does
not want to die.[3]—" I wanted to die." Why ? Because you were three times victorious ?—If you
believe me, he wanted to commit parricide himself;
if you believe him, he wanted me to commit parricide.[4]—What sort of a defendant is it whose sole
defence is that he was unworthy to live ?—I say that
his father was so hateful to him that he wanted to kill
him; he confesses his father was so hateful to him
that he wanted to die.

[1] For Mithridates' precautions against poison, see App.
Mithr. 111. For his matricide, *C.* 7.1.15 n.

[2] For Demosthenes' suicide see Plut. *Dem.* 29–30; it had
nothing to do with Philip.

[3] i.e. he is defending himself at this trial.

[4] By (on the son's story) allowing him to die.

6   Non puto vos exigere divisionem, cum coniecturalis 301M
sit controversia. Habet tamen dissimilem ceteris
coniecturam et duplicem; non quomodo solet aut
inter duos reos, cum alterum coarguimus, aut inter
duo crimina, cum alterum probamus, ut id alterius
fiat probatio, tamquam cum dicimus adulteram fuisse
ut credatur propter hoc etiam venefica: *in uno homine
coniectura duplex* est. Quaerimus enim *utrum* venenum
in suam mortem an in patris paraverit.

7   Si hoc colore dici placet pro adulescente quo dixit
Latro, ut nihil mutaret voces, sed diceret: " mori
volui taedio abdicationum et infelicitatis adsiduae,
cum in hoc tantum sordes ponerem ut cum maiore
tormento positas resumerem et absolutio mihi uni
non finis esset periculi sed initium," incipit praeter
coniecturam et illa prima vulgaris in eiusmodi controversiis et pertrita quaestio incurrere, an venenum
habere in mortem suam liceat.

Albucius illo colore pro adulescente dixit, non
fuisse venenum. Cum putarem, inquit, odio me esse
patri meo, volui experiri adfectum eius, quomodo
mentionem mortis meae ferret; itaque palam et ita
ut interveniret pater tenui. Fuscus Arellius eodem

---

[1] Concerning facts, not value-judgements.
[2] Cf. *C.* 6.6 n.
[3] Apparently of the theme: Latro accepts that poison was
involved, Albucius and others deny it.

I don't imagine you're demanding a division, this 6
being a conjectural case.[1] But the " conjecture " it
involves is unusual and two-fold; two-fold not, as
generally happens, because there are two defendants,
when we have to prove one guilty, or two charges,
where we have to prove one so that it can serve as a
proof for the other, as when we say that a woman has
been an adulteress to make people believe she is
therefore also a poisoner.[2] *This* two-fold conjecture
concerns one and the same man; for we are enquiring
whether he prepared the poison to kill himself or his
father.

You may decide to use the *colour* on behalf of the 7
youth that Latro used; he made no change in the
wording,[3] but merely said: " I wanted to die because
I was tired of disinheritances and continual misfortune [4]—I only took off my mourning clothes to
put them on again with yet more pain, and acquittal
for me (and only me) was not the end of my dangers
but the beginning of them." In that case, beside the
conjecture, the well-known and banal first question
common in that type of *controversia* begins to come
up: Is it legal to possess poison in order to kill oneself ?

Albucius used the *colour* for the youth that it wasn't
poison. " As I thought my father hated me, I wanted
to test out his attitude, to see how he would take the
idea of my death; that was why I held the poison
openly and in such a way that my father would catch
me." Arellius Fuscus used the same *colour*, but in a

[4] Elaborated in *Decl.* p. 313.8 *seq.* Lehnert (e.g. " victus
sum . . . absolutionibus meis "). The mourning clothes were
worn by a defendant to arouse pity.

colore usus est, sed aliter; non dixit: experiri patrem
volui, sed: ut miserabilem me patri facerem.

8　　Murredius pro cetero suo stupore dixit medicamentum se parasse ad somnum, quia adsiduae sollici-
tudines vigiliarum sibi consuetudinem ⟨fecerint. A
parte patris⟩[1] colorem et Publilianam sententiam
dedit: abdicationes, inquit, suas veneno diluit; et
iterum: mortem, inquit, meam effudit. Memini
Moschum, ⟨cum⟩[2] loqueretur de hoc genere sententiarum, quo infecta iam erant adulescentulorum
omnium ingenia, queri de Publilio quasi ille [iam][3]
hanc insaniam introduxisset. Cassius Severus, summus Publili amator, aiebat non illius hoc vitium esse,
sed eorum qui illum ex parte qua transire deberent
mitarentur, ⟨non imitarentur⟩[4] quae apud eum
melius essent dicta quam apud quemquam comicum
tragicumque aut Romanum aut Graecum; ut illum
versum quo aiebat unum versum inveniri non posse
meliorem:

　　tam dest avaro quod habet quam quod non habet;

et illum de eadem re dictum:

　　desunt luxuriae multa, avaritiae omnia;

302M (margin)

---

[1] *Supplied by Bursian.*
[2] *Supplied by Kiessling.*
[3] *Deleted by Baumm.*
[4] *Supplied by Bursian.*

---

[1] See the Index of Names.　Seneca means (as the following
discussion makes clear) sayings that depend on clever mani-

different way. He didn't say: "I wanted to test out my father," but "in order to make my father pity me."

Murredius, in accordance with his general stupidity, 8 said he had prepared a sleeping-draught, because constant anxieties had made him insomniac. On the side of the father, he gave a *colour*, with an epigram worthy of Publilius: [1] " He mixed in with the poison the times I had disinherited him "; and again: " It was my death he poured on the ground." I remember that Moschus, speaking of this type of epigram, which had infected all the bright young men even in those days, complained of Publilius for introducing this foolish feature. Cassius Severus, a great lover of Publilius, said it wasn't his fault, but the fault of those who imitated the side of Publilius that they should have passed by, while failing to imitate things that were better put by Publilius than by any comic or tragic writer, Greek or Roman [2]—for example, one verse which could not (according to Cassius) be matched by any other single line:

" The greedy lack what they have as much as what they do not have "; [3]

and this on the same subject:

" Luxury lacks much, avarice everything "; [4]

pulation of language, sometimes puns. For their form see W. Meyer, *Sitz. München (phil.-hist. Classe)* 2 (1872), 559–60.

[2] The younger Seneca comments similarly in *Ep.* 8.8 and *Tranq.* 11.8. Cf. also Gell. 17.14.

[3] Publilius Syrus *Sent.* 628 Meyer (quoted also by Quintilian 8.5.6 and 9.3.64).

[4] 236 Meyer (cf. also Sen. *Ep.* 108.9).

et illos versus qui huic quoque ter abdicato possent convenire:

o vita misero longa, felici brevis!

et plurimos deinceps versus referebat Publili diser-
9 tissimos. Deinde auctorem huius viti, quod ex
captione unius verbi plura significantis nascitur, 303M
aiebat Pomponium Atellanarum scriptorem fuisse,
a quo primum ad Laberium transisse hoc studium
imitando,[1] deinde ad Ciceronem, qui illud ad virtutem transtulisset. Nam ut transeam innumera-
bilia quae Cicero in orationibus aut in sermone dixit
ex ⟨ea⟩ [2] nota, ut non referam a Laberio dicta, cum
mimi eius, quidquid modo tolerabile habent, tale
habeant, id quod Cicero in . . . *Laberium divus
Iulius ludis suis mimum produxit, deinde equestri
illum ordini reddidit; iussit ire sessum in equestria;
omnes ita se coartaverunt ut venientem non reciperent.
Cicero male audiebat tamquam nec Pompeio certus amicus
nec Caesari, sed utriusque adulator. Multos tunc in
senatum legerat Caesar, et ut repleret exhaustum bello
civili ordinem et ut eis qui bene de partibus meruerant
gratiam referret. Cicero in utramque rem iocatus ⟨est⟩; [3]
misit enim ad Laberium transeuntem: recepissem te nisi*

---

[1] imitando *Gertz:* imitandi.
[2] *Supplied by Haase.*
[3] *Supplied by Schultingh.*

and (verses [1] that might fit our thrice-disinherited son too):

" O life—long for the wretched, short for the happy! "

And he went on to recall in turn many of Publilius' cleverest lines. Then he said that the author of 9 this vice—the one arising from a play on a single word that means more than one thing—was the writer of Atellans, Pomponius. The habit spread by imitation first to Laberius, then to Cicero; and it was he who brought it to the level of a virtue. I may pass over innumerable things said by Cicero in that vein, in both speeches and conversation, and also over sayings of Laberius, for his mimes, so far as they do have anything tolerable in them, derive it from this feature, as Cicero . . . The blessed Julius Caesar [2] presented Laberius as a mime at some games of his, then assigned him equestrian rank; he told him to go and sit in the knights' seats—and everyone huddled up so as not to let the newcomer in. Cicero used to be abused for being a firm friend of neither Pompey nor Caesar, though a flatterer of both. Caesar had at this time drafted many people into the senate, to fill up a class that had been drained by the civil wars, and also to pay off men who had deserved well by his party. Cicero made a joke about both these things [3] —he sent a message as Laberius passed: " I should

---

[1] 438 Meyer. The use of the plural suggests that the whole context of the line is alluded to.

[2] The story recurs in Macrob. *Sat.* 2.3.10; 7.3.8.

[3] Laberius' plight and Caesar's packing of the senate (cf. Macrob. 2.3.10): Cicero's fickleness is mentioned to lead up to the second joke.

anguste sederem. Laberius ad Ciceronem remisit: atqui soles duabus sellis sedere. Uterque elegantissime, 10 sed neuter in hoc genere servat modum. Ab his huius studii diffusa est in plures imitatio.

Sed ut ad controversiam redeam, Cassius Severus aiebat placere sibi illum colorem: mori volui; et quasdam dixit inter disputandum sententias: Tertio, inquit, cum abdicarer, aiebam: nihil tanti est; 304M infelicem hanc animam, quam totiens exagitat pater et infestat, semel recipiat. Sed illud rursus dice- bam mihi: serva istam animam: facies quod voles absolutus. Quare ergo nunc non moreris? dicet aliquis. Primum non semper idem miseris libet; nonnumquam iuvat cum fortuna sua concurrere et illam fatigare. Deinde vis verum quare non moriar interim? quia puto te velle.

Otho Iunius ineptam sententiam videbatur dixisse: non multum interest mea; aut enim me aut filium meum voluit occidere.

IV

Mater Caeca Filium Retinens

Liberi parentes alant aut vinciantur.

Quidam, cum haberet uxorem et ex ea filium, peregre profectus est. A piratis captus scripsit

84

have let you in—but I was rather cramped in my seat." Laberius sent a message back to Cicero: " Yet you generally sit on two seats." Both sayings are very witty, but neither man can restrain himself in this field. From them imitation of this habit 10 spread widely.

But to get back to the *controversia.* Cassius Severus said he liked this *colour*: " I wanted to die," and he spoke various epigrams during his arguments: " When I was disinherited the third time, I said: It's not worth it. Let my father once for all have this wretched life that he so often hounds and harries. But on the other hand I also said: Preserve this life. Once acquitted, you will be able to do what you will. Someone will say: Why then do you not die *now*? First, the miserable don't always like the same things. Sometimes they take pleasure in getting to grips with their luck and trying to tire it out. Again, do you want the true reason why I don't die for the moment? Because I think you wish me to."

Junius Otho was thought to have produced a foolish epigram: " It makes little difference to me: he wanted to kill either me—or my son."

4

The Blind Mother Who would not let Her Son Go

Children must support their parents, or be imprisoned.[1]

A man with a wife and a son by her set out abroad. Captured by pirates, he wrote to his

[1] See *C.* 1.1 n.

de redemptione epistulas uxori et filio. Uxor
flendo oculos perdidit. Filium euntem ad redemptionem patris alumenta poscit; non reman-
entem alligari volt.

1 CESTI PII. *Non est quod mulieris adfectum lege
aestimetis qua minatur; omnia facit ne filius alligetur.
Navigaturus reliquit uxori filium; nec adhuc caeca erat.*

ALBUCI SILI. †Deduxite filium†;[1] itaque tene,
complectere. Audeo dicere, hoc par ne piratae
quidem dividerent. Si vellet filium alligari, pateretur
ire quo properat. Ergo tu, adulescens, matri tuae 305M
ne decem mensum quidem alumenta reddes? Si
pascere non vis matrem, expecta saltem ut efferas.

TRIARI. Legem attulit qua catenas minatur,
causam qua timet.

MARCELLI AESERNINI. Si perseveras, me quoque
ad piratas trahe: impetrabo ab illis alimenta; et
virum meum pascunt.

FULVI SPARSI. Mater, si non pascitur, peritura
est; pater, etiamsi non redimitur, tamen pascitur.

IULI BASSI. Patri tuo supersunt et oculi et alumenta.

---

[1] *So AB* (-cite *V*).

---

[1] More complex themes involving blinded mothers and lost
husbands appear in *Decl.* 6 and 16.
[2] By preventing him going to the pirates (cf. Albucius and
Triarius below).
[3] Text and sense unclear.
[4] Period of gestation. For the inclusive reckoning see

wife and son about a ransom. The wife's weeping blinded her. She asks support from her son
as he goes off to ransom his father; she demands
that he should be imprisoned because he will not
stay.[1]

For the mother

CESTIUS PIUS. You should not judge the woman's 1
emotions by the law she is using to threaten her son;
she is doing everything she can to avoid her son being
imprisoned.[2]—When the husband sailed, he left his
son to look after his wife; she wasn't yet blind, either.

ALBUCIUS SILUS. . . .[3] so hold him, embrace him.
—I venture to say this: even pirates could not
separate this couple.—If she wanted her son to be
bound, she would let him go to the place he is hurrying
off to.—Will you not, then, young man, repay your
mother the food you owe her even for ten months?[4]—
If you don't want to feed your mother, you might at
least wait to bury her.

TRIARIUS. She has adduced a law that makes her
threaten chains—and a reason that makes her fear
them.[5]

MARCELLUS AESERNINUS. If you persist, drag me
too to the pirates: I will get support from them—
they are feeding my husband too.

FULVIUS SPARSUS. The mother will die if she is not
fed; the father is being fed, even without a ransom.

JULIUS BASSUS. Your father still has eyes, and
food.

H. J. Rose, *The Eclogues of Vergil* (University of California,
1942), 254 n. 9, to which add Pomponius 55–6 Ribbeck.
    [5] From the pirates.

2   Altera pars. CESTI PII. Matrem meam imitari
volo: amare me meos docuit. *Unius vinculis duos
alligat.* Si matris exemplo pius esse voluero, etiam
oculos patri debeo.

ARELLI FUSCI patris. Desertorem tuum apud
patrem invenies.

VARI GEMINI. Qualis fortuna est! cui *victo, mater,
catenas denuntias, victori ad piratas eundum est.* Omnia
licet patri praestem, meliorem tamen habuit uxorem.
Quam multi me putant, quia nolo ad patrem redimendum ire, nunc cum matre conludere!

FULVI SPARSI. Matri nihil timeo si eam apud vos
relinquo: patri quid non timeo si eum apud piratas
relinquo?

BUTEONIS. Oculos certe eruam mihi ne plus marito
praestiterit uxor.

3   Latro hanc controversiam quasi tota offici esset
declamavit; nullas quaestiones iuris inseruit, sed
comparavit inter se incommoda patris et matris et
tamquam thesim dixit: utrum ad redimendum potius 306M
captum patrem ire filius deberet an ad alendam caecam matrem subsistere; et sic eam divisit ut diceret:
hoc quod pater desiderat ⟨inutile est matri; hoc
quod mater desiderat⟩ [1] utile est patri. Novissime

_____

[1] *Supplied by Thomas.*

88

The other side

CESTIUS PIUS. I want to do the same as my 2
mother; she taught me to love my family.—She
binds two with the chains of one.[1]—If I wish to be as
loving as my mother's precedent suggests, I owe even
my eyes to my father.

ARELLIUS FUSCUS SENIOR. You will find your
deserter son—with his father.

VARIUS GEMINUS. Such is my fortune! If I lose,
mother, you threaten me with chains, if I win I must
go to the pirates.—Even if I do everything for my
father, he had a wife who was better.—How many
imagine that I am now conniving with my mother,
because I don't want to go to redeem my father!

FULVIUS SPARSUS. I have no fears for my mother if
I leave her in your [2] hands; I have every fear for my
father if I leave him in the hands of pirates.

BUTEO. At least I shall pluck out my eyes—so that
I shan't have done less for my father than a wife did
for her husband.

Latro declaimed this *controversia* as though it were 3
solely concerned with duty. He put in no legal
questions, but contrasted the losses suffered by father
and mother, and made a sort of general topic [3] of the
following: Ought a son to go to ransom a captive
father or stay to support a blind mother? He divided
it thus: What the father needs is disadvantageous to
the mother; what the mother needs is advantageous

[1] By restraining me.

[2] Addressing the jury, as representing the whole people.

[3] A *thesis* was a generalised statement, discussed as part of
philosophical training: see Austin on Quintilian 12.2.25.

tractavit ne patrem quidem velle; utique, si sciat matrem in hac esse fortuna, non passurum.

Buteo fatuam quaestionem moverat primam: an lex quae de alendis parentibus lata esset ad patres tantum pertineret. Illis omnia privilegia data et ipsam poenam non alentium signum esse non muliebris potestatis. Res est ineptior quam ut coarguenda sit; itaque transeo; illud unum quod dicebat Pollio Asinius referam: numquam debere temptari in causa verecunda inprobam quaestionem.

4 Hispo Romanius illam movit quaestionem: an lex de alendis parentibus non pertineret ad matres vivis patribus. *Filius*, inquit, *familiae nulli poterit servire nisi patri;* omni alia servitute liber est. Puta enim te *alumenta petere ab eo quem pater mittat peregre*, quem navigare iubeat: *primae partes sunt patris, secundae matris.* Albucius non iuris illam fecit quaestionem sed aequitatis, ita tamen ut et iuris adiungeret [et]:[1] matris prius esse ⟨quam⟩[2] patris officium.

Silo Pompeius illam fecit quaestionem: an, *quotiens duobus communio esset, potestas eius tota fieret qui praesens esset.* Puta, inquit, servum te esse communem: huic domino servies qui praesens est. Puta fundum esse communem: is fructus percipiet 307M qui praesens est. Illam quaestionem huic duram subiecit: an nunc pater nullum ius in filium habeat. Quomodo, inquit, iura civis non habet qui liberi homi-

[1] *Deleted by Müller.*
[2] *Supplied by Müller.*

to the father. Finally, he handled the idea that not
even the father wanted the son to go—surely, if he
knew the mother was in such a plight, he would not
allow it.

Buteo had brought up a silly first question: Did
the law brought in on the support of parents apply
only to fathers? "Fathers have all the privileges
conferred on them, and the very penalty exacted from
those who do not give support is a proof that this is
not a power held by women." The idea is too absurd
to be refuted; and so I forbear to do so, merely men-
tioning something said by Asinius Pollio: "You
should never try an outrageous question in a respectable case."

Romanius Hispo raised the question: Did the law 4
about supporting parents apply to mothers while the
father is still alive? "The son who is a minor will be
subject only to his father; he is free of all other
dependence. For suppose you are seeking support
from a son whom his father is sending abroad or
ordering to go to sea: the father comes first, the
mother second." Albucius made this a question not
of law but of equity—though he added a legal one,
that duty to a mother is prior to duty to a father.

Pompeius Silo made a question of this: When two
people have something in common, is control over it
altogether in the hands of the one who is on the spot?
"Suppose you are a slave held in common; you
will serve the master who is present. Suppose an
estate is owned in common; the owner who is present
will get the profit." To this he subjoined a hard
topic: Has the father now any rights over his son?
"Just as one who hasn't a free man's rights hasn't

nis non habet, ⟨ita qui civis non habet nec⟩ [1] patris
habet; ille nullam in te potestatem habet, mater in
totius legis possessione est; iam non commune illi
ius in te sed proprium est.

5   Varius Geminus sic divisit: an non semper filius
cogi possit ut matrem alat; deinde: an nunc cogen-
dus non sit. Non semper, inquit, filius cogitur.
Transeo illos qui non possunt, aegros et inutiles;
aliquis ad propellendum hostem proficiscitur, in
cuius unius militia posita est salus publica: hunc
retinebit mater? Puta legatum de summa rei
publicae, puta ⟨de⟩ foedere: [2] huic ⟨manus⟩ [3]
mater iniciet? ⟨Et⟩ [4] per partes comparando utrumque officium, *Ille,* inquit, *peregre est, tu domi; ille
captus, tu libera; ille inter piratas, tu inter civis; ille
alligatus, tu soluta* es. *At tu caeca es: ille* hoc *infelicior quod videt;* quid enim videt? ⟨notas⟩ [5] capti-
vitatis suae *et caedes et volnera et cruces eorum qui non
redimuntur. At periculosum est. Quam multi nihil
pro patribus periculosum putarunt!*

   In epilogis vehemens fuit Apollonius Graecus; [6]
⟨At periculosum est.⟩[7]   Nihil non; et domi manere 308.
et flere.

6   Latro dixit pro matre summisse et leniter agendum.
Non enim, *inquit, vindictam sed misericordiam quaerit,*

---

[1] *Supplied by Madvig.*
[2] de foedere *Schultingh:* foederis.
[3] *Supplied by Konitzer.*
[4] *Supplied by Schultingh.*
[5] *Supplied by Madvig.*

citizen rights, so someone who hasn't citizen rights hasn't a father's rights either. He has no power over you; your mother is in possession of all the rights under the law; now she has over you not a shared authority but one that is truly her own."

Varius Geminus made the following division: 5 Can a son always be forced to support his mother? Then: Should he be forced on this occasion? " A son is not always forced. Not to speak of those who cannot for reasons of illness and incapacity: suppose someone sets off to repulse the enemy, someone in whose prowess alone is placed the safety of the state, will *he* be kept back by his mother? Suppose he is an ambassador on high state business, dealing (for example) with a treaty: will his mother lay hands on *him*?" He compared the two duties detail by detail: " He is abroad, you are at home; he is captive, you are free; he is among pirates, you among your fellow-citizens; he is in chains, you are unchained. 'But you are blind.' Well, he is the more unhappy because he can see. For *what* does he see? Signs of his captivity, slaughter, wounds, the crosses erected for the unransomed. 'But it is dangerous.' How many have regarded nothing as dangerous in the service of their fathers!"

In epilogues much force was shown by the Greek Apollonius: " ' But it is dangerous.' Everything is —for example, staying at home and weeping."

Latro said the case for the mother should be put 6 mildly and with restraint. " What she seeks is not

---

⁶ in—Graecus *appears in the MSS after* passurum (§3): *the words were transposed by Müller.*
⁷ *Supplied by the editor, after Müller.*

et cum eo adulescente consistit in quo *ita exigit pieta-*
tem ut impediat. Aiebat itaque verbis quoque horridio-
ribus abstinendum quotiens talis materia incidisset;
ipsam orationem ad habitum eius quem movere
volumus adfectus molliendam. In epilogis nos de
industria vocem quoque infringere et vultum deicere
et dare operam ne dissimilis orationi sit orator;
conpositionem quoque illis mitiorem convenire.

Calvus, qui diu cum Cicerone iniquissimam litem de
principatu eloquentiae habuit, usque eo violentus *actor*
et *concitatus fuit ut in media eius actione* surgeret
Vatinius reus et *exclamaret: rogo vos, iudices: num,*
7 *si iste disertus est, ideo me damnari oportet?* Idem
postea, cum videret a clientibus Catonis, rei sui,
Pollionem Asinium circumventum in foro caedi,
inponi se supra cippum iussit—erat enim parvolus
statura, propter quod etiam Catullus in hendecasyl-
labis vocat illum " salaputium disertum "—et iuravit,
si quam iniuriam Cato Pollioni Asinio accusatori suo
fecisset, se in eum iuraturum calumniam; nec umquam postea Pollio a Catone advocatisque eius aut
re aut verbo violatus est. Solebat praeterea ex-
cedere subsellia sua et inpetu latus usque in adversariorum partem transcurrere. Et carmina quoque

---

[1] That is, in connection with his father.

[2] For more on style and delivery in the peroration, see
Quintilian 11.3.170 *seq.*

[3] " I have found those who preferred Calvus to all others "
(Quintilian 10.1.115). These would be the plain-speaking
" Atticists " combatted by Cicero, e.g. in the *Orator* and

revenge but pity, and she is at law with a young man so situated that in demanding his affection she obstructs it." [1]   He said, therefore, that one should abstain even from over-rough words, whenever this sort of theme comes up; the style itself should be toned down to match the kind of emotion we want to arouse.   In the perorations we even make our voices break on purpose, bow our heads and ensure the speaker doesn't clash with what he is speaking; moreover, epilogues are suited by a gentler rhythm.[2]

Calvus, who for a long time waged a most unequal contest with Cicero for the supremacy in oratory,[3] was so violent and passionate a pleader that in the middle of a speech of his the defendant Vatinius got up and exclaimed: " I ask you, judges—just because *he* is eloquent, must *I* be convicted ? "   It was Calvus, 7 too, who another time, seeing Asinius Pollio surrounded and beaten up in the forum by clients of the man Calvus was defending, Cato,[4] had himself put up on a pillar—he was a short man, hence Catullus' description of him in a hendecasyllabic poem [5] as an " eloquent manikin "—and swore that if Cato did any injury to his accuser, Asinius Pollio, he would bring a charge against him.[6]   And never after that was Pollio harmed in word or deed by Cato and his supporters. Besides this, Calvus used to leave his own benches, and carried by the impulse of the moment would rush

Brutus.   Testimonia and bibliography, with Calvus' oratorical fragments, in E. Malcovati, *Oratorum Romanorum Fragmenta* [2], 492 *seq.*

[4] For this trial (54 B.C.) see Malcovati, *op. cit.*, 518–19.

[5] Catullus 53.5.

[6] More literally: " he would swear he brought no false accusation against him ": see *C.* 2.1.34 n.

eius, quamvis iocosa sint, plena sunt ingentis animi. 309M
Dicit de Pompeio:

> digito caput uno
> scalpit.   quid credas hunc sibi velle? virum.

8 Conpositio quoque eius in actionibus ad exemplum
Demosthenis viget: nihil in illa placidum, nihil lene
est, omnia excitata et fluctuantia. Hic tamen in
epilogo, quem pro Messio tunc tertio causam dicente
habuit, non tantum leniter componit sed ⟨sum-
misse⟩,[1] cum dicit: " credite mihi, non est turpe
misereri," et omnia in illo epilogo fere non tantum
emollitae conpositionis sunt sed infractae.

  In hac controversia Publilianam sententiam dedit
Festus quidam rhetor, staturae pusillae, in quem
Euctemon, homo venustissimi ingeni, Graece dixit:
antequam te viderem, nesciebam rhetoras victoriatos
esse. Fuit autem Festi sententia: " Captus est,
inquit, pater." Si te capti movent, et haec capta est.
Et quasi non intellexissemus, ait: nescitis dici " captos
9 luminibus "? Et illud dixit: Mitte istam epistulam
infructuosam. Odisse illam debes: haec est quae 310M
matrem tuam excaecavit. Et illam falsissimam in

---

[1] *Supplied by Müller.*

[1] A practice criticised by Quintilian 11.3.133.
[2] For the poetic fragments see Morel's *Fragmenta Poetarum Latinorum*, 84–7.
[3] Cf. *C.* 10.1.8 (= frg. 18 Morel). For the gesture see Juv. 9.133 and Sen. *Ep.* 52.12.
[4] The two are linked again in Plin. *Ep.* 1.2.2.

right to his opponents' side of the court.[1]   His poetry,
too, though not serious, is full of great spirit.[2]   He
says of Pompey:

> " With one finger he scratches
> His head. What do you think he wants?   A man." [3]

Further, his forensic style is vigorous on the model of 8
Demosthenes,[4] with nothing sedate or gentle about it
—everything   excited   and   stormy.   Yet,   in   the
peroration he spoke for Messius in his third trial,[5] he
uses a gentle and even submissive style.   He says:
" Believe me, there is nothing shameful about pity."
And virtually everything in that peroration has a soft
and even womanly rhythm.

In this *controversia* an epigram of the Publilian [6]
kind was spoken by a rhetorician called Festus.   He
was a tiny man, of whom Euctemon, who had a very
pretty wit, said in Greek: " Before I saw you, I didn't
realise   there   were   sixpenny [7] rhetoricians."   Well,
Festus' epigram was: " My father is taken prisoner,
he says.   Well, if those who are taken move your
pity, this woman is taken too."   And as though we
hadn't understood he said: " Surely you know that
one talks of people being taken in their eyes?" [8]
He also said: " Forget that fruitless letter.   You 9
ought to hate it; it is what blinded your mother."
Also that quite ill-founded epigram on which many

[5] 54 B.C. (Malcovati, 499).

[6] See *C.* 7.3.8 *seq.*

[7] The *victoriatus* was a small silver coin.   For this transference to size, Thomas compares the use of ἡμιωβελιαῖος in
Xen. *Mem.* 1.3.12.

[8] Cf. Liv. 9.29.11; the more usual phrase for " blinded "
was " oculis captus."

quam multi inciderunt: propter hoc ipsum, inquit, magis flebilis est quod non potest flere; et iterum: lacrimae, inquit, matri desunt, causae supersunt; tamquam caeci flere non soleant.

Memini Crispum quendam, anticum rhetorem, in illa controversia viri fortis, qui tertium filium retinet cum alter filius in tyrannicidio perdidisset oculos, alter in acie manus: Exsurgite nunc, viva cadavera, rogate pro patre. Sed quid ego meos derideo? alter quos roget non videt, alter quibus roget non habet.

10 Multis conpositio belle sonantis sententiae imposuit; itaque memini Latronem Porcium, ut exprobraret hanc audiendi scholasticis neglegentiam, maxime quia Triarius conpositione verborum belle cadentium multos scholasticos delectabat, omnes decipiebat, in quadam controversia, cum magna phrasi flueret[1] et concitata, sic locum clusisse: inter sepulchra monumenta sunt; et cum scholastici maximo clamore laudarent, invectus est in eos, ut debuit, et hoc effecit ut in relicum etiam quae bene dicta erant tardius laudarent, dum insidias verentur.

Glycon dixit: παράθει, μῆτερ, ἐπιλαβοῦ τέκνου· ταλαίπωρε, οὐδὲ βλέπεις, ἂν κρατήσῃς. εἴ μέ, φησιν, οὐ τρέφεις ἐπίμεινον ἵνα θάψῃς. 311

---

[1] phrasi flueret *Thomas, Madvig:* quasi fl(u)erent.

---

[1] Cf. *C*. 4.1: " There is no better cause . . . ," and esp. Sen. *Phoen*. 240: " All that was left was tears: and even these I have snatched from myself " (the blind Oedipus speaks).

stumbled: " She is the more to be wept for because she cannot weep," [1] and again: " My mother has no tears—but many reasons for them "—as though the blind usually don't weep.

I remember one Crispus, a declaimer of the old days, in the *controversia* about the hero who keeps his third son at home after his first son had lost his sight killing a tyrant and the second his hands in battle, say: " Arise now, living corpses, beg on your father's behalf. But why do I mock my sons? One cannot see from whom he is to beg, the other has nothing with which to beg."

Many have found themselves deceived by the 10 rhythm of a well-sounding epigram. Thus I recall Porcius Latro—in order to reproach the schoolmen with this carelessness in listening, particularly because Triarius used to please many in the schools, and take them all in, by his arrangement of pretty word-cadences—finishing off a passage in some *controversia*, when he was flowing along with splendid and passionate diction, with these words: " Among the tombs there are memorials." [2] And when the schoolmen shouted their applause, he weighed into them, as was only right, and made sure that in future they expressed their appreciation even of good sayings rather more slowly, in their fear of a trap.

Glycon said: " Hurry, mother, take hold of your child. Wretched woman, you cannot see him even if you win." [3]—She says: " If you don't feed me, stay here—to bury me." [4]

---

[2] Virtually (and intentionally) meaningless.
[3] Or: " *do* catch him firmly " [Warmington].
[4] Cf. §1 Albucius.

Hybreas in hac controversia dixit: τέκνον, κἄν με φεύγῃς, καταλήψομαί σε ἐπαιτοῦσα. Hoc quibusdam corruptum videbatur, Romanius tamen . . .

V

QUINQUENNIS TESTIS IN PROCURATOREM

Mortua quidam uxore, ex qua filium habebat, duxit aliam: sustulit ex ea filium. Habebat procuratorem in domo speciosum. Cum frequenter essent iurgia novercae et privigno, iussit eum semigrare: ille trans parietem habitationem conduxit. Rumor erat de adulterio procuratoris et matris familiae. Quodam tempore pater familiae in cubiculo occisus inventus est, uxor volnerata, communis paries perfossus; placuit propinquis quaeri a filio quinquenni, qui una dormierat, quem percussorem cognosceret; ille procuratorem digito denotavit. Accusat filius procuratorem caedis, ille filium parricidi.

1 ARELLI FUSCI patris. *Ut audivi clamorem, si qua est fides, deprensos* a patre *adulteros putavi.* Quis ferret te voluntariam testem in forum venientem,

Hybreas said in this *controversia*: " Son, even if you leave me, I will overtake you with my entreaties." Some thought this in bad taste, but Romanius . . .

5

THE FIVE-YEAR-OLD WHO TESTIFIED
AGAINST THE AGENT

A man lost his wife, by whom he had a son, remarried and raised a son by his second wife. He had a good-looking agent in his household. The step-mother and step-son quarrelled frequently, and he ordered his son to move; he rented a house next door. There was a rumour of adultery between the agent and the mother. One day the father was found killed in his bedroom, his wife injured and the party-wall dug through.[1] The relations decided to ask the five-year-old son who had slept in the same room whom he recognised as the assassin; he identified the agent by pointing at him. The (elder) son accuses the agent of murder, while the agent accuses the son of parricide.[2]

For the son

ARELLIUS FUSCUS SENIOR. If you will believe me, 1 when I heard a shout I thought my father had caught his wife in adultery.—Who would tolerate you coming

---

[1] Bornecque points out that what some of the declaimers (e.g. Bassus in §5) say suggests that the theme originally mentioned that the murderer was seen to have a light.

[2] This mutual accusation was known as *anticategoria* (see Adamietz on Quintilian 3.10.4).—Slightly similar themes appear in *Decl.* 1–2.

etiamsi venires dictura pro filio? Miserrime puer,
quamvis ⟨ipse⟩ [1] pericliter, plus tamen pro te timeo:
nimium fraternis insistis vestigiis; itaque iam tibi
cum matre non convenit. Quamdiu mater vixit,
pater me fuit procuratore contentus. Non facile 312M
fit parricidium. Vis scire quantum natura possit?
etiam infans pro fratre loquitur.

TRIARI. Vivo patre adultera, moriente conscia,
mortuo testis. Aliquis uno teste contentus est:
*dabo puerum. Aliquis non est uno teste contentus: dabo
populum. Obicit privigno parricidium, filio mendacium.*
2 Intrat procurator qua solebat. *Dic, puer, quis
patrem tuum occiderit, dic audaciter; eundem nominas
quem populus. Nox placet sceleri: prorsus adulteri
tempus.* Habui patrem tam bonum ut, cum uxorem
habere vellet, tamen me novercam habere noluerit.
Quo mihi lumen? tantum admissuro nefas optanda
nox est. " Quid " inquit " ante peccavi? " Dis-
simile est: memento enim de homicida quaeri;
potest tirocinium esse homicidium, parricidium non
potest. Lumen attulisti ut discerneres illic quem
leviter volnerare deberes. Videmus adactum in

---

[1] *Supplied by Kiessling.*

---

[1] Let alone against a step-son. Arellius alludes to the ban
on convicted adulteresses giving evidence (*Dig.* 22.5.18).

[2] There is perhaps a play on the root meaning of *infans*
(" unable to talk "). " Infancy " was thought to last as
much as seven years (Isid. *Etym.* 11.2.2).

[3] Who spread the rumour.

[4] i.e. for the son and the agent. The son doesn't need to
find anything in the past record of the agent, because murder

as a voluntary witness to the court, even if you came to speak on a son's behalf ?[1]—Miserable child, whatever my own danger, I fear more for you. You tread too closely in your brother's footsteps: that is why you already disagree with your mother.—While my mother lived, my father was content to use *me* as his agent.—Parricide is no easy matter. If you want to know the power of natural ties: even a child[2] is ready to speak on his brother's behalf.

TRIARIUS. Adulteress while my father lived, accomplice in his death, witness after his death.—If one witness is enough, I will put up the child; if one is not enough, I will put up the people.[3]—She charges her step-son with parricide, her son with a lie.—The agent comes in—the way he usually came. —Say, child, who killed your father, say it boldly; 2 you give the same name as the people.—Night is to the liking of crime—that is precisely the time for adultery.—I had so good a father that, though he wanted a wife, he didn't want me to have a step-mother.—What should I want light for ? Darkness is something to be prayed for by a man who intends such a crime.—" What wrong have I done up to now ? " That is not the same thing;[4] remember this is a trial for homicide : homicide may be a practice run— not so parricide.—You brought a light to make out there the one you had to wound—slightly.[5]—We see

may be a first crime. Not so parricide (see *C.* 7.3.1 n.); cf. below §6 Triarius.

[5] The implication, as often below, is that the wounding of the woman was a cover. In the next epigram the son says *he* would have killed his step-mother, not scratched her. So below §4 Albucius.

⟨patris⟩[1] praecordia gladium: sic ego novercam volnerassem. Frater, quaero, an videris procuratorem novissima nocte; nihil de prioribus quaero.

3   VIBI GALLI.   Ego taceam de adulterio quod persequitur etiam populus? ego taceam de parricidio quod persequitur etiam puer? Testor vos, iudices, salvom patrem reliqui. *O magnam in contrarium saeculi* nostri *perversitatem! inventus est qui patrem posset occidere, novercam non posset.* Etiamsi quis occidere patrem non potest, novercam potest.

SEPULLI BASSI.   Dum perfodio parietem, aliquis sentiet. Cuius vis levissimum esse somnum? pueri 313M an senis an mediae aetatis? Pueri? frater sentiet. Senis? pater. Mediae aetatis? noverca. Quaererem quam sordida domo natus esset, si ullam habuisset: nunc inquisitionem nostram humilitate effugit. Non miror si nescis quam difficile sit patrem occidere, cum incertum habeas patrem.

4   ALBUCI SILI.   Quaero a te, mulier, an filio tuo credendum putes? Liceat mihi nutrire puerum: nec cum matre illi nec cum tutore conveniet. Tres in cubiculo sunt: patrem occidis, puerum contemnis,

---

[1] *Supplied by Gertz.*

the sword plunged in my father's heart; that is how *I* would have wounded my step-mother.—I ask you, brother, did you see the agent on the last night?—I don't enquire about previous ones.

VIBIUS GALLUS. Am *I* to remain silent about an 3 adultery that even the people denounces? About a parricide that even a child denounces?—I call you to witness, judges, I left my father safe and sound.— What a topsy-turvy situation, and one that runs counter to the tendencies of the age!—someone has been found capable of killing a father but sparing a step-mother.—Even someone who can't kill a father can kill a step-mother.

SEPULLIUS BASSUS. While I am digging through the wall, someone will hear me. Whom do you want to be the lightest sleeper? A child, an old person or someone of middle age? A child?—then my brother will hear. An old person?—my father. Someone of middle age?—my step-mother.—I would ask what a low family he came from—if he had one: as it is he escapes our enquiry thanks to the meanness of his birth.—I'm not surprised if you don't know how difficult it is to kill a father, seeing there is so much doubt about yours.

ALBUCIUS SILUS. I ask you, woman, whether you 4 think your son should be believed.—Let *me* look after the child—he will not get on with either his mother or his guardian.[1]—There are three people in the room;

---

[1] On the death of the father, the child would come under the control, not of his mother, but of a *tutor*: the declaimer assumes it would be the agent (cf. §15 Hermagoras). For methods of choosing *tutores* see B. Nicholas, *An Introduction to Roman Law* (Oxford, 1962), 90–1.

adulteram non times. Singuli se servi liberique
offerebant puero; ⟨ego⟩ [1] stabam ante omnis, percussor latebat post adulteram. Quid ante peccavi?
cuius uxorem corrupi? Quod si fecissem, hominem
occidere possem, patrem non possem. Bonos habeo
testes. Timeo huic [2] in aliena potestate. Aspice
corpus patris: quam gravis plaga, quam alte adac-
tus est gladius! Sic ego novercam percussissem.

CESTI PII. Adulterum te esse non unum testem dabo, non corruptum, dabo multos, dabo etiam pueros.
Patrem tam graviter percussi quam debui novercam,
novercam ⟨ne⟩ [3] sic quidem quemadmodum patrem?

5   IULI BASSI. Tibi fuit necessarium lumen ne eam
occideres propter quam occidebas; mihi supervacuum
erat, ne instrumento parricidi detegerem parricidium.
Si rerum natura pateretur, obliviscendum erat mihi
patris dum occiderem. Maiore licentia quae non   314M
videmus agimus, et, quamvis non minor sit atrocitas
facinoris, formido minor est. Si patrem occidi,
totus mihi lectus purgandus est; cui parcam parricida
non habeo. Non possum gloriari ultione patris;
frater illam meus occupavit.

---

[1] *Supplied by Gertz.*
[2] huic *Bornecque:* hunc.
[3] *Supplied by the editio Hervageniana (1557).*

---

[1] Demonstrating my confidence and innocence.
[2] Point unclear: the people may be meant (cf. §1).

you kill the father, you ignore the child, you have no fear of your lover.—Slaves and freemen offered themselves one at a time to the child for identification; I stood in front of all,[1] the assassin hid behind his lover. —What have I done wrong before this? Whose wife have I seduced? If I *had* done so, I should be able to kill a man—but not my father.—My witnesses are good.[2]—I fear for this child, who is in the power of another.[3]—Look at my father's body: how grievous the wound is, how deep the sword was plunged in! That is how *I* should have struck my step-mother.

CESTIUS PIUS. I will not provide a single or a corrupt witness to your adultery—I will provide many, including even children.—Did I strike my father, as heavily as I should have struck my step-mother? Did I fail to strike my step-mother even as heavily as my father?

JULIUS BASSUS. *You* needed a light to avoid killing 5 the woman responsible for your killing; it was superfluous for *me*—in case the means to the parricide should lay it bare.[4] If nature allowed it, I had to forget my father while I killed. We are freer to do what we cannot see. The atrocity of the deed may be no less; but it arouses less fear in the doer.—If I killed my father, I have to clean up the whole bed;[5] if I am a parricide, I can spare no-one.—I cannot boast of avenging my father; my brother has got in first with that.

The agent's, as *tutor*.
[4] i.e. in case the light, in showing my father's face, made me shrink from his murder.
[5] By killing the step-mother, who would be a witness against him.

BLANDI. Quam difficile est filio patrem vulnerare et quam facile privigno novercam occidere!

6   VARI GEMINI. "Patrem "inquit" occidisti." Testor vos, iudices, nihil leviter hae manus faciunt. Utrum nolui te occidere, ⟨an⟩ non habui potestatem? Atqui vulnerata est: leviter vulnerata es; [1] quam diligenter servata es! Tu testimonium dic et *ostende istud non vulnus, sed argumentum. Ostende vulnus: percussor ille quam timuit ne occideret!*

PORCI LATRONIS. Quare lumen adfero? Fortius parricidium faciam si non videro patrem. Occidere aliquis patrem ante [quam] [2] novercam potest, novercam ne post patrem quidem potest?

TRIARI. Quis parricidio puras manus servat, et inde incipit quo pervenire difficile est?

7   DIVISIO. Has controversias, quae et accusationem ⟨habent et defensionem⟩, [3] non eodem ordine omnes declamaverunt. Quidam fuerunt qui ante defenderent quam accusarent, ex quibus Latro fuit. Fuscus Arellius: debet, inquit, reus in epilogo desinere. Optime autem epilogum defensioni contexit; et homines magis defendenti quam accusanti favent. Ultima sit pars quae iudicem faventem possit dimittere.

Quidam permiscuerunt accusationem ac defen-

---

[1] *The passage, severely dislocated in the manuscripts, is printed as restored by Kiessling.*
[2] *Deleted by Müller.*
[3] *Supplied by Gertz.*

315N

BLANDUS. How difficult it is for a son to wound a father! How easy for a step-son to kill a step-mother!

VARIUS GEMINUS. "You killed your father." I 6 swear to you, judges, these hands do nothing lightly.[1] —Was it that I didn't want to kill you, or that I couldn't do it?—"But she was wounded." You were lightly wounded. How carefully you were preserved! Give evidence, show us that wound—or rather that piece of proof. Show us the wound: how frightened the assassin was in case he killed!

PORCIUS LATRO. Why am I carrying a light? I shall do my parricide more boldly if I don't see my father.—Can someone be capable of killing his father before his step-mother—but not his step-mother, even after his father?

TRIARIUS. Who keeps his hands unstained until he commits parricide?—and begins at a point so difficult to reach?

Division

These *controversiae* combining accusation and 7 defence were not declaimed by everyone in the same order. There were those who defended before accusing, among them Latro. Arellius Fuscus said: "In the peroration the accused should be over and done with." He is right to make the peroration follow on the defence—men feel more favour to defence than to accusation. The last part should be one that can leave the judges in a favourable mood.

Some mixed accusation and defence, comparing the

---

[1] They would not, then, have merely scratched the step-mother.

sionem, ut comparationem duorum reorum inirent,
et crimen simul reppulissent statim transferrent;
ex quibus fuit Cestius. Hoc non semper expedit.
Utique ei qui inbecilliorem partem habet non est
utile comminus congredi; facilius latent quae non
comparantur.

8   In hac controversia non sunt duo sed[1] tres rei;
noverca enim procuratori coniungitur. Itaque a fili
parte utique aiebat prius accusandum, quia unum
deberet crimen defendere, duo obicere, et adulteri
et caedis.

Si qua sunt ex utraque parte difficilia, non colorem
sed argumentationem desiderant; itaque, ne modum
excedam, praeteribo.

Circa vulnus novercae quidam bellas res dixerunt,
quidam ineptas, immo multi ineptas. Prius illa
quae belle dicta sunt referam.

9   Fuscus ait: destricta levi vulnere est cutis; non
credas factum manu privigni, credas amatoris.

Passienus ait: *sic leviter te vulneravit dextera illa cui
nec paries obstitit nec pater?*

Varius Geminus dixit: da ferrum testi meo:
fortius feriet.

Cestius dixit, cum descripsisset quam leve vulnus
esset: nocueras, inquit, mihi si amicae tuae nocere
potuisses.

---

[1] non—sed *Müller:* et duo *AB:* duo et *V.*

---

[1] Cf. Quintilian 7.2.22. Seneca means that a speaker would
divide the comparison up into several points.   After defending

two defendants and " transferring " a charge as soon
as they had repelled it.[1]   Among these was Cestius.
This is not always a good idea.   Particularly for the
one who has the weaker case, it is inexpedient to
come to close grips; details that are not matched together are more easily hidden.

In this *controversia* there are not two but three 8
accused; for along with the agent goes the step-
mother.   And this was why he [2] said that at least on
the side of the son one should place accusation first,
because he had one charge to refute, two to bring—
for adultery and murder.

Any awkward points on either side require not a
colour but argumentation; so to keep my account
short, I shall pass over the *colours*.

On the step-mother's wound there were some nice
remarks, some foolish—or rather, many foolish.
First for the pretty ones:

Fuscus said: " Her skin was scratched by a light 9
wound; you would suppose it the work of a lover's
hand, not a step-son's."

Passienus said: " Did the hand that neither wall
nor father could withstand wound you so slightly ? "

Varius Geminus said: " Give my witness [3] a sword
—*he* will strike more boldly."

Cestius, after describing the superficial nature of
the wound, said: " You would have harmed me [4]—if
you could have brought yourself to harm your lover."

his own client on each point, he would turn it against the
other accused.

[2] Hardly Arellius or Cestius.   A name seems to be missing.
[3] The five-year-old.
[4] i.e. harmed my case: the slightness of the wound is
suspicious.

Brutus Bruttedius cotidiano verbo significanter 316M
usus est: rivalem, inquit, occidit, amicam sauciavit.

Hispo Romanius eiusdem generis rem dixit:
ostende, noverca, ostende istud quod amator tuus
vellicavit.

Bassus Sepullius dixit: maritum occidit, adulteram
strinxit.

10 Ex illis qui res ineptas dixerant primus ibi ante
omnis Musa voster, qui cum vulnus novercae descripsisset adiecit: at, hercules, pater meus tamquam
paries perfossus est.

Murredius: patrocinium putat esse causae suae
quod sanguinem misit.

Nepos Licinius ait: non est istud vulnus, sed
ludentis adulteri morsus.

Saenianus ex illa stultorum nota sententiam pro-
tulit: non vulneravit, inquit, novercam sed viri sui
sanguine aspersit; cum illa vulnerata ponatur.

11 *Vinicius, exactissimi vir ingeni,* qui *nec dicere res
ineptas nec ferre poterat,* solebat hanc sententiam
Saeniani deridere et similem illi referre in oratione
dictam Montani Votieni. Saenianus in hac eadem
controversia dixerat: *nihil puero est teste certius,*
utique quinquenni; *nam et ad eos pervenit annos ut*

---

[1] *rivalis* must be the " everyday word," as *amica* appears
above without comment. Seneca uses the word himself in
C. 2.6.12. For its restriction to rivalry in love, see *Anti-
barbarus* s.v. *rivalitas.* Also O. Rebling, *Versuch einer
Charakteristik der römischen Umgangssprache* (Kiel, 1883),
44–5.

Bruttedius Brutus used an everyday word with emphasis: " He killed his rival,[1] and wounded his mistress."

Romanius Hispo said something of the same kind:[2] " Show us, step-mother, show us where your lover pinched you."

Sepullius Bassus said: " He killed the husband, grazed the mistress."

Of those who said foolish things, " first before all "[3] 10 was your friend Musa, who, after describing the step-mother's wound, added: " But, by heaven, my *father* was pierced just like the wall."

Murredius: " He thinks it a support for his case that he let blood."[4]

Licinius Nepos said: " That is no wound—it is the bite of a playful lover."

Saenianus produced an epigram with that hallmark of stupidity: " He didn't wound the step-mother— he splashed her with the blood of her husband "— though in fact in the theme she is said to have been wounded.

Vinicius, a man of extreme precision of mind, who 11 could neither speak nor tolerate foolish things, used to make fun of another epigram of Saenianus', and to compare it with one spoken in a speech of Votienus Montanus. Saenianus had said in this same *controversia*: " Nothing is more reliable than a child as witness, especially a five-year-old: he has reached

[2] Unless this epigram is out of place, Seneca must be commenting on the " everyday word " *vellico*.

[3] A jocular quotation from Virg. *Aen.* 2.40.

[4] *mittere sanguinem* is the phrase for letting blood medically (so Celsus 2.10.1).

intellegat, et nondum ad eos quibus fingat. Haec finitio, inquit, ridicula est: "nihil est puero teste certius, utique quinquenni"; puta nec si quadrimus puer testis est nec si sex annorum. Illud venustissime adiciebat: putes, inquit, aliquid agi: omnia in hac sententia circumspecti hominis sunt, finitio, exceptio; nihil est autem amabilius quam diligens stultitia.

12 Montani Votieni sententiam huic aiebat esse 317M similem et deridebat hanc: insomne et experrectum est animal canis, utique catenarius, paratus. Erat autem non aequos ipsi Montano. Accusaverat illum apud Caesarem, a colonia Narbonensi rogatus. At Montanus adeo toto animo scholasticus erat ut eodem die quo accusatus est a Vinicio diceret: "delectavit[1] me Vinici actio"; et sententias eius referebat. Eleganter illi dixit Surdinus: rogo: numquid putas illum alteram partem declamasse?

Gravis scholasticos morbus invasit: exempla cum didicerunt, volunt illa ad aliquod controversiae 13 thema redigere. Hoc quomodo aliquando faciendum est, cum res patitur, ita ineptissimum est luctari cum materia et longe arcessere, sic quomodo fecit in hac controversia Musa, qui, cum diceret pro filio locum de indulgentia liberorum in patres, venit ad

---

[1] diceret: delectavit *Madvig:* dicectauit.

the age where he can understand, but not yet the age where he can invent." [1] " This definition," said Vinicius, " is absurd: ' Nothing is more reliable than a child as witness, especially a five-year-old '! Not if the witness is a child of four or six ? " He added, very nicely: " You might suppose something was at stake. Everything in this epigram betokens the circumspect man—the definition, the limitation: but nothing is more attractive than scrupulous stupidity."

The epigram of Votienus Montanus which he said 12 was similar to this he also derided: " The dog is an unsleeping and wakeful animal, particularly one on a chain, at the ready." But he wasn't altogether fair to Montanus as a man. He had accused him before the emperor, appearing for the colony of Narbo.[2] But Montanus was so utterly a schoolman that the same day he was accused by Vinicius he said: " I enjoyed Vinicius' speech," and retailed some epigrams from it. Surdinus said wittily to him: " I say, do you really think he was simply declaiming the other side ? "

A serious disease has seized on the schoolmen. Having learnt up instances, they want to force them into some *controversia* theme. This is permissible 13 sometimes when the subject allows of it; but it is very silly to struggle against one's material and go to great lengths for one's examples, as did Musa in this *controversia*. Speaking for the son the commonplace on the

---

[1] Cf. Quintilian 5.7.36: " Oratory has much to do in the case of evidence from children: one side will say that they have no powers of invention, the other that they have no judgement."

[2] Montanus' home town.

filium Croesi et ait: mutus in periculo patris naturalia vocis inpedimenta perrupit, qui plus quam quinquennio tacuerat. Quia quinquennis puer ponitur, putavit ubicumque nominatum esset quinquennium sententiam fieri, quia Latroni bene cesserat, qui, cum elusisset vulnus exiguum, dixit: aspicite istam vix apparentem cicatricem; rogo vos: non putetis puerulum fecisse et ne puerulum quidem quinquennem?

14 Gallus Vibius inprobam dixit sententiam cum caedem describeret: occidit, inquit, maritum, novercam laesit, puero pepercit: etiamnunc putabat suum. Valde enim puero Cestius aiebat parcendum; 318M itaque dixit, cum laudaret eius testimonium: procuratore ⟨me⟩ [1] natus es. Hermagoras hunc sensum decentius posuit: κατὰ τὸν ἀδελφὸν ἢ μή;

Blandi sententia laudabatur, cum descripsisset a puero demonstratum procuratorem: digitum multa significantem!

15 Euctemon dixit: μητρυιά, χρηστὸν εὗρον μάρτυρα. ὦ παιδίον εὐσεβές· ὦ παιδίον †ἄξιον τῆς σῆς† [2] μητρός, ὅλον δὲ πατρός.

Murredius mimico genere fatuam sententiam dixit,

---

[1] procuratore me *Madvig:* procuratore(m).
[2] *So the editors; the MSS have* αξιο ιηϲ η *or similar. I have translated what seems to be the sense.*

---

[1] The story is told by Val. Max. 5.4 ext. 6, precisely under the heading of " Affection towards parents."
[2] As he would be once the guardianship began (see on §4):

affection of children for their fathers, he arrived at Croesus' son, and said: " Though he had been dumb for more than five years, when peril threatened his father he broke through the natural impediments to his voice." [1] Just because the boy is five in the theme, he imagined that whenever five years were mentioned it counted as an epigram—for Latro had been successful in saying, after mocking the tiny wound: " Look at this scar—one can scarcely see it. I ask you: wouldn't you imagine a child had done it—and not even a five-year-old? "

Vibius Gallus produced an outrageous epigram 14 when describing the murder: " He killed the father, he wounded the step-mother, he spared the boy: he already thought of the boy as his own." [2] Cestius, indeed, said the boy should be spared at all costs; this is why, when praising his evidence, he said: " You were born while *I* was agent." [3] Hermagoras put this idea more appropriately: " According to his brother—or not? " [4]

Blandus' epigram was praised; when he had described the child pointing out the agent, he said: " What an informative finger! "

Euctemon said: " Step-mother, I have found an 15 excellent witness. Good little child!—child with no share in your mother—wholly your father's."

Murredius employed a ridiculous epigram of the

the further hint—that the agent was the natural father—is what Seneca, and Cestius, disapproved.

[3] The implication is that the child was born before the agent arrived (cf. §1 for the son having been agent), and so was not his son.

[4] The context is unclear. But the " idea " expressed by Hermagoras is probably Vibius Gallus', not Cestius'.

cum dixisset novercam disputare contra filii sui
testimonium: facit, inquit, quod solet: pro amatore
sanguini suo non parcit.

Nicocrates Lacon aridus et exucus declamator
dixit: τοῦ μὲν ἰδίου μάρτυρος ἐφείσατο, τοῦ δ᾽ ἐμοῦ
κατεφρόνησεν.

Hermagoras, cum miserabilem dixisset pueri condicionem esse, qui infestae novercae et procuratori
redderetur, dixit iam procuratorem clamare: οὐκ
ἔστιν ἡμέτερος.

VI

Demens qui Servo Filiam Iunxit

Tyrannus permisit servis dominis interemptis
dominas suas rapere. Profugerunt principes
civitatis; inter eos qui filium et filiam habebat   319
profectus est peregre. Cum omnes servi dominas
suas vitiassent, servos eius virginem servavit.
Occiso tyranno reversi sunt principes; in crucem
servos sustulerunt; ille manu misit et filiam con-
locavit. Accusatur a filio dementiae.

1 ARGENTARI. *Haberemus solacium si has nuptias
tyrannus fecisset, non pater.* Habe hunc illi honorem:

---

[1] i.e. Publilian (see *C*. 7.3.8 *seq.*). There is a double meaning
of *sanguis*—" blood " (with allusion to the wound) and
" blood-relation."

[2] Wife and child respectively: cf. §4 " There are three
people . . ."

mime variety,[1] after saying that the step-mother was arguing against her own son's testimony: " She is acting as she usually does; on her lover's behalf, she does not spare her blood."

Nicocrates the Spartan, a dry and sapless declaimer, said: " He spared his own witness, and despised mine." [2]

Hermagoras, having said how wretched the child's plight was—for he was to be handed over to a hostile step-mother and the agent—said that the agent was already shouting: " He is not ours."

6

THE MADMAN WHO MARRIED HIS DAUGHTER TO A SLAVE

A tyrant gave permission to slaves to kill their masters and rape their mistresses.[3] The chief men of the state fled; among them one who had a son and a daughter set off abroad. Though all the other slaves raped their mistresses, this man's slave kept the girl inviolate. When the tyrant had been killed, the chief men returned, and crucified their slaves. But this man manumitted his slave, and gave him his daughter in marriage. His son accuses him of insanity.[4]

For the son

ARGENTARIUS. We should have some consolation 1 if it had been the tyrant who brought about this

---

[3] Compare the licence allowed to slaves at Volsinium according to Val. Max. 9.1 ext. 2.
[4] See *C.* 2.3 n.

fac dotalem, sine dominam custodiat. *Sanum putatis esse qui maluit tyrannum imitari quam servum?* Pater noster honestis parentibus natus—qui enim aliter condicionem matris nostrae habere potuisset, si tantum ingenuus fuisset?

2 CESTI PII. Soror, opto tibi perpetuam sterilitatem. Cum dicerem: "manu mittamus servum," aiebat: "expectemus sororis nuptias." Ergo tibi, soror, ut honestos habeas liberos adulterandum est? *Fecit se similem tyranno, filiam raptis, libertum cruciariis. Plus servo dominus permisit quam tyrannus. Qui facit has nuptias aut insanus est aut tyrannus.* Quis hoc potest credere, optandum filiae fuisse ne finiretur tyrannis, ne rediret pater? Si interrogavero patrem quod gravissimum in tyrannide fuerit scelus, si sanus est respondebit: quod dominae servis conlocatae sunt.

3 FULVI SPARSI. Eligitur maritus quem sanus pater dotalem dedisset. Gener tuus ipsis nuptiis crucem meruit. *Egregium generum, in quo nihil est gloriosius quam quod inter cruciarios non est!* Gravissima ipsi quoque servo facta est iniuria: dominam suam illi non licuit servare virginem.

---

[1] For the special circumstances of slaves given as part of a woman's dowry, see W. W. Buckland, *The Roman Law of Slavery* (Cambridge, 1908), 262 *seq.*

[2] But not marry her.

[3] i.e. making his daughter marry a slave rather than (as the slave had) maintaining her honour.

marriage, not my father.—Let him have the honour of being made a dowry slave,[1] let him be guard to his mistress.[2]—Do you regard as sane a man who preferred acting like a tyrant to acting like a slave? [3]—Our father, born of honourable parents—for how otherwise could he have won the hand of our mother, if he had merely been free-born?

CESTIUS PIUS. Sister, I pray you will be perpetually 2 barren.—When I said: " Let us free the slave," he [4] said: " Let us wait for your sister's marriage." [5]—Must you then, sister, commit adultery if you want to have respectable children?—He has made himself like the tyrant, his daughter like the women who were raped, his freedman like the slaves who were crucified.—The master has allowed his slave more licence than the tyrant did.—A man who makes such a match is either madman or tyrant.—Who can believe that a daughter should have had to pray that the tyranny should not end, that her father should not return from exile?—If I ask my father what the worst outrage during the tyranny was, he will reply, if he is sane: " The marrying off of mistresses to their slaves."

FULVIUS SPARSUS. The chosen husband is one 3 whom a sane father would have given her as a dowry slave.—Your son-in-law has deserved crucifixion just because of his marriage.—An excellent son-in-law, whose main claim to fame is that he is not one of the crucified.—The slave himself has been seriously wronged: he has not been *allowed* to preserve his mistress' virginity.

[4] The father.
[5] For the freeing of slaves on wedding-days, cf. §3 Blandus, §15 Cestius.

Blandi. Fecit etiam servo iniuriam, cui detraxit
abstinentiae gloriam. Nuptiis suis manu missus est. 320M
O matrimonium omni adulterio turpius!

4 Iuli Bassi. Liberata re publica quod me tristem
vidistis, nolite mirari: nobis etiamnunc vivit tyrannus.
Virginitatem, quam sub tyranno servaverat, perdidit
sub patre. Dic, furcifer: cui sororem meam virginem servasti? Dic, si placet: "mihi." Non
vitiavit, inquit, cum liceret illi. *Itane iste nuptiis*
dignus est quia indignus est cruce? ⟨Vel servus⟩ ¹ ex
cella sua in dominae migrabit cubiculum, vel domina
ex cubiculo suo migrabit in cellam.

5 Corneli Hispani. *Melioris condicionis sunt vitiatae*
quam virgo: illis tamen *mutare nuptias contigit.*
Quare, tyrannicida, praemium accepisti? etiamnunc
aliqua ex edicto tyranni nupta est. Qui edictum
tyranni fugerat redit cum edicto. Dementia hoc
patris factum est, ut tyrannum accusare non posset.
Quid? ille, inquit, filiam meam virginem alteri servavit? Nunc maritus est qui sub tyranno quoque
nihil amplius potuit quam raptor esse. Is qui dotalis
destinatus erat custos relictus est. Propositum est
edictum quod ne ferremus fugimus. Nihil per totum
publicae servitutis spatium indignius visum est, nihil
dis hominibusque minus ferendum. Itaque tyrannus

---

¹ *Supplied by C. F. W. Müller.*

Blandus. He has done his slave too a wrong—by taking away his boast of continence.—He has been manumitted at his own marriage.—What a marriage! —more shameful than any adultery.

Julius Bassus. Don't be surprised if you saw me 4 looking sad when the state was freed; even now *we* have a tyrant alive.—She has lost under her father the virginity she had preserved under the tyrant.—Tell me, jail-bird: whom did you keep my sister virgin for? Say, if you will: " Myself."—" He did not violate her when he could have done." Does he deserve the match just because he doesn't deserve the cross?—The slave will leave his cell for his mistress' bedroom—or the mistress her bedroom for his cell.

Cornelius Hispanus. The women who were raped 5 are in a better plight than the ones who remained virgin: *they* at least have had the chance to change their partners.—Why did the tyrannicide get his reward? Even now a woman has been married according to the tyrant's edict.—A man who had fled the tyrant's edict returns—with the edict.—My father's madness means that he could not accuse the tyrant.[1]—" What? " he says, " did he preserve my daughter's virginity for another to enjoy? "—Now he is a husband—one who even under the tyrant could be no more than a ravisher. The man who had been marked out as part of her dowry has been left as her guardian.—An edict was promulgated—we fled so as not to have to endure it. Nothing during the whole period of the people's slavery was thought more wicked, more intolerable to gods and men. And so it was after *this* that the tyrant got killed.—The girl

[1] Having acted in the same way.

post hoc occisus est.　Desponsa est puella; omnia ex
edicto tyranni facta sunt.

6　ALBUCI SILI.　Egregius gener, cuius haec una
gloria est, quod comparatus cruciariis frugalior est.
Melius servus custodit dominam quam pater filiam.　321M
*Propitius pater ita filiam suam collocavit quemadmodum
iratus tyrannus alienas.*　Inimici tibi nepotes precan-
tur.　*Cum sanus pater fuit, ne has videret nuptias fugit.*
Parum putatis magnum argumentum dementiae
quod egit tyrannum in mortem, patres in exilium,
servos in crucem?　Quomodo qui sic fugis sic
conlocas?　Honestius exul es quam socer.　Si voles
invenire generi tui propinquos, ad crucem eundum
est.

7　ARELLI FUSCI patris.　Ex servo gener, [et]¹ ex
domina uxor, ex domino socer factus est.　Quis has
nuptias non tyranni putet?　Patrem tyranni criminibus accuso, tyrannum patris.　Quid de tyranno
querar? patri similis est.　Quid de patre non querar?
tyranno similis est.　*Miserrima soror, sub tyranno
patrem desiderabas, sub patre tyrannum desideras.*　Id
in filia tua coegisti quod tyrannus tantum permiserat.
Nunc nobis, pater, si sanus es, exulandum est.　Quid
enim miserius accidere potest quam is status in
libertate quem ceteri vix ferunt in servitute?　Fugimus ne serviremus.　Felicitatem nostram in calami-

¹ *Deleted by C. F. W. Müller.*

---

¹ Or perhaps: "What complaint can I make . . . What
complaint can I not make."

has been betrothed: everything has been done in accordance with the edict of the tyrant.

ALBUCIUS SILUS. What a fine son-in-law: his only 6 boast is that he is more respectable—when compared with crucified slaves.—The slave looked after his mistress better than the father his daughter.—The kind father has married off his own daughter the way the angry tyrant married off other people's.—Your enemies pray for you to have grandchildren.—When my father was sane, he went into exile so as not to have to put up with the sight of this marriage.—Do you regard as an insufficient proof of madness something that has brought a tyrant to death, fathers to exile, slaves to the cross?—If you go into exile like that, how can you marry off your daughter like this? —It is more honourable for you to be an exile than a father-in-law.—If you want to discover your son-in-law's relatives, you must go to the cross.

ARELLIUS FUSCUS SENIOR. The slave has become 7 the son-in-law; his mistress has become his wife; his master has become his father-in-law. Who would not suppose this a marriage arranged by the tyrant? —I accuse my father for the tyrant's crimes, the tyrant for my father's crimes. How complain of the tyrant? He is like my father. How not complain [1] of my father? He is like the tyrant. Wretched sister, under the tyrant you missed your father, under your father you miss the tyrant.—You have forced on your daughter something the tyrant merely permitted.—Now, father, if you are sane we must go into exile: for what could be more wretched than a state of affairs in a free community that the rest scarcely tolerate in slavery?—We fled so as not to be slaves.—

tatem convertit; aliquanto enim fuit satius cum
ceteris contumeliam ferre quam liberatis omnibus
solos in tyrannidem reici. Servo libertatem dedit,
filiae servitutem. Servo filiam dedit, innocentiam
abstulit. Nescio quid sibi velit quod servi meritum
laudat; tyrannum enim laudare debebat. Servus 3221
noster ⟨non est⟩[1] stultus: tergus ⟨et⟩ caput suum
deliciis praesentibus praetulit. Si dixerit se exti-
muisse tantum nefas, laudabo et hanc illi etiamnunc
8 optabo mentem. Ceterae honestos invenerunt sibi
viros; haec talem habet quales illae in tyrannide
habuerunt. Soror mea ancillulae paelex est, et,
ut domina nuberet, conserva de cellula est eiecta.
Nullum in tyranno maius scelus fuit quam quod tibi
libuit imitari. O te, soror, miseram, quod ista non
sub tyranno passa es! iam enim pati desisses. Hoc tu
putas praemium esse: quia dominam non violavit,
violet quantum volet. Iste vero, ut dices, iniuriam
tibi fecit quia adfinitatem tuam moratus est. Si non
cessasset, iam fortasse ex illo nepotes haberemus.
Habeamus generum, si possumus, parem ⟨vel⟩[2]
similem; si minus, non erubescendum, cui cognatus

[1] *Supplied by Müller.*
[2] *Supplied by Müller.*

He has converted our good fortune into disaster. For it was rather better to endure outrage with everyone else for company than for us alone to be plunged back into tyranny when all have been freed.—He has given his slave freedom, his daughter slavery. He has given his daughter to a slave, and taken his innocence away from him.—I don't know what he means by praising the merits of his slave; he ought to have been praising the tyrant.[1]—Our slave is no fool; he preferred his hide and his head to the pleasures of the moment. If he says he was afraid to do such a wicked deed, I will praise him, and pray that he shows such an attitude even now.—All the other women have found themselves respectable husbands; this one has a husband like those *they* had under the tyranny.—My sister is rival of a slave-girl, and, so that the mistress could marry, a fellow-slave had to be ejected from his cell.—The tyrant did nothing worse than what you were pleased to imitate.—How unlucky you are, sister, not to have suffered this fate under the tyrant—for then you would have ceased to suffer it by now.—You regard this as his reward: because he did not rape his mistress, let him rape her as much as he likes.—But he, you will say, did you an injury by delaying his marriage-connection with you.[2] If he had not held back, by now, perhaps, we should have grandchildren by him.—Let us have, if possible, a son-in-law who is equal or like us; if not, let us have one for whom we do not need to blush, one

[1] Having acted similarly.

[2] Sarcastic: the son represents his father as so enthusiastic about the match that he complains it was not arranged earlier, under the tyrant.

sit aliquis, cui sacra aliqua et penetralia in quae
deducatur uxor, quem adiungamus ad domum, non
quem ex censu deleamus.

9   PORCI LATRONIS. Qui omnia tuleramus, hoc
fugimus. Vocat servum et, quia crucem non meruerat, mereri iubet. Itane, furcifer, tu potuisti
dominam complecti? Putasti aut semper tyrannum   323
victurum aut semper afuturum [1] patrem? Felicis-
simae videbuntur quibus contigerat raptus tyrannicus.
Ita sine dubio beneficium dedit, quod custodit dominam a stupro, se a cruce. Cum infelici face ad dotalem suum nova nupta deduceretur, si qua fides est,
exhorrui, quasi repositum esset edictum. Cogitabam
quem sorori virum eligerem. Simpliciter fatebor:
fastidiebam iam eas condiciones quae ante profec-
tionem fuerant; aiebam: illo tempore et aliae virgines erant. "Non vitiavit" inquit "sub tyrannide." O nos felices, si ne nunc quidem!

10   TRIARI. Age, hoc *non est praemium, unum spectare
omnium cruces?* Certum habeo, si habuisset tyrannus
filiam, non scripsisset edictum. Indicit festum
diem, aperiri iubet maiorum imagines, cum maxime
tegendae sunt.

VARI GEMINI. Eadem hora et libertum fecit et
generum. Hoc fecisti quod tyrannus non cogit,

---

[1] afuturum *Otto:* futurum.

---

[1] Answer, No: the implication (as in the previous epigram)
seems to be that the slave realised the tyranny would end (cf.
Latro's *colour* in §14), and only for this reason did not rape
the girl.

[2] Now there will be less competition.

with a relative or two, things he holds sacred, a household shrine to take his wife home to: one we can add to our household, not strike off the roll.

PORCIUS LATRO. We endured everything—but in 9 face of *this* we fled.—He summons the slave, and, because he had not hitherto deserved crucifixion, orders him to deserve it now.—Is this, jail-bird, the way you were able to embrace your mistress?—Did you think the tyrant would live for ever, or the father be away for ever?[1]—The women who got raped on the *tyrant's* orders will be thought most fortunate.— This, of course, was the service he performed: he saved his mistress from rape, and himself from the cross.—When, by the light of ill-omened torches, the new bride was led to marry her dowry slave, I shivered —if you will believe me—as though the edict had been renewed.—I was wondering whom to choose as my sister's husband. I will be frank: I was by now scorning the matches in prospect before our departure; I said to myself: " *Then* there were *other* virgins."[2]—" He didn't violate her under the tyranny." How happy we would be if he didn't now, either!

TRIARIUS. Well, doesn't this count as a reward— 10 to be the sole spectator of the crucifixion of all?—I am convinced that if the tyrant had had a daughter he wouldn't have written the edict.[3]—He announces the festive day, orders the busts of his ancestors to be put on view—just when they ought to be veiled.

VARIUS GEMINUS. The same moment made him both freedman and son-in-law.—You have done something that a tyrant does not enforce except

[3] Why then should a father put the edict into force again?

nisi cum irascitur, servos ne tunc quidem facit cum cogitur. Generum habes: qualem? ut illi laudationem suam reddam, nempe frugi servum. Servis tuis paritura fratres ⟨est⟩.[1] Quantum ad expositionem rerum pertinet, sunt quidem acerba tyrannidis mala, tamen tristiora exponam quae post tyrannidem gesta sunt. Non dubitabam quin esset tyrannicidae nuptura. Si sub tyranno vitiata esset, solacium haberemus hoc: non tibi uni accidit. Nondum occisum tyrannum puto, etiamnunc tyrannicas nuptias video. 324↑

11 MARULLI. Nunc sciam an merito libertatem acceperis, si liber non merueris crucem. Hoc quod obicio qui in pluribus fecit occisus est.

P. VINICI. Nunc in domo nostra matrimonium est cuius me puderet etiamsi raptus esset. Quam miseros putatis, iudices, esse quibus duo quae miserrima sunt optanda fuerunt, tyrannus et raptor? Una genero tuo commendatio est, quod se aliquando ista puella putavit indignum.

VALLI SYRIACI. In ea condicione, iudices, sumus ut consolari debeamus sororem quod aut rapta non sit aut nupserit. Et tamen quid ille meruit, quamdiu per dominum licuit innocentissimus servus?

12 SEPULLI BASSI. Nuptias clausa domo fecimus.

---

[1] *Supplied by Müller.*

---

[1] Actually the law *permitted* rape (cf. Latro's emphasis in §13).

when he is angry—and what a slave won't do even when he is forced.[1]—You have a son-in-law. What sort? A good slave, indeed—I must give him his due.—She will bear brothers for your slaves.—As to the narration of the facts, the evils of tyranny are bitter—but more terrible still are the actions following the tyranny: and it is of these I have to tell.—I had no doubt that she would marry the tyrannicide.—If she had been violated under the tyrant, we should have the consolation: " You aren't the only one this happened to."—I don't believe the tyrant is killed yet —I still see a marriage of the tyrant's type.

MARULLUS. Now I shall find out whether you 11 deserved your freedom—by seeing if you do not deserve crucifixion now you are free.—The man[2] who did what I am complaining of in the case of more than one girl has been killed.

PUBLIUS VINICIUS. Now we have in the family a marriage which I should be ashamed of even if it were a rape.—How wretched, judges, do you imagine people are who have had to pray for the two most wretched things—a tyrant and a ravisher?[3]—Your son-in-law has one thing in his favour: at one time he thought himself unworthy of this girl.

VALLIUS SYRIACUS. We are in such a plight, judges, that we have to console my sister either for not being raped or for getting married.—Yet what has he deserved, this slave who was altogether innocent, so long as his master allowed him to be?

SEPULLIUS BASSUS. We held the marriage behind 12

[2] i.e. the tyrant.
[3] In preference to a father and a husband (cf. §7 " Wretched sister . . .").

In contubernium deducta servi domina est: ita iste dexteram sororis meae nisi dum manu mittitur non contigit.

POLLIONIS ASINI. Inter nuptiales fescenninos in crucem generi nostri iocabantur. Miserrimum me diem egisse memini quo servire coepit res publica, miserrimum ⟨me⟩ [1] diem egisse memini quo in exilium fugimus: inter hos dies sororis nuptias numero. Miserrima soror, fortasse vernularum tuorum noverca es. Pater, volo ducere uxorem: dic quam mihi ex ancillis despondeas.

Contra. ALBUCI SILI. Servavit dominam. *Si quis tyranno indicasset, solus in cruce pependisset.*

13   DIVISIO. Latro in has quaestiones divisit: an, etiamsi non debuit filiam sic collocare, damnari tamen ob hoc non possit dementiae. Licet, inquit, mihi filiam meam cui velim conlocare: isto modo et 325 repudium ⟨cum⟩ [2] remisero genero accusabor. Male conlocavi filiam: et multi alii. Quid tibi videntur hi qui abducunt filias suas †avari†? Sed male ⟨conlocavi⟩ [3] eam: nec ob hoc damnabor. Tu patrem debes dementem accusare, non sanum regere. Ego istud an sine ratione fecerim videbimus: satis est si sana mente feci.

  [1] *Supplied by C. F. W. Müller.*
  [2] *Supplied by Bursian.*
  [3] *Supplied here by Müller.*

----

  [1] The " Fescennine jesting " of Catullus 61.120.
  [2] The father curries favour by promising more sane actions in future.
  [3] i.e. neither action is fit subject for accusation. But the text is doubtful.

closed doors. The mistress was escorted—to cohabit with her slave. So it was that this man never touched my sister's hand, except when he was manumitted.

ASINIUS POLLIO. Amid the licentious jesting of the wedding,[1] they made jokes about the crucifixion of our son-in-law.—I remember it as a bad day for me when the state began to be enslaved, a bad day when we went into exile; I count my sister's wedding-day comparable with those.—Wretched sister, perhaps you are step-mother to your own home-bred slaves.— Father, I wish to marry: tell me which of the slave-girls you betroth to me.

The other side

ALBUCIUS SILUS. He saved his mistress. If anyone had informed on him to the tyrant, he would have been the only one to get crucified.

Division

Latro distinguished these questions: Even if he [13] ought not to have married off his daughter thus, can he be convicted of madness for it? " I can marry my daughter to whoever I wish; on these principles I shall also be accused when I tell my son-in-law to leave my daughter.[2] I have made a bad marriage for my daughter—but then so have many others. What do you think of people who remove their daughters from their husbands?[3] But I have made a bad marriage for her: I shan't get condemned for *that*. You must accuse your father when he is mad— not control his actions when he is sane. We shall see if I did it for no good reason: but it suffices if I did it while of sound mind."

Deinde: an sic filiam conlocare debuerit. Hoc in haec divisit: an, etiamsi bene meruit servus, non tamen sic illi referenda fuerit gratia. Deinde: an bene meruerit; de facto servi primum disputavit, deinde de animo. Factum quale est? *dominam non stupravit. Auge beneficia: nec dominum occidit nec* adulter domino *venenum dedit. Non est beneficium scelere abstinere.* Et tyrannus permisit dominas rapere, non coegit. Deinde hoc beneficium eius quod laudas serva: alioqui iniuriam fecit, si non subducta est iniuriae, sed reservata; tunc tamen solacium fuisset cum multis pati. Denique, *quod aliae in tyrannide passae sunt, haec in libertate; ceterae absentibus suis, haec praesentibus; in aliis stuprum vocabatur, in hac matrimonium;* in aliis finis expectabatur iniuriae, in hac nullus; denique illarum stupratores suffixi sunt, huius manu missus est. Deinde de animo servi.

14 Latro colorem a fili parte, quare non vitiasset servos, hunc fecit: *timuisse illum supplicium, scisse futurum ut liberata re publica* omnes *poenas qui contaminassent* dominas suas *darent; et adventare* iam *tempus ultimum tyrannidi videbatur,* cum ad summam perducta ⟨esset⟩ rabiem, quae numquam nisi ex desperatione fit. Itaque cum videret, inquit, suffigi cruci servos, clamabat: hoc ego futurum sciebam. In ultima oratione Latro dixit: servi quoque nomine tecum

326M

---

¹ Cf. Cic. *Phil.* 2.5: '' quale autem beneficium est quod te abstinueris nefario scelere? ''

Then: Should he have married his daughter off thus? This he sub-divided: Even if the slave deserved well, should he have been rewarded like this? Then: *Did* he deserve well? He discussed first the slave's action, then his motives. " What kind of thing did he do? He did not rape his mistress. Increase his services—he did not kill his master, seduce his master's wife, then give his master poison. It is no service to abstain from crime.[1] And the tyrant *allowed* rape of mistresses—he did not enforce it. Then, you should preserve this service of his that you praise; otherwise he did wrong in saving her up for a wrong rather than removing her from it, though *then* she would have had the consolation of suffering along with many others. Finally, the girl has suffered in a free state what others suffered under a tyranny; the others in the absence of their family, she in its presence; for the rest it was called rape, for her the name is marriage. The others could look forward to an end of the wrong, she cannot. *Their* ravishers were crucified, hers has been manumitted." Then he discussed the slave's motives.

Latro gave this *colour* on the side of the son to 14 explain why the slave had not raped his mistress: he was afraid of punishment, he knew that when the state was freed all those who had violated their mistresses would pay the penalty. He could see that the final stage of the tyranny was approaching, since it had reached its highest pitch of madness—something that happens only as a result of desperation. " So when he saw slaves being crucified, he shouted: ' I knew it would happen.' " At the end of his speech, Latro said: " I can find fault with you in the name of

queri possum, qui eum qui frugi fuerat nequam fecisti.

Albucius hoc colore usus est: inmatura erat[1] puella nec adhuc iniuriae idonea, et ideo illam non abduximus, quia aetatis beneficio tyrannidem sentire non poterat.

15 Cestius dixit: ego plane non sum detracturus servo suam laudem: habuit bonam mentem; speravit posse fieri ut, si virginem servasset, nuptiis dominae manu mitteretur.

Varius Geminus ait: fortasse amicam habebat, hac delectatus non ⟨est; nam⟩[2] quidam virginum concubitum refugiunt. Fortasse scit illam non esse passuram et, illud quod nequam quoque servos interdum frugi facit, malam fortunam timuit. Et hanc sententiam, quae valde circumlata est, adiecit: an enim furcifer auderet cum domina concumbere nisi illi pater permisisset? Et illud dixit: Ad hoc, pater, ab exilio rediebas? In exilium ergo quid fugimus?

16 Buteo voluit videri re vera mente lapsum patrem et in narratione hoc dixit: Quam maestus venit domum ab edicto tyranni! quantum in sinu filiae flevit! Puto illo tempore mentem esse concussam.

Varius Geminus de abstinentia ⟨servi⟩[3] sic: 327l Contaminare dominam suam et trahere in cellam non est ausus. Nisi forte hoc modo mavis narrem: iam tunc sperare sororis nuptias coeperat.

---

[1] erat *Bursian:* etiam.
[2] *Supplied by Gertz.*
[3] *Supplied by Thomas.*

the slave too—you made him wicked when he had been good."

Albucius employed this *colour*: the girl was still not grown up, not yet ripe for violation. "We did not take her away with us just because thanks to her age she could not feel the effects of the tyranny."

Cestius said: "I definitely do not propose to 15 deprive the slave of the credit that is his due. He had good intentions; he hoped it could turn out that, if he kept her a virgin, he might be manumitted when she got married."

Varius Geminus said: "Perhaps he had a mistress and didn't like this woman. Some people avoid sleeping with a virgin. Perhaps he knew that she would not put up with it, and feared bad fortune to come—something that at times makes even bad slaves good." And he added this epigram, which was widely publicised: "Would a jail-bird dare to sleep with his mistress unless the father [1] had permitted it?" And he also said: "Is it to this that you returned from exile, father? Why then did we go into exile?"

Buteo wanted it to appear that the father really 16 had gone out of his mind, and in his narration he said: "How sad he was when he came home after hearing the tyrant's edict! How he wept in his daughter's bosom! I think that was when his mind became unhinged."

Varius Geminus on the slave's continence: "He didn't dare to violate his mistress and drag her into his cell. Unless you prefer an account like this: Even then he was beginning to entertain hopes of marrying my sister."

[1] And not merely the tyrant.

17   A parte patris magis defensione opus esse dicebat
Latro quam colore. Varius Geminus factum ipsum
defendit: magnos viros fecisse ut libertinas uxores
ducerent. *M. Cato*, inquit, *coloni sui filiam duxit
uxorem.* " Sed ingenuam." Respondeo: sed Cato;
plus interest inter te et Catonem quam inter libertum et colonum. Quam multa commoda haberet
subiectus et obsequens maritus: *non petulantiam
timebit, non verborum contumeliam, non paelicem, non
repudium.* Filiam meam domi semper habebo; quam
eo magis desidero quod adeo diu ab illa afui. Deinde
factum liberti laudavit.

18   Albucius et philosophatus est: dixit *neminem
natura liberum esse, neminem servum; haec postea nomina
singulis inposuisse Fortunam.* Denique, inquit, scis
et nos nuper servos fuisse. Rettulit *Servium regem.*

      Silo Pompeius hoc colore usus dixit: exhaustum
tyrannidis iniuriis patrimonium; non habuisse se
dotem quam daret.

      Argentarius voluit videri puella volente se fecisse.
Visa est, inquit, indulgere illi; certe debuit.

19   Gavius Sabinus hoc colore usus est, ut, in quantum
posset, dignitatem suam destrueret et humilitatem
confiteretur. Et ideo, inquit, facilius potuit non
vitiari quia nemo in domum nostram oculos derige-
bat. Nec sciebam quid [1] facerem, cui conlocarem: 328

----

¹ nec sciebam quid *conjectured by Müller after Gertz:* et
fueram inquit.

----

¹ Plutarch (*Cat. Mai.* 24) describes Cato's second wife as the
daughter of a former secretary.
² A constant idea in the first century A.D.: cf. Sen. *Ep.* 31.11

On the father's side, Latro said there was need of a 17
defence rather than of a *colour*. Varius Geminus
defended the actual deed: great men had married
freedwomen. " Marcus Cato married the daughter
of one of his farmers.[1] ' But *she* was freeborn.' I
reply: it was Cato who married her—and there is
more difference between you and Cato than there is
between a freedman and a farmer. How many
advantages there would be in an inferior and obedient
husband! She will have no need to fear viciousness,
verbal insult, a rival, a divorce. I shall always have
my daughter at home. And I need her the more that
I have been parted from her so long." Then he
praised the action of the freedman.

Albucius also philosophised: he said no-one is 18
naturally free or slave. These are titles imposed
later on individuals by fortune.[2] " Lastly, you know
that we too were recently [3] slaves." He brought up
the case of King Servius.

Pompeius Silo used this *colour*: His estate had been
exhausted as a result of the wrongs done under the
tyranny; he had no dowry to give her.

Argentarius wanted it to be thought that he had
acted with the girl's approval. " She seemed to
favour him. Certainly she should have done."

Gavius Sabinus used a *colour* that involved, as far as 19
possible, diminishing the father's dignity and acknowledging his lowness. " She could escape the more
easily from violation because no-one was casting an
eye on our house. I didn't know what to do, whom

and 47.10, *Ben.* 3.28.1; also *C.* 1.6.4, where King Servius
recurs.
  [3] Under the tyranny.

quaerendus mihi erat gener aliquis libertinus. Quid
ergo? alieno potius liberto? Hunc iam novi; scio
cuius in nos adfectus sit; si moriar, scio me meam
filiam apud hunc tuto relicturum. Et hanc sententiam adiecit, quae valde excepta est: eum non con-
tempsi generum qui tyrannum contempserat.

20   Accaus Postumius hoc colore usus est: Nihil est,
inquit, invidia periculosius; hanc sapientes viri velut
pestiferam vitandam esse praecipiunt: hanc vitavi.
Ingens invidia erat: " hic nunc nobis obicit fortunam
liberorum nostrorum." Oderant filiam meam femi-
nae, me patres, quasi publici mali segregem expro-
bratorem; quo uno modo honeste potui, feci filiam
meam ceteris similem, fortunam meam publicae
parem: sic [1] detracta omnis invidia est; filiam non
habeo honestiorem quam vos, servum frugaliorem
habui quam vos.

21   Hispo Romanius dixerat: maritum autem ego istum
vocem raptorem serotinum? Verbum hoc quasi apud
antiquos non usurpatum quibusdam displicebat.
Eiusdem verbi significatione, ut extra reprehensionem
esset, usus est Gavius Sabinus cum diceret nondum
esse consummatam adversus servos publicam vindictam: etiamnunc in domo nostra residuus raptor 329M
est.

22   Saturninus Furius, qui Volesum condemnavit,
maius nomen in foro quam in declamationibus habuit;
solebat tamen tam honeste declamare ut scires illum

---

[1] parem: sic *Gertz:* partis.

to marry her to. I had to look for some freedman as my son-in-law. Well, was it to be someone else's for preference? I know this one; I know his feelings towards us; if I die, I know I shall be leaving my daughter in good hands." And he added this highly acclaimed epigram: " I did not despise as son-in-law one who had despised a tyrant."

Postumius Accaus' *colour* was: " Nothing is more 20 dangerous than envy. Philosophers instruct us to avoid it like poison;[1] I have avoided it. My unpopularity was great. People said: ' Now this man reproaches us with the luck of our children.' Women hated my daughter, fathers hated me as apart from the public trouble—and as reproaching it in others. The only honourable course open to me I have taken— I have made my daughter like the others, my fortune like that of everybody else. Thus I have got rid of all unpopularity; I do not have a daughter more respectable than you—though I had a slave more honourable than you had."

Romanius Hispo had said: " But am I to give the 21 name of husband to this tardy ravisher? " The word *serotinus*,[2] not having been employed in the old days, displeased some. To escape criticism, Gavius Sabinus used a periphrasis for the word, when saying that public punishment of the slaves was not yet complete: " There is still, in our household, a ravisher left over."

Furius Saturninus, who got Volesus convicted, had 22 a greater reputation in the courts than in declamation. But he used to declaim so well that you could

---

[1] Cf. the (Stoic) argument in Cic. *Tusc.* 3.21: " non cadit . . . invidere in sapientem."

[2] Here used for the first time in extant literature?

huic materiae non minus idoneum esse sed minus familiarem. Is in hac controversia, cum L. Lamiae filio declamaret, dixit sententiam: ὁ μὲν πατὴρ χείρων γέγονεν τυράννου, ὁ δὲ δοῦλος ἑαυτοῦ.

Ex tabellis emptionis multi sententiam trahere temptaverunt. Albucius dixit: Profer mihi tabellas. Quid hoc est? generum socer mancipio accepit. 23 Triarius dixit: "fugitivum, erronem non esse": ita, si malum auctorem habemus, gener noster fugitivus est? Blandus dixit: Relegamus auctoritatis tabellas: "furtis noxaque solutum." Haec generi nostri laudatio est. Gallio dixit: Furtis noxaque solutus est . . .[1] Sparsus dixit: Ostende tabellas. Quid nobis cum isto genero? Prior dominus promisit fugitivum non esse. Gratulor vobis, posteri: patrem fugitivum non habebitis. Varius Geminus dixit: "Erronem non esse"; adicio fugitivum non esse, adicio noxa furtisque solutum. Numquid de 24 generi tui nobilitate detraxi? Pollio aiebat ridere se quod declamatores decrevissent hunc utique empticium esse.

Mirari vos puto quod in hac controversia omnes declamatores mentis suae fuerint. Non fuerunt. Nepos Mamilius, cum hortaretur libertum ad repudium sororis, dixit: refer nobis gratiam: et tu sororem meam manu mitte. Nepos Licinius illi non cessit;

---

[1] *Lacuna marked by R. G. Austin.*

tell that he was less at home with this type of material rather than less suited to it. In this *controversia*, declaiming before the son of Lucius Lamia, he produced the epigram: " The father has turned out worse than the tyrant—the slave worse than himself."

Many tried to get an epigram out of the documents of the slave's purchase.[1] Albucius said: " Produce me the documents. What is this? A father has got a son-in-law by deed of purchase." Triarius said: " ' He 23 is not a runaway or a vagrant.' Then if the vendor is not to be trusted, we have a runaway for a son-in-law? " Blandus said: " Let us go over the documents of title again. ' He is free from thefts and guilt.' Such is the praise accorded to our son-in-law." Gallio said: " He is free of thefts and guilt." . . . Sparsus said: " Show us the documents. What have we to do with such a son-in-law? His former master guaranteed he was no runaway. I congratulate the progeny: they will not have a runaway for their father." Varius Geminus said: " ' He is no vagrant.' I add that he is no runaway, that he is free of guilt and thefts. Have I removed any of your son-in-law's claims to nobility? " Pollio said he used to 24 be amused because the declaimers decided he could only be a bought slave.

You must be feeling surprised, I imagine, that in this *controversia* all the declaimers remained in their right minds. But in fact they did not. Mamilius Nepos, encouraging the freedman to divorce his sister, said: " Do *us* a service: *you*, manumit my sister."

---

[1] " In the purchase of slaves a guarantee is normally given that he is healthy and free from thefts or liability " (Varro *Res Rust.* 2.10.5); Gell. 4.2.1; Buckland, *op. cit.*, 52 *seq.*

THE ELDER SENECA

dixit enim: in illa subsellia *transite servi, transite liberti,* 330
empta cognatio. Et cum illum sensum elegantem et
ab omnibus iactatum subripuisset: " soror, opto tibi
sterilitatem," adiecit: nec est quod mireris me
timere partum tuum: ⟨certum⟩[1] habeo sic nasci
tyrannos.

VII

CAVETE PRODITOREM

Proditionis sit actio.

Pater et filius imperium petierunt; praelatus
est patri filius. Bellum commisit cum hoste;
captus est. Missi sunt decem legati ad redimendum imperatorem. Euntibus illis occurrit
pater cum auro; dixit filium suum crucifixum esse
et sero se aurum ad redemptionem tulisse. Illi
pervenerunt ad crucifixum imperatorem; quibus ille dixit: " cavete proditionem." Accusatur pater proditionis.

1 ALBUCI SILI. Quid desideratis ultra? *imperator
supplicium tulit, proditor pretium. Tristiorem istum
vidimus cum filius imperator renuntiatus est quam cum*

[1] *Supplied by Schultingh.*

---

[1] Those of the father.
[2] See above, §2.
[3] At Rome this would have formed part of the complex of

144

Licinius Nepos was not to be outdone by him; he said: "Slaves and freedmen, cross to the opposite benches,[1] you relations he has bought." And, filching a pretty idea bandied about by everybody: "Sister, I pray for you to be barren,"[2] he added: "You shouldn't be surprised that I fear your offspring; I am sure this is the way tyrants are bred."

7

BEWARE THE TRAITOR

An action may lie for treachery.[3]

A father and son sought a command. The son was chosen in preference to his father. He went to war with the enemy, and was captured. Ten ambassadors were despatched to ransom the general. The father met them with some gold on their way. He said that his son had been crucified and that he had arrived with the gold too late to ransom him. They got there to find the general on the cross. He said to them: "Beware treachery." The father is accused of treachery.[4]

Against the father

ALBUCIUS SILUS. What more do you want? The 1 general has his punishment, the traitor his price.— We saw him sadder when his son was declared general

maiestas offences; the word *actio*, inapplicable in Rome, suggests that the Greek γραφὴ προδοσίας is the starting-point. See Bonner, 110–11.

[4] The case is discussed by Quintilian 7.1.29–30 (cf. *RLM* p. 376.38 *seq.*).

captus. Redde rationem *quemadmodum redieris tutus,
senex solus cum auro, cum etiam imperatores capiantur.*
Imperator adulescens renuntiatus est omnibus laetis
praeter patrem.

2 CESTI PII. *Plus accepit auri quam quod posset
abscondi. Nolite mirari: et imperatorem et filium
vendiderat. " Cavete proditionem": iam comitiis cavi-
mus. Abstulissent tibi aurum hostes, nisi dedissent.* 331M
Cum de redemptione ageretur, omnes in curia fuerunt
praeter competitorem. *" Cavete proditionem" indicium
fuit morientis breve, fili verecundum.*

BLANDI. *Quomodo te dimiserunt? si nihil aliud, et
ducem genuisti et dux esse voluisti.* Si non decrevera-
mus, consilium nostrum expectari debuit; si decre-
veramus, officium.

ARELLI FUSCI patris. Unde tam graves paterni
sinus? numquid ossa fili reportantur? Expectat
videlicet iudicia vestra reus: tamquam nesciat quid
de illo sentiatis. Non tu semel apud hostem fuisti,
sed nos semel legatos misimus. Imperator non audet
nominare te tamquam patrem.

3 IUNI GALLIONIS. Fuit adulescens optimus, vere-
cundissimus, qui patri suo cessisset si salva pietate

---

[1] These should have been reasons for the enemy killing him:
cf. §7 " Why did the enemy . . ."

[2] That is, on the sending of a ransom. Instead, the father
had gone on his own initiative.

[3] Or perhaps: " to wait to be given the job."

than when he was taken prisoner.—Explain to us how
you managed to return safely, an old man, alone and
carrying gold, at a time when even generals are being
captured.—The young man was declared general to
the delight of everyone—except his father.

CESTIUS PIUS. He received more gold than he 2
could conceal. No wonder: he had sold a general
and a son.—" Beware of treachery." We have already done so—at the elections.—The enemy would
have taken away your gold—but then it was they
who gave it to you.—When there was discussion
about the ransom, everyone was in the senate-house
except the boy's rival.—" Beware treachery "—the
disclosure was brief, for he was dying, and respect-
fully phrased, for he was a son.

BLANDUS. How was it they let you go? If nothing
else, you begot the general, and wanted to be general
yourself.[1]—If we had not passed the decree, it was
his duty to await our discussion;[2] if we had, it was
his duty to await its being carried out.[3]

ARELLIUS FUSCUS SENIOR. How do the father's
pockets come to be so heavy? Can it be that he is
bringing back his son's bones?—Here he is, the
accused man, awaiting your judgement: as if he
didn't know what you think of him.[4]—It is not only
once you have been in the country of the enemy [5]—
but *we* only sent an embassy once.—The general does
not dare name you—for you are his father.

JUNIUS GALLIO. He was an excellent and most 3
modest young man, who would have yielded to his

---

[4] From the result of the election.

[5] Continued betrayal is also hinted at by Gallio in §4 (" You
must not say . . .") and by Hispo in §12.

potuisset. Iterum nobis inter vos, patrem et filium,
iudicandum est. *Candidatus processit contra patrem:* si
silentium eius intellegere scissemus, *et tunc nobis vere-
cunde indicaverat.* Habebas apud hostes auctoritatem:
apparebat te rei publicae irasci. *Legati nostri aurum
ferebant, pater auferebat.* Dixeras illos sero venturos;
non pervenerunt sero: imperatorem nostrum con-
venerunt. Imperator istum accusat, nos subscribi-
mus. Hoc fuit imperatoris nostri testamentum.
4 " Obice " inquit " aliqua ante actae vitae crimina."
Non possum: verecundum conpetitorem habuisti;
multum tacebat. Quod possum tibi maius crimen
obicere? *filius tibi tuus credi rem publicam noluit.* Non 332Ν
est quod dicas: quem misi ad hostes? tamquam ipse
ire non possis. Cur tam cito reverteris? diutius nos
contra filium rogasti quam pro filio hostem. *Non
immobilis stetisti, non illic quasi et ipse adfixus haesisti?
Quid tam cito recedis? Etiamnunc vivit, etiamnunc loquitur.* Recessurus interroga si quid velit mandare.
5 *Voce proditionem coarguit, silentio proditorem.* Intellego quanto istum periculo offendam. Quemadmodum enim iste accusationem vindicabit? cruce.

---

¹ *Pietas* is normally expressed in affection towards one's
father, so this epigram sounds paradoxical. But there was a
higher duty, to one's country, that is primarily meant here.
² Against his father, at the election: but he preferred not
to attack his competitor (cf. §4 " I cannot do it . . ." and §6
" I have nothing . . ."). Nevertheless, it is argued, his

father if he could have done so without neglecting his duty.[1]—For a second time we must judge between father and son.—He stood as candidate against his father; if we had known how to interpret his silence, he gave us information [2] with all diffidence on that occasion also.—You had weight with the enemy; it was clear you were angry with your country.—Our ambassadors were taking gold with them, the father was taking it back.—You had said [3] they would come too late; they did not arrive too late—they met our general.—It is the general who accuses him—we are seconding the charge.—This was our general's last will and testament.—"Reproach me with crimes in [4] my past career." I cannot do it—you had a diffident opponent, and he kept very quiet. What crime can I charge you with greater than this—that your own son didn't want the state entrusted to you?—You must not say: "Whom did I send to the enemy?"—as though you are incapable of going yourself.—Why do you come back so soon? You spent longer imploring us against your son than imploring the enemy for him. Did you not stand unmoving, did you not stick there, as though fixed—as he was? Why do you come back so soon? He still lives, still speaks. As you are about to leave, ask him if he has any instructions.—By his words he proved treachery; by his silence he proved the traitor.—I know well the [5] danger I run in offending him. For how will he revenge himself for the accusation? By the cross.[4]—

silence on the subject should have been seen as an accusation against his father.
    [3] When the ransom was discussed.
    [4] As he had avenged his defeat on his son.

Omnibus argumentis premitur: dabo qui viderint, dabo qui audierint, dabo aurum, dabo testem et, ne quid de dignitate dubitari possit, imperatorem. De hoc utrum volet dicat: " inimicus est " ⟨vel " filius est "⟩.[1] Hunc indicavit. Utrum tantum auri erat ut appareret etiam non quaerentibus, an tam suspectus eras ut quemvis illa vox[2] admoneret " proditionem cavete "? Optimus adulescens, *optimus imperator*, qui *rei publicae curam agere ne in cruce quidem desiit! Dignum te non putavit filius cui diceret: " cave proditionem."*

6   VARI GEMINI.   Nolite omnia expectare ab accusatore et occupato et verecundo: reum intellegite; crimina audistis.   Quaeris ante actae vitae crimina? Non habeo: nihil tibi umquam filius obicere voluit. Tam cito lassatae preces tuae sunt?   Quid faciet miser? *nec imperator potest tacere proditionem nec filius* 333M *loqui proditorem.*

7   PORCI LATRONIS.   Quid ab ista ⟨proditione securum⟩[3] est quae pervenit iam usque ad ducem? Vereor ne tam sero caveamus quam imperator noster, qui non ante intellexit proditionem quam proditus est; nec umquam praesentius periculum fuit: res publica sine imperatore est, proditor sine custode.

---

[1] *Supplied by Gertz: more may be lacking.*
[2] quemvis illa vox *Müller:* quamuis quamuos *AV:* quamuis *B.*
[3] *Supplied by Bursian.*

He is sunk by all the proofs: I shall produce people
who saw, people who heard, I shall produce the gold,
I shall produce a witness—who will be, to remove any
possibility of doubt as to his worth, the general himself. Let him say of him whichever he will—" he is
my enemy " or " he is my son." [1]—It was this man he
alluded to.[2] Was there so much gold that it was
obvious even without investigation, or were you so
suspect that anyone at all could be tipped off by the
words: " Beware treachery "?—Excellent youth,
excellent general, who did not stop caring for his
country even on the cross!—Your son did not think
you worthy to be told: " Beware treachery."

VARIUS GEMINUS. Do not expect all the details 6
from an accuser [3] who is at once pre-occupied and
respectful. You must understand who the guilty
man is; you have heard the charges.—Do you ask
what your earlier life has against it? I have nothing
to say—your son never wished to reproach you with
anything.—Were your prayers exhausted so soon?—
What will the wretched youth do? As general, he
cannot keep quiet about treachery; as son, he cannot
speak of the traitor.

PORCIUS LATRO. What can be free from that 7
treachery of yours, when it has already affected a
general? I fear we may be too late in guarding against
it, just as our general was—he didn't realise the
treachery afoot until he fell victim to it. Danger has
never come closer; the state has no general, the

---

[1] In neither case is his treachery justified. But the text is
doubtful.
[2] i.e. the son, by his words, meant his father.
[3] The son, on the cross.

Quid est quare tibi hostes pepercerint? et imperatoris nostri pater es et aurum habes et legatus non es. Si tibi dicam: "*expecta dum legati mittantur;* filius tibi publice remittetur," *dices:* "paternus *adfectus non sustinet moram;* rapit me desiderium fili; *etiamsi redimere vivum non potero, saltem mortuum redimam; numquam tam durus hostis fuit ut paternis lacrimis non*
8 *flecteretur.*" Ut ignoscam tibi quod tam cito isti, obiciam quod tam cito redisti. Dic quid dixerit tibi: an nihil cum patre voluit loqui? "*Cavete proditionem.*" *Hoc dixit:* videte *ne quis* nocte *insciis custodibus exeat, ne quis ignorante re publica ad hostem perveniat, ne quis ex hostium castris gravis auro revertatur. Nihil deest indicio.* Si quid *de proditione* quaeritis, *imperator vobis dicet;* si quid *de proditore, legati.*

9 Pars altera. ARELLI FUSCI. Quantum est pretium quo vendo ut filium pater spectem in cruce, filius patrem de cruce, tanti et imperatorem et parricidium vendidi? Gratulabantur omnes repulso magis quam designato nimis ambitiose. Nunc paenitet. Et filium et patriam vendidit: tam exiguum auri 334 accepit ut unus senex portare posset?

traitor no guard.—Why did the enemy spare you? You are our general's father, you carry gold, and you are not an ambassador.—If I say to you: " Wait till ambassadors are sent, your son will be returned to you by the state," you will say: " A father's emotions brook no delay; I am carried away by the loss I feel for my son; even if I cannot ransom him alive, I shall at least ransom him dead. No enemy was ever so hard that he could not be moved by a father's tears." Even if I forgive you for going so soon, I shall object 8 to your coming back so quickly.—Tell us what he told you—or did he perhaps not want to speak to his father?—" Beware treachery." This is what he meant: make sure no-one goes out at night without the guards knowing, no-one goes to the enemy without the knowledge of the state, no-one returns from the enemy camp weighed down with gold.[1]—There is nothing missing in the information. If you have any queries about the treachery, the general will tell you; if you have any about the traitor, the ambassadors.

The other side

ARELLIUS FUSCUS. Did I receive for the sale of a 9 general and ⟨my consent to⟩ a parricide the price I, as a father, ask for seeing my son on the cross—and for my son seeing his father from the cross?[2]— Everyone congratulated me on my defeat—rather than my son on an appointment that he owed to excessive canvassing. Now I am sorry.—He sold his son and his country; did he receive so small a quantity of gold that a single old man could carry it?

[1] Cf. Virg. *Ecl.* 1.35: " gravis aere."
[2] A tortuous epigram; but the answer is clearly " no."

10   In hac controversia, etiamsi coniecturalis est et habet quasi certum tritumque iter, fuit tamen aliqua inter declamantis dissensio. *Latro* semper contrahebat et quidquid poterat tuto relinquere praeteriebat. Itaque et quaestionum numerum minuebat et locos numquam attrahebat; illos quoque quos occupaverat non diu dicebat sed valenter. Hoc erat itaque praeceptum eius, quaedam declamatorem tamquam praetorem facere debere minuendae litis causa. Quod in hac controversia fecit; *non* enim *curavit dicere nullam factam esse proditionem, sed se proditorem non esse.* Et *suspectus, inquit, iudici est qui plus quam se defendit,* et nolo, inquit, cum fili voce pugnare, ut imperatorem et filium mentitum dicam, praesertim cum odium adversus filium obiciatur patri.

Albucius in duas partes declamationem divisit: primum negavit ullam esse proditionem, deinde: ut esset, ad se non pertinere.

11   Colorem contra patrem Silo Pompeius hunc introduxit: odio illum rei publicae a qua repulsus erat fecisse, et odio ipsius fili, quem oderat et quia competierat et quia vicerat.

Varius Geminus dixit statim petisse patrem hoc proposito imperium, ut proderet, hominem avarum et lucro inhiantem, et, quia noti mores eius erant, victum ab eo competitore a quo vinci fas non erat

In this *controversia*, though it is " conjectural "[1] 10 and has a fixed and well-trodden path, the declaimers nevertheless showed some divergencies. Latro used always to abbreviate,[2] passing by everything that he could safely leave out. Hence he used to reduce the number of questions and never dragged in commonplaces. Nor did he develop the ones he did fasten on for any length of time, though he did develop them forcibly. So this was his precept, that the declaimer, like the praetor,[3] should take some steps to disburden the case. So, in this *controversia*, he did not trouble to say that no treachery had taken place, merely that he was no traitor. "The judge feels suspicious of someone who goes beyond defending his own person, and I don't want to quarrel with the son's words, saying that a general and son lied—especially as the father is being reproached with hating the son."

Albucius divided the declamation into two parts, first saying there was no treachery, secondly that even if there were it had nothing to do with him.

Pompeius Silo introduced this *colour* against the 11 father: the father had acted out of hatred for a country that had rebuffed him, and even for a son he loathed both for competing and for defeating him.

Varius Geminus said that right from the start the father had stood for command with treacherous intentions. He was a greedy man, eager for gain, and, because his character was generally known, he was defeated by a rival to whom only someone of the

---

[1] Cf. *C.* 7.3.6 and n.
[2] Cf. *C.* 2.3.12–13.
[3] Presiding magistrate in court.

nisi hominem turpissimum. Ante comitia, inquit, 33⁵
paratus fuerat pecuniam dare ut filium vinceret;[1]
post comitia paratus erat pecuniam accipere[2] ut
filium perderet. Ut captus est dux, aiebamus, inquit: " non potest hoc sine proditione fieri." Ex-
cusavimus nos imperatori: diximus perseverasse
ad redemptionem, quamvis[3] deterruisset pater.
Hoc loco ille respondit: " cavete proditionem."

12   Blandus dixit aegre ferentem pudorem repulsae
voluisse occidi filium ut in eius locum substitueretur
ipse.

Hispo Romanius: Ultionem, inquit, suam hosti
vendidit. Tam facile, inquit, exit nocte, pervenit
ad hostes, redit, ut scires illum non tunc primum
fecisse.

Argentarius dixit: Perfer ad senatum mandata
fili tui. Necesse est tibi multa dixerit; legatis quoque
aliqua mandavit; fortasse proditoris nomen patri
dixit; indica nobis. " Nihil dixit" inquit " mihi."
Sublata omnis *quaestio est. Quaeritis quem dixerit?
Videte cui nihil dixerit.*

13   Pro patre de *comitiis* hic color Latronis fuit: ne quis
filium meum vinceret timui; itaque professus sum
ut auctoritate mea deterrerem futuros conpetitores;
deinde ipse *filio meo cessi.*

[1] vinceret *Novák:* perderet *BV:* perdideret *A.*
[2] dare—accipere *Otto, Gertz:* accipere—dare.
[3] quamvis *early editors:* quam.

lowest character could properly succumb.[1] " Before
the elections he had been ready to give money to
defeat his son; after the elections he was ready to
take money to destroy his son. When the general
was captured, we said: This is impossible without
treachery. We excused ourselves to the general; we
said we had gone on trying to ransom him even though
his father had tried to put us off.[2] It was at this point
that he replied: Beware treachery."

Blandus said that he had taken the shame of defeat 12
badly and wanted his son to be killed so that he himself might take his place.

Romanius Hispo said: " He sold his revenge to the
enemy. He went out by night and came to the
enemy and returned so easily that you could tell this
wasn't the first time he'd done it."

Argentarius said: " Carry to the senate your son's
instructions. He must have said a lot to you—even
to the embassy he gave some instructions. Perhaps
he told his father the name of the traitor: reveal it to
us. ' He said nothing to me.' The whole question is
settled. You ask whom he meant? Look at the
man he said nothing to." [3]

On the father's side Latro's *colour* on the elections 13
was: " I was afraid someone might defeat my son.
And so I put up my name so as to deter prospective
candidates by the authority of my name. Then I let
my son win."

---

[1] i.e. the father should properly have won, granted his
seniority; but his character weighed against him.
[2] Cf. §3 " You had said . . ."
[3] This depends on an ambiguity of *dicere* = " to mean " and
" to say."

Albucius hoc colore usus est: Aiebant, inquit, alii imperatorem fieri debere ⟨adulescentem⟩,[1] qualis Scipio fuisset, alii senem, qualis Maximus [fuit];[2] ⟨adulescentem acriter pugnaturum⟩,[3] senem nihil temere facturum. Utriusque populo copiam 336 feci.

Cestius hoc colore usus est: Noveram vitium fili mei; sciebam esse acrem adulescentem, fortem, sed inconsideratum, temerarium. Itaque petii et rei publicae causa ⟨et⟩[4] fili mei, quem idoneum ad tantum sustinendum onus non putabam.

14 Fuscus Arellius dixit in hoc se competisse, ut hostium animi frangerentur cum audissent posse rem publicam vel in una domo ducem eligere.

Hispo Romanius simpliciter putavit agendum: inepti, inquit, hi colores sunt, cum ponantur competitores. Hoc itaque egit colore, ut quereretur de exitu comitiorum: adulescentulos omnis conspirasse, quasi de aetatis comparatione ageretur; facile itaque victum senem non ambientem. De me, inquit, queri non potestis; clamavi: "non est vobis utilis huius aetatis imperator." Mansit, inquit, illi et post comitia eadem contumacia: nihil referebat ad patrem, nihil communicabat; itaque captus est. Et cum descripsisset quam imperite disposuisset aciem, quemadmodum inexploratis locorum insidiis oppressa eius

---

[1] *Supplied here by the editor (before* imperatorem *by Kiessling).*
[2] *Deleted by Novák.*
[3] *Supplied by Müller, following Vahlen.*
[4] *Supplied by Schultingh.*

Albucius used this *colour*: " Some said the general should be a young man, like Scipio, others an old man, like Maximus;[1] a young man would fight energetically, an old man would do nothing rash. I let the people have a choice between the two."

Cestius used this *colour*: " I knew my son's failing, I knew him to be a bold, brave youth, but a reckless and impulsive one. So I stood for the sake both of my country and of my son, for I didn't think him suitable to bear such a great burden."

Arellius Fuscus said he had stood as a rival candi- 14 date to shatter enemy morale when they heard that the state could confine its choice of a general even to a single household.

Romanius Hispo thought the course taken should be straightforward. " These *colours* are absurd, because the theme makes father and son true competitors." He therefore adopted the *colour* of complaining of the result of the election; all the young men had got together, as though what was in question were a comparison of ages—hence the easy defeat of an old man, who did no canvassing. " You cannot complain of me. I cried: A general so young is no use to you." Even after the elections the son was equally wilful—he consulted his father on nothing, told him nothing: hence his capture. After describing how his inexperience had shown itself in his arrangement of the battle-line, how his rash moves had been punished because he did not trouble to investigate the traps set by the terrain, he added:

[1] Scipio Africanus the elder was general in Spain at the age of 26; Fabius Maximus was well over sixty at Cannae.

temeritas esset, adiecit: hoc erat quod vobis clam-
abam: " ducem senem eligite."

15 Otho Iunius pater praesagiis quibusdam et in-
somniis hanc fortunam praenuntiantibus agitatum
se competisse dixit. Erat autem ex somniatoribus
Otho: ubicumque illum defecerat color, somnium
narrabat.

De eo quod inscio senatu egressus est, Latro sic
coloravit: *decretum non expectasse, sed amentem et* 337[1]
attonitum protinus procurrisse.

Albucius hoc colore usus est: semper de duce cito
constitui. Longum erat expectare; *ad summam,*
festinavi nec occurri.

16 Varius Geminus dixit maluisse solum ire; *hostes*
enim auctoritate legatorum non moveri, at *lacrimis*
patrum saepe flecti.

Silo Pompeius ait: putavi utilius esse privata
illum pecunia redimi; minoris enim posse aestimari
quam si tamquam imperator redimeretur.

Argentarius ait: Nihil tam iniquom erat quam
legatos ad redemptionem mitti; numquam enim
reddidissent quem sic desiderari publice iudicassent.
Itaque praecucurri rogaturus et hoc dicturus: exercitus contemnit illum, res publica relinquit.[2]

17 Blandus ait: cogitanti mihi quid facerem, contentus essem paternis lacrimis an comitatu publico
preces meas adiuvarem, tandem venit in mentem
Troianum regem ad redemptionem fili sine legatis
isse et cum auro.[3]

---

[1] Cf. *C.* 2.1.33.
[2] Probably corrupt: the decision alluded to should be the
senate's rather than the father's.
[3] Priam to ransom Hector (Hom. *Il.* 24).

" This is why I shouted at you: Choose an old man for general."

Junius Otho senior said he had become a competitor 15 because he had been troubled by certain omens and dreams that foretold this turn of events. Otho was one of the dreamers; wherever he was at a loss for a *colour*, he told of a dream.[1]

On the fact that he had left the country without the senate's knowledge, Latro used this *colour*: he had not waited for the decree, but had rushed out at once, bewildered and crazed.

Albucius used this *colour*: one always makes a quick decision about a general.[2] " It was a long business to wait; in short, I hurried—but I came too late."

Varius Geminus said he had preferred to go alone; 16 for enemies are not moved by the prestige of ambassadors, but they are often influenced by a father's tears.

Pompeius Silo said: " I thought it more expedient that he should be ransomed with private money: he could be assessed for less than if he were ransomed qua general."

Argentarius said: " Nothing was so maladroit as for ambassadors to be sent to ransom the general. The enemy would never have given back one whom they judged to be so missed by the state. So I hurried on in advance to ask, and to say: He is despised by the army, abandoned by the state."

Blandus said: " I was wondering what to do; 17 should I be content to shed a father's tears, or should I aid my entreaties with a state retinue? Finally it occurred to me that a Trojan king [3] went to redeem his son alone, without an embassy but with gold."

Sepullius Bassus ait non expectasse se curiam, quia putaverit futuros qui redimendum negarent, quod factum apud Romanos saepius erat; itaque ante se voluisse redimere quam posset aliquid de non redimendo constitui.

Cestius dixit: non quaesivi secretos tramites et occultum iter: proditor eadem via veni qua legati.

18 De voce fili colorem Albucius hunc fecit: pudebat illum, inquit, quod captus erat; quaerebat aliquod fortunae suae patrocinium; voluit videri non culpa sua sed proditione hoc sibi accidisse; itaque nomen adicere non potuit.

Fuscus Arellius dixit alienatum iam suppliciis animum et errantem has voces effudisse sine argumentis, sine reo.

Varius Geminus omnia complexus est: Potest, inquit, propter hoc, potest propter illud; ego vobis idem suadeo: cavete proditionem. Hoc si cavere vultis, imperatores senes facite.

19 Illud et in hac controversia et in omni vitandum aiebat Cestius, quotiens aliqua vox poneretur, ne ad illam quasi ad sententiam decurreremus. Sicut in hac apud Cestium quidam auditor eius hoc modo coepit: "ut verbis ducis vestri, iudices, incipiam, cavete proditionem"; sic finivit declamationem ut diceret: "finio[1] quibus vitam finit imperator: cavete proditionem." Hoc sententiae genus *Cestius*

---

[1] finio *Wachsmuth:* in.

Sepullius Bassus said he had not waited for the senate because he had thought it would be said that his son should not be ransomed—something that had quite frequently happened at Rome.[1] So he wanted to redeem him before anything could be decided about *not* redeeming him.

Cestius said: " I did not seek out secret paths, a hidden route. I, the traitor, went the same way as the ambassadors."

On the words of the son Albucius produced this 18 *colour*: " He was ashamed for having been captured. He was looking for some way to excuse his ill-fortune; he wanted it to be thought to have befallen him not through his own fault but because of treachery; this explains why he could add no name."

Arellius Fuscus said his mind had already been disordered by his crucifixion. He had poured out these words in his delirium with no proof, no individual accusation.

Varius Geminus put everything in: " Perhaps it is for this reason, perhaps for that. *I* give you the same advice: Beware treachery. And if you want to beware it, you must make old men generals."

Cestius said that in this *controversia*, and in all 19 others where some phrase was quoted in the theme, one should avoid rushing to the phrase as though it formed an epigram. For instance, on our present theme one of Cestius' audience once began thus: " To start with the words of your general, judges: Beware treachery," and finished the declamation by saying: " I end with the words with which your general ended his life: Beware treachery." Cestius called this kind

[1] For an instance see *C*. 5.7 with n.

echo vocabat et ⟨sic⟩ [1] dicenti discipulo statim ex-
clamabat: *ἱμερτὴν ἠχώ*: ut *in illa suasoria* in qua
*deliberat Alexander an Oceanum naviget cum exaudita
vox esset:* " *quousque invicte?* " ab ⟨hac⟩ [2] ipsa voce
quidam coepit declamare et in hac desit; ait illi
Cestius desinenti: *ἔν σοι μὲν λήξω, σέο δ' ἄρξομαι.*
Et alteri, cum *descriptis Alexandri victoriis, gentibus
perdomitis, novissime poneret:* " *quousque invicte?* ",
exclamavit Cestius: *tu autem quousque?*

20   Otho pater hoc colore usus est pro patre: dixit
hoc [3] molestum fuisse imperatori, quod illum suffixum
legati intuebantur; itaque, ut ab hoc illos spectaculo
abigeret [4] et exoneraret verecundiam suam, id 339
dixisse quo audito festinarent. Itaque dixisse illum
non " caveant proditionem," sed " cavete," quasi
ipsis legatis esset periculum ne proderentur.

[1] *Supplied by the editor.*
[2] *Supplied by Otto.*
[3] hoc *ed.:* enim.
[4] abigeret *Konitzer:* uigeret *AB:* urgeret *V.*

of epigram " echo," and when a student used it he would call out at once: " What a lovely echo! " So in the *suasoria* where Alexander deliberates whether to sail the Ocean, though a voice had been heard saying: " How much longer, unconquered one? "[1] someone began to declaim from these very words and finished with them. When he was finishing, Cestius said to him: " With you shall I finish, and from you start." [2] To another when, after a description of Alexander's victories and the nations he had conquered, he put at the end: " How much longer, unconquered one? " Cestius exclaimed: " How about *you*—how much longer? "

Otho senior used this *colour* for the father: he said 20 that the general had been upset to have the ambassadors gazing at him nailed up, and in order to drive them from the scene and relieve his shame, had said something that would make them hurry off as soon as they heard it. And this was why he said not: " Let them beware treachery," but " Beware," implying that the ambassadors themselves were in danger of betrayal.

[1] Cf. the very similar theme in *S.* 1.
[2] Hom. *Il.* 9.97.

VIII

Mutanda Optio Raptore Convicto

Rapta raptoris aut mortem aut indotatas
nuptias optet.

Rapta producta nuptias optavit. Qui dicebatur raptor negavit se rapuisse. Iudicio victus
vult ducere; illa optionem repetit.

1   Albuci Sili. Praeterquam quod in omni dis-
crimine periculosa libertas est, meruit puella ut
taceremus: misericors in nos etiam antequam roga-
remus fuit. Inhumana libertas est si vincimus
⟨adversus uxorem, si vincimur⟩ [1] adversus iudicem.
Non oportet tibi amplius quam semel licere optare.
Omnis nimia potentia saluberrime in brevitatem
constringetur. Qui potest condemnare, possit semel;
qui potest occidere, possit semel; aut, si qua iteratio
recipi potest, in paenitentiam mortis recipienda est.
Proponite vobis illam *supplici* invisam [2] *faciem, carni-*

---

[1] *Supplied by the editor after Shackleton Bailey.*
[2] invisam *Thomas:* causam.

---

[1] Cf. *C.* 1.5 n.
[2] The theme recurs in *Decl.* 309; parallels are noted below.
[3] That is, he will not attack the girl (cf. the *sermo* to *Decl.*
309: " actio debebit huius adulescentis esse summissa ").

8

THE CHANGE OF CHOICE TO BE MADE AFTER THE CONVICTION OF A RAVISHER

A girl who has been raped may choose either marriage to her ravisher without a dowry or his death.[1]

A girl who had been raped was brought to court and asked for marriage. The alleged ravisher said he was not responsible. The judgement has gone against him; he is ready to marry her—but she wants to have her choice over again.[2]

For the ravisher

ALBUCIUS SILUS. Apart from the fact that at any 1 crisis freedom of speech has its dangers, the girl has deserved my silence;[3] she showed me pity even before I entreated her.—Freedom of speech is cruel when directed against a wife (as she will be if I win), dangerous when directed against a judge (as she will be if I lose).—You shouldn't have the right to choose more than once. All excessive power will be best restricted to a short time.[4] One who can condemn should have the power only once; one who can kill should have the power only once; or, if any repetition can be allowed, it should be allowed for the purpose of having second thoughts on the choice of death. Imagine the ghastly spectacle of execution, the

[4] Cf. *Decl.* p. 217.24 *seq.* Ritter, and below, §7 " Nothing is so in accord . . ."

ficem, securem: hoc semel licere nimium est. " Exorata
sum, condo gladium; irata sum, repeto optionem."
At non semel mori satius est? Occides iam non 340
vitiatorem sed virum.

2 PORCI LATRONIS. Periculosius est negare raptum
quam commisisse? *In hanc perturbationem adulescens
perductus erat ut ignoraret quid fecisset.* Non refugie-
bat tamen puellae nuptias; favebat tantum sibi, ut
innocens duceret. Itaque nihil aliud petit quam
libertatem ut honestius duceret. Ita apud vos,
iudices, tutius est peccare quam erubescere? Dig-
nior poena erat si id peccasset quod meminisse posset. Exsurge, adulescens, et sine ullo respectu
pudoris ad pedes te puellae demitte; accedite et
vos, amici propinquique, et tu mater ac pater. Quid
est, puella? ecquid te horum lacrimae movent?
Non, inquit; ad [illum]¹ magistratum veniat. Non
dissimulo: metuo te, puella, si nusquam rogari vis
nisi ubi occidere potes. *Gravius punior nunc, cum
me peccasse pudet, quam cum peccavi.* Quae post
iniuriam ignoscit, post misericordiam ⟨irascitur⟩.²

3 CESTI PII. Venit ad vos vestro beneficio retenturus
puellae beneficium. *Optavit nuptias; neque adhuc*

---

¹ *Deleted by the editor.*
² *Supplied by Bursian.*

executioner, the axe: that this should be allowed *once* is excessive.—" I am won over, I sheathe my sword; I am angry, I want my choice again." But is it not better to die once ? [1]—You will be killing your husband this time, not your ravisher.

PORCIUS LATRO. Is it more perilous to deny a rape 2 than to have committed one ?—The youth had been thrown into such confusion that he didn't know what he had done. But he did not shrink from marriage to the girl; he was merely thinking of himself—ensuring that he married as an innocent man. So he asked nothing more than freedom to marry under more honourable circumstances.[2]— Is it then in your eyes, judges, safer to sin than to be ashamed ?—He would deserve punishment more if he had done some wrong that he could remember.—Get up, young man, and, with no thought of shame, throw yourself at the girl's feet. You too, friends and relations, approach, mother and father too. What is it, girl; are you not moved by their tears ? " No," she says, " let him face the magistrate." I will be frank—I fear you, girl, if you refuse to receive entreaties except in a place where you have the power to kill.—I am more harshly punished now, when I am ashamed of having done wrong, than when I *did* wrong.—A woman who forgives after receiving an injury is getting angry after feeling pity.

CESTIUS PIUS. He comes before you to ask to be 3 allowed to keep, by your favour, the favour he received from the girl.—She chose marriage—without

---

[1] And have it over with.
[2] Cf. *Decl.* p. 218.9 Ritter, and below, §4 " I was acting . . .," as well as elsewhere in our declamation.

sciebat quam verecundum maritum esset habitura.
Vitiatorem dimisisti; virum occides? Aiebat iudex:
Quid habes quod tam pertinaciter neges? nuptias
optat. *Minus est ergo quod vitiavit quam quod negavit?*

Q. HATERI. "Non sum" inquit "optatura mortem, sed volo mihi licere et mortem optare." Quam
potestas ista delectat crudelis est.

BLANDI. *Ergo nos iniuriam periculosius negavimus*
quam fecimus?

4   IUNI GALLIONIS. *Quadam nocte—quid dicam? iam*
non negare non pudet: nox, vinum, error—quid irasceris,
puella? iam negare non audeo. Non diligenter causa
mea acta est: dum nihil timetis, facilius me puellae 341M
credidistis. Confitendum est vitium nostrum: nos
nuptiis moram fecimus. Sive adhuc non esset
vitiata sive esset, visa digna matrimonio quae hominem non posset occidere. Tibi consulebam, ne
dicereris vitiatori nupta. Si per te licuisset, honestiorem maritum habuisses. Tu negasti? o hominem
inpudentem! ita tu non ante magistratus tribunal,
in conspectu populi, in medio foro clamitasti: "ego
virginem rapui"? Neminem habere tam obse-
quentem maritum potes: hic iam nihil negabit.

---

[1] In that he was unready to marry qua ravisher.
[2] Cf. *Decl.* p. 218.20 Ritter.—The result was the com-
placency complained of in §4 "My case . . ." Cf. §5 Vibius
Gallus and especially §11 Argentarius.
[3] Cf. *Decl.* p. 216.4 *seq.* Ritter; Ter. *Adelph.* 470; and
below, §10.
[4] Considering what had happened when he tried to deny it
before.

yet knowing how modest [1] a husband she was to have. —You let your ravisher go—will you kill your husband?—The judge said: " What reason have you to deny it so stubbornly? Her choice is marriage." [2] —Is it then less serious that he ravished her than that he denied it?

QUINTUS HATERIUS. " I don't propose to choose death," she says, " but I want to have the right to choose even death." A woman who takes pleasure in *that* privilege is cruel.

BLANDUS. Have I then run more danger in denying the deed than in doing it?

JUNIUS GALLIO. One night—what am I to say? 4 Now I am not ashamed to affirm it: night, wine, a mistake [3]—why are you angry, girl? *Now* I dare not deny it.[4]—My case was not carefully put. Fearing nothing, you [5] entrusted me to the girl too easily.—I must confess my fault: I have delayed the wedding. —Whether or not she had been raped up to now, she seemed to be worth marrying—this woman who could not bring herself to kill a man.—I was acting in your interests, in case you should be called the wife of a ravisher. If you had allowed it, you could have had a more respectable husband.—Did you deny it? Brazen fellow! Did you then not shout before the magistrate's tribunal, in view of the people, in mid-forum: " I raped the girl "? [6]—You can have no husband so obedient—this man will never deny anything now.

---

[5] The judges, who found him guilty secure in the belief that she would spare him.
[6] Sarcasm.

5   VARI GEMINI. Exponam vobis rerum ordinem sic tamquam ab eo didicerim qui quid fecerit nescit.[1]

VIBI GALLI. Ubi estis qui dicebatis: " nihil interest tua, confitere "? Confitetur, quia honestius putasti raptori nubere. " Sit " inquit " mihi heres si quis intra decem menses natus fuerit." [3] Numquid negat? Surge, adulescens, dic: " rapui, vitiavi "; incipe scire quod nescis.[4] Miraris si tibi non credit? multum est de quo timet.

6   Pars altera. P. ASPRENATIS. Nescio utro *iudicio* adversarius fuerit inprobior. *Priore id egit ne quam omnino poenam stupri penderet; hoc id agit ut ipse optet* ex duobus a lege constitutis suppliciis utrum velit pendere; fatetur enim se inpune habere maluisse quam ducere uxorem, uxorem ducere malle quam mori. Antea legem vitiationis evertere conatus est, nunc transferre volt: advocatos rogat, iudices rogat, omnis potius quam vitiatam. *Utinam non hoc illum liberaret metu, quod iudicis suae clementiam novit.* Clamabat se innocentem esse: si quid peccasset, 342N

---

[1] Cf. *Decl.* p. 215.12 Ritter. The Latin does not seem to bear what would be the natural meaning: " as I learned . . ."

[2] See n. on 7.4.1.

[3] The youth is now in favour of marriage; his declaration " Let any child . . ." might be a hint that he agrees he raped the girl.

[4] The youth's counsel suggests (ironically) that he confess, and " remember " what he is unaware of.

CONTROVERSIAE 7. 8.5–6

VARIUS GEMINUS. I will tell you of the course of 5 events, as if I learned it from one who doesn't know what it was he did.[1]

VIBIUS GALLUS. Where are those of you who said: " It makes no difference to you, confess "?—He confesses—because you thought it more respectable to marry a ravisher.—" Let any child born within ten [2] months be my heir." Is that a denial?[3]—Rise, young man, and say: " I raped her, I violated her." Begin to know what you do not know.[4]—Are you surprised he doesn't believe you? He has much to fear.[5]

The other side

PUBLIUS ASPRENAS. I don't know at which trial my 6 adversary has behaved more outrageously. At the first the aim of his plea was that he should pay no penalty at all for his rape. In this one, his aim is himself to choose which of the two penalties determined by the law he wants to pay; for he acknowledges that formerly he preferred going unpunished to marrying a wife, but that now he prefers marrying a wife to dying. Previously he tried to subvert the law of rape, now he wants to turn it to his own ends; he begs the counsel, he begs the judge, everyone rather than the girl who was raped.—If only he wasn't freed from fear by the knowledge of how merciful his judge [6] is!—He cried that he was innocent, that he did not refuse to die if he had done

---

[5] This apparently takes us back to the period just after the rape and before the choice. The man does not believe the girl's version of the rape (which he " cannot remember ").

[6] The girl.

mori non recusare. Aderat raptori populus, nec
quicquam magis suspectam faciebat vitiatae causam
quam lenitas optionis. Si iam tibi de stupro tuo
liquet, *est quaedam proxima innocentiae verecundia,
praebere se legibus;* tu vero [ne][1] meruisti quidem
mortem illa infitiatione. Ignorasti an peccasses?
innocens esse voluisti? Causam habes. Revertere
ad parentes, puella, quoniam quidem totiens iam
rogas, quae rogari ipsa debueras.

7   Latro tres fecit quaestiones: an illa, interrogavit,
optio iusta fuerit. Non fuit, inquit, iusta; non enim
constabat te raptorem esse. Nihil refert, inquit, an
negaverit. Erat enim raptor, etiamsi negabat, et
ita iusta fuit optio. An, si iniusta optio fuit, revocari
possit. Optio, inquit, semel puellae datur; immuta-
bilis est simul emissa est. *Iudex quam tulit* de reo
*tabellam revocare non potest; quaesitor non mutabit
pronuntiationem* suam. *Nihil tam civile, tam utile
est, quam brevem potestatem esse quae magna est.* Si
volet et alteram optionem suam revocare et deinde
tertiam, numquam constabit quid futurum sit, cum
illa quod optaverit possit sequenti semper optione
rescindere. Tertiam fecit quaestionem: an, si

---

[1] *Deleted by Shackleton Bailey.*

---

[1] She would have been more severe if she really *had* been
raped.

[2] i.e. from the court (instead of being begged by the ravisher
to spare him).

any wrong. The people was on the side of the ravisher, and nothing more prejudiced the case of the raped girl than the mildness of her choice.[1]—If you are now clear about the outrage you did, there is a kind of modesty, the next best thing to innocence, in offering oneself to the law; but *you* have actually deserved death by that denial of yours.—Did you not know whether you had sinned? Did you want to be innocent? You have good reason to.—Return to your parents, girl, since now you are having to beg such a lot,[2] though you yourself should have been the one to be begged.

Latro put three questions. He asked: Was the choice legal? " No—for it was not yet established that you were the ravisher." [3] " It makes no difference whether he denied it. He was the ravisher, even if he denied it, and so the choice was legal." If the choice *was* illegal, can it be taken back? " The girl is given one choice; it is immutable as soon as it is uttered.[4] A judge cannot take back a vote he casts on an accused; an investigating magistrate will not change his sentence. Nothing is so in accord with civilised practice and expediency than that great power should be brief. If she wants to take her second choice back as well and then her third, it will never be agreed what is to happen, since she can always annul her choice by a subsequent choice." His third question was: If a choice can sometimes be

---

[3] Cf. *Decl.* p. 217.5 Ritter. Latro proceeds to give the opposite case.
[4] *ibid.* p. 218.2.

potest revocari aliquando optio, nunc debeat. Hic defensio adulescentis, qui negavit se vitiasse.

8 Fuscus et ordinem mutavit quaestionum et numerum auxit; fecit enim primam quaestionem: 343M an rapta non possit amplius optare quam semel. Potest, inquit; *lex* enim *non adicit quotiens optet, sed ex quibus: " aut hoc " inquit " aut illud "; non adicit " ne amplius quam semel."* Contra ait: lex te iubet alterutrum optare; tu *hodie si mortem optabis, facies quod numquam factum est: utrumque optaveris.* Etiamsi non licet, inquit, amplius quam semel [et mortem optabis et nuptias],[1] ego nondum optavi; optio est enim quae legitime fit: illa non est facta legitime. Si praetor defuisset, numquid optionem vocares? [si rapta defuisset][2] Raptor defuit: non est ista optio; sermo est. An proximo iudicio confirmata sit optio. Raptor ait: agebatur apud iudices utrum deberet rata esse optio ⟨an⟩[3] non; iudicata est rata esse debere: rata sit. Non, inquit puella; quaesitum est enim an ego in raptorem ius haberem; iudicatum est habere me: uti debeo. Non possum ante legem habere quam raptorem. Novissimam quaestionem fecit aequitatis: an rata debeat esse optio.

9 Passienus hanc ultimam partem sic dividebat: an, si adulescens malo adversus puellam animo infitiatus est raptum, ut nuptias effugeret, dignus sit qui iterum fortunam subeat optionis recusatae. Deinde: an malo animo fecerit.

---

[1] *Deleted by Bursian.*
[2] *Deleted by the editor.*
[3] *Supplied by Gronovius.*

taken back, should it be now? Here came a defence of the young man, who denied that he had violated the girl.

Fuscus changed the order of questions and in- 8 creased their number. His first was: Can a ravished girl choose more than once? " She can; the law does not add how often she is to choose, but merely says what she is to choose from. It says ' either this or that '—it doesn't go on to say: ' not more than once.' " The opposite view is: " The law orders you to choose one or the other; if you choose death today, you will do something unprecedented—you will have chosen both." " Even if it is not permissible to choose more than once, I haven't yet chosen; a choice is a choice when it is made legally—this choice was not. If the praetor had been absent, would you call it a choice? In fact, there was no ravisher. That is no choice—it is mere words." Was the choice rati-fied by the previous trial? The ravisher says: " The judges had to say whether the choice was to stand or not. It was decided that it should—let it so stand." [1] " No," says the girl, " for what was at stake was whether I had a right over the ravisher. It was judged that I have. I must use it. I cannot appeal to the law before I have a ravisher." Fuscus' last question was one of equity: Should the choice stand?

Passienus divided this last part like this: If the 9 young man acted with bad intentions towards the girl in denying the rape, in order to escape marriage, does he deserve to undergo a second time the chances of a choice he has refused once? Then: *were* his inten-tions bad?

[1] *ibid.* p. 217.18.

Varius Geminus ultimae quaestioni vel parti, in qua quid debeat fieri quaeritur, duo haec adiciebat, quae posse [1] quaeri putabat: an, si puella pro certo 344M adulescentis mortem optatura est, non debeat illi permitti optio tam crudeliter usurae sua potestate; deinde: an mortem optatura sit. Quid est, inquit, quare velis optare nisi quod nuptias non vis? ⟨An vis?⟩ [2] Hoc non tantum patimur sed rogamus.

10 Color pro adulescente introductus est a Latrone talis ut diceret se ebrium fuisse et ignorare quid fecerit: hodie quoque magis credere de facto suo quam scire; recusasse autem non ne duceret uxorem sed ut sua voluntate duceret; et iudices non audisse sollicitos: faciles fuisse, quasi de nuptiis ageretur.

Varius Geminus raptum confessus est, et dixit nihil esse tam contrarium adulescenti quam etiamnunc negare: non tantum raptam sed iudicem offendet.

Cestius nec Latronem secutus est dicentem nescisse se hodieque nescire nec Varium Geminum confitentem, sed [non] [3] rapuisse apertius negavit. Verum, inquit, inveniri non poterat; iudices illam sententiam secuti sunt: si rapuit, indignum est puellam inultam esse; si non rapuit, non est indignum fieri illum maritum.

Silo Pompeius dixit adulescentem verecundum

---

[1] posse *Kiessling:* per se.
[2] *Supplied by Thomas.*
[3] *Deleted by Faber.*

Varius Geminus, to the last question or part, where the question is: What ought to be done, added these two, which he thought bore asking: If the girl is definitely going to choose the young man's death, should a choice be allowed to someone who proposed to use her power so cruelly? Then: *Does* she propose to choose death? "Why should you want to choose unless because you do not want marriage?[1] Or do you? We not only put up with that—we ask it."

Latro introduced a *colour* for the youth that in- 10 volved his saying he had been drunk and didn't know what he had done; even today he had more belief than knowledge of his action; but he had denied it not in order to avoid marriage but in order to marry of his own will. The judges hadn't listened carefully —they had been easily persuaded, on the assumption that it was marriage that was in question.

Varius Geminus confessed to the rape, and said that nothing was so prejudicial to the youth as to go on denying it even now: " He will offend the judge as well as the girl."

Cestius followed neither Latro's line that he had not known anything and knew nothing even now, nor Varius Geminus' of confessing, but instead said more openly [2] that he had not raped. " The truth could not be determined. The judges followed this line of thought: If he raped it is outrageous that the girl should not be avenged, if he did not, it is not outrageous that he should be her husband."

Pompeius Silo said that the youth, being naturally

[1] *ibid.* p. 218.27.
[2] Sc. than Latro.

natura et rustici pudoris non sustinuisse confessionem. Non placebat Latroni ⟨hic⟩ [1] color: minus, inquit, ignoscetur illi si scit se rapuisse et sciens mentitus est. Contradicebat Silo ⟨non⟩ [2] posse ulli fidem fieri aliquem nescire an rapuerit.

11 Hispanus Cornelius: Non subducere illi, inquit, 345M maritum volui, sed honestiorem dare. Digna est, inquit, tam misericors puella quae non videatur nupsisse raptori.

Hispo Romanius ait illos sodales qui illum nocte inpulerant circumstetisse et dixisse: non est quam rapuisti; alia fuit. Timuit ne illi quam rapuerat faceret iniuriam.

Argentarius dixit: Vellem mortem optasses: non esset hic raptor iudicatus. Non causa tua illum ⟨vicit⟩ [3] sed optio, dum unusquisque iudex dicit: "Quid habet quod tantopere recuset? putes de capite agi; et ipse ait se non nolle ducere uxorem, sed titulum recusare. Nempe victus ducet uxorem. Non est sollicite de eo iudicandum cui damnato gratulandum est."

Silo hoc colore usus est: confusum adulescentem subito et tanto tumultu parum sibi constitisse; et negasse quia perturbatus erat, ⟨et⟩ [4] perseverasse quia negaverat.

[1] *Supplied by Gertz.*
[2] *Supplied by Kiessling.*
[3] *Supplied by Madvig.*
[4] *Supplied by Haase.*

bashful and having a countryman's sense of shame, had not been up to confessing. Latro didn't like this *colour*: " He will be forgiven less readily if he knows he raped and told a lie in that knowledge." Silo answered that no-one can be believed to be unaware whether he has committed rape.

Cornelius Hispanus: " I didn't want to deprive her 11 of a husband, but to give her a more respectable one. So compassionate a girl deserves not to be thought to have married a ravisher."

Romanius Hispo said that the companions who had egged him on by night surrounded him [1] and said: " This is not the girl you raped—it was another." He was afraid of acting wrongly by the girl he *had* raped.

Argentarius said: " I could wish you had chosen death; this man would not then have been adjudged a ravisher. It is not the case you brought that over-came him, but your choice—each of the judges was saying: ' What reason has he to be so vehement in his denials? You would think it a matter of life and death. He himself says he is ready to marry the girl, though not labelled a seducer. Surely he will marry her if he is defeated. We don't need to judge with any care the case of one who, if he is condemned, deserves congratulations.' " [2]

Silo used this *colour*: in the sudden tumult the young man was bewildered and lost control of himself; he denied because he was confused—and went on denying because he had started by denying.

---

[1] In court, at the first trial.
[2] Cf. *Decl.* p. 218.22 Ritter: " id pronuntiaverunt in quo victus gratias ageret."

EXCERPTA

CONTROVERSIARUM

LIBRI OCTAVI

I

Orbata Post Laqueum Sacrilega

Magistratus de confessa sumat supplicium.

Amisso quaedam viro et duobus liberis suspendit se. Incidit ei laqueum tertius filius. Illa,
cum sacrilegio facto sacrilegus quaereretur,
dixit magistratui se fecisse sacrilegium. Vult
magistratus tamquam de confessa supplicium
sumere; filius contradicit.

Facio, iudices, in foro quod domi feci: matrem mori
prohibeo. Quomodo, inquit, fecisti? quo loco quae
sustuleras condidisti? Haerebat nec quicquam sacrilegi nisi poenam noverat. Amissis duobus liberis
sacrilega sibi videbatur quod vivebat. Non ad-

---

[1] i.e. theft of sacred objects.
[2] The law reflects Roman and particularly Greek legal
practice (Bonner, 103). It recurs (with the more non-
committal masculine *confesso*) in the very similar theme of

EXCERPTS FROM BOOK 8

1

The Bereaved Woman Who Committed Sacrilege [1] after Hanging Herself

A magistrate may execute a woman
who confesses to a crime.[2]

A woman, having lost her husband and two
children, hung herself. The third son cut her
down. A sacrilege had taken place, and there
was a search for the guilty party. The woman
told the magistrate she had committed the sacrilege. The magistrate wants to execute her as
confessedly guilty. The son speaks against him.

For the son: Judges, I am doing in court what I did
at home—I am preventing my mother dying.—" How
did you do it? " they asked her. " Where did you
hide what you stole? " She was at a loss, and knew
nothing of sacrilege except the punishment for it.—
Having lost two sons, she thought herself sacrilegious

Calp. Flacc. 42: cf. *Decl.* 314. The *supplicium* would not
normally be capital, but I have translated " execute " because
this gives point to the present theme.

futurus veni, sed servaturus. Alii pro reis rogant, ego rogabo ream. Nullum habet accusator nisi in subselliis meis testem. Non est confessio nisi cum 360 accusator eruit, negat rea, tortor expressit. Fertur quaedam viso contra spem filio expirasse. Si ad mortem agit matres magnum gaudium, quid magnus dolor? Mater, habes non mediocre solacium: vides aliquid et deos perdere. Magis deos miseri quam beati colunt. Non fecit sacrilegium mulier, non fecit anus, non fecit orbata, non fecit quae custoditur, non fecit quae confitetur. Irata, inquit, dis sacrilegium potuit committere. Frangitur calamitosis animus et ipsa se infelicitas damnat, et hoc condicio humana vel pessimum habet, quod Fortuna quos miseros fecit etiam superstitiosos facit. Diligentius dii coluntur irati. Quis ergo fecit? Unde scire possum qui matrem custodii? Ago causam legum, ne carnificem quem sacrilegis minantur calamitosis adhibeant. Deos ita coluit ut quae pro tam multis timeret.

Pars altera.[1] Confessio conscientiae vox est. Confessio coacti et quae fecit agnoscentis verbum est. Omnium vox erat: " sacrilegus [2] latere non

---

[1] *These words appear in the manuscripts after* verbum est: *they were transposed by Gronovius.*
[2] sacrilegus *Bornecque:* sacrilegium.

---

[1] See Livy 22.7.13; Gell. 3.15.4.
[2] Cf. Sen. *Agam.* 694: " miseris colendos maxime superos putem."

to go on living.—I am here not to defend her, but to save her.—Some beg on behalf of the accused: *I* shall beg the accused herself.—The accuser has no witness —except on my benches.—There is no confession except when the accuser elicits it, the accused denies it, the torturer has extorted it.—It is said that a woman once expired after seeing her son unexpectedly.[1] If great joy drives mothers to die, what of great grief?—Mother, you have a great consolation: you see that even the gods suffer losses.— The wretched worship the gods more than the fortunate.[2]—This sacrilege was not the crime of a woman, an old woman, a bereaved woman, one under custody,[3] one who confesses.—" She might have committed sacrilege out of anger with the gods." In disaster the spirit gets broken. Misfortune dooms itself, and quite the worst thing about the human lot is that those whom Fortune has made miserable it makes superstitious as well. The gods are worshipped with more care when they show anger.— Who then did the deed? How can I know? I was looking after my mother.—I am pleading in the name of the laws, for fear they may bring to bear on the wretched the executioner with which they threaten the sacrilegious.—She worshipped the gods, as you expect of one who had so many reasons [4] to fear them.

The other side: Confession is the voice of conscience. Confession is the utterance of one under constraint, one who acknowledges what he has done.—Everyone was saying: " The temple-robber will not be able to

[3] That of her son, as we learn below.
[4] i.e. so large a family.

poterit; quisquis est, non ipse bonum exitum faciet,
non quisquam suorum; etsi nemo fuerit accusator,
ipse narrabit." Concita processit, velut diis ipsis
persequentibus; "feci" inquit. Supplicium de ea
vel nunc exigamus homines de qua dii olim exigere
coeperunt. Violatorum numinum maiestate con-
pulsa est ut mori et vellet et deberet et non posset. 361
Incisus est laqueus. Ita putabas te, sacrilega,
secreto mori posse? Omnia fecit ut taceret quae
ne confiteretur etiam mori voluit. Si crimen
quaeritis, factum est sacrilegium, si sacrilegum, fatetur. Facti quaeritis causam? Si priusquam amit-
teret liberos, avara ⟨fuit⟩; si postquam amisit, irata.

II

PHIDIAS AMISSIS MANIBUS

Sacrilego manus praecidantur.

Elii ab Atheniensibus Phidian acceperunt ut
his Iovem Olympium faceret, pacto interposito
ut aut Phidian aut centum talenta redderent.
Perfecto Iove Elii Phidian aurum rapuisse
dixerunt et manus tamquam sacrilego prae-

---

[1] The objection is that the gods seem to have shown their
favour, the reply that they want to have the woman die—
more publicly.

stay hidden; whoever he is, he will come to no good end, nor will any of his family; even if there is no-one to accuse him, he will tell the tale himself." She came forth in perturbation, as though the gods themselves were harrying her. " I did it," she said. Let us humans now exact punishment from a woman whom the gods have long since started to punish. She was driven by the sanctity of the powers she had violated to want to die, to have a duty to die, to fail to die.—" The noose was cut." [1] Did you, sacrilegious woman, think you could die in private like that?—She did everything to keep silent—she was ready even to die so as not to have to confess.—If it is a crime you are looking for, sacrilege has been committed; if it is a culprit, she confesses. Are you looking for a motive for the act? If she did it before she lost her children, she was greedy; if afterwards, she was angry.

2

How Phidias Lost His Hands

The sacrilegious shall have their hands cut off.[2]

The Eleans got Phidias from the Athenians to make a statue of the Olympian Zeus for them, promising to return either Phidias or a hundred talents. When the statue was complete, the Eleans said Phidias had stolen some gold. They cut off his hands for sacrilege and sent him back

---

[2] Sacrilege (i.e. theft of sacred objects), though punished severely, was not given this penalty either in Greece or at Rome (Bonner, 106).

ciderunt, truncatum Atheniensibus reddunt.
Petunt Athenienses centum talenta. Contra-
dicunt.

Iam Phidian commodare non possumus. Tunc
demum illa maiestas exprimi potest cum animus
opera prospexit, manus duxit. Ante sibi quam operi
Iovem fecit. Sacrilegi vos estis, qui praecidistis
consecratas manus. Primum sanguinem deus sui
vidit artificis. Testor Iovem, proprium iam Phidiae
deum. Ars alios in miseria sustinet, te miserrimum
fecit. Paciscendum Phidian manus fecerant. Sine 362
eo Phidian nos recepturos putatis sine quo vos accep-
turi non fuistis? Commodavimus qui facere posset
deos, recepimus qui ne adorare quidem possit. Non
pudet vos Iovem debere sacrilego? Superest homo,
sed artifex periit. Poenam nobis Phidiae, non
Phidian redditis. Manus quae solebant deos facere
nunc ne homines quidem rogare possunt. Talem
fecit Iovem ut hoc eius opus Elii esse ultimum vellent.
Manus commodavimus, manus reposcimus. Elius
est testis, Elius accusator, Elius iudex, Atheniensis
tantum reus. Invoco deos, et illos quos fecit Phidias

---

[1] Phidias *did* make such a statue for the Eleans (e.g. Paus.
5.10.2). Philochoros (328 *FGH* 121) states that there was a

mutilated to the Athenians. The Athenians ask
for the hundred talents. The Eleans dispute it.[1]

For the Athenians: Now we are not in a position to
lend Phidias.—The majesty of Zeus can only be
represented when the mind has seen the work in
advance, and the hand has shaped it. Phidias made
Zeus for himself before making his statue.—It is
you who commit sacrilege, in cutting off those sacred
hands.—The first blood the god saw was that of the
craftsman who made him.—I call to witness Zeus,
now Phidias' personal deity.—Others are sustained in
their misery by art—you it has made most miserable
of all.—It was because of his hands that the bargain
concerning Phidias was worth making; do you
imagine we are ready to take back Phidias lacking
something but for which you would not have taken
him?—We lent you a man who could make gods—we
have received back a man who can't even worship
them.—Aren't you ashamed to be indebted for your
Zeus to a temple-robber? [2]—The man survives, but
the artist has perished.—You are returning to us not
Phidias but the penalty inflicted on him.—The hands
that used to make gods now cannot even beg men.—
He made a Zeus so fine that the Eleans wanted this to
be his last creation.—We lent you his hands—and it is
his hands we ask back.—Witness, accuser, judge are
Eleans—the only Athenian is the defendant.—I call
on the gods whom Phidias made—and those he might

story he was executed for embezzlement by the Eleans; Plut.
Per. **31** has a different story. See Jacoby's full discussion
ad loc.

[2] Sarcastic.

et illos quos facere potuit. Recepimus Phidian: confiteor, si possumus commodare.

Pars altera. Habuimus aurum olim sacrum, habuimus ebur; sacrae materiae artificem quaesivimus. Disposueramus quidem ut aliis quoque templis simulacra Phidias faceret, sed non erat tam necesse ornare deos quam vindicare.

III

INFAMIS IN NURUM

Duorum iuvenum pater uni uxorem dedit, quo peregre profecto infamari coepit socer in nurum. Maritus reversus abduxit ancillam uxoris et torsit. Illa in tormentis periit. Maritus incerto quid quaesierit se suspendit. Imperat alteri filio pater ut eandem ducat; nolentem abdicat.

Duc, inquit, fratris uxorem. Si hoc fieri potest, adulterum frater invenit. Haec est mihi causa abdicationis quae fratri mortis fuit. Duc, inquit, fratris uxorem. Temptari me, si qua est fides, credidi. Mulier, si nubere lugenti potes, facis ut de te omnia credantur. Cogor eam ducere quae

---

[1] i.e. if I am capable of doing that, I was capable of being the seducer.

[2] i.e. the woman (cf. below: ". . . the cause of my disinheritance . . .").

have made.—" We have had Phidias back ": yes, if we are still in a position to lend him.

The other side: We possessed gold that had long been sacred, we possessed ivory; it was to work holy materials that we looked for a craftsman.—We had certainly intended that Phidias should make images for other temples too—but it was more vital to avenge the gods than to decorate their temples.

3

THE MAN SLANDERED IN CONNECTION WITH HIS DAUGHTER-IN-LAW

The father of two youths provided one of them with a wife. The son went abroad, and the father began to be slandered in connection with his daughter-in-law. The husband returned, took one of his wife's servants and put her to the torture, under which she died. The husband, without revealing what he had been looking for, hung himself. The father orders the second son to marry the same woman; he refuses, and is disinherited.

For the son: " Marry your brother's wife." If that is possible, my brother has found the adulterer he was looking for.[1]—The reason[2] for my disinheritance is the reason for my brother's death.—" Marry your brother's wife." If you will believe me, I thought I was being put to the test.—Woman, if you are capable of marrying a man weighed down by grief, you make it possible to believe anything of you.—I am forced

mihi abdicationis est causa, populo rumoris, viro mortis. Legi iam uxorem quae, si peregrinatio inciderit, mecum peregrinari velit, quae, si viro aliquid acciderit, nubere alii nolit. Qui me abdicari audiunt, putant fratrem de me aliquid suspicatum.

Pars altera. Obiecisti mihi ultimum nefas et quod qui tantum suspicatus est noluit vivere. Inpulsu tuo frater torsit ancillam, et, quia nihil repperit, falsas suspiciones morte expiavit.

IV

Homicida in Se

Homicida insepultus abiciatur.

Quidam se occidit; petitur ut insepultus abiciatur. Contradicitur.

Adferre sibi coactus est manus assiduis malis. Summam infelicitatum suarum in hoc removit, quod existimabat licere misero mori. Infelicissime adu- 364 lescens, cum te prohiberi etiam sepultura video, mirari desino quod peristi. Tales inimicos habes ut etiam mortuum persequantur. Facilius miserum

---

[1] The brother.

[2] Bonner (pp. 100–1) argues that this may have been an obsolete Roman law: but it sounds appreciably more Greek. However, the situation is in any case fictional, because suicides were left unburied also, and there would have in practice been

to marry the cause of my disinheritance, the people's talk, her husband's death.—I have already chosen a wife who would be willing to travel with me if I have to travel, and unwilling to marry again if something fatal happens to her husband.—People who hear that I am getting disinherited think that my brother was suspicious of *me*.

The other side: You reproached me with the most extreme of sins—one [1] who merely suspected it was unwilling to go on living.—It was on your instigation that your brother tortured the slave-girl; finding nothing, he paid for his false suspicions by his death.

4

The Self-Murderer

Homicides shall be cast out unburied.[2]

A man killed himself. A demand is made for him to be cast out unburied. Objection is raised.

For the suicide: It was by unending misfortunes that he was forced to lay hands on himself.—He banished the worst of his troubles, because he thought an unfortunate man has the right to die.—Wretched youth, when I see you barred even from burial I cease to be surprised that you perished. You have the sort of enemies that harry even the dead.—Fortune con-

---

no need for the appeal to the " law " about homicide. Clearly, the point is the discussion whether suicide is to count as homicide (cf. Quintilian 7.3.7). But the declaimers preferred to attack or defend suicide itself.

quam sceleratum Fortuna vincit. Sumpsisti hoc ferrum, Cato, et quam invidiosum, quod Catonem occideris. Curti, perdideras sepulturam nisi in morte repperisses. Quid est in vita miserius quam mori velle? quid in morte quam non posse sepeliri? Quis miretur eum mori voluisse quem fugientem quoque Fortuna persequitur? Omnibus natura sepulturam dedit: naufragos idem fluctus qui expulit ⟨sepelit⟩; suffixorum corpora crucibus in sepulturam suam defluunt; eos qui vivi uruntur poena funerat. Irascere interfectori, sed miserere interfecti. Homicida, inquit, est, quia se occidit. Huic irasceris pro quo irasceris? Non aliud Scaevolae Mucio cognomen dedit et capto contra Porsennam regem libertatem reliquit quam vilitas sui. Non aliud Codrum illum ceteris imperatoribus exemplum dedit quam quod positis imperatoris insignibus ad mortem cucurrit, nec ullo maior dux fuit quam quod se ducem non esse mentitus est. Non postulo ut gloriosum mori sed ⟨ut⟩ tutum sit. Non magis crudeles sunt qui volentes vivere occidunt quam qui volentes mori non sinunt. Curtius deiciendo se in praecipitem locum fatum sepulturae miscuit; cele- 365

---

¹ Cato Uticensis was the most famous Roman suicide: cf. below and on *S.* 6.2.

² M. Curtius' feat is described in Livy 7.6.1 *seq.*

³ A topic touched on in Sen. *Ep.* 92.35, citing Maecenas: " nec tumulum curo: sepelit natura relictos."

⁴ As they rot.

⁵ For the story see Flor. 1.10.5–6 and Livy 2.12.1 *seq.*, with

quers the wretched more easily than the wicked.—
You took up that sword, Cato—and how loathsome a
sword, seeing that it was Cato you killed! [1]—Curtius,
you would have lost your chance of burial if you had
not found it in death.[2]—What is there more wretched
in life than to wish to die? What in death than to be
unable to find burial?—Is there any wonder that one
whom Fortune tracks down even as he runs away
should have wanted to die?—Nature gives everyone a
burial; [3] the same wave that ejected the shipwrecked
from their vessel covers them over; the bodies of the
crucified flow down [4] from their crosses into their
graves; those who are burned alive are given funeral
by their punishment.—Get angry with the killer—but
pity the victim.—" He is a homicide—he killed himself." Are you then angry with a man on whose
behalf you are angry?—What gave Mucius Scaevola
his name,[5] and left him free, though a prisoner, in the
face of King Porsenna, was his contempt for his own
life. What made the great Codrus an example to all
other generals was that he laid aside his general's
insignia and ran to his death: he was most splendidly
a leader in pretending not to be one.[6]—I don't ask
that death be glorious—merely that it should be undisturbed.—There is equal cruelty in killing those
who wish to live and forcing life on those who wish to
die.[7]—Curtius, by throwing himself into an abyss,
found death and burial at the same moment. Cato

Ogilvie's notes: cf. also Sen. *Ep.* 66.51, *Ben.* 7.15.2. The
" name " referred to is Scaevola (" left-handed ").

[6] The story is in e.g. Val. Max. 5.6 ext. 1.

[7] A frequent thought: e.g. Hor. *Ars Poet.* 467: " invitum
qui servat idem facit occidenti "; Sen. *Phoen.* 98–9, *Herc.
Fur.* 513.

bratur Cato: huic miserrimo quod aliquid non
ignave de spiritu suo statuit tantum inpune sit.
Etiam vulnera infelicis in crimen scrutantur. Aestimate an vivere licuerit cui ne mori quidem licuit.

Pars altera. Facinus indignum si inveniuntur
manus quae sepeliant eum quem occiderunt suae.
Sumpsit gladium, video ardentes oculos—in quem,
nescio; quod solum scio, scelus cogitat. Nescio
cuius sibi criminis conscius confugit ad mortem,
cuius inter scelera etiam hoc est, quod damnari non
potest. Contra hos inventum est ut aliquid post
mortem timerent: non timent mortem. Nihil non
ausurus fuit qui se potuit occidere.

V

Fortis Nolens ad Patrem Fortem Redire

Abdicavit quidam filium; ille tacuit. Fortiter
fecit; petit praemio ad patrem reditum; pater
contradixit. Postea pater fortiter fecit; petit
ad se filii reditum; filius contradicit.

Ego fortior sum: post tuam pugnam pugnavimus,
post meam vicimus. Revertere, dignam te domum

has his fame. At least let there be no question of punishing *this* poor man for making a not ignoble decision about his own life.—They even examine the wretched man's wounds in order to make a charge out of them.—Judge whether he was allowed to live—he wasn't even allowed to die.

The other side: It is a dreadful outrage if hands are found to bury one whom his own hands killed.—He took up his sword—I see his glaring eyes. I don't know at whom they glare—all I know is that it is a crime he has in mind.—Some guilty conscience made him take refuge in death; one of his crimes is that he cannot be convicted.—It was for people like this that the fear of something after death was devised—death itself they do not fear.—One capable of killing himself might have dared anything.

5

THE HERO SON WHO WOULD NOT RETURN
TO HIS HERO FATHER

A man disinherited his son, who did not protest. The son became a hero, and for his reward [1] sought to return to his father. His father spoke against the idea. Later, the father became a hero; he seeks the return of his son; his son speaks against it.

For the father: I am the braver: after your fight, we went on fighting, after mine we were victorious.—

Cf. *C.* 10.2 n.

feci. Isti oculi mei sunt, istae manus meae sunt, ista contumacia mea est. Si mereor praemium, mihi date, si non mereor, isti suum reddite. " Ego " inquit " eadem lege praemium non accepi." Hoc est unde abdicatus es, quod putas nihil inter te et patrem interesse. Post tam similia opera, si tantum commilito esses, patrem me adoptare debueras. Admoneo te, iuvenis : hoc praemium qui recusaverat petit. " Timeo ne me iterum abdices." Commissurum me putas ut iterum rogem ? Bello graviore pugnavi, quo necesse fuit etiam senibus militare, quo fortes esse non potuerunt etiam qui priore bello fuerant. Ille annos suos exercuit, ego vici meos. Tu fregisti bellum, ego sustuli. Quanta adhortatio iuvenum fui senex fortis! Utrique nostrum praemium reddite. Militavi senex, militavi exanguis, militavi qui iam vicarium dederam. Uterque nostrum cum rogatur fastidit, cum relinquitur rogat. Quid nos suspicari cogis quod non vis in paternam domum venire nisi tuo praemio ? Turpe erat virum fortem nisi a patre coacto non recipi.

Pars altera. Quid me captivum ex libero cupis ? quid ignominiae subicis virum fortem ? quid efficis

366M

---

[1] i.e. yours. The similarity of the two is stressed again below: " Both of us . . ."

[2] The result in either case being the same. Cf. below: " Give us both our prizes."

[3] The father, that is; and the same may in the end happen to the son.

Return; I have made our house worthy of you.—
Those [1] eyes are mine, those hands mine, that stub-
bornness mine.—If I deserve a prize, give it to me; if
I do not, let him have his.[2]—" I did not receive *my*
prize, under the same law." That is why you were
disinherited—because you think there is no difference
between you and your father.—After such similar
exploits, you should have adopted me as your father
even if you had been merely my companion-in-arms.
—Take note, young man, he who had refused this prize
is in search of it.[3]—" I am afraid you may disinherit
me a second time." Do you imagine I shall put
myself in the position where I have to beg you a
second time?—I fought in a more serious war, one in
which even old men had to campaign and even the
heroes of the earlier war could not be heroic.—*He* put
his years to use, *I* overcame mine. You broke the
back of the war, I obliterated it.—How well I, an old
hero, served as an exhortation to the young!—Give
us both our prizes.—I fought as an old man, I fought
when feeble, I fought despite having already provided
a substitute.[4]—Both of us are scornful when we are
asked—both of us ask when we are abandoned.—
What do you force me to suspect if you won't come
into your father's household except as *your* prize? [5]—
It was shameful for a hero to be taken back by his
father only against his father's will.[6]

The other side: Why do you want to turn me from
free man into prisoner? Why humiliate a hero?

---

[4] His son, in the earlier war.
[5] The answer to this is not altogether clear.
[6] But now, when his father wishes it, the case is different.

ut possit abdicari? "Meus" inquit "es filius."
Quid opus est praemio, si tuus sum?

VI

Pauper Naufragus Divitis Socer

Vitiata vitiatoris aut mortem aut indotatas
nuptias petat.

Dives pauperem de nuptiis filiae interpellavit
tertio; ter pauper negavit. Profectus cum
filia naufragio expulsus est in divitis fundum;   367
appellavit illum dives de nuptiis filiae; pauper
tacuit et flevit. Dives nuptias fecit. Redierunt
in urbem; vult pauper educere puellam ad
magistratus. Dives contradicit.

Educatur ad magistratus puella. Quid times?
certe uxor est tua. Queri nec de morte poteris si
hanc puella maluerit. Nemo umquam raptor serius
perit. Ut litus agnovi, naufragus in altum natavi.
Quid times, si exorasti? Accessit ad me primum;
"filiam tuam ducere volo" inquit "uxorem." Non
flevi; tunc enim licuit negare. Nuptias filiae tamquam naufragium meum flevi. Naufragus plus de

---

[1] See *C.* 1.5 n.
[2] That is, to carry out her choice.
[3] i.e. you should be confident that she will choose marriage.
—For a reply, see below: "There is no righteousness . . ."
[4] Contrast the position after the wreck.

Why put him in a position where he may be disinherited?—" You are my son." What need of a prize if I belong to you?

6

THE SHIPWRECKED PAUPER WHO BECAME FATHER-IN-LAW OF A RICH MAN

A girl who has been raped may choose either marriage to her ravisher without a dowry or his death.[1]

A rich man asked a poor man for his daughter in marriage three times; three times the poor man refused. He set out abroad with his daughter, and was shipwrecked and cast up on the rich man's land. The rich man asked for his daughter's hand; the poor man wept, but said nothing. The rich man married her. They returned to the city. The poor man wants to take the girl before the magistrates;[2] the rich man objects.

For the father: Let the girl go before the magistrates. What are you afraid of? She is undoubtedly your wife.[3]—You won't be able to complain even of death if that is what the girl chooses.—No ravisher's death was ever so late.—When I recognised the shore, I swam out into deep water, despite my shipwreck.— What are you afraid of, if you have talked her over?— On the first occasion he came to me, and said: " I want to marry your daughter." I did not weep; for *then*[4] I was in a position to refuse him.—I wept for my daughter's wedding as though for my shipwreck.—

litore queror.   Inter naufragium [quidem][1] et nuptias ne una quidem nox interfuit.   Differ nuptias
dum flere socer desinat.   Putat me iam filiam commisisse sibi, cum hic se necdum committat uxori.
Lacrimis inter verba manantibus venio: talis et
filiae nuptiis fui.   Si rapta est, cur optionem recusas?
si uxor est, cur times?   Loquor ubi primum licet.
Procul a conspectu reliqueram patriam, nondum
tamen possessionem divitis praeterieram.   Subito
fluctibus inhorruit mare ac discordes in perniciem
nostram flavere venti; demissa nox caelo est et
tantum fulminibus dies redditus; inter caelum ter-
ramque dubii pependimus.   Adhuc tamen bene,
iudices, navigamus; naufragium maius restat in
litore.   Erat in summis montium iugis ardua divitis 368
specula: illic iste naufragiorum reliquias conputabat,
illic vectigal infelix et quantum sibi iratum redderet
mare.   Interrogavit[2] de nuptiis filiae cum adhuc
pulsaret aures meas fluctus; feci quod debui: et
captus et naufragus inimico stuprum lacrimis negavi.

___

[1] *Deleted by Gertz.*
[2] interrogavit *ed.:* interrogo *M* (*corrected to* interrogat).

___

[1] i.e. he does not wish her to have a choice, because he is
fearful of the outcome.
[2] Before the court.

Though I have been shipwrecked, the place where I landed is a worse cause for complaint.—Between wreck and marriage not even a single night intervened.—Put off the wedding until the father-in-law stops crying.—He thinks I have now entrusted him with my daughter—though he doesn't yet entrust himself to his wife.[1]—I come,[2] tears flowing as I speak: this is what I was like at my daughter's wedding too.—If she was raped, why do you refuse to let her have a choice? If she is your wife, what have you to fear?—I take the first chance I have to speak. —I had left my country far out of sight—but I hadn't yet got past the rich man's estates. Suddenly the sea bristled with waves, winds blew that battled to destroy us;[3] night fell from the sky, and day returned only with the flashes of lightning. We hung in suspense between sky and land. But up to this point, judges, our voyage is prosperous: a worse shipwreck awaits us on the shore.—On the highest ridge of the mountains there was a lofty look-out post [4] owned by the rich man; there he used to reckon up the remains of wrecks, the tribute of misery, the toll exacted for him by the anger of the sea.—He asked about marrying my daughter while the beat of the waves still sounded in my ears; I did what I had to do: prisoner and shipwrecked, I refused my enemy an outrage on her—with my tears.

---

[3] For storms in general, see *C.* 7.1.4 n.: for the battle of the winds, Morford, *op. cit.*, 40–2.

[4] For such eyries, Bornecque compares Sen. *Ep.* 89.21. For wreckers, see L. Friedländer, *Roman Life and Manners*[7] (transl. L. A. Magnus), 1.282–3, citing e.g. Manil. 5.401, 434–5.

THE ELDER SENECA

Delicatus dives, qui amare etiam inter naufragia potest! Matrimonii celebritatem remoti angulo ruris abscondis; ibi facis nuptias quo nemo nisi naufragus venit. Lacrima semper indicium est inoptatae rei; lacrimae pignora sunt nolentium et repugnantis animi vultus index. Nemo umquam quod cupit deflet. Lacrimae coacti doloris intra praecordia et intolerabilis silentii eruptio. Sic ille qui super cinerem deflet patrimonium odit incendium; sic qui naufragium deflet maria detestatur. Fletus humanarum necessitatum verecunda execratio est. Tuae nunc sunt partes, puella; discedo et, quod prius etiam feci, taceo. Si nupta es, habes quod optes, si vitiata, quod imperes.

Pars altera. Naufragum duo sacratissima inter homines acceperunt, hospitium et adfinitas: alterum praestiti, alterum etiam rogavi. Oblatas conciliante Fortuna nuptias, quod erat amantis, saepius rogavi, quod festinantis non distuli. Quid hic raptoris est, nisi quod indotatam duxi? Errat socer qui putat mihi cariorem futuram puellam si me potuerit occidere. Quid enim superest? preces meae, quas totiens adhibui, an istius lacrimae, quas movi? Nihil mihi inimicus obicere praeter matrimonium 369] potest. Magnus est amor qui ex misericordia venit. Fundebamus lacrimas ex paenitentia discidii prioris,

---

[1] Perhaps: "the ceremony, that should have been crowded."

[2] These are the final words of a speech: the girl must now make her *optio*.

[3] This is a *colour* explaining away the father's tears.

204

—Pernickety rich man, capable of love even amid shipwrecks!—You hide the crowded [1] wedding ceremony in a remote corner of the countryside; you hold the marriage where only the shipwrecked come. —A tear is always the sign of the undesired; tears are the guarantee of unwillingness, the face shows the rebelliousness of the mind. No-one ever weeps at what he desires. Tears are the bursting forth of a grief that has been suppressed in the heart, a silence that can be endured no longer. This is how the man who bewails his property amid its ashes shows his hatred of fire; this is how the man who has a shipwreck to lament curses the sea. Weeping is a curse laid, with self-restraint, on the exigencies that afflict men.—Now it is your turn, girl; I am going away,[2] and, as once before, I am silent. If you are married, you can make a choice; if you were raped, you can give an order.

The other side: The shipwrecked man was greeted by the two holiest ties that unite men, hospitality and the bond of family; I provided one, and begged for the other.—I asked often, as a lover should, for a marriage offered me by the match-making of Fortune, and, as a man in haste should, I brooked no delay. What is there here of the ravisher—except that I married her without a dowry?—Her father is wrong in supposing that the girl will be dearer to me if she gets the right to kill me.—For what remains? My prayers?—I have used *them* often; or his tears?—I have moved *them*.—All my enemy can accuse me of is marriage.—Great is the love that arises out of pity.— We shed tears [3] out of repentance for our former

nec plura aut me proloqui aut istum respondere
passae sunt mentes gaudiis occupatae. Nulla in-
tegritas tantum sibi etiam explorata confidit ut
causam velit dicere. Si interrogaveris filiam, partem
legis inputaturus es; si non interrogaveris, legem.
Si genero vitam daturus esset, etiam innocentiam
reliquisset. Quaeritis quid dum fleret fecerit?
Non negavit; et solebat negare, si nollet. Mortem
optaturus est; non enim potest eas partes legis
desiderare quas habet.

quarrel, and hearts pre-occupied by joy did not allow me to speak out—or him to reply.—There is no righteousness, however well-tested, that is so self-confident that it *wants* to plead its case.—If you proceed to ask your daughter, you will be chalking up half the law; if you do not, you will be chalking up the whole.[1]—If he were ready to grant his son-in-law life, he would have left him his innocence too.[2]—Do you ask what he was doing when he wept? He wasn't saying no—and he was used to saying no if he didn't want something.—He is going to choose death; he cannot feel the need of the part of the law he already possesses.

[1] Meaning (apparently): If you force the daughter to make a choice, you can take the credit for renouncing half the law (that concerning death); if you do not, you can take the credit for renouncing the whole law (i.e. a choice either way).

[2] He has taken away his innocence by bringing the case; and he must be proposing to advise his daughter to choose death, otherwise he would not have brought the case: cf. below " He is going . . ." and *C.* 7.8.9. For the exercise of the *optio* by the father, see Quintilian 4.2.68: " He raped the girl—but the *father* will not thereby be given the choice." But naturally the father's advice would carry weight with the girl: " it is incredible that your daughter would have chosen marriage except at your wish " (*Decl.* p. 355.10 Ritter).

LIBER NONUS

SENECA NOVATO, ⟨SENECAE⟩,[1] MELAE FILIIS SALUTEM.

1 Iam videbar promissum meum implesse; circumspiciebam tamen num quid me praeterisset. Ultro
Votieni Montani mentionem intulistis; et velim
vos subinde aliqua nomina mihi offerre, quibus
evocetur memoria mea, quae quomodo senilis per se
marcet, admonita et aliquando lacessita facile se
colliget.

Montanus Votienus adeo numquam ostentationis
declamavit causa ut ne exercitationis quidem declamaverit. Rationem quaerenti mihi ait: Utram
vis? honestam an veram? Si honestam, . . ., ⟨si
veram⟩,[2] ne male adsuescam. Qui declamationem
parat, scribit non ut vincat sed ut placeat. Omnia

---

[1] *Supplied by Kiessling.*
[2] *Lacuna recognised, and these words supplied, by Thomas.*

BOOK 9

PREFACE

Seneca to his sons Novatus, Seneca and Mela
greetings

Just now I thought I had done all I promised—but 1
I was looking around to see if I had forgotten anything. Without any prompting you brought up
Votienus Montanus: and indeed I should like you to
keep suggesting names in order to jog my memory.
I am an old man, and my memory unprompted is failing; but if it is given its cue and prodded from time
to time, it will easily pull itself together.

Votienus Montanus never declaimed for show—in
fact he never declaimed even for exercise. When I
asked why, he said: "Which do you want, the
respectable reason or the true one? If the respectable . . .;[1] if the true one, I don't want to get into
bad habits.[2] If you prepare a declamation beforehand, you write not to win but to please. You look

---

[1] Presumably that he felt unsuited to declamation: cf. *C.* 3
pr. 14.
[2] For Votienus' assault on declamation, compare in detail
Cassius Severus' in *C.* 3 pr. 8 *seq.*, with my notes.

itaque lenocinia [ita] [1] conquirit; argumentationes, quia molestae sunt et minimum habent floris, relinquit; sententiis, explicationibus audientis delinire 371M contentus est. Cupit enim se approbare, non causam.

2 Sequitur autem hoc usque in forum declamatores vitium, ut necessaria deserant dum speciosa sectantur. Accedit etiam illud, quod adversarios quamvis fatuos fingunt: respondent illis et quae volunt et cum volunt. Praeterea nihil est quod errorem aliquo damno castiget; stultitia eorum gratuita est. Vix itaque in foro futurus periculosus stupor discuti potest, qui crevit dum tutus est. Quid quod laudationibus crebris sustinentur et memoria illorum adsuevit certis intervallis quiescere? Cum ventum est in forum et desiit illos ad omnem gestum plausus excipere, aut deficiunt aut labant.

3 Adice nunc quod ⟨memoria⟩ illis [2] nullius interventu excutitur: nemo ridet, nemo ex industria obloquitur, familiares sunt omnium vultus. In foro, ut nihil aliud, ipsum illos forum turbat. Hoc quod vulgo narratur an verum sit tu melius potes scire: Latronem Porcium, declamatoriae virtutis unicum exemplum, cum pro reo in Hispania Rustico Porcio, propinquo suo, diceret, usque eo esse confusum ut a soloecismo inciperet, nec ante potuisse confirmari

---

[1] *Deleted by Haase, Bursian.*
[2] memoria (animus *C. F. W. Müller: perhaps* mens?) illis *ed.:* ab illis.

out all possible allurements; you throw arguments overboard, because they are bothersome and much too sober; you rest content with cajoling the audience with epigrams and developments. Your aim is to win approval for yourself rather than for the case.

" Now declaimers are dogged right into the courts 2 by this fault of leaving out what is necessary and making for the attractive. Further, they make out their opponents to be as silly as they like; they give them replies as they will and when they will. Further, error never gets punished by any harm done —their folly costs them nothing. So a dullness that grew well in safe surroundings isn't easy to throw off, though in court it spells danger. Declaimers, too, are kept going by frequent applause,[1] and their memories are used to taking a rest at fixed intervals. When they get into court, and cheers cease to attend their every gesture, they fail or collapse.

" Moreover, in the schools there are no interrup- 3 tions to put their memory out; no-one laughs, no-one purposely contradicts, every face is well-known.[2] In the courts, apart from anything else, they are disturbed by the court itself. You are in a better position than I to know what truth there is in the popular tale [3] that Porcius Latro, unsurpassed pattern of excellence in declamation, when speaking for a relation, Porcius Rusticus, on trial in Spain, was so confused that he began with a solecism, and—so great

---

[1] For applause in declamation-schools, see Quintilian 2.2.9 seq., 8.5.13–14, with E. Norden, Antike Kunstprosa, 1.274–5.
[2] For the contrasting unfriendly atmosphere in court see Quintilian 12.6.5; Tac. Dial. 34.
[3] Told also by Quintilian 10.5.18.

⟨tectum⟩ ac parietem desiderantem quam impetravit ut iudicium ex foro in basilicam transferretur.

4   Usque eo ingenia in scholasticis exercitationibus delicate nutriuntur ut clamorem silentium risum, caelum denique pati nesciant. Non est autem utilis 372M exercitatio nisi quae operi simillima est in quod exercet; itaque durior solet esse vero certamine. Gladiatores gravioribus armis discunt quam pugnant; diutius illos magister armatos quam adversarius retinet. Athletae binos simul ac ternos fatigant ut facilius singulis resistant. Cursores, quom intra exiguum spatium de velocitate eorum iudicetur, id saepe in exercitationem decurrunt quod semel decursuri sunt in certamine. Multiplicatur ex industria labor quo condiscimus ut levetur quo decerni-

5 mus. In scholasticis declamationibus contra evenit: omnia molliora et solutiora sunt. In foro partem accipiunt, in schola eligunt; illic iudici blandiuntur, hic inperant; illic inter fremitum consonantis turbae intendendus animus est, vox ad aures iudicis perferenda, hic ex vultu dicentis pendent omnium vultus. Itaque velut ex umbroso et obscuro prodeuntes loco clarae lucis fulgor obcaecat, sic istos e scholis in forum transeuntes omnia tamquam nova et inusitata perturbant, nec ante in oratorem conroborantur quam

---

[1] Cf. Quintilian 10.5.20, with Peterson's n.

was his need of ceiling and four walls—couldn't regain his self-confidence before he made a successful application to have the trial transferred from the forum to a basilica.

" Students are so coddled and pampered in the 4 exercises of the declamation school that they cannot tolerate noise, silence, laughter, even the open air. But no exercise is any use unless it very closely resembles the activity for which it is a preparation. This is why it is often more demanding than the real thing: gladiators train on heavier weapons than those used in combat,[1] their trainer keeps them longer in arms than will their opponents; wrestlers tire out two or three at a time in order to be able to stand up easily to one; runners, though their speed is to be tested over a tiny stretch of track, for training purposes cover many times a course they will have to run once only in the real contest. The labour of learning is purposely increased in order to lighten the labour of the decisive test. But the opposite is true 5 of declamation in the schools; everything is softer and more casual. In the court they take the role they are given, in the school they choose it. There they have to coax the judge, here they give him orders. There they have to concentrate, and struggle to make their voices reach the judge's ears amid the competing hubbub of the throng; here every face hangs on the face of the speaker. Men going out of a dark shady place are blinded by the dazzle of broad daylight; similarly as pupils pass from the schools to the forum, they are put off by the novelty and unfamiliarity of everything, and they can only be hardened off into orators after they have had many

multis perdomiti contumeliis puerilem animum
scholasticis deliciis languidum vero labore durarunt.
Lepidus, vir egregius et qui declamatorio non
studio . . .

I

CIMON INGRATUS CALLIAE

Adulterum cum adultera qui deprenderit, dum
utrumque corpus interficiat, sine fraude sit.
Ingrati sit actio.

Miltiades, peculatus damnatus, in carcere
alligatus decessit; Cimon, filius eius, ut eum sep-
eliret, vicarium se pro corpore patris dedit.
Callias dives sordide natus redemit eum a re
publica et pecuniam solvit; filiam ei suam
collocavit, quam ille deprensam in adulterio de-
precante patre occidit. Ingrati reus est.

1 ALBUCI SILI. Non movet me periculum meum:
semper nos in malis nostris non fortunam sed causam
spectavimus. Non dubito quin Callias redempturus
fuerit Miltiaden si iam habuisset filiam nubilem.

MUSAE. Alius aliud pati non potest. *Mihi adulterium carcer est.*

---

[1] Cf. *C.* 1.4 n.
[2] Cf. *C.* 2.5 n.
[3] Miltiades was fined in 489 B.C. for deceiving the Athenian
people; he then died, but the fine was paid by his son Cimon.
Callias married Cimon's sister Elpinice. All else is fiction
(*RE* s.v. Kimon, col. 439), though one not confined to Seneca.
Nearest to him are Ephorus (see Jacoby 70 *FGH* 64) and
Diodorus (10.30.1; 10.32), who give Cimon's marriage to an

insults to chasten them, and real work to toughen
juvenile minds relaxed by the spoiling they get in the
schools. Lepidus, an excellent man, and one who
. . . not . . . declamatory enthusiasm . . ."

1

HOW CIMON WAS UNGRATEFUL TO CALLIAS

Whoever catches an adulterer with his mistress
in the act, provided that he kills both, may go free.[1]
An action may lie for ingratitude.[2]

Miltiades, convicted of embezzlement, was
imprisoned and died. His son Cimon gave himself as substitute for his father's body so that it
could be buried. Callias, a rich man of low
birth, ransomed him from the state and paid the
money; he married his daughter to him. Cimon
caught her in adultery, and killed her despite her
father's pleas. He is accused of ingratitude.[3]

For Cimon

ALBUCIUS SILUS. I am not moved by my own 1
danger; always amid my troubles I have had regard
not to fortune but to motive.[4]—I am sure that Callias
would have been willing to redeem Miltiades if he
had had a daughter ready for marriage *then*.

MUSA. Different people find different things intolerable. For me adultery is a prison.

unnamed rich wife as the reason for his being able to pay. For
the imprisonment of Cimon, see e.g. Val. Max. 5.3 ext. 3, 5.4
ext. 2 and *Decl.* p. 191.29 Ritter.
  [4] Lucan 3.303: " et causas, non fata, sequi."

ARELLI FUSCI patris. Nihil, inquit, filiae plus possum dare quam Cimonem virum. Quando mihi ex eo contingent nepotes? *Ferrum a lege mihi traditum ad vindictam pudicitiae proiciam? Perdidisti pecuniam, Callia, si tales solvisti manus.* Damnatus peculatus nihil aliud heredi suo reliquit quam se patrem.

2 CESTI PII. *Non potest generosus animus contumeliam pati.* Merito tu ex Cimone habere nepotes concupisti. Quid magis in me probasti quam carcerem? Non sum innocentior quam pater, ne infelicior quidem; *hoc unum interest inter parentis et fili fortunam quod illius calamitatium exitus fuit carcer, mearum initium.* Exponam vobis quam in neminem meorum ingratus sim. *Unus Miltiadis census inventus est Cimon filius;* ne hic quidem quicquam habuit quod daret pro patre praeter se. Poteram in Cynaegiri domo sperare nuptias, poteram in Callimachi, nec verebar ne Cynaegirus suas pluris aestimaret manus. *Redemptus Cimon redemptoris felicitas est.*

3 VOTIENI MONTANI. Facis iam ut dicam: non accepi *beneficium* aut reddidi.[1] Certius *reddam cum tam honeste desideraris quam dedisti. Ego adulteros dimit-*

374M

---

[1] aut reddidi *Gronovius:* alter reddidit.

---

[1] Hands capable of neglecting the punishment for adultery.
[2] i.e. prison was honourable, and Callias' service in freeing him negligible.

ARELLIUS FUSCUS SENIOR. " I cannot do better than Cimon as a husband for my daughter. When shall I have grandsons by him? "—The law gave me the sword in defence of chastity; am I to throw it away? You have wasted your money, Callias, if these were the hands [1] you thought you were freeing. —Convicted of embezzlement, he left his heir nothing—except himself for a father.

CESTIUS PIUS. A noble spirit cannot brook insult. 2 —You were quite right in wishing to have grandsons by Cimon.—What did you find more praiseworthy in me than my imprisonment? [2]—I am not more innocent than my father, not even more unfortunate; the one difference between the fortunes of father and son is that prison was the end of *his* troubles, the start of mine.—I will relate to you how I am not ungrateful to any relation of mine.[3]—Miltiades' one asset proved to be his son Cimon: and he too had nothing to give in exchange for his father except himself.—I could have hoped for marriage into the house of Cynaegiros or Callimachus, and I had no fear that Cynaegiros would reckon his own hands worth more.[4] —The ransom of Cimon is a stroke of good fortune— for the ransomer.

VOTIENUS MONTANUS. You force me to say: " I 3 have received no service—or I have reciprocated it." —I shall reciprocate it more surely if you ask for a service from me in as honourable a spirit as you did me

---

[3] Particularly, he means, his father, whose name must be protected.

[4] Cynaegiros had his hand(s) cut off at Marathon (Hdt. 6.114), a fact that greatly struck the declaimers: see Bonner, *A.J.P.* 87 (1966), 281 *seq.*

tam? quid aliud facerem si alligatas haberem manus?
Egit me attonitum dolor. Non mehercules me exorasset Miltiades pater. Nihil Calliae debeo nisi
liber sum.[1] Est vir egregius Callias, est misericors;
sed utinam tantum adversus bonos! Maior iniuria
est si nunc manus Cimonis alligantur quam fuit
beneficium quod tunc solutae sunt. Non iste ini-
quiore animo filiam amisit quam ego uxorem, sed
aequiore animo inpudicam pati voluit. Vis tu divitias tuas abscondere cum in eos incideris qui men-
dicitate censentur? Nihil habet domus nostra
melius quod ostendat quam paupertatem. Da
pecuniam Miltiadi qua damnationem luat: nocens
erit; da Cimoni qua patrem redimat: pius non erit. 375

4   VIBI GALLI. Nullo mihi felicior videor quam quod
Miltiadis pretium fui. Alligatus iacebat Persicae
potentiae vindex, libertatis publicae adsertor, alligatus iacebat crimen ingratae civitatis. Adulteram
dimittam? patiar adulteram qui non tam glorior
quod filius sum Miltiadis quam quod vicarius?
Quid? tu poenam putas pro Miltiade alligari? Si
adulterum solum occidero, exulandum est. Quid

---

[1] liber sum *early edd.:* libertum.

---

[1] i.e. what was the good of you freeing me if I am to let
adulterers off?

one.—Am I to let adulterers go free? Wouldn't I do that if I had my hands *tied*? [1]—I was bewildered, driven on by my grief.—God help me, my father Miltiades himself would not have talked me out of it. —I owe nothing to Callias unless I am a free agent.[2]— Callias is an excellent man, he is compassionate; would that his compassion extended only to the good! —It is a greater injustice if Cimon's hands are tied now than it was a service for them to be freed then.— I was as distressed to lose my wife as he to lose his daughter: but he was willing to put up with her lack of chastity with less distress.—Don't you want to hide your riches when you fall in with men whose reputation rests on their poverty?—Our house has nothing better to show off than its poverty.—Give Miltiades money to get off his conviction: he will be guilty. Give Cimon money to ransom his father: he will not be displaying affection.[3]

VIBIUS GALLUS. I count myself fortunate in 4 nothing so much as having been the price for Miltiades.—There lay, in chains, the scourge of the power of Persia, champion of the people's freedom. There he lay in chains, a reproach to an ungrateful country.—Am I to let an adulteress go? Shall I wink at a wife's deceptions?—I who boast of being son of Miltiades, and, still more, his deputy.—What, do you regard it as a *punishment* to be imprisoned in place of Miltiades?—If I kill only the man who deceived me in adultery, I must go into exile.

[2] i.e. if I am free, I can act as I like; if I am not free, I owe nothing to Callias for getting me out of prison.

[3] Presumably part of a *locus* on the importance of motive as compared with mere riches.

faciam? Occidam? plus quam praestitisti exigis: pro carcere exilium. Non occidam? plus quam praestitisti exigis: unum beneficium dedisti, duo petis. *Uterque magnum beneficium dedistis et statim dum datis recepistis: Cimon quod Miltiadem redemit, tu quod Cimonem.* Videbatur mihi omnis maiorum meorum circa me turba fremere dicentium: ubi sunt illae manus quae solvere Miltiadem? Non mihi occurrit indulgentia uxoris, non Callias socer, non ullius aut rei aut benefici memoria; feci quod soleo, nihil aliud respexi quam patrem.

5   MENTONIS. Cogita adulteros esse pro quibus rogas, cogita qualium misereri soleas: *turpe est ab eodem dimitti et adulteros et Cimonem. Ego sum qui referre gratiam ne mortuis quidem desino: ita mihi veros habere liberos contingat; quod quantum esset Miltiades expertus est.*

6   PORCI LATRONIS. Ego adulteros dimittam? Ardet cupiditate vindictae animus. Has manus continere non posset Miltiades, quas alligare potuit. Si in hoc solutus sum, redde me carceri. Ille Graeciae servator et vindex Persarum orientisque domitor, cui modo tam insignem triumphum Fortuna de hoste detulerat, damnatus est peculatus, ob hoc videlicet ipsum, ut innocentia eius, quae alioqui latere potuerat, ipsa damnatione ostenderetur. Damnatus est innocens. Quisquis[1] in civitate misericors est, nunc occasio misericordiae venit:[2]   376

---

[1] quisquis *Müller:* quis.
[2] venit *early edd.:* inuenit.

---

[1] i.e. the man and not the woman.
[2] The sparing of both offenders.

What am I to do? Kill him?[1] You are asking more than you gave—exile compared with prison. Not kill? You are asking more than you gave: you gave one boon, you ask two back.[2]—You[3] have both of you conferred a great benefit, and immediately in conferring it received one: Cimon in ransoming Miltiades, Callias in ransoming Cimon.—I thought I heard the whole crowd of my ancestors clamouring around me, saying: " Where are the hands that freed Miltiades? " I did not think of my love for my wife, of my father-in-law Callias, any thing or any service; I did what I always do—I thought only of my father.

MENTO. Reflect that it is adulterers you beg for, 5 reflect on the sort of person you normally pity; it is a disgrace that the same man should release both a pair of adulterers—and Cimon.—I'm a person who does not cease to be thankful, even to the dead, so may I have true sons: how much *that* meant, Miltiades found.

PORCIUS LATRO. Am *I* to let adulterers go? My 6 mind is ablaze with passion for revenge. Miltiades himself could not have restrained these hands—though he was able to have them bound.—If this is why I was freed, send me back to prison.—That saviour of Greece, scourge of the Persians, tamer of the Orient, whom Fortune had just granted so signal a triumph over the foe, was convicted of embezzlement, pre- cisely, no doubt, in order that his innocence, which might otherwise have lain hidden, should be shown up by his very conviction.—He was convicted despite his innocence. Whoever is merciful in this country has

[3] Cimon and Callias are addressed by the advocate. Each received a *beneficium* in the fame accruing from the act.

Miltiades redimendus est. Redemi corpus tuum, Miltiade, ne funeri quidem interfuturus in quod me ipsum impenderam. Misereor accusatoris mei non quia perdidit filiam sed quia habuit. *Dignus erat Callias tales habere quales redemit.* Quodsi me in hanc stuprorum patientiam redemisti, matrimonio carcerem praefero. Honestius patri alligor quam adultero solvor. Ut audivi esse qui pecuniam numeraret, miratus sum fuisse in civitate nostra quemquam qui Cimonem redimere quam Miltiaden maluisset. Ego ne patrem quidem meum nisi innocens fuisset redemissem.

7   BLANDI. Obiciat licet vincula, numquam tamen efficiet ut non magis carcere glorier quam matrimonio. Diversi sunt hominum adfectus: tu fortasse, Callia, vincula non potes ferre; ego adulteram uxorem. Effugient ergo adulteri tamquam alligatas Cimonis manus?

ARGENTARI. Redemptum me protinus appellare coepit de filiae nuptiis. " Statim " inquam " Callias experitur an gratus sim." †Habes in Callias sine Cimone.†   Pro una rogat, duos eripit.

FULVI SPARSI. *Dic nunc: " ego te carceri exemi,"* 37 *dum ego respondeam: " ego me carceri tradidi."* *Numquam effici poterit ut melius actum putem quod a Callia redemptus sum quam quod pro Miltiade alligatus.* Filia tua abstulit tibi generum Cimonem. Ductus

---

[1] Text quite uncertain.

an opportunity to show it now; Miltiades requires a ransom.—Miltiades, I ransomed your body, myself destined not to be present even at the funeral on which I had spent—myself.—I pity my accuser, not for losing his daughter but for having ever had her. Callias deserved to have offspring like the man he ransomed.—But if it was to tolerate such outrages that you ransomed me, I prefer prison to marriage. It is more honourable for me to be imprisoned to the advantage of a father than to be freed to the advantage of an adulterer.—When I heard there was someone prepared to pay up, I was astonished that anyone in our country preferred ransoming Cimon rather than Miltiades.—*I* should not have ransomed even my father unless he had been innocent.

BLANDUS. He may make a reproach of my chains 7 —but he will never make me glory less in my imprisonment than in my marriage.—Men's feelings differ; *you*, Callias, perhaps, cannot stand being chained; *I* cannot stand an adulterous wife.—Shall adulterers, then, escape Cimon's hands, as though they were still bound?

ARGENTARIUS. As soon as I was ransomed, he started to make overtures about my marrying his daughter. I said to myself: "Callias is testing out right from the start whether I am grateful." . . .[1] —He is begging for the life of one—but the effect is to save two from death.

FULVIUS SPARSUS. Say now: "*I* got you out of prison"—so long as you let *me* reply: "*I* put myself in it." I shall never think I did better to be ransomed by Callias than to be imprisoned for Miltiades. —Your daughter has stolen from you the blessing of

est pater meus in carcerem etiamnunc captivis suis plenum.

8 IUNI GALLIONIS. Beneficium, inquit, tibi dedi quod filiam tibi collocavi. Nunc vere, Miltiade, graviorem fortunam carcere sustines: Callias tecum ⟨nepotes⟩ [1] communicare dignatus est. *Ego me redemptum putabam; filiae istius emptus sum.* Steterunt ante oculos meos maiorum imagines emissusque sede sua Miltiades maiestate imperatoria refulsit et iterum meas invocavit manus.

IULI BASSI. *Calliae filiam* uxorem *duxi: hanc tibi, pater, iniuriam feci, dum ingratus esse nolo.* Placeas tibi licet et istas iactes divitias: tantidem tamen redemi patrem quanti a te redemptus sum.

9 DIVISIO. Latro in has quaestiones divisit: an non quisquis gratiam non rettulit cum posset ingrati teneatur. Multa, inquit, interveniunt propter quae non debeam facere etiamsi possum. Si non tenetur quisquis non rettulit gratiam cum posset, an hic teneatur. Hoc in haec divisit: *an possit ob id damnari quod lege fecit;* deinde: an facere debuerit; novissume: an, si adfectu et indignatione ablatus non fuit in sua potestate, ignoscendum illi sit. Hoc non 378 tamquam quaestionem sed, ut illi mos erat, pro

---

[1] *Supplied by Gertz.*

---

[1] Cimon paid his own body; Callias paid the market price for Cimon.
[2] Cf. *C.* 2.3.15.

having Cimon as your son-in-law.—My father was taken to a prison which was still full of the prisoners he took.

JUNIUS GALLIO. " I did you a service in marrying 8 my daughter to you." Now indeed, Miltiades, you suffer a fate worse than prison: Callias has condescended to share his grandchildren with you.—I thought I had been bought off my imprisonment; I had been bought—for his daughter.—Before my eyes stood the ghosts of my ancestors; and there, emerging from his resting place, was Miltiades, ablaze in his glory as general, once again summoning my hands to his aid.

JULIUS BASSUS. I married Callias' daughter; this was the wrong I did you, father, through not wanting to be ungrateful.—You may feel pleased with yourself, you may boast of those riches of yours: but I ransomed my father for the same price [1] for which I was ransomed by you.

Division

Latro divided into the following questions: Is 9 everyone who has failed to repay a service when able to repay it liable on a charge of ingratitude? " Many things crop up which mean I should not do it even if I can." If not everyone is culpable for failing to repay a service though he could, is this man? This he subdivided: Can he be condemned for something he did according to the law? Secondly, Ought he to have done it? Lastly: If he was not in control of himself as a result of emotion and anger, should he be forgiven? This Latro did not treat as a question, but, as usual with him,[2] as a piece of development or a

10 tractatione aut loco. Montanus Votienus quaestionem hanc adiecit: an gratiam rettulerit Cimon Calliae. Rettuli, inquit: filiam tuam uxorem ⟨duxi⟩,[1] filia tua Miltiadis nurus facta est. Non putas beneficium communes cum Miltiade nepotes?

Gallio illam quaestionem duram movit, sed diligenter executus est, quae solet esse in ingrati controversiis prima: an beneficium acceperit. Non erat, inquit, mihi poena in carcere esse: mea voluntate illo perveneram. Ita putas me libentius in cubiculo meo iacuisse? Nullus tunc erat locus Athenis honestior quam qui Miltiaden habuerat. Deinde et illam subiunxit quaestionem: an teneatur is qui beneficium accepit quod non petit. Non rogavi, inquit, te; dedisti istud iactationi tuae: putasti ad gloriam tuam pertinere. Ita tu non accepisses beneficium si tibi solvere Miltiaden contigisset?

11 Silo Pompeius a parte Calliae *duo beneficia se dixit dedisse, quod redemisset et quod egenti filiam conlocasset.* Hoc quod secundum posuit nemo alius pro beneficio inputavit, in quo adeo non est dubium an beneficium non dederit ut dubium sit an receperit.

Brutus Bruttedius illas praeterea quaestiones fecit: an, si sua causa fecit hoc Callias, ut redimeret, Cimoni sit beneficium. *Beneficium* enim *est,* inquit, *quod totum eius causa praestatur in quem confertur. Ubi* 37⟨9⟩ *aliquis ex eo* aut *sperat quid aut praeparat, non* est *beneficium, consilium est.* Hoc diu executus est et

¹ *Supplied by Otto.*

commonplace. Votienus Montanus added this ques- 10
tion: Did Cimon repay Callias? " I did," he says.
" I married your daughter, and your daughter became
daughter-in-law of Miltiades. Don't you think it a
benefit to have grandchildren in common with Miltiades ? "

Gallio brought up a tricky question, though he
worked it out carefully. It is one that is usually put
first in *controversiae* concerning ingratitude: Did he
receive a service? " It was no punishment for me to
be in prison. I had come there at my own request.
Do you imagine I took more pleasure in lying in my
bedroom? There was at that time no place in Athens
more honourable than that which Miltiades had
occupied." Next he put the question: Is a man
liable if he has received a service he did not seek?
" I didn't ask you; you gave it—to serve your own
pride. You thought it would advance your prestige.
Would *you* then have received no favour if *you* had had
the luck to free Miltiades? "

Pompeius Silo, for Callias, said he had conferred 11
two benefits, ransoming Cimon and giving him his
daughter's hand when he was poor. This second
point no-one else claimed as a benefit. There is no
question that he conferred no favour here—the
question is whether he in fact received one.

Bruttedius Brutus produced these further questions: If Callias' ransoming of Cimon was done to
serve his own interests, does it count as a service to
Cimon? " A service is something that is done
wholly for the sake of the man on whom it is conferred. When someone hopes or plans something
from it, it is no service—it is a scheme." He de-

argumentis et exemplis. Deinde: an sua causa
Callias fecerit. Voluisti, inquit, opinionem sordium
inlustri facto effugere; petisti ex hoc aeternam memoriam. Non magis poterat ignotum esse a quo
Cimon solutus esset quam pro quo alligatus. Voluisti
habere generum nobilem, pium.

Hispo Romanius duram quaestionem fecit: an
rettulerit gratiam hoc ipso, quod occidit. *Liberavi
te*, inquit, *summo dedecore; invito tibi beneficium dedi.*
Non est quod mireris; nam *et tu me non rogantem
redemisti. Hoc loco Verginios et* illos patres *qui filias
vitiatas occiderunt, qui incluserunt.*

12   *Color et Gallioni et Latroni et Montano placuit ut
nihil in Callian diceretur contumeliose, et redemptorem
et socerum et infelicem.* Cestius multa ⟨ut⟩ [1] in avarum et feneratorem et mensularium et lenonem dixit,
dum vult illud probare, reddidisse se beneficium quod
talem socerum habere sustinuisset.

Latro dixit: Filiam tuam dimittam? Quid
adultero faciam? Pro una rogas, duos eripis. Hanc
Hybreas aliter dixit sententiam: σοὶ δέ, μοιχέ, τί
ποιήσω; μὴ καὶ σοῦ Καλλίας πατήρ ἐστιν; Haec tota
diversa sententia est a priore, etiamsi ex eadem est
petita materia.

Illa non est similis sed eadem quam dixit prior
Adaeus, rhetor ex Asianis non proiecti nominis,

---

[1] *Supplied here by the editor.*

veloped this for some time with arguments and examples. Then: *Did* Callias do it for his own sake? "You wanted to escape a reputation for mean birth by doing a glorious deed; you looked for eternal fame from it. One could no more be ignorant of the man who ransomed Cimon than of the man for whom Cimon was imprisoned. You wanted to have a son-in-law at once noble and loving."

Romanius Hispo posed a harsh question: Did he repay by his very killing? "I freed you from the height of disgrace; I did you a service against your will. You need not be surprised: *you* ransomed me without my asking you to." Here he brought in the Verginii, and fathers who have killed or imprisoned their violated daughters.

Gallio, Latro and Montanus favoured the *colour* of 12 saying nothing to insult Callias, who was Cimon's ransomer, his father-in-law and a man in trouble. Cestius had a lot to say against Callias, as being greedy, a usurer, a money-changer, a pimp; his intention was to prove Cimon had repaid his debt in tolerating a father-in-law like this.

Latro said: "Am I to let your daughter go? What am I to do with her lover? You are begging for the life of one—but getting two off." [1] Hybreas put this epigram differently: "What shall I do with you, adulterer? Surely Callias isn't *your* father too?" This epigram is totally different from the earlier one, even though it is taken from the same material.

Another one, as spoken first by Adaeus, an Asian rhetorician of no little repute, and then by Arellius

[1] Cf. above, §7.

deinde Arellius Fuscus: ἀχάριστός σοι δοκῶ, Καλλία; 380
13 οὐκ οἶδας ποῦ μοι τὴν χάριν ἔδωκας; Hanc sic
mutavit Arellius Fuscus: non dices me, Callia, ingratum: unde redemeris cogita. Memini deinde
Fuscum, cum haec Adaei sententia obiceretur, non
infitiari transtulisse se eam in Latinum; et aiebat non
commendationis id se aut furti, sed exercitationis
causa facere. Do, inquit, operam ut cum optimis
sententiis certem, nec illas corrumpere conor sed
vincere. *Multa oratores, historici, poetae Romani a
Graecis dicta non subripuerunt sed provocaverunt.*[1] Tunc
deinde rettulit aliquam *Thucydidis sententiam:* δειναὶ
γὰρ αἱ εὐπραξίαι συγκρύψαι καὶ συσκιάσαι τὰ
ἑκάστων ἁμαρτήματα, deinde *Sallustianam: res
secundae mire sunt vitiis obtentui. Cum sit praecipua in
Thucydide virtus brevitas, hac eum Sallustius vicit et in suis
illum castris cecidit;* nam in sententia Graeca tam brevi
habes *quae salvo sensu detrahas: deme vel* συγκρύψαι *vel*
συσκιάσαι, *deme* ἑκάστων: *constabit sensus, etiamsi
non aeque comptus, aeque tamen integer. At ex Sallusti
sententia nihil demi sine detrimento sensus potest.*

14   *T. autem Livius tam iniquus Sallustio fuit ut hanc*

<hr/>

[1] *This sentence appears only in E: it was placed here by
Castiglioni.*

<hr/>

[1] In a glorious place: cf. above, §10 "There was at that
time . . ." and §15 Dorion.
[2] For translation practice see Quintilian 10.5.2 *seq.*, with
Peterson's notes.
[3] In fact taken from a much less concise writer, the unknown

Fuscus, is not merely similar but just the same: " Do
you think me ungrateful, Callias? Don't you know
where I was [1] when you rendered me your service? "
Arellius Fuscus' version was: " You will not call me 13
ungrateful, Callias: reflect where you ransomed me
from." I remember that afterwards Fuscus, when
challenged with this epigram of Adaeus', did not
deny that he had translated it into Latin; he said he
did so not to win credit for it or as a plagiarism but for
practice.[2] " I strive to rival the best epigrams; I
don't try to spoil them but to beat them. Roman
orators, historians and poets have not stolen but vied
with many sayings of the Greeks." Then he quoted
an epigram of Thucydides': " Success is wonderfully
good at hiding and shading over everybody's faults,"[3]
followed by Sallust's version: " Success is a wonder-
ful screen for vice."[4] Thucydides' primary virtue is
brevity, but Sallust has beaten him at it and defeated
him on his own ground. The Greek epigram is
certainly short, but there are words one can remove
without harm to the sense; take out " hiding " or
" shading," [5] take out " everybody's "—and the sense
will remain, not perhaps so pretty, but equally complete. But from Sallust's epigram nothing can be
removed without spoiling the sense.

Livy, however, was unjust enough to Sallust to 14

author of the pseudo-Demosthenes *in Ep. Phil.* 13, drawn
from the genuine *Ol.* 2.20. See D. Guilbert, *Les études clas-
siques* 25 (1957), 296–9.

[4] *Hist.* 1.55.24 Maurenbrecher.

[5] Indeed, Demosthenes himself only had " hiding ":
" shading " is the addition of his imitator. As to " everybody's," ps.-Demosthenes gave " of men," Demosthenes
" such."

*ipsam sententiam et tamquam translatam et tamquam
corruptam dum transfertur obiceret Sallustio. Nec* hoc
amore Thucydidis facit, ut illum praeferat, sed laudat 381[1]
*quem non timet et facilius putat posse a se Sallustium
vinci si ante a Thucydide vincatur.*

Cestius colorem pro Callia hunc habuit: *obiecit*
ultro Cimoni *quod passus esset uxorem* suam *adulteram
fieri, quod non custodisset, quod expectasset dum superveniret pater* ut *spectator calamitatis suae* fieret. Iam,
inquit, etiamsi dimiseris, ingratus es. *Ego non
expectaveram dum rogarer.*[2]

15   Hispo Romanius hunc colorem secutus est: dixit
adulescentem tumidum et nobilitatis suae cogitatione
insolentem invisa habuisse beneficia sua, *moleste
ferentem socerum suum dici Callian;* itaque omnem
operam dedisse ut *mores puellae in vitia non tantum labi
pateretur sed ipse impelleret,* ut haberet iustam dimittendi causam. *Nanctum occasionem non intermisisse,*
expectasse tamen dum superveniret pater. Hoc
secum cogitasse: expectat me; vult mecum pares
rationes facere. Fecisset, si non ostendisset patri
adulteram filiam.

---

[1] See R. Syme, *Sallust* (Cambridge, 1964), 289. Sallust's
Thucydidean tendencies were well-known; Livy wanted history
to be more expansive (cf. the contrast in Quintilian 2.5.19).
[2] i.e. now that I have had to ask you to spare her: I released
you without being asked. Callias is represented as speaking
before the killing of the girl.

criticise him both for translating the epigram and for
spoiling it in translation. He doesn't prefer Thucydides out of any love for him; he is praising someone
he does not fear, and thinks he may the more easily
overcome Sallust if Thucydides overcomes him first.[1]

Cestius had this *colour* for Callias. Going on the
offensive, he accused Cimon of having allowed his
wife to be seduced, of not having guarded her, of
having waited till the father should come on the scene
to be spectator of his own disaster. " You are ungrateful already [2] even if you let her go. *I* did not
wait to be asked."

Romanius Hispo pursued the following *colour*: he 15
said the youth was boastful and arrogant in the con-
sciousness of his noble birth. He had loathed the
favour done him, and was aggrieved that Callias
should be called his father-in-law. So he had made
every effort not only to allow the girl's morals to go
astray but even to give them a push, so as to have a
legitimate excuse for getting rid of her. He had got
his opportunity, and he had not wasted it, though he
had waited till the father came in. His [3] reflections
were: " He is waiting for me; he wants to level
accounts with me." " And he would have levelled
them if he had not shown her father his daughter in
adultery." [4]

---

[3] The father's, on entering the bedroom.
[4] Thereby tipping the scales against Cimon. Otherwise
Callias' service (so much resented by Cimon) and Cimon's
killing of the daughter would have exactly balanced. Now
Callias is " one up." This sentence is perhaps a quotation
from Hispo's declamation or a comment of Seneca's; probably
not part of Callias' reflections.

Gargonius in hac controversia foedo genere cacozeliae usus dixit: istud publicum adulterium est, sub
Miltiadis trophaeis concumbere.

Dorion, cum descripsisset gloriae sibi fuisse
carcerem, numquam non se illam fortunam ostentasse,
dixit: ὅτε εἰσῆλθεν Καλλίας, τὰς πέδας ἀπεκάλυψα.

Hybreas dixit: συγγνώμην ἔχε μοι . . .

II

FLAMININUS IN CENA REUM PUNIENS

Maiestatis laesae sit actio.

Flamininus proconsul inter cenam a meretrice
rogatus, quae aiebat se numquam vidisse hominem decollari, unum ex damnatis occidit.
Accusatur laesae maiestatis.

1 MENTONIS. Iam etiam perituri dormiebant. Pera-
gitur totus ordo supplici, ne quid se meretrix negaret
vidisse. O miserum, si quis meretricem offendit!
o miseram matrem familiae, si quoius formae meretrix invidet! Nihil petenti praetor negaturus est.

---

¹ For the Roman view of *maiestas*, see Bonner, 108–9.

² Two versions are given of the escapade of L. Quinctius
Flamininus in Livy 39.42–3. Livy believes the account of
Cato, who inveighed against Flamininus in 184 B.C., and is
scornful of the "fabula sine auctore edita" put about by
Valerius Antias. The declamation follows Valerius (as do Cic.
Sen. 42, Val. Max. 2.9.3); Livy, rejecting him, took the
opportunity for some declamation of his own ("inter pocula

Gargonius in this *controversia* showed a disgusting type of bad taste in saying: " This is an adultery against the state, to have sex under the trophies of Miltiades."

Dorion, having described how prison had been a boast to Cimon, and how he had always shown off about his fortune in that respect, said: " When Callias came in, I uncovered my chains."

Hybreas said: " Pardon me. . . ."

2

How Flamininus Executed a Criminal at Dinner

An action shall lie for *lèse-majesté*.[1]

Flamininus, when proconsul, was once asked a favour by a whore while dining. She said she had never seen a man's head being cut off. He had a condemned criminal killed.[2] He is accused of *lèse-majesté*.

Against Flamininus

Mento. By now even the men in the death cell 1 were asleep.—The whole routine of execution is gone through, so that the whore could not say she had not seen it all.—I pity anyone who offends the whore! I pity any wife whose beauty the whore envies! The praetor will deny her nothing she asks for.[3]

atque epulas, ubi libare diis dapes, ubi bene precari mos esset, ad spectaculum scorti procacis, in sinu consulis recubantis, mactatam humanam victimam esse et cruore mensam respersam! ").

[3] She might have a rival beauty accused: cf. §2 " An accuser was ready . . ."

MUSAE. Hic est Flamininus qui exiturus in provinciam uxorem a porta dimisit.

ARGENTARI. *Obicio luxuriam*, obicio *histrioniam*, ⟨obicio⟩ [1] *iocos: an* vos [revixerunt] [2] *in convivio nihil aliud nisi occiditis?* Qui in carcere vixerunt in convivio perierunt.

2 BLANDI. Feriatur in foro; omnes videant, meretrix audiat. Reliquiae praetoris unco trahebantur. Maiestatem laesam dixissem si exeunti tibi lictor a conspectu meretricem non summovisset.

VIBI RUFI. Paratus erat accusator cum commentariis, aiebat, si quid meretrix desiderabat.[3] In hoc tecum uxorem non misimus? Ut salva provincia sit, optemus meretrici bonam mentem? Dedimus tibi legatum, dedimus quaestorem, ut tu cum meretrice cenares? Meretrix uxoris loco accubuit, immo praetoris.

3 P. ASPRENATIS. *Uni fortasse osculo donavit homicidium.* Etiam *carnifices cenaturi manus abluunt.*

PORCI LATRONIS. Ne a sobrio quidem lictore percussus est. *Non inquiro in totum annum: una nocte contentus sum.* "Bibe, lictor, ut fortius ferias." Ecquid intellegitis quemadmodum damnatus sit

383

---

[1] *Supplied by Otto.*
[2] *Deleted by Kiessling.*
[3] desiderabat *Gronovius:* -erarit. *Perhaps* desideraret (*so* Warmington).

---

[1] He was in fact proconsul, as the theme states; but there are parallels for the usage. *reliquiae* in the context of a meal would normally mean "left-overs."
[2] Used to dispose of the executed (see Mayor on Juv. 10.66).

MUSA. This is the Flamininus who, when going out to his province, took leave of his wife at the city gate.

ARGENTARIUS. I accuse him of debauchery, of play-acting, of buffoonery: or does your sort do nothing at your supper-parties except kill?—Those who survived in a cell died at a dinner.

BLANDUS. Let him be struck down in the forum: 2 let everyone see it—and the whore *hear* of it.—What the praetor [1] left was dragged away on the hook.[2]—I should have called it *lèse-majesté* if the lictor [3] had failed to get a whore out of your sight as you left.

VIBIUS RUFUS. An accuser was ready with his note-book, he used to say, should the whore have any requirements.—Was it for this we did not send your wife with you? [4]—To make sure the province is un-harmed, must we pray for the good intentions of—a whore?—Did we give you a legate, a quaestor, so that you could dine with—a whore?—A whore reclined in the wife's place—or rather, in the praetor's.[5]

PUBLIUS ASPRENAS. He gave her a murder—in 3 return, maybe, for a single kiss.—Even executioners wash their hands before dinner.[6]

PORCIUS LATRO. It wasn't even a sober lictor who struck the blow.—I do not enquire into the whole year: one night gives me enough scope.—" Drink, lictor: you will strike the more bravely."—Can't you realise how someone killed in this fashion must have

---

[3] Cf. *C.* 1.2.3 n.

[4] For this practice cf. above, §1 Musa, and Tac. *Ann.* 3.33.2 with Furneaux's note.

[5] i.e. she took his decisions for him.

[6] And don't expect to dirty them during it.

qui sic occisus est? Qui scio an, in cuius gratiam
occisus est, in eiusdem etiam damnatus sit? Quantum tibi populus Romanus dederat, tantum tu meretrici dedisti. Si negaret, quos testes haberem?
Quis enim in illo convivio fuit quoi esset credendum?
*Facilius est ut qui alia meretrici dederit homicidium
neget quam ut qui hoc quoque dederit quicquam.* ⟨" Num-
quam⟩ [1] vidi." Nimirum numquam istud mulierum
oculis ostendi solet, aut ista iam saepe vidisset.

4 IULI BASSI. Inter temulentas reliquias sumptuo-
sissimae cenae et fastidiosos ob ebrietatem cibos
modo excisum humanum caput fertur; inter purga-
menta et iactus cenantium et sparsam in convivio
scobem humanus sanguis everritur. Gratulor sorti
tuae, provincia, quod desiderante tale spectaculum
meretrice plenum carcerem damnatis habuisti.
Servum si verberari voluisses, extra convivium abduxisses.

ROMANI HISPONIS. Quis ferret te si in triclinio
tuo iudicium coegisses? Scelus est in convivio 384
damnare hominem: quid occidere? Ad arbitrium
meretricis de reis pronuntiasti: nisi forte facilius in
honorem eius decollas quam iudicas.

5 FULVI SPARSI. *Contactam sanguine humano mensam*
loquor, *strictas in triclinio secures: quis credat ista*
aut *concupisse meretricem aut fecisse praetorem?* Cadaver, secures, sanguinem loquor: quis inter haec de

---

[1] *Supplied by Thomas.*

---

[1] Roman speakers enjoyed descriptions of debauched
feasts: a notable example from Caelius appears in Quintilian
4.2.123–4.
[2] Otherwise an innocent man would have had to serve.

got condemned?—Maybe he was condemned to
please the same person he was killed to please.—
Everything you had been granted by the Roman
people you granted to a whore.—If he denied it, what
witnesses should I have? Who was there at that
party that one could trust?—It is easier for a man
who has given other things to a whore to deny her a
killing than for a man who has given even a killing to
deny her anything at all.—" I have never seen . . ."
This is something not usually placed before a woman's
eyes—otherwise *she* would have seen it often.

JULIUS BASSUS. Amid the sodden remains of a 4
lavish feast,[1] amid food that drunkenness rejected,
they carry the head of a man, newly lopped off.
Together with the filth and litter of the diners, together with the sawdust scattered during the banquet,
is swept up human blood.—I congratulate you on
your luck, province: when a whore felt in need of
such a spectacle, you had your prison full of condemned prisoners.[2]—If you had wanted a slave
flogged, you would have had him taken outside the
dining room.

ROMANIUS HISPO. Who would tolerate your behaviour if you had held a trial in your dining-room?
It is a crime to condemn a man at a party—how much
worse to kill?—It was at the whim of a whore that
you pronounced sentence on accused men, unless you
are readier to behead men for her sake than to judge
them.

FULVIUS SPARSUS. I have to tell of a table defiled 5
with human blood, of axes bared in a dining-room:
who would believe that a whore wanted such things—
or that a praetor did them? I have to tell of a body,

convivio cogitat? " Hominem " inquit " occidi numquam vidi." Quid?[1] Flaminino praetore omnia
alia vidisti?

SILONIS POMPEI. Virum nobilissimum et tantis
honoribus functum turpiter meretrix clementem
fecisset: crudelem fecit. " Numquam vidi "; adice,
si vis: " nec alio praetore videre potero."

6   ALBUCI SILI. Si quis autem est, iudices, qui
desideret ut praetoris referam crudelitatem, quot
praeter hunc iugulaverit, quot innoxios damnaverit,
quot carcere incluserit, huic ego me satis facturum
esse polliceor: uno convivio cum sua praetura reum
evolvam.   Instituuntur ab isto in provincia epulae et
magnifico apparatu exstruitur convivium; distin-
guuntur argenteis poculis aurea. Quid multa, iudices? convivii eius apparatum sensit provincia.
Extrahitur quidam e carcere in convivium praetoris,
cui stupenti misero meretrix arridet.   Interim *virgae
promuntur et victuma crudelitatis ante mensam ac deos
trucidatur.   Me miserum, imperi Romani terrore lusisti.*

7 O qui crudelitate omnis superasti tyrannos! soli
tibi inter epulas voluptati est morientium gemitus:
hic ultimus apparatus cenae fuit. In eodem tri- 385
clinio video praetorem amatorem, scortum avidum
caedis; et[2] meretrix praetori, praetor provinciae
imperat.[3] Constituitur catenatus, qui, cum lan-
guentis praetoris istius aspexit oculos, existimans
ipsum praetoris beneficio dimitti, gratias isti agens

---

[1] quid *ed.:* alio quid *AB:* alio quem *V.*
[2] scortum avidum caedis; et *Brzoska:* scorta c(a)edis set
(or sed) *BV:* scorta uidisset *A.   The text is very doubtful.*
[3] imperat *Bursian:* imperato *AB:* imperat in conuiuio *V.*

240

axes, blood: who can think of a feast amidst all this?
—" I have never seen a man killed." Did you then
see everything else under the magistracy of
Flamininus?

POMPEIUS SILO. It would have been shameful for
a whore to make a fine nobleman—one who had held
such high office—lenient: *she* made him cruel.—" I
have never seen . . ." Go on to say, please: "and I
shan't be able to see it when someone else is praetor."

ALBUCIUS SILUS. But if anyone, judges, wants me 6
to tell of the praetor's cruelty, how many besides this
man he slaughtered, how many innocent men he
condemned, how many he shut up in prison, I promise
that I shall satisfy such an enquirer: in one party I
shall unroll the story of the accused and his praetor-
ship.—In his province he organises a banquet. The
feast is lavishly arranged with splendid appointments;
silver cups are set off by gold ones. What more need
I say, judges? The province felt the preparation of
that banquet, to its cost.—A man is hauled from the
prison and taken to the praetor's party; the whore
smiles on the poor dazed wretch. Rods are produced,
and the victim of sadism is slaughtered before the
table and before the gods. Alas, you have made a
game out of the terror inspired by the empire of
Rome. In sadistic practices you have surpassed 7
every tyrant! You alone find pleasure at dinner in
the groans of the dying; this was the final touch to
the feast.—I see reclining together the love-sick
praetor, and a whore greedy for a death; the whore
rules the praetor, the praetor the province.—They
place there a man in chains; seeing the drooping eyes
of that praetor, and thinking that he is being released

et utrisque manibus mensam tenens " di tibi "
inquit " immortales parem gratiam referant." Qui-
cumque in eodem accubabant triclinio, alius ubertim
demisso capite flebat, alius avertebat ab illa crudelitate oculos, alius ridebat, quo gratior esset meretrici.

8 Hic iste inter varios convivarum vultus submo-
veri iubet et miserum stare ad praebendas cervices
immotum: interim distinguitur mora poculis. Ne
sobri quidem carnificis manu civis Romanus occisus
est. Non veto quominus securi percutiatur: illud
rogo, *legi potius quam scorto cadat.* Memento ter-
rorem imperio quaeri, non oblectamenta mulierculis.
Quid ego nunc referam, iudices, ludorum genera,
saltationes, et illud dedecoris certamen, praetorne
se mollius moveret an meretrix?

9 CAPITONIS. *Exsurgite* nunc *Bruti, Horatii, Decii et
cetera imperi decora: vestri fasces, vestrae secures* in
quantum, pro bone Iuppiter, dedecus recciderunt!
istis *obscenae puellae iocantur.* Quid? si, per deos
inmortales, nullo sollemni die populo inspectante in
foro convivium habuisses, non minuisses maiestatem
imperii nostri? Atqui quid interest convivium in
forum an forum in convivium attrahas?   386]

10 Deinde descripsit quanto aliter[1] in foro decol-
letur. Ascendit praetor tribunal inspectante pro-

---

[1] quanto aliter *C. F. W. Müller:* qualiter.

---

[1] The speaker pretends to point to the *fasces*, that would, in
a real court, accompany the praetor.

by his favour, he thanks him. Holding the table
in both hands, he says: " May the immortal gods repay you the like! "—Of those who sat in the same
room, one wept floods of tears with bowed head,
another averted his eyes from the cruel sight, a third
laughed—to keep in with the whore. Here, amid 8
these different expressions on the faces of the guests,
the praetor orders room to be made, orders the
wretched man to stand quietly and offer his neck to
the blow. Meanwhile the pause is marked by cups
of wine. A Roman citizen was killed—and by the
hand of an executioner who was not even sober.—I
don't say that he should not be struck by the axe;
but I do ask that he fall victim to the law rather than
a prostitute.—Remember that the aim of your power
is terror, not diversions for frivolous women.—Why,
judges, should I tell you now of their various amuse-
ments, their dances, their contest in shame to see
whether the praetor or the whore capered more in-
decently?

CAPITO. Arise now, you Brutuses, Horatii, Decii, 9
and all the other glorious names of our empire. To
what disgraceful depths, by heaven, have sunk your
rods, your axes! Obscene girls make jest with *these*.[1]
—If, by God, you had held a feast in the forum, with
the people watching, on a working day, would you
not have detracted from the majesty of our empire?
Yet what is the difference between taking a feast into
the forum and the forum into a feast?

Capito went on to describe how different is the 10
manner of beheading in the forum.[2] " The praetor

[2] Cicero makes play with the horror of such a scene in *Rab.
Perd.* 11 *seq.*

vincia; noxio post terga deligantur manus, stat
intento ac tristi omnium vultu; fit a praecone silentium; adhibentur deinde legituma verba; canitur ex
altera parte classicum. Numquid vobis videor
describere convivales iocos? Heu quam dissimiles
exitus initiis habes! Accusavit te eques Romanus,
iudicaverunt equites Romani, praetor damnatum
pronuntiavit, occidit meretrix.

11 BUTEONIS. Ut iste cum amica cenaret iucundius
homo occisus est. Numquid, iudices, [quod]¹ pro
rostris vidistis praetorem cum meretrice cenantem?

VOTIENI MONTANI. Qui sic convivatur quomodo
irascitur? Damnaturi iurant nihil se gratiae, nihil
precibus dare: postulo ut in hanc legem iures.
Maiestas populi Romani per omnes nationes, per
omnis diffusa provincias, in sinu meretricum iacet; ea
imperat praetori nostro quae prostitit, cuius osculo
nemo se abstinuit nisi qui pepercit suo. Convivas
tuos ipse narra: fuere, credo, tribuni, fuere praefecti,
fuere equites Romani: †cum his ergo praetor.† ²

12 CASSI SEVERI. Ne de servo quidem aut captivo

¹ iudices *Novák:* iudi (*or* uidi) quod.
² " with these then the praetor . . ."

244

ascends the tribunal, beneath the gaze of the province. The guilty man's hands are tied behind his back; he stands there, as all look intently and grimly on. Silence is enforced by the herald. Then the ritual words are pronounced.[1] The trumpet sounds from the other side. Is this, do you think, the description of a dinner-table jest?"—How different your beginning from your end! You were accused by a Roman knight, judged by Roman knights,[2] pronounced guilty by a praetor: killed by a whore.

BUTEO. Someone was killed—so that *this* man 11 could have a nicer dinner with his girl-friend.—Have you, judges, seen a praetor dining with a whore on the rostrum?[3]

VOTIENUS MONTANUS. If he is like this at a party, what is he like when he is angry?—Judges about to pass sentence swear they are conceding nothing to bias or to entreaty:[4] I demand that *you* swear by this law.—The majesty of the Roman empire, spread through all nations and all provinces, lies in the lap of whores; the ruler of our praetor is a common prostitute, whose lips no-one has scrupled to enjoy—unless he shrank from polluting his own.—Tell us yourself about your guests; they were, I feel sure, tribunes, prefects,[5] Roman knights. . . .

CASSIUS SEVERUS. Not even a slave or a captive 12

---

[1] Cf. below on §21.

[2] Presumably members of the governor's *consilium*.

[3] Platform for public speeches in the forum at Rome.

[4] For the pledge taken by the judge see A. H. J. Greenidge, *The Legal Procedure of Cicero's Time* (Oxford, 1901), 270.

[5] A title conferred by governors on friends among their staff: see Caesar *B.G.* 1.39.2, and G. H. Stevenson, *Roman Provincial Administration* (Blackwell, 1939), 87.

omni loco aut omni genere aut per quos libebit aut 387]
cum libebit supplicium sumi fas est, adhibeturque
ad ea magistratus ob custodiam, non ob laetitiam.

TRIARI. Quo crimine damnatus erat? caedis.
Non tamen in convivio occiderat. Animadverte
diligenter, meretrix, ne iterum homicidium roges.

13 Montanus Votienus has putabat quaestiones esse:
an quidquid [1] in magistratu peccavit proconsul vindicari possit maiestatis lege. Reus enim qui tueri
se facto non potest, ad ius confugit, et dicit hac se
lege non [2] teneri. Non quidquid peccavit aliquis in
magistratu maiestatem laedit. Puta aliquem dum
magistratus est patrem suum occidere, veneno uxorem suam necare: puto, non hac lege causam dicet,
sed aliis, parricidii et veneficii. Vis scire non a quo
fiat ad rem pertinere sed quid fiat? Privatus potest
accusari maiestatis laesae, si quid fecit quo maiestatem populi Romani laederet. Puta, amicam habet
proconsul: ideo maiestatis damnabitur? Quod amplius est dico: puta, matronam corrumpit dum proconsul est: adulterii causam dicet, non maiestatis.

14 Singula, inquit, aestima quae obicis. Si tantum
amicam habuisset, numquid accusares? Si anim-
advertisset in aliquem nullo rogante, numquid
accusari posset? Si non omne non recte factum hac

---

[1] quidquid *Faber:* quid quis.
[2] lege non *early editors:* non lege.

---

[1] The next victim might be the guilty proconsul.
[2] This is called *tralatio*, "transference": cf. Quintilian
3.6.68 *seq.*, 83.
[3] As Bonner, 109 points out, Montanus exploits the vague-
ness of the concept of *maiestas*: cf. Cic. *de Orat.* 2.107 for a
case that hinged on the meaning of the word.

may properly be executed just anywhere or in any way or by whom or at what time you like. If a magistrate is made to attend, it is to oversee it, not to amuse himself.

TRIARIUS. What charge had he been convicted on? Murder. But *he* hadn't murdered at a party. Beware, whore, of asking a second time for the death of a man.[1]

Votienus Montanus thought the questions were as 13 follows: Can *any* crime committed by a proconsul during his magistracy be punished under the law concerning *lèse-majesté*? For a defendant who cannot defend himself by appeal to the facts has resort to legal points, saying he is not subject to the law in question.[2] "Not every wrong done by someone during his magistracy harms the majesty of the state.[3] Suppose someone kills his father or poisons his wife during his term of office; he will, surely, plead his cause not under this law, but under others, those on parricide and poisoning. If you want to convince yourself that what matters is not the author of the crime but the crime itself, observe that a private citizen may be accused of *lèse-majesté*, if he has done something to harm the majesty of the Roman people. Suppose that a proconsul has a girlfriend: will he then be condemned for *lèse-majesté*? Suppose, further, that he seduces a married woman during his proconsulship. He will plead on a charge of adultery, not of *lèse-majesté*. Weigh the charges 14 you bring individually. If he had merely had a girlfriend, you wouldn't, surely, accuse him? If he had executed a man without anyone requesting it, there could surely be no charge against him." If not every

247

lege vindicari potest, an id quod sub auctoritate 388
publica geritur. Nam cum adulterium committit,
cum veneficium, tamquam civis peccat; cum animadvertit, auctoritate publica utitur, *in eo* autem
quod sub praetexto publicae maiestatis agitur, quidquid
peccatur maiestatis actione vindicandum est. Dic enim
mihi, si, cum animadvertere debeat [non] [1] legitimo
cultu ac more sollemni usus, interdiu tribunal
conscenderit convivali veste, si, cum classicum
canere debeat, symphoniam canere iusserit, non
laedet maiestatem? Atqui quod fecit foedius est:
et comparavit.

15   Deinde, si potest vindicari maiestatis lege id quod
proconsul maiestatis publicae et iure et apparatu
usus [2] peccavit, an hoc possit. Non potest, inquit;
nihil enim detractum est populi Romani magnitudini.
Is laedit populi Romani maiestatem qui aliquid
publico nomine facit: *tamquam legatus falsa mandata*
adfert, sic audiuntur tamquam illa populus Romanus
dederit; imperator foedus percussit, videtur populus
Romanus percussisse et continetur indigno *foedere.*
Nunc nec viribus quicquam populi Romani *detractum*
est nec opinioni; ⟨homini⟩ [3] enim inputatur si quid

---

[1] *Deleted by Gertz.*
[2] apparatu usus *Madvig:* apparatus est.
[3] *Supplied by Gertz.*

illegal action can be punished under this law, can an action which is done on public authority? " When he commits an adultery, a poisoning, he sins as a private citizen. When he executes a man, he is exercising public authority. But any wrong done under the show of public authority is to be punished by an action for *lèse-majesté*. Tell me: if, when he ought to carry out sentences of death in the prescribed dress and according to the ritual, he ascends the tribunal by day in a dinner suit: if, when the trumpet ought to sound, he orders a band to strike up: will he not be harming the majesty of the Roman people? Yet what he did do is even more foul." And he proceeded to make a comparison.

Next: If the law of *lèse-majesté* can cover a wrong 15 done by a proconsul in the exercise of the rights of the state and employing its paraphernalia, does it cover this case? " It does not. For there has been no detraction from the greatness of the Roman people. The majesty of the Roman people is harmed by someone when he acts in the name of the state. Suppose an ambassador brings forged instructions, they get listened to as though the Roman people had sent them. Suppose a general has negotiated a treaty; the Roman people is thought to have made it, and is held to it even if it is degrading.[1] In the present case, neither the power nor the prestige of the Roman people has suffered any loss; if he did anything, it is marked up against the man, not the

---

[1] Bonner cites the case of C. Popilius Laenas, accused of *maiestas* for entering into an improper treaty (*ad Her.* 1.25, with Kayser's note).

fecit, non populo Romano. *At ex te ceteros aestimant.*
Non: nam *et ante hunc alii fuerunt ex quibus aestimari* 389
possit et post hunc erunt; et *singulorum vitia nemo*
16 *urbibus adscribit.* Attamen factum ipsum turpe est.
Sed ⟨et⟩ [1] multa alia, nec ideo illis maiestas laeditur.
Nemo paene sine vitio est: ille iracundus est, ille
libidinosus; non tamen, si quid in aliquo mutatum
malis, eo statim maiestas laeditur. Deinde ad facti
ipsius aestimationem venit et dixit haec obici, quod
meretricem habuit, quod aliquem in domo occidit,
quod nocte, quod in convivio, quod rogante meretrice.
17 Silo Pompeius has adiecit quaestiones: an, si
quod facere ei licuit fecit, non possit maiestatis lege
accusari. Potest, inquit; haec enim lex quid opor-
teat quaerit, aliae quid liceat. Licet ire in lupanar;
si praecedentibus fascibus praetor deducetur in
lupanar, maiestatem laedet, etiamsi [2] quod licet
fecerit. Licet qua quis velit veste uti; si praetor
ius in veste servili vel muliebri dixerit, violabit maiestatem. Deinde illam fecit quaestionem: an hoc
facere ei licuerit. Non licuit, inquit, illo loco aut
illo tempore aut ex illa causa occidere. Quaedam
quae licent tempore et loco mutato non licent.
18 De colore [inquit] [3] quaeritur quo uti debeat is qui
pro Flaminino dicit. *Quaedam controversiae sunt in*
quibus factum defendi potest, excusari non potest; ex
quibus est et haec. Non possumus efficere ut ⟨reus⟩ [4]

---

[1] *Supplied by Kiessling.*
[2] etiamsi *Müller:* et.
[3] *Deleted by Müller.*
[4] *Supplied by Gertz.*

Roman people. 'But they judge other Romans from you.' No: for there have been others, before this man, from whom assessment may be made; and after him there will be still more. And no-one ascribes to cities the faults of individuals. 'But the act itself is 16 disgraceful.' Yes, but so are many others, without necessarily impairing the majesty of the state. Almost no-one is faultless; one man is choleric, another lustful; just because you might prefer a man to be in some respect different from what he is, majesty is not thereby necessarily harmed." Then he came to assess the actual act. He said the charges were: keeping a whore, and killing someone indoors, at night, at a party, at the request of the whore.

Pompeius Silo added these questions: If he did 17 something he had the right to do, can he be accused under the law on *lèse-majesté*? "Yes; this law is concerned with what *should* be done, others with what is allowed. One is allowed to go into a brothel; but if a praetor, preceded by his axes, is escorted into a brothel, he will be harming majesty even though he is doing something he is allowed to do. One is allowed to wear what dress one likes; but if a praetor acts as judge in the clothing of a slave or a woman, he will be impairing majesty." Next he put the question: *Was* he allowed to do this? "No, he was not allowed to kill in that place, at that time, for that reason. Some things that are permissible become impermissible if time and place alter."

What *colour* should be used in defence of Flamin- 18 inus? Some *controversiae*—and this is one—allow defence of an act but not excuse for it. We cannot stop the accused from being censured because of this;

THE ELDER SENECA

propter hoc non sit reprehendendus; *non speramus* 390
ut illum iudex probet sed ut dimittat; itaque sic agere
debemus tamquam pro facto non emendato, non scelerato
tamen. Itaque negabat se pro Flaminino narratu-
rum Montanus, sed iis quae obiciuntur responsurum.

19 Aiebat autem illam sententiam Rufi Vibii colorem
actionis esse: bonum se animum habere pro reo
in quo *libido omnis intra meretricem esset, crudelitas intra*
carcerem. Ipse Montanus illum locum pulcherrime
tractavit, quam *multa populus Romanus in suis impera-*
toribus tulerit: in Gurgite luxuriam, *in Manlio in-*
potentiam, cui non nocuit *et filium et victorem occidere,*
in Sulla crudelitatem, in Lucullo luxuriam, in multis
avaritiam. ⟨In hoc⟩,[1] inquit, praetore, cum illi
constiterit abstinentia, diligentia, ne excutiatis
quomodo una nocte cenaverit. Utrum tamen, inquit, iniquius est? [quod][2] *obiciunt quod damnatus*
perierit meretrici, postulant proconsulem perire damnato.

20 Colorem Fuscus Arellius hunc introduxit: ebrium
fuisse nec scisse quid fecerit. Silo Pompeius hoc
colore usus est: *non putavit,* inquit, *in rem pertinere*
ubi aut quando periret qui perire deberet. Triarius inep-
tum introduxit colorem: Sermo erat, inquit, in convivio contemni nimiam praetoris lenitatem; alios
fuisse proconsules, qui cotidie animadverterent,

---

[1] *Supplied by Gertz.*
[2] *Deleted by Faber.*

---

[1] Cf. *C.* 10.3.8.
[2] Compare Sen. *Clem.* 1.12.1–2; Lucan 2.139–232.

our hope is not that the judge will approve of him but
that he will acquit him. Therefore we must plead as
for an act which is not wicked but not faultless.
Hence Montanus said he would not give a narration
on behalf of Flamininus, but would merely reply to the
charges. He did say, however, that a *colour* for the 19
case was provided by a *mot* of Vibius Rufus—that he
felt confident for an accused person whose lust was
confined to a whore and whose cruelty to a prison.
Montanus himself dealt splendidly with the topic of
how much the Roman people have tolerated in their
generals—in Gurges luxury, in Manlius lack of self-
control (Manlius was not harmed by killing his victorious son [1]), in Sulla cruelty,[2] in Lucullus luxury,[3]
in many avarice. " As to this praetor—since he undoubtedly possessed restraint and diligence—do not
examine how he dined on one single night. But the
charge is the death of a condemned criminal for the
sake of a whore; what is demanded is the death of a
praetor for the sake of a condemned criminal.
Which is more unfair? "

Arellius Fuscus introduced this *colour*: he had been 20
drunk, and hadn't known what he was doing.
Pompeius Silo used this one: he didn't think it
mattered where or when a man doomed to die did in
fact die. Triarius brought in a silly *colour*: there was
a conversation at the party about the scorn felt for the
praetor's excessive leniency;[4] other proconsuls had
carried out executions every day, while in this one's

[3] Lucullus' luxurious life was notorious: see e.g. Vell. Pat.
2.33.4.
[4] Valerius Antias' version was that the praetor was boasting
of his severity.

huius anno nullum esse occisum. Dixit aliquis ex
convivis: " ego numquam [iratus] [1] ⟨vidi hominem 39⟩
occidi⟩." Dixit et mulier: " et ego numquam."
Iratus quod clementia sua contemptui esset, " cura-
bo" inquit " sciant non deesse mihi ⟨severitatem."
Adducitur⟩ [2] sceleratus, quem videre lucem ultra non
oportet. *Occisus est quis? damnatus; ubi? in praetorio;
quo tempore? est enim ullum quo nocens perire non debeat?*
21 Gallus Vibius dixit: Meretrix oravit. Timebam
mehercules ne exorasset ut aut indemnatus occideretur aut damnatus viveret.

Ex altera parte multa bene dicta sunt, multa corrupte: in descriptione suplici utique illi qui voluerunt omnia legitima suplici verba in sententias
trahere in vitia inciderunt, tamquam dixit Triarius:
" Summove." Audis, lictor? Summove a praetore
meretricem. Hoc non male. Adiecit: " Verbera."
Sed vide ne virgae tuae pocula nostra disturbent.
" Despolia." Meretrix, agnoscis hoc verbum? certe
provincia agnoscit.
22 Silo Pompeius, homo qui iudicio censebatur, et
ipse ad hanc descriptionem accessit, minimum tamen
mali fecit; ait: animadvertit meretrix; " age
lege "; quicquam enim lege hic agitur?

[1] *Deleted by Bursian, who supplied the following words.*
[2] *Supplied by Madvig.*

---

[1] For the formula see Livy 1.26.6, with Ogilvie's notes.
summovere was the normal word for the clearing of a space and
the removal of the undesirable (above, §2, and *C.* 1.2.3), but it
does not appear in Livy. Nor does *despolia*—but stripping
was a natural preliminary to the scourging (cf. Petr. 30.7), and

year of office no-one had been killed. One of the guests said: " I have never seen a man killed." The woman too said: " Nor I." Angry that his clemency should be an object for ridicule, he said: " I will make sure they realise I *can* be severe." A criminal was brought in, one who didn't deserve to see the light of day any longer. " Who was killed? A condemned criminal. Where? In the residence of the praetor. When? Is there any time when a guilty man ought not to die?" Vibius Gallus said: 21 " The whore implored me. In fact I was afraid she would request either the death of a man who had never been sentenced or the life of a man who had been sentenced—and win her request."

On the other side, many good things were said, many in bad taste. In the description of the execution, anyway, faults attended those who wanted to bring in all the ritual words of execution [1] to form epigrams. For instance, Triarius said: " ' Remove.' Do you hear, lictor? Remove the whore from the praetor." This is not bad. He added: " ' Strike.' But make sure your rods don't smash our glasses. ' Strip.' Whore, do you recognise the word? Certainly the province does."

Pompeius Silo, a man celebrated for his judgement, 22 also essayed this description, though he did least harm with it, thus: " The whore orders the execution. ' Act according to the law.' [2] Is *anything* done according to the law *here*? "

is brought in here for the double sense " undress " and " plunder."

[2] The herald's instruction to the lictor at an execution: cf. Liv. 26.15.9.

Hispanus dixit: " age lege "tibi dicitur, Flaminine: vive sine meretrice, cena sine carnifice.

Argentarius in quae solebat schemata minuta tractationem violentissime infregit: " Age lege " scis, inquit, quid dicat? interdiu age, in foro age. Stupet lictor; idem dicit quod meretrix tua: hoc numquam se vidisse. [1]

Montanus Votienus dixit: *percussurus lictor ad praetorem respexit, praetor ad meretricem.*

23 Vibius Gallus dixit: lictori quia bene percusserat propinatum est.

Illud, quod tamquam Latronis circumfertur, non esse Latronis pro testimonio dico et Latronem a sententia inepte tumultuosa vindico; ipse enim audivi Florum quendam, auditorem Latronis, dicentem non apud Latronem. Neque enim illi mos erat quemquam audire declamantem; declamabat ipse tantum et aiebat se non esse magistrum sed exemplum; nec ulli alii contigisse scio quam apud Graecos Niceti, apud Romanos Latroni, ut discipuli non audiri desiderarent sed contenti essent audire. Initio contumeliae causa a deridentibus discipuli Latronis auditores vocabantur; deinde in usu verbum esse coepit et promiscue poni pro discipulo auditor. Hoc erat non patientiam suam sed eloquentiam vendere.

24 Ut ad Florum revertar, ille dixit in Flaminino: refulsit inter privata pocula publicae securis acies; inter temulentas ebriorum reliquias humanum everritur caput. Numquam Latro sic composuisset ut,

---

[1] Cf. §4 Bassus.

Hispanus said: " ' Act according to the law.' It is you that's being addressed, Flamininus: live without a whore, dine without an executioner."

Argentarius violently broke up the treatment with his usual fragmented figures. " ' Act according to the law.' You know the meaning of that? Act by day, act in the forum. The lictor is aghast—he says the same as your whore: he has never seen such a thing."

Votienus Montanus said: " As he was about to strike, the lictor looked to the praetor—and the praetor to the whore."

Vibius Gallus said: " Because he had struck a good 23 blow, they drank a toast to the lictor."

There is an epigram attributed to Latro, which I swear is not his—and I want to save Latro from an incongruously melodramatic saying; for I personally heard it spoken by one Florus, a pupil of Latro's, though not in Latro's presence. Indeed, Latro would never hear anyone declaim—he merely declaimed himself, saying he was a model, not a school-teacher. To my knowledge only Nicetes among the Greeks and Latro among the Romans had the luck to find pupils content to listen without demanding to be listened to. At first, detractors called Latro's pupils " listeners " as an insult; later the word got into general currency, and " listener " was used freely instead of " pupil." This was a case of selling one's oratory, not one's patience.

To return to Florus, he said about Flamininus: 24 " Amid private goblets shone out the edge of a public axe; amid the sodden remnants left behind by drunks is swept up a human head." [1] Latro would never

quia publicam securem dicturus erat, diceret privata
pocula, nec in tam mollem conpositionem sententia
eius evanuisset; nec tam incredibilis umquam
figuras concipiebat ut in ipso triclinio inter lectos et 39°
†loco† et mensas percussum describeret.

Ille, cum in hac controversia descripsisset atroci-
tatem supplicii, adiecit: Quid exhorruistis, iudices?
Meretricios lusus loquor. Et illam dixit minus
notam sententiam, sed non minus bonam: in socium
nostrum praetor populi Romani animadvertit in
privato, nocte, tumultuario tribunali, ebrius fortasse,
ne calciatus quidem, nisi si ut omnia spectaret meretrix diligenter exegit.

25 Rufus Vibius erat qui antiquo genere diceret;
belle cessit illi sententia sordidioris notae: praetor
ad occidendum hominem soleas poposcit. Altera
eiusdem generis, sed non eiusdem successus sententia: cum deplorasset condicionem violatam
maiestatis et consuetudinem maiorum descripsisset,
qua semper voluissent ad supplicium ⟨luce⟩ [1] ad-
vocari, sententiam dixit: at nunc a praetore lege
actum est ad lucernam. Pollio tamen Asinius
aiebat hanc se sententiam recipere.

26 *Livius de oratoribus qui verba antiqua et sordida
consectantur et orationis obscuritatem severitatem putant*

---

[1] *Supplied by Müller.*

---

[1] Wearing slippers or sandals (see below) rather than proper
shoes. Compare Cicero's indignation about the " soleatus
praetor " in *Verr.* 5.86: and see Denniston on *Phil.* 2.76.

have tolerated such a juxtaposition, saying " private goblets " just because he proposed to mention " a public axe." Nor would an epigram of Latro's have disappeared amid such effeminacy of rhythm. He never dreamed up such incredible figures to describe a man executed in the very dining-room amid couches and . . . and tables.

Latro, after describing in this *controversia* the savagery of the execution, added: " Why blench, judges? I am merely speaking of the playfulness of a whore." And he spoke a less celebrated though equally good epigram: " An ally of ours was executed by a praetor of the Roman people in private, at night, on an improvised tribunal, when he was perhaps drunk and not even properly shod [1]—or maybe he did everything in due form so that the whore could have a complete performance to view."

Vibius Rufus was a man who spoke in the old way; 25 he scored well with an epigram of a rather vulgar kind: " The praetor called for his slippers to kill a man." Here is another of the same sort,[2] which was less successful. After deploring the violation of the majesty of Rome and describing the practice of our ancestors, according to which they had always insisted on summons to execution coming in daylight, he spoke this epigram: " But now a praetor has ' acted according to the law ' by lamp-light." However, Asinius Pollio said he did not rule out this epigram.

Livy said that the rhetorician Miltiades had an 26 elegant saying on orators who go out in search of old vulgar words and think that obscurity in a speech

[2] Seneca seems to allude to the everyday words *solea* and *lucerna*.

aiebat Miltiaden rhetorem eleganter dixisse: ἐπὶ τὸ δεξιὸν μαίνονται. *Tamen in his etiamsi minus est insaniae minus spei est; illi qui tument, illi qui abundantia laborant, plus habent furoris, sed plus et corporis;* 394 *semper* autem *ad sanitatem proclivius est quod potest detractione curari; illi succurri non potest qui simul et insanit et deficit.*

27   Sed ne hoc genus furoris protegere videar, in Flaminino tumidissime *dixit Murredius:* praetorem nostrum in illa ferali cena saginatum meretricis sinu excitavit ictus securis.[1] Et illud *tetracolon: serviebat forum cubiculo, praetor meretrici, carcer convivio, dies nocti. Novissima pars sine sensu dicta est, ut impleretur numerus;*[2] *quem enim sensum habet: " serviebat dies nocti"? Hanc ideo sententiam rettuli quia et in tricolis et in omnibus huius generis sententiis curamus ut numerus constet, non curamus an sensus. Omnia autem* genera *corruptarum* quoque *sententiarum de industria pono, quia facilius et quid imitandum et quid vitandum sit docemur exemplo.*

----

[1] ictus securis *Novák, Gertz:* successuri.
[2] numerus *Bursian:* sensus E (*omitted in other MSS*).

----

[1] If this text is right, there is an allusion to Plat. *Phaedr.* 266A, where Socrates refers to an earlier speech of his as conducting " us to the forms of madness which lay on the right-hand side " (Hackforth's translation). I have used the ambiguity of the English " right " to lead up to " they may be less mad." Further discussion in W. Lebek, *Verba Prisca* (Göttingen, 1970), 201–5.

[2] Cf. Quintilian 2.4.5–6 on the need for exuberance rather than aridity in the budding orator.

makes it austere: "They are mad—in the right direction."[1] Nevertheless, though they may be less mad, they arouse less hope; those who are puffed out and whose trouble is abundance are more mad—but they have more body. Now something that can be remedied by removal is always more likely to regain health—but there is no help for the man who is at once mad and feeble.[2]

But I don't want to be thought to be covering up 27 for this kind of madness, so I will quote a highly flatulent remark of Murredius on Flamininus: "A praetor of Rome, fattened up in that funeral feast, was roused from a whore's lap by the blow of an axe." Also the tetracolon:[3] "The forum was slave of the bedroom, the praetor of the whore, the prison of a party, day of night." The last words were nonsense, designed to fill out the rhythm.[4] For what is the sense in "Day was slave of night?"[5] I have quoted this epigram just because in tricola and all epigrams of this kind we take care about the establishment of the rhythm—but not of the sense. Indeed, I purposely quote all kinds even of decadent epigrams; it is easier for us to learn by example both what to imitate and what to avoid.

[3] Cf. *C.* 2.4.12: *tetracola* are sentences with four parallel clauses. See E. Norden, *Antike Kunstprosa* 1.289–90.

[4] *carcer convivio* would have an inferior rhythmic clausula; *-ō diēs nōctī* gives the favourite cretic type. But it is conceivable that Seneca means: "to make up the number (i.e. four)." So too with *numerus* below.

[5] Cf. Sen. *Agam.* 35–6 (another tetracolon): "avo parentem (pro nefas), patri virum, / gnatis nepotes miscui, nocti diem" (with rather more point).

28　Ecce et illud genus cacozeliae est, quod amaritudinem verborum quasi adgravaturam res petit;
ut in hac controversia Licinius Nepos dixit: reus
damnatus est legi, perit fornici. Et illud quod
Saenianus dixit habet sui generis insaniam: cum
diceret nocte non debere sumi supplicium, post
longam descriptionem †cum†: nunc ne victumae
quidem occiduntur.

29　Et ad hanc controversiam Graeci porrexerunt
manum. Dixit in hac Nicetes: ὡς δ᾽ ἤκουσαν ὅτι 39
συμπόσιόν ἐστιν, ἤριζον.

Euctemon dixit: πάντες ἐνόμιζον ὅτι †ЄCΛΤΟ†.[1]
Glaucippus Cappadox, cum cenam luxuriosam descripsisset indignam maiestate praetoris, adiecit:
διηγήσομαι νῦν καὶ τὸν κῶμον. Hoc idem elegantius
dixit Adaeus, cum descripsisset cenam nocturnam:
ὡς ἐρωτικὸς ὁ κῶμος.

Nicetes dixit: " οὐδέποτε τεθέαμαι ἀναιρούμενον."
ἂν ἡ πόλις εὐτυχῇ, οὐδὲ ὄψῃ.

Artemon eodem loco aliam dixit sententiam:
" οὐδέποτε τεθέαμαι ἀναιρούμενον." γύναι,
†ΤΟΥΤШΛΛΝΟΥ ΑЄICIC†.[2]

Glycon dixit: ὡς δὲ ἀπηγγέλη τοῖς ἐν τῷ
δεσμωτηρίῳ· " πότος ἐστὶ καὶ ἑταίρα καὶ ἄνεσις,"[3]
ἀνέκραγέ τις τάλας· ἐμὲ ἄπαγε, ἐγὼ γὰρ ἀδίκως
κατεκρίθην.

---

[1] I have translated Thomas' ἐλέλυτο.
[2] I have translated Bursian's doubtful οὐ κώμου δέησις.
[3] καὶ ἄνεσις Gertz: ΚΑΗЄCIC.

---

[1] For wide variations in the use of cacozelia see Russell on
" Longinus " 3.4.

There is also a variety of bad taste [1] that looks for 28 bitter words in order to make the facts appear worse. Thus in this *controversia* Licinius Nepos said: " The accused was condemned for the law's sake, and died for a brothel's." A remark of Saenianus, too, has its own kind of insanity. Saying that executions ought not be carried out by night, and after a long description: " *Now* not even victims [2] are killed."

The Greeks tried their hand at this *controversia* too. 29 In it Nicetes said: " But when they heard there was a party, they began to dispute." [3]

Euctemon said: " Everyone thought he had been released."

Glaucippus, a Cappadocian, having described the luxurious banquet as being unworthy of the dignity of a praetor, added: " Now I will describe the carousal too." The same thing was more elegantly put by Adaeus, after a description of the night feast: " What a loving revel! "

Nicetes said: " ' I have never seen a man killed.' If the city is lucky, you won't in future."

Artemon, at the same point, had a different epigram: " ' I have never seen a man killed.' Woman, there is no need of a debauch."

Glycon said: " When the prisoners were told: ' There is a party and a prostitute and high jinks,' one poor chap shouted: ' Take me—*I* was unjustly condemned.' " [4]

---

[2] i.e. sacrificial animals.

[3] The prisoners, that is: for their topic of dispute, see Glycon's epigram below.

[4] And so deserve a break. But in fact he was to die, equally unjustly.

III

Expositum Repetens ex Duobus

Per vim metumque gesta ne sint rata.
Pacta conventa legibus facta rata sint.
Expositum qui agnoverit solutis
alimentis recipiat.

Quidam duos filios expositos sustulit, educavit.
Quaerenti patri naturali pollicitus est se indica-   396
turum ubi essent si sibi alterum ex illis dedisset.
Pactum interpositum est.   Reddit illi duos filios,
repetit unum.

1   ARELLI FUSCI patris.   Aecum est ut *cum alienis
dividamus liberos quos non dividimus cum matribus?*
Si alterum nobis [1] abstuleris, utrumque habebis.
Quid faciam? *utrumque genui, utrumque desideravi, pro
utroque pactus sum.*

ALBUCI SILI. *Una nati sunt, una expositi, una
educati; redditi* potissimum *distrahuntur.   Distraxit*

[1] nobis *Gertz:* non.

---

[1] See *C.* 4.8 n., and Bonner, 114–15.
[2] Bonner (p. 125) compares Cic. *Off.* 3.92: " Are agreements
and promises always to be kept?—those that, in the words of
the praetors, are not the result of force or fraud."
[3] Bonner (pp. 125–7) argues that the law reflects Roman
rather than Greek legal practice.   Quintilian knows of it
(7.1.14 and 9.2.89); cf. *Decl.* 278 and *RLM* p. 343.11.

3

THE MAN WHO ASKED FOR ONE OF TWO EXPOSED BOYS BACK

Acts motivated by force or fear shall not be valid.[1]
Agreements made according to the law shall stand.[2]
A man who acknowledges a child he has exposed
may take him back after paying for his upbringing.[3]

> A man took in and educated two boys [4] who
> had been exposed. When the natural father
> made enquiries, the foster-father promised he
> would reveal where they were if he was given
> one of them. They struck a bargain. He gives
> him back his two sons—and seeks one for himself.

For the natural father

ARELLIUS FUSCUS SENIOR. Is it fair that we should 1
divide with outsiders children whom we do not divide
with mothers? [5]—If you take one away from me, you
will have both.[6]—What am I to do? I begot both, I
missed both, I bargained for both.[7]

ALBUCIUS SILUS. They were born together,
exposed together, brought up together; they are
being separated just when they have been given

---

[4] Twins, we gather from e.g. §§1 and 3.

[5] One doesn't share out twins between their parents: why
with an outsider?

[6] They are " inseparable ": cf. §3 " I shall have either two
or neither."

[7] The rhetoric of the tricolon seems to lead to a mis-state-
ment of the facts.

*illos Fortuna aliquando a parentibus, numquam ab
ipsis.* Miseremini, iudices: gravis indiciva est.

2 IUNI GALLIONIS. *Duos exposui quia alterum eligere
non poteram.* Periclitor ne qui cum duobus liberis in
iudicium veni sine ullo revertar; nam quem perdam
eligere non possum. Causa pacti mei fuit ut haberem filios, consummatio ut perderem. Pro filiis tibi
debeo, non filios: pete quantum vis pro disciplinis,
inputa quantum vis pro alumentis; licet plus petas
dum ⟨ne⟩ minus reddas. Maiores nostri viderunt
quam effusa esset indulgentia pro suis timentium,
quam parata quidquid posceretur dare; itaque pro
3 patre lex [non]¹ cum educatore pacta est. Non
potui obligari de eis qui in mea potestate non erant.
Si ex aequo dividimus, habeatur utriusque ratio:
habeam ego tamdiu duos quamdiu tu habuisti. 397
Nolite timere, pueri, non diducam vos: aut utrumque habebo aut neutrum. *In auctione fratres quamvis hostilis hasta non dividit. Plus quiddam est gemi-
nos esse quam fratres, perdit uterque gratiam suam nisi
cum altero est.*

4 FULVI SPARSI. *Ignoscere* mihi adversarius *debet
meos retinenti cum ipse alienos concupiscat.* Repetit

¹ *Deleted in ed. Frobeniana (1515).*

back.—Chance once separated them from their parents, never from each other.—Show pity, judges; the informer's reward is a heavy one to bear! [1]

JUNIUS GALLIO. I exposed both just because I 2 could not choose between them. My danger is that, though I came to court with two sons, I may return home with none: for I cannot choose which to lose.— The motive for my bargain was to have sons, its outcome that I lost them.—I owe you money for my sons, not my sons themselves; ask as much as you like for their rearing, send in as big a bill as you like for their keep; you may ask more, so long as you don't give less back.—Our ancestors saw how extravagant is the affection of those who fear for their children, how ready it is to give whatever it is asked; and so the law made an agreement with the foster-father on behalf of the father.[2]—I could not have put 3 myself under an obligation in respect of children who were not under my control.—If we are making an equal division, let account be taken of both of us: let *me* have two for as long as *you* had two.—Don't be afraid, children, I won't separate you; I shall have either two or neither.—At an auction the spear,[3] however unfriendly, does not divide brothers.—It is rather more to be twins than brothers—both lose their charm if they are separated.

FULVIUS SPARSUS. My opponent must forgive me 4 trying to keep my own children—*he* after all covets

---

[1] Paying the "informer" (the foster-father) his price is hard.

[2] i.e. the terms of the law insist on *both* being returned and preclude any bargain dictated by fear and love.

[3] Planted at public auctions, where slaves might be on sale.

quos adhuc habuit, retineo quos modo agnovi. *Agnitio dividet quos iunxit etiam expositio?*

CORNELI HISPANI. Dic uter obsequentior sit, uter indulgentior. " Uterque ⟨aeque⟩ " [1] inquis. Miraris si tam pios dividere non possum? *Omnia pro filio paciscor praeter filium.*

5 VOTIENI MONTANI. Ego vero ne patrocinium quidem habebo: si tam facile liberos remitto, libenter exposui. Reddere est istud liberos an eripere? Utroque modo perdendi erant, vel paciscenti vel neganti. *Pactus sum flens, tremens, tamquam cum exponerem.*

CESTI PII. Ne dividerem filios, una exposui. Iste quoque duos sustulit, qui tantum uno contentus est. Iterum cogor exponere.

6 Contra. IUNI GALLIONIS. Expeditae partes vestrae sunt: *utrumque potestis ex hoc iudicio patrem dimittere.*

MENTONIS. *Iste adsuevit carere liberis, ego, etiamsi unum accipiam,* tamen *necesse est torquear: duobus adsuevi.* Quidquid umquam commisi—et habes domi quos de me interroges—, nihil umquam sine illis feci nisi indicium. *Vim vocas quae te patrem fecit?*

---

[1] *Supplied by Gertz.*

---

[1] If I did not agree, I should not find out their whereabouts. If I did, I should lose both in losing one (cf. p. 265 n. 6).
[2] The foster-father originally took in two, though by now

other people's.—He wants to have back children he has had all this time. I am trying to keep ones I have only just recognised.—Shall recognition divide children whom even exposure kept together?

CORNELIUS HISPANUS. Say which of the two is the more obedient, which the more affectionate. " Both equally," you say. Are you surprised if I cannot separate two such dutiful children?—I will agree to give anything for my son—except my son.

VOTIENUS MONTANUS. I shall not even have a 5 defence of my conduct: if I resign children so easily, I must have been glad to expose them.—Is this returning children or snatching them away?—Either way I had to lose them, whether I agreed to the bargain or not.[1]—I made the bargain weeping, trembling, just like when I exposed them.

CESTIUS PIUS. It was in order not to separate the children that I exposed them together.—He also took in two—even though he is content with only one.[2]—I am being forced to expose them a second time.

Against

JUNIUS GALLIO. Your role, judges, is simple: you 6 can send both of us away from this court fathers.

MENTO. *He* is used to being without children, *I* am doomed to torment even if I get one. I am used to two.—Whatever I have done at any time—and you have at home with you witnesses [3] to my behaviour— I have never done anything without consulting them —except informing you about them.—Do you call it

he is satisfied with one; why should not the natural father also start with two?

[3] The twins.

Sine herede ero qui paulo ante habui filios duos
tales ut ex illis vel unus cuilubet satis sit?

POMPEI SILONIS. Videte quam modeste agam:
ego sustuli, ego educavi, ego reddidi; iste eligat.

7 VIBI RUFI. " Salvi sunt " inquam " liberi tui ":
post hanc vim meam iste me osculatus est.

PASSIENI. Cedo mihi tabulas testamenti: plures
in testamento habeo quam in pacto. Hoc testamentum delere non cogito; si meos filios heredes
facere non possum, tuos faciam. Preces meas ad
filios transferam; hoc enim nomen licebit, puto,
mihi usurpare dum litigo.

ARELLI FUSCI patris. Fertis hoc, optimi iuvenes?
Ego vos expositos sustuli, ego educavi, ego aegro-
tantibus adsedi; senem me fecistis, et relinquitis?

ARGENTARI. *In ista vi duos filios perdidi.*

8 DIVISIO. Latro sic divisit: ⟨an⟩ [1] in re vis aut
necessitas sit. Nulla, inquit, vis est; *arma lex et
vincula et ultimum periculum conplectitur*, quorum nihil
fuit in tua persona. Ille ait: *Vis* est *et necessitas*
ubi velim nolim subcumbendum est mihi. *Tum*
autem necesse *mihi* ⟨*erat*⟩; [2] *non enim poteram habere
alterum filium nisi alterum promisissem.* Respondetur:
Primum non est vis ubi aliquid expediendae rei causa

---

[1] *Supplied by Faber.*
[2] *Supplied by Otto (comparing E).*

force, when it made you a father?—Shall I be without an heir, I who not long ago had two sons so good that even one of them is enough for anybody?

POMPEIUS SILO. See how modest is my attitude; *I* took them in, *I* brought them up, *I* have given them back: let *him* choose.

VIBIUS RUFUS. "Your sons are safe," I said. 7 After this act of " force " on my part, he kissed me.

PASSIENUS. Hand me my will: I find here more children than the agreement allows me. I do not have a mind to tear up this will; if I cannot make my sons my heirs, I will make your sons.—I shall turn my prayers towards my sons; for I can, I suppose, use this name so long as I am still in court.

ARELLIUS FUSCUS SENIOR. Can you bear this, excellent youths? I took you in when you were exposed, I brought you up, I sat by you in your illnesses. You have made an old man of me: do you abandon me?

ARGENTARIUS. Thanks to that " force " I have lost two sons.

Division

Latro made the following division: Is this a case of 8 force or necessity? "There is no force here; the law relates to force of arms, imprisonment and extreme danger: none of these was present in your case. He says: ' Force and necessity are present where willy-nilly I have to give in.[1] Now, on that occasion I *did* have to: I couldn't have one son unless I promised the other.' The reply is: ' First, there is no force where something has to be tolerated to get a

[1] Bonner points out that Ulpian (*Dig.* 4.2.1) supports this wide view of *vis*.

patiendum est, sed ratio: tamquam non possum domum habere nisi hanc emero; nulla alia venalis
est; hanc occasionem vidit venditor et premit. Non
tamen hanc emptionem rescindes, alioqui in infinitum
calumnia excedet. ⟨Deinde⟩[1] dicat[2] alius: necesse
mihi erat. Tibi necesse? Carere primum etiamnunc poteras; deinde et alia via poteras invenire,
sperare alium indicem. An aliter invenire non
poteras? Ergo hoc tibi plus praestiti.   399M

9   An, si in re vis et necessitas est, ita tantum rescin-
dantur quae per vim et necessitatem gesta sunt si
vis et necessitas a paciscente adhibita est. Nihil,
inquit, mea an tu cogaris si non a me cogeris; meam
culpam esse oportet ut mea poena sit. Non, inquit;
neque enim lex adhibenti vim irascitur sed passo
succurrit, et iniquum illi videtur id ratum esse quod
aliquis non quia voluit pactus est sed quia coactus
est. Nihil autem refert, inquam, per quem illi
necesse fuerit; iniquum enim quod rescinditur facit
fortuna eius qui passus est, non persona facientis.

Deinde: an ab hoc vis admota sit. Tu, inquit,
mihi vim admovisti, qui non aliter indicabas quam
si pactus essem. Non est, inquit, admovere vim
aliquid sub certa condicione promittere. Si qua
vis est, a te tibi adhibita est, quod exponere . . . et

---

[1] *Supplied by Gertz.*
[2] dicat *Schultingh:* dicet.

---

[1] The foster-father clearly argued that the other put force
on himself (cf. §11) by exposing the children in the first place.

matter settled—this is merely good sense. For example, if I cannot have a house unless I buy this one—no other is for sale, the seller has seen his opportunity and is putting the pressure on. Still, you won't be able to invalidate this sale, or else quibbles will be extended *ad infinitum*. Secondly, another man may say: " I had to." Had *you*? First of all, you could still have gone without. Secondly, you could have tried to find them by another route, hoped for another informant. Or could you not find them any other way? Then all the greater the service I was doing you.' "

If there *is* force or necessity present, can actions 9 done as a result of force and necessity only be annulled if the force and necessity were applied by the bargainer? " It is nothing to do with me whether you are forced—if you aren't forced by *me*; if I am to be punished, the fault must be mine." " No. The law is not angry with the man applying the force; it merely comes to the aid of one who has suffered by it, and regards it as unfair that something should stand when one party agreed to it not because he wanted to but because he was forced to. It makes no odds, I repeat, who caused him to be forced; for what is annulled is made unfair by the fortunes of the man who suffered, not the person of the agent."

Then: *Did* this man apply force? " You applied force to me in consenting to give the information only if I agreed." " Promising something on conditions is not applying force. If any force comes into it, it was applied by you to yourself, because . . . to expose . . ."[1] *He* had come to release himself from a

ad exonerandum se venisse, ut tantum patri redderet quantum educatori superfuisset.

10 Pro educatore Gallio hunc colorem secutus est: se misericordia motum. Cum viderem, inquit, orbum sine herede, dixi mihi ipse: quid avidus es? possumus duo patres esse. Et dixit illam amabilem sententiam: do itaque nunc poenas misericors.

Montanus Votienus sic coepit: si quis me videt, iudices, modo duorum liberorum patrem, nunc solitudine periclitantem, certum habeo, dicit crudelem indicem. Et summisse cum adversario egit: rogavit ut altero contentus esset; et illam sumpsit contradictionem: nescio, inquit, utrum ⟨eligam⟩,[1] et dixit: mihi crede, qui illos optume novi: utrumvis elige; ideo sic pactus sum, quia nihil intererat.

11 Hispo Romanius erat natura qui asperiorem dicendi viam sequeretur; itaque hoc colore egit, ut inveheretur tamquam in malum patrem et diceret crudeliter exponentem, perfide recipientem. In hoc, inquit, repetit, non quia habere vult sed quia eripere; irascitur mihi quod [duo][2] educavi, quod indicavi. Et cum descripsisset saevitiam exponentis, adiecit: Etiamnunc mihi videtur eiusdem animi, eiusdem duritiae, quia nihil putat se debere ei qui liberos suos educavit. Durus est pater, crudelis

400

---

[1] *Supplied by Gertz.*
[2] *Deleted by Müller.*

burden, to give back to the father as much as had
proved excessive for the foster-father.

For the foster-father Gallio pursued this *colour*: he 10
had been influenced by pity. "When I saw this
man, childless and heirless, I said to myself: ' Why
be greedy? We can both be fathers.' " And he
spoke the attractive epigram: "So now I pay the
penalty for my pity."

Votienus Montanus began like this: "If, judges,
anyone sees me now in solitude and danger, when just
now I was father of two children, I am sure [1] he will
say I was cruel to give the information." He pleaded
in a restrained fashion with his opponent. He begged
him to be content with one of the two; and he posed
the following objection: "I don't know which to
choose," replying to it: "Believe me, I know them
very well. Choose whichever you like. This is why
I made the bargain in these terms—there was no
difference between them."

Romanius Hispo was a man naturally disposed to 11
pursue the harsher course in a speech. So the *colour*
of his plea was to inveigh against the father as being
wicked. He had been cruel to expose the children,
treacherous in taking them back. " He seeks to get
them back not because he wants to have them but
because he wants to filch them from another. He is
angry because I brought them up and gave him the
information." After describing the savagery of the
exposure, he added: "Even now he seems to me to
be of the same mind, equally harsh—for he thinks he
owes nothing to the man who reared his children. He
is a harsh and cruel father; do not believe that he can

[1] Irony: or perhaps he implies " cruel to myself " (cf. §11).

est; nolite credere ex illa feritate tam subitam mutationem. Sinite me in filio uno non experiri.

Dixerat ⟨Cestius⟩[1] in hac controversia in illa quaestione qua dicebat se non[2] vim adhibuisse: Quid ergo? quis adhibuit vim? Tu tibi. Non est quod dicat aliquis: quis sibi ipse vim adhibet? Solet fieri; ecce ego ipse mihi nocui. Et illud dixerat: Placet mihi in inritum revocari quae gesta sunt. Quid do ne indicaverim?

12 Argentarius dixit ex altera parte miseriorem se nunc esse quam cum ignoraret suos; et cum tormenta paterni animi descripsisset, ait: Etiamnunc 401M pacisci volo. Quid do ut liberos meos recipiam? quid do ne agnoverim?

Indignabatur Cestius detorqueri ab illo totiens et mutari sententias suas. Quid putatis, aiebat, Argentarium esse? Cesti simius est. Solebat et Graece dicere: ὁ πίθηκός μου. Fuerat enim Argentarius Cesti auditor et erat imitator. Aiebat invicem: quid putatis esse Cestium nisi Cesti cinerem? et sic solebat iurare: "per manes praeceptoris mei 13 Cesti," cum Cestius viveret. Omnibus autem insistebat Cesti vestigiis: aeque ex tempore dicebat, aeque contumeliose multa interponebat; illud tamen

[1] *Supplied by Bursian.*
[2] non *Novák:* nequa.

change so quickly from such brutality. Allow me not to have to make the experiment—in the case of one son." [1]

Cestius had said in this *controversia*, on the question where he claimed he had applied no force: " Well then? Who applied force? *You*—to yourself. No-one need say: ' Who can apply force to himself? ' It is a common occurrence—look, *I* have harmed myself." And he had also said: " I am happy that what has been done should be annulled. What would I give not to have revealed the information? "

Argentarius, on the other side, said he was now 12 more wretched than when he did not know about his sons; after describing the agonies of a father's feelings, he said: " I still want to bargain. What would I give to take back my sons? What would I give not to have recognised them? " [2]

Cestius was angry that Argentarius so often twisted and changed his epigrams, and he said: " What do you think Argentarius is? He is Cestius' ape." He also used to say " my ape " in Greek. For Argentarius had been a pupil of Cestius', and was still his imitator. He said in return: " What do you think Cestius is but the ashes of Cestius? " And he used to swear " by the ghost of my teacher Cestius " while Cestius was still alive. All the same, he used to 13 tread in all Cestius' footsteps; he spoke extempore just like him, and put in many insulting comments in

[1] The one who, according to the bargain, would go to the foster-father.

[2] These two questions contrast the father's two states—his blissful ignorance previously, and his present knowledge—which leaves him longing to have both sons.

optima fide praestitit, cum uterque Graecus esset,
ut numquam Graece declamaret, ⟨et⟩ [1] illos semper
admiraretur qui, non [fuerunt] [2] contenti unius linguae eloquentia, cum Latine declamaverant, toga
posita sumpto pallio quasi persona mutata rediebant
et Graece declamabant; ex quibus fuit *Sabinus
Clodius, in quem uno die et Graece et Latine declamantem*
14 *multa urbane dicta sunt. Dixit Haterius quibusdam
querentibus pusillas mercedes eum accepisse cum duas
res doceret: numquam magnas mercedes accepisse eos
qui hermeneumata docerent. Maecenas dixit:* Τυδείδην
δ᾽ οὐκ ἂν γνοίης, ποτέροισι μετείη. *Cassius Severus*
venustissimam rem ex omnibus: qui *ab auditione eius
cum rediret, interrogatus quomodo dixisset, respondit:
male* καὶ κακῶς. 402.

Glycon dixit: ἂν ἀμφοτέρους μοι μὴ ἀποδῷς,
ἀπολέσεις αὐτῶν τὸ δίδυμον.

Gallio autem elegantissime dixit a parte patris,
cum ultima per testamenti figuram tractaret:
quandoque ego mortuus ero, tunc mihi heres sit: vis
interrogem uter?

Triarius dixit a parte educatoris: ergo ego tollere
potui, educare potui, tacere non potui?

---

[1] *Supplied by Müller.*
[2] *Deleted by Gertz and Madvig.*

---

[1] The toga was the sign of Roman citizenship, the *pallium*
of Greek blood: see Sherwin-White on Plin. *Ep.* 4.11.3.
Compare bilingual Fuscus (*S.* 4.5).

just the same way. But he was very loyal to the principle of never declaiming in Greek, though both he and Cestius were Greeks, and was always astonished at those who, not content with eloquence in one language, would, after declaiming in Latin, take off their togas, put on cloaks, return, as it were, with a change of mask, and declaim in Greek.[1] One of these was Clodius Sabinus, about whom many witty remarks were made when he declaimed in Latin and Greek on the same day. When some people were deploring that Sabinus got trifling pay even though he taught two things, Haterius said: " People who teach translation have never got a lot of money." Maecenas said: " You could not tell which side the son of Tydeus was fighting on."[2] Cassius Severus said the prettiest thing of all. Coming back from listening to Sabinus and being asked how his speech had gone, he replied: " Badly—*et mal.*"

Glycon said: " If you don't give me both, you will destroy their twinness."

Gallio said very neatly on the father's side, when he was treating the final section by employing the figure of a will: " When I shall be dead, then let my heir be:[3] do you want me to have to *ask* which ? "

Triarius said, for the foster-father: " Then I could take them in, I could rear them—but I could not keep quiet about them ? "[4]

---

[2] *Il.* 5.85: ". . . with the Trojans or the Achaeans: for he ran about the plain like a river in flood."

[3] For the form of a will, see Gaius 2.117 " TITIUS HERES ESTO."

[4] For this regret, see §11 " What would I give . . ."

IV

A FILIO IN ARCE PULSATUS

Qui patrem pulsaverit, manus ei praecidantur.

Tyrannus patrem in arcem cum duobus filiis accersit; inperavit adulescentibus ut patrem caederent. Alter ex his praecipitavit se, alter cecidit. Postea in amicitiam tyranni receptus est. Occiso tyranno praemium accepit. Petuntur manus eius; pater defendit.

1 CESTI PII. *Felicior essem si plures reos defenderem.*

TRIARI. Haec vulnera quae in ore videtis meo postea feci quam dimissus sum.

IUNI GALLIONIS. Gratias ago filio quod me non reliquit solum tyranno. Quod manus illius passus sum [1] ego iussi; itaque crimini meo adsum. " Amicus " inquit " tyranni fuit." Age, hoc tantum filius meus in arce simulavit? Procumbo ad genua vestra, iudices, ille contumax qui cum vapularem non rogavi.

2 MUSAE. Occisus est tyrannus; a quo putatis 403

---

[1] passus sum *Otto:* usum.

---

[1] Bonner, 96–7. The law is doubtless a fiction so far as classical Greek and Roman practice was concerned; it appears in *Decl.* 358, 362, 372 and Theon *Rhet. Gr.* 2.130 Spengel.

[2] i.e. if both sons were alive.

[3] Perhaps at the funeral: cf. §5 Mento.

4

THE MAN STRUCK BY HIS SON IN THE CASTLE

A son who strikes his father shall have his hands cut off.[1]

A tyrant summoned a man and his two sons to his castle; he ordered the youths to beat their father. One of them threw himself from the height, the other beat his father. Later he became one of the circle of the tyrant, killed him and received the reward. His hands are sought; his father defends him.

For the father

CESTIUS PIUS. I should be more fortunate if I had more defendants to appear for.[2] 1

TRIARIUS. These wounds which you see on my face I inflicted,[3] after I was released.

JUNIUS GALLIO. I thank my son for not leaving me isolated before the tyrant.[4]—If I suffered at his hands, it was because *I* gave the order; thus it is a deed of my own I am defending.—" He was a friend of the tyrant." Look, was this the only time that my son pretended in the castle?[5]—I fall at your knees, judges, that stubborn man who did not beg for mercy when he was beaten.

MUSA. The tyrant was killed. By whom, do you 2

---

[4] i.e. for not jumping out of the window also.
[5] Both the beating and the friendship with the tyrant were part of the son's plot against the tyrant: cf. §3 " Harden your heart . . ."; §11 Latro; §22 Mento.

THE ELDER SENECA

nisi ab eo qui patrem pulsare [non][1] poterat?
*Praecidetis tyrannicidae manus? Quid hoc est? integer
tyrannus iacet.* Praecisas tyrannicidae manus arci
praefigite. Non vindicem filium propter quem ne a
tyranno quidem inpune vapulavi? Postquam occupavit arcem, secuti sunt illum homicidae, secuti
venefici, secutus quisquis patrem pulsare poterat.
Necesse fuit patrem caedere, tam hercules *quam* necesse
fuit *spoliare templa, virgines rapere.* Aiebam: fili,
fortius feri; tyrannus spectat. Si talis erat filius
meus qualem describitis, nescio cui magis expedierit
tyrannum vivere. *O quantum istis debemus manibus
per quas iam nihil necesse est!* Occidit tyrannum: sic
huius iratae manus feriunt. Cum occideret tyrannum, aiebat: "frater te ferit, pater ferit." Sic
feriunt qui volunt. Tecum, fili inconsideratae pietatis, queror: ⟨non⟩[2] validius patrem cecidisti quam
iussit tyrannus. Iratus iacenti ipsas cadaveris manus
in me ingessi.

3   FULVI SPARSI. *Tales fuerunt ex quibus posset alter
tyrannum contemnere, alter occidere.*

IULI BASSI. Conpressas fili manus in os meum in-
pegi, caedentem consolatus sum.

PORCI LATRONIS. "Caede" inquit "patrem";

---

[1] *Deleted by Bursian.*
[2] *Supplied by the editor.*

---

[1] The tyrant.
[2] The son had to behave like an ordinary follower of the
tyrant in furtherance of the plot.
[3] Because dangerous to both father and son: cf. §5 "'Son,'
I said . . .''

think, if not the man who could bring himself to beat his father?—Will you cut off the hands of one who killed the tyrant? What is this? The *tyrant* lies unmutilated.—Hang up the severed hands of the tyrant's killer before the castle.—Am I to fail to defend a son thanks to whom not even a tyrant could get away with striking me?—After he [1] took over the castle, he was followed by homicides, poisoners, anyone capable of striking his father.—It was compulsory to strike one's father, to be sure, just as it was compulsory to despoil temples, rape virgins.[2]—I said: " Son, strike more boldly: the tyrant is watching."— If my son was as you describe him, I cannot think of anyone for whom it was more expedient that the tyrant should live.—O how much we owe to these hands; thanks to them we now have nothing imposed on us.—He killed the tyrant: that is how his hands strike when they are angry.—As he killed the tyrant, he said: " My brother strikes you, my father strikes you." That is the way people strike when they *want* to.—My son, I deplore your thoughtless [3] affection; you did not strike your father harder than the tyrant ordered.—Angered with the other son as he lay there, I made even the corpse's hands strike me.[4]

FULVIUS SPARSUS. My sons were such that one was 3 capable of despising a tyrant, the other of killing him.

JULIUS BASSUS. I made my son's clenched fist dash against my mouth, and consoled him as he flogged.

PORCIUS LATRO. " Flog your father." While I

[4] Because I preferred the one son's beating to the other dying: cf. §4 " Which of my sons . . ." (to which the answer is: the second), " So may I die . . .," etc.

dum ego neglegens sum, occupavit ⟨*praecipitare*⟩ [1] 404

se ex arce *filius. Hoc non est patri parcere, sed sibi.*
Dura, fili; ad tyrannum tibi per patrem eundum est.

4   BLANDI. Ut vidi tyrannicidam ex arce descen-
dentem, nihil prius quam manus osculatus sum.
Tenent ecce cruentum tyranni caput; nunc illas
praecidite.[2]

POMPEI SILONIS. *Utrum ex filiis meis probatis? alter*
se occidit, alter tyrannum. Nemo ius habet in istas
manus, meae sunt; istae etiam cum tyranno ser-
virent mihi paruerunt. Ita mihi superstite filio mori
liceat ut ego illum qui mori maluit parricidam vocavi.

ARELLI FUSCI patris. Rogo vos per securitatem
publicam, per modo restitutae libertatis laetitiam,
per coniuges liberosque vestros. Nemo tam sup-
pliciter audit me rogantem cum vapularem. Quam
languidae caedentis manus erant! non putarem illum
posse tyrannicidium facere. Istae mihi salutares
porrexerunt cibos, istae potiones; numquam tamen
indulgentiores sensi manus quam cum me caederent.

5   VOTIENI MONTANI. " Pereat " inquit " potius."
Cum sint qui tam fortiter loquantur, vix inventus est
qui tyrannum occideret. Fili, fortius, inquam,
feri, ne nos colludere tyrannus intellegat. *Suspensas*
leviter admovebat manus; filius simulabat ictus, pater
gemitus. Si qua est fides, iratus filium extuli quod

---

[1] *Supplied by Bursian, comparing E.*
[2] *This epigram appears in the MSS at the end of §3: it was*
transposed by Bursian.

wasn't watching, my son got in first by throwing himself from the castle walls. This is not sparing one's father—it's sparing oneself.—Harden your heart, my son: to get to the tyrant you must go by way of your father.

BLANDUS. When I saw the tyrannicide coming 4 down from the castle, it was his hands I kissed before anything else. Look, they hold the bloody head of the tyrant. *Now* cut *them* off!

POMPEIUS SILO. Which of my sons do you approve? One has killed himself, the other the tyrant. —No-one has power over these hands—they belong to *me*: they obeyed *me*[1] even when they were enslaved to the tyrant.—So may I die before my son, I actually termed the son who preferred to die a parricide.

ARELLIUS FUSCUS SENIOR. I beg you by the safety of the state, by the pleasure we take in the liberty now restored to us, by your wives and children—no-one heard me begging and suppliant like this when I got beaten.—How feeble his hands as he struck me! I shouldn't have supposed him capable of killing a tyrant. These hands have held out food and drink to succour me; but I have never felt them more affectionate towards me than when they flogged me.

VOTIENUS MONTANUS. "Rather let him perish." 5 There are those who speak as boldly as that—but it was difficult to find one ready to kill the tyrant.— "Son," I said, "strike harder, so that the tyrant doesn't realise we are in collusion."—He was checking his hands and bringing them down lightly: the son was pretending to strike, the father to groan.—If you

[1] By beating me, as I preferred.

me non ceciderat. *Necessitas magnum humanae
inbecillitatis patrocinium* est: *haec excusat Saguntinos,
quamvis non ceciderint patres sed occiderint;* haec
excusat Romanos, quos ad servilem dilectum Can- 405
nensis ruina conpulit; quae quidquid coegit defendit.
Ille quoque mihi ⟨*non*⟩[1] *pepercisset si* unicus fuisset.
Ille me fratri relinquebat: ⟨*relinqueret*⟩[2] *hic tyranno?*
" Etiamnunc "inquit" in facie tua vulnera apparent."
Fili, nocet tibi quod tam cito occidisti tyrannum.

MENTONIS. Quaeritis quis haec fecerit vulnera?
Ille cuius in funere me cecidi. Ita mihi libero et
vivere contingat et mori, ita oculos meos fili manus
operiant, ut ego inter liberos meos fortior steti.

6   Ex altera parte. ARELLI FUSCI patris. *Tamdiu
cecidit patrem donec placeret tyranno satelles.* Quid?
tu tyrannicidium facere non potes nisi in parricidio
exercueris manus? " Pater "inquit " adest." Malo; non enim tantum patrem, etiam patronum cecidisti.

IULI BASSI. Quoniam usque eo saeculum mutatum
est ut parricidae pater adsit, nos istius advocationi
adsimus?[3] Defendit quamvis nocentem: ecquid

[1] *Supplied by Faber.*
[2] *Supplied by Wachsmuth.*
[3] adsimus *ed.*: adsum *AV*: adsumus *B*.

---

[1] See *C.* 4.4, and Juvenal 15.93 *seq.* on the necessity that
forced the Vascones to cannibalism.
[2] Cf. *Decl.* p. 405.29 Ritter: " sic Saguntini fecerunt parricidium."
[3] Cf. *C.* 5.7 n.

will believe me, I buried my son feeling angry that he
had not beaten me.—Necessity is a great defence for
feeble humanity: [1] this is the excuse for the people of
Saguntum: though *they* killed their fathers rather
than flogged them.[2] This is the excuse of the
Romans, who were driven by the disaster at Cannae
to recruit slaves.[3] Necessity defends what it has enforced.—He [4] too would not have spared me if he had
been the only son. He was leaving me to his
brother; was *he* to leave me to the tyrant?—" Even
now your wounds show on your face." Son, it goes
against you that you killed the tyrant so swiftly.[5]

MENTO. Do you ask who caused these wounds?
The son at whose funeral I struck myself.—May I
live and die a free man, may the hands of my son close
my eyes—I, standing there between my sons, was
more brave than either.

The other side

ARELLIUS FUSCUS SENIOR. He struck his father for
as long as the tyrant demanded of his hireling.—How
is this? Can't you slay a tyrant unless you have exer-
cised your hands on your father?—" My father is
defending me." All the better for me: you beat
your counsel as well as your father.

JULIUS BASSUS. Just because things are so topsy-
turvy that a father is speaking in favour of a parricide,
are *we* to support his defence?—He defends him even

----

[4] The dead son (also the subject of "was leaving" in the
next sentence).

[5] So swiftly that the scars had no time to disappear; the
prompt killing of the tyrant is (the father implies) a point in
favour of the son.

agnoscitis indulgentiam? Illius est pater qui maluit
perire quam patrem caedere. †Infelix causam suam
cum fratre iungebat.† Exclamat iste: nihil illi
mandavi; ego tibi et pro illo satis faciam? "Ut
validius caederem, *pro re publica*" inquit "*feci.*"
Vis tu pudorem habere nec *inputare idem et rei publicae*   406
et tyranno? "Pater" inquit "mihi adest." At
mehercules frater non adesset. *Habuisti quod tyranno
iactares: frater maluit mori.* Quisquis caedendus
erat saevius, isti tradebatur. "Tyrannum" inquit
"occidi." At patrem quantulo minus quam occidisti?

7   POMPEI SILONIS. Gaudeo in subselliis istius esse
patrem. Quomodo enim aliter efficere potuissem ut
vulnera eius videretis? Nunc multum refert mea
ubi sit: ab hac parte crimen obicitur, ab illa ostendi-
tur. Gravior esse testis solet qui a reo surgit. Talis
prorsus pater quem nemo alius posset caedere nisi
⟨qui⟩ [1] amicus esse posset tyranni. *Perit ne parricidium* aut *faceret aut videret:* in illo praecipitio non
minus, inquam, fratrem fugit quam tyrannum.

8   CORNELI HISPANI. Descendebat cruentus pater,
vexato laceratoque ore vix agnoscendus; putares duos

----

[1] *Supplied by Wachsmuth.*

----

[1] i.e. the trait ran in the family. The next sentence is an
earlier instance.
[2] Point unclear. The meaning may be that the youth tried to
claim that he was as innocent as his dead brother (by means
of the alleged plot: see p. 281 n. 5 above).

though he is guilty. Don't you find this kindness familiar?[1] He is the father of the son who preferred death to beating his father.—The unhappy youth equated his brother's cause with his own.[2]—He cries: " I gave him no orders. Must *I* render you satisfaction for him too? "[3]—" It was for the state that I struck harder." How about thinking of your self-respect, and not claiming credit with both the state and a tyrant for the same action?—" My father is defending me." But to be sure your brother would not be defending you.—You had something to boast of to the tyrant: your brother preferred death.— Anyone who was to receive a particularly severe flogging would be handed over to this man.—" I killed the tyrant." How near you came to killing your father!

POMPEIUS SILO. I rejoice that his father is on *his* benches. How otherwise could I have managed to let you see his wounds? As it is, it makes a great difference to me where he sits; on this side the charge is levelled, on that it is demonstrated. And a witness who appears on the defendant's side tends to be taken more seriously.—He was indeed such a father that the only person capable of beating him was one capable of becoming the friend of the tyrant.—He perished to avoid doing or seeing parricide; indeed, on that precipice, he fled from his brother as much as from the tyrant.

CORNELIUS HISPANUS. The father came down 8 blood-stained, scarcely recognisable with his bruised and torn face; you would have thought there had

---

[3] Apparently the father is represented as saying to the tyrant (or to the second son when he flogged him): *I* didn't tell my son to commit suicide—must I pay for his offence also?

fuisse qui cecidissent. Fecit quod debebat qui patrem ceciderat: amicum occidit.

Cesti Pii. "Ego" inquit "caesus sum; *poenam remitto.*" *Mirarer nisi pro tam bono patre fuisset qui mori vellet.* Dignus est quem invitum vindicetis. Quid ?[1] apud nos tantum crudeles patres vindicantur ? "Pater" inquit "iussit." Ergo frater tuus impius fuit, qui patri non paruit ? Si quando lente parebant satellites, aiebat tyrannus: non spectastis quemadmodum patrem ceciderit ? "Qui patrem ceciderit, manus eius praecidantur." Hanc legem moriens laudavit tyrannus. Novissime inter filium 40 et patrem tyrannus intercessit.

9 ⟨Divisio. Latro sic divisit:⟩[2] an non quisquis patrem ceciderit puniatur. *In lege, inquit, nihil excipitur. Sed multa quamvis non excipiantur intelleguntur, et scriptum legis angustum, interpretatio diffusa est;* quaedam vero tam manifesta sunt ut nullam cautionem desiderent: nam *quid interest lege excipere ne fraudi sit ei qui per insaniam patrem pulsavit, cum illi non supplicio sed remedio opus sit?* Quid opus est caveri lege *ne puniatur infans si pulsaverit patrem?* Quid opus est lege caveri ne puniatur si quis vi patrem sopitum et subita corporis gravitate conlapsum ex-

---

[1] quid? *Otto:* qui.
[2] *Supplied by Schultingh, Müller.*

---

[1] And so would beat *you* even more ferociously (cf. §6 " Anyone who was . . .").

been two beating him.—He did what one would expect of a man who had beaten his father: he killed his friend.

Cestius Pius. " It is *I* who was beaten, and I waive the penalty." I should have been surprised had there been no son willing to die for so good a father. He deserves to be avenged by you even against his will. In this country is it only cruel fathers who get revenge?—" My father ordered me to." Was your brother then wicked in disobeying his father?—If ever his men were slow to obey, the tyrant would say: " Didn't you see how he beat his father?"[1]—" The son who beats his father shall have his hands cut off." This was the law the tyrant quoted as he died.[2]—At the last the tyrant had to intervene between father and son.[3]

Division

Latro's division went like this: Should all those who beat their fathers be punished? " There is no exception mentioned in the law.[4] But many exceptions are understood, even if not explicitly stated. The words of the law are restricted, its interpretation spreads wide. But some things are so obvious that they require no clause to cover them. What is the use of legally excepting from liability one who has struck his father while mad—and so needs not punishment but cure? What need of a provision in the law not to have a baby punished if he strikes his father? Or suppose someone forcibly awakes a father who is un-

---

[2] This would seem to make a better point *for* the son.
[3] i.e. he had to restrain the son's cruelty.
[4] Cf. Theon *Rhet. Gr.* 2.130.30 Spengel.

citavit, cum illa non iniuria sed medicina fuerit?
Nondum de propria sed de communi causa loquor.
Si efficio ut qui [1] cecidit patrem possit absolvi, pro hoc
animosius agam, ut dignus sit supplicio nisi praemio
fuerit.

10 Si non quisquis patrem pulsavit puniri debet, ⟨an
hic debeat⟩.[2] Hanc quaestionem in partes plures
divisit: an tutus sit qui tyranno iubente fecit. Cogi-
tate quam multa tyrannus exegerit. Pro publica
innocentia est non licere hoc quoque tyrannis, ut nos
faciant nocentes. *Hoc qui cogente tyranno fecit miserior
fuit ipso vapulante. Illa non dicitur inpudica quae
arcessita est a tyranno; ille non [3] dicitur sacrilegus qui* 408
*deorum inmortalium dona manibus suis tulit ad tyran-
num,* aut qui funestas tyranni imagines inter effigies
11 deorum immortalium consecravit. An tutus sit qui
patre iubente fecit. Non cecidit sed paruit. Et illud
dixit in narratione: stabat contumax fraterno vultu;
intellexi non posse cogi a tyranno. An tutus sit
qui pro patria fecit; an hic pro patria fecerit, id est:
an illo iam tempore cogitationem tyrannicidi habuerit,

---

[1] ut qui *ed. after Bursian:* si quis qui.
[2] *Supplied by Konitzer.*
[3] dicitur—ille non *reconstructed from E by the ed. after
Bursian, Opitz: the words are omitted in the main MSS.*

---

[1] A flamboyant way of saying the son deserves reward, not
punishment.

conscious and has collapsed in a sudden faint—this being not an injury but a remedy? So far I am talking in generalities, and not about the particular case. If I can establish that someone who has beaten his father *can* be acquitted, I shall plead with the more self-confidence on behalf of this man, proving that he deserves to be punished if he does not deserve the reward." [1]

If not everyone who has struck his father should be 10 punished, does *this* man deserve punishment? Latro divided this question into several parts: Is a man free of danger if he acted on the orders of a tyrant? "Consider how many things the tyrant demanded. It is in the interests of public innocence that tyrants should not be allowed this right too—to make us guilty.[2] The man who did this on the compulsion of the tyrant was more wretched than the man who got beaten. A woman who has been sent for by a tyrant is not called unchaste; a man is not called sacrilegious if he has taken to the tyrant gifts dedicated to the immortal gods, or who has consecrated ill-omened likenesses of the tyrant among statues of the immortal gods." Is a man free of danger if he acted on 11 his father's orders? "He did not flog—he obeyed." In the narrative, he also said: "He stood there, obstinately, looking just like his brother. I realised he [3] could not be coerced by the tyrant." Is a man free of danger if he acted on behalf of his country? *Did* this man act on behalf of his country? That is, did he already at that time have a plan to kill the

---

[2] Cf. Sen. *Phoen.* 367–8: " hoc leve est quod sum nocens: / feci nocentes ": and often elsewhere.

[3] Any more than his dead brother.

et hoc animo ceciderit ut aditum sibi faceret ad amicitiam tyranni.

Montanus et illam quaestionem ultimam fecit: an, etiamsi quid peccatum est, tanto merito redemptum sit.

12 Gallio illam quaestionem primam fecit: an *ultio caesi patris nullius sit nisi patris.* Invitum, inquit, me non vindicabis. *Si a quolibet alieno caesus essem et nollem agere iniuriarum, nemo nomine meo ageret. Atqui nihil interest: poena maior est eius qui cecidit, ius idem eius qui caesus est.* Contra ait omnibus actionem dari; non enim privatam iniuriam esse sed publicam; itaque †nec taxatione† defungi damnatum aut iniuriarum poena, sed manus perdere; ad omnes patres pertinere hoc exemplum, ad omnes filios, ad ipsam rem publicam: tales esse qui fiant tyranni, certe qui tyrannorum amici.

13 Et ultimas fecit has quaestiones: an si pio animo fecit non teneatur; an pio animo fecerit. Et illi 409 quaestioni Latronis, " an tutus sit qui patre volente fecit," nunc, inquit, fingis in fili patrocinium, sed tunc noluisti; et adiecit: Ne dixerit idem voluisse patrem quod tyrannum. Quaeritis utri paruerit? tyrannus illum amavit tamquam sibi paruisset. *" Pater " inquit " voluit ": sed frater noluit. " Pater " inquit " voluit ": ita tu non tyranno tantum sed etiam*

---

[1] Cf. *C.* 4.1 n.

tyrant and did he flog with the intention of thereby opening the way for himself into the tyrant's circle?

Montanus had a further question for his final one: Even if there was a wrong done, has it been compensated by so great a service?

Gallio made the first question: Is the avenging of a 12 father being beaten a matter for anyone but the father himself? " You will not avenge me if I do not wish it. If I had been beaten by any outsider whatever, and didn't want to bring an action for injury,[1] no-one would sue in my name. But there is no difference; the son who flogged receives a more severe penalty, but the rights of the man flogged are just the same." On the other hand, Gallio said that going to law is open to all; this is a public wrong, not a private one. That is why someone condemned for it does not get away with an assessment or a punishment for assault and battery, but must lose his hands. All fathers (went on Gallio) are affected by this precedent—so are all sons and the state itself. People like this become tyrants—or at least friends of tyrants.

His last questions were these: Is he liable if he 13 acted from good motives? *Did* he act with a good motive? To Latro's question, Is a man free of danger if he acted on his father's wishes, he replied: " *Now* you are ready to produce fictions to defend your son: but *then* you didn't want to." He added: " Let him not say his father wanted the same as the tyrant. Do you ask which of the two he obeyed? The tyrant loved him, as if he had obeyed *him*. ' My father wished it.' But your brother did not. ' My father wished it.' Did your father then think you a

patri dignus parricidio visus es? Cum descripsisset
impium in fratrem, impium in patrem, adiecit:
tyrannum quoque tunc cum amare deberes occidisti.

14 Montanus partem accusatoris declamavit et hoc
colore usus est: indulgentissimum fuisse in liberos
patrem; nimiam eius pietatem tyranno notam fuisse;
itaque illum, qui quaereret pudicis dolorem ex in-
pudicitia, contumacibus ex servitute, piissimo patri
tormentum quaesisse ex filiorum impietate; et
induxit illum animose loquentem qui iussus est prior
patrem caedere: " Quid si non cecidero? " inquit;
" quid facturus es? Torquebis? occides? Plus
est quod imperas quam quod minaris." Certamen
erat in uno homine utrum plus posset natura an tyrannus. " Caede " inquit: " non caedo "; " verbera ": " non ferio." Haec fratre audiente. Et
illud dixit: cum promitteret amicitiam tyrannus,
magis praemium extimuit tyrannici imperi quam imperium. Et cum descripsisset cicatrices pulsati
patris et deformem adhuc faciem, dixit: ab utroque
caesum putes.

15 Montanus tamen aiebat nihil posse melius dici
⟨quam quod Marcellus Marcius dixit⟩:[1] ex hac 410
parte tyrannus iubet, ex altera lex vetat: morieris
nisi[2] cecideris; morere ne caedas.

Cestius dixit: Tyrannus imperat ut patrem caedas:
non est novum. Noluisti facere: laudaturum me

[1] *Supplied by Gertz (cf. 9.6.18).*
[2] nisi *Schenkl:* si.

fit person to commit parricide, just as the tyrant
did?" After describing his lack of affection towards
his brother and his father, he added: "You killed the
tyrant, too, just when you should have felt love for
him."

Montanus, declaiming the accuser's part, used this 14
colour: the father had been very fond of his children;
his extreme affection was known to the tyrant; and
so the tyrant, who sought to inflict pain on the chaste
by means of unchasteness, on the stubborn by means
of servitude, sought to torture a most affectionate
father by means of his sons' lack of affection. He
introduced the son who was first told to beat his
father saying spiritedly: "What if I refuse to beat
him? What will you do? Torture? Kill? What
you order is worse than what you threaten." "There
was a contest within one man to see which had more
power, nature or the tyrant. 'Strike.' 'No.'
'Flog.' 'No.' This in the hearing of his brother."
He also said: "When the tyrant offered friendship,
he feared the reward offered for obeying the tyrant's
order more than the order itself." Describing the
scars left on the father by the beating, and his still
mutilated face, he said: "One would think both sons
had beaten him."

But Montanus used to say nothing could be better 15
put than a saying of Marcius Marcellus: "On one
side the tyrant orders, on the other the law forbids.
You will die unless you flog; die so as not to flog."

Cestius said: "The tyrant orders you to beat your
father: there is nothing new here.[1] You did not wish

---

[1] Because the other brother has already been given the
order—and showed his unwillingness more effectively.

putas? Ego vero non laudo; alterius ista gloria
est: tu fratrem imitatus es!

Argentarius dixit: tu *patrem cecidisti cum et legem
nosses et fratrem.*

Montanus dixit: parricida, [voluisti][1] violasti
patris corpus, fratris beneficium.

16   Ab altera parte hoc colore omnes declamaverunt,
tamquam patre iubente fecisset.

Triarius dixit: in fili mei manus incucurri.

Bassus Iulius dixit: ego me fili mei manibus cecidi.

Haterius dixit: ago gratias tyranno quod alterum
filium meum custodiri iussit, ne mori posset.

Cestius ait in narratione: Tyrannus iubet caedere,
exposita tormenta sunt; quid faciat? Moriatur,
inquis.   Hoc dicis: ne caedat patrem, occidat.

Fuscus Arellius dixit: conplecti volo istas manus
optume de me etiam ante tyrannicidium meritas.

Gallio dixit: viderit quantum tibi se putet debere
res publica; ego plus me quam illam debere tibi
iudico: difficilius est quod me iubente fecisti.

Montanus Votienus dixit in narratione: si perseveras, fili, fratrem sequar: videris utrum caedere
patrem malis an occidere.

17   Hanc controversiam et ab Asilio Sabino bene decla-
mari memini.   Describe, inquit, describe tyrannum
occisum et te cum ingenti gloria ex arce deductum.

---

[1] *Deleted by Bursian.*

---

[1] i.e. kill himself out of remorse.
[2] By grief: cf. below, Votienus (where the implication is
rather of suicide).   The play on words *caedat/occidat* is hardly
to be translated.

to do it: do you want me to praise you? *I* don't praise you, this glory belongs to the other—*you* merely imitated your brother."

Argentarius said: " You beat your father, though you knew what the law said—and what your brother did."

Montanus said: " Parricide, you did outrage to your father's body and your brother's good deed."

On the other side, every declaimer used the *colour* 16 that he had acted on the orders of his father.

Triarius said: " I ran on to my son's hands."

Julius Bassus said: " I beat myself, with my son's hands."

Haterius said: " I thank the tyrant for ordering my second son to be guarded so that he could not die."[1]

Cestius said in his narrative: " The tyrant orders him to flog, the tortures are laid out; what is he to do? ' Let him die,' you say. What you mean is: ' Let him kill his father,[2] so as not to beat him.' "

Arellius Fuscus said: " I wish to grasp the hands that served me well even before the tyrant was killed."

Gallio said: " The state can decide how much it thinks it owes you; in *my* judgement *I* owe you more than the state does; what you did on *my* orders was more difficult."

Votienus Montanus said in his narrative: " If you persist, son, I shall follow your brother; you had better make up your mind whether you prefer to beat your father or to kill him."

I recall the *controversia* being declaimed well by 17 Asilius Sabinus also. " Describe," he said, " describe the killing of the tyrant, and how you were escorted

O te parricidam, nisi post tyrannicidium quoque 411
intellegis quanto frater tuus honestius perierit quam
tu occideris. Illud non probavi, quod multa in re
severa temptavit salse dicere. Erat autem urban-
issimus homo, ut vobis saepe narravi, ut quidquid
in eloquentia illi deerat urbanitate pensaret.

18 Memini illum, cum Syriacus Vallius, homo disertus,
accusaret et videretur laturus calumniam, tristem
circa coronam iudici obversari et totiens occurrere
eunti Syriaco et quaerere quid haberet spei, deinde
post iudicium, cum Syriacus gratias illi ageret quod
tantam curam sui egisset: at mehercules, inquit,
timebam ne uno rhetore plus haberemus.

Et testis productus cum interrogatus esset an
accepisset a patre . . . sestertia, dixit accepisse;
an haberet: ⟨scire se⟩ [1] negavit; deinde interrogatus an calumniam haberet, ipse, inquit, neglegentiam meam nosti: an habeam nescio, accepisse
me scio.

Et in Domitium, nobilissimum virum, in consulatu
cum thermas prospicientis viam Sacram aedificasset
⟨et⟩ [2] coepisset deinde rhetores circumire et declamare: ego, inquit, sciebam hoc te facturum et
matri tuae querenti de tua desidia dixeram: πρῶτον
κολυμβᾶν, δεύτερον δὲ γράμματα.

[1] *Supplied by Shackleton Bailey.*
[2] *Supplied by Kiessling.*

---

[1] For *calumnia* see *C.* 2.1.34 n.
[2] For Syriacus, if condemned, would have had to give up his
forensic career: see *C.* 7 pr. 7 n.

from the castle with great pomp. O you are indeed
a parricide if, even after slaying the tyrant, you fail to
realise how much more honourable was your brother's
death than your own killing." But I *didn't* approve
of his trying to jest so frequently on a serious subject;
but he was a very witty man, as I have often told you,
and so he made up by his wit for any deficiency in his
eloquence.

I remember that, when Vallius Syriacus, an accom- 18
plished speaker, was prosecuting, and seemed likely
to be declared to have brought a malicious charge,[1]
Sabinus went round the crowd in court showing a long
face, and every time he met Syriacus on *his* circuit
asked him about his prospects; then after the trial,
when Syriacus thanked him for being so considerate,
he said: " Actually, I was afraid we should have one
more rhetorician." [2]

Once as a witness, when he was asked whether he
had received . . . sesterces from a father, he said he
had. Had he got them?—" I don't know." Then
he was asked whether he " had a calumny." [3] " *You*
know how careless I am," he said. " I don't know if
I have it, but I know I received it."

Against Domitius, a nobleman who during his consulship had built baths overlooking the Sacred Way
and then proceeded to go round the rhetors and
declaim, he said: " I knew you'd do this, and I'd said
to your mother when she complained of your laziness:
' First diving—then letters.' " [4]

---

[3] i.e. the penalty for *calumnia*: see previous note.
[4] An iambic verse, based on the Greek proverb alluded
to in Plat. *Laws* 689D: " they know neither how to read nor
how to swim."

19 Duas eius urbanas res praeterire non possum. *Secutus erat in* provinciam *Cretam Occium* Flammam *proconsulem. Graeci coeperunt in theatro postulare ut Sabinus maximum magistratum gereret. Mos autem est barbam et capillum magistratui Cretensium summittere.* 412[1] *Surrexit Sabinus et silentium manu fecit;* deinde *ait: hunc magistratum ego Romae bis gessi. Bis enim reus causam dixerat. Graeci non intellexerunt, sed bene precati Caesari petebant ut illum honorem Sabinus et tertio gereret.*

20 Postea deinde offendit illos tota comitum cohors: oppressi sunt in templo ab omni multitudine, quae postulabat ut Romam Sabinus cum Turdo proficisce-retur: erat inter infames maxime et invisos homines Turdus. Cum Turdus promitteret iturum se, ut inde posset exire, Sabinus silentio facto ait: ego ad Caesarem non sum iturus cum mattea. Postea hoc Sabino *cum causam diceret* obiectum est. Multa illum diserte dixisse memini cum introductus esset ex carcere in senatum postulaturus ut diaria acci-peret. Tunc dixit de fame questus: nihil onerosum a vobis peto, sed ut me aut mori velitis aut vivere. Et illud dixit: nolite, inquam, superbe audire homi-nem calamitosum:

saepe qui misereri potuit misericordiam rogat.

21 Et cum dixisset Seianianos locupletes in carcere esse: homo, inquit, adhuc indemnatus, ut possim vivere

---

[1] Where defendants grew their hair to emphasise their plight (so in bereavement: *C.* 4.1 n.).

[2] *Turdus* = Thrush. The Romans were fond of eating

I can't miss two witticisms of his. He had accom- 19
panied the proconsul Occius Flamma to his province,
Crete. The Greeks began to demand in the theatre
that Sabinus should have the highest powers. Now
in Crete magistrates customarily wear beard and hair
long. Sabinus got up, and gestured for silence.
Then he said: "I have twice carried out this office in
Rome." For he had twice been accused in court.[1]
The Greeks did not understand, but showered bless-
ings on the emperor, and begged that Sabinus should
have the honour a third time too.

Later, the Greeks were offended by the whole 20
troop of camp-followers. These were besieged in a
temple by the whole mob, which demanded that
Sabinus should go to Rome with Turdus—Turdus
being one of the most infamous and hated of them.
Turdus promised to go, so as to get out of the temple.
Sabinus called for silence and said: "I don't propose
to go to the emperor with a tit-bit." [2] Later this was
made a charge against Sabinus at his trial. I remember he made many clever remarks when he had
been brought in from prison to the senate to ask to
receive his daily rations. It was then that he said,
while complaining of hunger: "I don't ask anything
difficult of you, merely that you allow me to die or to
live." He also said: "Do not, I say, listen haughtily
to one smitten by disaster. 'Often he who might
have pitied has to ask for pity.'" [3] Saying that there 21
were rich followers of Sejanus in the jail, he added:
"*I* haven't yet been convicted—yet I have to ask

birds of the thrush-family, especially it seems fieldfares, as
delicacies.
[3] *Frg. Com. Inc.* 76 Ribbeck[2].

parricidas panem rogo. Cum movisset homines
et flebili oratione et diserta, redit tamen ad sales:
rogavit ut in lautumias transferretur: non est, inquit,
quod *quemquam vestrum decipiat nomen ipsum lautumiae;*
illa enim minime lauta res est.   413]

Hoc rettuli ut et ipsum hominem ex aliqua parte
nossetis et illud sciretis, quam difficile esset naturam
suam effugere. Quomodo posset ab illo obtineri ne
in declamationibus iocaretur qui *iocabatur in miseriis*
ac periculis suis, in quibus iocari eum non debuisse quis
nescit, potuisse quis credit?

22   Murredius non degeneravit in hac controversia;
nam colorem stultissimum induxit: voluit, inquit,
et hic sequi fratris exemplum: dum retineo, dum
luctor, visus est patrem cecidisse.

Unum ex his quos audivi declamantis scio Men-
tonem usum non patrono patre sed advocato;
ipsum tyrannicidam induxit dicentem et ⟨hoc⟩ [1]
colore usus est: non iussum se a patre, quia aiebat
incredibile omnibus videri patrem coram tyranno
caedi se iussisse, sed inisse se parricidi consilium ut
per hoc ad amicitiam perveniret, per amicitiam ad
tyrannicidium. Haec eius sententia laudata est

[1] *Supplied by Thomas.*

---

[1] i.e. his well-to-do fellow prisoners.
[2] Used as a prison in Rome, as well as in Syracuse: see
Varr. *Ling. Lat.* 5.151.
[3] Quintilian, on the other hand, thought jokes would be a
good thing in declamation: see 2.10.9 and 6.3.15.

parricides [1] for bread to keep me alive." He moved
people by his pitiful and eloquent speech, but he
returned to jesting: he asked to be transferred to the
stone-quarries.[2] "None of you need be deceived by
the word stone-quarry (*lautumia*): the actual thing is
far from cushy (*lauta*)."

I have related this to you so that you could get to
know the man himself a little, and see how difficult he
found it to escape from his own nature. How could
he be got to steer clear of jokes in his declamations,[3]
this man who used to jest amid his troubles and
dangers? We all know he shouldn't have joked in
those circumstances, but no-one believes that he was
capable of it.

Murredius remained himself in this *controversia*, 22
bringing in a very silly *colour*: "He too wanted to
follow his brother's example; it was while I was holding him back and struggling with him that he looked
to have beaten his father."

Alone of declaimers I heard, I know that Mento
used the father not as defence counsel but merely as
a supporter.[4] He introduced the tyrant-killer himself speaking, and employed this *colour*: he had not
been ordered by his father (because he said everyone
thought it incredible that a father should have ordered
his own beating before a tyrant), but had agreed to a
parricide in order by these means to come into the
tyrant's circle—and thence to the killing of the
tyrant. The following epigram was praised, when he

---

[4] For the distinction see the pseudo-Asconius p. 190.4
Stangl: "One who defends in court is called either *patronus*,
if he is an orator, or *advocatus* if he advises on legal points or
is giving a friend the benefit of his presence."

cum describeret se patri manus adferentem: nihil
in toto tyrannicidio difficilius feci. Et illud dixit:
iam tum factum esset tyrannicidium si me frater non
dereliquisset. Et illud dixit: vos ego tunc respexi,
templa leges rem publicam; nam si me tantum spec-
tassem, facile tyrannidem effugissem illa qua frater
effugerat.

V

414.

PRIVIGNUS AB AVO RAPTUS NOVERCAE

De vi sit actio.

Quidam duos filios sub noverca amisit: dubia
cruditatis et veneni signa insecuta sunt. Tertium filium eius maternus avus rapuit, qui ad
visendos aegros non fuerat admissus. Quaerenti patri per praeconem dixit apud se esse.
Accusatur de vi.

1 IUNI GALLIONIS. Violentus et inpotens senex
hominem liberum sinu meo rapui. Quod servare
tibi difficile est avo dona. Quotiens, miserrume

---

[1] Cf. §1 " I thank my son . . ."
[2] See Bonner, 115. The word *actio* points towards the
Greek δίκη βιαίων. In Rome the *Lex Iulia de vi* would have
been appropriate in *C.* 5.6 (*Dig.* 48.6.3.4), less so here, where

described himself raising his hands against his father: " I had nothing more difficult to do during the whole of my killing of the tyrant." And he also said: " The tyrannicide would have been done on the spot if my brother hadn't left me in the lurch."[1] Again: " Then I thought of you, the temples, the laws, the state. If I had regarded only myself, I should easily have escaped the tyranny—by the route my brother had used."

5

The Boy who was Seized from his Step-mother by his Grandfather

An action may lie for violence.[2]

A man lost his two sons, who had a step-mother: the attendant symptoms suggested either indigestion or poison.[3] The third son was removed by his mother's father, who had not been let in to visit the sick children. When the father made enquiries through a crier, the grand-father said the boy was at his house. He is accused of violence.

For the grandfather

Junius Gallio. A " violent and uncontrollable old man," I snatched a free person away in the fold of my cloak.—Give to grandfather what you find it difficult to keep safe.—How often, wretched child, will you

the child was " raped " only in a very limited sense: observe the scorn of " raptor " in §3 Vibius Rufus.
[3] Cf. *C.* 6.6 n.

THE ELDER SENECA

puer, audies ⟨a⟩ noverca: " quis es tu? fugitive,
reductus es? " *Habui filiam, quamvis iste unum filium
habeat, fecundam.* Quam indulgenter puerperia divisit! Natus est filius, dixit: " filius hic meus est ";
natus est alter, dixit: " hic patris est "; natus est
tertius, dixit: " hic avi est." Cum quaereret iste
filium, erant qui suaderent et dicerent: " tace,
meruit excludi."

CESTI PII. Quam causam rapiendi habui inpotens
senex? Numquid fratres eius occideram? Ignos-
cite mihi si tantum filiae meae mandata narro: hanc
solam ex meis morientem vidi. Habui filiam: de
omnibus meis habeo dicendum " habui." Vaga-
batur lugubri sordidaque praetexta; omnes illius
miserebantur, quosdam etiam dicentis audivi: " quid?
iste puer matrem non habet? patrem non habet?
avum non habet? "

2   ARELLI FUSCI patris. Tres filios filiae meae debes,
unum mihi; *sine apud me nutriatur. Quid times?
ne non admittare cum veneris?* Exposuisse hactenus
iuvat; iam nunc fortuna aut noverca narranda est.
Ut vidit me, haesit complexibus meis puer; oscula-
bar miser, interrogabam de fratribus; dum interrogo, dum fleo, perveneram domum. Rogo ne hoc
causam meam peiorem fecerit, quod ille quem rapui
unicus erat.

---

[1] As though he were some slave.
[2] Cf. Catullus 62.62–4.
[3] As the grandfather had been.

hear your step-mother say: " Who are you ? They've
brought you back again then, runaway ? " [1]—I had a
daughter who was fertile—yet he has only one son.—
How kindly she divided up her offspring! When one
son was born, she said: " This is my son." A second
son was born, and she said: " This is his father's."
A third was born, she said: " This is his grandfather's." [2]—When he was looking for his son, some
people advised me: " Keep quiet—he deserves to be
kept out of the house." [3]

Cestius Pius. What motive had I, an " uncontrollable old man," to take him away ? Had I
killed his brothers ?—Forgive me if I tell you only of
my daughter's last instructions: she was the one
member of my family I saw dying.—I had a daughter;
of all my family I have to say: " I had."—He
wandered the streets in a dirty mourning toga;
everybody pitied him—I even heard people saying:
" What ? This child has no mother ? No father ?
No grandfather ? "

Arellius Fuscus Senior. You are beholden to my 2
daughter for three sons, to me for one. Let him be
reared at my house. What are you afraid of ? Not
being let in when you come to visit ?—So far my
story [4] has given me pleasure; now I must tell of
fortune—or a step-mother.—When the child saw me,
he clung to my embrace; I kissed him sadly, asked
him about his brothers. While I was questioning
him in tears, I found I had arrived home.—I ask that
my case be not weakened by the fact that the son I
took away was the only one.[5]

[4] Of the marriage, and the birth of the children.
[5] He means that this in fact strengthens the case.

3   VOTIENI MONTANI.   Mitte sis [1] praeconem; adice
illi omnia insignia: "hic puer matrem perdidit,
fratres amisit, novercam habet": adfirmo tibi, non
indicabit quisquis faverit.   Erras et vehementer
erras: *filios quos perdidisti non quaeris, quem quaeris
non perdidisti.*   Utra tandem iustior querella est?
pater ab avo unum repetit, avus duos a patre.

VIBI RUFI.   Raptor ille et inpotens, dum moriuntur
nepotes mei, ad ianuam steti: *plus habeo quod avo
quam quod reo timendum sit.*

4   FULVI SPARSI.   Unus perit, alter perit: totiens
fortunam accusas, numquam novercam.   Facinus
indignum! puer ad supplicium indiciva patris quaeritur.   *Ad aegrotantem nepotem veni, non sum admissus:
haec vera vis fuit.*

ARGENTARI.   "Noverca [2] quos conscios habuit?"
Nescio: domi non fui.   Amissa filia volui aliquem   416M
adoptare ex nepotibus, sed aiebam: Quid necesse
est?   Quotiens videre volam, in domum veniam,
quotiens volam, domum abducam.   Agamus tamquam adfines: tres habes filios, dividamus; et vide
quam non inprobam divisionem desiderem: ex

---

[1] mitte sis *Gertz:* mittis.
[2] noverca *Thomas:* per.

---

[1] e.g. his *bulla* (plate of gold hung around neck), as means of
identification: cf. Hor. *Epod.* 5.12.

VOTIENUS MONTANUS. Send the crier, if you will; 3
let him take with him all his finery: [1] " This child has
lost his mother and his brothers; he has a step-
mother." I can tell you, anyone who is on his side
will give no information.[2]—You are wrong, badly
wrong: you are not looking for [3] the sons you have
lost—and you haven't lost the one you are looking
for.—Which is the juster complaint? The father
asks one son back from the grandfather, the grandfather asks two back from the father.

VIBIUS RUFUS. A " violent kidnapper," I stood at
the door while my grandchildren died; I have more
to fear as grandfather than as accused.

FULVIUS SPARSUS. One perished, a second perished; 4
each time you accuse fortune—never the step-
mother.—What a disgrace! They are looking for a
boy to punish him [4]—and the father gets the informer's reward.—I came to see my grandson when
he was ill, and they would not let me in—that is real
violence.

ARGENTARIUS. " Who were the step-mother's accomplices? " *I* don't know—*I* wasn't in the house.—
When my daughter died, I wanted to adopt one of
my grandchildren; but I kept saying to myself:
" Why need I? Whenever I want to see them, I
shall come to the house; whenever I want to, I shall
take them back to mine."—Let us behave like relations. You have three sons—let us divide them.
And see how fair is the division I want. Out of three

---

[2] They won't want him returned: cf. §16.
[3] The father makes no attempt to investigate their deaths;
or perhaps this *quaeris* at least = " miss."
[4] By returning him to the clutches of his step-mother.

tribus unum posco. Utinam omnis quos perdidit quaereret!

5 BLANDI. Cum tradere vellem puerum, nescio quis exclamavit: " puer, nunc peristi." Nihil vobis subtraham; quidni? praeconi quoque omnia indicavi.

MENTONIS. Rapui nepotem, habeo; redderem si pater quaereret.

6 DIVISIO. Montanus Votienus in has quaestiones divisit: an in re vis sit. *Nulla*, inquit, *vis est: quae arma, quam pugnam, quae vulnera habet? Volo* mihi *describi comitatum istius tumultus:* quae turba *est unus* puer *et unus senex? Rapuisti, inquit, filium meum: immo nepotem suum sustulit, immo venientem non potuit excludere.* An, si pro illo fuit fieri vim quoi facta dicitur, non teneatur qui fecit. Vis iniuriosa damnatur; solet enim esse et salutaris. *Cum latrones aliquem obsiderent, si* perfodissem villam, *armata manu coniugem liberos* eius *rapuissem,* accusari posset *beneficium meum? Et medici alligant et corporibus nostris ut medeantur vim adferunt.* An pro illo fuerit rapi. Hoc loco accusatio novercae et insectatio patris tam patienter suos perdentis.

7 Gallio et illam quaestionem fecit et prius sumendam quaestionem putavit ex persona quam ex re:

---

[1] And not the step-mother.
[2] The raising of a *turba* was also covered by the *Lex Iulia* (*Dig.* 48.6.3.1).
[3] Whether it *was* in the child's interest: see §8.

I ask only for one.—I only wish he were looking for all the sons he lost!

BLANDUS. When I was ready to hand over the boy, 5 someone shouted: "Now you've had it, boy."—I won't keep anything from you—why should I? I told even the crier everything.

MENTO. I took my grandson, and have him. I would give him back if it were the father [1] who is looking for him.

Division

Votienus Montanus divided into the following 6 questions: Is there violence in this case? "There is none. What weapons, what fight, what wounds does the case present? I wish someone would describe to me the crowd involved in this riot: what sort of a mob [2] is one boy and one old man? 'You kidnapped my child.' On the contrary, he took his own grandson: or rather he could not keep him out when he came." If it was in the interests of the alleged victim for the violence to be done, is its author liable? "Injurious violence gets condemned—but violence may also be salutary. When robbers lay siege to someone's house, could my good deed be subject to accusation if I broke into the house and took his wife and children away by force of arms? Doctors too tie people up, and apply force to our limbs in order to heal." *Was* it in this child's interests to be removed? Here he accused the step-mother, and inveighed against a father who lost his children with so little protest.

Gallio did pose this question.[3] But he had another 7 one, drawn from the person, which he thought should

an cum avo nepotis nomine agi possit; non magis, inquit, quam cum patre fili nomine, non magis quam cum matre. *Habet sua iura natura, et hoc inter avum patremque interest, quod avo suos servare licet, patri et occidere. Non potes,* inquit, sic *mecum agere tamquam cum alieno,* ut dicas: " quid tibi cum illo? quis es tu? " cuius intestati filius tuus heres futurus est, quem dementem alligaturus est. Quaedam iura non lege sed natura nobis attributa. Nepotem suum avus peccantem aliquid et inter pueriles iocos petulantius lascivientem feriet, nec iniuriarum quisquam cum illo aget.

8   Et ultimam illam Gallio fecit, cum tractasset illa: " licet mihi ut prosim vim facere," deinde: " huic profuit ": an avo ignoscendum sit cum pro nepote adfectu ablatus fecerit. Hoc loco tractavit quam indignum esset damnari illum ob hoc.

Latro duas ultumas quaestiones aliter posuit et plus conplexus est: etiamsi vim fecit, an tamen damnari non possit si bono animo fecerit; ⟨deinde: an bono animo fecerit.⟩ [1] Ait enim et de animo fieri controversiam avo et dicere patrem: *non ut nepotem servaret fecit, sed ut infamaret uxorem* meam *tamquam veneficam, me* tamquam *veneficae emancipatum,* quoi male liberi sui committerentur.

---

[1] *Supplied by Müller after Schultingh.*

---

[1] i.e. act as my *curator (C.* 2.3 n.).

417

be taken before the one drawn from the circumstances: Can one litigate with a grandfather in the
name of a grandson? " No—any more than with a
father or with a mother in the name of a son. Nature
has rights of its own, and the only difference between
father and grandfather is that a grandfather may
keep his grandsons safe, the father may even kill his
sons. You cannot," he went on, " sue me as though
I were an outsider, saying: ' What have you to do
with him? Who are you?' After all, if I die
intestate, your son will be my heir. If I go mad, he
will be my restrainer.[1] Some rights are given to us
not by law but by nature. A grandfather can strike
his grandson if he does something naughty and rags
about too violently in his childish play, without anyone suing him for damages."

After dealing with the point that he was allowed to 8
do violence in order to do good, then with the point
that it *was* to the good of the child, Gallio posed his
last question: Should this grandfather be forgiven for
something he did when carried away by his feelings
for his grandson? Here he dealt with the topic of
how wicked it was for him to be condemned for this.

Latro put the last two questions differently, and got
more in. Even if he did do violence, can he nevertheless be convicted if he acted from good motives?
Next: *Did* he act from good motives? He said that
the father's dispute with the grandfather turned on
motive, the father asserting that the grandfather
acted not to save his grandson but to slander the
present wife as a poisoner, and the father as a
poisoner's catspaw to whom it was wrong to leave
custody of his own children.

9   Colore ergo Latro hoc eodem usus est pro patre,
ut diceret *ne viva quidem uxore* bene *sibi cum socero
convenisse, mortua vero professas inimicitias* illum ges-
sisse secum. *Languente puero venisse* illum *cum* 418
convicio, cum vociferatione, nefaria et dicentem et
auspicantem: auctores amicos fuisse [1] ne admitteret
hominem non ad officium nepotum sed ad invidiam
et contumeliam generi venientem, *qui ad sanos nepotes
numquam dignatus esset accedere;* medicos vero suasisse
ne veniret et puerum confunderet et impleret
suspicionibus.

10   Silonis Pompei color fuit, ut Latroni videbatur, qui
controversiae repugnaret; dixit enim venisse avum
ad inbecillum puerum. Ad aegros non semper admitti, utique ad eos qui graviter aegrotent; saepe
et patrem non admissum; sic avo quoque intempestive
venienti dictum: "nunc non potes"; statim cum
convicio abisse. In altero idem fecisse. Latro
aiebat hunc colorem optumum esse si res ita esset,
sed recipi non posse, quia ponatur: "non est admissus"; sub hoc themate intellegere nos non hoc
illi dictum: "nunc non potes," sed "ex toto non
potes."

11   Gallio utrumque miscuit et hoc colore, qui videri
potest alioqui thema evertere, paratius [2] usus est.
Dictum est, inquit, illi: "Quiescit puer, paulum
commorare; medici vetuerunt quemquam admitti.

---

[1] fuisse *Bursian:* se.
[2] paratius *Müller:* partius.

---

[1] Latro's and Silo's *colours:* "this *colour*" is Silo's.

This, then, was Latro's *colour* for the father, to say 9
that even when his first wife was alive, he had not got
on well with his father-in-law, while after her death
the father-in-law had been an acknowledged enemy.
When the child was ill, the father-in-law came
abusing him, shouting, his words and intentions
abominable. He had been advised by his friends not
to admit a man who came not to do his duty by his
grandsons but to insult his son-in-law and make him
odious: after all, when his grandsons had been well,
he had never condescended to come and see them.
The doctors, further, had advised that the grandfather should not come and upset the boy by filling
him with suspicions.

Pompeius Silo's *colour* was, in Latro's view, one that 10
conflicted with the theme: he said the grandfather
had come to see the child at a time when he lacked
strength. Admission to sick beds is not always
granted, especially where the patient is gravely ill:
often even the father is not admitted. So when the
grandfather came so inopportunely, he was told:
" Not now," and he went away at once with abuse on
his lips. The same thing happened in the case of the
second child. Latro said this was an excellent *colour*
if it conformed with the facts, but that it could not be
accepted because we have in the theme: " he was
not admitted "; and with this theme one has to
understand that what was said to the grandfather was
not " Not now " but " Not at all."

Gallio mixed both [1] together, and used this *colour*, 11
which may otherwise be thought to subvert the
theme, more skilfully. " The grandfather was told:
' The boy is resting, wait a little while. The doctors

Scitis solere illos dicere: nec si pater venerit."
Protinus iste clamare coepit: "testor me non admitti" et tantum non tabellis signatis denuntiare.
Avum distuleram, accusatorem exclusi. Iterum,
inquit, venit cum convicio: "iam unum occidistis,
alterum occiditis." Nihil est miserius quam ubi
aliquoi ex miseria sua invidia quaeritur.

Non est admissus, cum diceret se nepotem suum 41⁹
non videre velle sed inspicere.

**sic egit: veni non ut istum accusarem sed ut me
defenderem.

†Gallio† hoc colore usus est: *non admisi* avum
quia dictum erat mihi hoc illum animo venire, ut raperet.

12   Ex altera parte colorem hunc Cestius induxit:
timuisse se de puero. ⟨Nec⟩ [1] frustra, inquit: duos
occiderat noverca. Et ait: vellem ad vos nocentior
venirem reus, vellem tres haberem.[2]

Argentarius hoc colore usus est: rogatum a puero
avum. Negabat, inquit, posse se vivere si in illa
relinqueretur domo.

Hispanus hoc colore usus est: affectu se ablatum.
Sustuli, inquit, nepotem meum; non potui satiari
osculis, non potui ab illo tam cito distrahi. Nolite
mirari: post longum tempus illum videram.

---

[1] *Supplied by Faber.*
[2] haberem *Kuhn, Gertz:* raperem.

have forbidden anyone to be let in—you know how they tend to say: " Not even if his father comes." ' He at once started to make a row: ' I call you to witness I am not let in,' and all but summoned me in due form. I had put off the grandfather—but it was an accuser I proved to have kept out. He came a second time, with abuse: ' You have already killed one— now you're killing another.' A man's misery is at its worst when it is made a means of getting him disliked."

He was not let in, for he said he wanted to examine his grandson, not see him.[1]

** pleaded like this: " I have come here not to accuse this man but to defend myself."

**'s *colour* was: " I did not let in the grandfather because I had been told that he was coming with the intention of taking the child."

On the other side, Cestius introduced this *colour*: 12 he had been frightened for the child. " Reasonably enough: the step-mother had killed two." And he said: " I could wish that I came before you a more guilty defendant, that I had three of my grandsons at home."

Argentarius used this *colour*: the grandfather had been asked by the child to take him: " He said he could not stay alive if he were left in that house."

Hispanus used this *colour*: he had been carried away by emotion. " I took up my grandson; I could not have enough of kissing him. I could not be torn from him so soon. Don't be surprised: it was a long time since I had seen him."

---

[1] The last sentence seems to represent a fragment of a different *colour*.

13   Albucius hoc colore usus est, ut diceret noluisse
illum in tam infausta domo educari, ex qua duo iam
fratres eius elati essent; ⟨ei⟩ qui postea decessit inter
causas moriendi casum fratris fuisse. Et servavit
hunc colorem, ne quid in novercam, ne quid in patrem
diceret; aiebat iustissimum futurum avum si tantum
defendere se voluisset. Quid ergo? quare rapuisti?
Amabam; huic maxime ab initio animum meum
addixeram. In domo vestra nihil praeter ipsam
domum timui. Si apud me duo decessissent, ex
domo illum mea transtulissem.

14   ⟨Montanus Votienus⟩ [1] Marcellum Marcium aiebat 420M
sic narrasse: Puer me secutus est. Non criminor
vobis illum; quidquid est, ⟨meo⟩ [2] potius quam illius
periculo fiat: ego rapui. " Ubi est? " inquit.
Vivit, salvus est: veni et cum voles aspice. " Redde "
inquit. †Suo ego asper;† [3] age, monstrabo si vis
quis ante me tibi filios abstulerit.

Varius Geminus eundem sensum dixit: *Quae est
ista* [aut] [4] *tam sera pietas, tam praepostera? Quaerere
tuos a tertio incipis.*

15   Montanus Votienus, homo rarissumi etiamsi non
emendatissimi ingeni, vitium suum, quod in orationibus non evitat, in scholasticis quoque evitare non
potuit, sed in orationibus, quia laxatior est materia,

---

[1] *Supplied by Bursian, Kiessling.*
[2] *Supplied by Nicotius.*
[3] *I have translated Müller's* non ego asper.
[4] *Deleted by the editor, comparing E.*

Albucius' *colour* was to say that he hadn't wanted 13
the child to be brought up in so ill-omened a house,
one from which his two brothers had already been
carried out to burial; among the reasons for the
death of the second was the fate of his brother. And
he kept to this *colour*, in such a way as to attack
neither the step-mother nor the father; he said the
grandfather would be on very firm ground if he was
content merely to defend himself. " ' Well then, why
did you take him?' I loved him; it was on this
boy that I had particularly set my heart from the
beginning. In your house I feared nothing except
the house itself. If two children had died in *my*
house, I should have moved the third elsewhere."

Votienus Montanus said that Marcius Marcellus' 14
narrative went like this: " The boy followed me.
I'm not trying to incriminate him in your eyes.
Whatever happens, may the peril be mine rather than
his—it was I who took him. ' Where is he?' says
his father. He is alive and well; come and look at
him whenever you wish.[1] ' Give him back.' *I* am
not a cruel man: come, I will show you if you like who
it was [2] who removed your sons, before me."

Varius Geminus had the same idea: " What is this
affection, so late in the day, so perverse? You look
for your children, starting only with the third."

Votienus Montanus, a man of rare though not fault- 15
less talent, could not avoid in school either the fault
that waylays him in his speeches; but in his speeches,
the material being more diffuse, one notices repetition

---

[1] The grandfather rubs in the contrast with the father's
behaviour.
[2] The step-mother, by killing them.

minus earundem rerum adnotatur iteratio; in scholasticis si eadem sunt quae dicuntur, quia pauca
sunt notantur. Memini illum pro Galla Numisia
apud centumviros tirocinium ponere. Ex uncia heres
erat patris sui Galla: obiciebatur illi veneficium.
Dixit rem disertissumam et omnibus saeculis dura-
turam, qua nescio an quicquam melius in eiusmodi
genere causarum dictum sit: uncia nec filiae debetur
nec veneficae. Non fuit contentus; adiecit: in
paternis tabulis filiae locus aut suus debetur aut
nullus. Etiamnunc adiecit: relinquis nocenti ni-
16 mium, innocenti parum. Ne sic quidem satiare se
potuit; adiecit: non potest filia tam anguste paternis
tabulis adhaerere, quas aut totas possidere debet aut
totas perdere, et plura multo, quae memoria non 421
repeto; ex eis quaedam in orationem contulit et
alia plura quam dixerat adiecit. Nihil non ex eis
bellum est, si solum sit; nihil non rursus ex eis alteri
obstat.

Idem in hac declamatione fecisse eum memini.
Erras, inquit, pater, et vehementer erras: quos
perdidisti non quaeris, quem quaeris non perdidisti.
Deinde: puer iste ⟨si⟩ [1] invenitur perit. Deinde:
quisquis puero favet ne inveniatur optet. Deinde:
puer, nisi avum sequitur, fratres secuturus est;

---

[1] *Supplied by Bursian.*

less: in declamation if the same things get said again, it shows, just because there are few things said. I recall that he made his début speaking for Galla Numisia before the centumviral court.[1] Galla was heiress to a twelfth of her father's estate, and was accused of poisoning him. Montanus said something very smart, that will never be forgotten— something perhaps unsurpassed in this sort of case: " A twelfth is the due neither of a daughter nor of a poisoner." [2] He wasn't satisfied, but added: " In her father's will a daughter should get her proper place—or no place at all." And still he went on: " You leave something which is too much if she is guilty, too little if she is innocent." Even then he 16 wasn't content—he went on: " A daughter cannot find so narrow a place in her father's will—she ought to have it all, or lose it all." And he said much more that I don't remember. He brought some of these sayings into his published speech, while adding much that he had not said. Every one of the dicta is pretty —or would be if it stood by itself; each one in turn gets in the way of the next.

I remember he did the same in this declamation. " You are wrong, father," he said, " badly wrong: you are not looking for the sons you have lost—and you haven't lost the one you are looking for." [3] Next: " This boy dies, if he is found." Then: " Whoever wishes the boy well should pray he may not be found." Then: " Unless the boy follows his

---

[1] Which dealt largely with testamentary cases.
[2] As a daughter she should get more; if she was a budding poisoner, she should have been left less.
[3] Above, §3.

desine quaerere quem si inveneris sic perdes ut invenire non possis. Et deinde: rapuit istum avos ne raperet noverca. Et deinde: unum tantum pater
17 ex liberis suis quaerit qui salvus est. Glycon hunc sensum semel dixit, sed genere corrupto: τοῦτο τὸ παιδίον ὅταν εὑρεθῇ τότε ἀπολεῖται. *Habet hoc Montanus vitium: sententias suas repetendo corrumpit; dum non est contentus unam rem semel bene dicere, efficit ne bene dixerit.* Et *propter hoc* et propter alia quibus orator potest poetae similis videri *solebat Scaurus Montanum inter oratores Ovidium vocare; nam et Ovidius nescit quod bene cessit relinquere.* Ne multa referam quae Montaniana Scaurus vocabat, uno hoc contentus ero: *cum Polyxene esset abducta ut ad tumulum Achillis immolaretur, Hecuba dicit:*

cinis ipse sepulti
in genus hoc pugnat.

Poterat hoc *contentus esse; adiecit:*

tumulo quoque sensimus hostem.

Nec hoc contentus est; *adiecit:*   422

Aeacidae fecunda fui.

Aiebat autem *Scaurus rem veram: non minus magnam virtutem esse scire dicere quam scire desinere.*

grandfather, he will end up following his brothers.
Stop looking for him; if you find him, you will lose
him—in such a way that you can never find him."
And then: " His grandfather took him—in case his
step-mother took him." And then: " The only one
of his sons the father is looking for is the one who is
safe." Glycon expressed this idea once, though his 17
expression shows bad taste: " This child will be lost
when he is found." Montanus' trouble is that he
spoils his own epigrams by repetition; because he is
not content to say a thing well once, he in the end
does not say it well at all. For this and other reasons
that make the orator comparable with the poet,
Scaurus used to call Montanus the Ovid among
orators; for Ovid too is incapable of leaving well
alone. Not to give many examples of what Scaurus
called " Montanisms," I will content myself with one:
when Polyxena had been led away to be sacrificed at
the tomb of Achilles, Hecuba says:[1]

> " Even the ashes of the buried man
> Fight our family."

That might have sufficed him. He added:

> " We felt our enemy, even in his grave."

He wasn't satisfied even with this, but went on:

> " I was fertile—for Achilles."

Scaurus was quite right in saying that to know how to
stop is as important a quality as to know how to speak.

[1] *Met.* 13.503 *seq.*

THE ELDER SENECA

VI

Filia Conscia in Veneno Privigni

Venefica torqueatur donec conscios indicet.

Quidam mortua uxore ex qua filium habebat, duxit alteram uxorem et ex ea filiam sustulit. Decessit adulescens; accusavit maritus novercam venefici. Damnata cum torqueretur dixit consciam sibi filiam esse. Petitur puella ad supplicium. Pater defendit.

1 Cesti Pii. Non est quod putetis has lacrimas aut filiae esse aut reae: fratrem ⟨flet⟩.[1] *Non prodesset tibi, puella, ne hoc quidem, quod te frater amavit, nisi mater odisset.* Hoc me occidisti, noverca, quod scisti consciam eligere. Paene dixi: ante actam eius vitam excutiamus.

Fulvi Sparsi. *Nefaria mulier, filiae quoque noverca, ne mori quidem potuit nisi ut occideret. Inter gladiatores quoque victoris condicio pessuma est cum moriente pugnantis. Nullum magis adversarium timeas quam qui vivere non potest, occidere potest.*

423M

---

[1] *Supplied by Bursian.*

---

[1] Bonner (p. 112) argues that this provision, though perhaps not a part of the *Lex Cornelia* on poisoning, reflects practice under the empire. But normally a free person could not be tortured. For the " law " see Quintilian 9.2.81 (applied to budding tyrants), and especially Calp. Flacc. 12, *Decl.* 381, two exactly similar cases (see Bornecque, *Déclamations*, 30 *seq.*).

[2] This being the real defence.

6

THE DAUGHTER INVOLVED IN THE POISONING OF THE STEP-SON

A woman who poisons shall be tortured till she reveals her accomplices.[1]

A man lost his wife, by whom he had a son, married again and raised a daughter by his new wife. The youth died; the husband accused the step-mother of poisoning him. On conviction she was tortured and said her daughter was her accomplice. The girl is to be executed. Her father defends her.

For the father

CESTIUS PIUS. Don't think these tears are shed for 1 her mother or because she is guilty; she is weeping for her brother.—If your mother did not hate you,[2] girl, it would be no help to you even that your brother loved you.—You killed me, step-mother, because you knew how to choose your accomplice.[3]—I almost said: let us examine her past record.[4]

FULVIUS SPARSUS. Wicked woman, step-mother even to her own daughter, she could not even die without killing. Even among gladiators the worst position for a victor is to have to fight a dying opponent. Fear no adversary more than one who cannot live—but can kill.

---

[3] Point unclear.
[4] A normal gambit, here inappropriate because of the child's age: cf. §14 " I reproached her . . ."

THE ELDER SENECA

2   VIBI GALLI. *Concitatissuma est in morte rabies, et desperatione ultima in furorem animus impellitur. Quaedam ferae tela ipsa commordent et ad mortis auctorem per vulnera sua ruunt.* Abscisa missione *gladiator quem armatus fugerat nudus insequitur. Praecipitati non quod impulit tantum trahunt sed quod occurrit,* et *naturali quodam deploratae mentis adfectu morientibus gratissimum est commori.*

3   VOTIENI MONTANI. Dum filium vindico, ubi gravissime mihi noceri posset ostendi. *Veneficio simile mendacium!* Si incredibile est parricidium ⟨in noverca⟩,[1] in sorore creditis? Non timeo ne quis hoc in sorore credat quod ego vix probavi in noverca. Natam mihi filiam quasi futuram pacis obsidem sustuli; aiebam: dum matris meminit, obliviscetur novercae. At illa *dum novercae meminit matris oblita est.* "Filia" inquit "mihi conscia est." Post hanc vocem remissa putares tormenta: similis facta torquenti est. Soror fratri venenum dedit? Quamdiu luctati sumus ut crederetur noverca privigno dedisse! Noverca, quod volueras consecuta es: damnasse iam paenitet.

    [1] *Supplied here by Opitz.*

---

    [1] Sen. *Agam.* 202: "mors misera non est commori cum quo velis."

    [2] I showed that I felt strongly for my children; my wife took advantage of this by hurting me by way of my daughter.

    [3] In the previous trial.—Montanus again repeats himself (*C.* 9.5.15): cf. also below "How long . . ."

VIBIUS GALLUS. Madness is most violent at the 2
point of death, and its last despair drives a mind to
fury. Some beasts snap at the very shaft that hits
them, and rush on amidst their own wounds at the
author of their death. When his chance of release is
removed, a gladiator will pursue naked the opponent
he had fled under arms. People falling down a cliff
take with them not only what pushed them but anything in their way. And, by a feeling natural to a
mind that is despaired of, the dying find it very
pleasant to have a companion in death.[1]

VOTIENUS MONTANUS. In avenging my son, I 3
showed where I could be hurt most.[2]—This lie is like a
poisoning!—In a step-mother parricide is incredible;
can you believe it of a sister? I have no fears that
anyone will believe of a sister what I could scarcely
prove in a step-mother.[3]—I acknowledged the
daughter born to me, as a hostage who would ensure
peace. I said to myself: " Remembering she is a
mother, she will forget she is a step-mother." In fact,
she remembered she was a step-mother and forgot she
was a mother.—" My daughter is my accomplice,"
she says. After such a speech you would imagine the
tortures were relaxed—she has become like the
torturer.[4]—Did the sister give her brother poison?
How long we had to struggle to get people to believe
a step-mother gave it to her step-son!—Step-mother,
you have got what you wanted; I am sorry now that
I had you convicted.

[4] Cf. *Decl.* p. 426.17 Ritter: " If nothing else, she is torturing the father by her information [read *indicio*]." Also §6
"*I* began to be the victim . . ."; §18 "She found a way . . .";
§20 " Perhaps so that she could exact . . ."

THE ELDER SENECA

4   ARGENTARI. Facio rem, iudices, non novam: liberos meos a noverca vindico. *Peto ne, quia filium vindi-
cavi, filiam perdam. Nisi succurritis, noverca vicit, ego
victus sum.* Duxi nescio peiorem uxorem an novercam. Hoc mihi carior est quod tam invisa matri
fuit.

CORNELI HISPANI. Si conscia esset, neminem
expectarem: scitis quemadmodum veneficam oderim. 424
Instabam tormentis, aiebam: morere peius quam
occidisti; non satis mihi ardere ignes videbantur, non
satis insidere verbera; dixi: si quid adicere tormentis
tuis possum, ⟨faciam; possum⟩,[1] puto: iubebo
filiam adferri; vocet hoc aliquis! Matrem quid
expavisti, puella? quid ad sinus meos refugisti?
quid extimuisti tamquam novercam?

5   MARULLI. *Ne inter supplicia quidem desit occidere:*
et hanc quisquam putet non potuisse venenum sine
conscia dare? Puella quae occidisse fratrem dicitur quid ante peccavit? Noverca quoque ante
privignum occidit quam filiam. Haec bonae spei
est; quaeritis argumentum? matri suae non placet.

ARELLI FUSCI. Etiam cineribus tuis infesta est

---

[1] *Supplied by Müller.*

ARGENTARIUS. Judges, I am doing something 4 familiar: I am defending my children from a step-mother.—What I ask is that I should not have to lose my daughter because I avenged my son.—If you [1] don't come to my rescue, the step-mother has won, I am defeated.—The woman I married—I don't know if she is more wicked as wife or step-mother.— The girl is the dearer to me that she was so hated by her mother.

CORNELIUS HISPANUS. If she were implicated, I should not wait for anyone [2]—you know how I hate a poisoner.—I pressed on with the tortures, saying: " Die more cruelly than you killed." The flames did not, to my mind, blaze fiercely enough, the lashes sink in sufficiently far. I said: " If I can add any-thing to your torments, I will do it. I think I can; I will order your daughter to be brought. Summon her here, someone. Why are you terrified of your mother, girl? Why flee to my bosom? Why dread her—as though she were *your* step-mother?

MARULLUS. Even amidst her punishment she did 5 not cease to kill: can it be doubted if such a woman was capable of giving poison without an accomplice? —This girl who is said to have killed her brother— what wrong has she done before? Even the step-mother killed her step-son before her daughter.[3]— The girl is a good prospect. You want proof? She displeases her mother.

ARELLIUS FUSCUS. Your step-mother threatens

---

[1] Judges.

[2] i.e. to accuse (the daughter).

[3] For the need to work slowly up to a parricide, see *C.* 7.3.1 n., and below §7 " Even if she . . .''

noverca; quod unum potest, persequitur sororem
tuam. Quid potest adhuc nosse nisi fratrem?
Prosit illi apud vos quod illam pater laudat, et *prosit quod
talis mater accusat.*

6　MENTONIS. Non misereris huius? miserior est
quam frater: ille habuit sine dubio novercam,
⟨haec matrem noverca peiorem⟩.[1]　" *Conscia* " inquit
" *est filia.*"　*Ego torqueri coepi, noverca torquere.*
Consecuta es, mulier, quod voluisti: solus omnium
magis sensi novercam cum perdidi.

PORCI LATRONIS. *Habui filium tam bonum ut illum
amare posset* etiam *noverca, nisi in eam incidisset quae
posset etiam filiam odisse.*　Hucine saecula recciderunt
ut parricidium puellare sit?　Ita si magnitudinem　425
rei non intellegit, num est idonea parricidio?　" Sed
veneficae " inquit " filia est."　Si parentes inspi-
ciuntur, cur non potius patri videatur similis, cui
placet, quam matri, cui displicet?　Denique non
recuso quo minus in illa vel matris exigatur imitatio:
illa cum huius aetatis esset nec noverca erat nec
venefica.

7　ALBUCI SILI. Duxi uxorem nullis adhuc in-
quinatam fabulis, nec miror innocentem tunc fuisse:
adhuc puella erat.

BLANDI. Ut scelerata sit, nempe matri suae
similis est; ante veneficium oportet faciat quam parricidium.　" Filia " inquit " conscia est."　Di te

---

[1] *Supplied by Müller after Spengel.*

---

[1] She cannot know how to poison; but she knows—and
loves—her brother.

[2] i.e. I felt what she could do on the point of death; most
step-mothers do their dirty work while alive.

even your ashes; she harries your sister—it is all she
can do.—What can she know, at her age, except her
brother? [1]—May it be to her credit in your eyes that
her father praises her, and that she is accused by a
mother of such a character.

MENTO. Don't you pity her? She is more un- 6
happy than her brother; *he*, it is true, had a step-
mother, *she* has a mother who is worse than a step-
mother.—" My daughter is my accomplice." *I*
began to be the victim, the step-mother the torturer.
—Woman, you have got what you wanted; alone of
all men, I felt a step-mother more when I lost her. [2]

PORCIUS LATRO. I had a son so good that even a
step-mother could have loved him—but he happened
on one capable of hating even her daughter.—Has it
come to this, that parricide is a girl's crime?—So if
she does not understand the magnitude of the matter,
does that make her suitable for parricide?—" But she
is a poisoner's daughter." If we are going to review
her parents, why should she not be thought to
resemble her father, who loves her, rather than her
mother, who hates her? Still, I don't reject the idea
of seeing in her the image even of her mother; *she* at
this age was neither step-mother nor poisoner. [3]

ALBUCIUS SILUS. I married a woman as yet un- 7
besmirched by any talk; and it is not surprising she
was innocent then—she was only a child. [4]

BLANDUS. Even if she is wicked, surely she
resembles her mother—and so has to do a poisoning
before a parricide.—" My daughter is my accom-

---

[3] Cf. *Decl.* p. 425.25 Ritter: " People of this age don't sin
—even when they are ⟨future⟩ step-mothers."
[4] As is the daughter.

perdant! etiam dum torqueris, occidis. *Servus tortus Catonem conscium furti dixit.* Quid agitis? *utrum plus creditis tormentis an Catoni?*

BUTEONIS. Si conscius a te, puella, quaereretur, nominato patrem. *Quod noverca tam sero, puella tam cito?* " Filia " inquit " conscia est." Male pereas! at ego te putabam unius novercam.

8 TRIARI. " Filia " inquit " tua conscia est." Videbatur sibi post hanc vocem vicisse. Amissum fratrem flevit in funere, totius populi lacrimas suis expressit; itaque illam noverca peius perire voluit quam privignum. " Filia " inquit " conscia est." Hoc ultumum fuit novercae veneficium.

Q. HATERI. Succurrite, quaeso, ne, cum torta sit quia filium meum occiderat, filiam etiam dum torquetur occiderit. Liberos effero semper unius mulieris aut mendacio aut veneno. Non flet quantum reae satis est. Quemadmodum illi extorquebo 426 lacrimas? Adferte mihi imaginem fratris; videte subito desiderio fletus concitatos: numquid talem vultum cum mater torqueretur habuit?

9 Pars altera. TRIARI. Si odissemus te, pateremur cum eiusmodi filia vivere. *Quarundam ferarum catuli cum rabie nascuntur; venena statim radicibus pestifera sunt.* Quantum illi ad scelera aetatis adiecit quod

---

[1] See on *C.* 10.1.8.
[2] Cf. *Decl.* p. 426.2 Ritter. The point of what follows is that the step-mother was being crueller towards her natural child than she had been towards her step-son.
[3] The accuser speaks for the state.
[4] Contrast *Decl.* p. 425.26 Ritter: " Small serpents do no harm "!

plice." God damn you! Even while you are tortured, you go on killing.—A slave under torture said Cato was implicated in a theft.[1] What are you on about? Do you prefer to believe the torture—or Cato?

BUTEO. If they torture *you* to find your accomplice, child, name your father.—Does a child do so promptly what a step-mother did so late in the day? —" My daughter is my accomplice." Curse you! I thought you step-mother to *one* child.

TRIARIUS. " Your daughter is my accomplice." 8 She thought she had won after she said that.—She wept for her lost brother at his funeral, and by her tears evoked the tears of the whole people.[2] That is why the step-mother wanted her to die more cruelly than her step-son.—" My daughter is my accomplice." This was the last time the step-mother poisoned.

QUINTUS HATERIUS. Come to my aid, I beg of you: or else, having been tortured for killing my son, she will kill my daughter too under the torture.—I keep burying my children thanks to the lie or the poison of a single woman.—She does not weep enough for a defendant. How make her cry? Bring me the portrait of her brother. See the weeping that her sudden sense of loss excites; did she look like that when her mother was tortured?

The other side

TRIARIUS. If we[3] hated you, we should let you 9 live with a daughter like that.—Some beasts have cubs that are savage from birth;[4] some plants are poisonous from the roots up.—Surely the fact that she

illam noverca peperit? *Quid illa quae fratrem in moram sequentis patris sparsit? Habes exemplum quod et sorori conveniat et virgini.*

10 DIVISIO. Cestius in duas partes coniecturam divisit, et primum quaesiit an illi conscia opus fuerit; deinde: si opus est aut fuit, an hanc habuerit. Non servavit autem modum; nam et illum locum diu tractavit: non posse sororem in mortem fratris impelli, et interim tam puellam voluit videri ut nulli esset idonea ministerio. Itaque elegantissime deridebat Montanus Votienus in hac controversia ineptias rhetorum, quod sic declamarent tamquam haec quae nominata est infans esset, nec intellegerent si talis esset ne futuram quidem ream. Itaque hoc debemus, inquit, nobis proponere: puellam eius aetatis in qua †et torta† credibile scelus. Illud quidem intolerabile esse aiebat: induxerat Cestius matrem dicentem filiae: " da fratri venenum," ⟨filiam respondentem: "mater, quid est venenum?"⟩ [1]

11 Triarius multo rem magis ineptam, quia non invenit illam sed conrupit; nam ex Cesti sententia 427 traxit; induxerat novercam dicentem: " do [2] fratri

---

[1] *Supplied by Bursian.*
[2] do *ed.*: da.

---

[1] The precedent as both (cf. *Decl.* p. 425.27 " virgo . . . soror ") is Medea, who tore her brother Absyrtos to pieces and left his limbs to delay the pursuit of Aeetes (Cic. *Imp. Pomp.* 22; Sen. *Med.* 173).
[2] The discussion of the facts of the case. See *Decl.* p. 426.3 Ritter for such a discussion.

was daughter of a step-mother gave her an advance in years as far as crime goes?—What of the woman who scattered her brother about to delay the pursuit of her father? There is a precedent to fit both sister and virgin.[1]

Division

Cestius divided the " conjecture "[2] into two parts, 10 first asking: Did she need an accomplice? Next, if she has or had need of one, did she use this girl as one? But he kept no sense of proportion: for he spent a long time treating the point that a sister cannot be driven to kill her brother, while at the same time wanting to make her out so young as to be incapable of rendering any kind of assistance. Hence in this *controversia* the very pretty play that Votienus Montanus made of the stupidities of the rhetoricians: they declaimed as though the accused were an infant,[3] not realising that if that was so she could not even stand trial. " Thus what we must represent to ourselves," he said, " is a girl of such an age as to make her committing a crime conceivable." He described as insupportable Cestius' picture of the mother saying to her daughter: " Give your brother poison " and the girl replying: " Mummy, what is poison? "[4]

Triarius said something that was much more silly— 11 because he didn't invent it, merely made it worse. Drawing on Cestius' epigram, he had pictured the

---

[3] Cf. *Decl.* p. 425.25 Ritter: " Bring out the defendant—from the lap of her nurse " (so below §13 " Nurse, lift up the accused ").

[4] So too *Decl.* p. 426.13 Ritter.

venenum"; fecit illam respondentem: " mater, et mihi da." Quid enim est tam absurdum quam matrem sic locutam cum puella: " do [1] fratri venenum"?

Non ferebat nec illam Triari sententiam, qua aliter Haterius usus est, cum ad epilogum pervenisset: Hoc loco debebat reus flere; num flet puella? Inveniam quemadmodum fleat; aliquis hoc imaginem fratris. Illa enim, si tam puella est ut dicat: " mater, quid est venenum?", non potest tantae pietatis esse ut eam imago fratris in lacrimas concitet.

Tantus autem error est in omnibus quidem studiis, ⟨sed⟩ [2] maxime in eloquentia, cuius regula incerta est, ut vitia quidam sua et intellegant et ament. 12 Cestius pueriliter se dixisse intellegebat: " mater, quid est venenum?"; deridebat enim Murredium qui hanc sententiam imitatus in epilogo, cum adloqui coepisset puellam et diceret: " compone te in periclitantium habitum, profunde lacrimas, manus ad genua dimitte, rea es," fecerat respondentem puellam: pater, quid est rea? Et aiebat Cestius: quod si ad deridendum me dixit, homo venustus fuit, et ego nunc scio me ineptam sententiam dicere; multa autem dico non quia mihi placent sed quia audientibus placitura sunt.

13   Et illud Rufi Vibi tolerabilius aiebat esse, sed et ipsum aliqua obiurgatione dignum: dixerat in

---

[1] do *ed.*: da.
[2] *Supplied by C. F. W. Müller, Gertz.*

step-mother saying: " I am giving your brother poison "; and then he made her reply: " Mother, give me some too." For what is so absurd as for a mother to say to her daughter: " I am giving your brother poison? "

Nor would he stand either for Triarius' epigram—adapted by Haterius [1]—at the start of the epilogue: " At this point an accused ought to have been crying. *Does* the girl cry? I shall discover a way to make her. Someone, bring here the picture of her brother." For if she is so much of a child that she can say: " Mother, what is poison? ", she cannot be so affectionate that her brother's picture could move her to tears.

All spheres of study, and especially eloquence, whose rules are not fixed, are subject to the great trap that some people both realise their own faults and love them. Cestius realised he had been childish 12 to say: " Mother, what is poison? " For he laughed at Murredius, who imitated this epigram in his epilogue. Starting to address the girl, he had said: " Make yourself look like one in danger of condemnation. Pour forth tears, put your hands on the judges' knees. You are a defendant." Then he had made the girl reply: " Father, what is a defendant? " Cestius said: " If he said this to mock me, he was a witty man—and *I* now realise that mine is a foolish epigram. However, there is much that I say not because I like it but because the audience will like it."

He said that a remark of Vibius Rufus' was more 13 bearable, though still worthy of some criticism;

[1] Above, §8.

epilogo: nutrix, ream tolle. Illud in Haterio, qui et promisit oratorem et praestitit, negabat se perferre, quod dixerat: haec rea non mittenda in exilium, 428 sed ferenda est; cum sciret, inquit, in exilium exportandos locari solere. Quid enim intellegi vult hac sententia? ex toto puellam ambulare non posse, ⟨an non posse⟩ [1] usque in exilium? Verum est, sed nec mater eius potuisset.

14 Silo a parte patris comparationem fecit inter se matris et filiae ⟨et⟩ [2] totam hac figura declamavit: Non sum, inquit, vobis dicturus qualis debeat esse venefica. Operam perdam si coepero describere debere esse aetate provectam, usu exercitatam, invisam viro, quae possit etiam filiam occidere. Supervacuum est uti pluribus verbis; in hac ipsa causa habemus veneficae exemplar. Comparemus inter se duas reas; nec est quod quaeratis aliquem qui cognitionem vestram per omnis comparationis partis ducat; ego vobis dicam quomodo illam accusaverim. Ego illi obieci ante actam vitam: vos huic 15 potestis obicere? Et sic omnia circumit et comparando defendit. Illam quaestiunculam, quae in prima parte tractata erat a quibusdam, " an illi utique opus fuisset conscia," sic transcucurrit: aiebat, inquit, tota actione rea: " dic quam consciam habuerim "; ego negabam opus illi fuisse; aiebam:

[1] *Supplied by Madvig.*
[2] *Supplied by Schultingh.*

Vibius in his epilogue had said: " Nurse, lift up the
accused." But he said he would not tolerate a saying
of Haterius, who promised to be an orator, and proved
himself one. He had said: " This defendant is not to
be sent into exile—she must be carried there." Yet
he knew, according to Cestius, that the transportation
of persons going into exile is let by contract. What
does he mean by this epigram? That the girl cannot
walk at all, or that she cannot walk as far as her place
of exile? The latter is true [1]—but then her mother
couldn't have, either.

Silo, for the father, introduced a comparison of 14
mother and daughter, and his whole declamation was
given this figure. " I am not going to tell you what
sort of woman a poisoner should be. I should be
wasting my time if I proceeded to describe how she
should be advanced in age, rich in experience,
detested by her husband, capable even of killing her
daughter. It is superfluous to say more; in this very
case we have the pattern of a poisoner. Let us compare the two defendants. Don't ask for someone to
take your enquiry through all the points of comparison: *I* will tell you how I accused her. *I* reproached her with her previous career: can *you* do
that to this girl?" He went through every point like
this, and made a defence out of his comparison. The 15
little question that some had dealt with in the first
part, viz. Had she *needed* an accomplice at all, he
skated over like this: " The defendant kept saying
throughout the trial: Tell me who my accomplice
was. *I* said she had not needed one; I said: ' You

[1] Because the place of exile would be too far away, and
perhaps an island.

in eadem domo eras, venenum notum erat, novercae occasio facilis conviventi, non eras suspecta, nemo te timebat †propter sororem†.

Ex altera parte hoc usus est colore: *novercam ideo venenum dedisse ut filia* sua *sola heres esset; eandem* 429N *illi et consciam fuisse* venefici et causam.

16 Omnes declamatores aiebat voluisse aliquid novi dicere illo loco quo nominabat noverca filiam consciam. Dixit, inquit, Hybreas: τί οὖν; ἐψεύσατο κατὰ τῆς ἰδίας θυγατρός; οὔκ· ἀλλὰ κατὰ τῆς ἐμῆς.

Hanc sententiam Fuscus Arellius, cum esset ex Asianis,[1] non casu dixit, sed transtulit ad verbum quidem: quid ergo? inquit, mentita est de filia sua? immo de mea.

Modestius hanc sententiam vertit Haterius: Quid ergo? mentita est? Quidni illa mentiretur de accusatoris sui filia?

17 Cestius dixit: nominavit privigni sui sororem.

Albucius dixit: quid habuit quod dubitaret an parceret filiae eius a quo occidebatur, sorori eius quem occiderat?

---

[1] Asianis *Schultingh:* asia.

342

were in the same house, the poison was well-known. A step-mother living with her step-son has every opportunity.[1] You were not suspected—no-one was afraid of you on the sister's behalf.' " [2]

On the other side, he used this *colour*: the step-mother had given her step-son poison so that her daughter should be sole heiress; the same girl had been both her accomplice in the poisoning and her motive.

He said that all the declaimers had wanted to say 16 something novel at the point where the step-mother named her daughter as her accomplice. According to him, Hybreas said: " What? Did she lie against her own daughter? No, against mine." [3]

It was not by chance that Arellius Fuscus spoke this epigram—for he was one of the Asians; indeed he translated word for word: " What? Did she lie about her daughter? No, about mine."

Haterius gave the epigram a more restrained turn: " What? Did she lie? Why should she not lie— about her accuser's daughter? "

Cestius said: " She named the sister of her step- 17 son." [4]

Albucius said: " What reason had she for hesitating whether to spare the daughter of one by whom she was being killed, the sister of one she had killed? "

---

[1] Cf. *Decl.* p. 426.7 Ritter.

[2] The last words are unclear.

[3] i.e. to get at me, she slandered the girl in her capacity as *my* child rather than her own; cf. above on §3 " In avenging my son . . ."

[4] This epigram gives allusively a motive for the mother to wish her own daughter ill; cf. also Nicetes' epigram in §18.

THE ELDER SENECA

Triarius dixit: Quid ergo? mater mentita est?
Tolle matris nomen: post damnationem noverca
est.

Blandus dixit: nominabo istam quae patri adfuit,
istam quae mortuo fratre ⟨flevit⟩,[1] torta[2] matre
non flevit.

Silo Pompeius dixit: " Filia " inquit " mihi
conscia est." Post hoc eundem vultum eius notavi
quem videram moriente privigno.

18   Montanus Votienus Marcellum Marcium, amicum
suum, cuius frequenter mentionem in scriptis suis
facit tamquam hominis diserti, aiebat hanc dixisse
sententiam: Invenit quomodo damnata accusaret,
moriens occideret, torta torqueret. Non est hoc
indicium, sed alterum novercae veneficium.

Latro dixerat, cum descripsisset tormenta: Instabam super caput non accusator sed tortor; ipse ignes
subiciebam, ipse ad intendendum eculeum manus
admovebam.   Ego non bibam sanguinem istius, non
eruam oculos?   Filium mihi eripuit; nisi citius illam 43
oppressissem, et filiam abstulisset.

Triarius dixit: cum accusarem, obieci veneficium;
in ultima parte inter preces meas excitavi puellam ad
ultionem fratris sui: haec res maxime iudices movit,
haec maxume novercam offendit.

Albucius dixit: postquam nominavit filiam, ad
me respexit: videlicet ut sciret an satis torsisset.

Nicetes egregie dixit in hoc eodem loco: συνοῖδέ
μοί, φησιν, ἡ θυγάτηρ· καὶ προσέθηκεν· ἡ τούτου.

[1] *Supplied by Faber.*
[2] torta *Gronovius:* a(c).

[1] The implication of the sentence so far in the Greek is: *my*
daughter.

344

Triarius said: "'What? Did a mother lie?' Get rid of the word mother; once she was condemned, she became a step-mother."

Blandus said: "I shall name the girl who stood by her father, who wept when her brother died, who did not weep when her mother was tortured."

Pompeius Silo said: "She said: My daughter is my accomplice. After this I noticed the same look on her face as I had seen when her step-son was dying."

Votienus Montanus said that his friend Marcius 18 Marcellus, whom he often mentions in his writings as an eloquent man, spoke this epigram: "She found a way to accuse though convicted, to kill while dying, to torture while under torture. This is no laying of information—it is a second poisoning by the step-mother."

Latro, describing the tortures, had said: "Standing over her, I urged on the work not as accuser but as torturer. *I* stoked the fire, *my* hands stretched the rack. Shall I not drink her blood, tear out her eyes? She took my son from me; if I hadn't crushed her first, she would have taken away my daughter too."

Triarius said: "When I was accusing her, I charged her with poisoning. In the last part of my speech, amidst my entreaties, I exhorted the girl to avenge her brother. That is what particularly influenced the judges—and particularly angered the step-mother."

Albucius said: "After she named her daughter, she looked at me, I suppose to find out whether she had tortured me enough."

At this same spot, Nicetes made an excellent remark: "She says: My accomplice is the daughter.[1] And she added: of this man."

345

THE ELDER SENECA

19　Montanus, cum diceret illum locum: quamvis
sceleratos parentes velle tamen innocentes liberos
suos esse, dixit: potest ista filiam veneficam fingere,
si potest facere; difficilius est liberos inquinare
quam perdere. Et illud: Favete saeculo, iudices,
cum ingentia scelera ferat, ne etiam inmatura tulerit;
favete ut nullum scelus commissum sit nisi quod
solet; favete ut potius noverca non desierit parricidium facere quam soror coeperit. Damnare illam
potui, effugere non potui. Sero fecisti, noverca:
si hoc ante dixisses, potuisti praevaricationem
pacisci; ⟨non⟩[1] recte cum damnareris animosa
eras. Recte nihil potes facere. Si qua est fides,
accusator insidias reae timui; nusquam a sinu meo
dimisi puellam, ipse omnes praegustavi cibos.
Incauta futuri mortalitas! postquam ad tortorem per-
duxi novercam, timere de filia desii.

20　Omnes illo colore usi sunt, a noverca nominatam　43
filiam in dolorem patris. Gallio plura dixit: fortasse, inquit, hanc nominavit ut veros conscios celaret,
fortasse ut, quia acerrume instabat accusator, hoc
metu territus finem tormentis inponeret, fortasse
nimio dolore tormentorum stupefacta nescit quid
loqueretur. Novissume dixit: fortasse *in hoc, ut*

[1] *Supplied by Schultingh.*

---

[1] If, as you allege, she made her daughter her accomplice,
then she was also capable of the easier crime—which I allege
—of pretending she was her accomplice.

Montanus, while on the topic that parents, however 19
criminal, want their children to be innocent, said:
" This woman is capable of falsely representing her
daughter as a poisoner if she is capable of making her
one.[1] It is more difficult to bring oneself to corrupt
one's children than to kill them." Also: " Look
favourably upon our time, judges, and decide that
though it produces great crimes, it has not also produced precocious ones. Decide that no crime has
been committed except the usual kind. Decide that
it was a case of a step-mother not stopping her career
of parricide rather than a sister beginning hers.—I
was able to get her convicted; I was not able to
escape her.—You acted too late, step-mother: if you
had said this before, you could have bargained for my
connivance; you were wrong to be noble [2] while you
were still being condemned. You do everything
wrong.—Believe me, I, the accuser, was afraid of the
wiles of the defendant; I never let the girl go out of
my lap, I tasted all her food in advance. How little
thought can men take for the future! Once I had
taken the step-mother to the torturer, I stopped fearing for my daughter."

Everyone used the *colour* that the step-mother 20
named the daughter to grieve the father. Gallio
went further: " Perhaps," he said, " she named this
girl in order to conceal her true accomplices, perhaps
—for the accuser was pressing hard—in order to make
him frightened and stop the torture; perhaps, rendered senseless by the extreme pain of the torture, she
did not know what she was saying." Lastly he said:

---

[2] By not alleging at the trial that the girl was your accomplice, and leaving it to the torture-session that followed.

quae *poenas venefici dabat accusationis exigeret*. Illum
sensum adiecit: Ex meis hoc adfectibus aestumo:
tunc cum ira, cum odio furerem, circumspiciebam
omnis ultionis vias oblitus innocentiae, si proprios
habuisset filios noverca, occidissem. In hanc ipsam
quotiens impetum facere volui! Sed propter hoc
a me tuta erat quod a matre non erat.

" Perhaps it was so that she could exact for the accusation the penalty she was paying for the poisoning." He added this idea: " I judge this from my own feelings: when, crazy with anger and hatred, I had forgotten innocence, and was looking about me for any road to revenge, had the step-mother had sons of her own, I should have killed them. How often I wanted to rush at this girl herself! But she was safe from me just because she was not safe from her mother."

LIBER DECIMUS

SENECA NOVATO, SENECAE, MELAE FILIIS SALUTEM.

1   Quod ultra mihi molesti sitis non est: interrogate
si qua vultis, et sinite me ab istis iuvenilibus studiis
ad senectutem meam reverti. Fatebor vobis, iam
res taedio est. Primo libenter adsilui velut optimam
vitae meae partem mihi reducturus: deinde iam me
pudet, tamquam diu non seriam rem agam. Hoc
habent scholasticorum studia: leviter tacta delec-
tant, contrectata et propius admota fastidio sunt.
Sinite ergo me semel exhaurire memoriam meam
et dimittite vel adactum iureiurando quo adfirmem
dixisse me quae scivi quaeque audivi quaeque ad
hanc rem pertinere iudicavi.   447

2   Pertinere autem ad rem non puto quomodo L.
Magius, gener T. Livi, declamaverit (quamvis aliquo
tempore suum populum habuerit, cum illum homines

---

[1] Contrast *C.* 1 pr. 1. But Seneca is posing, for he went on
to write the *Suasoriae.*

BOOK 10

PREFACE

Seneca to his sons Novatus, Seneca and Mela
GREETINGS

You must trouble me no further: ask, if you have 1
any request, and let me get back from these youthful
pursuits to my old age.[1] I will confess to you: by
now I am tired of the whole thing. At first I leapt
willingly at the idea, proposing to bring back to
myself the best part of my life. More recently I have
begun to be ashamed of a long period of trifling.
This is what the studies of the schoolmen are like: if
you touch lightly on them, they please; if you handle
them and get nearer to them, they pall. Allow me,
then, to dredge my memory once for all, and after
that let me go—bound, if you like, by an oath [2] that I
have said what I knew and what I have heard and
what I judged to be relevant to this matter.

I don't think it *is* relevant to describe how Lucius 2
Magius, son-in-law to Livy, declaimed (though for a
time he had his public, for, though people didn't praise

[2] Perhaps part of the formula used in the swearing in of
witnesses (C. J. Fordyce, *C.R.* 52 [1938], 59).

non in ipsius honorem laudarent, sed in soceri ferrent),
quomodo L. Asprenas aut Quintilianus senex
declamaverit: transeo istos, quorum fama cum ipsis
extincta est. De Scauro si me interrogatis, cum
illum mecum audieritis, iniqui estis. Non novi
quemquam cuius ingenio populus Romanus per-
tinacius ignoverit. Dicebat neglegenter: saepe
causam in ipsis subselliis, saepe dum amicitur disce-
bat; deinde litiganti similior quam agenti cupiebat
evocare aliquam vocem adversariorum et in alter-
cationem pervenire: vires suas noverat. Nihil
erat illo venustius, nihil paratius: genus dicendi
antiquum, verborum quoque non vulgarium gravitas,
ipse voltus habitusque corporis mire ad auctoritatem
3 oratoriam aptatus. Sed ex his omnibus sciri potest
non quantum oratorem praestaret [ignarus] [1] Scaurus,
sed quantum desereret. Pleraeque actiones malae,
in omnibus tamen aliquod magni neglectique ingeni vestigium extabat. Raro aliqua actio bona, 448M
sed quam fortunae imputares: eo illum longa, immo
perpetua desidia perduxerat ut nihil curare vellet,
nihil posset. Orationes septem edidit, quae deinde
⟨ex⟩ [2] senatus consulto combustae sunt. Bene cum
illo ignis egerat, sed extant libelli qui cum fama eius
pugnant, multo quidem solutiores ipsis actionibus;

[1] ignarus *AB:* ignaris *V: omitted in M.*
[2] *Supplied by C. F. W. Müller.*

him for his own sake, they put up with him for the sake of his father-in-law), or how Lucius Asprenas or the old Quintilian declaimed. I pass over these men, whose fame died with them. If you ask me about Scaurus, you are cheating,[1] for you were with me when I heard him. I don't know anyone for whose talents the Roman people made such obstinate allowance. He spoke negligently; he often used to get a case up on the very benches of the court-room,[2] or while he was dressing. Again, he was more like a litigant than a counsel—he longed to provoke some hasty word from his opponents and get into a dispute: he knew his strength. Nothing more agreeable or quick-witted than he. His style of oratory was old-fashioned; his vocabulary, too, impressive and far from trite. His very countenance and mien were wonderfully suited to add to his weight as an orator. But from all this we may realise not how great an 3 orator Scaurus made, but what a great one he refused to be. Most of his speeches were bad, but all had some obvious trace of a great neglected talent. Rarely was a speech of his good—and when it was you might attribute it to good fortune. His persistent and indeed perpetual sloth had brought him to such a plight that he was neither able nor willing to take trouble about anything. He published seven speeches, later burnt at the senate's decree. The fire served him well. But there remain sketches[3] to fight against his reputation—and indeed they are

---

[1] Cf. *C.* 1 pr. 4.

[2] Note the warning of Quintilian 12.8.2.

[3] Apparently notes used in working up the speech: cf. Cicero's *commentarii* (Quintilian 10.7.30).

illas enim, cum destitueret cura, calor adiuvabat; hi caloris minus habent, neglegentiae non minus. Declamantem audivimus, et novissume quidem M. Lepido ita ut, quod difficillimum erat, sibi displiceret.

4 De T. Labieno interrogatis? Declamavit non quidem populo, sed egregie. Non admittebat populum et quia nondum haec consuetudo erat inducta et quia putabat turpe ac frivolae iactationis. Adfectabat enim censorium supercilium, cum alius animo esset: magnus orator, qui multa impedimenta eluctatus ad famam ingeni confitentibus magis hominibus pervenerat quam volentibus. Summa egestas 449 erat, summa infamia, summum odium. Magna autem debet esse eloquentia quae invitis placeat, et cum ingenia favor hominum ostendat, favor alat, quantam vim esse oportet quae inter obstantia erumpat! Nemo erat qui non, cum homini omnia obiceret, ingenio multum tribueret.

5 Color orationis antiquae, vigor novae, cultus inter nostrum ac prius saeculum medius, ut illum posset utraque pars sibi vindicare. Libertas tanta ut libertatis nomen excederet, et quia passim ordines hominesque laniabat Rabienus vocaretur. Animus inter vitia ingens et ad similitudinem ingeni sui violentus

---

[1] See *C.* 4 pr. 2 n.
[2] With a play on *rabies*, " madness."

even more listless than the actual speeches; for *they* were assisted by the heat of delivery, though he neglected to give them care, while the notes have less heat without being any less negligent. We heard him declaiming, last of all before Marcus Lepidus, in such a manner that even Scaurus himself was dissatisfied—a difficult feat.

Do you enquire about Titus Labienus? He was an 4 outstanding declaimer, though not one who performed in public. He didn't let the public in, both because this custom had not yet been introduced [1] and because he thought it shameful and indicative of a boastful frivolity. For he pretended to the severity of a censor, though his character was quite other; he was a great orator who had wrestled his way through many obstacles to arrive at a reputation for genius amid the grudging acknowledgement of men rather than their consent. He was very poor, very notorious, very hated. But great indeed must be the eloquence that pleases even the reluctant; and since it is the favour of men that marks out genius, their favour that nourishes it, how great must be the force that can burst through all obstacles to its course! There was no-one who did not grant much to the talent—while accusing the *man* of every crime.

His tone was that of the old oratory, his vigour that 5 of the new, his ornament midway between our age and the preceding one: so that he could be claimed by both sides. His freedom of speech was so great that it passed the bounds of freedom: and because he savaged all ranks and men alike, he was known as Rabienus.[2] Amid all his faults, he had a great spirit —one that was, like his genius, violent; despite the

et qui Pompeianos spiritus nondum in tanta pace
posuisset.

In hoc primum excogitata est nova poena; effectum
est enim per inimicos ut omnes eius libri combur15eren-
tur: res nova et invisitata supplicium de studiis sumi.

6 Bono hercules publico ista in poenas ingeniorum versa [1] crudelitas post Ciceronem inventa est; quid
enim futurum fuit si triumviris libuisset et ingenium
Ciceronis proscribere? Sunt di inmortales lenti quidem sed certi vindices generis humani, et magna
exempla in caput invenientium regerunt, ac ius- 450
tissima patiendi vice quod quisque alieno excogitavit
supplicio saepe expiat suo. Quae vos, dementissimi
homines, tanta vecordia agitat? Parum videlicet in
poenas notae crudelitatis est: conquirite in vosmet
ipsos nova quibus pereatis, et si quid ab omni patientia
rerum natura subduxit, sicut ingenium memoriam-
que nominis, invenite quemadmodum reducatis ad
7 eadem corporis mala. Facem studiis subdere et in
monumenta disciplinarum animadvertere quanta
et quam non contenta cetera materia saevitia est!
Di melius, quod eo saeculo ista ingeniorum supplicia
coeperunt quo ingenia desierant! Eius qui hanc in

---

[1] ingeniorum versa *Wachsmuth:* ingeniosa.

depth of the prevailing peace, it had not yet laid down its Pompeian[1] passions.

It was for him that there was first devised a new punishment: his enemies saw to it that all his books were burnt.[2] It was an unheard of novelty that punishment should be exacted from literature. Certainly it was to everyone's advantage that this cruelty that turns on genius was devised later than the time of Cicero; for what would have happened if the triumvirs had been pleased to proscribe Cicero's talent as well as Cicero?[3] The immortal gods are slow but sure to punish the human race; they make severe penalties recoil on the heads of their devisers— by a well-merited exchange of suffering, what a man has worked out to punish others often comes home to roost on himself. What appalling mania harries these madmen? I suppose familiar cruelties are insufficient punishment. Go ahead, look for fresh ways to perish —yourselves: and as for anything that nature has removed from all suffering—genius, and the memory of a name—find a way of subjecting it too to the ills that afflict the body. How great is the savagery that puts a match to literature, and wreaks its vengeance on monuments of learning; how unsatisfied with its other victims! Thank god that these punishments for genius began in an age when genius had come to

---

[1] Natural in a (presumed) relation of a notable Pompeian, another Titus Labienus (for whom see R. Syme, *The Roman Revolution*, 67-8).

[2] The fate of works of Scaurus (see above) and Cremutius Cordus (Sen. *Marc.* 1.3). For Tacitus' comments on such burnings see *Agr.* 2.1 and especially *Ann.* 4.35.

[3] Compare the theme of *S.* 7 (where see esp. §11).

scripta Labieni sententiam dixerat postea viventis
adhuc scripta conbusta sunt: iam non malo exemplo
quia suo.

Non tulit hanc Labienus contumeliam nec superstes
esse ingenio suo voluit, sed in monimenta se maiorum
suorum ferri iussit atque ita includi, veritus scilicet
ne ignis qui nomini suo subiectus erat corpori nega-
retur: non finivit tantum se ipse sed etiam sepelivit.

8   Memini aliquando, cum recitaret historiam, mag- 45
nam partem illum libri convolvisse et dixisse: haec
quae transeo post mortem meam legentur. Quanta
in illis libertas fuit quam etiam Labienus extimuit!
Cassi Severi, hominis Labieno invisissimi, belle
dicta res ferebatur illo tempore quo libri Labieni ex
senatus consulto urebantur: nunc me, inquit, vivum
uri oportet, qui illos edidici. Monstrabo bellum
vobis libellum quem a Gallione vestro petatis.
Recitavit rescriptum Labieno pro Bathyllo Mae-
cenatis, in quo suspicietis adulescentis animum
illos dentes ad mordendum provocantis.

9   ⟨Nunc⟩ [1] autem, puto, iam nihil quod interrogetis
restat. Musa rhetor, quem interdum solebatis
audire, licet Mela meus contrahat frontem, multum
habuit ingeni, nihil cordis: omnia usque ad ultimum
tumorem perducta, ut non extra sanitatem sed extra
naturam essent. Quis enim ferat hominem de

  [1] *Supplied by Kiessling.*

an end! [1] The man [2] who had pronounced this judgement on Labienus' writings lived to see his own writings burnt: no longer an evil penalty, once it became
his.

Labienus did not take this insult lying down, nor
did he wish to outlive his own genius. He had himself carried to the tombs of his ancestors and walled
up, fearing, I suppose, that the flames that had been
put to his glory might be denied to his body: he not
only finished his own life—he buried himself.

I remember that once, when he was reciting his 8
history, Labienus rolled up a good deal of the book,
saying: "The parts I pass over will be read after my
death." How great must have been their outspokenness if even Labienus was frightened of it! A
pretty saying of Cassius Severus, a great enemy of
Labienus', was in circulation at the time when
Labienus' books were burnt at the decree of the
senate: "*I* ought to be burnt alive now—I have
those books by heart." Here is a nice book for you
to ask for from your friend Gallio: he read out once a
reply to Labienus on behalf of Bathyllus, Maecenas'
freedman, a speech in which you will admire the spirit
of a youth prepared to provoke *those* teeth to bite.

Now, I think, there is nothing left for you to ask. 9
The rhetorician Musa, whom you used sometimes to
hear, had—however much my son Mela may frown—
much talent, but no sense: everything was taken to
an extreme of bombast, so as to be beyond nature as
well as beyond reason. Who would put up with a

[1] For this view of the decadence after Cicero see *C*. 1 pr. 6–7.
[2] Cassius Severus (I take it), for the burning of whose books
see Suet. *Cal*. 16.

siphonibus dicentem " caelo repluunt " et de spar-
sionibus " odoratos imbres " et in cultum viridarium [1]
" caelatas silvas " et in picturam " nemora sur-
gentia "? aut illud quod de subitis mortibus memini 45:
eum dicentem cum vos me illo perduxissetis : " Quidquid avium volitat, quidquid piscium natat, quidquid
ferarum discurrit, nostris sepelitur ventribus. Quaere
nunc cur subito moriamur : mortibus vivimus."
10 Non ergo, etiamsi iam manu missus erat, debuit de
corio eius nobis satis fieri ? Nec sum ex iudicibus
severissimis qui omnia ad exactam regulam derigam : [2]
multa donanda ingeniis puto ; sed donanda vitia,
non portenta sunt. Si qua tamen tolerabiliter dicta
sunt, non subtraham, licet non plura videantur : vos
subiciatis.

Moschus non incommode dixit, sed ipse sibi
nocuit ; nam dum nihil non schemate dicere cupit,
oratio eius non figurata erat sed prava. Itaque
non inurbane Pacatus rhetor, cum illi Massiliae mane
occurrisset, schemate illum salutavit : " poteram "
inquit " dicere : ave, Mosche." Ipse ab eloquentia
multum aberat ; natus ad contumelias omnium ingeniis inurendas, nulli non inpressit aliquid quod
11 effugere non posset. Ille Passieno prima eius syllaba 45
in Graecum mutata obscenum nomen inposuit, ille

---

[1] viridarium *Kiessling :* uiridium *ABV :* uirilium *M.*
[2] derigam *Kiessling :* redicam *AB :* -igam *V :* -icant *M.*

man saying of siphons: " They rain back at the sky,"
and about sprays:[1] " perfumed showers," or using
the phrase " chiselled forests " of a spruce garden,
and " springing glades " of a picture? Or what I
remember him saying of sudden deaths one day when
you took me along to listen to him: " Every bird that
flies, every fish that swims, every beast that roams
finds burial in our stomachs.[2] *Now* ask why we die
suddenly: it is on deaths that we live." Should he 10
not have paid us for that with his hide, even if he *had*
already been manumitted? I'm not one of those
very rigid judges, determined to direct everything by
a precise rule. I think that many concessions must
be made to genius—but it is faults, not monstrosities
that we must concede. However, if he did say anything tolerably, I won't suppress it, though there
doesn't seem to be much: *you* can prompt me.

Moschus spoke not badly, but he was his own worst
enemy: he burned to say everything by means of a
figure, with the result that his oratory was not figured
but warped. And so it was not without wit that the
rhetorician Pacatus, meeting him one morning in
Marseille, greeted him with a figure: " I could have
said: Hail, Moschus."[3] *He* was far from eloquent;
born to brand insults on the talents of all, he saddled
everyone with something that could not be escaped.
It was he who gave Passienus an obscene name by 11
changing the first syllable of his name into Greek.[4]

---

[1] Used for sweetening the air in a theatre.

[2] Bonner (*A.J.P.* 87 [1966], 273) compares Lucan 10.155 *seq.*

[3] Cf. Quintilian's figure " possum dicere . . ." (9.2.47).

[4] Perhaps with a play on $\pi\alpha\sigma\chi$-, $\pi\alpha\theta$-, giving homosexual
overtones. Romans enjoyed puns on names (Quintilian
6.3.53).

THE ELDER SENECA

Sparso dixit scholam communem cum rhetore quodam, declamatore subtili sed arido,[1] habenti: tu
potes controversiam intellegere, qui non intellegis te
laterem lavare? Sparsus autem dicebat violenter,
sed dure. Ad imitationem se Latronis derexerat,
nec tamen umquam similis illi erat, nisi cum eadem
diceret. Utebatur suis verbis, Latronis sententiis.

12 Cum Basso certamen illi fuit, quem vos quoque
audistis, homine diserto, cui demptam velles quam
consectabatur amaritudinem et simulationem actionis
oratoriae. Nihil est indecentius quam ubi scholasticus forum quod non novit imitatur. Amabam
itaque Capitonem, cuius declamatio est de Popillio,
quae misero Latroni subicitur: bona fide scholasticus erat, in his declamationibus quae bene illi cesserunt nulli non post primum tetradeum praeferendus.

13 Primum tetradeum quod faciam quaeritis? La- 454
tronis, Fusci, Albuci, Gallionis. Hi quotiens con-
flixissent, penes Latronem gloria fuisset, penes
Gallionem palma; reliquos ut vobis videbitur con-
ponite: ego vobis omnium feci potestatem. Hos
minus nobiles sinite in partem abire, Paternum et
Moderatum, Fabium et si quis est nec clari nominis
nec ignoti. Cum vobis ad satietatem vestram me
praestiterim, permittite [me][2] mihi et aliquos quos

[1] *These four words (but with* declamatori*) appear in the manuscripts after* inposuit: *they were transposed by Gertz.*
[2] *Deleted by Madvig.*

It was he who said to Sparsus, who kept a school together with a certain rhetorician, who was an acute but dry declaimer: " Can *you* understand a *contro-versia*—when you don't understand that you're wash-ing bricks ? " [1] As for Sparsus, he spoke violently but harshly. He had set himself to imitate Latro—but he never resembled him except when he said the same things. He would use his own words, but Latro's ideas.

He was a rival of Bassus, whom *you* have listened to 12 as well as I: an eloquent man, whom one could have wished to have done without the bitterness he affected and without his imitation of an orator's delivery. Nothing is more indecorous than when a schoolman imitates the practices of the forum—of which he knows nothing. That is why I liked Capito, whose declamation on Popillius [2] gets palmed off on to the wretched Latro; he was a genuine schoolman, and in his successful declamations superior to all after the first quartet.

You ask whom I make the first quartet? Latro, 13 Fuscus, Albucius, Gallio. In every clash between them, Latro would have got the glory—but Gallio the prize. Rank the rest as you will: I have given you the chance to judge them all. Let the obscurer ones go their own way—Paternus and Moderatus, Fabius and anyone else who is neither famous nor unknown. But since I have given you my services to the point of sating you, let me produce from up my sleeve some

---

[1] i.e. attempting the impossible (Otto, *Sprichwörter*, 187): I suppose in trying to make a school pay with so unsatisfactory a partner, whose dryness, of course, is part of the point.

[2] *C.* 7.2.5 *seq.*

non nostis ex sinu proferre, quibus quo minus ad famam pervenirent non ingenium defuit sed locus.

14 Bene declamavit Gavius Silo, cui Caesar Augustus, cum frequenter causas agentem in Tarraconensi colonia audisset, plenum testimonium reddidit; dixit enim: "numquam audivi patrem familiae disertiorem." Erat qui patrem familiae praeferret, oratorem subduceret: partem esse eloquentiae putabat eloquentiam abscondere.

Solebat declamare studiose et Turrinus Clodius, cuius filius fraterno vobis amore coniunctus est, adulescens summae eloquentiae futurus nisi mallet 455] exercere quantum habet quam consequi quantum 15 potest. Sed Turrinus pater multum viribus dempserat dum Apollodorum sequitur ac summam legem dicendi sectam putat; tantum tamen superfuit illi virium quantum valeret etiamsi ars abesset. Sententias dicebat excitatas, insidiosas, aliquid petentis. Numquam non de colore Latroni controversiam fecit. Latro numquam solebat disputare in convivio aut alio quam quo declamare poterat tempore. Dicebat quosdam esse colores prima facie duros et asperos: eos non posse nisi actione probari. Negabat itaque ulli se placere posse nisi totum; nosse enim semet [1] suas vires et illarum fiducia aliis metuenda et praerupta audere; multa se non persuadere iudici

---

[1] nosse enim semet *Müller:* nossent seet (seeis *M*).

---

[1] Seneca proceeds to discuss some declaimers from his native province. Its remoteness is seen as a disdavantage: cf. what is said of Turrinus in §16.

others you *don't* know—ones who lacked the background[1] rather than the talent to arrive at fame.

Gavius Silo was a good declaimer. He was paid a 14 fine tribute by the emperor Augustus, who had heard him pleading a good many times in the colony of Tarraco. He said: " I've never heard a more eloquent family man." Silo was the sort of person to put forward the father of the family and keep the orator in the background; he thought it part of eloquence to hide one's eloquence.[2]

Clodius Turrinus, too, used to put a lot into his declamation; his son you regard with a brotherly affection—a youth who would master the highest eloquence if he did not prefer to practise what he has rather than to acquire what he is capable of. But the 15 elder Turrinus had removed a good deal of his own force by following Apollodorus[3] and regarding his sect as the supreme rule of oratory: but he had enough strength left over to be effective even in the absence of art. His epigrams were vigorous, wily and pointed. He always used to discuss the topic of the *colour* with Latro. Latro never used to debate at supper or at any other time when he could not declaim. He used to say some *colours* are at first sight hard and harsh—they can only win acceptance in the course of a speech. He said he could only please as a whole; he knew his own strength, and relying on it ventured on things that were perilous and frightening to others. In many matters he did not persuade the judge, but imposed on him.

---

[2] For art hiding art, see Colson's notes in his edition of Quintilian Book 1, pp. 142, 179.

[3] *C.* 2.1.36 n.

16 sed auferre. Turrinus contra nihil probare nisi tutum; non quia inbecillus erat sed quia circumspec- 456M tus. Causas nemo diligentius proposuit, nemo respondit paratius; et pecuniam itaque et dignitatem, quam primam in provincia Hispania habuit, eloquentiae debuit. Natus quidem erat patre splendidissimo, avo divi Iuli hospite, sed civili bello attenuatas domus nobilis vires excitavit, et ita ad summam perduxit dignitatem ut, si quid illi defuerit, scias locum defuisse.

Inde filius quoque eius, id est meus—numquam enim illum a vobis distinxi—, habet in dicendo controversiam paternam diligentiam, qua vires ingenii sui ex industria retundit. Hoc et in ipso genere vitae sequitur, ad summa evasurus iuvenis nisi modicis contentus esset, et ideo dignus est cuius tam modestis cupiditatibus Fortuna praestet fidem.

Horum nomina non me a nimio favore sed a certo posuisse iudicio scietis cum sententias eorum rettulero aut pares notissimorum auctorum sententiis aut praeferendas.

Turrinus, on the other hand, approved nothing that 16 was risky: not because he was feeble, but because he was cautious. No-one put forward cases more carefully, no-one replied with more readiness: so it was that he owed to his eloquence his wealth and his pre-eminent prestige in the province of Spain. His father was highly distinguished, his grandfather had entertained the blessed Julius. His house, noble as it was, had been weakened in the civil wars, but Turrinus brought it back to life, and raised it to the highest honours—so that, if he lacked anything, it was, you should realise, the right place to display his quality.

As a result, his son—or rather mine, for I have never made any distinction between him and you—has his father's careful approach to declamation, and thus purposely blunts the edge of his talent. This is the young man's way even in his private life: he would get to the top if he weren't unambitious; so he deserves that Fortune should smile on his so moderate desires.

Once I have recounted their epigrams, which are equal or perhaps superior to those of the most renowned authors, you will see that I have set down the names of these men not out of excess of enthusiasm for them, but on the basis of a considered judgement.

THE ELDER SENECA

I

<small>Lugens Divitem Sequens Filius Pauperis</small>

Iniuriarum sit actio.

Quidam, cum haberet filium et divitem inimicum, occisus inspoliatus inventus est. Adulescens sordidatus divitem sequebatur; dives 457M
eduxit in ius eum et postulavit ut si quid suspi-
caretur accusaret se. Pauper ait: "accusabo
cum potero" et nihilominus sordidatus divitem
sequebatur. Cum peteret honores dives, repulsus accusat iniuriarum pauperem.

1   <small>Vibi Galli.</small> *Gratias* ago *diviti quod quos odit iam
reos facere contentus est.* Interdiu nobis publico
interdicitur; quaerite quid nocte fiat. *"Non am-
bulabis" inquit "eadem via* qua ego, *non calcabis
vestigia mea, non offeres delicatis oculis sordidam vestem,
non flebis invito me, non tacebis":* perieramus si hic
magistratus esset.

  <small>Albuci Sili.</small> *Quod sordidatus fui, luctus est; quod
flevi, pietatis* est; *quod non accusavi, timoris* est; *quod*

<small>[1] Parallelled in *Rhet. Gr.* 4.235.32 Walz.
[2] See Bonner, 115–16. The extension to defamation is in
accordance with Roman practice: see *Dig.* 47.10.15.27, where</small>

1

THE GRIEVING POOR MAN'S SON WHO FOLLOWED THE RICH MAN [1]

An action may lie for injury.[2]

A man who had a son and a rich enemy was found killed, though not robbed. The youth, dressed in mourning, began to follow the rich man about. The rich man took him to court, and demanded that if he had any suspicions he should accuse him. The poor man said: " I shall accuse when I can," and continued to follow the rich man in mourning clothes just the same. The rich man stood for office, but was rejected; he accuses the poor man of injury.

For the son

VIBIUS GALLUS. I am grateful to the rich man that 1 nowadays he is satisfied to bring those he hates to court.[3]—By day I am barred from appearing in public; ask yourselves what may happen at night.—" You shall not walk," he says, " on the same road as I, nor tread in my footsteps, nor afford my fastidious eyes the sight of your black clothes, nor weep or keep silent if I do not wish it." I should be dead if this man were magistrate.

ALBUCIUS SILUS. That I was in mourning is due to grief; that I wept, to affection; that I did not accuse

" wearing mourning clothes to arouse unpopularity against a person " is one of the examples given.

[3] Rather than to kill them. The next epigram implies just this danger.

repulsus est, vestrum est. Non taceam, qui adhuc vivo quod tacui? Nostis populi loquacis suspiciones. Quare iste *honores illo vivo numquam petit?* Ego vero omnes quaeso, omnes, ut me in inquisitione paternae mortis adiuvent; et ad tua genua, dives, venissem nisi timerem ne invidiam tibi fieri diceres; et iam pridem hoc animo sequor: occasionem loquendi capto, nec mehercules possum dicere inhumanitate tua fieri quod non audeo, sed *vitium me meum sequitur: taceo. Utinam hoc vitium habuisset et pater!* Dum libere loquitur, multos offendit; neque enim, puto, te solum in civitate habuit inimicum. Ut iste ait, causam meam populo probavi.

2   Iuli Bassi. *Quando* autem *istis divitibus non sordidati sumus?* " *Accusa* " *inquit. Pauper divitem,* lugens candidatum ego accusem? *Ambulare mihi meo ar-* 458 *bitrio non licet.* In ius vocavit: " *reum* " *inquit* " *me perage, perora." Quis haec loquentem auderet accusare? " Cur me " inquit " sequeris? " Quasi aliud iter pauperes, aliud divites habeant.*

Cesti Pii. Non essem reus si accusare possem. Barba demissa, sordidatus cum criminibus meis ad vos veni. Omnia licet fiant, non desinam inquirere

---

[1] That of the judges, who, as voters, had prevented the rich man getting office.

[2] Whereas the father, being outspoken (see below), had been killed for abusing the rich man, and, as the next epigram suggests, to remove an obstacle to his candidacy.

[3] The rich man, apparently, during his narration.

[4] That is, our clothes are always dark and shabby compared

you, to fear; that he was rejected is *your* doing.[1]—Am
I not to keep silent—I who am still alive because I
kept silent? [2]—You know the suspicions entertained
by a gossipy people: " Why did he never seek office
while the father was alive? "—Now I beg everyone,
yes everyone, to aid me in the investigation of my
father's death: I should have come to your knees too,
rich man, if I weren't afraid you'd say it caused you
unpopularity. This is why I've been following you
about so long: I'm looking for the opportunity to
speak to you. And I cannot say that it is the result
of your cruelty that I do not dare; but my usual fault
dogs me—I keep silent. Would that my father too
had had this fault! By speaking freely, he caused
much offence—for I don't suppose *you* were the only
enemy he had in the state.—Just as he says,[3] I proved
my case before the people.

JULIUS BASSUS. When are we *not* in mourning in 2
the eyes of these rich men? [4]—" Accuse me," he
says. Am I, a poor man, to accuse a rich man, am I,
mourning, to accuse a candidate for office? [5] I cannot
even walk where I will.—He called me to law, said:
" Prosecute me to the bitter end, plead your case
through." Who would venture to accuse one who
talks thus?—" Why do you follow me? " As if poor
men had one street, rich men another.

CESTIUS PIUS. I should not be defending myself if
I were capable of accusing.—Beard untrimmed and
in mourning, I have come—together with what is

with the rich man's: cf. the *pullatus circulus* of Quintilian
2.12.10 (cf. Plin. *Ep.* 7.17.9 and Suet. *Aug.* 40).
[5] This too is a matter of dress: the poor man is in mourning
clothes, a *candidatus* (as his name implies) wore a white toga.

percussorem et fortasse iam inveni. Cum subito pater meus in media civitate—quid me intueris? quid observas quid dicam?—subductus est.

3   ARELLI FUSCI. Incedere magno comitatu, splendido cultu, non est fortunae meae; ista divites possunt; satis est si vivimus. Cum inspoliatum cadaver [meum][1] inventum sit, quis fuerit *percussor* nescio: *quisquis fuit, quasi dives spolia contempsit.* " Quare " inquit " me sequeris per publicum? " Facinus indignum commissum est: dives et pauper eadem via incessimus.

MOSCHI. " Accusa " inquit. Ubi est qui primo coeperat? ⟨" Cur " inquit " me sequeris?"⟩[2] Vellem pater meus quoque a te non discessisset: viveret. " Quare " inquit " me reum non facis? " Quia accusatorem me non times. *Mortuo patre meo—timeo enim ne quis sibi iniuriam fieri putet si dixero " occiso."* Occisus est pater meus—a quo? si permittitis, nescio.

4   IUNI GALLIONIS. " *Sordidatus* es " inquit; " *fles.*" *Quid aliud facere possum filius occisi pauperis?* Pater 459M meus in media civitate salvis legibus occisus est. Quis hoc sine lacrimis narrare possit? Non deponam has sordes nisi invenero cui induam. Quis occidit patrem meum? nescio. Nihil amplius testari potes quam hanc vocem meam: adhuc nescio. Delibero

[1] *Deleted by the editor.*
[2] *Supplied by Thomas.*

---

[1] i.e. his mourning clothes, which he wears qua defendant as well as because of his father's death.
[2] Cf. Bassus' epigram in §13.

charged against me.[1]   Whatever may happen, I shall
not stop looking for the murderer—perhaps I have
already found him.— . . . when suddenly, in the
middle of the city, my father—why do you look at me,
why watch what I am going to say?—was removed.

ARELLIUS FUSCUS.   Those of my rank cannot go in 3
great state, wearing bright clothes—*that* is possible
for the rich: it is enough for us to be alive.—Since the
body was found unrobbed, I don't know who the
assassin was: but whoever he was, he resembled a
rich man in despising loot.—" Why do you follow me
in public? "   A wicked crime has been committed:
we, a rich man and a poor man, have gone along the
same road.[2]

MOSCHUS.   " Accuse me," he says.   What became
of the man who began to?—" Why keep following
me? "   I wish my *father* hadn't left your side; he'd
still be alive.—" Why not take me to court? "   Because you have no fear of my accusations.—My father
once dead—I'm afraid someone may think it an injury to him if I say " killed " . . . —My father was
killed—by whom?   If I am permitted to say so, I don't
know.

JUNIUS GALLIO.   " You are in mourning; you 4
weep."   What else can I do, I, the son of a poor man
who has been killed?   My father was murdered in
mid-city, though the laws still stood.   Who could
even tell the story without tears?—I shall not take
off these dark clothes unless I find someone I can put
them on to.[3]—Who killed my father?   I don't know.
You can swear to no more than that I said [4] that.

---

[3] As defendant.
[4] i.e. at the first trial.

interim cui [1] illam induam vestem quam patri meo
reliquit percussor. " Cur me sequeris?" Magistratus post terga sua non summovent.

5 FULVI SPARSI. *Quid* iste *accusanti fecisset qui
persequitur tacentem?* " *Cur non agis?* " *Quia adeo
non metuis ut cogas* tecum agi. Numquid nunc
tibi iniuriam facio *sordidatus? quod reo licet, lugenti
non licet?* Quid potui patri meo minus praestare?
in honorem eius vestem mutavi.

ARGENTARI. Non vis patrem meum fleam?
lacessere nos ultro non solebas.

CLODI TURRINI patris. " Quare " inquit " sordes
sumpsisti?" Quid ergo? *ne lugebo quidem quem
vindicare non possum?* Nulli iniuriam facio nisi patri,
quem adhuc tacitus fleo.

6 PORCI LATRONIS. Cuius inter necessarium ita
crudeliter interempti patris dolorem nihil fortius est
quam quod gemit. " Accusa " inquit " me." Unde
tam securus es? Invenisse videris quis alius occiderit. *Non erat in illo praeda quam grassator seque-
tur,* sed *erat summa virtus,* sed erat, firmissimum ino- 460
piae [2] munimentum, *contumax adversus fastidium
divitiarum innocentia: haec ab inimico spolia petita sunt.*

---

[1] cui *Müller:* et.
[2] inopiae *Kiessling:* i(g)noti.

---

[1] Compare the previous epigram: the speaker imagines the
same dark clothes worn by the victim as passing to the
murderer in court.

And I still don't know. Meanwhile I am considering whom I am to clothe in the suit his assassin did not take from my father.[1]—" Why do you follow me ? " Even magistrates do not clear the streets *behind* their backs.

FULVIUS SPARSUS. What would he have done if I had been accusing him, considering that he harasses me even when I keep quiet ?—" Why not sue ? " Because you are so confident that you hope to force me to sue you.—Surely I do you no injury now, in *these* mourning clothes ? Is one who grieves not allowed what a defendant is allowed ?—What less could I do for my father ? It was out of respect for him that I changed my clothes.

ARGENTARIUS. Don't you want me to weep for my father ? You didn't use to take the first step in provocation in the old days.[2]

CLODIUS TURRINUS SENIOR. " Why have you put on mourning ? " What—am I not to grieve for one I cannot avenge ? I do no-one injury except my father—for whom I still weep, in silence.

PORCIUS LATRO. Amid his inevitable grief for a father so cruelly slain, he can do nothing more brave than to groan.—" Accuse me," he says. Why are you so confident ? You sound as though you have identified another man as the murderer.—He had no spoils that a highwayman might seek, but he had the highest virtue, he had what is the surest protection of poverty—innocence obstinate in the face of proud riches : *these* were the spoils his enemy was

---

[2] Cf. §6 " He exults . . ." The father is represented as the stronger character, with a hold over the rich man (cf. the remarks of the populace mentioned by Albucius in §1).

Nescio quomodo miserum esse inter miserias iuvat,
et plerumque omnis dolor per lacrimas effluit. Nimium funere nostro exultat: non solebat vivo illo
provocare nos ut reus fieret. Si quis omnium mortalium miserrimi inter necessarias super occisum
patrem lacrimas ita creditam adhuc inertiam miratus
est, in hac indignitate praesentis periculi omnem
suam ponat admirationem. Si pauper accusandi
divitis animos non sumpsit, miramini? quia tacet,
7 reus est. Per has lacrimas, per hunc squalorem,
per haec necessaria omnibus periclitantibus instrumenta non invidiosum vestrae misericordiae praemium petimus, ut absoluto sic esse tamquam reo
liceat. Potens iste et gratiosus, quod ne ipse
quidem negat, dives fuit et qui nihil umquam putaret
sibi timendum, etiam reo. Crescere deinde in dies
odium alterius inpotentia, alterius libertate. Dives
nihil aliud quam ⟨nocentes⟩[1] nos pauperes existimare,
nos nihil aliud quam innocentes, inter cotidianas
acies semper invicti. *Quis de* nostra interim *morte
cogitaverit nescio: quod dissimulari non potest, scio quis
optaverit.* Venit iste cum turba clientium ac para-
sitorum et adversus paupertatem totam regiam suam 46]
effundit. "Cur me non accusas, non postulas?"
Vix temperabat quin diceret: "quid ego in te accusatorem non audeam qui occidendum curavi eum

---

[1] *Supplied by Novák.*

---

[1] For more on tears, see *C.* 8.6.
[2] The rich man and the poor father.

after.—Amid troubles there is a kind of pleasure in being troubled—and generally all grief flows out in the form of tears.[1]—He exults excessively in our bereavement; he didn't use to provoke us to accuse him while my father lived.—People may have felt surprise at what has hitherto been regarded as sloth on the part of the most wretched of all mortals in the midst of the tears inevitably shed over a slain father; but they may lay aside all their surprise in the face of the monstrousness of my present danger. Is it any wonder to you that a poor man hasn't summoned up the courage to accuse a rich man? He keeps quiet, yet finds himself accused.—I beg you by these 7 tears, by this filthy garb, by these trappings that are essential for all those on trial, I ask you a favour that your pity will not grudge: that when I am acquitted I may continue to dress as I do now as a defendant.— This rich man was powerful and influential, as he him- self acknowledges: he thought he could never have anything to be afraid of, even if he were accused. Then hatred for him grew day by day, thanks to the violence of the one and the outspokenness of the other.[2] The rich man thought us poor men nothing but harmful; we thought ourselves nothing but harm- less. And amid these daily battles we were always the victors. I don't know who, meanwhile, plotted our death: I do know who prayed for it—*that* cannot be hidden.—He comes with his throng of clients and parasites, and pours out the riches of his whole palace to crush the poor.—" Why don't you accuse me, take me to court? " He could scarcely stop himself say- ing: " What would *I* not dare to do to you if you accuse me—I who arranged the killing of a man who

377

THE ELDER SENECA

8 qui tantum mecum litigaverat? " Civitates plerumque finitimae inter repentinam discordiam bello tument: inter civilia certamina tantum in ultionem satis est quantum quisque ad male dicendum occupavit. Macerio qua violentia in absentiam Metelli strepit! M. Cato Pulchro obiciente furtorum crimina audivit. Quae maior indignitas illius saeculi esse potuit quam aut Pulcher accusator aut reus Cato! In Cn. Pompeium terra marique victorem fuit qui carmen conponeret, uno, ut ait, digito caput scalpentem; fuit aliquis qui licentia carminis tres auratos currus contemneret. M. Bruti †sacratissimi† [1] eum eloquentia lacerat, cum quidem eius civili sanguine non inquinatas solum manus sed infectas ait; atque ille tamen, cum tres consulatus ac tres triumphos scinderet, adeo non timuit ne esset reus ut etiam disertus esse curaverit. Solus hic est in nostra civitate innocentior Catone, nobilior Metello, Pompeio fortior.

9 Latro sic divisit: an in re iniuria sit. Nulla, 462 inquit, iniuria est ⟨si⟩ [2] sordidatus sum: quam multi faciunt! Omnia iniuriae genera ⟨lege⟩ [3]

[1] I have translated Müller's sceleratissimi ⟨calumniatoris⟩.
[2] Supplied by Gertz.
[3] Supplied by Bursian.

---

[1] For the feud of C. Atinius Labeo Macerio against Q. Metellus Macedonicus, see the Index of Names under Atinius.
[2] For Clodius' attacks on Cato for misappropriating money in Cyprus see Plut. Cat. Min. 45.1.
[3] Calvus: see C. 7.4.7.

378

merely quarrelled with me? "—Generally neighbour- 8
ing cities, when a sudden quarrel arises, are bursting
to go to war; in civil strife sufficient revenge is taken
by the man who has got his insult in first. How
violently Macerio inveighed against the absence of
Metellus![1] Marcus Cato had to listen to Pulcher
levelling a charge of theft.[2] What greater indignity
for that age than for Pulcher to accuse, or Cato to be
accused! There was a man[3] capable of composing a
lampoon against Pompey, victor on land and sea, who
(as it said) scratched his head with one finger: a man
capable of using the licence of a poem to make mock
of three golden chariots.[4] He was torn by the
eloquence of that most wicked of slanderers, Marcus
Brutus,[5] who said that his hands were stained and
even steeped in civil blood. Yet though he was
attacking three consulships and three triumphs, he
was so far from being afraid of being accused that he
even took the trouble to be eloquent. *This*[6] is the
only man in our state who is more innocent than Cato,
more noble than Metellus, more brave than Pompey.

Division

Latro's division went like this: Is there an injury in 9
the case? "There is no injury if I am in mourning:
how many do it! The law specifies all the types of

---

[4] Three triumphs. See Plut. *Pomp.* 45 on the occasion of
the third (61 B.C.).

[5] For Brutus' attacks on Pompey see *ORF*, 463. For his
hatred of the general R. Syme, *The Roman Revolution*, 58.

[6] Latro says sarcastically that the rich man can claim
immunity from criticism, being so far superior to these great
personages.

conprehensa sunt: pulsare non licet, convicium facere contra bonos mores non licet.

Hoc loco Scaurus dixit: nova formula iniuriarum componitur: " quod ille contra bonos mores flevit."

Etiamsi in re iniuria est, an si non malo animo facit tutus sit; an malo animo faciat. Hoc Latro in duas quaestiones divisit: an, si credidit ab hoc patrem suum occisum et propter hoc secutus est, ignoscendum illi sit; deinde: an crediderit.

Gallio illam fecit primam quaestionem: an, quod licet cuique facere si facit, iniuriarum non teneatur. Licet, inquit, flere, licet ambulare qua velis, licet vestem quam velis sumere. ⟨Sed⟩ [1] nihil, inquit, licet in alienam invidiam facere. Sordidatus es, non queror; sed si sordes tuae invidiam mihi concitant, queror.

10   De colore quaesitum est: quidam aperte invecti sunt in divitem, quidam ex toto nihil dixerunt, quidam secuti sunt mediam viam. Cum praeter haec nihil sit, Latro volebat videri invenisse quartum genus, ut hoc modo in divitem diceret: tu quidem non fecisti, sed tamen ego habui causas propter quas possem decipi et de te aliquid frustra suspicari: quia inimicus eras, quia inspoliatus pater inventus est, et cetera. Hoc est autem medium illud genus nec dimittendi divitem nec accusandi; nam et dimittere 46

___
[1] *Supplied by Faber.*

injury: one cannot strike another, one may not abuse contrary to good morals." [1]

It was at this point that Scaurus said: " A new wording for injuries is being formulated: That he did weep contrary to good morals."

Even if there is an injury in the case, is he safe from condemnation if he does not act with evil intent? *Does* he act with evil intent? This Latro divided into two questions: If he believed the rich man had killed his father and if he was following him for that reason, is he to be forgiven? Next: *Did* he believe it?

Gallio made this the first question: If a man does something that everybody is entitled to do, is he liable to a charge of doing an injury? " It is permitted to weep, to walk where you like, to dress as you like." " But," the reply is, " one is not permitted to act in such a way as to arouse hatred against another. You are in mourning—I do not complain; but if your mourning arouses hatred for me, I do complain."

Questions were raised about the *colour*. Some openly attacked the rich man, some said nothing at all against him, some took a middle way. Though there is no course apart from these three, Latro wanted the prestige of discovering a fourth type; this involved addressing the rich man as follows: " No, *you* didn't do it, but all the same *I* had reasons for being misled and for entertaining false suspicions about you: you were my enemy, my father was found unrobbed," and so on. But this in fact is the middle course, that of neither letting the rich man off nor accusing him: he ought not to let him off, despite

[1] For these two aspects of " injury " see Gaius 3.220.

non debet quem distulit, et accusare propter hoc
ipsum non debet, quia distulit.

11   Albucius nihil dixit in divitem; hoc colore declamavit: Committit, inquit, iniuriam si quem non
postulavit accusat. *Quare, inquit, sequeris me?
Ut aliquando mei miserearis, ut desinas afflictam domum
persequi,* ut scias me in hoc habitu accusare non posse,
ut concupiscas gloriam vindicatae mortis. Tu solus
potes, si voles, invenire quis occiderit, tu accusare.
"At me quidam propter hoc suspectum habent."
Potes discutere istam suspicionem: quaere quis
fecerit. " *Ut scias* " inquit " *te invidiam mihi facere,
cum dixissem: accusa me, non negasti* te accusaturum,
sed respondisti: accusabo, cum potero." Ignosce
mihi, non magis quemquam adhuc accusare possum
quam absolvere: quaero quis fecerit. Haec levia
argumenta sunt, vana sunt quae alios tangunt;
*quod inimicus es, quod ille inspoliatus inventus est, non
est quare accusem, est quare suspicer.*

12   Rufus Vibius hoc pro colore posuit: sordidatus
sum, lugeo; sequor te ut tutior sim; timeo nescio
quem illum qui patrem meum occidit; scio me quamdiu tecum fuero perire non posse.

Dum hunc colorem sequitur Murredius, ineptissime
dixit: Quare te sequor? pater meus quia solus in-
ambulabat occisus est.

Moschi color non placebat Gallioni: sequor, inquit, ut inveniam quis fecerit; hoc mecum cogito:

---

[1] It is not clear why this is so foolish.

having put off the accusation, and he ought not to accuse him, just because he *has* put the accusation off.

Albucius said nothing against the rich man. His **11** declamation had the following *colour*: " ' To accuse someone without having prosecuted him is to commit an injury. Why do you follow me? ' he says. So that you should at last take pity on me, should cease to persecute a prostrate household, should realise that I cannot in this plight accuse you, should covet the glory of avenging a death. You alone, if you will, can find the man who killed him, you alone can accuse him. ' But some people regard me as suspect because of this.' You can dispel that suspicion: look for the man responsible. ' If you want to see that you are causing me unpopularity, remember that when I said: Accuse me, you didn't say you wouldn't, but instead you replied: I will accuse when I can.' Forgive me, I can no more accuse anyone yet than acquit him: I am looking for the man responsible. Mine are feeble proofs—but the ones that weigh against other people are empty. You are my enemy, he was found unrobbed; I have here no reason to accuse you—but I do have reason to suspect."

Vibius Rufus used this as a *colour*: " I am in **12** mourning—I grieve. I follow you so as to be safer. I am afraid of whoever it was who killed my father; I know that I cannot perish so long as I am with you."

Following this *colour*, Murredius said, very foolishly:[1] " Why do I follow you? My father was killed because he walked the streets alone."

Moschus' *colour* displeased Gallio. " I follow you," said Moschus, " to find who did the deed. This is my

quisquis est ille qui fecit, volet hoc inimico inputare, ad divitem veniet. Multo, inquit, hoc iniuriosius est si inquirendi causa facit, si non tantum in convicium sed periculum divitis sequitur.

Gallio subtiliter agendum putavit et ad positionem controversiae colorem actionis derigendum, ut 464r diceret: Suspicor a te patrem meum occisum. Quis enim illum alius magis oderat? quis tam potens alius est? Vestem sine dubio alius nescio quis percussor concupierat. Dicet aliquis: quid ergo? si inimicus est, protinus interfector est? Non; ideo non accuso.

13 Hispo Romanius palam accusavit et dixit non causam sibi desse sed vires; et hanc sententiam in prooemio magno cum adsensu hominum dixit: *eum accusatorem habeo qui se reum non esse miratur.*

Bassus Iulius in hac controversia dixit: " quare me sequeris per publicum? " Facinus indignum, iudices, factum est: pauper et dives eandem terram calcavimus. Consectari autem solebat res sordidas et inveniebat qui illas unice suspicerent. Memini illum declamantem [declarasse][1] controversiam de lenone, qui decem iuvenibus denuntiavit ne[2] in lupanar accederent, et foveam igne repletam terra

[1] *Deleted by C. F. W. Müller.*
[2] ne *early editors:* de.

[1] Apparently by helping the true criminal in his attempt to

train of thought: whoever did it will want to lay the blame on an enemy of mine, and he will come to the rich man." "It is much more injurious," said Gallio, "if he does this in order to make his investigations, if he follows the rich man not only to insult him but to endanger him." [1]

Gallio thought that one should employ finesse, and adapt the *colour* of the speech to the theme of the *controversia*, saying: "I suspect that you killed my father. Who else hated him more than you? Who else is so influential? Without doubt, some other murderer would have coveted his clothes. Someone may object: 'Well? If he is your enemy, does that straightaway make him the killer?' No: that is just why I make no accusation."

Romanius Hispo made open accusations, and said 13 that he lacked not the motive to bring a charge but the strength to carry it through. And he placed in his proem an epigram that was highly applauded: "I have an accuser who is surprised that he is not the defendant."

Julius Bassus said on this subject: "'Why do you follow me in public?' Judges, a dreadful crime has been committed: we, a poor man and a rich, have trodden the same ground." He used to go in for vulgarity, and found people to admire that above all else. I remember him declaiming a *controversia* [2] on a pimp who forbade ten youths to go into a brothel. The young men slipped into a pit filled with fire

---

incriminate the rich man. But *inputare* may = "claim credit for."

[2] For the declamation see Calp. Flacc. 5 and *RLM* p. 83.1: and in a rather different form *Rhet. Gr.* 2.135 Spengel.

superiecta obruit, in quam adulescentibus lapsis et consumptis accusatur rei publicae laesae. Audit illum declamantem Albucius, fastidiosus auditor eorum quibus invidere poterat; admirabatur hanc Bassi sententiam: non mehercules te ferrem si

14 canem ad ostium alligasses. Idem Latronis illas sententias aiebat tumidas magis esse quam fortes, 465 quae summa hominum admiratione circumfere-bantur: legunt argumenta patres et ossa liberorum coniectura dividunt; et illam: produc istam sacer-dotem [1] tuam; et illam: supra cineres liberorum nostrorum lupanar ⟨solo⟩ [2] aequandum [3] est. Ipse autem laudabat haec utique ⟨quae⟩ [4] docuerat. Nam in hac ipsa controversia, ne Bassus videretur aliquid dixisse sordidius, dixit ipse: itane sic peribunt de-

15 cem iuvenes propter dipondios tuos?

Euctemon a fili parte, cum patrem suum narrasset solum sine comite oppressum et occisum, dixit: διὰ τοῦτο ἀσφαλέστατόν ἐστιν μετὰ πλουσίων περιπα-τεῖν. Et idem: διὰ τί σιγῶ; ὁ πατήρ μου λέγων ἀπέθανεν.

Hermagoras dixit: κτίσωμεν ἰδίᾳ, ὦ πένητες, πόλιν· οἱ γὰρ πλούσιοι τὴν αὐτ⟨ῶν . . .⟩. [5] Illud in narratione: ὑπὸ τίνος ἀνηρέθη οὐκ οἶδα. εἶχεν ἐχθροὺς φύσει παρρησιαστὴς κακηγορεῖν δυνάμενος.

---

[1] produc istam sacerdotem *Shackleton Bailey:* producta(m) sacerdotes.
[2] *Supplied by Bursian.*
[3] aequandum *Müller:* dequantum.
[4] utique quae *Bursian:* utiqua.
[5] *I have translated Linde's supplement* ἔχουσιν.

---

[1] Let alone protecting his house with a pit.

and concealed with earth, which the pimp had prepared, and were burned up; the pimp is accused of
harming the state. He was heard declaiming by
Albucius, who was liable to listen with scorn to things
that he might feel jealous about; he liked this epigram of Bassus': "I should not tolerate you if you had
tied up a dog at the door." [1]   This same man said that 14
Latro's epigrams, that were being circulated with
great admiration, were bombastic rather than force-
ful: "The fathers pick out their proofs, and use conjecture to make division of their children's bones." [2]
Also: "Bring out your priestess!" [3]   And: "Over
the ashes of our children, the brothel must be rased
to the ground." But he did at least praise the things
he had inspired himself: for in this same *controversia*
—making sure that Bassus shouldn't be thought to
have said anything more vulgar—Albucius himself
said: "Are ten youths to perish because of your
two-pences?"

Euctemon, on the son's side, having narrated how 15
his father had been caught alone, with no companions, and murdered, said: "That is why it is safest
to go about with rich men." He also said: "Why
am I silent? My father spoke—and died."

Hermagoras said: "Let us poor men found a city
separately: the rich have one of their own." [4]   And
in his narration: "I don't know who killed him. He
had enemies, for he was by nature outspoken and
could be abusive."

---

[2] Latro describes the search for the remnants of the bodies
with rhetorical *double entendre*.

[3] i.e. the prostitute you guard so carefully.

[4] For they exclude poor men from the existing city.

Artemon dixit: ὅταν εὕρω τὸν φονέα, τότ᾽ αὖ 46•
γράψομαι· καὶ τότε δή, ἂν εὕρω πένητα.

II

FORTIS NON CEDENS FORTI PATRI

Vir fortis quod volet praemium optet; si plures
erunt, iudicio contendant.

Pater et filius fortiter fecerunt. Petit pater
a filio sibi cederet; ille non vult. Iudicio con-
tendit; vicit patrem. Praemio statuas patri
petivit. Abdicatur.

1 IUNI GALLIONIS. *Dubito quid de eventu huiusce iudici
optem cum crimen meum sit vicisse.* Videtis quemadmodum in hoc quoque iudicio opera sua iactet: et
miratur quisquam si hoc patre natus gloriae cupidior
est? Faciles habetis partes: viros fortes iungite.
Dissidemus quia nimium similes sumus. Cum ex-
iremus in aciem, aiebat: si adulescens essem, nemo
pugnaret fortius. Maiorum quoque suorum virtutes referebat, sed omnibus se praeferebat. Cum
ad aetatem tuam pervenero, non contendam cum
ullo, quamvis ⟨sit⟩,[1] si exemplum tuum sequi voluero,

---

[1] *Supplied by Thomas.*

---

[1] A law common, with variations, in declamation: parallels
in Bonner, 88. No real life counterpart is known.
[2] The nearest parallel is *Decl.* 258.

Artemon said: "When I find the killer, I shall accuse him: and I'll do it even if it's a poor man I find."

2

THE HEROIC SON WHO WOULD NOT YIELD TO HIS HEROIC FATHER

A hero may choose the reward he wishes; if there are more heroes than one, they must dispute the point at law.[1]

A father and his son acted heroically. The father asked the son to give way to him. He was not prepared to. He disputed the point at law and defeated his father. As his reward he asked for statues to be erected to his father. His father disinherits him.[2]

For the son

JUNIUS GALLIO. I am doubtful what result to pray 1 for in this trial—for what I am accused of is having won.—You see how in this trial too he boasts of his own deeds; does anyone wonder if a son of such a father is over-eager for glory?—Your [3] role is easy: bring two brave men together.—We are quarrelling because we are too alike.—When we went out to fight, he used to say: "If I were a young man, no-one would fight more bravely." And he would recount the brave deeds of his ancestors, putting himself, however, before them all.—When I reach your age, I shall not dispute with anyone: though, if I choose to

[3] The judges'.

389

2 etiam cum filio contendendum.[1] Quia *patriae iudicium habeo, patris perdidi*. Dicam abdicanti: " non
luxuriabor, non amabo." Hanc emendationem criminum meorum non possum promittere: ⟨" non fortiter
pugnabo ";⟩ [2] ego vero pugnabo et fortiter et fortissime. *Vidi patrem* iam senem *loricam induentem:*
multum est *pugnare cum exemplo. Iudicium vocat* 46
quo pater et filius spolia contulimus? Ecce commilito
ego tibi possum cedere, seni non possum. Quod
contendi, legis, quod vici, iudicum, quod pugnavi,
patris est. Volui cedere; concurrerunt iuvenes,
aetatis causa agebatur: *vici non filius patrem, sed
iuvenis senem. Ego vici, sed omnes patri gratulati sunt.*

3 Parui adulescens magnis exemplis. Deceptus sum
dum *cogito* mecum *Horatium Etruscas acies corpore
suo summoventem* et Mucium in hostili ara manum
urentem et dum *te, Deci, cogito, qui et ipse noluisti
patri cedere.* Transibo in subsellia tua, complectar
invitum: licet repugnes, fortior sum.

[1] contendendum *Thomas:* con(di)tendam.
[2] *Supplied by the ed. after Gertz.*

---

[1] The objection to the son being that he had thwarted his
father in a trial (see §10): cf. below §4 " Do you call . . ."
[2] That is, apparently, it is your age, not your being my
companion in battle, that prevents my yielding to you.

follow your example, I have to dispute even with my son.—It is because I have the judgement of my 2 country on my side that I have lost my father's.—I shall say to him as he disinherits me: "I shall not be dissolute. I shall indulge in no amours." *One* reform of my misdeeds I cannot promise: "I shall not fight bravely." I *will* fight bravely, most bravely. —I saw my father, now an old man, putting on a breastplate; it is a great thing to fight with an example at one's side.—Does he call it a trial [1]—a father and son comparing their booty?—Look, I, your companion in arms, can yield to you—but I cannot yield to an old man.[2]—That I disputed is due to the law, that I won is due to the judges, that I fought is due to my father.—I wanted to give way. The young men flocked, it was my age-group whose cause was at stake. I won, not as son over father, but as young man over old.—*I* won—but everyone congratulated my father.—I was a young man with great 3 precedents to follow. I was deceived as I thought to myself of Horatius using his body to keep off the Etruscan ranks,[3] and Mucius burning his hand on an enemy altar,[4] and Decius, who, like me, was unwilling to yield to his father.[5]—I will come over to your benches, I will embrace you against your will; even if you fight back, I am the stronger.[6]

---

[3] For the famous deed at the bridge see, e.g. Val. Max. 3.2.1; Livy 2.10; Sen. *Ep.* 120.7.

[4] Cf. *C.* 8.4 n.

[5] For the Decii devoting themselves for the state, see Val. Max. 5.6.5–6; Sen. *Ep.* 67.9. Gallio merely means that the son was unwilling to be less brave than his father.

[6] There is a play on the double sense of *fortis*.

4   FULVI SPARSI.   Necesse fuit mihi fortiter militare:
pugnandum habebam non imperatori tantum sed patri.
Si tu vicisses, diceretur: patri cessit; abdicationem
enim timuit.   Solebas semper optare ut contingeret
tibi filium habere meliorem.   Iudicium vocas duplicem domus nostrae triumphum?

5   CLODI TURRINI.   Tu Mucio diceres: "non est
quod ostendas istam manum"?   tu Scipioni post
deletam Carthaginem: "tace"?   Loquax est virtus
nec ostendit se tantum sed ingerit.   Aiunt ecce
nunc quidam: cessit pater filio, et in hoc abdicat ut
videatur verum fuisse certamen.   Opta, pater, ut et
a nepote vincaris.   "Postea" inquit "pugnare
fortiter poteris."   Unde scio?   Vulneribus me senem
feci.   Quis te felicior?   tu omnes vicisti, te filius.
Quanto honestius modo pater et filius inter se
contenderunt, honestiorem facturus victum uter   46
6   vicisset!   Dubito quid faciam.   Taceam?   sed silentium videtur confessio.   Narrem virtutes meas?
sed illud quoque mihi novum accidit, quod uni mihi
abdicato eas narrare non ⟨prodest⟩.[1]   Processi in
aciem coram patre: fortiter, inquit, pugna; turpe
est adulescenti vinci a sene.   *Avidus sum gloriae:
hoc si vitium est, paternum est.*   Fortis sum: numquid

----

[1] *Supplied by Bursian.*

Fulvius Sparsus. I had to be a brave soldier; I 4 had to fight not only for my commander but for my father.—If you had won, people would be saying: "He yielded to his father because he was afraid of being disinherited."—You always used to pray to be lucky enough to have a son better than yourself.—Do you call the double triumph of our house a trial?

Clodius Turrinus. Would you say to Mucius: 5 "Do not show your hand"? To Scipio after the destruction of Carthage: "Be silent"? Virtue cannot but speak; it shows itself, even thrusts itself forward.—See, now people are saying: "The father gave way to the son, and is disinheriting him to make it look as though it was a real contest."—Pray, father, that you may be defeated by your grandson too.—"*You* can be a hero later." How do I know? I have made myself an old man by my wounds.—Who is luckier than you? *You* have overcome all—and your son has overcome *you*.—How much more honourable was the contest of father and son a while back:[1] the victor in it was destined to add to the glory of the loser.—I don't know what to do. Keep 6 quiet? But silence looks like confession. Tell of my feats? But here too is a fresh affliction for me—I alone, on being disinherited, find no profit in telling of such things.—I went to battle alongside my father. "Fight bravely," he said. "It is shameful for a young man to be surpassed by an old."—I am greedy for glory; if that is a vice, it is one I have inherited from my father.—I am brave; surely you have no

---

[1] That is, in the previous contest, when the father's victory would have reflected credit on the son and the son's on the father: cf. Turrinus in §14.

THE ELDER SENECA

improbas, pater? At iam abdicabis si dixero:
fortissimus sum. Dicam tamen audaciter: "fortissimus sum "nec timeo in ea civitate hoc crimen in
qua fortes etiam senes novimus.

7   IULI BASSI. Ad te quoque ignominiae meae
pars redundat: *pudeat* te, *pater, si a filio abdicando
victus es.*

ARELLI FUSCI patris. Ignosce, iuvenis erravi:
ambitiosus non ero cum senex fuero.

GAVI SILONIS. Utrum putas vicisse? *ego praemium*
tantum *habeo, tu et praemium et virum fortem.*

8   ⟨DIVISIO. ** sic divisit: an filius abdicari possit
propter id quod⟩ [1] permittente lege fecit. Nemo,
⟨inquit⟩,[2] in eadem re et habet legem et timet.
Contra ait: si quid fecerit quod non licet, lex vindicabit; si quid quod licet sed non oportet pater.
Non quaeritur de scelere filii, sed de officio. Deinde:
utatur sua quisque lege; tibi illud licuit, et mihi
hoc licet. Abdicare liberos liceat. Est aliqua lex
quae filio patrem praeferat. Si potest abdicari
etiam propter id quod lege permittente fecit, an
abdicari etiam propter hoc non possit, ⟨propter⟩ [3] 46:
quod praemium accepit. Non potest, inquit, in ea
re privatim puniri in qua publice honoratur. Eidem

[1] *Supplied by Schultingh, Müller.*
[2] nemo inquit *Schultingh:* immo.
[3] *Supplied by Schott.*

---

[1] Unlike you.
[2] Your son (if he remains in your household).
[3] The son's action was legal. But the father's, as well as
the actual law just quoted, has a moral law in its favour also.

objection to that, father? Yet now you propose to disinherit me if I say I am bravest of all. But I shall say it boldly: " I am bravest of all." I am not frightened of this charge in a city where we know of bravery even in the old.

JULIUS BASSUS. Part of my disgrace falls upon you 7 too; you should be ashamed, father, if you have been defeated by a son who deserves disinheriting.

ARELLIUS FUSCUS SENIOR. Forgive me, I am young and I have gone astray; I shall not be ambitious when I grow old.[1]

GAVIUS SILO. Whom do you regard as the victor? *I* have merely my prize, *you* have both the prize and a hero.[2]

Division

** 's division was as follows: Can a son be dis- 8 inherited for something he did in accordance with the law? " No-one, in one and the same matter, has the law on his side and also fears the law." On the other side he said: " If he does something that is not allowed, the law will punish him; if he does something that is allowed but that should not be done, his father will punish him. The enquiry concerns not a sin done by the son, but his duties." Then: " Let each make use of the law that favours him. You were allowed that, I am allowed this. ' One may disinherit children.' And there is a law that puts the father above the son."[3] If he can be disinherited even for a legal action, can he be disinherited even for an action for which he has received a prize? " He cannot be punished privately for an action that brings him public honour. You cannot have the same

rei non potest et praemium dari et nota denuntiari.
Cetera iura puta paterno imperio subiecta esse: hoc
ius maius est ceteris, quo de victoria, de summa
virtute quaeritur. Non potes propter hanc legem
filium abdicare propter quam a filio victus es.

9   Si potest abdicari, an debeat. Hoc ⟨in haec⟩ [1]
divisit: an, etiamsi non debuit cum patre contendere,
ignoscendum tamen sit, si adulescens gloriae cupiditate lapsus est; deinde: an contendere debuerit.
Tibi, inquit, et honestum erat certamen et tutum:
quid est enim gloriosius quam aut virum fortem vincere aut a filio vinci? Si non debuisset contendere,
non vicisset. Et potuit fieri ut, si hic tibi cessisset,
alius aliquis ad certamen procederet, qui nunc non
processit quia sciebat nihil sibi profuturum si te
vicisset, cum deberet a filio tuo vinci. Nulla laus
tua fuisset; apparuisset enim illam victoriam non
viri fortis fuisse sed patris. *Silentio virtutes vestrae
transissent:* nunc *inlustratae sunt, dum conferuntur.*

10 Turrinus hoc loco belle dixit: Plures tibi invidere
coeperunt, postquam victus es. Itaque novi generis
res accidit: filius vicerat; omnes aiebant: o felicem
patrem!

Novissimam quaestionem fecit: an, etiamsi quid
iudicio peccavit, praemio emendaverit. Hoc loco
dixit Gallio illam sententiam quae valde excepta est:

[1] *Supplied by Müller, Otto.*

---

[1] That is, to you qua father, not qua brave man. The case
of a third contestant is no longer in question.

thing rewarded by a prize *and* threatened with disgrace. Suppose all other rights are subject to a
father's rule: *this* right is greater than the rest, that
by which enquiry is made as to victory and the
extremities of courage. You cannot disinherit a son
because of the law that enabled him to defeat you."

If he can be disinherited, should he be? He 9
divided this into the following: Even if he ought not
to have disputed with his father, should he nevertheless be forgiven if, being a young man, he has gone
astray through greed for glory? Then: Ought he
have disputed it? " For you the contest was both
honourable and safe; for what is more glorious than
either to defeat a brave man or to be defeated by
one's son? If he ought not to have competed, he
would not have won. And it might have been that if
he had given in to you some other person would have
come into the contest, someone who, as it was, did
not enter it because he knew it would do him no good
to beat you, because he must lose to your son. No
praise would have accrued to you: for it would have
been obvious that victory belonged not to the hero
but to the father.[1] Your exploits would have been
passed over in silence; now their brilliance has been
shown up, by the comparison."

Here Turrinus had a pretty saying: " Many began 10
to envy you—after you were beaten. Hence a
novelty: the son had won, but everyone said: Lucky
father."

The last question he made: Even if he did do
wrong by going to law, did he make amends by the
prize he chose? Here Gallio spoke an epigram that
was rapturously received. After begging forgiveness

cum diu deprecatus esset, ait: Si nihil profecero, quid
me facturum putas? ad templa iturum aut ad deos 470M
supplicem? Ad statuas tuas confugiam.

11   Silo Pompeius temptavit et in hac controversia illam
quaestionem quam in omnibus virorum fortium abdicationibus putabat esse temptandam: an vir fortis
abdicari possit; aiebat in nulla magis controversia
illam posse tractari. Non potes, inquit, eum abdicare qui te potest vincere. Miraris si patri hac lege
subducitur qui ⟨ei⟩ [1] et comparatur et praefertur?

12   Colorem pro adulescente Gallio illum induxit:
⟨Concurrerunt ad⟩ [2] me, inquit, iuvenes: aetatis
causa agi videbatur. Cum dubitarem, exaudivi [3]
nescio quem dicentem: nihil agis; ego tibi cedo,
illi non cedo.

Cestius hoc colore usus est: putasse se ipsi patri
honestius hoc esse, certe domui, laudes utriusque in
foro inspici.

Montanus Votienus ait: Cogitavi non quid im-
perares sed quid praecepisses: dixeras semper, cum
me hortareris ad gloriam, ut nulli cederem. Invi-
diosa omnibus in illo iudicio fortuna tua videbatur,
cum quaereretur utrum pugnasses felicius an
genuisses. Non est quod me putes visum illis fortiorem: decepti sunt, pater; *iudicaverunt non quod erat*
sed quod te malle crediderunt.

[1] qui ei *Jahn:* qua.
[2] *Supplied by Müller.*
[3] exaudivi *Bursian:* exordi.

for some time, he said: " If I beg to no avail, what do you think I shall do? Go to the temples or the gods as suppliant? No, I shall flee for refuge to your statues."

Pompeius Silo tried in this *controversia* too the 11 question which he thought should be tried in all cases involving the disinheriting of heroes: Can a hero be disinherited? He said that this could be handled nowhere better than in this case. " You cannot disinherit him, for he can defeat you. Are you surprised if by this law the father loses his power over a son who is compared to him—and found superior? "

Gallio introduced this *colour* for the youth: " The 12 youths flocked to me. It was, it seemed, the cause of youth that was at stake. I hesitated, then heard someone saying: ' You are wasting your time. I concede to you—but not to him.' "[1]

Cestius used this *colour*: he had thought it more honourable for the father himself, and certainly for the family, that the praises of both should be reviewed in the forum.

Votienus Montanus said: " I thought not of your present orders but of your past precepts; you had always said, when spurring me on to glory, that I should yield to none. At that trial your good fortune was regarded by all as enviable, for the point at dispute was whether you had been luckier in fighting or in begetting. Don't imagine they thought me the braver. They were misled, father: they decided not according to the facts, but according to what they believed you preferred."

---

[1] i.e. if the son conceded, an alternative rival would appear —and beat the father (cf. §9).

13   Argentarius ait: Occasionem benefici quaesivi,
non concupivi accipere praemium. *Honor ad utrum-*
que pervenit: alter praemium habet, alter accepit.   471M

Fuscus Arellius pater ait: Si navigare imperasses,
per hibernos fluctus egissem ratem; si peregrinari,
nihil fuisset iubente te durum. Hanc rem impera-
bas difficilem forti viro, vinci.

Blandus hoc colore narravit: pater mihi obicit
quod illi in una re non cesserim; ego multiplicabo
crimina mea: numquam illi quotiens recte faciendum
fuit cessi, semper volui videri frugalior, videri volui
laboriosior; nam cum ad vires ventum erat, etiam
ipse cedebat: non ego illum vincebam, sed aetas.

14   Turrinus hoc colore usus est: Volui, inquit, cedere,
sed erant qui dicerent non licere; hoc enim [nobis] [1]
modo legem saluberrimam tolli. Disputaturi contra
praemium patris videbantur et dicturi: non licet
inter se cedere fortibus; non ipsorum tantum causa
agitur, sed publica; omnium interest scire quis sit
fortissimus. His vocibus hominum missus sum ad
id certamen in quo ad istum utraque pertineret
victoria. Quid putatis me dicturum? fortiorem me
visum? Falsum est, cum hoc quoque, quod ego
fortis eram, istius esset. Quid ergo? quare vicerim
quaeritis? Visum est ad ruborem totius iuventutis

---

[1] *Deleted by early editors.*

Argentarius said: " I sought an opportunity to do 13
a good turn—I didn't covet the prize. Both of us
have attained honour: one has the prize,[1] the other
received it."

Arellius Fuscus senior said: " If you had told me
to go to sea, I should have steered my ship through
stormy waves. If you had told me to travel, I should
have found nothing hard when you ordered it. But
what you did order was something a brave man finds
difficult—to be overcome."

Blandus' narration used this *colour*: " My father
reproaches me with not giving way to him in one
matter. *I* will increase the number of charges
against me: I never yielded to him when it was a
question of doing right—I always wanted to be
thought more honest, more industrious; for when it
came to strength, it was *he* who gave way: age
defeated him, not I."

This was the *colour* Turrinus used: " I wanted to 14
give way. But people told me that it was not
allowed—for that was the way to nullify a highly
salutary law. They seemed ready to dispute the
award of the prize to my father, and to use the argument: ' Heroes may not give way to each other. It
isn't their case alone that is at issue, but that of the
state. It is in everybody's interests to know who is
the bravest.' I was pushed by remarks like this into
a contest where the victory of either of us would
belong to my father. What do you think I am going
to say? That I was thought the braver? It is not
true, for *my* bravery too was thanks to him. Well
then, you ask why I won? People thought it would

---

[1] The father has the statues. This is the good turn.

pertinere, neminem pugnasse fortius quam senem. Et cum dixisset se praemia in patrem contulisse, dixit: vici te, pater, sed nempe vici tibi.

15 Albucius hoc colore narravit: nolui, inquit, videri per collusionem patri titulum fortissimi viri contigisse: non cessi ante iudicium ut in iudicio cederem, et feci nihil aliud quam laudavi patrem, virtutes eius rettuli; visus sum propter hoc ipsum praemio dignus.

16 Silo Gavius ait: Solebas mihi, pater, insignium virorum exempla narrare, quaedam etiam domestica; 472 aiebas: avom fortem virum habuisti; vide ut sis fortior. Processi tecum in aciem nec illic . . .; ubi rediimus, omnis gloria in una domo erat. Volebat res publica fortes viros recognoscere. O quantam ego cupiditatem gloriae in patre meo vidi, quam iuvenilem! contendere me vetabat imperio, iubebat exemplo. Ventum est in iudicium: omnium quas ego novi res invidiosissima quaerebatur de patre meo: utrum fortior esset an felicior.

17 Moschus hoc colore narravit: ⟨Erant qui⟩ accederent et dicerent: roga patrem tuum cedat tibi: non est utile rei publicae excitari hostium animos; excitabuntur si scierint neminem in hac civitate esse fortiorem quam senem. Illi me coegerunt, quasi tum quoque aliquid praestaturus essem rei publicae,

bring shame on the whole of our youth if it were decided that no-one had fought more bravely than an old man." And after saying he had conferred prizes on his father, he said: " I defeated you, father—but in fact it was for *you* that I won."

Albucius' narration employed this *colour*: " I 15 didn't want it to be thought that the title of bravest had gone to my father by collusion. I didn't give way before the trial so that I could give way *at* the trial: and I did nothing beyond praise my father and recount his deeds. It was just because of this that I was thought worthy of the prize."

Gavius Silo said: " Father, you used to tell me of 16 the feats of famous men, some actually taken from our family records. You would say: ' You had a hero for your grandfather: make sure *you* are braver.' I went into battle with you—and there too . . .¹ When we returned, the whole of the glory was confined to one household. The state wished to review its heroes. How great, how typical of a young man was the thirst for glory I saw in my father! He used his power to forbid me to compete, but his example to order me. We came to court: the most enviable question I know was raised about my father—was he more brave, or more fortunate ? "

Moschus used this *colour* for his narration: " People 17 came up and said: Ask your father to give way to you; it is not in the interests of the state that the spirits of our enemies should be raised—as they will be if they learn that no-one in this country is braver than an old man. They forced me to go to trial—as if on this occasion too I had a service to do the state.

¹ ⟨you continued to exhort me⟩ (?).

venire in iudicium: in quo quid habeo? ego iudicatus sum iuvenior.

Mento dixit: timeo ne ob hoc ipsum patri vilior fiam [ego]; [1] scimus quam gloriosus sit.

18 Triarius hoc colore usus est: in iudicio volui tibi cedere, ut non imperasse videreris sed vicisse, et cessi: defunctorie causam meam egi; †sed notum sit illum cedere quia parum est illi non putabat.† [2]

473

Nicetes in hac controversia dixit: εἰ ὁ πάππος ὑπὸ τῆς φύσεως ἀποδοθεὶς ἡμῖν παρέστη τῷ τότε δικαστηρίῳ, οὐκ ἂν εἶπεν·

τίς νύ μοι ἡμέρη ἥδε, θεοὶ φίλοι. ἦ μάλα χαίρω

⟨υἱός θ' υἱω⟩νός τ' ἀρετῆς πέρι δῆριν ἔχουσιν;

et: πολλὸν δ' ὅγε πατρὸς ἀμείνων.

19 Scaurus hunc sensum aliter dixit: O si avos meus interesset iudicio, quam libenter spectaret et discordiam nostram! Clamasset mihi: non est quod cedas; ipse mihi numquam cessit.

Labienus partem patris declamavit et dixit: Quod etiam deterioribus licet, *nolo habitare cum ad-*

---

[1] *Deleted by the editor.*

[2] *I have translated Müller's* sed notum sit filium non cedere quia parem se illi non putabat. *But the words should perhaps be deleted as the remains of a commentator's gloss explaining in what sense the son " yielded."*

What was the result there? *I* was judged the younger." [1]

Mento said: " I am afraid I may become cheaper in my father's eyes for this very reason; [2] we all know how much he loves glory."

Triarius used this *colour*: " I wanted to give way to 18 you at the trial, so that you might be thought not to have ordered it but to have won—and I did give way. I pleaded my case cursorily; but let it be known that the son does not yield because he didn't think himself his father's equal." [3]

Nicetes said in this *controversia*: " If Nature had given us back my grandfather to be present at that trial, would he not have said:

' What a day is this for me, dear gods! I rejoice
    indeed—
My son and grandson quarrel over bravery ' '";

and

" ' far better he than his father.' " [4]

Scaurus put this idea differently: " O, if my grand- 19 father were present at the trial, how glad he would be to see even our discord! He would have shouted to me: You should not yield—*he* never yielded to me."

Labienus, declaiming the father's part, said: " I don't want to live with my adversary—that is a favour

---

[1] i.e. there was no reflection on the father's courage; the son had a natural advantage in his youth.

[2] i.e. for conceding to my father. These words would be spoken at or before the first trial.

[3] Text and sense uncertain.

[4] Hom. *Od.* 24.514–5; *Il.* 6.479.

*versario meo: non capit idem contubernium fortem virum
et victum. " Statuam" inquit " tibi posui": immo, ne
possem umquam victum me oblivisci, ignominiam meam
in aes incidisti.*

III

Demens Quod Mori Coegerit Filiam

Dementiae sit actio.

Bello civili quaedam virum secuta est, cum in
diversa parte haberet patrem et fratrem. Victis
partibus suis et occiso marito venit ad patrem;
non recepta in domum dixit: quemadmodum
tibi vis satis faciam? Ille respondit: morere.
Suspendit se ante ianuam eius: accusatur pater
a filio dementiae.

474

1   Porci Latronis. *Sic sibi satis fieri ne victor quidem
voluit:* excusavit victos, quin restituit. Quoniam
reposcis vitam quam dedisti, accipe. *Nullum fuit
in proscriptione mulierculae caput.*

Moschi. *Inquinasti filiae sanguine penates. Quam-
quam quid* ego *dico penates, tamquam in domo perierit?
Adlatum ad se Caesar Pompei caput flevit: hoc ille
propter filiam praestitit.*

---

[1] See *C.* 2.3 n.
[2] *C.* 4.8 with n.
[3] For scene and sentiments cf. Val. Max. 5.1.10: " At the
sight Caesar forgot his feud, put on the look of a father-in-law,
and shed for Pompey the tears due from himself and from his
own daughter [i.e. Julia]."   Lucan (9.1035 *seq.*) is more cynical.

allowed even to inferior persons. The same lodgings
cannot hold a hero and a loser. ' I erected a statue
to you.' Say rather that, in order that I could never
forget my defeat, you carved my disgrace in bronze."

3

THE MAN ACCUSED OF BEING MAD FOR FORCING
HIS DAUGHTER TO DIE

An action may lie for madness.[1]

In the civil wars, a woman refused to desert
her husband, though her father and brother were
on the other side. Her own side defeated and
her husband killed, she came to her father; he
would not admit her into his house. She said:
" How do you want me to make amends to you? "
He replied: " Die! " She hanged herself before
his door. The father is accused of madness by
his son.

For the son

PORCIUS LATRO. Not even the victor wanted 1
amends to be made him like this; *he* pardoned the
defeated, even restored them.[2]—" Since you demand
back the life you gave, take it."—No woman's life
was doomed in the proscriptions.

MOSCHUS. You have stained the household gods
with the blood of your daughter. But why do I say
" household gods? "—as if she perished *inside* the
house.—Caesar wept when the head of Pompey was
brought to him; this was the tribute he paid for his
daughter's sake.[3]

THE ELDER SENECA

Arelli Fusci. " *Quemadmodum tibi vis satis fa-ciam?* " Hoc ipso satis fecisse debuerat. Filiam habuit *piam et in maritum et in patrem: alterum usque in mortem secuta est, alteri etiam per mortem satis fecit.* Quam *periculose istum offendo, qui* simul irasci coepit *nescit ignoscere!*

2 Clodi Turrini patris. " *Morere.*" Quid aliud meruerat si satis facere nollet? Nisi occupasses, soror, fortasse pater tibi satis fecisset. Hoc, certum habeo, unusquisque vestrum suadebat puellae: " ad iratum patrem venis; in quas potes te compone blanditias; roga, deprecare; si nihil proficies, habes quemad-modum cogas: morituram te denuntia." Hoc quod ignovisti, victor, ad viros pertinet: illi tibi gratias agunt; nam feminas ne si irascereris quidem proscripsisses. " Quare secuta est virum? " Adeo tibi vetera exempla exciderunt bonarum coniugum, in quae filiam tuam solebas sanus hortari? Aliqua spiritum viri redemit suo, aliqua se super ardentis rogum misit. Inpendisset se puella viro nisi ser- 47⁸ vasset patri.

3 Fulvi Sparsi. Filia ante limen paternum in cruore suo volutatur. Quid exhorruistis? paterna satisfactio est. Nostis domus nostrae legem: aut vincendum

---

[1] By killing yourself.
[2] *C.* 2.2.1 n.

408

ARELLIUS FUSCUS. "How do you want me to make you amends?" She should have made amends by asking this very question.—He had a daughter who loved both her husband and her father; the one she followed till his death, the other she made amends to even by dying.—How perilous it is for me to offend a man who, once he gets angry, does not know how to forgive!

CLODIUS TURRINUS SENIOR. "Die." What else 2 would she have deserved if she had *refused* to make amends?—If you hadn't got in first,[1] sister, perhaps our father would have made *you* amends.—This, I feel sure, is what every one of you advised the girl: "You are going to an angry father; prepare yourself for such wheedlings as you are capable of. Beg, ask his pardon. If you don't succeed, you have a means of forcing his hand—threaten to kill yourself."—Your pardon, victor, has to do with men; they thank you. For you would not have proscribed women even if you had been angry.—"Why did she follow her husband?" Have you so totally forgotten the ancient instances of faithful wives,[2] to emulate which you used to exhort your daughter—when you were sane? One bartered her life for her husband's, another flung herself on his blazing pyre. This girl would have forfeited herself for her husband—if she hadn't been keeping herself for her father.

FULVIUS SPARSUS. A daughter writhes in her own 3 blood before her father's threshold. Why shiver? This is known as "making amends to a father."— You know the rule in our house: I must either win [3]

[3] For the son, his case had to be won; for the daughter, the war.

mihi aut moriendum est. Qualis est ista satisfactio qua filia exoratum sibi patrem non sentit?

ALBUCI SILI. Utrae meliores partes essent, soli videbantur iudicare di posse. " Si vis satis facere mihi, morere." Quod ad me attinet, irascare malo. Si parricidium ⟨esset⟩ fuisse [1] in diversis partibus, numquam *defendisset* apud Caesarem *Ligarium Cicero*. M. Tulli, *quam leve iudicasti crimen de quo confessus es!* Dona filiam, si misericors es, deprecanti; si hostis, edicto; si pater, naturae; si iudex, causae; si iratus es, fratri.

4 BUTEONIS. *Ante ipsum limen domus decessit, ne dubitari posset* utrum *marito perisset an patri.* Ubi istud vidisti? ubi audisti? Nego te istuc in bello didicisse.

MARULLI. " *Meruerat*" *inquit* " mori." *Etiamnunc accusas? certe iam tibi satis factum est.* O novum monstrum! irato victore vivendum est, exorato patre moriendum est.

PASSIENI. Utinam intervenissem: non satis fecisses sola patri. Furiosum te dicerem si pro genero non rogasses. *Secutus est gener diversas partes, uxor suas.*

---

[1] esset fuisse *Bursian:* fuisset.

---

[1] By the action she took to appease him.
[2] He confessed, on Ligarius' behalf, to having fought against Caesar: *Lig.* 1–2, cf. *S.* 6.13.
[3] That restoring the proscribed.

or die.—What sort of amends are these—where the daughter doesn't even live to see her father appeased? [1]

ALBUCIUS SILUS. Only the gods seemed able to judge which side was the better.—" If you want to make me amends, die." As for me, I prefer you to go on being angry.—If it were an act of parricide to have adhered to the other side, Cicero would never have defended Ligarius before Caesar. Marcus Tullius, how slight you must have thought a crime to which you confessed! [2]—If you are merciful, concede the life of your daughter to her prayers; if you are her enemy, to the edict; [3] if you are her father, to your natural feelings; if you are her judge, to her case; if you are angry, to her brother.

BUTEO. She died just by the threshold of his [4] house, so that there should be no doubt whether she had perished for her husband or for her father.— Where have you seen, where heard such a thing? I declare that you cannot have learnt this even in the wars.

MARULLUS. " She deserved to die." Are you *still* accusing her? Surely by *now* she has made you amends?—O strange prodigy! The victor is angry: she may live. Her father has been talked over: she must die.

PASSIENUS. Would that I had come on the scene: you would not have been alone in making amends to father.—I should call you crazy if you had not put in a word for your son-in-law.[4]—Your son-in-law adhered to the other side, his wife to her own.[5]

[4] Let alone condemning your daughter.
[5] Because it was her husband's.

THE ELDER SENECA

5 LABIENI. Hoc obsequio consequatur denique ut intra domum moriatur. M. Cato, quo viro nihil speciosius civilis tempestas abstulit, potuit beneficio Caesaris vivere, si ullius voluisset. *Optima civilis belli defensio oblivio est.*

MUSAE. Allato ad se capite Cn. Pompei Caesar avertisse oculos dicitur, quod tu ne in morte filiae 476 quidem fecisti.

CORNELI HISPANI. Pervagata est illa crudelis belli fortuna omnem ordinem, usque in infimae plebis supplicia descendit; nihil in civitate nostra immune a victoris ira praeter feminas fuit: hanc laudem miserae urbi servare licuit. Aut pater noster aut victor insanit.

6 MENTONIS. Semel repulsa iterum redit, iterum repulsa tertio rogat, non fatigatur, scit exorari etiam hostes. O te crudelem, nisi iam tibi etiam pro genero satis factum est! Non ignoro in quanto periculo sim: nescit placari iratus et voce etiam filiae excanduit.

TRIARI. An non exoraretur victor cum pro filio ⟨rogaret⟩[1] pater? " *Morere.*" *Illi quoque quibus animadvertere in damnatos necesse est non dicunt " occide," non " morere," sed " age lege ": crudelitatem imperi verbo mitiore subducunt.*

7 DIVISIO. Latro usus est in hac controversia illa calcata quaestione: an possit dementiae agi cum

---

[1] *Supplied by Bursian.*

---

[1] *C.* 9.2.22 n.

LABIENUS. Let her, by this act of obedience, at 5
least win the right to die *inside* the house.—Marcus
Cato, the most brilliant victim of the storm of the
civil war, could have lived by the favour of Caesar—if
he had been willing to live by anyone's favour.—The
best defence against civil war is to forget it.

MUSA. When Pompey's head was brought to him,
Caesar is said to have averted his eyes; *you* didn't do
that even at the death of your daughter.

CORNELIUS HISPANUS. The cruel chance of war
stalked through every rank, descending to execute
even the lowest classes. Nothing in our state was
immune from the wrath of the victor—except
women: *that* praise our wretched city was permitted
to retain.—Either our father or the victor is crazy.

MENTO. Repelled once, she returns a second time; 6
again repelled, she begs yet a third time. She does
not grow tired; she knows that even enemies can be
talked round.—How cruel you are if by now you have
not received amends for your son-in-law too!—I well
know what great peril I am in; once he is angry, he
cannot be placated—even at the sound of his
daughter's voice he flared up.

TRIARIUS. Would not the victor be won over if a
father begged for his son?—" Die." Those whose
duty it is to execute condemned criminals do not say
" Kill " or " Die " but " Act according to the law." [1]
They use a milder word to lessen the cruelty of the
command.

Division

Latro used in this *controversia* the banal question: 7
Can a suit for madness be brought against a father for

413

patre ob ullam aliam rem quam ob dementiam. Inpotens sum, crudelis sum, inmitis, non tamen demens.
Mores tuos patri debes adprobare, non patris regere.
Dic: desipis, nihil intellegis; ego sanitatis meae,
si potuero, argumenta colligam; dicam: in senatu
non stulte sententiam dixi. Quid tibi videor fecisse
dementer? partes male egi? *Multa debes dementiae*
signa colligere; damnare non potes patrem propter 477M
verba, immo propter verbum.

8   Si damnari dementiae aliquis pater, etiam non
demens, ob aliquod inprobandum factum potest, an
hic possit. Hoc in duo divisit: an, etiamsi hoc animo
dixit ut filiam mori vellet, damnandus tamen non sit.
Hic accusatio filiae contrarias partes et patri ⟨et
fratri⟩[1] sequentis, cum illam ipsa natura publicis
excepisset malis. *Animadvertit Manlius in filium*
et victorem, animadvertit Brutus in liberos non factos
hostes sed futuros: vide an sub his exemplis patri fortius
9 *loqui liceat.* Deinde: an non eo animo dixerit ut
illam mori vellet. Dixi, inquit, iratus, cum vellem
castigare, non occidere.

Turrinus Clodius belle dixit: nolite mirari si
durioribus verbis utor; non sum processurus ultra
verba, minabor, deinde ignoscam: fecit et victor.

10   Gallio et illam quaestionem fecit: an non ob hoc
puella perierit, quod pater illi tam dure responderit.

---

[1] *Supplied by Otto.*

---

[1] *C.* 9.2.19.

anything other than madness? " I am violent, I am cruel, harsh, but not mad. What you must do is to justify *your* behaviour in your father's eyes—not rule *his*. Say: You have no sense, you understand nothing. If I can, I shall collect proofs of my sanity. I shall say: In the senate I have given my views sensibly. What is it you think I have done as a result of madness? Have I played my part badly? You must accumulate many proofs of madness; you cannot get a father convicted just for words—or rather just for a single word."

If a father, though not mad, can be convicted of 8 madness for some discreditable act, can this father? This he sub-divided into two: Even if he spoke with the intention that his daughter should die, should he be convicted? Here came accusations directed against the daughter for following a side opposite to her father's and brother's, though her very sex kept her out of reach of public calamity. " Manlius executed his son—when he was victorious; [1] Brutus executed sons who were not yet enemies but intended to become enemies. [2] Consider in the light of these parallels whether a father may not *speak* a little strongly." Next: *Did* he speak with the intention 9 that his daughter should die? " I spoke in anger, wanting to reproach, not to kill."

Clodius Turrinus said prettily: " Don't be surprised that I use somewhat harsh words. I shall not go beyond words. I shall threaten—then pardon: that is what the victor did."

Gallio added the question: Did the girl die because 10 her father gave her such a harsh reply? " No. She

[2] For the conspiracy alluded to in *C*. 3.9.

Perit, inquit, propter desiderium viri; alioqui unius
verbi amaritudinem morte pensasset? Immo mulier
praeceps, temeraria, insano flagrans amore et
attonita, quem virum patre relicto secuta fuerat,
†res viso† [1] consecuta est.

11 Silo Pompeius huic quaestioni praeponebat illam,
ex qua in hanc transitus fit: an, etiamsi propter hoc
verbum patris perit, damnari tamen pater non debeat:
nec enim eventus imputari debet cuiusque rei, sed
consilium. Si post hoc verbum puella vixisset, 478M
numquid patrem dementiae damnare posses? Atque post hoc verbum si quid factum est, non a patre
sed a puella factum est. Non oportet autem illius
temeritatem dementiam videri patris. Post hanc
quaestionem faciebat illam: an ob hoc perierit.

12 Color a parte accusatoris simplex est. ⟨Latro⟩ [2]
ait patrem durum fuisse, crudelem, bono publico
hunc non fuisse partium ducem. Dixit, inquit, eo
vultu, ea adfirmatione, ut videretur non iubere
tantum sed occidere.

Hoc loco dixit Turrinus Clodius: hoc post bellum,
immo post edictum? et adiecit: nunc intellegit res
publica, imperator, quantum tibi debeat, cui sine
sanguine satis factum est.

. . . omnes enim dixerunt patre nolente illam
perisse. [3]

---

[1] *I have translated Gertz'* patre invito.
[2] *Supplied by Müller.*
[3] perisse *Gertz:* dixisse.

died because she missed her husband. Would she otherwise have thought one bitter word had to be paid for by her death? Rather, this rash headstrong woman, burning with a crazy love, out of her mind, followed against her father's wishes the husband she had left her father to follow."

Pompeius Silo prefaced this question with another 11 that provides a transition to it: Even if she died because of this word uttered by her father, should her father be convicted? " For a man is not to be made responsible for the result of every action, but for his intentions. If the girl had gone on living after this word was spoken, surely you couldn't get her father convicted of madness? And anything done after the word was spoken was done not by the father but by the girl. But her rashness should not be equated with her father's madness." After this question he raised the other: *Did* she die because of this?

The *colour* on the accuser's side is straightforward. 12 Latro said the father had been harsh and cruel; it was lucky for the state that he had not been the leader of his party. " He spoke with an expression and an emphasis that made him seem not merely to be ordering but to be killing."

Here Clodius Turrinus said: " Did this take place after the war—no, after the edict? " And he added: " Now the state realises, emperor, how much it owes to you. Amends were made to *you* without bloodshed."

. . .[1] for all said that she died against her father's wishes.

[1] In the lacuna, Seneca will have turned to the *colour* for the father.

13 Gallio dixit: Nondum mihi videbatur scire quid
meruisset. Volui illam intellegere crimen suum.

Cestius hoc colore: *Contumaciter*, inquit, *rogavit,
sic quomodo periit*, non vultu demisso, non summissio-
ribus verbis, nondum tamquam victa: *nihil agnovi
filiae, nihil victae.* Primum quare *ad me non fratrem*
suum *mittit? An etiamnunc fratri irascitur?*

14 Argentarius ait: Nos ducem exoravimus, quorum
liberi in diversis partibus fuerant; diximus: ignosce;
nobis ⟨licebit⟩ severis [1] esse si licuerit esse securis.
Quid peccavi quod filiam ex hostium castris venientem non primo verbo recepi?   479

Turrinus Clodius ait: Volui fratrem sorori dare
beneficium: " eo durius loquar ut ille me pro sorore
sua deprecetur." Primum *quare me solum rogat,
cum debeat duobus satis facere?*

Silo Gavius dixit: volui illam mora torqueri:
sine, inquam, et iterum et tertio roget: ne mitissi-
mus quidem victor statim ignovit.

15 Labienus ait: Non sum statim exoratus, et si
vixisset non essem fractus proximis precibus eius,
ne tertio quidem rogatus aut quarto. " At *victor
cito exoratus est.*" Noli mirari: *facilius est ignoscere
bello quam parricidio.*

---

[1] licebit severis *ed. after Müller:* eueris.

---

[1] Thoughts of father on return of daughter. So too in
Turrinus' *colour* in §14.

Gallio said: " I didn't think she yet realised her 13
deserts. I wanted her to understand her crime."

Cestius used this *colour*: " She begged defiantly,
just as she died, face not cast down, words not meek,
as if she had not yet been defeated. I recognised in
her nothing of my daughter, nothing of a loser."—
" Why, first of all, does she not send her brother to
me?[1] Is she still angry with him? "

Argentarius said: " We asked pardon of the 14
general, those of us who had had children on the
other side. We said: Forgive; we can be stern if we
can be secure." [2]—" What have I done wrong if my
first word to a daughter who came from the enemy
camp was not a welcome? "

Clodius Turrinus said: " I wanted her brother to
do his sister a good turn. I said to myself: ' I shall
speak rather harshly so that he has to beg me for his
sister's life.' "—" First, why does she beg me alone
when she has two to make amends to? "

Gavius Silo said: " I wanted her to be tortured by
the delay. Let her (I said to myself) ask twice, a
third time: even the gentlest victor does [3] not pardon
at once."

Labienus said: " I was not immediately appeased, 15
and, if she had lived, I should not have been swayed
by her next prayers, nor even if I had been asked a
third or fourth time. ' But the victor was swiftly won
over.' No wonder: war is easier to forgive than
parricide."

[2] Assured, that is, that their children would not forfeit
their lives, they would feel free to punish them themselves.

[3] Or perhaps " did not," with specific reference to the victor
of the civil war.

Hispanus de morte eius hoc dixit: *Etiam morte patri quaesivit invidiam.* Iterum illam nobis vir abduxit.

Albucius ait: Tuto me [ait] [1] putavi loqui fortius; non dubitavi enim quin frater illi dicturus esset: non est quod timeas: exorabitur; si difficilior erit, ego illum rogabo; et si rogasses, adulescens, fecissem. Non magis tibi ego quicquam ⟨negassem⟩ [2] quam sorori tuae maritus.

16 Montanus Votienus dixit: non est quod putes illam cecidisse irae patris: cui vixerat perit, illi [3] se cui addixit inpendit. Et eundem sensum in argumentis, cum dixisset *non propter patrem illam perisse:* " Quid ergo ? " inquis " propter quem ? " *Scis illam unum habuisse pro quo mori posset.*

IV

48

MENDICI DEBILITATI

Rei publicae laesae sit actio.

Quidam expositos debilitabat et debilitatos mendicare cogebat ac mercedem exigebat ab eis. Rei publicae laesae accusatur.

1 PORCI LATRONIS. Aestimate quale sit scelus istius, in quo laesi *patres, ne liberos* suos *aut agnoscant aut*

---

[1] *Deleted by Gertz.*
[2] *Supplied by Madvig.*
[3] illi *Bornecque:* ille.

---

[1] Bonner, 97–8. It seems doubtful whether there was a special law on harming the state in either Greece or Rome.

420

Hispanus had this to say about her death: " Even by her death she sought to make her father hated."— "This is the second time her husband has deprived us of her."

Albucius said: " I thought it was safe to speak boldly; I did not doubt that her brother would have said to her: ' Don't be afraid, he will be won over. If he is a little difficult, *I* will beg him.' And if you *had* asked, young man, I should have done it; I should not have denied you anything, any more than her husband denied your sister."

Votienus Montanus said: " Don't imagine she fell 16 victim to her father's anger; she died for the man she had lived for, sacrificed herself for the man to whom she had devoted herself." He put the same idea among his arguments, after saying she did not die because of her father: " ' Well, you ask, for whom did she die? ' You know she had only one man for whom she could die."

4

THE CRIPPLED BEGGARS

An action may lie for harming the state.[1]

A man used to cripple children who had been exposed, forcing them to be beggars and demanding a fee from them. He is accused of harming the state.

Against the man

PORCIUS LATRO. Consider the nature of this man's 1 crime, as a result of which injured fathers, rather than

recipiant, etiam confessas iniurias tacent. *Vectigalis isti crudelitas* fuit *eo magis quod omnes praeter istum misericordes sumus*. Mendicares nisi tot mendicos fecisses. *Effecit* scelestus iste *ut* novo more *nihil esset miserius expositis quam tolli, parentibus quam agnoscere.*

2   CASSI SEVERI. Hinc caeci innitentes baculis vagantur, hinc trunca bracchia circumferunt, huic convulsi pedum articuli sunt et extorti tali, huic elisa crura, illius inviolatis pedibus cruribusque femina contudit: aliter in quemque saeviens ossifragus iste alterius bracchia amputat, alterius enervat, alium distorquet, alium delumbat, *alterius diminutas scapulas in deforme tuber extundit* et risum e [1] crudelitate captat. *Produc*, agedum, *familiam* semivivam, tremulam, debilem, caecam, mancam, famelicam; ostende nobis captivos tuos. *Volo* mehercules *nosse* illum specum tuum, *illam humanarum calamitatium officinam*, illud 48 infantium spoliarium. *Sua cuique calamitas tamquam ars adsignatur:* huic recta membra sunt, et, si nemo moratur,[2] proceritas emicabit: ita frangantur ut humo se adlevare non possit, sed pedum crurumque resolutis vertebris reptet. Huic ⟨lingua velox, oculi acuti⟩:[3] extirpentur radicitus. Huic speciosa facies est: potest formonsus mendicus esse; reliqua mem-

---

[1] e *Gertz:* in.
[2] moratur *Müller:* naturae.
[3] *Supplied by Shackleton Bailey.*

have to recognise or take back their children, keep quiet even after they have confessedly been wronged.—His cruelty paid the better because we all feel pity—except him.—*You* would be a beggar if you had not made beggars out of so many!—This wicked man produced a novel situation, where nothing was more calamitous to the exposed than to be reared or to their parents than to recognise them.

CASSIUS SEVERUS. Here roam the blind, leaning on 2 sticks, here others carry round stumps of arms. This child has had the joints of his feet torn, his ankles wrenched; this has had his legs crushed. Another's thighs he has smashed, though leaving feet and legs unharmed. Finding a different savagery for each, this bone-breaker cuts off the arms of one, slices the sinews of another's; one he twists, another he castrates. In yet another he stunts the shoulder-blades, beating them into an ugly hump, looking for a laugh from his cruelty. Come on, bring out your troop half-alive, shaking, feeble, blind, crippled, starving; show us your prisoners. I want to get to know that cave of yours, that factory in human misery, that stripping-place [1] for children. Each has his misery assigned him, like a trade. This child has straight limbs, and, if no-one holds them back, he will shoot up tall: let those limbs be broken in such a way that he can't raise himself from the ground, but creeps about, the joints of feet and legs enfeebled. This child has a ready tongue and sharp eyes: let them be torn out by the roots. This child has a pretty face—he can make

---

[1] The *spoliarium* was the place where slain gladiators were stripped.

bra inutilia sint, ut Fortunae iniquitas in beneficia sua saevientis magis hominum animos percellat. ⟨Sic⟩[1] sine satellitibus tyrannus calamitates humanas dispensat.

3   Vibi Galli. *Intuemini* debilia infelicium membra nescio qua tabe consumpta, illi praecisas manus, *illi erutos oculos, illi fractos pedes. Quid exhorrescitis? sic iste miseretur.* Tot membra franguntur ut unum ventrem impleant, et—o *novom monstrum!—integer alitur, debiles alunt.*

  Albuci Sili. *" Perissent " inquit. Ita non infelicius supersunt* quam perituri fuerant? *" Perissent " inquit. Interroga patres utrum maluerint.* Eruantur, inquit, oculi illius, illius praecidantur manus. *Quid si aliquis ex istis futurus est vir fortis? quid si tyrannicida? quid si sacerdos? Nec,* puto, *incredibilia* in hac turba[2] *loquor;* certe *ex hac fortuna origo Romanae* 48 *gentis apparuit.* Egregius educator *plus acceptum crudelitati quam expensum misericordiae refert.*

4   Triari. " Perissent " inquit. Puto, expertus es nos non esse crudeles; tamen nemo non nostrum, cum istis stipem porrigeret, mortem precatus est. Surge tu, debilis: conatur et corruit. Surge tu, mute: sed quid excitaris? rogare non potes. Surge tu, caece: sed ad quorum eas genua nescis. O te

---

[1] *Supplied by Bursian.*
[2] turba *Otto:* fortuna.

---

[1] Who had to be unmutilated (*C.* 4.2).
[2] Romulus and Remus having been exposed before rescue

a handsome beggar: but let the rest of his limbs be useless, so that the cruelty of Fortune, savaging the gifts it gave, may touch the hearts of men more poignantly. This is how this tyrant without a bodyguard distributes human disasters.

VIBIUS GALLUS. Look at the wretches, their limbs 3 weakened and wasted by I know not what disease, hands cut off, eyes plucked out, feet broken. Why do you shudder? This is the way he shows his pity. —So many limbs smashed—to fill one belly; and— strange prodigy!—a whole man gets fed, cripples do the feeding.

ALBUCIUS SILUS. "They would have perished." Don't they suffer more in surviving like this than if they had perished? "They would have perished." Ask the fathers which *they* preferred.—"Let this one's eyes be torn out, that one's hands be amputated." What if one of these is destined to be a hero? Or a tyrannicide? Or a priest?[1] And what I say is not incredible, surely, where there is such a crowd; at least it was from people as wretched as these that the origin of the Roman nation sprang.[2]— This excellent foster-father has more cruelty to his credit than pity to his debit.

TRIARIUS. "They would have perished." I think 4 you know by experience that we are not cruel: yet every one of us, when holding out alms to these wretches, prayed they might die.—Get up, cripple: he tries, and falls over. Get up, dumb man. But why stir yourself—you cannot beg. Get up, blind man; but you don't know to whose knees you go.

by the wolf (for which see §4 Triarius and §9 Sparsus): cf. §5 Hispanus.

inter omnis debiles ante hoc iudicium felicissimum, quod istum dominum non videbas, in hoc iudicio infelicissimum, quod istum reum non vides! *Expositos aluerunt etiam ferae, satis futurae mites si praeterissent.*

5 CORNELI HISPANI. Ergo, si illis temporibus iste carnifex apparuisset, conditorem suum Roma non haberet. Timeo ne hoc prosit reo, quod nemo ex istis quemquam videri volt suum.

IULI BASSI. Intuemini utramque partem, et ei succurrite quae miserabilior est. Liceat videre mercedarios tuos: hic caecus est, hic debilis, hic mutus. His tu mori non permittis? Vis in te iudices more tuo misericordes sint, tuo exemplo?

ARGENTARI. *Quorum cum ubique audiantur preces, in sua tantum causa cessant.* " Adiciamus aliquid ad quaestum: deme huic oculos, illi manus."

6 ARELLI FUSCI patris. " *Praecidatur* " inquit " *lingua: genus est rogandi rogare non posse.*" *Miseremini omnium,*[1] *iudices; misereri* etiam *singulorum soletis.*

CESTI PII. Ut hanc causam susciperem, ne ab eis quidem rogatus sum pro quibus ago. Quid enim miseri rogare sciunt nisi stipem? Quid infelix iste 483 peccavit aliud quam quod natus est?

CLODI TURRINI patris. Age, si quis agnoverit

---

[1] omnium *E:* horum *ABV.*

Of all the cripples, you were most fortunate before this trial—because you could not see this master of yours: though at this trial you are most unfortunate, because you cannot see this man in the dock.— Exposed babes have been fed even by wild beasts, who would have been kind enough if they had merely passed them by.

CORNELIUS HISPANUS. So if this butcher had ap- 5 peared in those days, Rome would have no founder.— I fear it may help the defendant that no-one wants any of these creatures to be thought to belong to him.

JULIUS BASSUS. Look at both sides, and rally to the one that seems the more to be pitied.—Let us see your paymasters: this one is blind, this crippled, this dumb. Are these the children you do not allow to die?—Do you want the judges to be merciful to you in *your* fashion, after *your* example?

ARGENTARIUS. Their prayers are heard every-where: they only keep quiet when their own case is at issue.[1]—" Let us add to our resources: remove this one's eyes, that one's hands."

ARELLIUS FUSCUS SENIOR. " Let his tongue be cut 6 out," he says. " To be unable to beg is one method of begging."—Pity them all, judges, for you are in the habit of pitying them even individually.[2]

CESTIUS PIUS. Not even those for whom I appear asked me to undertake this case. For what do these wretches know how to ask except alms?—What did this wretch [3] do wrong—except to be born?

CLODIUS TURRINUS SENIOR. Look, suppose someone

---

[1] Cf. §6 Turrinus ". . . ask something for yourselves."
[2] i.e. in giving alms.
[3] One of the beggars, not the master.

suum, petes alimenta tamquam alueris? Non est
quod timeas: nemo agnoscet. O miserum, si quis
alimenta suo dat! o miserum, si negat! Ita *nos
istis vindictam negaturos putas, quibus ne id quidem
negamus quod tibi daturi sunt? Et, quod indignissimum
est, cum tam crudelis sit, misericordia publica vivit.
Venite, miseri, et hodie primum vobis rogate.*

7 MENTONIS. Errant miseri circa parentum suorum
domos, et fortasse aliquis a patre alumenta non
impetrat. Nulli plus reddunt integra mancipia.
" Cur tu tam exiguum refers? Mutus es? Haec
causa esse [1] poterat ut non rogares, ut non acciperes?
Spiritum tibi non relinquerem nisi crudelior futurus
essem relinquendo." " *Tibi cotidiana captura non
respondet. Apparet te nondum* hominibus *satis miserum
videri.*"

GAVI SILONIS. " Tu " inquit " in illa vicinia
mendicabis, tu ad ⟨illud⟩ [2] limen accedes "—et crude-
lissime miseris parentium domos monstrat. " Hic
non facile stipem impetrat: etiamnunc aliquid illi
detrahatur."

8 IUNI GALLIONIS. " Serva oculos ut videat quem
roget; serva manus ut habeat quibus stipem accipiat." 484M
*Occurrunt nuptiis dira omina, sacris publicis tristia
auspicia;* feriatis maxime ac sollemnibus *et in hilaritates*

---

[1] mutus—esse *Müller:* uitus est equas.
[2] *Supplied by Jahn.*

recognises his own son. Will you then demand the cost of rearing him,[1] as though you *had* reared him? Don't be afraid. No-one *will* recognise them.—Unhappy the man who gives alms to his own child, unhappy the man who refuses them!—Do you suppose we shall deny these people revenge when we don't deny them even the money they have to pass on to you?—And, worst of all, despite his cruelty, he owes his living to the compassion of the public.—Come, wretches, today for the first time ask something for yourselves.

MENTO. The poor creatures wander round their 7 parents' homes, and, maybe, one of them fails to get alms from his father.—No-one makes more profit out of slaves who are sound of limb.—" Why do *you* bring back so little? You are dumb? Was that any reason for not begging, for not receiving? I shouldn't leave you your life—except that leaving it is the crueller course."—" Your daily takings don't come up to scratch. It's obvious people don't yet think you pitiable enough."

GAVIUS SILO. " *You* shall beg in that district, go to that door "; and, in an extreme of cruelty, he points out to the wretches the houses of their parents.— " This one doesn't get alms easily; let him have something more pulled off him."

JUNIUS GALLIO. " Preserve his eyes, so he can see 8 whom he is begging from; preserve his hands, so he has something to take alms with."—They present themselves as evil omens at marriages, as gloomy signs at public sacrifices; particularly on holidays, days traditionally dedicated to cheerfulness, these

[1] Cf. the law in *C.* 9.3.

429

dicatis diebus semianimes isti greges oberrant. A te
fortasse aliquis acceptam stipem portat ad deos.

FULVI SPARSI. Scio, iudices, variis quemque causis
ad accusandum solere compelli: quosdam ambitio
gloriae quam ex damnato petierunt provocavit, alios
odia et simultates protraxerunt; non dubito fuisse
quosdam qui praemium peterent: ego omnibus
ceteros inpellentibus causis vaco; quae enim gloria
est in tam sordido reo? quae simultates ut non eas
quoque contraxisse pudeat? aut quod praemium
9 cum *istum alant qui se alere non possunt? Non* is *est
qui rogare nesciat; etiam docere solet.* Quos adfectus
vestros optare debeam, nescio: si misericordiae
propiores fueritis, crimina rei vobis ostendam; si
severitati, reum. Hunc nos publice pascimus.
Exigi a te talio ⟨non potest⟩ :¹ *non habes totidem membra quot debes.* Oblita feritatis, placida velut fetibus
suis ubera praebuisse fertur. Sic lupa venit ad infantes: expectemus hominem? Gratulor tibi, Roma,
quod in conditores tuos homo non incidit. *Ergo tu,
cum de publica misericordia cogitares, tam crudelis esse* 485M
10 potuisti? Proxima, inquit, die hic plurimum
rettulit: faciendus est huic similis alter; hic satis
rettulit: fiat et alius miser ad hoc exemplum. Ite

¹ *Supplied by Bursian.*

---

¹ Text uncertain. The point may lie in the double sense of
stips as " alms for the poor " and " gift to the gods."
² *Delatores* received a proportion of the estates of their convicted victims.

flocks of half-dead creatures intrude.—Someone, maybe, bears to the gods an offering received from *you*.[1]

FULVIUS SPARSUS. I know, judges, that men are driven into accusation by differing motives; some have been lured on by ambition for the fame they seek from a conviction, others drawn by hatreds and feuds; I do not doubt that some have been in search of rewards.[2] *I* do not have the motives that impel others. What glory is there in convicting so base a defendant? What feuds that would not themselves be shaming to contract? What reward, when the man is fed by those who cannot feed themselves?— It's not that he doesn't know how to beg; he's used even to teaching it.—What feelings on your part I should hope for I don't know; if you are more prone to pity, I will show you the crimes of the accused; if to severity, I will show you the accused.—*This* is the man we are feeding at the public expense.—Tooth-for-tooth [3] cannot be exacted from *you*: you do not possess as many limbs as you owe.—Forgetting her wildness, she is said to have quietly offered her dugs as though to her own offspring. This is how a wolf comes to babies; are we to wait for a *man*? [4]—I congratulate you, Rome, that a *man* did not happen on your founders.—Were *you* then capable of such cruelty, even though you had the mercy of the people in mind? [5]—" This one," he says, " brought home the most yesterday; another must be made to resemble him. This one brought home enough; let another be made pitiable according to this pattern."—" Go,"

---

[3] For *talio* see *C.* 3.1 n.
[4] For a man, judging by the present case, would be less kind.
[5] Even though your plans relied on the public giving alms.

nunc, inquit, et alimenta mihi quaerite. Tu, inquit,
qui oculos non habes, per oculos rogato; tu, inquit,
qui manus perdidisti, per manus rogato; tu per illa
membra quae trahis debilia; per ea quisque quae
non habet ambiat. *O miseros qui sic rogant, miseriores qui sic rogantur!* Ecce nescio quis: Meus,
inquit, filius, si viveret, huic fortassis similis esset.
Numquid ego meum transeo? Alius: Potuit, inquit, meus in eundem incidere dominum. Quid si
incidit? *Omnes omnibus stipem congerunt, dum unusquisque timet ne suo neget.*

Pars altera. ARELLI FUSCI. "*Debilitasti*" inquit.
Plus illis patres nocuerant.

11   Latro sic divisit: an laesa sit res publica. Primum,
inquit, crimen constare oportet, deinde tunc reum
quaeri. An laesa sit res publica, non solet argumentis probari; manifesta statim rei publicae damna
sunt, si muri diruti sunt, si classis incensa est, si
exercitus amissus, si vectigalia deminuta: hoc
damnum, quod tu obicis, ⟨quis⟩[1] videbat? Dic
mihi: quando rem publicam laesit? Cum unum
expositum debilitavit? atqui etiam qui occidit unum,
non tamen rei publicae laesae tenetur, sed caedis;
etiam qui duos, etiam qui plures: dic mihi quis 486M
numerus efficiat ut laesa videatur res publica. Duo

[1] *Supplied by Schultingh.*

he says to them, " and seek food for me. *You* have no eyes: beg invoking your eyes. *You* have lost your hands: beg invoking your hands. *You* invoke the limbs which you drag crippled behind you. Let each solicit invoking the parts of him that he does not have." Wretched men, to have to ask thus: more wretched those who are asked thus! One here is saying to himself: " My son, if he lived, would perhaps resemble this child. Can it be my son that I am passing by? " Another says: " My son could have fallen into the hands of the same master. What if he did? " They all give alms to them all: for each is afraid he may be refusing his own son.

The other side

ARELLIUS FUSCUS SENIOR. " You crippled them." Their fathers had harmed them more.

Division

Latro's division was as follows: Has the state been 11 harmed? " First the crime has to be established: only then can one look for a defendant. Whether the state has been harmed is not normally proved by arguments; the loss to the state is immediately obvious if the walls have been destroyed, the fleet burned, the army wiped out, the revenues diminished.[1] But who saw this loss that you reproach him with? Tell me, when did he harm the state? When he crippled one exposed child? Yet even the *killer* of one man is not liable for harming the state but for murder; so with two, so with several. Tell me what number makes it obvious that the state has been

[1] Cf. *Decl.* p. 62,20 Ritter.

debilitantur: nondum res publica ⟨laesa est[1] . . .⟩.
[iuvenes qui suadere infantes perdidit et infelices][2]
Potuerunt, inquit, duces fieri. Potuerunt et sacrilegi esse et homicidae, potuerunt et perire. Attamen
crudelem rem facit. ⟨Facit⟩[3] *et lanista qui iuvenes
cogit ad gladium, nec damnatur rei publicae laesae, et
leno qui cogit invitas pati stuprum, nec laedit rem publicam. Ego non laudari reum desidero, sed absolvi;
noceat hoc illi, cum honores petet. Potest aliquis et non
esse homo honestus et esse innocens reus.*

12   Deinde: an, si laesa est res publica, ab hoc laesa
sit. Non a me, inquit, sed a parentibus qui proiec-
erunt. Hic crudelis, *ut multum illis abstulerit, vitam
reddidit.* Contra ait: illi singulos exponunt, tu
omnes debilitas: illi spem, tu instrumenta vivendi
detrahis.

Deinde: an teneatur rei publicae laesae si fecit
quod ei facere licet. Non potest, inquit, ulla res
lege damnari quae lege permittitur. Si domum
meam diruo, numquid dicis me rem publicam
laedere? Et poteras describere quam inhumanum
sit illos parietes maiorum in nostram usque perductos   487
memoriam in hostilem modum deici. Si in agris
meis arbusta succidere velim . . .

13   Deinde: an hoc non licuerit illi facere. Licuit,
inquit; expositi in nullo numero sunt, servi sunt;

---

[1] *Supplied by Vahlen.*
[2] *Deleted by the editor.*
[3] *Supplied by Wachsmuth.*

harmed.[1] Two get crippled; the state hasn't yet been harmed . . . 'They might have become generals.' They *might* have committed sacrilege, or murder; they might even have died. 'Yet he is acting cruelly.' So is a trainer who forces young men to run on the sword—but *he* isn't convicted of harming the state; so is a pander who forces unwilling girls into the sexual act—yet *he* does not harm the state. I don't look for the accused to be praised; I look for him to be acquitted. Let this go against him when he stands for magistracies. You can be wrongly accused without being a decent man."

Next: If the state has been harmed, was it he that 12 harmed it? "He says that it wasn't he that did the harm, but the parents who threw out their babies. This cruel man may have deprived them of much; but he did restore them their lives." On the other side he said: "*They* expose one child at a time, *you* cripple the lot; *they* remove hope of life, *you* its means."

Next: Is he liable to a charge of harming the state if he did something that is not illegal? "Nothing can be condemned by law when law permits it. If I destroy my house, can you say I am harming the state? Yet you might have gone on about how cruel it is to have those walls, built by our ancestors and preserved to our day, cast down as if by the enemy. If I were to want to cut down trees on my estate . . ."

Next: *Was* he permitted to do this? "He was. 13 The exposed don't count, they are slaves; this the

[1] This is the fallacy of the diminishing heap (Hor. *Ep.* 2.1.47).

hoc educatori [1] visum est. Denique si non licet, habent legem: talionis agere singuli possunt, iniuriarum possunt. *Rei publicae* quidem *laesae non potest agi eorum nomine qui extra rem publicam sunt;* non potest pro omnibus agi pro quibus singulis non potest.

14   Scio quosdam putare quaestionem esse: an possit a privato homine laedi res publica; Sparsum certe ita declamare memini. Quod si quisquam recipit, et illam recipiet: an a muliere possit, an a sene, an a paupere possit; quorum nihil umquam quaeritur, sed dici tamen solet; quomodo cum illa quaestio tractatur: an res publica laesa sit, totiens reus inter argumenta non laesae rei publicae dicit: ne potuit quidem laedi a privato, a paupere, ab aegro, ab absenti.

Gallio fecit et illam quaestionem: an in expositis laedi possit res publica. Non potest, inquit, res publica laedi [possit] [2] ⟨nisi⟩ [3] in aliqua sui parte; haec nulla rei publicae pars est; non in censu illos invenies, non in testamentis. Sed haec quoque in illam incurrit: an res publica laesa sit; dicitur enim: ne laedi quidem potuit in eis quos non habebat.

15   Pro illo qui debilitabat expositos pauci admodum 488 dixerunt. Dixit Gallio et hoc colore usus est: *egentem hominem et qui ne se quidem alere nedum alios posset sustulisse* eos qui iam *relicti* sine spe vix spiritum traherent, *quibus non iniuria fieret si aliquid detra-*

---

[1] hoc educatori *Müller:* haec iugatori.
[2] *Deleted by Kiessling.*
[3] *Supplied by Kiessling, Madvig.*

man who reared them saw. And if it is illegal, they have a law to appeal to—they can sue individually for tooth-for-tooth or for injury. But there can be no action for harming the state in the name of persons who are outside the state; no action can be brought in favour of the whole of a group when it cannot for individuals within it."

I know that some regard as a question: Can the state be harmed by a private citizen? At least I recall Sparsus declaiming on these lines. Anyone who accepts that will also accept the question: Can it be harmed by a woman, an old man, a pauper? None of these is in fact ever made a question, though they are often mentioned, as when the question, Has the state been harmed, is dealt with, the defendant invariably puts among the proofs that the state has not been harmed the assertion that it could not in fact have *been* harmed by a private citizen, a pauper, a sick man, one in absence.

Gallio also raised the question: Can the state be harmed in connection with exposed persons? "It cannot be harmed except in respect of some part of itself. *This* is no part of the state; you will not find these people in the census-roll, in wills." But this too comes under: Has the state been harmed? For one says: "It could not in fact have *been* harmed in respect of those who were not members of it."

Very few spoke for the man who crippled exposed children. Gallio did so, using this *colour*: a man in need, who could not feed himself, let alone others, reared children already abandoned, without hope, all but dead, children who suffered no injury if they were deprived of some limb, but were done a kindness if

heretur, sed beneficium daretur si vita servaretur. Faciant invidiam, ⟨dicant⟩ [1] *alicui oculos desse, alicui manus, dicant illos per hunc tam misere vivere, dum fateantur per hunc vivere.* Gallio illud quoque in argumentis temptavit: adeo, inquit, haec res non nocuit rei publicae ut possit videri etiam profuisse: pauciores erunt qui exponant filios.

16 Turrinus Clodius hoc colore usus est: multos patres exponere solitos inutiles partus. Nascuntur, inquit, quidam statim aliqua corporis parte mulcati, infirmi et in nullam spem idonei, quos parentes sui proiciunt magis quam exponunt; aliqui etiam vernulas aut omine infausto editos aut corpore invalidos abiciunt. Ex his aliquos hic sustulit, et eas partes quae cuique possent miserabiliores esse manu sua abstulit: stipem rogant et *unius misericordia vivunt, omnium aluntur.* At res foeda est mendicos habere, a mendicis ali, inter debiles versari. Age, non pudet vos ex hoc producere contubernio reum ⟨a⟩ quo dicatis laesam rem publicam? Et sic descendit ad argumenta, ut diceret: quomodo hic potuit laedere?

17 Silo Pompeius illo colore usus est: misericordem hunc fuisse, voluisse vitam dare, sed non potuisse alere; itaque eo conpulsum ut unusquisque aliquam partem corporis pro toto dependeret. 489

Labienus tam diserte declamavit partem eius qui debilitabat expositos quam nemo alteram partem, cum illam omnes disertissimi viri velut ad experi-

---

[1] *Supplied by Thomas.*

their life were preserved. " Let people stir up ill-feeling, say that one lacks eyes, another hands, say that it is thanks to this man that they live such a wretched life—so long as they acknowledge that they owe life itself to him." Gallio also tried this argument out among his others: " Far from harming the state, this practice may be thought even to have been of advantage to it; there will be fewer prepared to expose their sons."

Clodius Turrinus used this *colour*: " Many fathers 16 are in the habit of exposing offspring who are no good. Some right from birth are damaged in some part of their bodies, weak and hopeless. Their parents throw them out rather than expose them. Some even cast out home-bred slave children, when they are born under an evil star or are physically weak. This man reared some in this category, and removed with his own hand parts capable of making each individual specially pitiful. They beg for alms; they owe their lives to the compassion of one man, their food to the compassion of all. ' But it is a disgusting thing to keep beggars, to be fed by beggars, to live among cripples.' Come now, are *you* not ashamed to extract a defendant from this crew to say he harmed the state ? " And he came round to the proofs with the question: How could he have harmed it ?

Pompeius Silo used this *colour*: the accused felt 17 pity; he wanted to give them their lives, but could not feed them. So he was compelled to make each pay some part of his body for the good of the whole.

Labienus declaimed in favour of the man who crippled exposed children more eloquently than anyone taking the other side—though all the most

mentum suarum virium dixerint. Illum autem locum vehementissime dixit: *Vacare homines huic cogitationi, ut curent quid homo mendicus inter mendicos faciat! Principes, inquit, viri contra naturam divitias suas exercent: castratorum greges habent, exoletos suos ut ad longiorem patientiam inpudicitiae idonei sint amputant, et, quia ipsos pudet viros esse, id agunt ut quam paucissimi sint. His nemo succurrit delicatis et for-*
18 *mosis debilibus. Curare vobis in mentem venit quis ex solitudine infantes auferat perituros nisi auferantur; non curatis quod solitudines suas isti beati ingenuorum ergastulis excolunt, non curatis quod iuvenum miserorum simplicitatem circumeunt et speciosissimum quemque ac maxime idoneum castris in ludum coniciunt.* In mentem vobis venit misereri horum quod membra non habeant; quidni illorum quod habent? Et hoc genere insectatus saeculi vitia egregia figura inquinatum et infamem reum maiorum criminum inpunitate defendit.

Celebris haec apud Graecos controversia est; multa ab illis pulchre dicta sunt, a quibus non abstinuerunt nostri manus, multa corrupte, quibus non cesserunt nec ipsi.

19   Dixit Glycon: καὶ τούτους τροφὰς αἰτεῖς, οὓς μὴ τρέφειν ἀσεβές ἐστιν;   49(

Hunc dixit sensum P. Asprenas eodem modo,

---

¹ Cf. Sen. *Ep.* 122.7: "Is not a life contrary to nature lived by those who make sure boyhood's glow lasts into a time not

eloquent men spoke for the accusation as if to try out their prowess. This was the passage he spoke with most emphasis: " To think that people have time to care what a beggar among beggars gets up to! Distinguished men use their wealth to combat nature:[1] they own troops of castrated youths, they cut their darlings, to fit them to submit to their lusts over a longer period; and because they are themselves ashamed of being men, they make sure that as few men exist as possible. No-one rushes to the aid of *these* pampered and pretty cripples. It occurs to you 18 to worry who is taking from lonely places children who would die if they were left there; you don't worry that the rich employ workhouses full of free-born men to cultivate their own lonely places, that they trick the naïveté of unfortunate youths, and throw into the gladiatorial school all the best looking, the most fit for combat. It occurs to you to pity *these* persons for not having limbs; why not pity *those*, for having them? " By these means he inveighed against the vices of the age, and by an excellent figure defended a stained and disgraced defendant by showing that greater crimes go unpunished.

This is a familiar *controversia* among the Greeks; they said many nice things that our declaimers haven't kept their hands off, and many things in bad taste (and the Romans haven't fallen short of *them* either).

Glycon said: " Do you ask food even from those 19 whom it is wicked to fail to feed? "

Publius Asprenas put this idea in the same way,

its own? What more pitiful—shall he never be a man, so as to submit to a man the longer? " For castration see Sen. *Ir.* 1.21.3 and Quintilian 5.12.17 *seq.*, with Mayor on Juv. 10.307.

uno verbo magis proprio usus: hos aliqui alimenta poscit quibus crudelis est qui negat? Circa hunc sensum est et ille a Quintiliano dictus: nescio utrumne vos miseriores dicam quod alimenta accipitis an huic quod datis; accipitis enim quia debiles estis, datis ei per quem debiles estis.

Adaeus rhetor: κλαίουσαι μητέρες ἠράνιζον, " εἰ μὲν ἐμός," λέγουσαι ⟨" ἵνα τρέφω⟩ [1] τὸν ἐμόν, εἰ δὲ ἀλλότριος, ἵνα καὶ τὸν ἐμὸν ἄλλοι."

20 Hunc sensum quidam Latini dixerunt, sed sic ut putem illos non mutuatos esse †arti† [2] hanc sententiam sed imitatos. Blandus dixit: Porrigit aliqua mendico rogata stipem, utique si peperit ⟨et⟩ [3] exposuit. O quam misera cogitatio porrigentis est: " hic fortasse meus est "!

Moschus dixit: aliqua, quia iam proiecit pluribus stipem, suo negat.

Arellius Fuscus dixit: alit rogata filium mater, misera si scit suum esse, misera si nescit.

Artemon dixit: τὰ μὲν τῶν ἄλλων εὔρωστα· πλεῖ, γεωργεῖ. τὰ δ᾽ ἡμέτερα ἀνάπηρα· τρέφει ἄρα τὸν ὁλόκληρον.

21 Hanc sententiam Latro Porcius virilius dixit, qui non potest ⟨de⟩ [4] furto suspectus esse; Graecos enim et contemnebat et ignorabat. Cum descripsisset 491 debiles artus omnium et alios incursantes, alios repentes, adiecit: pro di boni! ab his aliquis alitur integer?

---

[1] *Supplied by Gertz.*
[2] arti *BV :* arci *A. I translate* Kiessling's *aperte.*
[3] *Supplied by Novák, Gertz.*
[4] *Supplied by Bursian.*

---

[1] *crudelis,* " cruel."

using one word more appropriate:[1] "Is someone demanding food from those whom it is cruel to deny food?" In this vein is also a saying of Quintilian: "I don't know whether I should call you more wretched for receiving alms or for having to give them to *him*; you receive them because you are cripples, you give them to the man who crippled you."

Adaeus the rhetorician: "Weeping mothers contributed, with this thought in their minds: 'If he is my son, I give in order to feed my son; if he is another's, so that the others may feed my son too.'"

Some of the Latin declaimers put over this idea, 20 but in such a way that I suppose they were imitating the epigram rather than borrowing it openly. Blandus said: "A woman hands alms to a beggar when she is asked—particularly if she has had a child, and exposed it. How wretched the thought as she hands the money over: 'Maybe this is my son'!"

Moschus said: "One woman, because she has already thrown alms to more than one child, refuses them to her own."

Arellius Fuscus said: "A mother is solicited, and gives alms to her son: poor woman, if she knows it to be hers, poor woman, if she does not know."

Artemon said: "The slaves of others are strong—they sail, they till the ground. Ours are cripples—therefore they support a man who is sound of limb."

Porcius Latro, who cannot be suspected of 21 plagiarism, for he both despised the Greeks and was ignorant of them, put this epigram more strongly. After describing the crippled limbs of all the children, how some ran up, some crawled, he added: "Good God! Is a whole man fed by *these*?"

Damas Scombros dixit: πάλαι μὲν ἐκθέτοις κίνδυνος ἦν τὸ ῥιφῆναι, νῦν δὲ τὸ τραφῆναι.

Hunc sensum Cestius transtulit: *effecisti*, inquit, *ut maius esset periculum educari quam exponi.*

Fuscus Arellius aliter dixit: illa adhuc in miserae sortis infantia *timebantur: ferae serpentesque et inimicus teneris artubus rigor et inopia; inter expositorum pericula non numerabamus educatorem.*

22 Glycon corruptam dixit sententiam: κρουσάτω τις τὴν θύραν τῶν ἐχόντων, ⟨ἵνα⟩ [1] προσαγάγῃ τις. Et illam: ἄγε, σὺ δὲ κλαῖε, σὺ δὲ θρήνει. ὦ κακῶν συμφωνιῶν. Sed nostri quoque bene insanierunt. Murredius dixit: producitur miserorum longus ordo, maior pars se sine se trahit. Et Licinius Nepos: ut solvendo sis, in poenas quotiens tibi renascendum est?

23 Illud Sparsus dixit quod non corruptum tantum sed contrarium dicebat esse Montanus: " solus plura habes membra quam tot hominibus reliquisti." Ita enim hic potest videri laesisse rem publicam si multi sunt debilitati; apparet autem non esse multos si plura habet membra quam debilitatis reliquit. Et illud aeque aiebat ab illo corrupte dictum: " prodierunt plures mendici quam membra."

Graecas sententias in hoc refero, ut possitis aesti- 492 mare primum quam facilis e Graeca eloquentia in

---

[1] *Supplied by Bursian.*

---

[1] Text and sense uncertain. The point may be that the cripples look so appalling that no-one would take them in, let alone the rich.
[2] By *talio.*

Damas Scombros said: "Once the danger for the exposed was being thrown out—now it is being reared."

Cestius translated this idea: "You have made it more dangerous to be reared than to be exposed."

Arellius Fuscus, rather differently, said: "Up to now the dangers to be feared by luckless infants have been wild beasts, snakes, the freezing cold that threatens tender limbs, and lack of food; we didn't use to reckon among the perils faced by the exposed the man who reared them."

Glycon spoke an epigram in bad taste: "Let some- 22 one knock at the door of the rich, to get taken in ";[1] and also: "Now *you* can cry, and *you* can wail. A horrid concert!" But our declaimers too have crossed well over into madness. Murredius said: "A long line of wretches is led forth, the greater part dragging themselves along in the absence of their own selves." And Licinius Nepos: "To be quit, how many times will you have to be reborn to pay the penalty?"[2]

Sparsus said something that Montanus described 23 as damaging to his case as well as in bad taste: "You by yourself have more limbs than you have left to such a crowd." For the man cannot be thought to have harmed the state unless many have been crippled—but it is clear that not many have if he has more limbs than he left to the cripples. Montanus said that another saying of Sparsus' was in equally bad taste: "There came forth more beggars than limbs."

I give Greek epigrams so that you may judge, first, how easily the passage from Greek to Latin eloquence

Latinam transitus sit et quam omne quod bene
dici potest commune omnibus gentibus sit, deinde ut
ingenia ingeniis conferatis et cogitetis Latinam linguam facultatis non minus habere, licentiae minus.

24   Labieni sententiam separavi, quia locuti de illa
homines erant: Sedet ad cotidianum diurnum et
mendicantium quaestus recognoscit: "Tu hodie
minus attulisti: cedo lora; gaudeo me non omnes
emancasse. Quid fles? quid rogas? Plus rettu-
lisses si sic rogasses." Dixit et illam sententiam:
date miseris quod unum percipere gaudium possunt:
aliquis ex illis damnatum istum videat, aliquis audiat.

Glycon dixit: [1] αὕτη μόνη τοῖς ταλαιπώροις χαρὰ
καταλέλειπται.

25   P. Vinicius, summus amator Ovidi, hunc aiebat
sensum disertissime apud Nasonem Ovidium esse
positum, quem ad fingendas similes sententias aiebat
memoria tenendum.   Occiso Achille hoc epiphonema
poni:

quod Priamus gaudere senex post Hectora posset,
hoc fuit.

Cassius Severus dixerat: ostende nobis captivos
⟨tuos⟩.[2] Iulius Bassus dixerat: ostende mercedarios
tuos.   Labienus commodius videbatur dixisse: os- 493M
tende nobis alumnos tuos.

----

[1] *The words* Glycon dixit *appear in the MSS after* μόνη, *and
were transposed by Gertz.*
[2] *Supplied by Schultingh.*

is made, and how every conceivable good saying is common to all races: then so that you can compare talents, and reflect that Latin has as much resource in expression—though less licence.

I have put Labienus' epigram separately because it had been a subject of discussion. The defendant sits before his day-book and goes over the profits made by the beggars: " *You* brought in less today. Get me the whip. I'm glad I didn't maim the lot.[1] Why do you weep? Why beg? You'd have brought more home if you had begged like this." He also spoke this epigram: " Give the wretches the one joy they can feel: let one of them see, another hear this man convicted." [2]

Glycon said: " This is the one joy left to the wretches."

Publius Vinicius, a great enthusiast for Ovid, said that this idea is put very cleverly in Ovid, and that Ovid's verse should be kept in mind with a view to the invention of similar epigrams. When Achilles has been killed, this exclamation is put in:

" This was the only joy that old Priam could feel
Now Hector was gone." [3]

Cassius Severus had said: " Show us your prisoners." Julius Bassus had said: " Show us your paymasters." [4] Labienus' epigram was thought more appropriate: " Show us your nurselings."

---

[1] i.e. there is still scope for further mutilation, and further profit (cf. §5 " Let us add . . .").
[2] According to the senses left to each.
[3] *Met.* 12.607–8. For *epiphonemata* see on *C.* 1 pr. 23.
[4] For these sayings see §§2 and 5.

P. Asprenas dixit, cum induxisset stipem porrigentem mendico: "o infelicem patrem!": et hoc qui dicit, ipse fortassis pater est.

V

PARRHASIUS ET PROMETHEUS

Laesae rei publicae sit actio.

Parrhasius, pictor Atheniensis, cum Philippus captivos Olynthios venderet, emit unum ex iis senem; perduxit Athenas; torsit et ad exemplar eius pinxit Promethea. Olynthius in tormentis perit. Ille tabulam in templo Minervae posuit. Accusatur rei publicae laesae.

1   GAVI SILONIS. Infelix *senex* vidit iacentis divulsae patriae ruinas; abstractus a coniuge, *abstractus a liberis, super exustae Olynthi cinerem stetit; iam ad figurandum Promethea satis tristis est.* Pro Iuppiter! —quem enim melius invocem adversus Parrhasium quam quem imitatus est?—Olynthium tantum picturae tuae excipio? *Nemo ut naufragum pingeret mersit.* Caeditur: "parum est" inquit; uritur:

---

[1] Cf. *C.* 10.4 n.

[2] For the capture of Olynthus and Athenian action towards its inhabitants see n. on *C.* 3.8.

[3] This will be sheer fiction: it is unlikely that Parrhasius was even alive in 348 B.C. No Prometheus is recorded among his works, but he was certainly concerned with realistic facial

Publius Asprenas said, after introducing a man giving alms to a beggar: " ' His poor father! '—and perhaps the speaker of these very words *is* the father! "

5

PARRHASIUS AND PROMETHEUS

An action may lie for harming the state.[1]

The Athenian painter Parrhasius purchased an old man from among the captives from Olynthus [2] put up for sale by Philip, and took him to Athens. He tortured him, and using him as a model painted a Prometheus. The Olynthian died under the torture. Parrhasius put the picture in the temple of Minerva; he is accused of harming the state.[3]

Against Parrhasius

GAVIUS SILO. The wretched old man has seen the 1 prostrate ruins of his torn country; snatched from wife and children, he has trodden underfoot the ashes of the burned Olynthus; now [4] he is miserable enough to pose for Prometheus.—Jupiter!—for what god could I better invoke against Parrhasius than the one he imitated? [5]—is it only this Olynthian I am trying to keep out of your paintings?—No-one plunged a man in the sea to paint him as shipwrecked.—He is

detail (*argutiae vultus* in Plin. *N.H.* 35.67) and interested in mythological subjects.
[4] Without being tortured.
[5] i.e. in " punishing Prometheus " (Jupiter = Zeus).

" etiamnunc parum est "; laniatur: " hoc " inquit " ⟨in⟩ irato Philippo satis est, sed nondum in irato 49 Iove."

IULI BASSI. Producitur puer: " supervacuum est " inquit; " nondum quantum satis sit Prometheo potest gemere." *Ultima Olynthi deprecatio est:* " Atheniensis, *redde me Philippo.*" Non est istud donum, sacrilegium est. " *Servus* " inquit " *meus fuit.*" *Putes Philippum loqui. Aedem Minervae tamquam castra Macedonum fugiunt.*

2 CLODI TURRINI. " *Parum* " inquit " *tristis est.*' *Aliquis Olynthius parum tristis est* nisi qui Atheniensem dominum sortitus est? *Vis [Parrhasi] tristem videre?* [1] Dabo tibi, Parrhasi, maiora tormenta: *duc illum ad iacentem Olynthum,* duc illo ubi liberos, ubi domum perdidit. *Scis certe quam tristem* illum *emeris. Olynthiis urbem aperuimus, templa praeclusimus? Ergo nemo Olynthius tortus esset si omnes illos Macedones emissent?* " *Torqueatur* ": hoc nec sub Philippo factum est. " *Moriatur* ": hoc nec sub Iove.

3 ARGENTARI. *Hoc hospitio Olynthius Athenis exceptus est?* Tantum porro Olynthium torsit Parrhasius?

---

[1] *This sentence is only given in the excerpta, which, however, do not have the next words; in view of this, Gertz was right to delete* Parrhasi.

flogged. " Not enough," says Parrhasius. He is
burned. " Still not enough." He is torn limb from
limb. " That is enough for Philip's anger—but not
enough for Jupiter's."

JULIUS BASSUS. A boy is brought forward. " It's
waste of time," says Parrhasius. " He isn't yet
capable of groaning as much as I need for Prometheus."—The Olynthian's last prayer is: " Athenian,
give me back to Philip."—This is no present [1]—it is
sacrilege.—" He was my slave." You might suppose
it was Philip talking.—People shun the temple of
Minerva as though it was the Macedonian camp.

CLODIUS TURRINUS. " He is not sad enough." Can 2
there be an Olynthian who is only sad enough if an
Athenian owner has fallen to his lot? [2]—Do you want
to see a sad man? I will give you, Parrhasius,
greater torments: take him to prostrate Olynthus,
take him to where he lost his children and home.—
Surely you know how sad he was when you bought
him? [3]—Have we opened our city to the Olynthians
only to close our temples to them?—Then would no
Olynthian have been tortured if Macedonians had
bought them all?—" Let him be tortured ": this was
not done even under Philip. " Let him die ": *this*
not even under Jupiter.[4]

ARGENTARIUS. Was an *Olynthian* given this sort of 3
reception in Athens?—Was it then only the Olyn-

---

[1] i.e. to the temple.

[2] Indignant question. The special relationship of Olynthus
and Athens would suggest the opposite: cf. §10 Latro.

[3] i.e. you don't need tortures to get the right expression.

[4] Prometheus survived his torments and lived to see Zeus
worsted.

Quid? non et oculos nostros torquet? Ibi ponit tabulam ubi fortasse nos tabulam foederis posuimus. *Hoc Promethea facere est, non pingere.* Aiebat tortoribus: " sic intendite, sic caedite, sic istum quem fecit cummaxime vultum servate, ne sitis ipsi exemplar."

4 CESTI PII. *" Emi " inquit. Immo, si Atheniensis es, redemisti.* Si nescis, Parrhasi, *in isto templo* pro *Olynthiis vota suscepimus:* ⟨ita⟩ [1] solventur? Crudelis *ille Graeciae carnifex istum tamen nihil amplius quam vendidit.* Producitur nobilis *senex, longa miseriarum tabe confectus,* reductis introrsus oculis, *tam tristis quam si iam tortus esset.* Ut admoveri sibi catenas vidit: "supervacuae sunt " inquit; " si ad alium dominum pervenissem, Athenas fugerem." Istud tibi in nullo Olynthio permitto, nisi si Lasthenen emeris.

5 TRIARI. Corrupisti duo maxima Promethei munera, ignem et hominem. *Quemcumque praeco flentem viderat, sciebat emptorem,* miserebantur omnes; et fortasse ipse Philippus reduci iussisset, nisi Atheniensem vidisset emptorem. . . . quod ego fabulosum esse non dubito. Sed utrum vult Parrhasius eligat: parum pie aut infamavit Iovem aut imitatus est.

---

[1] *Supplied by Müller.*

---

[1] Temples being commonly used for keeping archives. There is play on two senses of the word *tabula.*
[2] i.e. redeemed him from Philip.
[3] Philip.
[4] Whose treachery (cf. §§11, 18) deserves such tortures.

thian that Parrhasius tortured? Does he not torture
our eyes too?—He puts a picture where, perhaps, we
have put the text of the treaty.[1]—This is *making* a
Prometheus, not painting one.—He said to the tor-
turers: " Stretch him like that, flog him like that,
keep his present expression just so—or I'll make a
model of *you*."

CESTIUS PIUS. " I bought him." Rather, if you 4
are an Athenian, you bought him back.[2]—In case you
don't know, Parrhasius, this is the temple where we
made our vows on behalf of the Olynthians: is this
how we are to pay them?—That cruel butcher of
Greece [3] did at least confine himself to *selling* this
man.—They bring forth a distinguished old man,
worn out by the long decay wrought by his troubles,
eyes sunken, as sad as if he had already been tortured.
When he saw the chains brought for him, he said:
" They are superfluous. If I had found myself under
a different master, it is Athens to which I should have
fled."—I don't allow you to do this to any Olynthian
—unless you buy Lasthenes.[4]

TRIARIUS. You have abused Prometheus' two 5
greatest gifts, fire and man.—Anyone the auctioneer
saw weeping he knew to be a buyer.[5]   Everybody felt
pity.   And maybe Philip himself would have ordered
him to be taken out of the sale if he hadn't seen the
purchaser was an Athenian.[6]— . . .[7] which I do not
doubt is a fiction.   But let Parrhasius choose which
he likes; he has shown lack of piety either in dis-

---

[5] Rather than, as one would expect, a slave for sale (παρὰ
προσδοκίαν).

[6] So assuming that he had fallen into good hands.

[7] Details of the Prometheus myth will have fallen out.

Clamabat iste: nondum satis tristis es, nondum satis, inquam, adiecisti ad priorem vultum. ⟨Num⟩[1] talis in auctione Philippus?

6 MUSAE. *Narraturus sum Olynthi senis ignes, verbera, tormenta: aliquis* nunc *me queri de Philippo putat.* Dii deaeque te perdant! misericordem Philippum fecisti. *Si isti creditis, iratum Iovem imitatus est, si nobis, iratum vicit Philippum.* Pinge Philippum 490 crure debili, oculo effosso, iugulo fracto, per tot damna a dis immortalibus tortum.

CORNELI HISPANI. Ultima membrorum tabe tormentis inmoritur. Parrhasi, quid agis? Non servas propositum; hoc supra Promethea est. *Tantum patiendum est pingente Parrhasio quantum irato Iove.*

7 ARELLI FUSCI patris. Pinge Promethea, sed homines facientem, sed ignis dividentem; pinge, sed inter munera potius quam inter tormenta. Inter altaria Olynthi senis crucem posuit. *Miserrime senex, aliquis fortassis ex servis tuis felicius servit;* utique felicior est quisquis Macedoni servit.

8 FULVI SPARSI. *Si ad succurrendum profectus es, queror quod unum emisti, si ad torquendum, queror quod ullum.* Utinam, Philippe, auctionem cum exceptione fecisses: ne quis Atheniensis emeret! Non vidit Phidias Iovem, fecit tamen velut tonantem;

---

[1] *Supplied by Müller, perhaps needlessly.*

gracing Jupiter or in imitating him.—This man cried:
"You aren't sad enough yet. You haven't yet
exaggerated your previous expression enough."
Was *Philip* like this at the sale?

Musa. I shall tell of fires, floggings, rackings 6
undergone by an old Olynthian: people suppose it is
Philip I am complaining of.—Gods and goddesses
damn you! You have made Philip seem merciful!—
If you believe *him*, he represented the anger of Jove;
if you believe *us*, he surpassed the anger of Philip.—
Paint Philip with crippled leg, eye knocked out, throat
scarred, with all the defects sent by the immortal
gods to torment him.[1]

Cornelius Hispanus. He dies under the torture,
his limbs finally worn away; Parrhasius, what are you
up to?—you aren't keeping to your plan: this goes
beyond Prometheus. There should be only as much
suffering when Parrhasius paints as when Jove is
angry!

Arellius Fuscus Senior. Paint Prometheus—but 7
paint him creating man, paint him distributing fire;
paint him, but amid his gifts rather than amid his
agonies.—Among the altars he has placed the cross
of an old Olynthian.—Most pitiable old man, perhaps
one of your own serfs has a more fortunate serfdom:
at least any slave of a Macedonian is more fortunate.

Fulvius Sparsus. If you went there [2] to bring 8
help, my complaint is that you bought only one; if to
torture, that you bought one.—Would you had
inserted a clause of exception into the terms of the
auction, Philip: No Athenian to buy!—Phidias never

---

[1] For Philip's defects see Dem. *de Cor.* 67.
[2] To the sale.

nec stetit ante oculos eius Minerva, dignus tamen illa arte animus et concepit deos et exhibuit. Quid facturi sumus si bellum volueris pingere? Diversas virorum statuemus acies et in mutua vulnera armabimus manus? Victos [1] sequentur victores? Revertentur cruenti? Ne Parrhasii manus temere ludat coloribus, internecione humana emendum

9 est? Si necesse est aliquem torqueri, eme nocentem servum, ut eodem tempore ⟨et⟩ [2] exemplum sumas 49 et supplicium. *Statuitur ex altera parte Parrhasius cum coloribus, ex altera tortor cum ignibus,* flagellis, eculeis. Ista aut videntem aut expectantem, Parrhasi, parum tristem putas? Dicebat miser: " Non prodidi patriam. Athenienses, si nihil merui, succurrite, si merui, reddite Philippo." *Inter ista Parrhasius dubium est studiosius pingat an saeviat.*

10 " Torque, verbera, ure ": sic iste carnifex colores temperat. Quid ais? parum tristis videtur quem Philippus vendidit, emit Parrhasius? " Etiamnunc torque, etiamnunc; bene habet, sic tene, hic vultus esse debuit lacerati, hic morientis."

Porci Latronis. Si videtur tibi, istis muneribus aram Misericordiae orna. Nemo ergo ex Olynthiis

---

[1] victos *Bursian, Madvig:* ducte *AB:* uicti *V.*
[2] *Supplied by Kiessling.*

saw Jove, but he nevertheless represented him as thundering; Minerva did not stand before his eyes, but his mind, that matched such superb technique, formed a concept of gods and put them on view.[1]— What are we to do if you decide to paint a war? Are we to arrange opposing ranks of men, and put weapons in their hands to wound each other? Shall victors pursue vanquished, to return covered in blood? That Parrhasius' hand need not play unguided over his colours, must the price be human carnage?—If someone must be tortured, buy a guilty slave, so that you can take likeness and vengeance at the same time.—On one side Parrhasius, with his colours, on the other the torturer, with his fires, whips, racks. Don't you think a man sad enough who sees these things or is waiting for their application?—The wretch said: "I did not betray my country; Athenians, if I have done no wrong, come to my help —and if I have done wrong, give me back to Philip." —Amidst all this, it is doubtful whether Parrhasius has more interest in painting or in sadism.—" Rack, whip, burn ": that's how this butcher mixes his colours.—What do you say? Do you regard a man sold by Philip and bought by Parrhasius as not sad enough?—" Torture him still, still; that's right, hold it so, this must have been the expression of a man torn and dying."

PORCIUS LATRO. Use gifts like this, if you will, to deck the altar of Mercy.[2]—Then does none of the

---

[1] Compare the discussion of imitation and imagination in Philostratus *Vit. Apoll.* 6.19: also Cicero *Orat.* 8–9.

[2] In the Athenian Agora (Paus. 1.17.1). For rhetorical use of the cult see Quintilian 5.11.38.

miserius servit quam qui Atheniensem dominum sortitus est? Miser, ubicumque Philippum non viderat, pacem putabat. " Alliga " inquit. Aiebat: " solutus apud Philippum fui."

11   ALBUCI SILI. Expecta dum Euthycrates aut Lasthenes capiantur. Phidias omnia opera sine tortore fecit. Philippus quoque vendidisse contentus est. *Producitur senex* nobilis, flens, *respiciens patriam: placuit isti vultus; habuit aliquid Promethei simile etiam ante tormenta.* Quam diligenter causam agit! ut Philippus Olynthio . . . non est, ego pecuniam perdidi; redi ad auctorem. Propter homines Prometheus distortus ⟨est⟩,[1] propter Promethea homines ne torseris. Philippus sic rogabatur: liceat Olynthios vivere. Parrhasius aliter rogandus: Olynthiis mori liceat. " Tristem volo facere." Nemo faciet si Philippus non fecit.

12   Hanc controversiam magna pars declamatorum sic dixit velut ⟨non⟩[2] controversiam divideret sed accusationem, quomodo solent ordinare actionem suam in foro qui primo loco accusant; in scholastica, quia non duobus dicitur locis, semper non dicendum tantum sed respondendum est. Obiciunt quod hominem torserit, quod Olynthium, quod deorum sup-

498

---

[1] *Supplied by Gertz.*
[2] velut non *Gertz after Faber:* ut.

---

[1] ⟨sad enough⟩?
[2] Rather than suffer further torment.
[3] i.e. by considering objections to one's case: Seneca com-

Olynthians endure a more pitiable slavery than the one whom the lot gave to an Athenian master?—Poor man, he thought there was peace where he saw no Philip.—" Chain him." " Under Philip, I wasn't in chains."

ALBUCIUS SILUS. Wait till Euthycrates or Las- 11 thenes is captured.—Phidias did all his work without employing a torturer.—Even Philip is satisfied with *selling.*—They bring forth a distinguished old man, weeping, looking back at his country. This man liked his face: he had something reminiscent of Prometheus even before being tortured.—How carefully he pleads his case! As Philip . . . the Olynthian . . .—" He is not . . .[1] I have wasted my money. Go back to your seller."—Prometheus was racked because of men: do not rack men because of Prometheus.—Philip was begged in these terms: " May the Olynthians live! " Parrhasius needs begging in another way: " May the Olynthians die! "[2] —" I want to make him sad." No-one will do that if Philip failed.

The majority of declaimers spoke this *controversia* 12 as if it was an accusation rather than a *controversia* they were dividing. Their arrangement was like that of those who in court make the first speech for the prosecution—while in a declamation one always has both to assert and to reply,[3] because one doesn't speak on both sides. They accuse Parrhasius of torturing a man, an Olynthian, of representing

plains that this was not done here (cf. below: " refute anything that *can* be said "). *duobus locis* may mean rather " twice." For similar passages see Quintilian 4.2.28, 5.13.50, 7.1.38.

plicia imitatus sit, quod tabulam in templo Minervae posuerit. Si Parrhasius responsurus non est,
satis bene dividunt. Nihil est autem turpius quam
aut eam controversiam declamare in qua nihil ab
altera parte responderi possit, aut non refellere si
responderi potest.

13   Gallio fere similem divisionem in Parrhasio habuit
ei quam habuerat in illa controversia cuius mentio
est in hoc ipso libro, de illo qui debilitabat expositos,
detractis quibusdam. Divisit autem sic: an laesa
sit res publica. Quid perdidit? inquit; nihil.
Nondum de iure controversiam facio. Perdidit
unum senem Olynthus. Fac Atheniensem: non
ages mecum rei publicae laesae si Atheniensem
senatorem occidero, sed caedis. "Ita; verum
opinio Athenarum corrumpitur; misericordia semper censi sumus." *Numquam unius ⟨male⟩* [1] *facto
publica fama corrumpitur; solidior est opinio Athenien-*   499M
14 *sium quam ut labefactari illo modo possit.* "Laesa
est" inquit "res publica." Laesa non ⟨est⟩,[2] ut
existimo. Aliquis Olynthio depositum negaverit:
videbitur hominem, non rem publicam laesisse.
Olynthiis hoc tribuisti, ut eodem loco essent quo
Athenienses. "*Laesisti*" inquit "*rem publicam quod
hanc picturam in templo posuisti.*" *Laedunt rem publi-*

---

[1] *Supplied by C. F. W. Müller, comparing E.*
[2] *Supplied by Schultingh.*

punishments inflicted by gods, of putting the picture
in the temple of Minerva. If Parrhasius is not going
to reply, their division is good enough. But nothing
is more disgraceful than to declaim a *controversia*
where nothing can be said in reply on the other side,
or to fail to refute anything that *can* be said.

Gallio's division in the case of Parrhasius was very 13
similar to the one he had used in the *controversia*
mentioned in this very book [1] about the man who
crippled exposed babies; but he removed various
points. His division went like this: Has the state
been harmed? " What has it lost? Nothing. For
the moment I'm not disputing the rights and wrongs
of the case. One old man has been lost—by Olynthus. Suppose he had been an Athenian. If I kill
an Athenian senator, you will not sue me for harming
the state, but for murder. ' Yes, but the prestige of
Athens has been impaired. We have always been
accounted merciful.' The reputation of a state is
never impaired by the crime of a single man; [2] the
prestige of the Athenians is too well-established to be
capable of being shaken thus. ' The state has been 14
harmed.' It has not, I think. Suppose someone
refuses to return to an Olynthian an article he has
deposited with him: he will be regarded as harming
the man, not the state. [You have given the Olynthians the privilege of equality with the Athenians.] [3]
' You have harmed the state by putting this picture
in the temple.' The state is harmed by those who

---

[1] See *C*. 10.4.14.
[2] Cf. *C*. 9.2.15.
[3] Clearly out of place. Gertz transposed the sentence to
follow " by Olynthus " in §13.

cam qu aliquid illi auferunt, non qui adiciunt, qui
diruunt templa, non qui ornant. *Peccaverunt ergo
et sacerdotes, qui tabulam receperunt. Quare tamen non
reciperent? Deorum adulteria picta sunt,* positae sunt
15 picturae Herculis liberos occidentis. Deinde: an
ob id accusari possit laesae rei publicae quod illi
facere licuit. Ea lege persequere quae ⟨facere⟩ [1]
non licuit. Dicis mihi: " hoc facere non oportet."
Huic rei aestimatio inmensa est. Itaque nulla vin-
dicta est; et id tantum punitur quod non licet.
Satis abundeque ⟨est⟩ si opifex rerum imperitus ad
legem innocens est. An hoc ei facere licuerit. Hoc
in illa dividitur: an Olynthius apud Atheniensem,
etiam antequam fieret decretum, ⟨servus esse non
potuerit⟩.[2] Servus, inquit, est meus, quem ego
belli iure ⟨possideo. Rata autem esse quae parta
sunt belli iure⟩ [2] vobis, Athenienses, expedit:
alioqui imperium vestrum in antiquos fines redigitur;
16 quidquid est, bello partum [et] [3] est. Contra
ait: Ille servos alii emptori potest esse, Atheniensi 500M
non. Quid enim si Atheniensem a Philippo emisses?
Atqui sciebas Olynthios coniunctos nobis esse foedere.
Ut scias, inquit, servos fuisse, decretum postea factum
est Atheniensium quo iuberentur et liberi et cives
esse. Quare hoc illis ius, si iam habebant, dabatur?

[1] quae facere *Gertz:* quia.
[2] *Supplied by Bursian.*
[3] *Deleted by Bursian.*

---

[1] The second sub-question comes halfway through §16.
[2] That giving citizen rights to the Olynthians, regarded as
being passed after the purchase.

take something away from it, not those who give it
something: those who destroy temples, not enrich
them. In that case, the priests who received the
picture were in the wrong also. But why should they
not accept it? There have been paintings of the
adulteries of the gods; and pictures of Hercules killing his children have been put in temples." Next: 15
Can he be accused of harming the state for doing
something he was allowed to do? "Use law to
proceed against illegalities. You say to me: 'One
ought not do this.' This principle leaves unlimited
room for value-judgements—hence there is no
punishment for such actions. Only what is illegal is
punished. It is quite enough if an artist, ignorant of
practical matters, is innocent before the law." *Was*
he permitted to do this? This is divided thus:[1]
Could an Olynthian have been a slave in an Athenian
household even before the decree[2] was passed? "He
is my slave; I possess him by right of war. It is in
your interests, Athenians, that what is won by right
of war should go unchallenged. Otherwise you find
your empire reduced to its former limits. Without
exception, it was won in war." On the other side he 16
said: "He can be the slave of any other purchaser—
but not of an Athenian. What if you had bought an
Athenian from Philip? Yet you knew the Olynthians are intimately bound to us by treaty." "To
show you," he[3] says, "that they had been slaves: a
decree of the Athenians was passed afterwards
making them free, with citizen rights. Why give
them this right if they already had it?" Next: Is it

---

[3] The contender on the other side (that for Parrhasius).
There is another dialogue after the next question is posed.

Deinde: an decreto hoc non contineatur, ut liberi
fiant, sed ut esse liberi iudicentur. Hoc censuimus,
Olynthios cives nostros esse: ita et ille civis noster
fuit. Non, inquit; nam decretum in futurum factum
est, non in praeteritum. Vis hoc scire? [uis] [1]
Num, quisquis Olynthium servum habuit, accusabitur
quod civem in sua servitute tenuerit? Si quis
tunc inter necessaria servilium officiorum ministeria
percussit aut cecidit, iniuriarum accusabitur? Atqui, quantum ad ius attinet, nihil interest occiderit
an ceciderit; nam aut nec caedere licuit aut ⟨et⟩ [2]
occidere.

17 ⟨Latro⟩ [3] a parte Parrhasii fecit hunc colorem:
emptum esse a Parrhasio senem inutilem, expiratu-
rum; si verum, inquit, vultis, non occidit illum, sed
deficientis et alioqui expiraturi morte usus est.
Torsit, inquit, tamen: si lucri causa, obice; nempe
huius crudelitatis pretium Athenae habent. In
argumentis dixit *quantum semper artibus licuisset:
medicos, ut vim ignotam morbi cognoscerent, viscera
rescidisse;* hodie cadaverum artus rescindi ut ner-
vorum articulorumque positio cognosci possit.

Albucius hoc colore: calamitosum fuisse, orbum,
palam mortem optantem: nec aliter illum Philippus 501M
vendidisset nisi putasset illi poenam esse vivere.

18 Silo Pompeius putabat commodius esse si hoc
animo isset ad auctionem Parrhasius, ut aliquem in

---

[1] *Deleted by Thomas.*
[2] *Supplied by Gertz.*
[3] *Supplied by Kiessling.*

a provision of the decree not that they should become free but that they should be judged to be already free? " We voted for the Olynthians to be citizens of our city; this is how *this* man became a citizen of ours." " No, for the decree was made for the future, not the past. Do you want proof? Will anyone who had an Olynthian slave now be accused of holding a citizen in slavery under him? Will anyone who struck or beat him then, in the inevitable routine of a slave's duties, be accused of causing injury? Yet as far as the law goes there is no difference between killing and beating; either it was not legal even to beat—or it was legal even to kill."

Latro, for Parrhasius, made a *colour* of this: 17 Parrhasius had bought an old man, useless and on the point of death. " If you want the truth, he did not kill him: he made use of the death of one who was failing and was going to die in any case. 'But he tortured him.' If it was for gain, make a charge of that; Athens of course fixes a price to pay for such cruelty." Among his arguments, he said how much licence the arts have always had. Doctors have laid bare the vital organs in order to investigate the secret potential of a disease; today the limbs of cadavers are opened up so that the position of sinews and joints can be ascertained.

Albucius used this *colour*: he was in distress, bereaved, openly praying for death. Philip would not have put him up for sale if he hadn't thought it a punishment for him to have to go on living.

Pompeius Silo thought it more suitable that 18 Parrhasius should be represented as having gone to the auction with the intention of buying someone for

hunc usum emeret. Poterit enim videri elegisse vilissimum et maxime inutilem.

Fusco Arellio placebat emptum quidem illum in alios usus, sed, cum deficeret et mori vellet, in id quod unum ex cadavere artifex ⟨petere⟩ [1] poterat inpensum.

Gallio ad neutrum se alligavit nec dixit quo animo emisset.

†Gallionis† color intolerabilis est; dixit enim ⟨se⟩ [2] senem ex noxiis Olynthiis emisse; quod si illi licet fingere, non video quare non eadem opera dicat et conscium proditionis Lastheni fuisse et se poenae causa torsisse.

19 Hispo Romanius ignorantia illum excusavit: pictor, inquit, intra officinam suam clausus, qui haec tantum vulgaria iura noverat, in servum nihil non domino licere, pictori nihil non pingere, mancipium suum operi suo impendit. " Non omnia " inquit " narras: Olynthius fuit ille qui perit." Quid autem ad rem pertinet cuius nationis servos fuerit? " Audes " inquit " servum dicere Olynthium? " Etiam, post bellum et ante decretum; alioqui quod vos illis beneficium dedistis, nisi quod iam illos nec torquere licet nec occidere?

Graeci nefas putaverunt pro Parrhasio dicere: omnes illum accusaverunt; in eosdem sensus in-
20 currerunt. Glycon dixit: πῦρ καὶ ἄνθρωπος, Προ-

---

[1] *Supplied by Gertz.*
[2] *Supplied by Müller.*

466

this purpose: he can then be supposed to have chosen a particularly cheap and useless man.

Arellius Fuscus decided that he had been bought for other uses, but that when he was failing and wanting to die he was exploited for the one use that an artist could look for from a corpse.

Gallio committed himself to neither line, and didn't say why he bought him.

** 's *colour* is intolerable: he said that he had bought the old man from among the guilty Olynthians. If he can invent that detail, I don't see why he doesn't on the same principle say the old man had been in the plot with Lasthenes and that Parrhasius tortured him as a punishment.

Romanius Hispo gave him the excuse of ignorance. 19 " A painter, shut up inside his studio, with no idea of the law in his head except the unsophisticated notion that everything is permitted between master and slave,[1] and that a painter may paint anything, exploited his own slave for his own work. 'You are suppressing something: the victim was an Olynthian.' What difference does the nationality of the slave make? ' Do you dare to call an Olynthian a slave?' Yes, after the war and before the decree; otherwise what good did you do them,[2] except that *now* it is illegal to torture and kill them? "

The Greeks thought it an abomination to speak for Parrhasius, and they all accused him, falling into the same ideas. Glycon said: " Fire and man, your own 20

---

[1] For restrictions on the originally unlimited power of master over slave see R. H. Barrow, *Slaves in the Roman Empire* (Methuen, 1928), 46–7.

[2] i.e. by passing the decree.

μηθεῦ, τὰ σά σε δῶρα βασανίζει. Triarius hoc ex aliqua parte, cum subriperet, inflexit. Hos aiebat 502M Severus Cassius qui hoc facerent similes sibi videri furibus alienis poculis ansas mutantibus. Multi sunt qui detracto verbo aut mutato aut adiecto putent se alienas sententias lucri fecisse. Triarius autem sic vertit: corrupisti duo maxima Promethei munera, ignem et hominem.

21 Sed et Graeci illam subrupuerunt: Euctemon qui dixit: Προμηθεῦ, ἐπὶ σέ τις πῦρ καὶ ἄνθρωπον; Sanius quam Glycon, Adaeus: Προμηθεῦ, σέ τις γράφων ἄνθρωπον ἀφανίζει. Damas corruptissime: δικαίως, Προμηθεῦ· διὰ τί γὰρ πῦρ ἔκλεπτες ἀνθρώπῳ; Craton furiosissime, qui dixit: Προμηθεῦ, νῦν ἔδει σε πῦρ κλέψαι. Hic est Craton, venustissimus homo et professus Asianus, qui bellum cum omnibus Atticis gerebat. Cum donaret illi Caesar talentum, in quo viginti quattuor sestertia sunt Atheniensium more: ἢ πρόσθες, φησίν, ἢ ἄφελ', ἵνα μὴ 'Αττικὸν ᾖ. Hic ⟨et⟩¹ Caesari, quod illum numquam nisi mense Decembri audiret, dixit: ὡς βαύνῳ μοι χρῆ; et cum commendaretur a Caesare Passieno nec curaret, interroganti quare non conplecteretur tanti viri gratiam: ἡλίου καίοντος λύχνον οὐχ ἅπτω. 503M

22 Saepe solebat apud Caesarem cum Timagene

¹ *Supplied by Schultingh.*

---

¹ See above, §5.
² i.e. to prevent the torturer using it (cf. Apaturius in §28). There is a similar conceit in Philostr. *Vit. Soph.* 602.

gifts, Prometheus, put you to the torture." Triarius,
filching this, gave it a slightly different turn. Cassius
Severus said people who behaved like this were in his
view like thieves who change the handles on other
people's cups. There are many who think they've
pocketed other people's epigrams by taking out,
changing or adding a word. However, Triarius'
twist was like this: " You have abused Prometheus'
two greatest gifts, fire and man." [1]

But the Greeks too pinched the *mot*. Thus 21
Euctemon said: " Prometheus, is someone using fire
and man on *you*? " In better taste than Glycon,
Adaeus said: " Prometheus, someone is painting you
—and destroying a man." Damas in the worst of
taste: " Quite fair, Prometheus. Why did you steal
fire to give it to man? " Craton said, dottily:
" Prometheus, *this* is the moment you should have
stolen fire." [2] This is the Craton, a very witty man
and professed Asianist, who waged war on everything
Attic. When the emperor gave him a talent, in
which there are according to Athenian practice
twenty-four sesterces, he said: " Either add something or take something off, to stop it being Attic."
He also said to the emperor, who only came to listen
to him in the month of December: " You are using
me as a furnace." And when he was commended by
the emperor to Passienus and didn't bother about it,
he said to someone [3] who asked why he didn't welcome the friendship of so great a man: " I don't light
the lamp when the sun is blazing."

He used often to clash before the emperor with 22

[3] Perhaps the emperor himself. The reply is modelled on
a proverb (Otto, *Sprichwörter*, 327).

confligere, homine acidae linguae et qui nimis liber erat: puto quia diu non fuerat. Ex captivo cocus, ex coco lecticarius, ex lecticario usque in amicitiam Caesaris enixus,[1] usque eo utramque fortunam contempsit, et in qua erat et in qua fuerat, ut, cum illi multis de causis iratus Caesar interdixisset domo, combureret historias rerum ab illo gestarum, quasi et ipse illi ingenio suo interdiceret: disertus homo et dicax, a quo multa inprobe sed venuste dicta.

Ne modum excedam excurrendo, ad Parrhasium revertor.

23   Nicetes dixit: εἰ πυρὶ ⟨καὶ⟩[2] σιδήρῳ ζωγραφοῦνται, τίνι τυραννοῦνται;

Hispo Romanius dixit: *ignis, ferrum, tormenta: pictoris ista an Philippi officina est?*

Sparsi sententia in descriptione picturae habet aliquid corrupti: " et, ubicumque sanguine opus est, humano utitur "; dixit enim quod fieri non potest.

Illum locum omnes temptaverunt: quid si volueris bellum pingere? quid si incendium? quid si parricidium? E Graecis Dorion furiose dixit: τίς Οἰδίπους ἔσται, τίς Ἀτρεύς; οὐ γράψεις γὰρ ἂν μὴ μύθους ἴδῃς ζῶντας. Sed nihil est quod minus ferri 24 possit quam quod a Metrodoro dictum est: μή μοι 504

---

[1] enixus *Thomas:* felix.
[2] *Supplied by Thomas.*

Timagenes, a man of acid tongue, and over-free with it (because, I imagine, he hadn't been free himself over a long period).[1] From a captive he had become a cook, from a cook a chair-carrier; from being a chair-carrier he had struggled into the friendship of the emperor. But he despised both his present and his past fortunes to such an extent that, when the emperor, angry with him on many counts, barred him from his house, he burned the histories he had written recounting the emperor's deeds, as though barring him, in his turn, from access to his genius. He was a fluent and witty man, who came out with many outrageous but attractive things.

Not to pass due measure in my digression, I return to Parrhasius:

Nicetes said: " If men are *painted* with fire and steel, what will a tyrant use on them? "

Romanius Hispo said: " Fire, steel, rackings: is this a painter's workshop—or Philip's? "

Sparsus' epigram in the description of the painting has an element of bad taste: " And wherever he needs blood, he uses human blood." [2] For what he said is impossible.

Everyone had a go at the topic, What if you decide to paint war, a fire, a parricide? Among the Greeks, Dorion insanely said: " Who shall be Oedipus, who Atreus? For you will not paint them unless you see their myths come alive." But nothing is more in-

[1] Timagenes first came to Rome from Alexandria as a captive. For his exclusion from Augustus' house see Sen. *Ir.* 3.23.5 *seq.*

[2] Professor R. G. Austin suggests that there may be an allusion to the use of " dragon's blood " as a pigment (cf. Plin. *N.H.* 33.116).

THE ELDER SENECA

Τρωάδας μηδὲ Νιόβην. ἐπίθες τὸ πῦρ· οὔπω μοι τὸν Προμηθέα ἀπέδωκεν.

Triarius dixit: nondum dignum irato Iove gemuisti.

Haterius dixit sanius: nondum vultus ad fabulam convenit. Et illud: Parrhasi, ut omnia fiant ad exemplum, vivat qui tortus est.

Sed si vultis audire supra quod non possit procedere insania, Licinius Nepos ait: si vultis digne punire Parrhasium, ipse se pingat.

25 Non minus stulte Aemilianus quidam Graecus rhetor, quod genus stultorum amabilissimum est, ex arido fatuus dixit: ἀποκτείνατε Παρράσιον, μὴ θελήσας γράφειν ἐξ ὑμῶν ἀρχέτυπον εὕρῃ.

Pausanias dixit: διὰ σέ, Παρράσιε, δεῖ τοὺς ἐκπορευομένους τοῦ ναοῦ ἀφαγνίσασθαι.

Otho pater, cum pro Parrhasio diceret, in hoc colore derisus est: quia conciderat, inquit, per proditores Olynthos, volui pingere iratum proditori suo Iovem.

Gargonius multo stultius quare Promethei Parrhasius supplicium pinxisset: ego, inquit, ardente Olyntho non odissem ignium auctorem?

26 Latronis illa celebris sententia est, quam Sparsus quoque subtractis quibusdam verbis dixit, in descriptione tormentorum: " Parrhasi, morior "; " sic tene." Hanc sententiam aiunt et Dioclen Carystium 50

---

[1] Cf. §2 n.
[2] i.e. use himself as a model.
[3] Addressed to the jury.

472

tolerable than Metrodorus': " Don't paint me the Trojan women or Niobe."—" Lay on the fire: he hasn't yet given me the Prometheus-look."

Triarius said: " Your groans aren't worthy of the anger of Jove—yet."

Haterius, more sanely, said: " His expression doesn't yet fit the story." Also: " Parrhasius, let the tortured man survive, so as to keep to the pattern in every detail." [1]

But if you want to hear something beyond which lunacy cannot go, Licinius Nepos said: " If you want to punish Parrhasius as he deserves, let him paint himself." [2]

No less absurdly a Greek rhetorician, Aemilianus— one of the most agreeable type of fools, those who pass from dryness to silliness—said: " Kill [3] Parrhasius, in case he wants to paint a picture and finds a model in one of you."

Pausanias said: " Because of you, Parrhasius, those *leaving* the temple have to purify themselves."

Otho senior, speaking for Parrhasius, was made fun of for using this *colour*: " Because Olynthus' fall had been due to treachery, I wanted to paint the anger of Jupiter with the man who betrayed *him*."

Much more stupidly, Gargonius, explaining why Parrhasius had painted the punishment of Prometheus, said: " While Olynthus burned, was I not to hate the originator of fire ? "

Here is a celebrated epigram of Latro's from the description of the tortures (it was used by Sparsus too, though *he* removed a few words): " ' Parrhasius, I am dying.' ' Hold it like that.' " They say that Diocles of Carystos put this epigram differently:

THE ELDER SENECA

dixisse non eodem modo: ἄπιστος ἡ ὑπεροψία · πρὸς
τὸ ἀρέσκον εἶδος ἐβόα· μένε.

27 Spyridion honeste ⟨dixisse⟩[1] Romanos fecit;
multo enim vehementius insanit quam nostri phre-
netici. Voluit videri volturios ad tabulam Parrhasi advolare, fabula eleganti ad turpem sententiam perductus. Traditur enim Zeuxin, ut puto,
pinxisse puerum uvam tenentem, et, cum tanta
esset similitudo uvae ut etiam faceret ⟨aves ad-
volare⟩[2] operi, quendam ex spectatoribus dixisse
aves male existimare de tabula; non fuisse enim
advolaturas ⟨si⟩ puer[3] similis esset. Zeuxin aiunt
oblevisse uvam et servasse id quod melius erat in
28 tabula, non quod similius. Spyridion aeque fami-
liariter in templum volturios subire putavit quam
passeres aut columbas; dixit[4] enim: σαρκοφάγα σοῦ
γ' ἡ γραφὴ ἠπάτα ζῷα.

Sed nolo Romanos in ulla re vinci; restituet aciem
Murredius, qui dixit: pinge Triptolemum, qui iunc-
tis draconibus sulcavit auras. Inter illos qui de
Prometheo corrupte aliquid dixerunt, et Apaturius
locum sibi vindicat; dixit enim: ὤφελε τὸ πῦρ εἰς
θεοὺς πάλιν κλαπῆναι.

[1] *Supplied by Bursian.*
[2] faceret aves advolare *ed. after Bursian:* facere.
[3] si puer *Titius:* uel.
[4] dixit *Gertz:* dixerit.

474

" His disdain is unbelievable. When the expression pleased, he shouted: ' Stay like that! ' "

Spyridion made the Romans look decent speakers: 27 he was much dottier even than *our* lunatics. He wanted it to be thought that vultures flew up to Parrhasius' picture. He was lured by a pretty story [1] into a shameful epigram. For it is related that Zeuxis (I think it was) painted a boy holding a bunch of grapes, and because the bunch was so realistic that it even made birds fly up to the picture, one of the spectators said the birds thought ill of the picture: they would not have flown up if the *boy* had been a good likeness. They say Zeuxis erased the grapes and kept what was best in his picture, not what was most like. Spyridion thought vultures come as 28 naturally into a temple as sparrows or doves; for he said: " *Your* picture deceived animals that eat flesh."

But I don't want the Romans to be beaten at anything. Murredius will restore the day. He said: " Paint Triptolemus, who ploughed the breezes with a team of dragons." [2] Among those who said something in bad taste on Prometheus, Apaturius too claims a place. For he said: " Would that fire had been stolen and given back to the gods! "

[1] Told in Plin. *N.H.* 35.66.
[2] For Triptolemus' chariot see Apollodorus 1.5.2, with Frazer's note. The word *sulcavit* is used in allusion to T. as the first ploughman.

VI

Fur Accusator Proditionis

Fur contione prohibeatur.

Quidam, cum divitem proditionis postulasset,
noctu parietem eius perfodit, et scrinium in quo
erant missae ab hostibus epistulae sustulit.
Damnatus est dives. Accusator contionari cum
vellet, a magistratu prohibitus agit iniuriarum.

1 Porci Latronis. *Id solum sustuli quod fur reliquisset. Nihil tam valde fur timui quam ne dominus
res suas non agnosceret.* Fac mihi invidiam, prode
furtum meum, age magistratui tamen isti gratias,
quod, cum ad illum furtum meum detulissem, furem
summoveri non iussit. *Ruentem civitatis statum unius
parietis ruina reposui.*

Moschi. Sollicitus erat ne quod perdiderat
quaereretur. *Indicium profiteor: multos furti conscios
habeo.* Ad illum tuli, illi ostendi.[1] Hoc furtum non
solus habeo. *Furtum est quod timet dominus agnoscere?*
Potui non esse pauper, habui quod magno venderem:

---

[1] tuli, illi ostendi *C. F. W. Müller, Thomas:* tuti illius
tendi.

---

[1] See Bonner, 105: the law is grounded in Greek and
Roman practice.
[2] i.e. I was no thief. The identification of the stolen goods
would clearly be a part of legal procedure; it is mentioned
elsewhere in this declamation: cf. also Sen. *Beat. Vit.* 23.2.

6

The Thief who Accused the Traitor

A thief shall be barred from public meetings.[1]

A man who had accused a rich man of treason dug through his wall at night and took a writing-case containing letters from the enemy. The rich man was convicted. When his accuser wanted to speak at a public meeting, he was barred by the magistrate. He sues him for injury.

For the accuser

Porcius Latro. I only took what a *thief* would 1 have left.—My worst fear as a " thief " was that the owner might not recognise his own property.[2]—Stir up hatred against me, noise my theft abroad, but thank this magistrate: when I took my booty to him, he didn't order the removal of the thief from his presence.—I made one wall totter—and restored thereby the tottering fortunes of the city.

Moschus. He was anxious in case a search was made for what he had lost.—I volunteer the information against me: in this theft I have many accomplices.—I took it to him, and showed him it.[3]—I am not the only one who has received these stolen goods.[4]—Can property be stolen if the owner is afraid to recognise it as his own ?—I could have ceased to be

---

[3] Again, not the action of a thief.
[4] i.e. the city profits from it; cf. the " many accomplices " above.

teneo ecce epistulas, in quibus manifesta proditionis argumenta sunt, in quibus hostium consilia. Te interrogo: si furtum est, repono.

MUSAE. Furtum vocas quod qui perdiderat negabat suum? Furtum feci, sed hostibus.

CLODI TURRINI. Furtum vocas *quod qui perdiderat* 507[1] *supplicium tulit, qui subripuerat praemium? Utri permisisses loqui si eodem tempore et fur venisset et dominus?* Potui rem publicam magno vendere vel proditori.

2 ARELLI FUSCI patris. *Mille navium duces furto Troiam cepistis. Si bene furto evertuntur urbes, quanto melius servantur!* Si non indicavero cuius sit, nemo agnoscet.

VIBI RUFI. Cuius ego si potuissem non parietem tantum, pectus ipsum perfodissem. Nondum totum consummavi officium: non est tam angusta res publica ut ab uno opprimi possit.

CESTI PII. Nolite a me omnia exigere quae scio; multa sunt, quaedam et in contione dicenda. Hoc furtum liberos vestros docete. Rogo vos, iudices, per furtum meum: quotiens furtum meum protuli, tacet dominus? Ego fur? ecce altera iniuria. Non

---

[1] The rich man is addressed; he clearly did *not* want the plans back.

poor: I had something I could sell for a good sum. Look, I have letters giving clear proofs of treason and the plans of the enemy.—I ask you:[1] if these are stolen goods, I put them back.

MUSA. Do you call property stolen where the loser denied it was his?—I stole—but from enemies.

CLODIUS TURRINUS. Do you call it stolen property where the loser has been punished, the thief rewarded?—Which of the two would you have allowed to speak if the thief and the owner had come along at the same time?—I could have sold the state for a large sum—even to the traitor.

ARELLIUS FUSCUS SENIOR. You commanders of a 2 thousand ships took Troy by a trick. If cities can properly be destroyed by means of a trick, how much more proper is it for them to be saved by such means![2]—If *I* don't lay information as to the owner, no-one will claim the property as his own.

VIBIUS RUFUS. If I could, I would have pierced his breast as well as his wall.—I haven't yet completed my duty; the state is not so tiny that it can be overcome by a single man.[3]

CESTIUS PIUS. Do not ask me to tell all I know; there is much—and some of it must even be told in the assembly.—Teach your children the story of this theft.[4]—I appeal to you, judges, in the name of my theft; whenever I have proclaimed my theft, does the owner keep quiet?—I a thief? Here is a second

---

[2] A play on the double sense of *furtum*, " stealing " and " trickery." Agamemnon and his friends took Troy by means of the Wooden Horse.

[3] i.e. there are other traitors to unmask.

[4] i.e. it was a meritorious action.

tu, inquit, perfodisti domum? Tace, ego novi ista melius. Narrare soleo. Non nego rem pretio . . .[1]

In forum veni, narravi nocturnam expeditionem 518 meam. Convenerant omnes tamquam ad contionem. Cur me summoves ante accusationem, cum nec proditores inauditi pereant? O furtum in contione narrandum! Proditoris vigilantissimum pectus et in exitia semper nostra sollicitum publica fata sopierant; ita etiam ministros eius alligaverat somnus ut mihi liceret eligere quod tollerem. Diruere mihi videbar hostium muros. Furtum vocas quo nihil melius anno tuo factum est? Nemo fur rem publicam cogitat. Nihil non licet pro re publica facere.

Pars altera. Quale illud, di, spectaculum fuit! Conposuerat inter se fortuna rei publicae furem et proditorem. Ut vidit inutile furtum suum, prodidit, ut vobis venderet quod nulli poterat, tam callidus fur ut etiam proditori posset inponere. Consilium videri volt infelicitatem furti sui. Lex, quae nocturnum furem occidi quoquo modo iubet, non de damnato tantum sed de fure loquitur; odit hoc vitium

[1] The declamation is from this point preserved only in the excerpta.

[1] Twelve Tables 8.12: " si nox furtum faxsit, si im occisit, iure caesus esto." Cf. e.g. Cic. *Mil.* 9.

injury.—" Didn't you break into the house? " Sh!
I know that better than you—I am used to telling the
story.—I do not deny . . . the affair . . . for a
price . . .

FROM THE EXCERPTA

I came to the forum, and narrated my nocturnal
raid. Everyone had assembled—as if it were a
public meeting.—Why get rid of me without any
accusation?—even traitors don't perish unheard.—O
theft that clamours to be told in the forum!—The
mind of the traitor, always most vigilant and anxious
for our destruction, had been put fast asleep by the
fate of our city; sleep had submerged even his
servants so far that I could choose what to take.—I
told myself that it was the walls of the enemy that I
was undermining.—Do you call it a theft, when no
better action has been performed in your year of
office?—No *thief* thinks of the state.—One may do
anything in the service of the state.

The other side

Ye gods, what a sight that was! The fortune of the
state had matched against each other a thief and a
traitor.—When he saw that his booty was without
value, he noised it abroad, so as to sell to you what he
could sell to no-one else: so clever a thief that he
could deceive even a traitor.—He wants the lack of
success of his theft to be thought a deep-laid plot.—
The law, which orders the killing of a thief at night by
any means,[1] speaks not merely of a convicted man but
of a thief pure and simple: it hates this crime—

nec inmerito: non multum abest a proditore. Sustulit non quod elegit, sed quod illi fatum publicae felicitatis obiecit. Uno tempore et proditorem nobis ostendit et furem, qui divitem conpilare quam damnare mallet. Effregit domum suspensa manu; elusit illum. Non tunc primum fecit. Sed sustulit non quod voluit, sed quod potuit. Bono exemplo damnatus est proditor, malo inventus.

reasonably, for it is not far removed from treachery.
—He took not what he chose, but what the destiny of
the state happily put in his way.—At one and the
same time he has shown us both a traitor and a thief [1]
who preferred to loot a rich man rather than get him
convicted.—He broke into the house with a light
touch; he out-manoeuvred him. That was not the
first time he did it.—But he took not what he wanted
but what he could.—The traitor was convicted—that
was a good precedent; he was found—that was a bad
one. [2]

[1] In the person of himself.
[2] Because of the method of discovery.

SUASORIARUM

LIBER

I

Deliberat Alexander an Oceanum naviget.[1]

1 . . . sinunt: cuicumque rei magnitudinem natura dederat, dedit et modum; nihil infinitum est nisi Oceanus. Aiunt fertiles in Oceano iacere terras ultraque Oceanum rursus alia litora, alium nasci orbem, nec usquam rerum naturam desinere, sed semper inde ubi desisse videatur novam exsurgere. Facile ista finguntur, quia Oceanus navigari non potest. Satis sit hactenus Alexandro vicisse qua mundo lucere satis est. Intra has terras caelum Hercules meruit. Stat immotum mare, quasi de- 520

---

[1] *Title supplied by a corrector of the Toledo MS.*

---

[1] For this *suasoria* cf. *C.* 7.7.19; the exact title of ours is uncertain, as the manuscripts are deficient at the start. It gave scope for raising the question of the nature of the Ocean (see §4: cf. Quintilian 7.4.2, Tac. *Agr.* 10.6) and the possibility of the existence of land beyond it (Quintilian 7.2.5). For some declaimers only death prevented Alexander from launch-

THE SUASORIAE

1

ALEXANDER DEBATES WHETHER TO SAIL THE OCEAN [1]

. . . allow: to whatever thing nature has granted [1] size she has granted a limit as well; nothing is infinite except the Ocean.—They say that in the Ocean there lie fertile lands, while beyond it in turn are born new shores, a new world: that nature stops nowhere— always it appears in a fresh guise just at the point where one thinks it had come to a halt. These are fictions easy of invention—for the Ocean cannot be sailed.—Let Alexander be content to have conquered as far as the world is content to have light. It was within the limits of the known world that Hercules won his claim to heaven.[2]—There, motionless, stands

ing forth (Lucan 10.36 *seq.*; cf. *ad Her.* 4.31): Curtius allows him to sacrifice to the gods of the sea at the Indus mouth without being tempted further (9.9.27), but he elsewhere indulges in declamatory topics very similar to those treated here.

[2] For Alexander's alleged rivalry with Hercules and Liber-Dionysus (cf. §2) see e.g. Curt. 9.2.29, 9.4.21; Sen. *Ben.* 1.13.1, 7.3.1; Arrian *Alex.* 4.10.6, 5.3.4: also W. W. Tarn, *Alexander the Great* 2 (Cambridge, 1950), 55–62.

ficientis in suo fine naturae pigra moles; novae ac
terribiles figurae, magna etiam Oceano portenta,
quae profunda ista vastitas nutrit, confusa lux alta
caligine et interceptus tenebris dies, ipsum vero
grave et defixum mare et aut nulla aut ignota
sidera. Ea est, Alexander, rerum natura: post
omnia Oceanus, post Oceanum nihil.

2   ARGENTARI. Resiste, orbis te tuus revocat; vicimus qua lucet. Nihil tantum est quod ego Alexandri
periculo petam.

POMPEI SILONIS. Venit ille dies, Alexander,
exoptatus quo tibi opera desset; idem sunt termini
et regni tui et mundi.

MOSCHI. Tempus est Alexandrum cum orbe et
cum sole desinere. Quod noveram vici; nunc con-
cupisco quod nescio. Quae tam ferae gentes fuerunt
quae non Alexandrum posito genu adorarint? qui
tam horridi montes quorum non iuga victor miles
calcaverit? Ultra Liberi patris trophaea consti-
timus. Non quaerimus orbem, sed amittimus.
Inmensum et humanae intemptatum experientiae
pelagus, totius orbis vinculum terrarumque custodia,
inagitata remigio vastitas, litora modo saeviente 521
fluctu inquieta, modo fugiente deserta; taetra caligo
fluctus premit, et nescio qui, quod humanis natura
subduxit oculis, aeterna nox obruit.

MUSAE. Foeda beluarum magnitudo et inmobile

---

[1] Tacitus describes the stillness of the northern seas in
similar terms at *Agr.* 10.5, *Germ.* 45.1. For the speaker here,
as for Lucan 5.443-4 and Curt. 9.4.18 (to be compared in other
details), the explanation is the inability of natural forces to
keep the ordinary tidal system working at the limits of the
world.

the sea,[1] an inert mass of nature failing, as it were, at its own limits: strange and frightening shapes, monsters great even for the Ocean, nurtured by that desolate depth, light plunged in the deepest gloom, day cut off by darkness, the sea itself heavy and stationary, stars either vanished or unfamiliar. Such, Alexander, is nature: beyond all, the Ocean; beyond the Ocean, nothing.

ARGENTARIUS. Stop: the world that is yours calls 2 you back. We have conquered wherever light shines. —There is nothing worth my seeking if the cost is peril to Alexander.

POMPEIUS SILO. Alexander, the longed-for day has come—the day on which nothing should remain for you to do. Your empire and the world have the same limits.

MOSCHUS. It is time for Alexander to come to a halt where world and sun halt.—"What I knew, I conquered. Now I desire what I do not know."— What tribes so barbarous that they have not worshipped Alexander on bended knee? What mountains so rude that their ridges have not been trodden by his victorious soldiery? We have halted beyond the trophies set up by Father Liber.—We are not in search of a world—we are losing one.—Here is a measureless sea, untried by human adventure, that encircles the whole world and guards the earth, a waste undisturbed by oars, shores now disquieted as the waves rage, now deserted as they retreat. A horrid darkness weighs on the breakers; strangely, what nature has removed from men's sight is shrouded by everlasting night.

MUSA. Loathsome the vast monsters, unmoving

profundum. Testatum est, Alexander, nihil ultra
esse quod vincas; revertere.

3 ALBUCI SILI. Terrae quoque suum finem habent,
et ipsius mundi aliquis occasus est; nihil infinitum
est; modum ⟨tu⟩ [1] magnitudini facere debes, quoniam Fortuna non facit. Magni pectoris est inter
secunda moderatio. Eundem Fortuna victoriae
tuae quem naturae finem facit: imperium tuum
cludit Oceanus. O quantum magnitudo tua rerum
quoque naturam supergressa est! Alexander orbi
magnus est, Alexandro orbis angustus est. Aliquis
etiam magnitudini modus est; non procedit ultra
spatia sua caelum, maria intra terminos suos agi-
tantur. Quidquid ad summum pervenit, incremento
non relinquit locum. Non magis quicquam ultra
Alexandrum novimus quam ultra Oceanum.

MARULLI. Maria sequimur, terras cui tradimus?
Orbem quem non novi quaero, quem vici relinquo.

4 FABIANI. Quid? ista toto pelago infusa caligo
navigantem tibi videtur admittere, quae prospicien-
tem quoque excludit? Non haec India est nec
ferarum terribilis ille conventus. Inmanes propone 522
beluas, aspice quibus procellis fluctibusque saeviat,
quas ad litora undas agat. Tantus ventorum con-
cursus, tanta convulsi funditus maris insania est;
nulla praesens navigantibus statio est, nihil salutare,
nihil notum; rudis et inperfecta natura penitus reces-

---

[1] *Supplied here by C. F. W. Müller, Köhler.*

---

[1] Cf. Sen. *Marc.* 23.3: "Whatever has reached its peak is
near its end."

[2] For the dangers which Alexander was turning his back on
see §4 *ad fin.*, §10.

the deep. Evidence is before you, Alexander, that nothing lies beyond for you to conquer. Go back.

ALBUCIUS SILUS. Even the earth has its end; the 3 very universe has its setting. Nothing is infinite. *You* must give greatness its limits, seeing that Fortune does not.—It is the sign of a great spirit to be moderate in prosperity.—Fortune makes the limit of your victories the same as the limit of nature: your empire is closed by the Ocean.—How far has your greatness surpassed even nature! Alexander is great for the earth: for Alexander the earth is cramped.— Even greatness has some end; the heavens do not proceed beyond their fixed limits, the seas toss within their bounds.—Whatever has reached its peak leaves no room for increase.[1]—We know nothing beyond Alexander, just as we know nothing beyond Ocean.

MARULLUS. We are in pursuit of the seas: to whom are we entrusting the land? [2]—" I am looking for a world I do not know, I am leaving the world I have conquered."

FABIANUS. Can you imagine that this darkness 4 cast over all the sea admits navigation when it excludes even the view ahead ?—This is not India, nor that fearful assembly of beasts.[3] Imagine the savage monsters. Look how the sea rages with squalls and waves, look at the breakers it drives shorewards: such is the conflict of the winds, such the raving of a sea churned up from its depths. Sailors have here no ready haven, nothing to save them, nothing they know. All that is primitive and incomplete in nature

[3] For terror at Indian beasts see Curt. 9.2.19. Fabianus means that the present situation is even worse—the beasts are " primitive and incomplete " and so more terrifying.

sit. Ista maria ne illi quidem petierunt qui fugiebant
Alexandrum. Sacrum quiddam terris natura circum-
fudit Oceanum. Illi qui iam siderum collegerunt
meatus et annuas hiemis atque aestatis vices ad
certam legem redegerunt, quibus nulla pars ignota
mundi est, de Oceano tamen dubitant, utrumne
terras velut vinculum cludat[1] an in suum colligatur
orbem et in hos per quos navigatur sinus quasi
spiramenta quaedam magnitudinis ⟨suae⟩[2] exaes-
tuet; ignem post se, cuius augmentum ipse sit,
habeat an spiritum. Quid agitis, conmilitones?
domitoremne generis humani, magnum Alexandrum,
eo dimittitis quod adhuc quid sit disputatur?
Memento, Alexander: matrem in orbe victo adhuc
magis quam pacato relinquis.

5   DIVISIO. Aiebat Cestius hoc genus suasoriarum   523M
⟨alibi⟩[3] aliter declamandum esse [quam suaden-
dum].[4] Non eodem modo in libera civitate dicendam
sententiam quo apud reges, quibus etiam quae
prosunt ita tamen ut delectent suadenda sunt. Et
inter reges ipsos esse discrimen: quosdam minus,
alios[5] magis veritatem pati;[6] Alexandrum ex iis

[1] cludat *Bursian:* pluat *AB:* circumpluat *V.*
[2] *Supplied by Schultingh.*
[3] *Supplied by Novák.*
[4] *Deleted by Faber.*
[5] alios *Novák:* aut.
[6] pati *Leo:* facti.

---

[1] The alternatives seem to be a round land-area with the
Ocean forming a fringe (Sen. *N.Q.* 3.29.7; Isid. 13.15.1), and
a vast circular Ocean with a small land-area, the gulfs in
which are like vents for the sea. For views on Ocean, see

has retreated to this far refuge. These seas were not the goal even of those who fled from Alexander. It was as something holy that the Ocean was poured round the world by nature. Those who have by now calculated the movements of the stars, and reduced to fixed laws the yearly changes of winter and summer, men to whom no part of the universe is a mystery, are still in doubt as to the Ocean. Does it shut off the earth like a band, or does it go round in a circle of its own, seething into those gulfs that are navigable as into breathing holes serving its great size?[1] Beyond it is there fire, which it itself goes to increase, or air? What are you about, fellow-soldiers? Are you letting the conqueror of the human race, great Alexander, enter something whose very nature is still in dispute?—Remember, Alexander: you are leaving your mother[2] in a world that is still subdued rather than pacified.

Division

Cestius used to say that this type of *suasoria* should 5 be declaimed differently in different places. " One's opinion should be stated in one way in a free country, in another before kings, who need to be given even salutary advice in such a way as to give them pleasure. And even among kings distinctions are to be made. Some can tolerate the truth better than others. Alexander is to be classed among those who are by

J. O. Thomson, *History of Ancient Geography* (Cambridge, 1948), e.g. 97–8, 163. For exhalations from the sea feeding heavenly bodies see the references collected by Pease on Cic. *Nat. Deor.* 2.40.

[2] Olympias.

esse quos superbissimos et supra mortalis animi
modum inflatos accepimus. Denique, ut alia dimit-
tantur argumenta, ipsa suasoria insolentiam eius
coarguit; orbis illum suus non capit.

Itaque nihil dicendum aiebat nisi cum summa
veneratione regis, ne accideret idem quod praeceptori
eius, amitino [1] Aristotelis, accidit, quem occidit
propter intempestive liberos sales; nam cum se
deum vellet videri et vulneratus esset, viso sanguine
eius philosophus mirari se dixerat quod non esset
ἰχώρ, οἷός πέρ τε ῥέει μακάρεσσι θεοῖσιν. Ille se 524M
ab hac urbanitate lancea vindicavit.

Eleganter in C. Cassi epistula quadam ad M.
Ciceronem missa positum: multum iocatur de
stultitia Cn. Pompei adulescentis, qui in Hispania
contraxit exercitum et ad Mundam acie victus est;
deinde ait: "nos quidem illum deridemus, sed
timeo ne ille nos gladio ἀντιμυκτηρίσῃ." In
omnibus regibus haec urbanitas extimescenda est.

6   Aiebat itaque apud Alexandrum esse ⟨sic⟩ [2] dicendam sententiam ut multa adulatione animus eius
permulceretur, servandum tamen aliquem modum,
ne non veneratio ⟨videretur sed adulatio⟩,[3] et accideret tale aliquid quale accidit Atheniensibus cum

---

[1] amitino *Bursian:* autem.
[2] *Supplied by Müller.*
[3] *Supplied by Otto.*

---

[1] Cf. §3 " For Alexander the earth is cramped." Many
parallels are listed by Edward *ad loc.* and Mayor on Juv. 10.168.
[2] Aristotle's cousin was Callisthenes, who was put to death
for conspiracy (Curt. 8.8.21) and certainly had a free tongue
(*id.* 8.5.13). It was Clitus, however, whom Alexander personally killed for insolence (*id.* 8.1.45), and the actual remark

tradition particularly proud, puffed up beyond mortal standards. Finally, leaving aside other proofs, the terms of the *suasoria* in themselves demonstrate his arrogance; the world that is his is not enough for him." [1]

Cestius accordingly used to say that nothing should be said that did not show the highest respect towards the king, in case the speaker should meet with the same fate as Alexander's tutor, a cousin of Aristotle,[2] whom the king killed because of a witticism that was both outspoken and untimely. Alexander wanted to be regarded as god; once he was wounded, and, seeing his blood, the tutor said he was surprised that it was not the " ichor, such as flows in the veins of the blessed gods." Alexander used the spear to get revenge for this joke.

The point is neatly made in a letter of Cassius to Cicero:[3] after a good deal of pleasantry about the stupidity of the young Pompey, who recruited an army in Spain and was defeated at the battle of Munda, he says: " Here we are deriding him—but I'm afraid he may have his sneer back—with his sword." In dealings with every king, one has to be shy of this sort of wit.

Cestius, then, used to say that in Alexander's 6 presence one's opinion must be given in such a way that his feelings were soothed by lavish flattery, though some moderation must be preserved so as to give an impression not of flattery but of due respect,

(based on *Iliad* 5.340) is often attributed to Alexander himself (e.g. Plut. *Alex.* 28): elsewhere to Anaxarchus (Diog. Laert. 9.60).

[3] Cic. *ad Fam.* 15.19.4, quoted by Seneca from memory.

THE ELDER SENECA

publicae eorum blanditiae non tantum deprehensae
sed castigatae sunt. Nam cum Antonius vellet
se Liberum patrem dici et hoc nomen statuis ⟨suis⟩ [1]
subscribi iuberet, habitu quoque et comitatu Liberum imitaretur, occurrerunt venienti ei Athenienses
cum coniugibus et liberis et Διόνυσον salutaverunt.
Belle illis cesserat si nasus Atticus ibi substitisset.
Dixerunt despondere ipsos in matrimonium illi
Minervam suam et rogaverunt ut duceret; Antonius 525M
ait ducturum, sed dotis nomine imperare se illis mille
talenta. Tum ex Graeculis quidam ait: κύριε, ὁ
Ζεὺς τὴν μητέρα σου Σεμέλην ἄπροικον εἶχεν. Huic
quidem impune fuit, sed Atheniensium sponsalia
mille talentis aestimata sunt. Quae cum exigeren-
tur, conplures contumeliosi libelli proponebantur,
quidam etiam ipsi Antonio tradebantur: sicut ille
qui subscriptus statuae eius fuit cum eodem tempore
et Octaviam uxorem haberet et Cleopatram: Ὀκτ-
αουία καὶ Ἀθηνᾶ Ἀντωνίῳ· res tuas tibi habe.
7 Bellissimam tamen rem Dellius dixit, quem Messala
Corvinus desultorem bellorum civilium vocat quia
ab Dolabella ad Cassium transiturus salutem sibi
pactus est si Dolabellam occidisset, a Cassio deinde
transit ad Antonium, novissime ab Antonio trans-
fugit ad Caesarem. Hic est Dellius cuius epistulae

[1] *Supplied by Gertz.*

[1] The story is given by Dio 48.39.2, and refers to Antony's
stay in Greece in 39–8 B.C. In *T.A.P.A.* 77 (1946), 146–50
A. E. Raubitschek publishes an inscription where Antony and
Octavia are made " benefactor Gods," perhaps as Dionysus
and Athena.

to avoid the fate of the Athenians on one occasion, when their publicly expressed blandishments were not only detected but punished. For Antony once [1] wanted to be known as Father Liber, ordering this name to be inscribed on the base of statues to him and aping Liber in his dress and attendants. Athenians came to him on his arrival with their wives and children, and saluted him as Dionysus. It would have been better for them if their Attic wit had stopped there. But they went on to say that they were offering him their Minerva in marriage, and asked him to marry her. Antony said that he would do so, but that as dowry he ordered them to contribute a thousand talents. Then one of the Greeklings said: " Lord, Zeus took your mother Semele without a dowry." *He* got away with that; but the Athenians' betrothal cost them a thousand talents. When the sum was demanded, several abusive lampoons were put about, and some even reached the eyes of Antony himself: for example the one written on the base of a statue of his because he had both Octavia and Cleopatra to wife: " Octavia and Athena to Antony: take your property." [2] The best thing was said by 7 Dellius. He was called by Messala Corvinus the " vaulter " of the civil wars,[3] because he deserted from Dolabella to Cassius on the promise of immunity if he killed Dolabella, then crossed from Cassius to Antony, and finally went over from Antony to Caesar.

[2] The formula for divorce (cf. *C*. 2.5.9 n.).
[3] The " vaulter " leapt from one galloping horse to another in the circus. Dellius had been Antony's envoy to Cleopatra: his career is recounted in R. Syme, *The Roman Revolution*, e.g. 267, 296.

ad Cleopatram lascivae feruntur. Cum Athenienses
tempus peterent ad pecuniam conferendam nec
exorarent, Dellius ait: at tamen dicito illos tibi
annua, bienni, trienni die debere.

Longius me fabellarum dulcedo produxit; itaque
ad propositum revertar.

8 Aiebat Cestius magnis cum laudibus Alexandri
hanc suasoriam esse dicendam; quam sic divisit 526M
ut primum diceret, etiamsi navigari posset Oceanus,
navigandum non esse; satis gloriae quaesitum;
regenda esse et disponenda quae in transitu vicisset;
consulendum militi tot [1] victoriis lasso; de matre illi
cogitandum; et alias causas complures subiecit.
Deinde illam quaestionem subiecit, ne navigari
quidem Oceanum posse.

9 Fabianus philosophus primam fecit quaestionem
eandem: etiamsi navigari posset Oceanus, navigandum non esse. At rationem aliam primam fecit:
modum inponendum esse rebus secundis. Hic
dixit sententiam: illa demum est magna felicitas
quae arbitrio suo constitit. Dixit deinde locum de
varietate fortunae et, cum descripsisset nihil esse
stabile, omnia fluitare et incertis motibus modo
attolli, modo deprimi, absorberi terras et maria
siccari, montes subsidere, deinde exempla regum ex
fastigio suo devolutorum, adiecit: " sine potius
rerum naturam quam fortunam tuam deficere."

[1] tot *ed. Romana (1585):* totius.

---

[1] That is, you can exact the sum (as with a returned dowry:
see *Epit. Ulp.* 6.8) in three annual instalments.
[2] Cf. Sen. *Tranq.* 10.6, esp. " nec fortunae arbitrium desin-
endi dare, sed ipsos . . . consistere."

This is the Dellius whose obscene letters to Cleopatra are in circulation. Now when the Athenians were asking time to get the money together, and not being given it, Dellius said: " Still, you can say they owe you this day next year, two years hence, three years hence." [1]

However, I have got too far from the point in my delight in stories. I must return to my theme.

Cestius used to say that this advice to Alexander 8 should be accompanied by the highest praises of him. His division went like this. First, even if the Ocean could be sailed, it should not be—Alexander had won enough glory; he should rule and put in order what he had conquered *en passant*, have some consideration for soldiers tired out by so many victories, and take thought for his mother: and he added several other reasons. Then he went on to argue that the Ocean could *not* be sailed.

Fabianus the philosopher put the same point first: 9 Even if the Ocean could be sailed, it should not be. But his first reason was different: a limit must be set to prosperity.[2] Here he spoke this epigram: " The only great felicity is that which stops of its own will." He then spoke the commonplace on the variability of Fortune. He described how nothing is stable, everything fluid, now raised, now depressed in unpredictable change, lands being swallowed, seas drained, mountains subsiding.[3] He gave examples of kings who have been tumbled from the height of their power. Then he added: " Allow nature rather than your fortune to run out."

---

[3] The ordinary *locus* on fortune (see e.g. Sen. *N.Q.* 3 pr. 7) is given a geographical twist.

10   Secundam quoque quaestionem aliter tractavit;
divisit enim illam sic ut primum negaret ullas in
Oceano aut trans Oceanum esse terras habitabiles.
Deinde: si essent, perveniri tamen ad illas non posse;
hic difficultatem navigationis, ignoti maris naturam
non patientem navigationis. Novissime: ut posset
perveniri, tanti tamen non esse. Hic dixit incerta
peti, certa deseri; descituras gentes si Alexandrum
rerum naturae terminos supergressum enotuisset; 527N
hic matrem, de qua dixit: quo modo illa trepidavit
etiam quod Granicum transiturus esset.

11   Glyconis celebris sententia est: τοῦτο οὐκ ἔστι
Σιμόεις οὐδὲ Γράνικος· τοῦτο εἰ μή τι κακὸν ἦν, οὐκ
ἂν ἔσχατον ἔκειτο. Hoc omnes imitari voluerunt.
Plution dixit: καὶ διὰ τοῦτο μέγιστόν ἐστιν, ὅτι
αὐτὸ μὲν μετὰ πάντα, μετὰ δὲ αὐτὸ οὐθέν. Artemon
dixit: βουλευόμεθα εἰ χρὴ περαιοῦσθαι. οὐ ταῖς
Ἑλλησποντίαις ἠόσιν ἐφεστῶτες οὐδ' ἐπὶ τῷ
Παμφυλίῳ πελάγει τὴν ἐμπρόθεσμον καραδοκοῦμεν
ἄμπωσιν· οὐδὲ Εὐφράτης τοῦτ' ἔστιν, οὐδὲ Ἰνδός,
ἀλλ' εἴτε γῆς τέρμα, εἴτε φύσεως ὅρος, εἴτε
πρεσβύτατον στοιχεῖον, εἴτε γένεσις θεῶν,
ἱερώτερόν ἐστιν ἢ κατὰ ναῦς ὕδωρ.[1]

Apaturius dixit: ἔνθα μὲν [1] ἡ ναῦς ἐκ μιᾶς φορᾶς
⟨εἰς⟩ ἀνατολάς, ἔνθα δὲ εἰς τὰς ἀοράτους δύσεις.

---

[1] ἔνθα μὲν *Gertz*: ΕΝΤΕΥΕΘ, or similar.

---

[1] Thales regarded water as in some sense the primal element
(Kirk and Raven, *The Presocratic Philosophers*, 87 *seq.*);

His treatment of the second point was also different. 10
His arrangement was first to say that there are no
habitable lands in the Ocean or beyond it, then that,
even if there were, they could not be reached.   Here
he spoke of the difficulty of navigation, the unknown
sea that was such as to permit of no sailing.   Finally,
even if it were possible to reach them, it was not
worth the trouble.   Here he said that uncertainty lay
ahead, certainty was being left behind.   The world
would rise in revolt if it became known that Alexander
had crossed nature's limits.   He brought in Alexander's mother, saying of her: " How she trembled
even when Alexander was going to cross the Granicus! "

Glycon's epigram is familiar: " This is not Simois 11
or Granicus.   If this were not an evil thing, it would
not lie at the end of the world."   Everyone wanted
to imitate this.   Plution said: " It is greatest just
because *it* is beyond all—and beyond *it* is nothing."
Artemon said: " We are discussing whether we
should sail across.   We are not standing on the shores
of the Hellespont, or the Pamphylian sea, awaiting the
ebb within its own time.   This is not Euphrates or
Indus, but the end of the world, the boundary of
nature, the oldest element or the origin of the gods: [1]
in any case, it is water too holy for ships."

Apaturius said: " This way the ship will go in one
course [2] to the dawn: that way to the unseen setting-
place of the sun."

Homer mentions Ocean as the θεῶν γένεσις in *Iliad* 14.201 (see
Kirk and Raven, 15).

[2] The Ocean being regarded as uninterrupted.

Cestius descripsit sic: fremit Oceanus quasi indignetur quod terras relinquas.

12   Corruptissimam rem omnium quae umquam dictae sunt ex quo homines diserti insanire coeperunt putabant Dorionis esse in metaphrasi dictam Homeri, 528M cum excaecatus Cyclops saxum in mare reiecit. Haec quo modo ex corruptis eo perveniant ut et magna et tamen sana sint aiebat Maecenas apud Vergilium intellegi posse. Tumidum est: ὄρους ὄρος ἀποσπᾶται. Vergilius quid ait? rapit

haud partem exiguam montis.

Ita magnitudini studet ⟨ut⟩ [1] non inprudenter discedat a fide. Est inflatum: καὶ χειρία βάλλεται νῆσος. Vergilius quid ait [qui] [2] de navibus?

credas innare revolsas
    Cycladas.

Non dicit hoc fieri sed videri. Propitiis auribus accipitur, quamvis incredibile sit, quod excusatur antequam dicitur.

13   Multo corruptiorem sententiam Menestrati cuiusdam, declamatoris non abiecti suis temporibus, nactus sum in hac ipsa suasoria, cum describeret beluarum in Oceano nascentium magnitudinem: . . . Efficit 529M haec sententia ut ignoscam Musae, qui dixit ipsis Charybdi et Scylla maius portentum: " Charybdis ipsius maris naufragium " et, ne in una re semel insaniret: " quid ibi potest esse salvi ubi ipsum mare perit ? "

    [1] studet ut *Gertz, Thomas:* scedat studet.
    [2] *Omitted in early editions.*

---

    [1] *Od.* 9.481–2: " He tore off the top of a great mountain

Cestius' description went like this: "The Ocean roars, as though angry that you are leaving the land behind."

It was generally agreed that the most decadent 12 thing said since the eloquent began to go mad was a remark of Dorion paraphrasing Homer, where the blinded Cyclops flings a rock into the sea.[1] Maecenas used to say that you could tell from Virgil how this, instead of being decadent, could be made grand and yet sane at the same time. It is bombastic to say: "Mountain is torn from mountain." So what does Virgil say? His character seizes "no small part of a mountain." He keeps size in mind without ill-advised departure from the truth. It is inflated to say: "and an island is picked up and flung." What does Virgil say of ships? "You might suppose there floated the Cyclades uptorn." He doesn't say it does happen—but that it seems to happen. However incredible it may be, anything excused before it is uttered is received with favour.

I have come across in this same *suasoria* a much 13 more decadent epigram by one Menestratus, a declaimer of some repute in his day, when he was describing the huge size of the monsters bred in the Ocean . . . The result of the epigram is that I am ready to forgive Musa for something more monstrous even than Scylla and Charybdis: "Charybdis, wrecker of the sea itself." And, so as to avoid an isolated folly on the same topic, he said: "What can be safe where even the sea perishes?"

---

[1] and threw it." Dorion gave a bombastic paraphrase, which Maecenas contrasts in two instalments with words of Virgil (*Aen.* 10.128, 8.691-2).

Damas ethicos induxit matrem loquentem, cum describeret adsidue prioribus periculis nova supervenisse: . . .

Barbarus dixit, cum introduxisset excusantem se exercitum Macedonum, hunc sensum: . . .

14 Fuscus Arellius dixit: testor ante orbem tibi tuum deesse quam militem.

Latro sedens hanc dixit; non excusavit militem, sed dixit: Duc, sequor; quis mihi promittit hostem, quis terram, quis diem, quis mare? Da ubi castra ponam, ubi signa inferam.[1] Reliqui parentes, reliqui liberos, commeatum peto; numquid inmature ab Oceano?

15 Latini declamatores in descriptione Oceani non nimis viguerunt; nam aut minus descripserunt aut ⟨nimis⟩ [2] curiose. Nemo illorum potuit tanto spiritu dicere quanto Pedo, qui ⟨in⟩ [3] navigante Germanico dicit:

> iamque vident [4] post terga diem solemque
>   relictum
> iam pridem, notis extorres finibus orbis,
> per non concessas audaces ire tenebras
> ad rerum metas extremaque litora mundi.
> nunc illum, pigris immania monstra sub undis

---

[1] inferam *Müller:* ponam.
[2] *Supplied by Haupt.*
[3] *Supplied by Thomas.*
[4] iamque vident—iam pridem *Kent after Withof:* iam pridem—iam quidem (quidam *A*).

---

[1] Cf. *C.* pr. 21. But the text is doubtful.
[2] This suggests that the epigram "I have parents . . ." was not Latro's.
[3] As opposed to the Ocean.

Damas, exploiting character, brought in words of Alexander's mother when describing how new dangers had piled themselves constantly on old: . . .

Barbarus, after introducing the Macedonian soldiers making excuses, expressed this idea: . . .

Arellius Fuscus said: " I swear that your world is 14 deserting you sooner than your soldiers."

Latro spoke this epigram while sitting down;[1] he did not excuse the soldiers,[2] but said: " Lead, I am following. Who offers me enemy, land, day, light, sea?[3] Give me somewhere to pitch camp and fight a battle."—" I have parents and children back home. I want some furlough: is it too soon, when I am on the shores of the Ocean? "

Latin declaimers were not particularly vigorous in 15 their description of the Ocean. They either described too little, or too fussily. None of them could match the verve of Pedo on Germanicus[4] at sea:

" And now they see day and sun long left behind;
  Banished from the familiar limits of the world
  They dare to pass through forbidden shades
  To the bounds of things, the remotest shores of
    the world.
  Now they think Ocean, that breeds beneath its
    sluggish waves

[4] We know of expeditions by the elder Germanicus (Tiberius' brother), the first Roman to sail in the North Sea (Suet. *Claud.* 1), and by his son (in A.D. 16: see Tac. *Ann.* 2.23–4, who comments on the imagination shown in narratives of the episode). The later is presumably in point here, for Pedo was one of the younger Germanicus' officers (*Ann.* 1.60). Information on the poem is assembled by V. Bongi, *Istituto Lombardo di scienze e lett. Rendiconti* (*Classe di Lettere*) ser. 3.13 (1949), 28–48.

qui ferat, Oceanum, qui saevas undique pristis 530
aequoreosque canes, ratibus consurgere prensis
(accumulat fragor ipse metus), iam sidere limo
navigia et rapido desertam flamine classem
seque feris credunt per inertia fata marinis
iam non felici laniandos sorte relinqui.[1]
atque aliquis prora caecum [2] sublimis ab alta
aera pugnaci luctatus rumpere visu,
ut nihil erepto valuit dinoscere mundo,
obstructa in talis effundit pectora [3] voces:
quo ferimur? fugit ipse dies orbemque relictum
ultima perpetuis claudit natura tenebris.
anne alio positas ultra sub cardine gentes
atque alium flabris [4] intactum quaerimus orbem?
di revocant rerumque vetant cognoscere finem
mortales oculos: aliena quid aequora remis
et sacras violamus aquas divumque quietas
turbamus sedes?

16 Ex Graecis declamatoribus nulli melius haec
suasoria processit quam Glyconi; sed non minus
multa magnifice dixit quam corrupte: utrorumque
faciam vobis potestatem. Et volebam vos experiri

---

[1] *The punctuation of this sentence is due to Gertz.*
[2] caecum *Haase, Haupt:* cedunt.
[3] obstructa in—pectora *Bursian:* obstructum—pectore.
[4] flabris *Haupt:* lib(e)ris.

Terrible monsters, savage sea-beasts everywhere,
And dogs [1] of the sea, is rising, taking the ships
  with it
(The very noise increases their fears): now they
  think the vessels
Are sinking in the mud, the fleet deserted by the
  swift wind,
Themselves left by indolent fate to the sea-beasts,
To be torn apart unhappily.
Someone high on the prow struggles to break
Through the blinding mist, his sight battling.
He can discern nothing—the world has been
  snatched away.
He pours his frustrated heart into words:
'Where are we being carried? Day itself is in
  flight,
Furthest nature shuts off in everlasting shadows
The world we have left. Are we looking for races
Beyond, in another clime, a new world untouched
  by breezes?
The Gods call us back, forbid us to know the end of
  creation
With mortal eyes. Why do our oars violate seas
  that are not ours,
Waters that are holy? Why do we disturb the
  quiet home of the Gods?'" [2]

No Greek declaimer had better success in this 16
suasoria than Glyco. But the decadent passages
were as frequent as the sublime. I shall let you
sample both. My intention was to try you out by

[1] Especially sharks.
[2] The immediate inspiration is Lucr. 3.18. For divine
objections to such voyages cf. Tac. *Germ.* 34.2.

non adiciendo iudicium meum nec separando a corruptis sana; potuisset [et] [1] enim fieri ut vos magis 531M
illa laudaretis quae insaniunt. At nihilo minus
poterit fieri quamvis distinxerim. Illa belle dixit:
. . . Sed fecit quod solebat, ut sententiam adiectione
supervacua atque tumida perderet; adiecit enim:
. . . Illud quosdam dubios iudici sui habet—ego
non dubito contra sententiam ferre—: ὑγίαινε γῆ,
ὑγίαινε ἥλιε· Μακεδόνες ἄρα χάος εἰσᾴσσουσι.

II

Trecenti Lacones contra Xersen missi, cum treceni ex omni Graecia missi fugissent, deliberant
an et ipsi fugiant.

1   ARELLI FUSCI patris. At, puto, rudis lecta aetas
et animus qui frangeretur metu, insuetaque arma
non passurae manus hebetataque senio aut vulneribus corpora. Quid dicam? potissimos Graeciae?
an Lacedaemonios? an electos? [2] An repetam tot
acies patrum totque excidia urbium, tot victarum
gentium spolia? et nunc produntur condita sine moe- 532M

---

[1] *Deleted by Kiessling, Madvig.*
[2] electos *Bursian:* eleos.

---

[1] Before the final stand of the Spartans (and others) at
Thermopylae in 480 B.C. there was a debate resulting in the
departure of contingents (not of three hundred apiece) from
other cities: Herodotus (7.219 *seq.*) argues that Leonidas
actually ordered this retreat. We hear of no further debate
among the Spartans. Their heroic defence of the pass

not adding my own views, and not separating the sound from the corrupt. It might have been that you praised the mad more. But that *may* happen even if I make a distinction. This was nicely said: . . . But as usual he spoiled his epigram with a superfluous and bombastic appendage. For he added: . . . Some people find it difficult to assess the following, though *I* don't hesitate to cast my vote against: "Farewell, land; farewell, sun. The Macedonians are darting off into Chaos."

2

THE THREE HUNDRED SPARTANS SENT AGAINST XERXES DELIBERATE WHETHER THEY TOO SHOULD RETREAT FOLLOWING THE FLIGHT OF THE CONTINGENTS OF THREE HUNDRED SENT FROM ALL OVER GREECE [1]

Against retreat

ARELLIUS FUSCUS SENIOR. No doubt the choice fell 1 on untried youth, on spirits liable to be shattered by fear, on hands unable to put up with weapons they found unfamiliar, on bodies dulled by age and wounds.[2]—What shall I call you? The flower of Greece? Spartans? The élite?—Need I go over all the battles fought by your ancestors, all the cities they destroyed, all the spoils from the peoples they

naturally attracted rhetoricians, who could expatiate on the feats of Xerxes (see the mocking list in Lucian *Rhet. Praec.* 18: Mayor on Juvenal 10.174, 182) and on Spartan bravery. Compare Sen. *Ben.* 6.31, elaborating on Herodotus 7.209.

[2] Sarcasm.

nibus templa? Pudet consilii nostri, pudet, etiamsi non fugimus, deliberasse talia. At cum tot milibus Xerses venit. O Lacedaemonii, ite adversus barbaros. Non refero opera vestra, non avos, non patres, quorum vobis [1] exemplo ab infantia surgit ingenium. Pudet Lacedaemonios sic adhortari. Loco [2] tuti sumus. Licet totum classe Orientem trahat, licet intuentibus [3] explicet inutilem numerum: hoc mare, quod tantum patet, ex vasto urguetur in minimum, insidiosis excipitur angustiis vixque minimo aditus navigio est, et huius quoque remigium arcet inquietum omne quod circumfluit mare, fallentia cursus vada altioribus internata, aspera scopulorum et cetera quae navigantium vota decipiunt. Pudet, inquam, Lacedaemonios et armatos quaerere quem-
2 admodum tuti sint. Non referam Persarum spolia? 533 certe super spolia nudus cadam. Sciet et alios habere nos trecentos qui sic non fugiant et sic cadant. Hunc sumite animum: nescio an vincere possimus; vinci non possumus. Haec non utique perituris refero; sed, [et] [4] si cadendum est, erratis si metuendam creditis mortem. Nulli natura in aeternum

---

[1] vobis *Kiessling:* non.
[2] loco *Novák:* filico.
[3] intuentibus *C. F. W. Müller, Madvig:* metuentibus.
[4] *Deleted by Schott.*

conquered? Are we *now* betraying temples built
with no walls to defend them?[1]—I am ashamed of
our deliberations: ashamed, even though we have not
fled, to have made this a topic of discussion.—It may
be said: look at all the thousands Xerxes has brought
with him. Spartans, advance against them: they are
barbarians.—I do not tell of your feats, of the grand-
fathers and fathers by whose example your spirit has
risen high since childhood. I am ashamed to have to
exhort Spartans like this. Our position ensures our
safety. He may drag with him the entire Orient on
his fleet, he may before your gaze deploy a force too
numerous to be useful; yet this sea, that opens out so
enormously wide, is here pressed into a narrow compass.[2] Treacherous are the straits that lead to it;
scarcely the smallest vessel can approach—and *its*
oars are kept away by the whole surrounding area of
disturbed sea, by the shallows amid deeper water that
deceive the advancing sailor, by the sharp rocks and
by all the other things that bring a navigator's prayers
to naught. I am ashamed, I repeat, that Spartans—
and in arms too—should be asking how they may find
safety.—Shall I not carry home the spoils of the 2
Persians? At least I shall fall amid spoils, myself
naked.—He will know that we have another three
hundred ready to stand like us and fall like us.—This
is the spirit you must adopt: we may not win—but we
cannot lose.—It is not to men necessarily doomed that
I say this; but if you have to fall, you are wrong if you
suppose that death is something to be feared. Nature

[1] For the lack of walls at Sparta see below, §§3, 5, 6, 16.
[2] See Herodotus 7.175–6 (and compare §8 *Description of
Thermopylae*).

spiritum dedit, statque nascentibus in finem vitae dies. Ex inbecilla enim nos materia deus orsus est; quippe minimis succidunt corpora. Indenuntiata sorte rapimur; sub eodem pueritia fato est, eadem iuventus causa cadit. Optamus quoque plerumque mortem; adeo in securam quietem recessus ex vita est. At gloriae nullus finis est proximique deos sic †ageses agunt†;[1] feminis quoque frequens hoc in mortem pro gloria iter est. Quid Lycurgum, quid interritos omni periculo, quos memoria sacravit, viros referam? Ut unum Othryadem excitem, adnumerare trecentis exempla possum.

3   Triari. Non pudet Laconas ne pugna quidem hostium sed fabula vinci? Magnum est, alimentum virtutis est nasci Laconem. Ad certam victoriam 534 omnes remansissent; ad certam mortem tantum Lacones. Ne sit Sparta lapidibus circumdata: ibi muros habet ubi viros. Melius revocabimus fugientes trecenos quam sequemur. Sed montes perforat, maria contegit. Numquam solido stetit superba felicitas, et ingentium imperiorum magna fastigia

---

[1] *So AB:* agessa satagunt *V: I have translated* sic cadentes sunt (*Müller*).

---

[1] Verg. *Aen.* 10.467: " stat sua cuique dies "; Sen. *Prov.* 5.7: " We are led on by fate, and the first hour after our birth laid down what time remains for each of us."

[2] Below, §16 n.

[3] The rumours, that is, of Xerxes' might: cf. §§4 and 6, and Sen. *Ben.* 6.31.1: " Another said the Greeks would turn tail at the first news of the arrival of Xerxes."

has granted no-one perpetual life, and the moment we are born the day that will end our life is fixed.[1] For it was of weak material that god fashioned us; our bodies succumb to the least accident. We are hurried off by a destiny that is not announced to us beforehand. Childhood is subject to the same fate, youth falls for the same reason. Often, indeed, we pray for death, so calm a retreat is it from life. But of glory there is no end; those who fall like this are nearest the gods. For women also this road to death is often a source of glory. No need to tell of Lycurgus, of men, deified by history, whom no danger appalled. I need only evoke Othryades[2] to give each of the three hundred a pattern.

TRIARIUS. Are Spartans not ashamed to be beaten 3 —not even in battle with the enemy, but by a myth about him?[3]—It is a great thing, and something that nurtures virtue, to be born a Spartan.—For certain victory, all would have stayed; for certain death, only Spartans.—Sparta does not need to be ringed with stone; where its men are, *there* are its walls.[4]— We shall do better to call back the contingents from each of the other cities than to follow them.—" But Xerxes tunnels mountains, bridges seas." [5] Arrogant prosperity never has firm ground to stand on; the

[4] Cf. Plut. *Apophth. Lac.* 210E (Agesilaos points to the Spartans in arms, and says: " These are the walls of Sparta "); Philostr. *Vit. Soph.* 514; and esp. Damas in §14 below (S. F. Bonner, *A.J.P.* 87 [1966], 283 n. 68).
[5] Xerxes was said to have cut a canal through the Athos peninsula (" velificatus Athos " for Juvenal) and bridged the Hellespont. For rhetorical play with these feats see p. 506 n. 1 above, and several epigrams below (e.g. §9 " Before we . . .": §17 " A man . . .").

oblivione fragilitatis humanae conlapsa sunt. Scias
licet ad finem non pervenisse quae ad invidiam perducta sunt. Maria terrasque, rerum naturam statione
mutavit sua: moriamur trecenti, ut hic primum
invenerit quod mutare non posset. Si tam demens
placiturum consilium erat, cur non potius in turba
fugimus?

4 PORCI LATRONIS. In hoc scilicet morati sumus, ut
agmen fugientium cogeremus? Rumori terga ver-
titis? Sciamus saltem quam ⟨fortis⟩ [1] sit iste quem
fugimus. Vix vel victoria dedecus elui potest; ut
omnia fortiter fiant, feliciter cadant, multum tamen
nomini nostro detractum est: iam Lacones an fuge-
remus deliberavimus. At enim moriemur! quantum
ad me quidem pertinet, post hanc deliberationem
nihil aliud timeo quam ne revertar. Arma nobis 535
fabulae excutiunt? Nunc, nunc pugnemus; latuis-
set virtus inter trecenos. [ceteri quidem fugerunt] [2]
Si me quidem interrogatis quid sentiam, et in nostrum
et in Graeciae patrocinium loquar: electi sumus, non
relicti.

5 GAVI SABINI. Turpe est cuilibet viro fugisse,
Laconi etiam deliberasse.

    MARULLI. In hoc restitimus, ne in turba fugien-
tium lateremus? Habent quemadmodum se ex-
cusent Graeciae treceni: "tutas Thermopylas puta-
vimus, cum relinqueremus illic Laconas."

    CESTI PII. Quam turpe esset fugere iudicastis,

---

[1] *Supplied by Müller.*
[2] *Transferred by the editor to § 7.*

---

[1] For the *locus de fortuna* see e.g. *C.* 2.1.1 and Index of
Commonplaces.

great peaks of vast empires fall because it is forgotten that men are feeble.[1]   What has been carried to a point that attracts jealousy is, you may be sure, cut short before its proper end.—He has moved seas, lands, nature itself from their positions: let us, the three hundred, die—so that he may prove to have found, for the first time, something he could not change.—If so crazy a counsel was going to prevail, why did we not flee with the bulk of the army?

PORCIUS LATRO.   Is it for *this* that we stayed—to 4 bring up the rear of those who fled?—Do you turn tail before a rumour?   Let us at least find out how brave is the man we flee.—Even victory can scarcely wash away the disgrace: though we play our parts bravely, though all turns out well, our reputation has been much diminished: it remains true that we, who are Spartans, have discussed the possibility of flight.— "But we shall die." As far as *I* am concerned, my one fear after this debate is lest we return.—Are our weapons knocked from our hands by a story?—*Now* let us fight, now: our bravery would have gone unnoticed when there were three hundred from each city here.—If you ask *me* my view, I shall speak for my own cause and for the cause of Greece: We have been chosen, not deserted.

GAVIUS SABINUS.   It is shameful for *any* man to 5 retreat: for a Spartan, even to talk of retreat.

MARULLUS.   Did we make a stand merely in order to avoid escaping notice in the mass of those who retreated?—Those contingents from the Greek cities have their excuse: "We thought Thermopylae was safe—for it was Spartans we left there."

CESTUS PIUS.   Spartans, you have given your judge-

Lacones, tam diu non fugiendo. Omnibus sua decora
sunt: Athenae eloquentia inclitae sunt, Thebae
sacris, Sparta armis. Ideo hanc Eurotas amnis
circumfluit, qui pueritiam indurat ad futurae militiae
patientiam; ideo Taygeti nemoris difficilia nisi
Laconibus iuga; ideo Hercule gloriamur deo [1]
operibus caelum merito; ideo muri nostri arma
6 sunt. O grave maiorum virtutis dedecus: Lacones se
numerant, non aestimant! Videamus quanta turba
sit, ut habeat certe Sparta etiamsi non fortes milites,
at nuntios veros. Ita ne bello quidem sed nuntio
vincimur? Merito hercules omnia contempsit quem
Lacones audire non sustinent. Si vincere Xersen 536
non licet, videre liceat; volo scire quid fugiam. Adhuc non sum ex ulla parte Atheniensium similis,
non muris nec educatione; nihil prius illorum imi-
tabor quam fugam?

7 POMPEI SILONIS. Xerses multos secum adducit,
Thermopylae paucos recipiunt. Erimus inter fortes
fugacissimi, inter fugaces tardissimi. Nihil refert
quantas gentes in orbem nostrum Oriens effuderit
quantumque nationum secum Xerses trahat; tot
ad nos pertinent quot locus ceperit.

---

[1] deo *Kiessling*: de.

---

[1] For a similar list see Manil. 4.687–8. Thebes was birth-
place of Dionysus, and had other religious associations.

[2] The royal house of Sparta proclaimed descent from
Hercules.

[3] For the contrast cf. Sen. *Helv.* 16.6: " si *numerare* funera

ment on the shame of flight by so long refusing to flee.
—Every city has its claim to fame: Athens is celebrated for eloquence, Thebes for religious ritual,
Sparta for war.[1] That is why the Eurotas river flows
around Sparta, the river that hardens our children to
withstand soldiering later. That is why the wooded
ridges of Taygetus are so difficult of access—for all
except Spartans. That is why we boast of Hercules,
the god who deserved heaven by his deeds.[2] That is
why our walls are our weapons.—Weighty is the dis- 6
grace brought on our ancestors' bravery!—Spartans
thinking of their numbers, not their valour.[3]—Let us
see how big the enemy host is: Sparta should at least
have truthful messengers, if it cannot have brave
soldiers.—Are we then conquered not by force of
arms but by a message? If Spartans cannot bear the
news of his coming, how right he was to despise
everything!—If it is not ours to beat Xerxes, let it be
ours to see him; I want to know what I am fleeing.—
Up to now, I am in no respect like the Athenians, in
walls or in upbringing. Am I to start by imitating
their flight?

Pompeius Silo. Xerxes brings many men with 7
him; Thermopylae has room for but a few. [We
shall be the most fugitive among the brave—and the
most tardy among the fugitives.][4] It makes no
difference how great are the nations that the East has
poured into our part of the world, how many peoples
Xerxes drags along with him. We have to do only
with the number this spot will hold.

Corneliae velles, amiserat decem, si *aestimare*, amiserat
Gracchos."
  [4] This sentence is misplaced; it may belong in §5 Marullus.

CORNELI HISPANI. Pro Sparta venimus, pro Graecia stemus; vincamus hostes, socios iam vicimus; sciat iste insolens barbarus nihil esse difficilius quam Laconis armati latus fodere. ⟨Ceteri quidem fugerunt.⟩[1] Ego vero quod discesserunt gaudeo; liberas nobis reliquere Thermopylas; nil erit quod virtuti nostrae se opponat, quod inserat; non latebit in turba Laco; quocumque Xerses aspexerit, Spartanos videbit.

8 BLANDI. Referam praecepta matrum: " aut in his aut cum his "? Minus turpe est a bello inermem reverti quam armatum fugere. Referam captivorum verba? Captus Laco " occide," inquit, " non servio." Non potuit capi si fugere voluisset. Describite terrores Persicos; omnia ista cum mitteremur audivimus. Videat trecentos Xerses, et sciat quanti bellum aestimatum sit, quanto aptus numero locus. Revertamur ne nuntii quidem nisi novissimi. Quis fugerit nescio; hos mihi Sparta commilitones dedit. DESCRIPTIO THERMOPYLARUM. Nunc me delectat quod fugerunt treceni; angustas mihi Thermopylas fecerunt.

9 Contra. CORNELI HISPANI. At ego maximum video dedecus futurum rei publicae nostrae si Xerses nihil prius in Graecia vicerit quam Laconas. Ne testem quidem virtutis nostrae habere possumus;

---

[1] *Transposed from § 4 by the editor, after Gertz.*

---

[1] Their shields, on which soldiers were carried to burial: see Plut. *Apophth. Lac.* 241F.

CORNELIUS HISPANUS. We came for Sparta: let us stay for Greece. Let us defeat our foes: we have already defeated our friends. Let this arrogant barbarian know that nothing is more difficult than to pierce the side of a Spartan in arms.—Certainly, the rest have gone. I am glad they have retreated; they have left Thermopylae free for us. There will be nothing to pit itself against our virtue, nothing to merge with it. The Spartan will not be lost in the throng: wherever Xerxes looks, he will see Spartans.

BLANDUS. Shall I repeat what our mothers told us: 8 "Either in them or with them"?[1] It is less shameful to return from war without arms than to flee in arms. Shall I repeat the words of captives? A Spartan, taken prisoner, said: "Kill me: *I* am no slave."[2] He couldn't have been captured if he had been ready to retreat.—Very well, relate the terrors aroused by the Persians: we heard all that when we were sent here.—Let Xerxes see the three hundred, and realise how we rated this war—and the number this place is suited to.—Let us not return even to tell the tale—unless we are the last.—Who fled, I do not know; *these* are the men Sparta gave to fight at my side.—*Description of Thermopylae.* Now I am glad that the other contingents have fled. They made Thermopylae too narrow for me.

The other side

CORNELIUS HISPANUS. Yet I see a great disgrace 9 befalling our state if Xerxes defeats Spartans before anyone else in Greece.—We cannot even have a wit-

[2] Cf. Sen. *Ep.* 77.14. Edward quotes parallels from Plutarch (e.g. 235B).

id de nobis credetur quod hostes narraverint. Habetis consilium meum; id est autem meum quod totius Graeciae. Si quis aliud suadet, non fortes vos vult esse sed perditos.

CLAUDI MARCELLI. Non vincent nos sed obruent. Satis fecimus nomini, ultumi cessimus; ante nos rerum natura victa est.

10 DIVISIO. Huius suasoriae feci mentionem non quia in ea subtilitatis erat aliquid quod vos excitare posset, sed ut sciretis quam nitide Fuscus dixisset vel quam licenter; ipse sententiam ⟨non⟩ [1] feram; vestri arbitrii erit utrum explicationes eius luxuriosas putetis an vegetas.[2] Pollio Asinius aiebat hoc non esse suadere sed ludere.[3] Recolo [4] nihil fuisse me 538 iuvene tam notum quam has explicationes Fusci, quas nemo nostrum non alius alia inclinatione vocis velut sua quisque modulatione cantabat. At quia semel in mentionem incidi Fusci, ex omnibus suasoriis celebres descriptiunculas subtexam, etiamsi nihil occurrerit quod quisquam alius nisi suasor dilexerit.

11 Divisione autem ⟨in⟩ hac suasoria Fuscus usus est illa volgari, ut diceret non esse honestum fugere etiamsi tutum esset; deinde: aeque periculosum esse fugere et pugnare; novissime: periculosius esse fugere: pugnantibus hostes timendos, fugientibus et hostes et suos.

Cestius primam partem sic transit, quasi nemo

---

[1] *Supplied by Schultingh.*
[2] vegetas *Gertz:* ut petas *A:* ut poetas *B:* ut poeta *V.*
[3] sed ludere *Gertz:* isciuidere.
[4] recolo *Bursian, Madvig:* ueuolo.

[1] But see Seneca's remarks in *C.* 2 pr. 1.

ness to testify to our bravery; what our enemies
relate of us will be the received version.—You have
my view—and it is the view of all Greece.   If anyone
tries to advise another course of action, he wants you
not heroic but dead.

   CLAUDIUS MARCELLUS.   They will not defeat us—
they will swamp us.—We have done enough to uphold
our reputation: we were the last to retreat.—Before
we were conquered, nature was conquered.

Division

I have mentioned this *suasoria* not because it con- 10
tained anything very subtle that might stimulate
you, but so that you could learn how brilliantly Fuscus
spoke—or how licentiously: *I* shall not vote on that
issue.[1]   It will be up to *you* to decide whether you
think his developments self-indulgent or lively.
Asinius Pollio used to say this was sport, not advice.
I recall that in my youth nothing was more familiar
than these developments of Fuscus'; all of us, with
differing inflexions of voice, used to intone them, each,
as it were, in his own key.   But now that I've got round
to speaking of Fuscus, I will append celebrated little
descriptive passages from all the *suasoriae*, even if
nothing turns up that anyone but a speaker of
suasoriae likes.

   In this *suasoria* Fuscus used the well-worn division: 11
It is wrong to retreat, even if it were safe.   Then, It
is as dangerous to retreat as to fight.   Lastly, It is
more dangerous to retreat.   Those who fight have the
enemy to fear; those who retreat have the enemy
and their own people to fear.

   Cestius passed over the first part as though there

dubitaret an turpe esset fugere; deinde illo transit, an non esset necesse. Haec sunt, inquit, quae vos confundunt: hostes, sociorum ⟨fuga, vestra ipsorum⟩ [1] paucitas.

Non quidem in hac suasoria, sed in hac materia disertissima illa fertur sententia Dorionis, cum posuisset hoc dixisse trecentis Leonidam quod puto etiam 539]
apud Herodotum esse: ⟨ἀριστοποιεῖσθε ὡς ἐν Ἅιδου δειπνησόμενοι⟩.

12   Sabinus Asilius, venustissimus inter rhetoras scurra, cum hanc sententiam Leonidae rettulisset, ait: ego illi ad prandium promisissem, ad cenam renuntiassem.

Attalus Stoicus, qui solum vertit a Seiano circumscriptus, magnae vir eloquentiae, ex his philosophis quos vestra aetas vidit longe et subtilissimus et facundissumus, cum tam magna et nobili sententia certavit et mihi dixisse videtur animosius quam prior: . . .

Occurrit mihi sensus in eiusmodi materia a Severo Cornelio dictus tamquam de Romanis nescio an parum fortiter. Edicta in posterum diem pugna epulantes milites inducit et ait:

                         stratique per herbam
         " hic meus est " dixere " dies."

_____

[1] *Supplied by Kiessling and Gertz.*

-----

[1] Not so. See however Diod. 11.9.4; Plut. *Apophth. Lac.* 225D; Val. Max. 3.2 ext. 3. Dorion's epigram may be incomplete.

[2] A similar play occurs in Sen. *Ep.* 82.21: " alacres et ad prandium illi promiserunt et ad cenam."

was no doubt of the shamefulness of flight. Then he went on to discuss whether it was necessary: " These," he said, " are the things that dismay you: the enemy, the flight of your allies, your own small numbers."

There is current a very clever epigram of Dorion (spoken, admittedly, not on this theme, but on this topic); he made Leonidas say to the three hundred what I think is also in Herodotus:[1] " Take breakfast: you will dine in Hades."

Asilius Sabinus, the most agreeable jester among the rhetoricians, after relating this remark of Leonidas', said: " *I* should have accepted for breakfast, but declined for dinner."[2] 12

Attalus the Stoic, who was banished thanks to the machinations of Sejanus, was a man of great eloquence, far the most subtle and at the same time the most articulate of the philosophers seen in your generation. He rivalled even that great and famous epigram, and his spirit, I think, even surpassed that of his predecessor, when he said: . . .

There occurs to me a thought on the same sort of subject spoken by Cornelius Severus. Considering that it concerns Romans, it perhaps betrays excessive cowardice. He represents soldiers dining when battle has been proclaimed for the following day, and says:

" Stretched on the grass,
They said: *This* is my day."[3]

---

[3] frg. 11 Morel. The phrase " meus dies est " (with the implication: " but tomorrow's fortunes are doubtful ") recurs in Sen. *Med.* 1017.

Elegantissime quidem adfectum animorum incerta sorte pendentium expressit, sed parum Romani animi servata est magnitudo; cenant enim tamquam crastinum desperent. Quantum illis Laconibus animi erat, qui non poterant dicere: "hic dies est meus."

13　Illud Porcellus grammaticus arguebat in hoc versu quasi soloecismum quod, cum plures induxisset, 540M diceret: "hic meus est dies," non: "hic noster est," et in sententia optima id accusabat quod erat optimum. Muta enim ut "noster" sit: peribit omnis versus elegantia, in quo hoc est decentissimum, quod ex communi sermone trahitur; nam quasi proverbii loco est: "hic dies meus est"; et, cum ad sensum rettuleris, ne grammaticorum quidem calumnia ab omnibus magnis ingeniis summovenda habebit locum; dixerunt enim non omnes simul tamquam in choro manum ducente grammatico, sed singuli ex iis: "hic meus est dies."

14　Sed ut revertar ad Leonidam et trecentos, pulcherrima illa fertur Glyconis sententia: . . .

In hac ipsa suasoria non sane refero memoria ⟨dignam⟩ [1] ullam sententiam Graeci cuiusquam nisi Damae: ποῖ φεύξεσθε, ὁπλῖται, τείχη;

De positione loci eleganter dixit Haterius, cum angustias loco facundissime descripsisset: natus trecentis locus.

------

[1] *Supplied by Kiessling.*

He put over in the most choice manner the emotions of men on a razor-edge of suspense; but he took too little account of the greatness of the Roman spirit: for they dine as if despairing of the morrow. How great was the spirit of those Spartans! *They* were incapable of saying: " This is my day."

The grammarian Porcellus used to brand as a 13 solecism Severus' saying in this line " this is my day " instead of " our day," when he had represented more than one as speaking.[1] Here Porcellus was finding fault with the best feature of an excellent epigram. Change it to " our day," and all the elegance of the verse will disappear: for its propriety lies in this phrase, which is taken from common idiom, " this is my day " being virtually a proverb. If you look to the sense, anyway, not even grammarians' pedantry (which should be kept away from all superior intellects) will maintain its ground: they didn't all speak together as in a choir under the direction of a grammarian, but each individual among them said: " This is my day."

But to return to Leonidas and the three hundred: 14 there is also current that very pretty epigram of Glycon's: . . .

In this same *suasoria* I recall no epigram of any Greek declaimer worthy of mention except Damas': " Where will you flee, hoplites, walls ? "

Haterius, after a fluent description of the narrowness of the place, said elegantly of the natural position of the spot: " A place made for three hundred."

---

[1] Quintilian 1.5.36 raises the question whether it is a solecism if you use the second person plural in summoning a single person.

Cestius, cum descripsisset honores quos habituri essent si pro patria cecidissent, adiecit: per sepulchra nostra iurabitur. Nicetes longe disertius hanc phantasiam movit et adiecit: . . . nisi antiquior Xerses fuisset quam Demosthenes † CIPTOY cui diceret†. Hanc suam dixit sententiam aut certe non depre- 541M hensam, cum descripsisset oportunitatem loci et tuta undique pugnantium latera et angustias a tergo positas, sed adversas hostibus: . . .

15 Potamon magnus declamator fuit Mitylenis, qui eodem tempore viguit quo Lesbocles magni nominis et nomini respondentis ingenii; in quibus quanta fuerit animorum diversitas in simili fortuna puto vobis indicandum, multo magis quia ad vitam pertinet quam si ad eloquentiam pertineret. Utrique filius eisdem diebus decessit: Lesbocles scholam solvit; nemo umquam amplius ⟨declamantem audivit; maiore⟩ [1] animo se gessit Potamon: a funere filii contulit se in scholam et declamavit. Utriusque tamen adfectum temperandum puto: hic durius tulit fortunam quam patrem decebat, ille mollius ⟨quam⟩ [2] virum.

16 Potamon, cum suasoriam de trecentis diceret, tractabat quam turpiter fecissent Lacones hoc ipsum, quod deliberassent de fuga, et sic novissime clausit: . . .

[1] *Supplied by the editor after Madvig and Müller.*
[2] *Supplied by Bursian.*

Cestius, having described the honours that would come their way if they died for their country, added: " They will swear by our graves." [1] Nicetes played much more elegantly on this fancy, adding: . . . had it not been that Xerxes was more ancient than Demosthenes . . . He spoke the following epigram (his own—or at least it has not been caught out as anyone else's) after describing the potentialities of the spot, with the flanks of the defenders secure in all directions, and a defile in their rear but in the enemy's way: . . .

Potamon was a great declaimer from Mytilene; he 15 flourished at the same time as Lesbocles, who had a high reputation and talents to match it. I think it's proper to tell you of their different reactions to similar circumstances,[2] much more proper because it is related to life than it would be if it were related to eloquence. Both lost a son at much the same time. Lesbocles closed his school; no-one ever again heard him declaim. Polemon showed more spirit. Straight from his son's funeral, he betook himself to his school and gave a declamation. I think the reactions of both require modification: one bore his affliction more stoutly than a father should, the other more weakly than a man should.

Potamon, when speaking the *suasoria* on the three 16 hundred, dealt with the shame inherent in Spartans debating retreat, and he finished off: . . .

[1] With an allusion to Demosthenes' famous oath in *de Cor.* 208 by those who died in the Persian Wars. The fragmentary sentence that follows clearly pointed out the anachronism involved in a use of Demosthenes' words in 480 B.C. (similarly in §22 about words of Caesar).

[2] Cf. *C.* 4 pr. 4–5.

Insanierunt in hac suasoria multi circa Othryadem: Murredius, qui dixit: fugerunt Athenienses;
non enim Othryadis nostri litteras didicerant. Gar- 542M
gonius dixit: Othryades, qui perit ut falleret, re-
vixit ut vinceret. Licinius Nepos: cum exemplo vobis
etiam mortuis vincendum fuit. Antonius Atticus
inter has pueriles sententias videtur palmam me-
ruisse; dixit enim: Othryades paene a sepulchro
victor digitis vulnera pressit ut trophaeo †Laconem†
inscriberet. O dignum Spartano atramentum! o
virum, cuius ne litterae quidem fuere sine sanguine!
Catius Crispus, municipalis ⟨rhetor⟩,[1] cacozelos dixit
post relatum exemplum Othryadis: aliud ceteros,
aliud Laconas decet; nos sine deliciis educamur, sine
muris vivimus, sine vita vincimus.

17   Seneca fuit, cuius nomen ad vos potuit pervenisse,
ingenii confusi ac turbulenti, qui cupiebat grandia
[dicere][2] adeo ut novissime morbo huius rei et
teneretur et rideretur; nam et servos nolebat habere
nisi grandes et argentea vasa non nisi grandia.
Credatis mihi velim non iocanti, eo pervenit insania
eius ut calceos quoque maiores sumeret, ficus non
esset nisi mariscas, concubinam ingentis staturae
haberet. Omnia grandia probanti inpositum est

[1] *Supplied by Edward.*
[2] *Deleted by Gertz.*

Many went off their heads in this *suasoria* on the topic of Othryades:[1] for instance, Murredius, who said: " The Athenians fled: they hadn't learnt the alphabet of our Othryades." Gargonius said: " Othryades, who perished to deceive, lived again to conquer." Licinius Nepos: " You had an example— you should have conquered even though dead." Antonius Atticus, I think, took the palm among these childish epigrams. He said: " Othryades, victor almost from the grave, pressed his fingers into his wounds in order to write . . . on the trophy. Ink worthy of a Spartan! What a man!—even his alphabet was steeped in blood." Catius Crispus, a small-town rhetorician, displayed bad taste in saying, after relating the story of Othryades: " One thing suits Spartans, another all other men. *We* are brought up without pampering; we live without walls; we conquer without life."

There was a Seneca whose name may be known to 17 you, a man of disordered and wild character, who had a passion for big things: to such an extent that he eventually succumbed to a positive disease in this matter, and became a laughing stock for it. He wanted to have only big slaves and big silver dishes. You must believe me—I'm quite serious: his madness went so far that he even wore shoes too big for him, ate no ordinary figs but only marisks,[2] and had a mistress of vast dimensions. As he approved every-

[1] For the story that Othryades revived on the battlefield after being left for dead and used his own blood to write " I won " on his shield, see Val. Max. 3.2 ext. 4; ps.-Plut. *Parall.* 306A; Ovid *Fast.* 2.665. Herodotus (1.82) is less extravagant.

[2] A coarse variety of fig.

cognomen vel, ut Messala ait, cognomentum, et 543M
vocari coepit Seneca Grandio.   Aliquando iuvene me
is in hac suasoria, cum posuisset contradictionem:
" at omnes qui missi erant a Graecia fugerunt,"
sublatis manibus, insistens summis digitis—sic enim
solebat, quo grandior fieret—exclamat: gaudeo,
gaudeo.   Mirantibus nobis quod tantum illi bonum
contigisset, adiecit: totus Xerses meus erit.   Item
dixit: iste, qui classibus suis maria subripuit, qui
terras circumscripsit, dilatavit profundum, novam
rerum naturae faciem imperat, ponat sane contra
caelum castra: commilitones habebo deos.

18   Saenianus multo potentius dixit: terras armis
obsidet, caelum sagittis, maria vinculis; Lacones,
nisi succurritis, mundus captus est.

Licentissimi [1] generis stultam sententiam referam
Victoris Statori, municipis mei, cuius fabulis memoria dignissimis aliquis ⟨delectetur.   Is huius⟩ [2]
suasoriae occasione sumpsit contradictionem: " at "
inquit " trecenti sumus "; et ita respondit: trecenti,
sed viri, sed armati, sed Lacones, sed ad Thermopylas; numquam vidi plures trecentos.

---

[1] licentissimi *Shackleton Bailey:* decentissimi.
[2] *Supplied by Vahlen and Madvig.*

---

[1] The purist (cf. *C.* 2.4.8 n.) Messala preferred the older word
(which appears only once in Cicero, but prevails in the
archaisers Sallust—and so Tacitus—and Gellius).
[2] Cf. Quintilian 2.3.8; Sen. *Ep.* 111.3.   For raised hands in

thing that was big, he was given a cognomen (or, as Messala puts it, a *cognomentum*),[1] and came to be known as Seneca Grandio. Once when I was a youth, during this *suasoria*, after posing the objection " But the Greek contingents have all fled," he raised his hands, stood on tip-toe (as he normally did in his desire to get bigger) [2] and shouted: " I am glad, I am glad! " We wondered what good fortune could have befallen him. Then he added: " Xerxes will be all mine." He also said: " A man who has stolen the seas with his fleets, who has set a limit to the earth, while extending the deep, who orders nature to put on a new look, can certainly fortify his camp against the sky: I shall have the gods in the ranks with me."

Saenianus said, much more forcefully: " He be- 18 sieges land with arms, heaven with arrows, seas with chains.[3] Unless you go to the rescue, Spartans, the universe is at his feet."

I will tell you a foolish epigram of a very decadent nature spoken by my fellow townsman Statorius Victor (his plays are noteworthy and may give some people pleasure). When this *suasoria* came up, he put forward the objection: " But there are only three hundred of us." His reply was: " Three hundred, yes—but men, but armed, but Spartans, but at Thermopylae; I have never seen three hundred so numerous."

oratory see Quintilian 2.12.9, 11.3.119 (declaimers seem to have prided themselves on the gesture).
[3] For Xerxes' chaining of the Hellespont see Herodotus 7.35.1 and Mayor on Juv. 10.182. The arrows derive from the story in Herod. 5.105, later exaggerated and transferred to Xerxes (see *S.* 5.4 and Diog. Laert. 1 pr. 9).

19 Latro in hac suasoria, cum tractasset omnia quae
materia capiebat, posse ipsos et vincere, posse certe 544M
invictos reverti [et] [1] beneficio loci, tum illam sententiam: si nihil aliud, erimus certe belli mora.
Postea memini auditorem Latronis Abronium Silo-
nem, patrem huius Silonis qui pantomimis fabulas
scripsit et ingenium grande non tantum deseruit sed
polluit, recitare carmen in quo agnovimus sensum
Latronis in his versibus:

> ite agite, ⟨o⟩ Danai, magnum paeana canentes,
> ite triumphantes: belli mora concidit Hector.

Tam diligentes tunc auditores erant, ne dicam tam
maligni, ut unum verbum [2] surripi non posset; at
nunc cuilibet orationes in Verrem tuto licet pro suis [3]
⟨dicere⟩.[4]

20 Sed, ut sciatis sensum bene dictum dici tamen posse
melius, notate prae ceteris quanto decentius Vergilius
dixerit hoc quod valde erat celebre, " belli mora
concidit Hector ":

> quidquid ad adversae cessatum est moenia Troiae,
> Hectoris Aeneaeque manu victoria Graium
> haesit.

Messala aiebat hic Vergilium debuisse desinere: 545M
quod sequitur

> et in decimum vestigia rettulit annum

---

[1] *Deleted by Kiessling.*
[2] unum verbum *Spengel:* unus uerba.
[3] suis *D, C. F. W. Müller:* sua *A:* suo *BV.*
[4] *Supplied here by the editor, elsewhere by Kiessling and
Müller.*

On this theme, Latro, after discussing all the points 19 the theme had room for—that they might even win, and could certainly return unbeaten, thanks to their position—then used the epigram: " At worst we shall put a brake on the war." [1]   Later I recall that Latro's pupil Abronius Silo, father of the Silo who wrote mime plays, thus profaning as well as neglecting his distinguished talents, recited a poem in which we recognised Latro's idea in the lines:

" Go forward, Greeks, singing a great paean:
  Go in triumph. Hector, brake on war, has fallen." [2]

So assiduous (not to say carping) were audiences in those days that not even a single word could be plagiarised. Nowadays anyone can pass off the Verrines for his own without being detected.

But, to let you see that a well-expressed idea can 20 all the same find a better expression, notice particularly how much more fittingly Virgil put this popular phrase: " Hector, brake on war, has fallen."

" Whatever pause there was by the walls of hostile Troy,
  It was by Hector's hand and Aeneas' that victory Was stayed for the Greeks." [3]

Messala used to say that Virgil should have stopped there, and that what follows

" and retreated from them till the tenth year "

---

[1] A popular phrase: see e.g. Sen. *Agam.* 211; Lucan 1.100.
[2] Morel, 120. This is a translation of *Iliad* 22.391–2, perhaps influenced by Virg. *Aen.* 6.657.
[3] *Aen.* 11.288 *seq.*

explementum esse; Maecenas hoc etiam priori conparabat.

Sed ut ad Thermopylas revertar, Diocles Carystius dixit: . . .

21 Apaturius dixit: . . .

Corvo rhetori testimonium stuporis reddendum est, qui dixit: " quidni, si iam Xerses ad nos suo mari navigat, fugiamus, antequam nobis terra subripiatur?" Hic est Corvus qui, cum temperaret[1] scholam Romae, Sosio illi qui Iudaeos subegerat declamavit controversiam de ea quae apud matronas disserebat liberos non esse tollendos et ob hoc accusatur rei publicae laesae. In hac controversia sententia eius haec ridebatur: " inter pyxides et redolentis animae medicamina constitit mitrata contio."

22 Sed, si vultis, historicum quoque vobis fatuum dabo. Tuscus ille qui Scaurum Mamercum, in quo Scaurorum familia extincta est, maiestatis reum fecerat, homo quam inprobi animi tam infelicis ingenii, cum hanc suasoriam declamaret, dixit: " expectemus, si nihil aliud hoc effecturi, ne insolens barbarus dicat: veni, vidi, vici," cum hoc post multos annos divus Iulius victo Pharnace dixerit.

Dorion dixit: ἄνδρες . . . Aiebat Nicocrates Lacedaemonius insignem hanc sententiam futuram 546M fuisse si media intercideretur.

23 Sed ne vos diutius infatuem, quia dixeram me

---

[1] temperaret *Gertz:* temptaret.

---

[1] Rich women (and effeminate men) would wear the *mitra* or turban.

is merely a stop-gap. Maecenas thought this as good
as what goes before.

But to return to Thermopylae, Diocles of Carystos
said: . . .

Apaturius said: . . .   21

An award for stupidity should go to the rhetorician
Corvus, who said: " If Xerxes is already sailing
against us over seas that belong to him, had we not
better flee before the earth is stolen from us? " It
was this Corvus who, while in charge of a school in
Rome, declaimed to the Sosius who had conquered
the Jews the *controversia* about the woman who
argued before matrons that children should not be
reared, and is therefore accused of harming the state.
On this theme one of Corvus' epigrams drew laughter:
" Amid the scent-pots and the breath-lozenges stood
the turbaned assembly." [1]

But if you like I'll let you have a crazy historian as 22
well. Tuscus (the same who had accused of treason
the Scaurus Mamercus in whom the Scauri clan came
to an end), a man of evil character and unenviable
talents,[2] said while declaiming this *suasoria*: " Let us
wait. We shall at least ensure that the arrogant
barbarian does not say: I came, I saw, I conquered."
In fact, it was many years later that Julius Caesar said
this, after his victory over Pharnaces.[3]

Dorion said: " Men, . . ." Nicocrates the Spartan
used to say that this epigram would have shown distinction if it had been cut short half-way.

But so as not to craze you further, I will end this 23

[2] Cf. Tac. *Ann.* 6.29 (A.D. 34), describing the trial.
[3] See Suet. *Jul.* 37: the words were used on placards in
Caesar's triumph over the King of Pontus (at Zela 47 B.C.).

Fusci Arelli explicationes subiecturum, hic finem
suasoriae faciam. Quarum nimius cultus et fracta
conpositio poterit vos offendere cum ad meam aetatem veneritis; interim ⟨non⟩ dubito quin nunc vos
ipsa quae offensura sunt vitia delectent.

III

Deliberat Agamemnon an Iphigeniam immolet
negante Calchante aliter navigari fas esse.

1 ARELLI FUSCI patris. Non in aliam condicionem
deus fudit aequora quam ne omnis ex voto iret dies;
nec ea sors mari tantum est: caelum specta,[1] non
sub eadem condicione sidera sunt? Alias negatis
imbribus exurunt solum, et miseri cremata agricolae
legunt semina, et haec interdum anno lex est;
alias serena clauduntur, et omnis dies caelum nubilo
gravat: subsidit solum, et creditum sibi terra non
retinet; alias incertus sideribus cursus est, et varian-
tur tempora, neque soles nimis urguent neque ultra 547M
debitum imbres cadunt: quidquid asperatum aestu
est, quidquid nimio diffluxit imbre, invicem tem-
peratur altero; sive ista natura disposuit, sive, ut
ferunt, luna cursu gerit—quae, sive plena lucis suae

---

[1] caelum specta *Haase:* ceterum ipsa.

---

[1] §10.
[2] The scene at Aulis is described in such famous passages as
Aesch. *Agam.* 40 *seq.*, Lucr. 1.95 *seq.*

suasoria here, for I have promised [1] to add developments by Fuscus. Their extreme ornamentation and effeminate rhythm may offend you when you reach my age. Meanwhile I am sure you will take pleasure in the very vices that will later grate on you.

3

AGAMEMNON DELIBERATES WHETHER TO SACRIFICE IPHIGENIA: FOR CALCHAS SAYS THAT OTHERWISE SAILING IS IMPERMISSIBLE [2]

Against the sacrifice

ARELLIUS FUSCUS SENIOR. God poured forth the [1] waters of the sea on the express understanding that not every day should go as we hope. And it is not only the sea that is thus limited: look at the sky—are not the stars subject to this same condition? [3] Sometimes they deny their rain and burn up the soil, and when the wretched farmers collect up the seed, it is burnt; such, at times, is the rule for a whole year. Sometimes the clear skies are hidden, every day weighs down the firmament with cloud; the soil sinks, the earth cannot keep what is entrusted to it. Sometimes the stars have uncertain courses, the weather varies; the sun is not too insistent, the rains do not fall beyond due measure: whatever has been made rough by heat, whatever dissolved by excessive rain, receives mutual blending from the other. Perhaps this is the law of nature; perhaps, as the story goes, the regulating factor is the course of the

---

[3] Cf. *C.* 2.5.8. For the following passage on extremes of weather cf. Sen. *Oed.* 41 *seq.*

est splendensque pariter adsurgit in cornua, imbres
prohibet, sive occurrente nubilo sordidiorem ostendit
orbem suum, non ante finit quam [in] [1] lucem reddit—,
sive ne lunae quidem ista potentia est, sed flatus,
qui occupavere, annum tenent: quidquid horum est,
extra iussum dei tutum fuit adultero mare. At non
potero vindicare adulteram. Prior est salus pudicae.
Ne quid huius virginitati timerem, persequebar
adulterum. Victa Troia virginibus hostium parcam.
Nihil adhuc virgo Priami timet.

2   CESTI PII. Vos ergo [adhunc],[2] di immortales, invoco: sic reclusuri estis maria? Obstate potius.
Ne Priami quidem liberos immolaturus es. Describe
nunc tempestatem. Omnia ista patimur nec parricidium fecimus. Quod hoc sacrum est virginis
deae templo virginem occidere? Libentius hanc
sacerdotem habebit quam victimam.

CORNELI HISPANI. Infestae sunt, inquit, tempestates et saeviunt maria, neque adhuc parricidium
feci. Ista maria, si numine suo deus regeret, adul-
teris clauderentur.

[1] *Deleted by Kiessling.*
[2] *Deleted by Ribbeck.*

---

[1] For the sources of this, see §5.
[2] Fuscus approaches the point. Weather is controlled by
natural forces, not the gods—and this is shown by the safe
passage granted to Paris when he carried off Helen. Fuscus
dismisses the supposed connection between the safety of a

moon—if her light is undimmed, and she rises with
equal resplendence to her horns, she prevents rain;
if she displays a duller orb as clouds encounter her, she
does not end the rain till she gives her light out once
more.[1]   Perhaps this is not in the power even of the
moon, but instead it is the prevailing winds which
hold the year in their grasp.   Whatever the case, it
was not on the orders of a god that the sea held no
perils for the adulterer.[2]—" But I shall not be able to
punish the adulteress."   The life of a chaste woman
comes first.—I was pursuing the adulterer so as not to
have to fear for the virginity of my daughter.[3]—When
Troy is conquered, I shall spare the daughters of the
enemy.[4]—*Priam's* maiden daughter as yet has nothing
to fear.

CESTIUS PIUS.   It is on you, then, that I call, im- 2
mortal gods: is this the way you propose to open the
sea to us?   I should rather you stood in our way.—
Even Priam's children you do not propose to sacrifice.
—*Now describe the storm.*[5]   We are suffering all this—
before committing parricide.—What is this rite, killing
a virgin in the temple of the virgin goddess?   She
will rather have the girl her priestess than her
victim.

CORNELIUS HISPANUS.   The storms are dangerous,
it is said, the seas rage: and I haven't yet committed
parricide.—If god's power ruled these waves, they
would be closed to *adulterers.*

voyage and the morals of the voyager, for which cf. below, §2
Hispanus, and *C.* 7.1.4 n.

[3] And now I have to fear for her life!

[4] Much more should I spare my own.

[5] A stage direction like " *Description of Thermopylae* " in
S. 2.8.

Marulli. Si non datur nobis ad bellum iter, revertamur ad liberos.

Argentari. Iterum in malum familiae nostrae fatale revolvimur: propter adulteram fratris liberi 548M pereunt. Ista mercede nolo illam reverti. At Priamus bellum pro adultero filio gerit.

3 Divisio. Hanc suasoriam sic divisit Fuscus ut diceret etiamsi aliter navigari non posset non esse faciendum. Hoc sic tractavit, ut negaret faciendum quia homicidium esset, quia parricidium, quia plus inpenderetur quam peteretur: peti ⟨Helenam⟩,[1] inpendi Iphigeniam; vindicari adulterium, committi parricidium. Deinde dixit, etiamsi non immolasset, navigaturum; illam enim moram naturae, maris et ventorum, esse: deorum voluntatem ab hominibus non intellegi.

Hoc Cestius diligenter divisit; dixit enim deos rebus humanis non interponere arbitrium suum; ut interponant, voluntatem eorum ab homine non intellegi; ut intellegatur, non posse fata revocari. Si non sint fata, nesciri futura; si sint, non posse mutari.

4 Silo Pompeius, etiamsi quod esset divinandi genus certum, auguriis negavit credendum: Quare ergo,

[1] *Supplied by Wehle.*

---

[1] Agamemnon's father Atreus had his wife Aerope seduced by Atreus' brother, Thyestes, and this resulted in the death (and eating) of Thyestes' children. So now Iphigenia is to die as a result of the seduction of her uncle's wife.

MARULLUS. If we can make no headway towards war, let us return to our children.

ARGENTARIUS. Once again we come back round to the evil fate that afflicts our family.[1] Because of an adulteress, a brother's children perish.—At that price I'll do without her [2] return.—Yet Priam is waging war on behalf of his adulterous son.[3]

Division

In his division of this *suasoria*, Fuscus first said that 3 even if sailing was otherwise impossible, they should not kill Iphigenia. His treatment was as follows: they should not do it because it was murder, because it was parricide, because the price paid was greater than the object sought—Helen was the object, Iphigenia the price; adultery was being avenged, and parricide committed. Then he said that Agamemnon would eventually set sail even if he did not make the sacrifice; there were natural causes for the delay, sea and winds; the will of the gods was inscrutable to mortals.

This point was carefully divided by Cestius; he said that gods do not make their wishes felt in human affairs; even if they do, men cannot know their will; even if men do know it, the fates are irrevocable. If there are no fates, the future is inscrutable; if there are, it cannot be changed.

Pompeius Silo said that even if there were some 4 sure method of divination, no belief should be placed

---

[2] Helen's.
[3] Agamemnon, then, should avoid killing his innocent daughter. The words are normally taken as an objection; but in that case one would expect a riposte.

si nescit Calchas, adfirmat? Primum [et][1] scire se
putat—hic communem locum dixit in omnes qui
hanc adfectarent scientiam—; deinde irascitur tibi,
invitus militat, quaerit sibi tam magno testimonio
apud omnes gentes fidem.

In ea descriptione ⟨quam⟩ primam in hac suasoria
posui[2] Fuscus Arellius Vergilii versus voluit imitari; 549M
valde autem longe petit et paene repugnante materia,
certe non desiderante, inseruit. Ait enim de luna:
" quae, sive plena lucis suae est splendensque pariter
assurgit in cornua, imbres prohibet, sive occupata
nubilo sordidiorem ostendit orbem suum, non ante
5 finit quam lucem reddit." At Vergilius haec quanto
et simplicius et beatius dixit:

> luna, revertentes cum primum colligit ignes,
> si nigrum obscuro comprenderit aera cornu,
> maximus agricolis pelagoque parabitur imber.

Et rursus:

> sin . . .
> pura nec obtunsis per caelum cornibus ibit.

Solebat autem Fuscus ex Vergilio multa trahere,
ut Maecenati imputaret; totiens enim pro beneficio narrabat in aliqua se Vergiliana descriptione

---

[1] *Deleted by Müller.*
[2] quam primam—posui *Bursian:* primum—potuit.

in augury. "Why, then, if Calchas is ignorant, does he make assertions? First of all, he thinks he *does* know"—here he spoke a commonplace against all those who pretended to such knowledge; "secondly, he is angry with you, he does not want to go to war; and he seeks universal recognition by so notable a token."

In the description which I put first in this *suasoria*, Arellius Fuscus wished to imitate certain lines of Virgil; but they were far from his point, and he put them in almost against the interests of his theme, which assuredly had no need of them. For he says of the moon: "if her light is undimmed, and she rises with equal resplendence to her horns,[1] she prevents rain; if she displays a duller orb as clouds seize upon her, she does not end the rain till she gives her light out once more." But how much more simply and 5 happily Virgil [2] put this:

"When first the moon collects her returning fires,
    Should she grasp dark air between her dimmed
        horns,
    Heavy rain will be in store for farmer and sailor."

And again:

"But if . . . she goes clear through the sky with
    unblunted horns . . ."

Fuscus used to take a lot from Virgil so as to win favour for it with Maecenas; he used often to tell how as a service to Maecenas he'd given pleasure in

[1] Cf. Virgil *Aen.* 10.275 "surgens in cornua cervus" describing a stag towering up.
[2] *Georg.* 1.427-9, 432-3.

placuisse; sicut in hac ipsa suasoria dixit: " cur iste
⟨in⟩ interpretis [1] ministerium placuit? cur hoc os
deus elegit? cur hoc sortitur potissimum pectus [2] quod
tanto numine impleat? " [3]   Aiebat se imitatum esse
Vergilianum " plena deo."

6   Solet autem Gallio noster hoc aptissime ponere. 550
Memini una nos ab auditione Nicetis ad Messalam
venisse.   Nicetes suo impetu valde Graecis placuerat.
Quaerebat a Gallione Messala quid illi visus esset
Nicetes. Gallio ait: " plena deo."   Quotiens audierat aliquem ex his declamatoribus quos scholastici
caldos vocant, statim dicebat: " plena deo."   Ipse
Messala numquam aliter illum ab novi hominis
auditione venientem interrogavit quam ut diceret:
" numquid plena deo? " Itaque hoc ipsi iam tam
7 familiare erat ut invito quoque excideret. Apud
Caesarem cum mentio esset de ingenio Hateri,
consuetudine prolapsus dixit: " et ille erat plena
deo." Quaerenti deinde quid hoc esse vellet,
versum Vergilii rettulit, et quomodo hoc semel sibi
apud Messalam excidisset et numquam ⟨non⟩ [4]
postea potuisset excidere. Tiberius ipse Theo-
doreus offendebatur Nicetis ingenio; itaque delectatus est fabula Gallionis.

¹ in interpretis *Leo:* inter eius.
² pectus *Madvig:* poetis.
³ impleat *Müller:* impie.
⁴ *Supplied by Schultingh.*

---

¹ i.e. why had Calchas been made interpreter of god to man?
² The words do not appear in our texts of Virgil. See O.
Ribbeck, *Rh.M.* 30 (1875), 626 n. 1; E. Norden, *Herm.* 28

connection with some Virgilian description. Thus in this very *suasoria* he said: " Why did *this* man find favour for the task of mediator ? [1] Why did the god choose *this* mouth ? Why does he light on *this* heart in particular to fill with such vast power ? " He said that he had imitated the Virgilian *plena deo*,[2] " she full of the God."

My friend Gallio often brings this phrase in very 6 nicely. I remember we once both visited Messala after listening to Nicetes. Nicetes' flood of words had much pleased the Greeks. Messala asked Gallio what he thought of Nicetes. " She's full of the god," said Gallio. Whenever he heard one of the declaimers that the schoolmen call " the hot ones," he used to say at once: " She's full of the god." In fact, Messala himself used invariably to phrase his question when Gallio arrived from hearing a new declaimer with these words: " Was she full of the god ? " Indeed, it was so habitual with Gallio that it used to drop from his lips despite himself. Once when the 7 emperor was present, and the conversation turned to the genius of Haterius, Gallio relapsed into habit, and said: " He too was full of the god, she was." The emperor asked what this meant, and Gallio recited the line of Virgil and told him how the phrase had once slipped out of him at Messala's and how it had been liable to slip out of him ever since. Tiberius himself, being a Theodorean,[3] used to be offended by Nicetes' manner, and so he much enjoyed Gallio's anecdote.

(1893), 506–11, suggests that they originally came in the description of the Sibyl in *Aen.* 6.45 *seq.*
[3] *C.* 2.1.36 n.

Hoc autem dicebat Gallio Nasoni suo valde placuisse; itaque fecisse illum quod in multis aliis versibus Vergilii fecerat, non subripiendi causa, sed palam mutuandi, hoc animo ut vellet agnosci; esse autem in tragoedia eius:

> feror huc illuc, vae, plena deo.

Iam, ⟨si⟩ [1] vultis, ad Fuscum revertar et descriptionibus eius vos statim satiabo, ac potissimum eis quas 551[in simili huius [2] tractatione posuit, cum diceret omnino non concessam futurorum scientiam.

IV

Deliberat Alexander Magnus an Babylona intret
cum denuntiatum esset illi responso auguris
periculum.

1 ARELLI FUSCI. Quis est qui futurorum scientiam sibi vindicet? Novae oportet sortis is sit qui iubente deo canat, non eodem contentus utero quo inprudentes nascimur; quandam imaginem dei praeferat qui iussa exhibeat dei. Sic est; tantum enim regem tantique rectorem orbis in metum cogit.

---

[1] *Supplied by Schultingh.*
[2] simili huius *Vahlen:* similitudinis.

---

[1] *Medea* (frg. 2 Ribbeck).
[2] Alexander died in Babylon in 323 B.C. For the disregarded warnings of the Chaldaean astrologers see e.g. Plut. *Alex.* 73, Arrian 7.16.5 *seq.* Seneca only cites this theme to

Gallio said that his friend Ovid had very much liked the phrase: and that as a result the poet did something he had done with many other lines of Virgil—with no thought of plagiarism, but meaning that his piece of open borrowing should be noticed. And in his tragedy [1] you may read:

" I am carried hither and thither, alas, full of the god."

Now, if you like, I'll return to Fuscus, and give you your fill of his descriptions without delay, particularly those he used in a similar development, when he was arguing that knowledge of the future is altogether denied to us.

4

ALEXANDER THE GREAT, WARNED OF DANGER
BY AN AUGUR, DELIBERATES WHETHER TO ENTER
BABYLON [2]

ARELLIUS FUSCUS.[3] What sort of man is he who 1 claims for himself knowledge of the future? Extraordinary must be the lot of the man who prophesies at the bidding of god; he cannot have been content with the same womb from which we ignorant mortals are born. There must be some overt sign of divinity in a man who reveals the orders of god. So it is: for he [4] compels so great a king, ruler of so vast a world,

bring in Arellius' development of it; for arguments against astrology see Sen. *Ep.* 88.14–15, Gell. 14.1.

[3] For Fuscus' remarks see L. Bieler, *Wien. Stud.* 53 (1935), 84–94.

[4] i.e. the augur.

THE ELDER SENECA

Magnus iste et supra humanae sortis habitum sit cui liceat terrere Alexandrum; ponat iste suos inter sidera patres et originem caelo trahat, agnoscat suum vatem deus; non eodem vitae fine aetatem agat,[1] extra omnem fatorum necessitatem caput sit quod gentibus futura praecipiat. Si vera sunt ista, quid ita non huic studio servit omnis aetas? Cur non ab infantia rerum naturam deosque qua licet visimus, cum pateant nobis sidera et interesse numinibus liceat? Quid ita ⟨in⟩[2] inutili desudamus facundia aut periculosis atteritur armis manus? An melius alio pignore quam futuri scientia ingenia 552 2 surrexerint? Qui vero in media se, ut praedicant, fatorum misere pignora, natales inquirunt et primam aevi horam omnium annorum habent nuntiam; quo ierint motu sidera, in quas discucurrerint partes, contrane dirus[3] steterit an placidus adfulserit Sol; [in][4] plenam lucem an initia surgentis acceperit, an abdiderit in noctem obscurum caput Luna; Saturnus nascentem ⟨ad cultum agrorum⟩,[5] an ad bella Mars militem, an negotiosum in quaestus Mercurius exceperit, an blanda adnuerit nascenti Venus, an ex humili in sublime Iuppiter tulerit, aestimant: tot circa unum caput tumultuantis deos!

---

[1] aetatem agat *Walter:* aetate magna.
[2] *Supplied by Novák.*
[3] dirus *Gertz:* deus.
[4] *Deleted by Thomas.*
[5] *Supplied by Konitzer.*

---

[1] Though *surgere* without qualification normally refers,

to feel fear. The man who can frighten Alexander must be great, high above the common lot of humanity; he must place his ancestors among the stars, trace his genealogy back to heaven; god must acknowledge him as his prophet. The personage who instructs men in the future cannot have the same bounds to his life, he must be placed outside all the restrictions imposed by fate. If all these prophecies are true, why do not men of every age apply themselves to this study? Why do we not, from infancy, penetrate to the gods and to nature along the road that is open to us, seeing that the stars lie before us and we can take our places beside divinities? Why do we thus sweat away at useless eloquence, why are our hands calloused by weapons that only bring us danger? Could talents have a better guarantee for their thriving than knowledge of what is to come? But those who have, as they put it, " launched them- 2 selves " into the mysterious certainties of fate enquire into birthdays, and regard the first hour of life as harbinger of all the years to follow. They work out what the movement of the stars was at that date, in what directions they scattered. Did the sun stand in ominous opposition, or shine on the scene calmly? Did the moon receive her light full, or was she at the beginning of her waxing,[1] or had she hidden her darkened head in night? Did Saturn welcome the new-born child to cultivate the fields, or Mars as a soldier for war, or Mercury as a businessman for profit, or did Venus nod graciously on the baby? Did Jupiter bear it from low to high? So many gods

when used of a heavenly body, to its rising, it must here refer to the waxing phase of the moon.

3 Futura nuntiant: plerosque ⟨diu⟩ [1] dixere victuros,
at nihil metuentis oppressit dies; aliis dedere finem
propincum, at illi superfuere agentes inutilis animas;
felices nascentibus annos spoponderunt, at Fortuna
in omnem properavit iniuriam. Incertae enim sortis
vivimus: unicuique ista pro ingenio finguntur, non
ex fide. Erit aliquis orbe toto locus qui te victorem
non viderit? Babylon ei cluditur cui patuit Oceanus?

4 DIVISIO. In hac suasoria nihil aliud tractasse 553M
Fuscum scio quam easdem quas supra rettuli quaestiones ad scientiam futuri pertinentis. Illud quod
nos delectavit praeterire non possum. Decla-
mitarat Fuscus Arellius controversiam de illa quae,
postquam ter mortuos pepererat, somniasse se dixit
ut in luco pareret. Valde in vos contumeliosus fuero
si totam controversiam, quam ego intellego me
dicere . . .[2] Fuscus, ⟨cum⟩[3] declamaret et a
parte avi non agnoscentis puerum tractaret locum
contra somnia et deorum providentiam et male de
magnitudine eorum dixisset mereri eum qui illos
circa puerperas mitteret, summis clamoribus illum
dixit Vergili versum:

> scilicet is superis labor est, ea cura quietos
> sollicitat.

[1] *Supplied by Gertz.*
[2] *The exact supplement is unclear.*
[3] *Supplied by Schultingh.*

---

[1] *Aen.* 4.379–80. Dido ironically dismisses Aeneas' claim
that gods and oracles demand his going to Italy.

bustling about one head! They announce the 3
future. Many, according to them, will live long—
yet their day has come suddenly upon them when
they feared nothing. To others they have assigned
an imminent end—yet they have survived to draw
breath that brings them no profit. They have
promised fortunate years to the new-born—yet
Fortune has hurried to do them every injury. For
the destiny under which we live is uncertain. These
are fictions devised for individuals as a show of clever-
ness, not from any belief in them.—Shall there be one
place in the whole world that has not seen you victorious? Is Babylon closed for the man to whom the
Ocean stood open?

Division

In this *suasoria* Fuscus, I know, dealt with nothing 4
else besides the questions related above about knowledge of the future. I cannot pass over something
that gave us pleasure. Fuscus had once declaimed
the *controversia* on the woman who after she had had
three stillborn babies said she had dreamed of giving
birth in a grove. I should be insulting you if ⟨I
expounded⟩ the whole *controversia*, for I know ⟨you
are familiar with it⟩. Fuscus' declamation was on
the side of the grandfather who would not recognise the son. Developing the commonplace against
dreams and divine providence, he said that anyone
who sent the gods out to minister at childbirths was
undervaluing their greatness. And amid loud applause he recited the line of Virgil: [1]

" Naturally that is a task for the gods, that is a care
    That troubles them in their calm."

5 Auditor Fusci quidam, cuius pudori parco, cum hanc
suasoriam de Alexandro ante Fuscum diceret, putavit
aeque belle poni eundem versum et dixit:

> scilicet is superis labor est, ea cura quietos
> sollicitat.

Fuscus illi ait: si hoc dixisses audiente Alexandro,
scisses apud Vergilium et illum versum esse:

> capulo tenus abdidit ensem.

Et quia soletis mihi molesti esse de Fusco, quid 554M
fuerit quare nemo videretur dixisse cultius, ingeram
vobis Fuscinas explicationes. Dicebat autem sua-
sorias libentissime et frequentius Graecas quam
Latinas.

Hybreas in hac suasoria dixit: οἷον ἔσχηκε
Βαβυλὼν μάντιν ὀχύρωμα.

V

Deliberant Athenienses an trophaea Persica
tollant, Xerse minante rediturum se nisi tolle-
rentur.

1 ARELLI FUSCI. Pudet me victoriae vestrae si sic
fugatum creditis Xersem ut reverti possit. Tot
caesa milia, nihil ex tanta acie relictum minanti nisi

---

[1] By not quoting his name: cf. Quintilian 6.3.64.
[2] *Aen.* 2.553.

A pupil of Fuscus', whose shame I will respect,[1] when 5 declaiming our *suasoria* on Alexander the Great before his master, thought that this same line could come in equally prettily here, and said:

> " Naturally that is a task for the gods, that is a care
>   That troubles them in their calm."

Fuscus said to him: " If you had said that in the hearing of Alexander you'd have been made aware there's another verse in Virgil:

> ' he buried the sword to its hilt.' "[2]

Now because you keep bothering me about Fuscus and why no-one was thought a more elegant speaker, I shall keep piling Fuscan delevopments on you. He was very ready to speak *suasoriae*, more frequently in Greek than Latin.

It was in this *suasoria* that Hybreas said: " What a shield Babylon has found in an augur!"[3]

5

XERXES HAS THREATENED TO RETURN UNLESS THE TROPHIES OF THE PERSIAN WAR ARE REMOVED: THE ATHENIANS DELIBERATE WHETHER TO DO SO[4]

ARELLIUS FUSCUS. I am ashamed of your victory if 1 you believe the rout of Xerxes was such as to leave him capable of returning. For all his threats, remember the thousands that were slain, remember how all that was left of that vast army was a force

---

[3] Though of course Alexander had conquered Babylon long before, in 331 B.C.

[4] This is altogether fictional.

quod vix fugientem sequi possit; totiens mersa
classis; quid Marathona, quid Salamina referam?
Pudet dicere: dubitamus adhuc an vicerimus.
Xerses veniet? Nescio quomodo languet circa
memoriam iacturae animus et disturbata arma non
repetit. Prior enim metus futuri pignus est, et
amissa ne audeat amissurum monent. Ut interdum
in gaudia surgit animus et spem ex praesenti meti-
tur, ita adversis frangitur. Omnis †est sit†[1]
animum dies ubi ignominia spem premit, ubi nullam
meminit aciem nisi qua fugerit; haeret circa damna
sua et quae male expertus est vota deponit. Si
venturus esset, non minaretur: suis ira ardet igni-   555M
2 bus et in pacta non solvitur. Non denuntiaret si
venturus esset, neque armaret nos nuntio nec in-
stigaret victricem Graeciam nec sollicitaret arma
felicia: magis superveniret inprovidis; nam et
⟨antea⟩[2] arma indenuntiata moverat. Quantum-
cumque Oriens valuit primo in Graeciam impetu
effusum est: hoc ille numero ferox et in deos arma
tulerat. Extincta tot ante Xersem milia, tot sub
ipso, iacent: nulli nisi qui fugerunt supersunt. Quid
dicam Salamina? quid Cynaegiron referam et te,
Polyzele? et hoc agitur, an vicerimus? Haec ego
trophaea dis posui, haec in totius conspectu Graeciae
statui, ne quis timeret Xersen minantem. Me

[1] I have translated Novák's compescit.
[2] Supplied here by Bursian.

---

[1] Not so: see Herodotus 7.131–3.
[2] i.e. in Darius' campaign that culminated in Marathon.

scarcely capable of escorting his flight, remember all
the times his fleet was sunk. There is no need to
dwell on Marathon, on Salamis. I am ashamed to
say it: we are still doubtful whether we were the
victors. Will Xerxes come? His mind is strangely
cast down as he ponders on his losses; it shrinks from
the thought of that rout. Former fear is a guarantee
of future fear; what he lost warns the man vulnerable
to further loss not to be daring. Just as a spirit is
sometimes uplifted at joy, and measures its hopes by
its present success, so it can be broken by adverse
fortune. Each day further restrains a man's spirit
when disgrace weighs heavily on hope, when he
remembers no battle where he was not put to flight;
he dwells on his defeats, and lays aside aspirations
whose outcome proved so unfortunate. If he were
going to come, he would utter no threats; anger
burns with its own fires, and does not die down into
bargaining. He would not warn us if he were going 2
to come: he would not arm us by his message, provoke victorious Greece, stir up arms that have tasted
success. Rather, he would come upon us when we
least expected it—after all, his previous attack was
made without warning.[1] All the strength of the East
was poured out in the first assault on Greece. Their
number inspired him with daring—he had taken up
arms even against the gods. Many thousands were
killed before Xerxes,[2] many under him: *they* lie dead,
only the fugitives survive. What of Salamis? What
of Cynaegiros and Polyzelos? And still the question
is raised, Did we win? I put up these trophies for
the gods, erected them in the sight of all Greece,
precisely in order that no-one should fear the threats

553

miserum! pugnante Xerse trophaea posui: fugiente tollam? Nunc Athenae vincimur: non tantum credetur redisse sed vicisse Xerses. Non potest
3 Xerses nisi per nos trophaea tollere. Credite mihi, difficile est attritas opes recolligere et spes fractas novare et ⟨ex⟩ [1] paenitenda acie in melioris eventus fiduciam surgere.

CESTI PII. Inferam, inquit, bellum. Alia mihi trophaea promittit. Potest maior venire quam victus est?

ARGENTARI. Non pudet vos? pluris trophaea vestra Xerses aestumat quam vos.

4 DIVISIO. Fuscus sic divisit: etiamsi venturus est Xerses nisi tollimus, non sunt trophaea tollenda: confessio servitutis est iussa facere. Si venerit, 556M vincemus: hoc non est diu colligendum; de eo dico " vincemus " quem vicimus. Sed ne veniet quidem: si venturus esset, non denuntiaret; fractus est et viribus et animo.

Cestius et illud adiecit, quod in prima parte tractavit, non licere Atheniensibus trophaea tollere: commune in illis ius totius Graeciae esse; commune bellum fuisse, communem victoriam.

Deinde ne fas quidem esse: numquam factum ut quisquam consecratis virtutis suae operibus manus

---

[1] *Supplied by Schultingh.*

---

[1] Or perhaps: Xerxes reckons your trophies more important than you do.
[2] This is probably the continuation of Cestius' division.

of Xerxes. Alas! When Xerxes fought, I put up
the trophies; am I to take them down when he flees?
Now we—Athens—are beaten: it will be believed
that Xerxes returned—and, worse, that he conquered.
Xerxes cannot take the trophies down unless we do it 3
for him. Believe me, it is hard to reassemble shattered forces, to renew broken hopes, to recover from
disgrace in battle and feel confidence in better luck.

CESTIUS PIUS. I will invade, he says. He is
promising me further trophies.—Can he come in
greater numbers than when he was defeated?

ARGENTARIUS. Are you not ashamed? Xerxes
reckons your trophies more important than yourselves.[1]

Division

This was Fuscus' division: "Even if Xerxes is 4
going to come unless we remove the trophies, we
should not remove them. It is a confession of slavery
to do what one is told. If he does come, we shall
conquer. There is no need for extended proof of
this point; I say 'We shall conquer him' of one
whom we have conquered. But he will not even
come. If he were going to come, he wouldn't
announce his intention. His strength and spirit are
broken."

Cestius added a point which he dealt with in the
first part, that it was not open to the Athenians to
remove the trophies: all Greece had a common
interest in them. The war had been shared by all,
and so had the victory.

Secondly,[2] it was not even allowable. It had never
happened that anyone raised his hand against the

adferret. Ista trophaea non sunt Atheniensium,
deorum sunt; illorum bellum fuit, illos Xerses vinculis, illos sagittis persequebatur. Hic omnia ad
impiam et superbam Xersis militiam pertinentia.

5 Quid ergo? bellum habebimus? habuimus. Et si
Xersem removeris, invenietur alius hostis: numquam magna imperia otiosa. Enumeratio [1] bellorum prospere ab Atheniensibus gestorum.

Deinde: non erit bellum; Xerses enim non veniet:
multo timidiores esse quom superbissimi fuerint.

Novissime: ut veniat, cum quibus veniet? Reliquias victoriae nostrae colliget; illos adducet quos
priore bello quasi inutiles [reliquias] noluit,[2] et si
qui ex fuga consecuti sunt. Nullum habet militem
nisi aut fastiditum aut victum.

6 Argentarius his duobus contentus fuit: aut non 557]
venturum Xersen aut non esse metuendum si venerit.
His solis institit, et illud dixit quod exceptum est:
" Tollite " inquit " trophaea." Si vicisti, quid
erubescis? si victus es, quid imperas? Locum movit
non inutiliter: iudicare quidem se neque Xersen
neque iam quemquam Persarum ausurum in Graeciam
effundi; sed eo magis trophaea ipsis tuenda, si quis
umquam illinc venturus hostis esset, ut conspectu
trophaeorum animi militum accenderentur, hostium
frangerentur.

[1] enumeratio *Kiessling, Haase:* enim *A:* omnium *BV.*
[2] noluit *Haase:* reliquias nouit.

[1] See *S.* 2 n. For the arrows and for the chains laid on the
Hellespont see *S.* 2.18 n.

hallowed symbols of his own courage. "These trophies belong not to the Athenians but to the gods. Theirs was the war, it was they whom Xerxes kept harassing with chains and arrows." Here he detailed everything to do with Xerxes' impious and arrogant campaign.[1]

"Well, then, shall we have to go to war? We have 5 been to war. And if you dispose of Xerxes, another enemy will turn up. Great empires are never at peace." List of wars successfully waged by the Athenians.

Then: "There will be no war. Xerxes will not come. When men have been particularly arrogant, they tend to show greater timidity."

Finally: "Even if he does come, who will accompany him? He will have to assemble the remnants from our victory. He will bring those whom he was unwilling to bring in the previous war, as being useless, together with any companions of his rout. He has no soldiers but the despised—or the defeated."

Argentarius was content with these two points: 6 Xerxes will either not come or, if he does come, he is not to be feared. He urged these alone, and voiced the following celebrated idea: "'Remove the trophies.' If you conquered, why blush? If you were conquered, why give orders?" He brought up one effective topic. He judged that neither Xerxes nor any future Persian would dare to pour his men into Greece. All the more reason, then, why the trophies must be maintained, in case of any invasion from that quarter, so that the sight of them should fire the spirit of the home soldiers, and break that of the enemy.

7   Blandus dixit: Repleat ipse prius Atho et maria
in antiquam faciem reducat.   Apparere vult posteris
quemadmodum venerit;   appareat quemadmodum
redierit.

Triarius omni dimissa divisione tantum exultavit
quod Xersen audiret venire: adesse ipsis novam victoriam, nova trophaea.

Silo Pompeius venusto genere sententiae usus est:
" Nisi tollitis " inquit " trophaea, ego veniam."
Hoc ait Xerses: nisi haec trophaea tollitis, alia po-
netis.

8   Alteram partem solus Gallio declamavit et hortans [1]
ad tollenda trophaea dixit gloriae nihil detrahi;
mansuram enim memoriam victoriae, quae perpetua
esset; ipsa trophaea et tempestatibus et aetate
consumi; bellum suscipiendum fuisse pro libertate,
pro coniugibus, pro liberis: pro re supervacua et
nihil nocitura si defieret non esse suscipiendum.
Hic dixit utique venturum Xersen et descripsit
adversus ipsos deos tumentem; deinde habere illum
magnas vires: neque omnes illum copias in Graeciam
perduxisse nec omnes in Graecia perdidisse; timen-
dam esse fortunae varietatem; exhaustas esse 558
Graeciae vires nec posse iam pati alterum bellum;
illi esse inmensam multitudinem hominum. Hoc
loco disertissimam sententiam dixit, ⟨dignam⟩ [2]
quae vel in oratione vel in historia ponatur: diutius
illi perire possunt quam nos vincere.

[1] hortans *Gertz:* (h)ortauit.
[2] *Supplied by Müller.*

Blandus said: " Let *him* first fill in Athos and 7
restore the sea to its old appearance.[1] He wants to
appear to posterity as he was when he came; let him
appear as he was when he went back."

Triarius rejected all division, merely exulting that
Xerxes was heard to be on his way: a new victory,
fresh trophies were at hand.

Pompeius Silo used a pretty type of epigram:
" ' Unless you remove the trophies I shall come.'
What Xerxes means is: ' Unless you remove these
trophies, you will have others to put up.' "

The other side was declaimed only by Gallio; in 8
advising them to remove the trophies, he said that
this was no detraction from their glory. The memory
of their victory was eternal and would remain.
Trophies themselves are worn by weather and the
passage of time. War had had to be undertaken in
the past in defence of freedom, of wives and children;[2] it should not now be undertaken for the sake
of something of no consequence, whose absence would
do no harm. Here he said that Xerxes would come
in any case, and he described him as swelling with
pride against the very gods. Then, Xerxes had great
power; he had not brought all his forces to Greece,
nor had he lost them all in Greece. The mutability
of fortune was to be feared. The strength of Greece
was exhausted, and could not now withstand a second
war, while Xerxes had an unmeasured multitude. At
this point he spoke a most eloquent epigram, that
deserved to find a place in oratory or history: " *They*
can go on dying for longer than *we* can go on winning."

[1] Cf. *S.* 2.3 n.
[2] With a possible reminiscence of Aeschylus *Persae* 402–5.

THE ELDER SENECA

VI

Deliberat Cicero an Antonium deprecetur.

1 Q. HATERI. Sciant posteri potuisse Antonio
servire rem publicam, non potuisse Ciceronem.
Laudandus erit tibi Antonius; in hac causa etiam
Ciceronem verba deficient. Crede mihi, cum diligenter te custodieris, faciet tamen Antonius quod
Cicero tacere non possit. Si intellegis, Cicero, non
dicit " roga ut vivas," sed " roga ut servias." Quemadmodum autem hunc senatum intrare poteris,
exhaustum crudeliter, repletum turpiter? Intrare
autem tu senatum voles in quo non Cn. Pompeium
visurus ⟨es⟩, non M. Catonem, non Lucullos, non
Hortensium, non Lentulum atque Marcellum, non
⟨tuos⟩,[1] tuos, inquam, consules Hirtium ac Pansam?
Cicero, quid in alieno saeculo tibi? iam nostra peracta ·
2 sunt. M. Cato, solus maximum vivendi moriendique
exemplum, mori maluit quam rogare—nec erat
Antonium rogaturus—et illas usque ad ultimum
diem puras a civili sanguine manus in pectus sacer-
rimum armavit. Scipio, cum gladium ⟨in⟩ pectus [2] 559M

---

[1] *Supplied by Gertz.*
[2] in pectus *Freinsheim:* ponitur *AV:* ponitus *B.*

---

[1] For this theme, and the next, related one, see Quintilian
3.8.46. They gave scope for allusions to words of Cicero,
some of which are noted below. Compare too Martial 5.69,
and *C.* 7.2.
[2] Even Cicero thought he was normally unlikely to find
words fail him: see *ad Fam.* 2.11.1, 13.63.1.
[3] Both Caesar (R. Syme, *The Roman Revolution,* c. 6) and

6

CICERO DELIBERATES WHETHER TO BEG
ANTONY'S PARDON [1]

QUINTUS HATERIUS. Let posterity know that if the 1
state was capable of being Antony's slave, Cicero was
not.—You will have to praise Antony: in such a cause
words will fail even Cicero.[2]—Believe me, however
carefully you guard your tongue, Antony will do
something about which Cicero cannot keep silent.—
If you understand him aright, Cicero, he is not saying: " Ask to live," but " Ask to be a slave."—How
will you be able to enter the senate in its present
plight, cruelly emptied and filled up to its shame?[3]
Will *you* even want to enter a senate where you will
not see Pompey, Cato, the Luculli, Hortensius,
Lentulus and Marcellus, or your—yes, your[4]—
consuls, Hirtius and Pansa? Cicero, what is there
left for you in a generation not your own? Now our
day is over.[5]—Cato, in himself the finest model of 2
how to live and how to die, preferred death to begging—and *he* had not Antony to beg; he put into
those hands, clean to the last of Roman blood, a sword
to plunge into his hallowed breast.[6] Scipio, having

Antony (*ibid.*, 196 *seq.*) had introduced their nominees into the
Senate.

[4] For Cicero's friendship with the consuls of 43 B.C., see *C.* 1
pr. 11 n.

[5] Cf. Cic. *ad Brut.* 8.2 Watt.

[6] Cato's suicide after Utica was a frequent theme for
rhetorical eulogy (Sen. *Ep.* 24.6). Particularly close to the
wording of our passage come Sen. *Ep.* 24.7, 67.13; more
generally, *Prov.* 2.9–10.

abdidisset, quaerentibus qui in navem transierant
militibus imperatorem " imperator " inquit " bene
se habet." Victus vocem victoris emisit. " Vetat "
inquis " ⟨me⟩ [1] Milo rogare iudices "; i nunc et
Antonium roga.

3 PORCI LATRONIS. Ergo loquitur umquam Cicero
ut non timeat Antonius, loquitur umquam Antonius
ut Cicero timeat? Civilis sanguinis Sullana sitis
in civitatem redit, et ad triumviralem hastam pro
vectigalibus civium Romanorum mortes locantur;
unius tabellae albo Pharsalica ac Mundensis Mutinen-
sisque ruina vincitur, consularia capita auro repen-
duntur: tuis verbis, Cicero, utendum est: " o
tempora, o mores! " Videbis ardentes crudelitate
simul ac superbia oculos; videbis illum non hominis
sed belli civilis vultum; videbis illas fauces per quas
bona Cn. Pompei transierunt, illa latera, illam totius
corporis gladiatoriam firmitatem; videbis illum pro
tribunali locum quem modo magister equitum, cui
ructare turpe erat, vomitu foedaverat: supplex acca-
dens genibus deprecaberis? Eo ore cui se debet 560M
salus publica humilia in adulationem verba sum-
mittes? Pudeat; Verres quoque proscriptus fortius
perit.

---

[1] *Supplied by Studemund.*

---

[1] For this story about P. Caecilius Metellus Scipio see Livy
Per. 114: declamatory treatment in Sen. *Ep.* 24.9, Val. Max.
3.2.13, *Decl.* p. 420.18 Ritter.
[2] A construction from Cic. *Mil.* 92, 105.
[3] At Rome the levying of taxes was put up for auction:
similarly the property of the proscribed was auctioned to middle-

stabbed himself, said to the soldiers who had boarded his ship to look for the general: " The general is well." Vanquished, he spoke with a victor's voice.[1] —" Milo," said Cicero, " forbids me to beg the judges." [2] Go ahead, beg *Antony*.

PORCIUS LATRO. Does then Cicero ever speak 3 without Antony feeling fear? Does Antony ever speak words that make Cicero feel fear?—Sulla's thirst for citizen blood has returned to the state; at the triumviral auctions the deaths of Romans are put up for sale like revenues.[3] One single notice-board surpasses the disaster of Pharsalus, of Munda, of Mutina. The heads of former consuls are weighed out for gold. One can only employ your own words, Cicero: " What a time! What behaviour! " [4]—You will see eyes ablaze with cruelty and arrogance; you will see not a human face, but the face of civil war; you will see the throat that gulped down the property of Pompey, the flanks, the gladiatorial strength of his whole body; you will see the place on the tribunal which on one occasion the Master of the Horse, for whom a belch would have been a disgrace, polluted with his vomit.[5] Will you fall at *his* feet and beg his pardon? With the lips to which the republic owes its life will you stoop to utter abject flatteries? You should be ashamed; even Verres in exile perished [6] more courageously.

men who would have hoped to make a profit on resale. Cf. esp. Sen. *Marc.* 20.5.

[4] *Cat.* 1.2 and elsewhere (Otto, *Sprichwörter*, 343).

[5] Ciceronian pastiche: see *Phil.* 2.63–4 (add *Verr.* 5.161).

[6] Verres was proscribed by Antony (Plin. *N.H.* 34.6), but died (according to Lact. *Inst. Div.* 2.4.37) later than Cicero.

4   CLAUDI MARCELLI AESERNINI.   Occurrat tibi Cato
tuus, cuius a te laudata mors est; quicquam ergo
tanti putas ut vitam Antonio debeas?

CESTI PII.   Si ad desiderium populi respicis, Cicero,
quandoque perieris parum vixisti; si ad res gestas,
satis vixisti; si ad iniurias Fortunae et praesentem rei
publicae statum, nimium diu vixisti; si ad memoriam
operum tuorum, semper victurus es.

POMPEI SILONIS.   Scias licet tibi non expedire
vivere si Antonius permittit ut vivas.   Tacebis ergo
proscribente Antonio et rem publicam laniante, et
ne gemitus quidem tuus liber erit?   Malo populus
Romanus mortuum Ciceronem quam vivum desideret.

5   TRIARI.   " Quae Charybdis est tam vorax?   Cha-
rybdim dixi, quae, si fuit, animal unum fuit?   Vix
me dius fidius Oceanus tot res tamque diversas uno
tempore absorbere potuisset."   Huic tu saevienti
putas Ciceronem posse subduci?

ARELLI FUSCI patris.   Ab armis ad arma discur-
ritur; foris victores domi trucidamur, domi nostro
sanguini intestinus hostis incubat; quis non hoc populi Romani statu Ciceronem ut vivat cogi putat?
Rogabis, Cicero, turpiter Antonium, ⟨rogabis⟩ ¹ 561M
frustra.   Non te ignobilis tumulus abscondet; ⟨nec⟩ ²

---

¹ *Supplied by Thomas.*
² *Supplied by Madvig.*

---

¹ See Schanz-Hosius, *Gesch. d. röm. Lit.*, 1.335.
² Inspired by Cic. *Marc.* 25, *Phil.* 1.38, *ad Fam.* 10.1.1.
³ Cf. Cic. *Phil.* 2.64.

CLAUDIUS MARCELLUS AESERNINUS. Remember 4
your friend Cato, whose death you praised.[1] Do
you think anything is worth the price of owing your
life to Antony?

CESTIUS PIUS. If you have regard to the sense of
public loss, you have lived too short a life whenever
you die; if to your deeds, you have lived long
enough;[2] if to the insults of fortune and the present
plight of the republic, you have lived too long; if to
the memory of your works, you will live for ever.

POMPEIUS SILO. You should know that it is not
expedient for you to live if it is Antony who gives you
the permission to live.—Will you then keep silent
while Antony carries out his proscriptions and savages
the republic? Will not even your groans be free?[3]—
I prefer the Roman people to feel the lack of Cicero
dead rather than Cicero alive.

TRIARIUS. " What Charybdis is so voracious? 5
Did I say Charybdis? If she existed, she was a single
creature. Scarcely, God help me, could the Ocean
itself have been able to suck down so many diverse
things at a single moment."[4] Do you imagine that
Cicero can be rescued from the fury of a man like that?

ARELLIUS FUSCUS SENIOR. We rush from war to
war. Victors abroad, we are butchered at home, at
home an internal foe battens on our blood. Who does
not think that with the Roman people in such a plight
Cicero is being forced to live?[5]—If you beg Antony,
Cicero, it will be a disgrace for you, and it will be in
vain.—It is no obscure grave that will receive you,

---

[4] From *Phil.* 2.67.
[5] i.e. (if this text is right) Cicero would rather die, and has
to be persuaded to live for the sake of the state.

idem virtutis tuae qui ⟨vitae⟩ [1] finis est.   Immortalis
humanorum operum custos memoria, qua magnis
viris vita perpetua est, in omnia te saecula sacratum
6 dabit; nihil aliud intercidet quam corpus fragilitatis
caducae, morbis obnoxium, casibus expositum,
proscriptionibus obiectum; animus vero divina
origine haustus, cui nec senectus ulla nec mors,
onerosi corporis vinculis exsolutus ad sedes suas et
cognata sidera recurret.   Et tamen, si ad aetatem
annorumque numquam observatum viris fortibus
numerum respicimus, sexaginta supergressus es,
nec potes non videri nimis vixisse qui moreris rei
publicae superstes.   Vidimus furentia toto orbe
civilia arma, et post Italicas Pharsaliasque acies
Romanum sanguinem hausit Aegyptus.   Quid in-
dignamur in Ciceronem Antonio licere quod in
Pompeium Alexandrino licuit spadoni? [2]   Sic occiduntur qui ad indignos confugiunt.
7   CORNELI HISPANI.   Proscriptus est ille qui tuam
sententiam secutus est.   Tota tabula tuae morti
proluditur.   Alter fratrem proscribi, alter avunculum
patitur: quid habes spei?   Ut Cicero periret, tot
parricidia facta sunt.   Repete agedum tot patro-

---

[1] *Supplied by Morgenstern.*
[2] spadoni *Gertz:* adnon *AB:* atnon *V.*

---

[1] Cf. Cic. *Sen.* 82, *Decl.* p. 37.11 Ritter, and for the passage
generally Vell. Pat. 2.66.5.
[2] Cf. Quintilian 12.2.28 (as emended by Stroux).   According
to Stoic belief, human souls, when purged of bodily ills, merged
in the divinity of the universe: see e.g. E. V. Arnold, *Roman
Stoicism* (1911), esp. 268 (with many parallels from Seneca the
philosopher).

nor does your virtue end with your life.[1] Memory, undying guardian of human works, through which great men attain to eternal life, will hand you down to all future generations, sacrosanct. Nothing will 6 die except the body, frail and fleeting, subject to disease, exposed to chance, open to proscription; the soul, which is drawn from divine origins, and knows neither old age nor death, will be freed from the shackles of the body that burdens it and dart back to its home, the stars to which it is akin.[2] And yet, if we look to your age, to the number of years that brave men never count up, you have passed sixty; you can only be thought to have lived too long, when you die a survivor of the republic.—We have seen civil strife raging throughout the world; after the battles in Italy and at Pharsalus, Egypt drained Roman blood. Why are we angry that Antony should have the same power over Cicero that an Alexandrian eunuch[3] had over Pompey? Such is the death of men who take refuge with those undeserving of their trust.

CORNELIUS HISPANUS. The man[4] who followed 7 your lead has been proscribed.—The whole list is but a prelude to your death. One lets his brother be listed, the other his uncle.[5] What hope have *you*? So many parricides committed just so that Cicero should die!—Go over, if you will, all those defences,

---

[3] Achillas, Pompey's killer.

[4] Text doubtful: Hispanus may be referring to the senate.

[5] Antony proscribed his uncle, Lepidus his brother (Vell. Pat. 2.67.3: Flor. 2.16.4). These concessions are represented as having forced Octavian's hand over Cicero (cf. Plut. *Cic.* 46).

cinia, tot clientelas, et maximum beneficiorum tuo- 562M
rum, ⟨consulatum⟩ [1] ipsum: iam intelleges Ciceronem
in mortem cogi posse, in preces non posse.

ARGENTARI. Explicantur triumviralis regni deli-
cata convivia, et popina tributo gentium instruitur;
ipse vino et somno marcidus deficientes oculos ad
capita proscriptorum levat. Iam ad ista non satis
est dicere: " hominem nequam! "

8   DIVISIO. Latro sic hanc divisit suasoriam: etiamsi
impetrare vitam ab Antonio potes, non est tanti
rogare; deinde: impetrare non potes. In priore
illa parte posuit turpe esse cuilibet Romano, nedum
Ciceroni, vitam rogare; hoc loco hominum qui ultro
mortem adprehendissent exempla posuit. Deinde:
vilis [illis] vita [2] futura ⟨est⟩ [3] et morte gravior
detracta libertate. Hic omnem acerbitatem servitutis futurae descripsit. Deinde: non futurum
fidei impetratae beneficium. Hic cum dixisset:
" aliquid erit quod Antonium offendat, aut factum
tuum aut dictum aut silentium aut vultus," adiecit
sententiam: †aut erit† placiturus es.

9   Albucius aliter divisit; primam partem fecit:
moriendum esse Ciceroni, etiamsi nemo proscriberet 563M

---

[1] *Supplied by Linde, Köhler.*
[2] vilis vita *C. F. W. Müller:* utilis (inutilis *V*) illis uita.
[3] *Supplied by Gertz.*

---

[1] Cf. *C.* 9.2.7.   For Antony's gluttony see e.g. *Phil.* 2.69,
3.20.
[2] *Phil.* 2.77.

all those favours to your clients, and—greatest of your services—your consulship itself: then you will see that if Cicero can be made to die, he cannot be made to beg.

ARGENTARIUS. The luxurious banquets of the triumvir kings are set forth, the kitchens equipped with the tribute of the world; he himself, reeling with wine and sleep, raises drooping eyes to the heads of those he proscribed.[1] In face of this it is not now enough to say: " Villain! "[2]

Division

Latro divided this *suasoria* thus: Even if you can 8 win your life from Antony, it is not worth the price. Then: You cannot win it. In the first part he placed the argument that it is shameful for any Roman, let alone Cicero, to beg for his life. Here he adduced examples of men who had sought death voluntarily. Then: Life will be worthless, harder than death, liberty once lost. Here he described all the bitterness of the slavery to come. Next: You will not reap the benefit of any assurance you win from him. Here, after saying: " There will be something to offend Antony, an action on your part, a word, a silence, a look,"[3] he added the epigram: ". . . you will please."

Albucius had a different division. He made the 9 first part: Cicero must die even if nobody proscribed

---

[3] With allusion to Cic. *ad Fam.* 10.1.1. The following epigram is textually uncertain. Seneca may have written *sic placiturus es*: "*That* (i.e. by offending Antony) is the way you will please " (by giving him a pretext to kill you). Cf. *C.*5.2.

eum. Hic insectatio temporum fuit. Deinde: moriendum esse illi sua sponte, quom moriendum esset etiamsi mori noluisset; graves odiorum causas esse; maximam causam proscriptionis ipsum esse Ciceronem. Et solus ex declamatoribus temptavit dicere non unum illi esse Antonium infestum. Hoc loco dixit illam sententiam: " si cui ex triumviris non es invisus, gravis es," et illam sententiam, quae valde excepta est: " roga, Cicero, exora unum, ut tribus servias."

10 Cestius sic divisit: mori tibi utile est, honestum est, necesse est, ut liber et inlibatae dignitatis consummes vitam. Hic illam sententiam dixit audacem: ut numereris cum Catone, qui servire ⟨ne⟩ [1] Antonio quidem nondum domino potuit. Marcellus hunc sensum de Catone melius: usque eone omnia cum fortuna populi Romani conversa sunt ut aliquis deliberet utrum satius sit vivere cum Antonio an mori cum Catone?

Sed ad divisionem Cesti revertamur. Dixit utile esse ne etiam cruciatus corporis pateretur: non simplici illum modo periturum si in Antonii manus [2] incidisset. In hac parte cum descripsisset contumelias insultantium Ciceroni et verbera et tormenta, dixit illam multum laudatam sententiam: tu mehercules, Cicero, cum veneris ad Antonium, mortem rogabis.

11 Varius Geminus sic divisit: hortarer te, si nunc alterutrum utique faciendum esset, aut moriendum

---

[1] *Supplied by Bursian.*
[2] manus *early editors:* manibus.

him. Here came an invective against the times.
Then: He should die of his own volition, seeing that
he had to die even if he did not wish to. There were
weighty reasons for hatred; the greatest cause of the
proscription was Cicero himself. And he alone of the
declaimers tried saying that Antony was not Cicero's
only enemy; it was here that he uttered the well-
known epigram: " Any of the triumvirs who does not
hate you finds you a burden," and the very popular
one: " Ask, Cicero, and beseech one man, only to
become the slave of three."

Cestius' division was as follows: It is expedient for 10
you to die, it is honourable, it is necessary if you are
to crown your life in freedom, dignity unimpaired.
Here he spoke the bold epigram: " That you may be
numbered with Cato, who was incapable of slavery
even before Antony became master." [1] Marcellus
produced a better idea on Cato: " Has everything so
changed along with the fortunes of the Roman people
that there should be debate whether it is better to
live with Antony or die with Cato ? "

But to return to Cestius' division. He said that it
was expedient for Cicero to die so that he should avoid
bodily tortures as well: his death would be no
straightforward one if he fell into the hands of
Antony. In this section, after describing the insults,
blows and tortures to be inflicted by Cicero's mockers,
he spoke the highly praised epigram: " When you
come before Antony, Cicero, you will beg—to die."

Varius Geminus divided· like this: " I should 11
advise you, if you *had* to choose now between death

---

[1] For this (not altogether certain) epigram, cf. §2 ". . . and
he had not Antony to beg."

aut rogandum, ut morereris potius quam rogares; 564㎆
et omnia conplexus est quae a ceteris dicta erant;
sed addidit et tertium; adhortatus est illum ad
fugam: illic esse M. Brutum, illic C. Cassium,
illic Sex. Pompeium. Et adiecit illam sententiam
quam Cassius Severus unice mirabatur: quid de-
ficimus? et res publica suos triumviros habet.
Deinde etiam quas petere posset regiones percu-
currit: Siciliam dixit vindicatam esse ab illo, Cili-
ciam a proconsule egregie administratam, familiares
studiis eius et Achaiam et Asiam, Deiotari regnum
obligatum beneficiis, Aegyptum et habere beneficii
memoriam et agere perfidiae paenitentiam. Sed
maxime illum in Asiam et in Macedoniam hortatus
est in Cassi et in Bruti castra. Itaque Cassius
Severus aiebat alios declamasse, Varium Geminum
vivum consilium dedisse.

12   Alteram partem pauci declamaverunt. Nemo
⟨paene⟩ [1] ausus est Ciceronem ad deprecandum Antonium hortari; bene de Ciceronis animo iudicaverunt. Geminus Varius declamavit alteram quoque partem et ait: Spero me Ciceroni meo persua-
surum ut velit vivere. Quod grandia loquitur et
dicit: "mors nec immatura consulari nec misera
sapienti," non movet · me: idiotam gerit; [2] ego

---

[1] *Supplied by Gertz.*
[2] gerit *Müller:* perit.

and begging pardon, to die rather than beg." And he included all the points made by the other declaimers, adding, however, a third: he exhorted him to flee. Brutus, Cassius and Sextus Pompeius had fled. And he added an epigram particularly admired by Cassius Severus: " Why do we lose heart? The republic too has its triumvirs."[1] Then he ran through all the regions Cicero could make for. Sicily had been avenged by him, Cilicia excellently administered under his governorship; Achaia and Asia were familiar from his student days.[2] Deiotarus' kingdom was bound to him by services rendered, Egypt remembered a benefit conferred—and also repented of an act of treachery.[3] But he especially urged him to go to the camp of Brutus and Cassius in Asia and Macedonia. Thus it was that Cassius Severus used to say that while others had declaimed Varius Geminus had given realistic advice.

Few declaimed the other side. Almost no-one 12 ventured to exhort Cicero to beg pardon of Antony: they had too high an opinion of Cicero's spirit. Varius Geminus declaimed this side as well as the other, saying: " I hope I will persuade my friend Cicero to consent to live. I am not moved by his fine talk, the way he says:[4] ' Death is not early for a former consul nor distressing for a wise man.' He is a private

---

[1] In the Republican leaders just mentioned.

[2] Cicero had prosecuted Verres, the plunderer of Sicily, in 70 B.C., and had been governor of Cilicia in 51 B.C. He had studied oratory in Athens and Asia Minor (*Brut.* 315).

[3] Cicero defended Deiotarus (45 B.C.), and aided Ptolemy Auletes in 56 B.C. Egypt had been the scene of Pompey's murder.

[4] *Cat.* 4.3, with *Phil.* 2.119 (cf. *C.* 7.2.10).

belle mores hominis novi: faciet, rogabit. Nam quod
ad servitutem pertinet, non recusabit; iam collum
tritum habet; et Pompeius illum et Caesar sube-
gerunt: veteranum mancipium videtis. Et com- 565
plura alia dixit scurrilia, ut illi mos erat.

13 Divisit sic ut diceret non turpiter rogaturum, non
frustra rogaturum. In priore parte illud posuit, non
esse turpe civem victorem rogari a victo. Hic quam
multi rogassent C. Caesarem, hic et Ligarium.
Deinde: ne iniquum quidem esse Ciceronem satis
facere, qui prior illum proscripsisset, qui hostem iudi-
casset: a reo semper nasci satisfactionem; audacter
rogaret.[1] Deinde: non pro vita illum, sed pro re
publica rogaturum: satis illum sibi vixisse, rei publicae parum. In sequenti parte dixit exorari solere
inimicos: ipsum exoratum [a][2] Vatinio [Gaio quoque
Verri][3] adfuisse. Facilius exorari Antonium posse,
qui cum tertio esset,[4] ne quis ⟨e⟩[5] tribus hanc tam
speciosam clementiae occasionem praeriperet. Fortasse ei irasci Antonium, qui ne tanti quidem illum
14 putasset quem rogaret. Fuga quam periculosa
esset cum descripsisset, adiecit quocumque pervenisset serviendum illi esse: ferendam esse aut
Cassii violentiam aut Bruti superbiam aut Pompei
stultitiam.

[1] audacter rogaret *Traube:* acda(c)to rogari.
[2] *Deleted by Müller.*
[3] *Deleted by the editor as an ill-informed gloss.*
[4] *This clause is very doubtful.*
[5] *Supplied by Faber.*

---

[1] Cf. Quintilian 3.8.46.

citizen now. *I* am pretty sure of the character of the man; he will do it, he will beg pardon. As to slavery, he will not refuse it; his neck is already worn— Pompey and Caesar have broken him in: you see before you an experienced slave." And, as usual, he had many other jeers to make.

His division was: if Cicero were to beg pardon, he 13 would do so with honour and with success. In the first section he placed the point that there is nothing shameful in the defeated begging pardon of a victorious fellow-citizen. Here he observed how many had begged pardon of Julius Caesar, for instance Ligarius. Nor, again, was it unfair that Cicero should make amends: he had been the first to proscribe Antony and dub him public enemy. Making amends should always start with the man on the defensive; let Cicero pluck up his courage—and ask. Again, he would not be pleading for his own life but for the republic.[1] He had lived long enough for himself—but not long enough for Rome. In the second section he said enemies are often won over; Cicero had been won over and had defended Vatinius.[2] Antony could be won over more easily; being only one of three, he would not want one of the other two to snatch from him so splendid an opportunity for clemency. Perhaps Antony was angry with Cicero for not thinking him worth begging. He described 14 how dangerous flight was, adding that Cicero must be a slave wherever he went: he had to put up with either Cassius' violence, Brutus' hauteur or Pompey's stupidity.

[2] For Cicero's speeches for and against Vatinius see Quintilian 11.1.73.

Quoniam in hanc suasoriam incidimus, non alienum puto indicare quomodo quisque se ex historicis 566N adversus memoriam Ciceronis gesserit. Nam, quin Cicero nec tam timidus fuerit ut rogaret Antonium nec tam stultus ut exorari posse eum speraret nemo dubitat, excepto Asinio Pollione, qui infestissimus famae Ciceronis permansit. Et is etiam occasionem scholasticis alterius suasoriae dedit; solent enim scholastici declamitare: deliberat Cicero an salutem promittente Antonio orationes suas comburat. Haec
15 inepte ficta cuilibet videri potest. Pollio vult illam veram videri; ita enim dixit in ea oratione quam pro Lamia edidit. ASINI POLLIONIS. Itaque numquam per Ciceronem mora fuit quin eiuraret suas [esse][1] quas cupidissime effuderat orationes in Antonium; multiplicesque numero et accuratius scriptas illis contrarias edere ac vel ipse palam pro contione recitare pollicebatur; adiecratque[2] his alia sordidiora multo, ut [tibi][3] facile liqueret hoc totum adeo falsum esse ut ne ipse quidem Pollio in historiis suis ponere ausus sit. Huic certe actioni eius pro Lamia qui interfuerunt, negant eum haec dixisse—nec enim mentiri sub triumvirorum conscientia sustinebat—sed postea conposuisse.
16 Nolo autem vos, iuvenes mei, contristari quod a declamatoribus ad historicos transeo: satis faciam

---

[1] *Deleted by Müller.*
[2] adiecratque *C. F. W. Müller:* ceteraque.
[3] *Deleted by Brakman.*

Since I have happened on this theme, it's not, I think, irrelevant to point out how each of the historians showed up in treating the memory of Cicero. All concede that Cicero was neither coward enough to plead with Antony, nor stupid enough to hope that Antony could be won over: all, that is, except Asinius Pollio,[1] who remained the most implacable enemy of Cicero's reputation. And he actually gave the schoolmen a handle for a second *suasoria*—for they often declaim on the theme: " Cicero deliberates whether to burn his speeches on Antony's promising him his life." [2] Anyone must realise that this is a crude fiction. Pollio wants to make us think it the truth. For this is what he said in his published speech for Lamia: " Thus Cicero never hesitated to go back on his passionate outpourings against Antony; he promised to produce, more carefully, many times more speeches in the opposite sense, and even to recite them personally at a public meeting." This together with other things much more shabby: from which it was quite clear that the whole was false —in fact even Pollio himself did not venture to find a place for it in his history. Indeed eye-witnesses of his speech for Lamia assert that he didn't say these things, not being prepared to lie when the triumvirs could show him up, but composed them later.

However, my dear young men, I don't want you to get depressed because I am passing from declamation to history. I will make amends to you:[3] though I

---

[1] For Pollio and Cicero see Quintilian 12.1.22 with Austin's n.

[2] See *S.* 7.

[3] i.e. by returning to declamation: see the end of this *suasoria*.

vobis. Sed [1] fortasse efficiam ut his sententiis lectis
solidis et verum habentibus ⟨robur a scholasticis⟩ [2]
recedatis; et, quia hoc [si tam] [3] recta via consequi   567M
non potero, decipere vos cogar, velut salutarem
daturus pueris potionem. Sumite pocula.

T. Livius [4] adeo retractationis consilium habuisse
Ciceronem non dicit ut neget tempus habuisse; ita
17 enim ait. T. LIVI. M. Cicero sub adventum triumvirorum urbe cesserat, pro certo habens, id quod erat,
non magis Antonio eripi se quam Caesari Cassium
et Brutum posse; primo in Tusculanum fugerat,
inde transversis itineribus in Formianum ut ab Caieta
navem conscensurus proficiscitur. Unde aliquotiens
in altum provectum cum modo venti adversi ret-
tulissent, modo ipse iactationem navis caeco volvente
fluctu pati non posset, taedium tandem eum et fugae
et vitae cepit, regressusque ad superiorem villam,
quae paulo plus mille passibus a mari abest, " moriar "
inquit " in patria saepe servata." Satis constat
servos fortiter fideliterque paratos fuisse ad dimi-
candum; ipsum deponi lecticam et quietos pati
quod sors iniqua cogeret iussisse. Prominenti ex
lectica praebentique inmotam cervicem caput prae-
cisum est. Nec ⟨id⟩ [5] satis stolidae crudelitati   568M
militum fuit: manus quoque scripsisse aliquid in

[1] sed *Gertz*: et.
[2] *Supplied by Castiglioni after Bursian.*
[3] *Deleted by the editor.*
[4] Sumite pocula. T. Livius *Müller:* sum(p)ti poculi
(populi *AB*) huius.
[5] *Supplied by Müller.*

may perhaps make you give up the schoolmen once
you've read these solid and truly powerful sentiments.
And, as I shan't be able to bring this about straight-
forwardly, I shall have to deceive you, like someone
wanting to give medicine to a child. Take up your
glasses.[1]

Livy is so far from saying that Cicero planned to
retract that he asserts he had not time to do so. This
is what he says:[2] " Marcus Cicero had left the city at 17
the approach of the triumvirs, rightly regarding it as
certain that he could no more be rescued from
Antony than Cassius and Brutus from Caesar.[3] First
he had fled to his estate at Tusculum, then cross-
country to his house at Formiae, intending to take
ship at Caieta. He put out to sea several times, but
sometimes the winds were against him and forced him
back, sometimes he himself could not put up with the
tossing of the vessel as it rolled on the dark ground-
swell. Finally he grew weary of flight and of life,
and, returning to the inland villa, which is little more
than a mile from the sea, he said: ' I shall die in the
country I so often saved.' There is no doubt that his
slaves bravely and loyally showed readiness to make a
fight of it; and that it was Cicero himself who ordered
them to put down the litter and suffer calmly the
compulsions of a harsh fate. He leaned from where
he sat, and offered his neck without a tremor; his
head was struck off. The soldiers, in their stupid
cruelty, were not satisfied. They cut off the hands,

[1] Cf. Lucr. 1.936–8 = 4.11–13.
[2] For accounts of Cicero's death see C. 7.2 n.
[3] i.e. Octavian, who, with Antony, defeated Brutus and
Cassius at Philippi.

Antonium exprobrantes praeciderunt. Ita relatum caput ad Antonium iussuque eius inter duas manus in rostris positum, ubi ille consul, ubi saepe consularis, ubi eo ipso anno adversus Antonium quanta nulla umquam humana vox cum admiratione eloquentiae auditus fuerat; vix attollentes lacrimis oculos humentes intueri truncata membra cives [1] poterant.

18 Bassus Aufidius et ipse nihil de animo Ciceronis dubitavit, quin fortiter se morti non praebuerit tantum sed obtulerit. AUFIDI BASSI. Cicero paulum remoto velo postquam armatos vidit, " ego vero consisto," ait; " accede, veterane, et, si hoc saltim potes recte facere, incide cervicem." Trementi deinde dubitantique: " quid si ad me " inquit " primum venissetis? "

19 Cremutius Cordus et ipse ait Ciceronem secum cogitasse utrumne Brutum an Cassium an Sex. Pompeium peteret; omnia illi displicuisse praeter mortem. CREMUTI CORDI. Quibus visis laetus Antonius, cum peractam proscriptionem suam dixisset esse, quippe non satiatus modo caedendis civibus sed differtus quoque, super rostra exponit. Itaque, quo saepius ille ingenti circumfusus turba processerat, quam [2] paulo ante coluerat piis contionibus, quibus multorum capita servaverat, ⟨eo⟩ [3] tum per artus sublatus [4] aliter ac solitus erat a civibus suis conspectus est, praependenti capiti orique eius inspersa 569

---

[1] cives *C. F. W. Müller:* ciuis.
[2] quam *ed.:* quae.
[3] *Supplied by Gertz.*
[4] sublatus *Gertz:* suos latus.

too, cursing them for having written attacks on Antony. The head was taken back to Antony, and, on his orders, placed between the two hands on the rostra, where as consul, and often as ex-consul, and in that very year attacking Antony, he had been heard amid such admiration for his eloquence as had rewarded no other human voice.[1] The Romans could scarcely bear to lift eyes wet with tears to look on his mutilated body."

Aufidius Bassus, too, had no doubts of the spirit of 18 Cicero: he was convinced that he had had the courage to expose and indeed to offer himself to death. "Cicero drew aside the curtain a little, and seeing the armed men said: '*I* am stopping here; approach, soldier, and if you can do *this* [2] properly cut off my head.' Then, as the soldier trembled and hesitated: 'What if you had come to me first?'"[3]

Cremutius Cordus, too, said Cicero pondered 19 whether to make for Brutus, Cassius or Sextus Pompeius—but only death found favour with him. "Seeing this Antony was glad. He said that his proscription was over, for he was sated, and indeed stuffed full of citizen blood; and he displayed Cicero on the rostra. And so, in the place to which he had so often gone, surrounded by a vast throng, which he had shortly before courted with the patriotic speeches that had been the salvation of so many, he was now raised, limb by limb, to be viewed by his fellow countrymen in a new state, blood spattered over his

---

[1] Cf. Juv. 10.120, with Mayor's notes.
[2] There being nothing proper (*rectum*) about assassination, the actual cut should be properly (*recte*) made.
[3] i.e. what if I had been your first victim?

sanie, brevi ante princeps senatus Romanique nominis titulus, tum pretium interfectoris sui. Praecipue tamen solvit pectora omnium in lacrimas gemi-
tusque visa ad caput eius deligata manus dextera,
divinae eloquentiae ministra; ceterorumque caedes
privatos luctus excitaverunt, illa una communem.

20 BRUTTEDI NIGRI. Elapsus interim altera parte
villae Cicero lectica per agros ferebatur; sed, ut
vidit adpropinquare notum sibi militem, Popillium
nomine, memor defensum a se laetiore vultu aspexit.
At ille victoribus id ipsum imputaturus occupat
facinus, caputque decisum nihil in ultimo fine vitae
facientis quod alterutram in partem posset notari
Antonio portat, oblitus se paulo ante defensum ab
illo. Et hic voluit positi in rostris capitis miserabilem faciem describere, sed magnitudine rei obrutus
21 est: [Bruttedi Nigri][1] Ut vero iussu Antonii inter
duas manus positum in rostris caput conspectum est,
quo totiens auditum erat loco, datae gemitu et
fletu maximo viro inferiae, nec, ut solet, vitam de-
positi in rostris corporis contio audivit sed ipsa
narravit. Nulla non pars fori aliquo actionis inclutae
signata vestigio erat; nemo non aliquod eius in se
meritum fatebatur: hoc certe publicum beneficium

---

[1] *Deleted by C. F. W. Müller, Morgenstern.*

lips and lolling head. Shortly before, he had been leader of the senate, glory of the Roman name: now he was merely a source of profit to his killer. What most set men weeping and wailing was the sight of his right hand, tied by the side of his head: the hand that had been the servant of that god-like eloquence. The murder of the others provoked private grief— this alone excited public mourning."

BRUTTEDIUS NIGER. " Meanwhile, slipping out at 20 the other side of the villa, Cicero was borne through the fields in a litter. But when he saw approaching him a soldier he knew, Popillius, his countenance lightened, for he remembered defending him in court. The soldier, however, proposing to make this a further point in his favour with the victors, wasted no time in committing his crime. Cicero, at this last moment of his life, did nothing that could be censured one way or the other. His head was cut off, and carried to Antony by the soldier, who forgot that Cicero had defended him shortly before." Bruttedius, too, wanted to enlarge on the pitiful appearance of the head on the rostra, but he was overcome by the magnitude of the task. " But when, on Antony's orders, 21 the head was placed for public viewing between the two hands on the rostra, where it had so often been heard, the great man was given his funeral offerings in groans and tears. The assembled people did not, as is customary, hear the biography of the body on the rostra, but *they* narrated it. Every part of the forum was marked by the memory of some glorious pleading; everyone had a benefit done him by Cicero to proclaim. There was no doubt of at least one service to Rome: he had put off that miserable

palam erat, illam miserrimi temporis servitutem a
Catilina dilatam in Antonium.

Quotiens magni alicuius ⟨viri⟩ [1] mors ab historicis 570M
narrata est, totiens fere consummatio totius vitae
et quasi funebris laudatio redditur. Hoc, semel aut
iterum a Thucydide factum, item in paucissimis
personis usurpatum a Sallustio, T. Livius benignus
omnibus magnis viris praestitit; sequentes historici
multo id effusius fecerunt. Ciceroni hoc, ut Graeco
22 verbo utar, ἐπιτάφιον Livius reddit. T. Livi.
Vixit tres et sexaginta annos, ut, si vis afuisset, ne
inmatura quidem mors videri possit. Ingenium et
operibus et praemiis operum felix, ipse fortunae diu
prosperae; sed in longo tenore felicitatis magnis
interim ictus vulneribus, exilio, ruina partium pro
quibus steterat, filiae morte, exitu tam tristi atque
acerbo, omnium adversorum nihil ut viro dignum erat
tulit praeter mortem, quae vere aestimanti minus
indigna videri potuit, quod a victore inimico ⟨nihil⟩ [2]
crudelius passus erat quam quod eiusdem fortunae
conpos ipse [3] fecisset. Si quis tamen virtutibus vitia
pensarit, vir magnus ac memorabilis fuit et in cuius
laudes exequendas Cicerone laudatore opus fuerit.
Ut est natura candidissimus omnium magnorum
ingeniorum aestimator T. Livius, plenissimum Ciceroni testimonium reddidit.

23 Cordi Cremuti non est operae pretium referre 571M
redditam Ciceroni laudationem; nihil enim in ea
Cicerone dignum est, ac ne hoc quidem, quod [paene] [4]

---

[1] *Supplied by Gronovius.*
[2] *Supplied by Müller.*
[3] conpos ipse *Lipsius:* conposito.
[4] *Deleted by the editor after Müller.*

servitude from the time of Catiline to that of
Antony."

Whenever historians relate the death of a great
man, they almost invariably give a summary of his
whole life and pronounce a kind of funeral eulogy.
This was done once or twice by Thucydides,[1] and
Sallust observed the practice in the case of a very few
personages. The generous Livy bestowed it on all
great men. Later historians have been much more
lavish. Here is—to use the Greek word—Livy's
" epitaph " on Cicero: " He lived sixty-three years: 22
so that if no force had been brought to bear his end
could not be thought premature. His genius was
fortunate in its works and their rewards; he himself
long enjoyed good luck. But during the long flow of
success he was from time to time afflicted with great
wounds, exile, the collapse of his party, the death of
his daughter and his own grievous and bitter end.
Yet of all these disasters he faced none but his death
as becomes a man: and even that to a truthful critic
might have seemed the less undeserved in that he
suffered at the hands of his victorious enemy no more
cruelly than he would have acted had he himself
enjoyed that good fortune. But, weighing his virtues
against his faults, he was a great and memorable man:
and to sing his praises one would need a Cicero for
eulogist." Livy, naturally the most fair-minded
judge of all great genius, gave Cicero his full meed of
praise.

It is not worth recording the eulogy accorded to 23
Cicero by Cremutius Cordus; nothing in it is worthy

---

[1] e.g. Pericles (2.65). For Sallust, see R. Syme, *Sallust*, 196.
For e.g. Tacitus, see Syme, *Tacitus*, 313.

maxime tolerabile est. CREMUTI CORDI. Proprias enim simultates deponendas interdum putabat, publicas numquam vi exercendas:[1] civis non solum magnitudine virtutum sed multitudine quoque conspiciendus. AUFIDI BASSI. Sic M. Cicero decessit, vir natus ad rei publicae salutem, quae diu defensa et administrata in senectute demum e manibus eius elabitur, hoc[2] ipsius vitio laesa, quod nihil in salutem eius aliud illi quam si caruisset Antonio placuit. Vixit sexaginta et tres annos, ita ut semper aut peteret alterum aut invicem peteretur, nullamque rem rarius quam diem illum quo nullius interesset ipsum mori vidit.

24   Pollio quoque Asinius, qui Verrem, Ciceronis reum, fortissime morientem tradidit, Ciceronis mortem solus ex omnibus maligne narrat, testimonium tamen quamvis invitus plenum ei reddidit. ASINI POLLIONIS. Huius ergo viri tot tantisque operibus mansuris in omne aevum praedicare de ingenio atque industria supervacuum ⟨est⟩.[3] Natura autem atque Fortuna pariter obsecuta est ei, si quidem facies decora ad senectutem prosperaque permansit valetudo; tum pax diutina, cuius instructus erat artibus, contigit; namque ad priscam severitatem iudiciis exactis maxima noxiorum multitudo provenit, quos 572M obstrictos patrocinio incolumes plerosque habebat; iam felicissima consulatus ei sors petendi et gerendi magno munere[4] deum, consilio ⟨suo⟩[5] industriaque.

---

[1] vi exercendas *Gertz, Müller:* uides credendam.
[2] hoc *Gertz:* non.
[3] supervacuum est *Schott:* superba.
[4] magno munere *Müller:* magna munera.
[5] *Supplied by Shackleton Bailey.*

of Cicero, not even this, which is more tolerable than the rest: " Private differences he thought should sometimes be laid aside: public ones should never be worked out by force. He was a citizen conspicuous alike for the greatness and the number of his virtues."

AUFIDIUS BASSUS. " So died Cicero, a man born to save the state. Long did he defend and administer it; then in his old age it finally slipped from his grasp, shattered by this personal mistake—his policy that it could only be saved if Antony were got rid of. He lived for sixty-three years, always attacking another or himself under attack; no sight was rarer for him than a day on which his death was in no-one's interest."

Asinius Pollio, too, who recorded the brave death 24 of Cicero's victim, Verres, is the only historian to relate Cicero's death in a carping tone; yet, however unwillingly, he gave him full praise. " This man's works, so many and so fine, will last for ever; and there is no need to pronounce on his genius and his industry. Nature and fortune smiled alike on him; for good looks and good health remained with him to old age. Further a long period of peace,[1] in whose arts he was well equipped, came his way. The forms of law were being enforced with antique vigour, and there was a great crop of guilty men, many of whom he defended successfully and so bound to himself. Thanks to the great favour of the gods and his own wisdom and energy, he was very fortunate in his candidature for and administration of the consulship.

---

[1] Between Sulla and the civil wars.

Utinam moderatius secundas res et fortius adversas
ferre potuisset! Namque utraeque cum evenerant
ei, mutari eas non posse rebatur. Inde sunt in-
vidiae tempestates coortae graves in eum certiorque
inimicis adgrediendi fiducia; maiore enim simultates adpetebat animo quam gerebat. Sed quando
mortalium nulli virtus perfecta contigit, qua maior
pars vitae atque ingenii stetit, ea iudicandum de
homine est. Atque ego ne miserandi quidem exitus
eum fuisse iudicarem, nisi ipse tam miseram mortem
25 putasset. Adfirmare vobis possum nihil esse in
historiis eius hoc quem rettuli loco disertius, ut mihi
tunc non laudasse Ciceronem sed certasse cum
Cicerone videatur. Nec hoc deterrendi causa dico
ne historias eius legere concupiscatis; concupiscite
et poenas Ciceroni dabitis.

Nemo tamen ex tot disertissimis viris melius
Ciceronis mortem deploravit quam Severus Cornelius.

26   CORNELI SEVERI

oraque magnanimum spirantia paene virorum
in rostris iacuere suis; sed enim abstulit omnis,
tamquam sola foret, rapti Ciceronis imago.
tunc redeunt animis ingentia consulis acta

---

[1] For (apparently) Pollio's malice elsewhere. But the
phrase is very strange (it should mean: " Cicero will punish
you ").

Would that he could have shown more temperateness
in prosperity, more stoutness in adversity! For when
either had befallen him, he could not visualise their
ever changing. Hence storm-clouds of hatred
gathered heavily over him, giving his enemies the
more confidence in their attacks on him—for he displayed more spirit in picking quarrels than in carrying
them through. But it has fallen to no mortal to be
perfectly virtuous: one must judge of a man in
accordance with the greater part of his life and
character. Indeed, *I* should not judge him as having
even met an end to be pitied, were it not that *he*
thought death so pitiable." I am ready to swear to 25
you that there is nothing in his history more eloquent
than the passage I have cited; Pollio, I think, here
not merely praises Cicero—he rivals him. I do not say
this to deter you from a strong desire to read his history.
Desire to do so—and you will make amends to Cicero.[1]

But none of all these eloquent men lamented the
death of Cicero more finely than Cornelius Severus:[2]

" The heads of great-hearted men, still almost 26
  breathing,
    Lay on the rostra that were theirs:[3] but all were
      swept away
    By the sight of the ravaged Cicero, as though he
      lay alone.
    Then they recalled the great deeds of his consul-
      ship,

[2] Morel, *Frag. poet. Lat.*, 118–19. Full commentary in
H. Homeyer, *Annales univ. Saraviensis (phil. Fak.)* 10 (1961),
327–34. Compare especially Cremutius Cordus in §19 above.
[3] Cf. Florus 2.16.

THE ELDER SENECA

iurataeque manus deprensaque foedera noxae
patriciumque nefas extinctum:[1] poena Cethegi   573M
deiectusque redit votis Catilina nefandis.
quid favor aut coetus, pleni quid honoribus anni
profuerant? sacris exculta quid artibus aetas?
abstulit una dies aevi decus, ictaque luctu
conticuit Latiae tristis facundia linguae.
unica sollicitis quondam tutela salusque,
egregium semper patriae caput, ille senatus
vindex, ille fori, legum ritusque togaeque,
publica vox saevis aeternum obmutuit armis.
informes voltus sparsamque cruore nefando
canitiem sacrasque manus operumque ministras
tantorum pedibus civis proiecta superbis
proculcavit ovans nec lubrica fata deosque
respexit.   nullo luet hoc Antonius aevo.
hoc nec in Emathio mitis victoria Perse
nec te, dire Syphax, non fecit ⟨in⟩ hoste Philippo;
inque triumphato ludibria cuncta Iugurtha
afuerunt, nostraeque cadens ferus Hannibal irae
membra tamen Stygias tulit inviolata sub umbras.

---

[1] extinctum *Gronovius:* est tunc.

---

[1] The conspiracy of Catiline (63 B.C.), in which Cethegus was involved.

The conspiracy, the wicked plot he uncovered,
The aristocrat's crime he smothered;[1] they recalled
Cethegus' punishment, Catiline cast down from his
impious hopes.
What availed his popularity with the mob, his years
Full of honour, his life adorned by sacred arts?
One day took away the glory of an age, and struck
by grief
The eloquence of the Latin tongue grew dumb with
sadness.
Once the sole guard and saviour of the distressed,
Always the glorious leader of his country, champion
Of the senate, bar, laws, ritual, civil life,
Voice of the public—now silenced for ever by cruel
arms.
The defaced countenance, white hairs horribly
sprinkled
With blood, the sacred hands, that had served such
great works,
His countryman threw down and trampled with
haughty feet,
In triumph, not thinking of fate's slipperiness
Or the gods. Antony will never pay in full for this.
Victory was kind, and never did such a thing
To Emathian Perses, dire Syphax or our enemy
Philip.[2]
When Jugurtha was led in triumph, there was
No mockery, and when fierce Hannibal fell to our
wrath
He took unharmed limbs down to the shades of
Styx."

[2] For these defeated enemies of Rome, see Index of Names.
With the whole context, cf. Juv. 10.286-8.

27   Non fraudabo municipem nostrum bono versu, ex 574M
quo hic multo melior Severi Cornelii processit:

> conticuit Latiae tristis facundia linguae.

Sextilius Ena fuit homo ingeniosus magis quam
eruditus, inaequalis poeta et plane quibusdam locis
talis quales esse Cicero Cordubenses poetas ait,
⟨pingue⟩ quiddam sonantis atque peregrinum. Is
hanc ipsam proscriptionem recitaturus in domo
Messalae Corvini Pollionem Asinium advocaverat et
in principio hunc versum non sine assensu recitavit:

> deflendus Cicero est Latiaeque silentia linguae.

Pollio Asinius non aequo animo tulit et ait: " Messala,
tu quid tibi liberum sit in domo tua videris; ego istum
auditurus non sum, cui mutus videor," atque ita
consurrexit. Enae interfuisse recitationi Severum
quoque Cornelium scio, cui non aeque displicuisse
hunc versum quam Pollioni apparet, quod meliorem
quidem sed non dissimilem illi et ipse conposuit.

Si hic desiero, scio futurum ut vos illo loco desinatis
legere quo ego a scholasticis recessi; ergo, ut librum
velitis usque ad umbilicum revolvere, adiciam suasoriam proximae [1] similem.

---

[1] *Warmington suggests* proxime *or* suasoriae proximam
similem.

I shall not deprive my fellow townsman of the credit 27
for a good line that gave rise to the even better one
by Cornelius Severus:

" The eloquence of the Latin tongue grew dumb
    with sadness."

Sextilius Ena was a man of talent rather than learning,
an uneven poet, and in some passages very like the
poets of Corduba as described by Cicero,[1] with " a
thick and foreign tone." Proposing to recite on the
subject of this same proscription in the house of
Messala Corvinus, he had invited Asinius Pollio. And
he started his recital with a line that was greeted with
some applause:

" I must lament Cicero and the silence of the Latin
    tongue."

Asinius Pollio did not take this lying down. He said:
" Messala, *you* can decide for yourself what goes on
in your own house; *I* do not propose to listen to
someone who thinks I am dumb "—and he immediately got up. I know that Cornelius Severus was
also present at Ena's recitation; and it's obvious that
he didn't dislike the line as much as Pollio, seeing that
he composed a similar, though better, line himself.

If I stop at this point, I know *you* will stop reading
where *I* abandoned the schoolmen;[2] so, to encourage
you to unwind the book right to the end of the roll, I
shall append a *suasoria* on a subject related to its
neighbour.

[1] *Arch.* 26.
[2] i.e. at §16.

VII

Deliberat Cicero an scripta sua conburat,
promittente Antonio incolumitatem si fecisset.

1 Q. Hateri. Non feres Antonium; intolerabilis in 575M
malo ingenio felicitas est nihilque cupientis magis
accendit quam prosperae turpitudinis conscientia.
Difficile est; non feres, inquam, et iterum inritare
inimicum in mortem tuam cupies. Quod ad me
quidem pertinet, multum a Cicerone absum; tamen
non taedet tantum me vitae meae sed pudet. Ne
propter hoc quidem ingenium tuum amas, quod illud
Antonius plus odit quam te? Remittere ait se tibi
ut vivas, commentus quemadmodum eripiat etiam
quod vixeras. Crudelior est pactio Antonii quam
proscriptio. Ingenium erat in quod nihil iuris habe-
rent triumviralia arma. Commentus est Antonius
quemadmodum, quod non poterat cum Cicerone
⟨proscribi, a Cicerone⟩ [1] proscriberetur. Hortarer
te, Cicero, ut vitam magni aestimares si libertas suum
haberet in civitate locum, si suum in libertate eloquentia, si non civili ense cervicibus luderetur; [2] nunc,
ut scias nihil esse melius quam mori, vitam tibi Antonius promittit. Pendet nefariae proscriptionis
tabula: tot praetorii, tot consulares, tot equestris
ordinis viri periere; nemo relinquitur nisi qui servire

[1] *Supplied by Müller, following Bursian.*
[2] luderetur *Bornecque:* luerentur.

7

QUINTUS HATERIUS.   You will not be able to put up   1
with Antony.   In an evil personality prosperity cannot be borne; nothing provokes the greedy more
than the realisation that their baseness is bearing
fruit.   It is difficult: you will not be able to put up
with him, I repeat, and you will long to goad your
enemy a second time to kill you.—As for me, I am far
from being Cicero: but *I* am ashamed of life as well as
tired of it.—Does not the fact that Antony hates your
genius more than he hates you make you love it the
more?—He says he gives you your life—but he has
found a way of stealing even your past from you.
Antony's bargain is more cruel than his proscription.
It was your genius against which the weapons of the
triumvirs were powerless.   Antony has devised a way
of making Cicero proscribe what could not be proscribed along with Cicero.—I should advise you,
Cicero, to rate your life high if freedom held its proper
place in the state, if eloquence held its proper place in
a free community, if our necks were not the sport
of our countrymen's swords.   As it is, Antony is
promising you your life—so you may be sure that
nothing is preferable to death.   There hangs the
notice proclaiming this wicked proscription: so many
ex-praetors, so many ex-consuls, so many men of
equestrian rank have died; no-one is left except those

[1] See *S.* 6 n., with *S.* 6.14.

THE ELDER SENECA

possit. Nescio an hoc tempore vivere velis, Cicero; nemo est cum quo velis. Merito hercules illo tempore vixisti quo Caesar ultro te rogavit ut viveres sine ulla pactione, quo tempore non quidem stabat res publica, sed in boni principis sinum ceciderat. 576M

2 CESTI PII. Numquid opinio me fefellit? Intellexit Antonius salvis eloquentiae monumentis non posse Ciceronem mori. Ad pactionem vocaris, qua pactione melior ante ⟨te⟩[1] pars tui petitur. Adcommoda mihi paulisper eloquentiam ⟨tuam⟩;[2] Ciceronem periturum rogo. Si te audissent Caesar et Pompeius, neque inissent turpem societatem neque diremissent; si uti umquam consilio tuo voluissent, neque Pompeius Caesar⟨em⟩ aluisset neque Pompeium violasset Caesar⟩.[3] Quid ⟨referam⟩[4] consulatum salutarem urbi, quid exilium consulatu honestius, quid provocatam inter initia adulescentiae libertate tirocinii tui Sullanam potentiam, quid Antonium avulsum ⟨a⟩[5] Catilina, rei publicae redditum? Ignosce, Cicero, ⟨si⟩[6] diu ista narravero: forsitan hoc die novissime audiuntur.

3 Si occidetur Cicero, iacebit inter Pompeium patrem

[1] ante te *Gertz:* inte.
[2] *Supplied by Schultingh.*
[3] *Supplied by Shackleton Bailey.*
[4] *Supplied by Müller.*
[5] *Supplied by Gronovius.*
[6] *Supplied by Schott.*

---

[1] Cf. Haterius in *S.* 6.1.
[2] After Pharsalus.

capable of being slaves. I do not know, Cicero, if you want to live at this time; no-one remains *with* whom you would wish to live.[1] You were surely right to decide to live when Caesar, without being begged, asked you to live, no terms laid down.[2] That was at a time when the republic was not standing, I agree— but at least it had fallen into the lap of a good master.

CESTIUS PIUS. Is my judgement at fault? Antony 2 has realised that so long as the products of Cicero's eloquence survive, Cicero cannot die. You are invited to come to terms, terms by which the better part of yourself is assaulted before you are. Lend me, for a while, your own eloquence: the Cicero I beg is doomed.—If Caesar and Pompey had listened to you, they would not have entered on their shameful alliance—or broken it;[3] if they had ever been ready to take your advice, Pompey would not have succoured Caesar, Caesar would not have done outrage to Pompey.—I need hardly speak of your consulship that saved the city, of your exile that was yet more honourable than your consulship, of the challenge to the dominance of Sulla that you offered in your extreme youth by the outspokenness of your earliest speeches,[4] of how Antonius was torn from Catiline and restored to the cause of the republic.[5] Forgive me, Cicero, if it takes a long time to narrate these events: perhaps today they are heard for the last time of all.—If Cicero is killed, he will lie alongside 3

[3] So Cicero claims (*Phil.* 2.24).
[4] Especially the *pro Roscio Amerino*, where Cicero attacks a favourite of Sulla's (80 B.C.).
[5] C. Antonius.

filiumque et Afranium, Petreium, Q. Catulum, M.
Antonium illum indignum hoc successore generis;
si servabitur, vivet inter Ventidios et Canidios et
Saxas: ita dubium est utrum satius sit cum illis iacere 577M
an cum his vivere? Pro uno homine iactura publica
pacisceris. Scio omne pretium iniquum esse quod
ille constituit: non emo tanti Ciceronis vitam quanti
vendit Antonius. Si hanc tibi pactionem ferret:
vives, sed eruentur oculi tibi, vives, sed debilita-
buntur pedes: etiamsi in alia damna corporis
praestares patientiam, excepisses tamen linguam.
Ubi est sacra illa vox tua: " mori enim naturae finis
est, non poena "? Hoc tibi uni non liquet? At
videris Antonio persuasisse. Adsere te potius
libertati et unum crimen inimico adice: fac moriendo
Antonium nocentiorem.

4   P. Asprenatis. Ut Antonius Ciceroni parcat,
Cicero in eloquentiam suam ipse animadvertet?
Quid autem tibi sub ista pactione promittitur? ut
Cn. Pompeius et M. Cato et ille antiquos resti-
tuatur rei publicae senatus, dignissimus apud quem
Cicero loqueretur? Multos care victuros animi
pusilli [1] contemptus oppressit; multos perituros
parati ad pereundum animi ipsa admiratio eripuit
et causa illis vivendi fuit fortiter mori. Permitte

---

[1] pusilli *C. F. W. Müller:* sui.

---

[1] Cf. Cestius in *S.* 6.10.

Pompey, father and son, Afranius, Petreius, Catulus,
Marcus Antonius (who did not deserve such a suc-
cessor to his name); if he is reprieved, he will live
alongside men like Ventidius, Canidius and Saxa.
Can there then be any doubt whether it is preferable
to lie dead with those or live with these? [1]—You are
purchasing the life of one man at the cost of a public
loss.—I know that any price fixed by that man is
unfair; I am not prepared to buy Cicero's life at a
price asked by Antony. If these were the terms he
offered: " You shall live—but your eyes will be
gouged out: you shall live—but your feet will be
crippled "—even if you were ready to tolerate other
mutilations, you would have made an exception of
your tongue. What has become of that revered
phrase of yours: " For to die is the end granted by
nature, not a punishment "? [2] Are *you* the only man
who does not realise its obvious truth? You may
think you have persuaded Antony. Claim your freedom, rather, and let your enemy have one crime the
more; die—and make Antony the guiltier.[3]

Publius Asprenas. That Antony may spare Cicero, 4
is Cicero to execute his own eloquence?—What do
you get out of this agreement? The restoration of
Pompey and Cato and the old senate of republican
days, worthiest audience for Cicero?—Many who
have been prepared to pay a high price for their lives
have been crushed by those who despised their lack
of spirit; many on the point of death have been
rescued by the very admiration felt for a brave man
ready to perish—they lived because they faced death

[2] *Mil.* 101.
[3] Cf. *C.* 9.4.10 n.

populo Romano contra Antonium liceri. ⟨Si⟩ [1]
scripta combusseris, Antonius paucos annos tibi
promittit: at, si non combusseris, [quam] populus
Romanus [2] omnes.

5   Pompei Silonis. Quale est ut perdamus eloquentiam Ciceronis, fidem sequamur Antonii? Mi- 578M
sericordiam tu istam vocas, supplicium sumptum
⟨de⟩ [3] Ciceronis ingenio? Credamus Antonio, Cicero,
si bene illi pecunias crediderunt faeneratores, si
bene pacem Brutus et Cassius. Hominem et vitio
naturae et licentia temporum insanientem, inter
scaenicos amores sanguine civili luxuriantem: hominem qui creditoribus suis oppigneravit rem publicam,
cuius gulae duorum principum bona, Caesaris ac
Pompei, non potuerunt satis facere! Tuis utar,
Cicero, verbis: " cara est cuiquam salus quam aut
dare aut eripere potest Antonius? " Non est tanti
servari Ciceronem ut servatum Antonio debeam.

6   Triari. Conpulsus aliquando populus Romanus
in eam necessitatem est ut nihil haberet praeter
Iovem obsessum et Camillum exulem; nullum tamen
fuit Camilli opus maius quam quod indignum putavit
viros ⟨Romanos⟩ [4] salutem pactioni debere. O

[1] liceri. Si *Gertz:* licet.
[2] populus Romanus *Schott:* quam populi Romani.
[3] *Supplied by Gronovius.*
[4] *Supplied by Müller.*

---

[1] Cf. Sen. *Tranq.* 11.4, esp. " saepe enim causa moriendi est timide mori."
[2] Antony was a notorious debtor (Plut. *Ant.* 2); Silo then

bravely.[1] Let the Roman people bid against
Antony: if you burn your writings, Antony promises
you a year or two; but if you do not burn them, the
Roman people promises you eternity.

POMPEIUS SILO. What a disaster to lose the 5
eloquence of Cicero, and to have to trust the good
faith of Antony!—Is that what you call pity—doing
Cicero's genius to death?—Let us trust Antony,
Cicero, if the usurers proved wise in trusting him with
money,[2] or Brutus and Cassius in trusting him with
peace: the demented product of faulty character and
the licence of the times, revelling in the blood of
Romans while conducting amours with actresses, a
man who gave the state as a pledge to his creditors,
whose greed could not be satisfied with the property
of two great men, Caesar and Pompey! To employ
your own words, Cicero: " Who holds life dear when
it is in the discretion of Antony to give it or take it
away ? "[3] If I have to owe Cicero's life to Antony,
it is not worth saving.

TRIARIUS. Once upon a time the Roman people 6
was in such straits that it could look only to Jupiter,
who was under siege, and Camillus, who was in
exile.[4] Yet Camillus' greatest service was to judge
it shameful that Romans should owe their safety to a

alludes to Antony's behaviour after the Ides of March, to his
mistress (Cic. *Phil.* 2.20, with Denniston's note), and to his
purchase of Pompey's (*Phil.* 2.71) and appropriation of
Caesar's estate.

[3] Not found in our texts of Cicero (though cf. *Phil.* 2.5 and
60): cf. *S.* 6.4.

[4] For Camillus' exile at Ardea during Brennus' attack on
Rome (390 B.C.) see Livy 5.32.6-9, 43.6 *seq.* (with Ogilvie's
notes).

gravem vitam, etiamsi sine pretio daretur! Antonius
hostis a re publica iudicatus nunc hostem rem publicam iudicat. Lepidus, ne quis illum putet male
Antonio collegam placuisse, alienae semper dementiae accessio, utriusque collegae mancipium, noster
⟨est⟩ [1] dominus.

7   ARGENTARI. Nihil Antonio credendum est. Men-
tior? Quid enim iste non potest qui occidere Ciceronem potest, qui servare nisi crudelius quam occidat
non potest? Ignoscere tu illum tibi putas qui ingenio tuo irascitur? Ab hoc tu speras vitam cui
nondum verba tua exciderunt? Ut corpus, quod
fragile et caducum est, servetur, pereat ingenium,
quod aeternum est? Ego mirabar si mors [2] crudelior 579M
8 esset Antonii venia. P. Scipionem a maioribus suis
desciscentem generosa mors in numerum Scipionum
reposuit. Mortem tibi remittit ut id pereat quod in
te solum inmortale est. Qualis est pactio? Aufer-
tur Ciceroni ingenium sine vita; promittuntur ⟨pro⟩ [3]
oblivione nominis tui pauci servitutis anni. Non ille
te vivere vult, sed facere ingenii tui superstitem:
vive [4]—ut Cicero audiat Lepidum, Cicero audiat
Antonium, nemo Ciceronem. Poteris perferre [5]

---

[1] *Supplied here by the editor.*
[2] mors *Gertz:* non.
[3] *Supplied by Schultingh.*
[4] vive *corrector of D:* uide.
[5] poteris perferre *Schultingh:* pateris perire.

bargain.—It is a burdensome life indeed that Cicero is being offered—even if it carried no price!—Antony has been judged an enemy by the state; now he judges the state his enemy.—In case anyone should suppose he has been an unsatisfactory colleague for Antony, Lepidus, that constant adjunct to the madness of another, that serf of both his colleagues, is now our master.[1]

ARGENTARIUS. Antony should be trusted in noth- 7 ing. Am I wrong? He is capable of anything if he is capable of killing Cicero and incapable of saving his life without greater cruelty than he would show in killing him. Do you suppose that he forgives you?— he is enraged by your genius. Do you hope for your life from a man who has not yet forgotten your words? That the body, which is frail and fleeting, should be saved, is the genius, which is eternal, to perish? I should be surprised if death proved more cruel than Antony's pardon.—Publius Scipio, who had 8 fallen below the standards of his ancestors, was returned to the ranks of the Scipios by a noble death.[2] —He reprieves you from death—at the cost of the death of the only part of you that is immortal. What sort of bargain is that? Cicero, without losing his life, is losing his genius. In exchange for the obliteration of your name, you are promised a few years of slavery. He does not want you to live—he wants you to outlive your genius. Live: the result will be that Cicero will listen to Lepidus and Antony, no-one will listen to Cicero. Will you be able to

[1] Lepidus was left in charge of Italy during the Philippi campaign.
[2] See *S.* 6.2.

ut quod Cicero optimum habet ante se efferat?
Sine durare post te ingenium tuum, perpetuam
Antonii proscriptionem.

ARELLI FUSCI patris. Quoad humanum genus in-
colume manserit, quamdiu suus litteris honor, suum
eloquentiae pretium erit, quamdiu rei publicae
nostrae aut fortuna steterit aut memoria duraverit,
admirabile posteris vigebit ingenium ⟨tuum⟩,[1] et
uno proscriptus saeculo proscribes Antonium omnibus.
Crede mihi, vilissima pars tui est quae tibi vel eripi
vel donari potest; ille verus est Cicero quem proscribi Antonius non putat nisi a Cicerone posse.
9 Non ille tibi remittit proscriptionem, sed tolli desiderat   580M
suam. Si fidem deceperit Antonius, morieris; si
praestiterit, servies. Quod ad me attinet, fallere
eum malo. Per te, M. Tulli, per quattuor et sexaginta annos pulchre actos, per salutarem rei publicae
consulatum, per aeternam, si pateris, ingenii tui
memoriam, per rem publicam, quae, ne quid te putes
carum illi relinquere, ante te perit, oro et obtestor
ne moriaris confessus quam nolueris mori.

10   Huius suasoriae alteram partem neminem scio
declamasse; omnes pro libris Ciceronis solliciti
fuerunt, nemo pro ipso, cum adeo illa pars non sit
mala ut Cicero, si haec condicio lata ei fuisset,
deliberaturus non fuerit. Itaque hanc suasoriam

---

[1] *Supplied by the corrector of D.*

tolerate Cicero burying what is best in him before he is buried himself? Let your genius survive you, to proscribe Antony for ever.

ARELLIUS FUSCUS SENIOR. So long as the human race survives, so long as literature has the honour due to it, eloquence its reward, so long as the fortune of our country holds or its memory is preserved, your genius shall flourish in the admiration of posterity.[1] Proscribed for a generation, you shall proscribe Antony for all generations.—Believe me, it is the least valuable part of you that can be taken from you or granted to you. The true Cicero is the one who Antony thinks can only be proscribed by Cicero.[2]— He is not reprieving *you* from proscription, but looking 9 for escape from his own.—If Antony breaks faith, you will die; if he keeps it, you will be a slave. As for me, I prefer his treachery.—I beg you, Cicero, by your sixty-four years nobly lived, by your consulship that saved the republic, by the memory of your genius (eternal, if you allow it to be so), by the republic, which—in case you should think you are leaving him anything you hold dear—has perished before you, I beseech you not to die acknowledging how little you wished to die.

I know of no-one who declaimed the other side in 10 this *suasoria*, everybody worrying about Cicero's books, no-one about Cicero: though in fact that side is not so bad that Cicero would have been unready to consider it if he had really been faced with these terms. So nobody declaimed this *suasoria* more

[1] Cf. Vell. Pat. 2.66.5, Sen. *Poly.* 2.6.
[2] Cf. §1.

nemo declamavit efficacius quam Silo Pompeius;
non enim ad illa speciosa se contulit ad quae Cestius,
qui dixit hoc gravius esse supplicium quam mortem,
et ideo hoc Antonium eligere; brevem vitam esse
homini, multo magis seni: itaque memoriae consulendum, quae magnis viris aeternitatem promitteret,
non qualibet mercede vitam redimendam esse.
Hic condiciones intolerabiles. ⟨Nihil tam intoler-
abile⟩ [1] esse quam monumenta ingenii sui ipsum
exurere. Iniuriam illum facturum populo Romano,
cuius linguam huc ipse [2] extulisset ut insolentis
Graeciae studia tanto antecederet eloquentia quanto 581M
fortuna; iniuriam facturum generi humano. Paenitentiam illum acturum tam care [3] spiritus empti, cum
in servitute senescendum fuisset ⟨et⟩ [4] in hoc unum
eloquentia utendum, ut laudaret Antonium. Male
cum illo agi: dari vitam, eripi ingenium.

11   Silo Pompeius sic egit ut diceret Antonium non
pacisci sed inludere: non esse illam condicionem sed
contumeliam; combustis enim libris nihilominus
occisurum; non esse tam stultum Antonium ut
putaret ad rem pertinere libros a Cicerone conburi,
cuius scripta per totum orbem terrarum celebrarentur,
nec hoc petere eum, quod posset ipse facere, nisi
forte non esset in scripta Ciceronis ei ius cui esset in
Ciceronem; quaeri nihil aliud quam ut ille Cicero
multa fortiter de mortis contemptu locutus ad turpes
condiciones perductus occideretur. Antonium illi

---

[1] *Supplied by Müller.*
[2] huc ipse *Gertz:* incipem *B:* inciuem *V.*
[3] tam care *Schott:* tangere.
[4] *Supplied by Bursian.*

---

[1] Cf. *C.* 1 pr. 6.

effectively than Pompeius Silo; he didn't resort to the
attractive points made by Cestius, who said that this
was a harsher punishment than death—hence
Antony's choice. A man, especially an old man,
could expect only a short life; and so regard must be
paid to fame, which promised eternal life to the great.
Life was not to be bought at any and every price.
Here the conditions were intolerable; no condition
could be so intolerable as to have personally to burn
the records of one's own genius. Cicero would be
doing wrong by the Roman people, whose language
he himself had raised so high that Rome excelled the
attainments of haughty Greece as much in eloquence
as in worldly success.[1] He would do wrong by the
human race. He would repent of breath so dearly
bought, for he would have to grow old in slavery,
and use his eloquence for only one thing, the
praises of Antony. He was being badly done by:
he was being given life—but being deprived of his
genius.

Pompeius Silo's procedure was to say that Antony 11
was not bargaining but taunting. This was no condition—it was an insult: for if he burned his books
Antony would kill him none the less; Antony was
not so stupid as to think it mattered for Cicero to
burn his books, for his writings were scattered all over
the world. Antony's real object was not this—after
all, he could do that for himself, unless perhaps he did
not possess over Cicero's books the power he possessed
over Cicero. His only aim was, before killing him, to
bring to shameful terms the Cicero who had uttered
so many brave sentiments on the subject of despising
death. Antony was not promising him his life on

non vitam cum condicione promittere, sed mortem sub infamia quaerere. Itaque quod turpiter postea passurus esset, nunc illum debere fortiter pati.

Et haec suasoria . . . insignita est. Dixit enim sententiam cacozeliae genere humillimo et sordidissimo, quod detractu aut adiectione syllabae facit sensum: " pro facinus indignum! peribit ergo quod Cicero scripsit, manebit quod Antonius proscripsit? "

12 Apud Cestium Pium rhetorem declamabat hanc suasoriam Surdinus, ingeniosus adulescens, a quo 582M Graecae fabulae eleganter in sermonem Latinum conversae sunt. Solebat dulces sententias dicere, frequentius tamen praedulces et infractas. In hac suasoria, cum iusiurandum bellis sensibus prioribus complexus esset, adiecit: " ita te legam." Cestius, homo nasutissimus, dissimulavit exaudisse se, ut adulescentem ornatum quasi inpudens ⟨esset⟩ [1] obiurgaret: " quid dixisti? quid? ita te fruar? " Erat autem Cestius nullius quidem ingenii ⟨amator⟩, [2] Ciceroni etiam infestus, quod illi non inpune cessit.

13 Nam cum M. Tullius, filius Ciceronis, Asiam obtineret, homo qui nihil ex paterno ingenio habuit praeter urbanitatem, cenabat apud eum Cestius. M. Tullio et natura memoriam ademerat, et ebrietas si quid ex ea supererat subducebat; subinde interrogabat quid ille vocaretur qui in imo recumberet, et cum saepe

---

[1] *Supplied by Müller.*
[2] *Supplied by Kiessling.*

---

[1] ?⟨" by the folly of declaimer X "⟩.
[2] This depends on the jingle *scripsit–proscripsit*.
[3] In *dulces–praedulces* it looks as if Seneca deliberately

conditions; he was after his death—with dishonour. Cicero should now suffer bravely what he would inevitably suffer later on—shamefully.

This *suasoria* too was marked . . .[1] For he spoke an epigram employing the lowest and most vulgar of bad taste—the type that works by adding or taking away a syllable: " Abominable deed! Shall then Cicero's script perish, Antony's proscript remain? "[2]

In the school of the rhetorician Cestius Pius, this *suasoria* was declaimed by Surdinus, a talented youth, who made elegant translations of Greek plays into Latin. He used to produce pleasant epigrams, but more often cloying and effeminate ones.[3] On this theme, after some pretty preliminary ideas in the form of an oath, he added: " So shall I read you." Cestius (witty fellow!) pretended he hadn't heard, so as to be able to tell off a distinguished young man for alleged immodesty: " What did you say? Eh? So shall I enjoy you? " Cestius, indeed, was an admirer of no talent, and felt positive hostility to Cicero [4]— and he didn't get away with that. For when the governor of Asia was Cicero's son, Marcus,[5] a man who possessed nothing of his father's talents except wit, Cestius once dined with him. Nature had stolen away Marcus' memory—and anything that remained was being filched by drunkenness. He kept asking the name of the guest on the bottom couch. The

mocks ("sweet" . . . "oversweet") the previous jingle *scripsit–proscripsit* in §11 (E.H.W.).

[4] Cf. *C.* 3 pr. 15 *seq.*

[5] Date unknown. See also R. Syme, *The Roman Revolution*, 303 n. 1.

subiectum illi nomen Cestii excidisset, novissime servus, ut aliqua nota memoriam eius faceret certiorem, interroganti domino quis ille esset qui in imo recumberet ait: " hic est Cestius, qui patrem tuum negabat litteras scisse "; adferri ocius flagra iussit, et Ciceroni, ut oportuit, de corio Cestii satis fecit.

14 Erat autem etiam ubi pietas non exigeret scordalus. Hybreae, disertissimi viri, filio male apud se causam agenti ait: ἡμεῖς οὖν πατέρων; Et, cum in quadam postulatione Hybreas patris sui totum 583M locum ad litteram omnibus agnoscentibus diceret, " age," inquit " non putas me didicisse patris mei: quousque tandem abutere, Catilina, patientia nostra ? "

Gargonius, ⟨fatuorum⟩ [1] amabilissimus, in hac suasoria dixit duas res quibus stultiores ne ipse quidem umquam dixerat; unam in principio: nam, cum coepisset scholasticorum frequentissimo iam more a iureiurando et dixisset multa, ait, ut quam primum tantum tumeat [2] quantum potest, " ita aut totus vivat Cicero aut totus moriatur ut ego quae hodie pro Ciceronis ingenio dixero nulla pactione delebo." Alteram rem dixit, cum exempla referret eorum qui fortiter perierant: " Iuba et Petreius mutuis vulneribus concucurrerunt et mortes faeneraverunt."

---

[1] *Supplied by Müller.*
[2] ait, ut quam—tumeat *Shackleton Bailey* (*but the passage is very uncertain*): ita quam—timeat.

---

[1] Hom. *Il.* 4.405: the familiar quotation is not complete in the Greek.

name Cestius was supplied a number of times, but he kept forgetting. Finally a slave, hoping to make his memory more retentive by giving it something to hang on to, said, when his master asked who that was on the lowest couch: " This is Cestius, who said your father didn't know his letters." Marcus called for scourges at the double, and, as was only right, avenged Cicero on the hide of Cestius.

Marcus, however, was quarrelsome even when 14 piety did not demand it. To the son of the eloquent Hybreas, who was making a mess of a case he was conducting before him, he said: " Do we, then, claim to be better than our fathers? " [1] And when in some application or other Hybreas spoke a whole passage from his father's writings to the letter and everyone recognised it, Marcus said: " Come now, do you think *I* haven't got off by heart my father's: How much longer, Catiline, will you abuse our patience? " [2]

Gargonius, most amiable of fools, said two things on this theme unsurpassed in stupidity even by himself. One came in his proem. He began, as school-men now frequently tend to, with an oath. This went on for some time. Then, so as to come as soon as possible to his point of maximum bombast, he added: " So may Cicero wholly live or wholly die, I assert I shall agree on no terms to destroy what I say today on the genius of Cicero." The other remark came when he was giving examples of courageous deaths: " Juba and Petreius [3] clashed with mutual wounds, and lent each other death."

[2] The famous first words of *Cat.* 1.
[3] For their suicide pact, see Sen. *Prov.* 2.10, Dio. 43.8.4.

FRAGMENTA

1. Novi vero et praecipue declamatores audacius nec mehercule sine motu quodam imaginantur, ut Seneca in controversia cuius summa est quod pater filium et novercam inducente altero filio in adulterio deprensos occidit: " duc, sequor: accipe hanc senilem manum et quocumque vis inprime," et post paulo: " Aspice " inquit " quod diu non credidisti. Ego vero non video: nox oboritur et crassa caligo." *Quint. 9.2.42.*

2. Nam et in totum iurare, nisi ubi necesse est, gravi viro parum convenit, et est a Seneca dictum eleganter non patronorum hoc esse sed testium. *Quint. 9.2.98.*

3. Et Seneca tradidit Iulium Montanum poetam solitum dicere involaturum se Vergilio quaedam, si et vocem posset et os et hypocrisin; eosdem enim versus ipso pronuntiante bene sonare, sine illo inanes esse mutosque. *Donat. Vita Vergilii, 29.*

FRAGMENTS*

RHETORICAL

1. Recent speakers, and especially declaimers, evoke pictures more boldly, and surely not without a certain verve. So Seneca, in the *controversia* whose theme roughly is that a father caught his son and his own second wife in adultery on the guidance of his other son and killed them: " Lead, I am following; take this old hand, and plant it wherever you like." And, a little further on: " Look, he says, at a sight you have long refused to believe. But I do *not* see it: night envelops me, and dense darkness." [1]

2. Swearing oaths in general is hardly suitable to the serious-minded, unless when it is essential; and Seneca wittily said that this is the duty of witnesses, not advocates.

3. Seneca related that the poet Julius Montanus used to say that he would have pilfered certain things [2] from Virgil if he could have pilfered his voice, tone and dramatic delivery as well; the same verses sounded well when Virgil himself recited them, whereas without him they were empty and expressionless.

* For these fragments see my Introduction, p. xxi.
[1] In each case (as Spalding's excellent note points out) the father is trying to shift responsibility to the son. For the " darkness " see Index of Colours, s.v. Emotion.
[2] Perhaps (as Mr. C. G. Hardie suggests to me) metrical effects, perhaps Virgilian phrases.

FRAGMENTA
HISTORIARUM

1. Seneca Romanae urbis tempora distribuit in aetates; primam enim dixit infantiam sub rege Romulo fuisse, a quo et genita et quasi educata sit Roma, deinde pueritiam sub ceteris regibus, a quibus 585M et aucta sit et disciplinis pluribus institutisque formata. At vero Tarquinio regnante, cum iam quasi adulta esse coepisset, servitium non tulisse, et reiecto superbae dominationis iugo maluisse legibus obtemperare quam regibus, cumque esset adulescentia eius fine Punici belli terminata, tum denique confirmatis viribus coepisse iuvenescere. Sublata enim Carthagine, quae diu aemula imperii fuit, manus suas in totum orbem terra marique porrexit, donec regibus cunctis et nationibus imperio subiugatis, cum iam bellorum materia deficeret, viribus suis male uteretur, quibus se ipsa confecit. Haec fuit prima eius senectus, cum bellis lacerata civilibus atque intestino malo pressa rursus ad regimen singularis imperii recidit quasi ad alteram infantiam revoluta. Amissa enim libertate, quam Bruto duce et auctore defenderat, ita consenuit tamquam sustentare se ipsa non valeret nisi adminiculo regentium uteretur. *Lactant. Inst. Div. 7.15.14.*

2. Seneca eum scribit intellecta defectione exemptum anulum quasi alicui traditurum parumper tenuisse, dein rursus aptasse digito et compressa

1. Seneca marked out the history of Rome in "ages."[1] First came her infancy under King Romulus, who brought Rome to birth and as it were reared her; then her childhood under the other kings, who increased her and trained her in various skills and customs. But during the reign of Tarquin, when Rome was already beginning to be grown up, she refused to put up with slavery, and throwing off the yoke of overweening tyranny preferred to obey laws rather than kings. Adolescence ended with the end of the Punic Wars; Rome's strength matured, and she began a flourishing prime at last. For on the destruction of Carthage, which had long rivalled her empire, she stretched out her hands to grasp the whole world, by land and sea, until she had brought all kings and races under her sway. There was now no scope left for war, but Rome used her strength ill—to wear down herself. This was her first old age; torn by civil war and oppressed by internal ills, she fell back into the control of one man—slipping into a sort of second babyhood. For she lost the liberty that she had defended under the leadership and instigation of Brutus, and grew senile, as though unable to carry herself upright unless she had the prop of kingship.

2. Seneca writes that he [Tiberius] took off his ring as he felt his weakness come on. He held it for a time, as if meaning to hand it over to someone, then put it

[1] Cf. Florus 1 pr. 4 *seq.*

sinistra manu iacuisse diu immobilem subitoque vocatis ministris ac nemine respondente consurrexisse nec procul a lectulo deficientibus viribus concidisse. *Suet. Tib. 73.*

back on his finger, clenched his left hand and lay for a long while without moving. Suddenly he called for servants; no-one replied. He got up, and fell not far from the bed, his strength failing.

INDEXES

INDEX OF NAMES

THIS Index is designed mainly with readers of the English in mind; but for those using the Latin text there are cross-references e.g. between *Aegyptus* and *Egypt*. In the case of the declaimers I have added in brackets anything we know about them from sources other than Seneca. For characterisations of them, see Bornecque, *Les Déclamations . . .*, 145–201; many are also dealt with in Schanz-Hosius. For the Greek declaimers, H. Buschmann, *Charakteristik d. griech. Rhetoren bei Rhetor Seneca* (Parchim, 1878). For the Spaniards, a series of articles by H. de la Ville de Mirmont in *Bulletin Hispanique* for 1910, 1912 and 1913. In general, W. Hoffa, *De Seneca patre quaestiones selectae* (Göttingen, 1909), 5–46. Illuminating remarks on many of the declaimers will be found scattered through the works of Sir Ronald Syme, e.g. his *Tacitus* (Oxford, 1958) and his " Personal names in Annales I–VI " (*J.R.S.* 39 [1949], 6–18 = *Ten Studies in Tacitus* [Oxford, 1970] c. 6). As to historical personages, I have given as much information as should elucidate the Senecan references. For their use as *exempla*, see Rolland, 47–53, and L. Lützen, *De priorum scriptorum argenteae latinitatis studiis scholasticis* (Eschwege, 1907), 17–25.

References are by *gens* name where that is known, with cross-references; brackets indicate which parts of the names are not used by Seneca. Entries in dark face direct attention to passages of particular interest, particularly for the biography of the declaimers.

ABRONIUS SILO, poet, pupil of Latro and father of mime-writer of the same name, *S.* 2.19

Accaus, *see* Postumius

Achaia, Roman province of Greece, *S.* 6.11

Achilles, death of, *C.* 10.4.25; tomb of, *C.* 9.5.17. *See also* Aeacides

Adaeus, Asian rhetor, *C.* 1.7.18; **9.1.12**; 9.2.29; 10.4.19; 10.5.21

Aeacides, i.e. Achilles, grandson of Aeacus, *C.* 9.5.17

INDEXES

INDEXES

INDEXES

by Cicero before Caesar (45 B.C.),
S. 6.11

(Q.) Dellius, efficient turncoat in
Roman civil wars, career of, *S.* 1.7

Demosthenes, Greek orator and poli-
tician, died by poison (322 B.C.)
after death of Alexander, *C.* 7.3.4;
resemblance of Calvus to, *C.* 7.4.8;
imitated by Nicetes, *S.* 2.14; cf.
also *C.* 9.1.13 n.

Diocles of Carystos, declaimer, *C.*
1.1.25; 1.3.12; 1.5.9; 1.8.15–16;
2.3.23; 2.6.13; 7.1.26; 10.5.26;
S. 2.20

Dionysius, father and son (the former teacher of Cicero's son), *C.*
1.4.11

Dionysius Atticus, follower of Apollodorus (from Pergamum, according
to Strabo 625; also mentioned by
Quintilian 3.1.18), *C.* 2.5.11

Dionysus, Greek god of wine =
Roman Liber, *S.* 1.6

Dolabella, *see* Cornelius

Domitius, unidentified nobleman,
builder of baths (perhaps = Cn.
Domitius Ahenobarbus, consul 32
B.C.), *C.* 9.4.18

Dorion, Greek declaimer, *C.* 1.8.16;
9.1.15; 10.5.23; *S.* 1.12; 2.11, 22

Egypt, *S.* 6.6, 11

Eleans, people of Elis in N.W.
Peloponnese, *C.* 8.2

Emathian, i.e. Macedonian, *S.* 6.26

Ena, *see* Sextilius

Etruscan forces, *C.* 10.2.3

Euctemon, Greek declaimer, *C.* 1.1.25;
7.4.8; 7.5.15; 9.2.29; 10.1.15;
10.5.21

Euphrates, river of Mesopotamia, *S.*
1.11

Eurotas, river encircling Sparta,
S. 2.5

Euthycrates, betrayer of Olynthus in
348 B.C., *C.* 10.5.11

Fabianus, *see* Papirius

(Paullus) Fabius Maximus, consul 11
B.C., intimate friend of Augustus
and Maecenas, declaimer, *C.* 2.4.9,
11–12; 10 pr. 13

(Q. Fabius) Maximus (Cunctator),
Roman general against Hannibal,
died 203 B.C., *C.* 7.7.13

(Q. Fabius Maximus) Gurges, consul
292, 276, 265 B.C. (for his luxury cf.
Juvenal 6.266, Macrob. *Sat.* 3.13.6),
C. 9.2.19

Fabricii, Roman family, *C.* 2.1.17–18

(C.) Fabricius Luscinus, incorrupt-
ible Roman general in Italian
wars and hero of struggle against
Pyrrhus (his incorruptibility became a commonplace, e.g. Sen. *Ep.*
120.6; Cic. *Parad.* 12; *Decl.* p.
93.21 Ritter; Mayor on Juv. 11.91),
C. 2.1.8, 29; 5.2; 7.2.7

Festus, rhetor, *C.* 7.4.8–9

Flamininus, *see* Quinctius

Flamma, *see* Occius

Flavus, *see* Alfius

Florus, declaimer, *C.* 9.2.23–4

Formiae, city on border of Latium
and Campania, *S.* 6.17

Fortune, personified, *C.* 1.1.5, 16–17;
2.5.2; 5.1; 7.1.3–4, 6; 7.3.1;
7.6.18; 8.1; 8.4; 8.6; 9.1.6; 9.3.1;
10 pr. 16; 10.4.2; *S.* 1.3; 4.3;
6.4, 24

Fulvius Sparsus, declaimer, *C.* 1.2.2;
1.3.3, 7; 1.4.3; 1.7.15; 2.5.10;
7.2.3; 7.4.1–2; 7.6.3, 23; 9.1.7;
9.2.5; 9.3.4; 9.4.3; 9.5.4; 9.6.1;
10 pr. 11–12; 10.1.5; 10.2.4;
10.3.3; 10.4.8–10, 14, 23; 10.5.8–
10, 23, 26

(M. Furius) Camillus, saviour of Rome
in Gallic invasions of 4th c. B.C.,
S. 7.6

Furius Saturninus, orator and declaimer, *C.* 7.6.22

Fuscus, *see* Arellius

Fusius, gladiator, *C.* 3 pr. 16

Galla, *see* Numisia

Gallio, *see* Junius

Gallus, *see* Asinius, Vibius

Gargonius, foolish declaimer (perhaps
identical with the pungent Gargonius of Hor. *Sat.* 1.2.27), *C.* 1.7.18;
9.1.15; 10.5.25; *S.* 2.16; 7.14

Gavius Sabinus, declaimer, *C.* 7.1.16;
7.2.1; 7.6.19, 21; *S.* 2.5

Gavius Silo, declaimer praised by
Augustus in Tarraco (26–5 B.C.),
C. **10 pr. 14**; 10.2.7, 16; 10.3.14;
10.4.7; 10.5.1

Geminus, *see* Varius

Germanicus (Julius Caesar), nephew of

625

INDEXES

INDEXES

Marathon, fined fifty talents for deceiving the people, father of Cimon, *C.* 9.1

Miltiades, Greek declaimer, *C.* 9.2.26

Minerva, Roman goddess equivalent to Athena, q.v., temple of, *C.* 10.5; patron of Athens, *S.* 1.6; sculpted by Phidias, *C.* 10.5.8

Minturnae, town on Via Appia, in a marsh near which Marius hid from Sulla's men in 88 B.C., *C.* 7.2.6

Mithridates, king of Pontus, defeated first by Lucullus (*C.* 7.1.15), finally by Pompey (63 B.C.: *C.* 7.2.7); his prophylactic diet left him immune to poison (*C.* 7.3.4)

Moderatus, declaimer, *C.* 10 pr. 13

Montanus, *see* Julius, Votienus

Moschus, *see* Volcacius

(C.) Mucius Scaevola, Roman who, failing to kill Porsenna, showed his fortitude by holding his hand in fire, *C.* 8.4; 10.2.3, 5

(L. Munatius) Plancus, friend of Latro, perhaps the consul of 42 B.C., *C.* 1.8.15

Munda, in Spain, scene of final battle between Caesar and the Pompeians (45 B.C.), *S.* 1.5; 6.3

Murredius, foolish declaimer, *C* 1.2.21, 23; 1.4.12; 7.2.14; 7.3.8; 7.5.10, 15; 9.2.27; 9.4.22; 9.6.12; 10.1.12; 10.4.22; 10.5.28; *S.* 2.16

Musa, rhetor, *C.* 7.1.14–16; 7.3.4; 7.5.10, 13; 9.1.1; 9.2.1; 9.4.2; **10 pr. 9–10**; 10.3.5; 10.5.6; 10.6.1; *S.* 1.2, 13

Mutina, modern Modena, besieged by Antony (43 B.C.), *S.* 6.3

Mytilene, on island of Lesbos, activities of Potamon at, *S.* 2.15

Narbo, Roman colony in S. France modern Narbonne, *C.* 7.5.12

Naso, *see* Ovidius

Nepos, *see* Licinius, Mamilius

Nero, eldest son of Germanicus and Agrippina, put to death A.D. 31, *C.* 2.3.23

Nicetes, Greek declaimer (placed by Jerome in 32 B.C.; a later Nicetes (Sacerdos) appears in Tac. *Dial.* 15 and elsewhere), *C.* 1.4.12; 1.5.9; 1.7.18; 1.8.13; 9.2.23, 29; 9.6.18; 10.2.18; 10.5.23; *S.* 2.14; **3.6–7**

Nicocrates, Spartan declaimer, *C.* 7.5.15; *S.* 2.22

Niger, *see* Bruttedius

Niobe, daughter of Tantalus who mourned her children until turned to stone, *C.* 10.5.24

L. (Nonius) Asprenas, declaimer, *C.* 10 pr. 2

P. (Nonius) Asprenas, declaimer, *C.* 1.1.5; 1.2.9–10; 1.4.2, 12; 1.8.4–6, 12; 2.2.4; 2.3.8, 18; 2.6.3; 7.8.6; 9.2.3; 10.4.19, 25; *S.* 7.4

Notus, south wind, *C.* 2.2.12

Novatus, *see* Annaeus

Numantia, on the Douro in Spain, resisted Rome till sacked by Scipio Aemilianus (133 B.C.), *C.* 1.8.12

Numisia Galla, defended by Votienus Montanus, *C.* 9.5.15

Occius Flamma, proconsul of Crete, *C.* 9.4.19

Ocean, sea thought to encircle the world, *C.* 7.7.19; *S.* 1; 4.3; 6.5

Octavia, wife of the triumvir Antony, *S.* 1.6

Oedipus, father-killer and husband of mother, *C.* 10.5.23

Olympia, in W. Greece, scene of games (*C.* 5.3), seat of Zeus (*C.* 8.2)

Olynthus, city of Chalcidic peninsula (N.E. Greece) which defied Philip of Macedon but was betrayed to him and destroyed (348 B.C.), *C.* 3.8; 10.5

Orient, brought to Greece by Xerxes, *S.* 2.1, 7; 5.2

Otho, *see* Junius

Othryades, hero of Thermopylae, *S.* 2.2, 16

(P.) Ovidius Naso, the poet Ovid (43 B.C.–A.D. 17), *C.* 1.2.22; **2.2.8–12**; 3.7; 7.1.27; 9.5.17; 10.4.25; *S.* 3.7

Pacatus, rhetor, *C.* 10 pr. 10–11

Palladium, sacred object preserved in temple of Vesta, *C.* 4.2

Pammenes, Greek declaimer (perhaps the eloquent orator mentioned by Cic. *Brut.* 332, *Orat.* 105), *C.* 1.4.7

Pamphylian sea, off Antalya, Turkey *S.* 1.11

Pansa, *see* Vibius

Papirius Fabianus, Sextian philo-

629

INDEXES

INDEXES

Tarquinius the Proud, last king of Rome, overthrown by L. Junius Brutus, *C.* 3.9; frg. hist. 1

Tarraco, Roman colony in Spain (modern Tarragona), *C.* 10 pr. 14

Taygetus, mountain ridge near Sparta, *S.* 2.5

(P. Terentius) Varro (Atacinus), born 82 B.C., poet drawn on by Virgil, *C.* 7.1.27

Thebes, *S.* 2.5

Theodorus of Gadara, teacher of Tiberius and rhetorical theorist, *C.* 2.1.36; *S.* 3.7

Theodotus, adviser of Ptolemy XIII and instigator of death of Pompey (48 B.C.), *C.* 2.4.8

Thermopylae, scene of heroic stand in central Greece by Spartans against Persians (480 B.C.), *S.* 2

Thracians, *C.* 6.5; (as type of gladiator) *C.* 3 pr. 10, 16

Thucydides, Athenian historian of 5th c. B.C., *C.* 9.1.13; *S.* 6.21

Thyestes, brother of Atreus, who served the flesh of his children up to him, *C.* 1.1.21

Tiberius, *see* Caesar

Timagenes, of Alexandria, historian and friend of Augustus, *C.* 10.5.22

Torquatus, *see* Manlius

Triarius, declaimer, *C.* 1.1.18; 1.2.21; 1.3.9, 12; 1.4.2; 1.5.2, 9; 1.6.11; 1.7.7; 2.1.15; 2.3.19, 21; 2.5.8; 7.1.8, 25; 7.2.4; 7.4.1, **10**; 7.5.1–2, 6; 7.6.10, 23; 9.2.12, 20–21; 9.3.14; 9.4.1, 16; 9.6.8–9, 11, 17–18; 10.2.18; 10.3.6; 10.4.4; 10.5.5, 20, 24; *S.* 2.3; 5.7; 6.5; 7.6

Triptolemus of Eleusis, who travelled in Demeter's chariot behind two dragons, teaching how to grow corn, *C.* 10.5.28

Troades, Trojan women (e.g. Hecuba, Andromache), whose sufferings Euripides depicted in the play of this name, *C.* 10.5.24

Troy, city of Asia, taken by Greeks in an expedition of a thousand ships, *C.* 10.6.2; *S.* 2.20; 3.1. King of, *see* Priam

Tubero, *see* Aelius

M. Tullius Cicero, 106–43 B.C., Roman orator and statesman, *C.* 1 pr. 6, 11–12; 1.4.7; 2 pr. 5; 2.4.4; 3 pr. 8, 15–17; 4 pr. 9; **7.2**; 7.3.9; 7.4.6; 10 pr. 6; 10.3.3; *S.* 1.5; **6; 7**

M. Tullius Cicero, son of the former, educated at Athens, consul suffectus 30 B.C., later proconsul of Asia, *C.* 1.4.11; *S.* 7.13–14

Turdus, friend of Occius Flamma, *C.* 9.4.20

Turrinus, *see* Clodius

Tusculum, city S.W. of Rome, *S.* 6.17

Tuscus, declaimer and historian (perhaps either the Cornelius or the Servilius of Tac. *Ann.* 6.29), *S.* 2.22

Tydides, son of Tydeus, i.e. Diomedes, *C.* 9.3.14

(C. Valerius) Catullus, Roman lyric and elegiac poet, on Calvus, *C.* 7.4.7

(M. Valerius) Messala Corvinus, 64 B.C.–A.D. 8, orator, statesman and purist, *C.* 2.4.8, 10; 3 pr. 14; *S.* 1.7; 2.17, 20; 3.6; 6.27

(L. Valerius Messala) Volesus, consul A.D. 5, successfully accused by Furius Saturninus, *C.* 7.6.22

Vallius Syriacus, declaimer (killed by Tiberius in A.D. 30), *C.* 1.1.11, 21; 2.1.34–6; 2.6.13; 7.6.11; 9.4.18

Varius Geminus, declaimer (a sublime orator according to Jerome), *C.* 4.8; 6.8; 7.1.18–19, 23, 26; 7.2.9, 13; 7.3.2, 4; 7.4.2, 5; 7.5.6, 9; 7.6.10, 15–17, 23; 7.7.6, 11, 16, 18; 7.8.5, 9–10; 9.5.14; *S.* 6.11–14

Varro, *see* Terentius

Varus, *see* Quinctilius

(P.) Vatinius, Caesarian tribune 59 B.C., prosecuted by Calvus in 54, *C.* 7.4.6; attacked, then defended, by Cicero (56, 54), *S.* 6.13

Ventidii, the like of P. Ventidius, partisan of Antony (died 38 B.C.), *S.* 7.3

Venus, goddess and planet, *S.* 4.2

P. Vergilius Maro, the poet Virgil (70–19 B.C.), *C.* 3 pr. 8; 7.1.27; *S.* 1.12; 2.20; 3.4–5, 7; 4.4–5; frg. 3; also cited *C.* 7.5.9

Verginia, killed by her father to save her from the lust of Appius

633

INDEXES

Claudius (cf. Livy 3.46 *seq.*), *C.* 1.5.3

Verginii, men of the type of the father of the former, *C.* 9.1.11

(C.) Verres, proconsul in Sicily (73–71 B.C.), then successfully prosecuted by Cicero, dying much later in the proscriptions of Antony, *C.* 7.2.4; *S.* 2.19; 6.3, 24

Vesta, Roman hearth-goddess, served by Vestal Virgins, *C.* 1.3; 4.2; 6.8; 7.2.7

Vibius Gallus, declaimer, *C.* 1.1.10; 1.3.6; 1.4.5; 2.1.9, 25–6; 2.6.3; 7.5.3, 14; 7.8.5; 9.1.4; 9.2.21, 23; 9.6.2; 10.1.1; 10.4.3

(C. Vibius) Pansa, consul 43 B.C. (when he died at Mutina), and friend of Cicero, *S.* 6.1

Vibius Rufus, declaimer (perhaps the consul suffectus of A.D. 16), *C.* 1.1.12; 1.2.21, 23; 1.4.10–12; 1.5.9; 1.7.10; 1.8.14; 2.1.2, 28; 2.3.8, 18; 2.6.10; 7.3.4; 9.2.2, 19, **25**; 9.3.7; 9.5.3; 9.6.13; 10.1.12; 10.6.2

Victor, *see* Statorius

L. Vinicius, distinguished extempore orator (perhaps the consul suffectus of 5 B.C., the son of the consul of 33 B.C.; the manuscripts give details of Vinicius' ancestry in too corrupt a form to be helpful), *C.* 2.5.19–20

P. Vinicius, declaimer and orator (perhaps the consul of A.D. 2, al-luded to in Tac. *Ann.* 3.11 and Sen. *Ep.* 40.9), *C.* 1.2.3; 1.4.11; 7.5.11–12; 7.6.11; 10.4.25

M. Vipsanius Agrippa, principal lieutenant of Augustus, whose daughter he married, *C.* 2.4.12–13

Virgil, *see* Vergilius

(Volcacius) Moschus, declaimer (of Pergamum; condemned on a poisoning charge and exiled to Marseille—Tac. *Ann.* 4.43; the name often appears in Seneca's MSS as Oscus), *C.* 2.3.4; 2.5.13; 7.3.8; 10 pr. 10; 10.1.3, 12; 10.2.17; 10.3.1; 10.4.20; 10.6.1; *S.* 1.2

Volesus, *see* Valerius

Votienus Montanus, declaimer (of Narbo; for his trial on a treason charge in A.D. 25 see Tac. *Ann.* 4.42; his death in the Balearics is recorded by Jerome under the year A.D. 27), *C.* 7.5.11–12; **9 pr.**; 9.1.3, 10, 12; 9.2.11, 13–16, 18–19, 22; 9.3.5, 10; 9.4.5, 11, 14–16; 9.5.3, 6, **14–17**; 9.6.10–11, 18–19; 10.2.12; 10.3.16; 10.4.23

Xerxes, king of Persia and invader of Greece (480 B.C.), *S.* 2; 5

Zeus, supreme Greek god, father of Dionysus, *S.* 1.6. *See also* Jupiter

Zeuxis, distinguished painter (*floruit* 400 B.C.), realism of, *C.* 10.5.27

II. INDEX OF COMMONPLACES, COLOURS AND RHETORICAL TERMS

THIS index makes no claim to completeness. In particular, very common words (e.g. *sententia*) are treated selectively; the references given aim to direct attention towards passages that throw light on the usage of the term. For wider coverage see H. Bardon, *Le vocabulaire de la critique littéraire chez Sénèque le rhéteur* (Paris, 1940). References are by volume and page. Those without volume number are to Vol. 1.

635

INDEXES

comparison, 309; 2.109–11, 341

compositio, 196, 390: 2.94, 96, 98, 258, 534

conclusio, 390

"conjecture," 133, 255: 2.79, 155, 337, 387

controversia, viii, 13, 241–9, 265, 385: 1.109, 251, 459–61

corruptus (and cognates), 234: 2.44, 100, 254, 260, 324, 336, 440, 444, 468, 470, 474, 500, 504, 506

declaimers, the best four, 2.363; "hot," 2.543

declamation, history of, vii–ix, 13, 203; contrasted with real-life legal oratory, 195, 377–91, 425; 2.13, 39, 141, 209–15, 321, 363, 459 (cf. 573); held in private, 423–5: 2.3, 355 (*contrast* 1.429); jests in, 379: 2.301, 305; criticism of, 385–91; 2.209–15

declamatoria lex, 430

delivery, 379: 2.95, 353, 363, 613 (*see* Gestures, Voice)

descriptions, xii, 109, 115, 197, 199, 233–5; 2.49, 255, 299, 435, 503, 517, 519, 537, 541, 545. Of cripples, 2.423–5; of executions, 2.243–5; of a feast, 2.239; of invasion by pirates, 149; of Ocean, 2.487, 489–91; 503–5; of the Tarpeian rock, 93, 99; of Thermopylae, 2.509, 517, 523, 525; of torture, 325: 2.345, 571; of storms, 2.21, 29, 47, 203, 537

developments (*explicationes*), 197, 235, 383: 2.49, 211, 519, 535, 551

digression, xii: 2.5

division, xvii–xviii, 41, 335, 429: 2.3, 79, 387, 459–61, 559

echo, 2.165

enthymemes, 23

epideixis, xiv

epigrams, *see sententia*

epilogue, xii, 171, 385, 429; 2.5, 93–5, 97, 109, 341

epiphonema, 22: 2.446

equity *v.* law, xviii, 43, 255, 289, 333, 335, 337, 339: 2.91, 177

ethicae controversiae, 264

ethicos, xi, 296, 306: 2.502

examples, xii, 31, 187, 263: 2.115, 229, 497, 569, 611

extempore oratory, 343, 381, 429: 2.5, 277

figures, 25, 57, 233, 311, 429: 2.7, 11–13, 39, 43, 257, 259, 279, 361; figured declamations, 47, 79, 231, 291, 295, 309, 311, 339, 355: 2.6 n., 341, 441

gestures, 491: 2.211, 529

hexis, 2.4

hypothesis, vii

imago (of vivid scene), 148 (*cf.* 2.612)

impetus, 428: 2.38, 542

laws, wording of, 77–9, 113, 441

membrum, 20, 286, 334

memory, *see* Index III

narration, xii, 57, 67, 83, 91, 95, 97, 115, 121, 173, 177, 197, 207, 245, 355, 357, 359, 385, 447, 475: 2.31, 41, 45, 47, 49, 65, 131, 137, 253, 293, 299, 309, 321, 387, 403

neologisms, 2.141

notes for speeches, 381 (*cf. also* 11: 2.353)

numerus = rhythm (?), 2.260

obscurity, 199: 2.259

paraphrase (*metaphrasis*), 2.501

pars = role (*q.v.*), *e.g.* 54

phantasia, 2.524

praefatio, xvii, 258 (*cf.* 20, 384: 2.2)

proem, xii, 57, 197, 385: 2.39, 47, 385, 611

propositio, 172: 2.4 (*cf.* 366)

proverb, 2.523 (*cf.* 1.350 n.)

questions, xvii, 21–3, 43, 131, 133, 283, 289: 2.5, 89, 91, 155

repetition, 2.321–5, 328 n.

rhetoricians, viii: 2.301

role, choice of, 2.213

scholastica, 13, 386: 2.12, 322, 458 (*cf.* 2.212)

scholasticus, viii (usually = virtuoso rhetorician; but perhaps = pupil at 1.260)

636

INDEXES

III. GENERAL INDEX

FIGURES in bold type signal the appearance of the topic in the theme of a declamation; further references within that declamation are not then given. References are by volume and page. Those without volume number are to Vol. 1.

INDEXES

INDEXES

torture, 163, **317**, 369, **515**: 2.185, **191**, 297, 299, **327**, **449**, 571

traders, **363**

translation, 2.45, 231–3, 279, 343, 445–7, 609

transvestism, **489**

treachery, 2.**145**, **477**

treaties, **513**: 2.453

tribunes (magistrates), 125–7, **419**; (army officers), 2.245

twins, 2.**265**

tyrants, tyrannicides, **151**, 283, **317**, **409**, **459**, **495**: 2.17, 99, **119**, **281**, 425, 615

unchastity, **89**, **489**, **523**: 2.293

unspecified offences, 389, **471**

verses, immoral, **523**

vices, 183, 229, 303, 351, 353, 355: 2.47 (see also Index II)

view, blocking of, **485**

violence, 395, **465**, **489**: 2.**265**, **307**; (at trials), **513**

votes, tied, 125, 271, **397**

war, 215, 347; right of, 2.463

weather, extremes of, 2.535

weeping, **415**, 435–9: 2.**201**, 377

wills, **363**, **419**, **499**, **509**: 2.149, 271, 279, 323, 437

witnesses, 2.43, 103, 115, 289, 351 n., 613 (see Perjury)

wives, rich, 141, 143–5; self-sacrifice by, 251, 263, 327: 2.409; and lust, 83; left behind by proconsuls, 2.237

women, ambitious, 325; garrulity of, 333 (see Chastity, Unchastity)

wreckers, 2.203

wrestling, 2.213 (see Pancratiasts)

youth, torpor and effeminacy of, 9

Printed in Great Britain by
Richard Clay (The Chaucer Press), Ltd.,
Bungay, Suffolk

THE LOEB CLASSICAL LIBRARY

VOLUMES ALREADY PUBLISHED

Latin Authors

AMMIANUS MARCELLINUS. Translated by J. C. Rolfe. 3 Vols.

APULEIUS: THE GOLDEN ASS (METAMORPHOSES). W. Adlington (1566). Revised by S. Gaselee.

ST. AUGUSTINE: CITY OF GOD. 7 Vols. Vol. I. G. E. McCracken. Vol. II. and VII. W. M. Green. Vol. III. D. Wiesen. Vol. IV. P. Levine. Vol. V. E. M. Sanford and W. M. Green. Vol. VI. W. C. Greene.

ST. AUGUSTINE, CONFESSIONS OF. W. Watts (1631). 2 Vols.

ST. AUGUSTINE, SELECT LETTERS. J. H. Baxter.

AUSONIUS. H. G. Evelyn White. 2 Vols.

BEDE. J. E. King. 2 Vols.

BOETHIUS: TRACTS and DE CONSOLATIONE PHILOSOPHIAE. REV. H. F. Stewart and E. K. Rand. Revised by S. J. Tester.

CAESAR: ALEXANDRIAN, AFRICAN and SPANISH WARS. A. G. Way.

CAESAR: CIVIL WARS. A. G. Peskett.

CAESAR: GALLIC WAR. H. J. Edwards.

CATO: DE RE RUSTICA; VARRO: DE RE RUSTICA. H. B. Ash and W. D. Hooper.

CATULLUS. F. W. Cornish; TIBULLUS. J. B. Postgate; PERVIGILIUM VENERIS. J. W. Mackail.

CELSUS: DE MEDICINA. W. G. Spencer. 3 Vols.

CICERO: BRUTUS, and ORATOR. G. L. Hendrickson and H. M. Hubbell.

[CICERO]: AD HERENNIUM. H. Caplan.

CICERO: DE ORATORE, etc. 2 Vols. Vol. I. DE ORATORE, Books I. and II. E. W. Sutton and H. Rackham. Vol. II. DE ORATORE, Book III. De Fato; Paradoxa Stoicorum; De Partitione Oratoria. H. Rackham.

CICERO: DE FINIBUS. H. Rackham.

CICERO: DE INVENTIONE, etc. H. M. Hubbell.

CICERO: DE NATURA DEORUM and ACADEMICA. H. Rackham.

CICERO: DE OFFICIIS. Walter Miller.

CICERO: DE REPUBLICA and DE LEGIBUS: SOMNIUM SCIPIONIS. Clinton W. Keyes.

2

Ovid: Heroides and Amores. Grant Showerman.
Ovid: Metamorphoses. F. J. Miller. 2 Vols.
Ovid: Tristia and Ex Ponto. A. L. Wheeler.
Persius. Cf. Juvenal.
Petronius. M. Heseltine; Seneca; Apocolocyntosis.
W. H. D. Rouse.
Phaedrus and Babrius (Greek). B. E. Perry.
Plautus. Paul Nixon. 5 Vols.
Pliny: Letters, Panegyricus. Betty Radice. 2 Vols.
Pliny: Natural History. Vols. I.–V. and IX. H. Rackham.
VI.–VIII. W. H. S. Jones. X. D. E. Eichholz. 10 Vols.
Propertius. H. E. Butler.
Prudentius. H. J. Thomson. 2 Vols.
Quintilian. H. E. Butler. 4 Vols.
Remains of Old Latin. E. H. Warmington. 4 Vols. Vol. I.
(Ennius and Caecilius.) Vol. II. (Livius, Naevius,
Pacuvius, Accius.) Vol. III. (Lucilius and Laws of XII
Tables.) Vol. IV. (Archaic Inscriptions.)
Sallust. J. C. Rolfe.
Scriptores Historiae Augustae. D. Magie. 3 Vols.
Seneca, The Elder: Controversiae, Suasoriae. M.
Winterbottom. 2 Vols.
Seneca: Apocolocyntosis. Cf. Petronius.
Seneca: Epistulae Morales. R. M. Gummere. 3 Vols.
Seneca: Moral Essays. J. W. Basore. 3 Vols.
Seneca: Tragedies. F. J. Miller. 2 Vols.
Seneca: Naturales Quaestiones. T. H. Corcoran. 2 Vols.
Sidonius: Poems and Letters. W. B. Anderson. 2 Vols.
Silius Italicus. J. D. Duff. 2 Vols.
Statius. J. H. Mozley. 2 Vols.
Suetonius. J. C. Rolfe. 2 Vols.
Tacitus: Dialogus. Sir Wm. Peterson. Agricola and
Germania. Maurice Hutton. Revised by M. Winterbottom,
R. M. Ogilvie, E. H. Warmington.
Tacitus: Histories and Annals. C. H. Moore and J. Jackson.
4 Vols.
Terence. John Sargeaunt. 2 Vols.
Tertullian: Apologia and De Spectaculis. T. R. Glover.
Minucius Felix. G. H. Rendall.
Valerius Flaccus. J. H. Mozley.
Varro: De Lingua Latina. R. G. Kent. 2 Vols.
Velleius Paterculus and Res Gestae Divi Augusti. F. W.
Shipley.
Virgil. H. R. Fairclough. 2 Vols.
Vitruvius: De Architectura. F. Granger. 2 Vols.

3

Greek Authors

ACHILLES TATIUS. S. Gaselee.

AELIAN: ON THE NATURE OF ANIMALS. A. F. Scholfield. 3 Vols.

AENEAS TACTICUS, ASCLEPIODOTUS and ONASANDER. The Illinois Greek Club.

AESCHINES. C. D. Adams.

AESCHYLUS. H. Weir Smyth. 2 Vols.

ALCIPHRON, AELIAN, PHILOSTRATUS: LETTERS. A. R. Benner and F. H. Fobes.

ANDOCIDES, ANTIPHON, Cf. MINOR ATTIC ORATORS.

APOLLODORUS. Sir James G. Frazer. 2 Vols.

APOLLONIUS RHODIUS. R. C. Seaton.

THE APOSTOLIC FATHERS. Kirsopp Lake. 2 Vols.

APPIAN: ROMAN HISTORY. Horace White. 4 Vols.

ARATUS. Cf. CALLIMACHUS.

ARISTIDES: ORATIONS. C. A. Behr. Vol. I.

ARISTOPHANES. Benjamin Bickley Rogers. 3 Vols. Verse trans.

ARISTOTLE: ART OF RHETORIC. J. H. Freese.

ARISTOTLE: ATHENIAN CONSTITUTION, EUDEMIAN ETHICS, VICES AND VIRTUES. H. Rackham.

ARISTOTLE: GENERATION OF ANIMALS. A. L. Peck.

ARISTOTLE: HISTORIA ANIMALIUM. A. L. Peck. Vols. I.–II.

ARISTOTLE: METAPHYSICS. H. Tredennick. 2 Vols.

ARISTOTLE: METEOROLOGICA. H. D. P. Lee.

ARISTOTLE: MINOR WORKS. W. S. Hett. On Colours, On Things Heard, On Physiognomies, On Plants, On Marvellous Things Heard, Mechanical Problems, On Indivisible Lines, On Situations and Names of Winds, On Melissus, Xenophanes, and Gorgias.

ARISTOTLE: NICOMACHEAN ETHICS. H. Rackham.

ARISTOTLE: OECONOMICA and MAGNA MORALIA. G. C. Armstrong; (with METAPHYSICS, Vol. II.).

ARISTOTLE: ON THE HEAVENS. W. K. C. Guthrie.

ARISTOTLE: ON THE SOUL. PARVA NATURALIA. ON BREATH. W. S. Hett.

ARISTOTLE: CATEGORIES, ON INTERPRETATION, PRIOR ANALYTICS. H. P. Cooke and H. Tredennick.

ARISTOTLE: POSTERIOR ANALYTICS, TOPICS. H. Tredennick and E. S. Forster.

ARISTOTLE: ON SOPHISTICAL REFUTATIONS.
On Coming to be and Passing Away, On the Cosmos. E. S. Forster and D. J. Furley.

ARISTOTLE: PARTS OF ANIMALS. A. L. Peck; MOTION AND PROGRESSION OF ANIMALS. E. S. Forster.

4

ARISTOTLE: PHYSICS. Rev. P. Wicksteed and F. M. Cornford. 2 Vols.
ARISTOTLE: POETICS and LONGINUS. W. Hamilton Fyfe; DEMETRIUS ON STYLE. W. Rhys Roberts.
ARISTOTLE: POLITICS. H. Rackham.
ARISTOTLE: PROBLEMS. W. S. Hett. 2 Vols.
ARISTOTLE: RHETORICA AD ALEXANDRUM (with PROBLEMS. Vol. II). H. Rackham.
ARRIAN: HISTORY OF ALEXANDER and INDICA. Rev. E. Iliffe Robson. 2 Vols.
ATHENAEUS: DEIPNOSOPHISTAE. C. B. Gulick. 7 Vols.
BABRIUS AND PHAEDRUS (Latin). B. E. Perry.
ST. BASIL: LETTERS. R. J. Deferrari. 4 Vols.
CALLIMACHUS: FRAGMENTS. C. A. Trypanis. MUSAEUS: HERO AND LEANDER. T. Gelzer and C. Whitman.
CALLIMACHUS, Hymns and Epigrams, and LYCOPHRON. A. W. Mair; ARATUS. G. R. Mair.
CLEMENT OF ALEXANDRIA. Rev. G. W. Butterworth.
COLLUTHUS. Cf. OPPIAN.
DAPHNIS AND CHLOE. Thornley's Translation revised by J. M. Edmonds: and PARTHENIUS. S. Gaselee.
DEMOSTHENES I.: OLYNTHIACS, PHILIPPICS and MINOR ORATIONS. I.-XVII. AND XX. J. H. Vince.
DEMOSTHENES II.: DE CORONA and DE FALSA LEGATIONE. C. A. Vince and J. H. Vince.
DEMOSTHENES III.: MEIDIAS, ANDROTION, ARISTOCRATES, TIMOCRATES and ARISTOGEITON, I. AND II. J. H. Vince.
DEMOSTHENES IV.-VI.: PRIVATE ORATIONS and IN NEAERAM. A. T. Murray.
DEMOSTHENES VII.: FUNERAL SPEECH, EROTIC ESSAY, EXORDIA and LETTERS. N. W. and N. J. DeWitt.
DIO CASSIUS: ROMAN HISTORY. E. Cary. 9 Vols.
DIO CHRYSOSTOM. J. W. Cohoon and H. Lamar Crosby. 5 Vols.
DIODORUS SICULUS. 12 Vols. Vols. I.-VI. C. H. Oldfather. Vol. VII. C. L. Sherman. Vol. VIII. C. B. Welles. Vols. IX. and X. R. M. Geer. Vol. XI. F. Walton. Vol. XII. F. Walton. General Index. R. M. Geer.
DIOGENES LAERTIUS. R. D. Hicks. 2 Vols. New Introduction by H. S. Long.
DIONYSIUS OF HALICARNASSUS: ROMAN ANTIQUITIES Spelman's translation revised by E. Cary. 7 Vols.
DIONYSIUS OF HALICARNASSUS: CRITICAL ESSAYS. S. Usher. 2 Vols.
EPICTETUS. W. A. Oldfather. 2 Vols.
EURIPIDES. A. S. Way. 4 Vols. Verse trans.
EUSEBIUS: ECCLESIASTICAL HISTORY. Kirsopp Lake and J. E. L. Oulton. 2 Vols.

5

GALEN: ON THE NATURAL FACULTIES. A. J. Brock.

THE GREEK ANTHOLOGY. W. R. Paton. 5 Vols.

GREEK ELEGY AND IAMBUS with the ANACREONTEA. J. M. Edmonds. 2 Vols.

THE GREEK BUCOLIC POETS (THEOCRITUS, BION, MOSCHUS). J. M. Edmonds.

GREEK MATHEMATICAL WORKS. Ivor Thomas. 2 Vols.

HERODES. Cf. THEOPHRASTUS: CHARACTERS.

HERODIAN. C. R. Whittaker. 2 Vols.

HERODOTUS. A. D. Godley. 4 Vols.

HESIOD AND THE HOMERIC HYMNS. H. G. Evelyn White.

HIPPOCRATES and the FRAGMENTS OF HERACLEITUS. W. H. S. Jones and E. T. Withington. 4 Vols.

HOMER: ILIAD. A. T. Murray. 2 Vols.

HOMER: ODYSSEY. A. T. Murray. 2 Vols.

ISAEUS. E. W. Forster.

ISOCRATES. George Norlin and LaRue Van Hook. 3 Vols.

[ST. JOHN DAMASCENE]: BARLAAM AND IOASAPH. Rev. G. R. Woodward, Harold Mattingly and D. M. Lang.

JOSEPHUS. 9 Vols. Vols. I.–IV. H. Thackeray. Vol. V. H. Thackeray and R. Marcus. Vols. VI.–VII. R. Marcus. Vol. VIII. R. Marcus and Allen Wikgren. Vol. IX. L. H. Feldman.

JULIAN. Wilmer Cave Wright. 3 Vols.

LIBANIUS. A. F. Norman. Vol. I.

LUCIAN. 8 Vols. Vols. I.–V. A. M. Harmon. Vol. VI. K. Kilburn. Vols. VII.–VIII. M. D. Macleod.

LYCOPHRON. Cf. CALLIMACHUS.

LYRA GRAECA. J. M. Edmonds. 3 Vols.

LYSIAS. W. R. M. Lamb.

MANETHO. W. G. Waddell: PTOLEMY: TETRABIBLOS. F. E. Robbins.

MARCUS AURELIUS. C. R. Haines.

MENANDER. F. G. Allison.

MINOR ATTIC ORATORS (ANTIPHON, ANDOCIDES, LYCURGUS, DEMADES, DINARCHUS, HYPERIDES). K. J. Maidment and J. O. Burtt. 2 Vols.

MUSAEUS: HERO AND LEANDER. Cf. CALLIMACHUS.

NONNOS: DIONYSIACA. W. H. D. Rouse. 3 Vols.

OPPIAN, COLLUTHUS, TRYPHIODORUS. A. W. Mair.

PAPYRI. NON-LITERARY SELECTIONS. A. S. Hunt and C. C. Edgar. 2 Vols. LITERARY SELECTIONS (Poetry). D. L. Page.

PARTHENIUS. Cf. DAPHNIS and CHLOE.

PAUSANIAS: DESCRIPTION OF GREECE. W. H. S. Jones. 4 Vols. and Companion Vol. arranged by R. E. Wycherley.

PHILO. 10 Vols. Vols. I.–V. F. H. Colson and Rev. G. H. Whitaker. Vols. VI.–IX. F. H. Colson. Vol. X. F. H. Colson and the Rev. J. W. Earp.

PHILO: two supplementary Vols. (*Translation only.*) Ralph Marcus.

PHILOSTRATUS: THE LIFE OF APOLLONIUS OF TYANA. F. C. Conybeare. 2 Vols.

PHILOSTRATUS: IMAGINES; CALLISTRATUS: DESCRIPTIONS. A. Fairbanks.

PHILOSTRATUS and EUNAPIUS: LIVES OF THE SOPHISTS. Wilmer Cave Wright.

PINDAR. Sir J. E. Sandys.

PLATO: CHARMIDES, ALCIBIADES, HIPPARCHUS, THE LOVERS, THEAGES, MINOS and EPINOMIS. W. R. M. Lamb.

PLATO: CRATYLUS, ZARMENIDES, GREATER HIPPIAS, LESSER HIPPIAS. H. N. Fowler.

PLATO: EUTHYPHRO, APOLOGY, CRITO, PHAEDO, PHAEDRUS. H. N. Fowler.

PLATO: LACHES, PROTAGORAS, MENO, EUTHYDEMUS. W. R. M. Lamb.

PLATO: LAWS. Rev. R. G. Bury. 2 Vols.

PLATO: LYSIS, SYMPOSIUM, GORGIAS. W. R. M. Lamb.

PLATO: REPUBLIC. Paul Shorey. 2 Vols.

PLATO: STATESMAN, PHILEBUS. H. N. Fowler; Ion. W. R. M. Lamb.

PLATO: THEAETETUS and SOPHIST. H. N. Fowler.

PLATO: TIMAEUS, CRITIAS, CLITOPHO, MENEXENUS, EPISTULAE. Rev. R. G. Bury.

PLOTINUS: A. H. Armstrong. Vols. I.–III.

PLUTARCH: MORALIA. 16 Vols. Vols. I.–V. F. C. Babbitt. Vol. VI. W. C. Helmbold. Vols. VII. and XIV. P. H. De Lacy and B. Einarson. Vol. VIII. P. A. Clement and H. B. Hoffleit. Vol. IX. E. L. Minar, Jr., F. H. Sandbach, W. C. Helmbold. Vol. X. H. N. Fowler. Vol. XI. L. Pearson and F. H. Sandbach. Vol. XII. H. Cherniss and W. C. Helmbold. Vol. XV. F. H. Sandbach.

PLUTARCH: THE PARALLEL LIVES. B. Perrin. 11 Vols.

POLYBIUS. W. R. Paton. 6 Vols.

PROCOPIUS: HISTORY OF THE WARS. H. B. Dewing. 7 Vols.

PTOLEMY: TETRABIBLOS. Cf. MANETHO.

QUINTUS SMYRNAEUS. A. S. Way. Verse trans.

SEXTUS EMPIRICUS. Rev. R. G. Bury. 4 Vols.

SOPHOCLES. F. Storr. 2 Vols. Verse trans.

STRABO: GEOGRAPHY. Horace L. Jones. 8 Vols.

THEOPHRASTUS: CHARACTERS. J. M. Edmonds. HERODES, etc. A. D. Knox

THEOPHRASTUS: ENQUIRY INTO PLANTS. Sir Arthur Hort, Bart. 2 Vols.
THUCYDIDES. C. F. Smith. 4 Vols.
TRYPHIODORUS. Cf. OPPIAN.
XENOPHON: CYROPAEDIA. Walter Miller. 2 Vols.
XENOPHON: HELLENICA. C. L. Brownson. 2 Vols.
XENOPHON: ANABASIS. C. L. Brownson.
XENOPHON: MEMORABILIA AND OECONOMICUS. E. C. Marchant. SYMPOSIUM AND APOLOGY. O. J. Todd.
XENOPHON: SCRIPTA MINORA. E. C. Marchant and G. W. Bowersock.

IN PREPARATION

Greek Authors

AELIAN: VARIA HISTORICA. C. Pritchet.
MUSAEUS: HERO AND LEANDER. T. Gelzer and C. H. Whitman.

Latin Authors

MANILIUS. G. P. Goold.

DESCRIPTIVE PROSPECTUS ON APPLICATION

CAMBRIDGE, MASS.   HARVARD UNIVERSITY PRESS
LONDON   WILLIAM HEINEMANN LTD

8